Recent Developments in Machine and Human Intelligence

S. Suman Rajest
Dhaanish Ahmed College of Engineering, India

Bhopendra Singh
Amity University, Dubai, UAE

Ahmed J. Obaid
University of Kufa, Iraq

R. Regin
SRM Institute of Science and Technology, Ramapuram, India

Karthikeyan Chinnusamy
Veritas, USA

A volume in the Advances in Computational Intelligence and Robotics (ACIR) Book Series

Published in the United States of America by
IGI Global
Engineering Science Reference (an imprint of IGI Global)
701 E. Chocolate Avenue
Hershey PA, USA 17033
Tel: 717-533-8845
Fax: 717-533-8661
E-mail: cust@igi-global.com
Web site: http://www.igi-global.com

Library of Congress Cataloging-in-Publication Data

Names: Rajest, S. Suman, 1988- editor. | Singh, Bhopendra, 1974- editor. |
  Obaid, Ahmed, 1983- editor. | R, Regin, 1985- editor. | Chinnusamy,
  Karthikeyan, 1973- editor.
Title: Recent developments in machine and human intelligence / edited by S.
  Suman Rajest, Bhopendra Singh, Ahmed Obaid, Regin R, Karthikeyan
  Chinnusamy.
Description: Hershey, PA : Engineering Science Reference, [2023] | Includes
  bibliographical references and index. | Summary: "For a long time,
  researchers in the fields of psychology and neuroscience have been
  interested in discovering ways to boost productivity in traditionally
  "healthy," "clinical," and "military" populations. However, one of the
  biggest challenges in reaching this objective is developing personalised
  performance phenotypes that can be used to build interventions that are
  specifically catered to each individual's needs. Impact: Thanks to AI's
  recent advancements, we can now create individualised training,
  preparation, and recovery plans that are tailored to each person's
  unique cognitive and biological profile. Concurrent AI advancements,
  especially in the psychological and neurological sciences, have
  demonstrated the importance of incorporating domain expertise and
  stakeholder inputs into the development of trustworthy AI. Value: This
  Patterns themed issue seeks original empirical work, literature reviews,
  and methodological papers that establish and validate precision
  artificial intelligence methods for human performance optimization, with
  a focus on modelling individual differences via state-of-the-art
  computational methods"-- Provided by publisher.
Identifiers: LCCN 2023011172 (print) | LCCN 2023011173 (ebook) | ISBN
  9781668491898 (h/c) | ISBN 9781668491904 (s/c) | ISBN 9781668491911
  (eISBN)
Subjects: LCSH: Knowledge, Theory of. | Intellect. | Artificial
  intelligence.
Classification: LCC BD143 .R43 2023 (print) | LCC BD143 (ebook) | DDC
  121--dc23/eng/20230509
LC record available at https://lccn.loc.gov/2023011172
LC ebook record available at https://lccn.loc.gov/2023011173

This book is published in the IGI Global book series Advances in Computational Intelligence and Robotics (ACIR) (ISSN: 2327-0411; eISSN: 2327-042X)

British Cataloguing in Publication Data
A Cataloguing in Publication record for this book is available from the British Library.

All work contributed to this book is new, previously-unpublished material. The views expressed in this book are those of the authors, but not necessarily of the publisher.

For electronic access to this publication, please contact: eresources@igi-global.com.

Advances in Computational Intelligence and Robotics (ACIR) Book Series

Ivan Giannoccaro
University of Salento, Italy

ISSN:2327-0411
EISSN:2327-042X

MISSION

While intelligence is traditionally a term applied to humans and human cognition, technology has progressed in such a way to allow for the development of intelligent systems able to simulate many human traits. With this new era of simulated and artificial intelligence, much research is needed in order to continue to advance the field and also to evaluate the ethical and societal concerns of the existence of artificial life and machine learning.

The **Advances in Computational Intelligence and Robotics (ACIR) Book Series** encourages scholarly discourse on all topics pertaining to evolutionary computing, artificial life, computational intelligence, machine learning, and robotics. ACIR presents the latest research being conducted on diverse topics in intelligence technologies with the goal of advancing knowledge and applications in this rapidly evolving field.

COVERAGE

- Fuzzy Systems
- Intelligent Control
- Machine Learning
- Agent technologies
- Cyborgs
- Brain Simulation
- Evolutionary Computing
- Pattern Recognition
- Heuristics
- Artificial Life

IGI Global is currently accepting manuscripts for publication within this series. To submit a proposal for a volume in this series, please contact our Acquisition Editors at Acquisitions@igi-global.com or visit: http://www.igi-global.com/publish/.

Titles in this Series

For a list of additional titles in this series, please visit: www.igi-global.com/book-series

Scalable and Distributed Machine Learning and Deep Learning Patterns
J. Joshua Thomas (UOW Malaysia KDU Penang University College, Malaysia) S. Harini (Vellore Institute of Technology, India) and V. Pattabiraman (Vellore Institute of Technology, India)
Engineering Science Reference • copyright 2023 • 286pp • H/C (ISBN: 9781668498040) • US $270.00 (our price)

Handbook of Research on Thrust Technologies' Effect on Image Processing
Binay Kumar Pandey (Department of Information Technology, College of Technology, Govind Ballabh Pant University of Agriculture and Technology, India) Digvijay Pandey (Department of Technical Education, Government of Uttar Pradesh, India) Rohit Anand (G.B. Pant DSEU Okhla-1 Campus, India & Government of NCT of Delhi, New Delhi, India) Deepak S. Mane (Performance Engineering Lab, Tata Research, Development, and Design Center, Australia) and Vinay Kumar Nassa (Rajarambapu Institute of Technology, India)
Engineering Science Reference • copyright 2023 • 542pp • H/C (ISBN: 9781668486184) • US $350.00 (our price)

Multi-Disciplinary Applications of Fog Computing Responsiveness in Real-Time
Debi Prasanna Acharjya (Vellore Institute of Technology, India) and Kauser Ahmed P. (Vellore Institute of Technology, India)
Engineering Science Reference • copyright 2023 • 280pp • H/C (ISBN: 9781668444665) • US $270.00 (our price)

Global Perspectives on Robotics and Autonomous Systems Development and Applications
Maki K. Habib (The American University in Cairo, Egypt)
Engineering Science Reference • copyright 2023 • 405pp • H/C (ISBN: 9781668477915) • US $360.00 (our price)

Stochastic Processes and Their Applications in Artificial Intelligence
Christo Ananth (Samarkand State University, Uzbekistan) N. Anbazhagan (Alagappa University, India) and Mark Goh (National University of Singapore, Singapore)
Engineering Science Reference • copyright 2023 • 220pp • H/C (ISBN: 9781668476796) • US $270.00 (our price)

Handbook of Research on Deep Learning Techniques for Cloud-Based Industrial IoT
P. Swarnalatha (Department of Information Security, School of Computer Science and Engineering, Vellore Institute of Technology, India) and S. Prabu (Department Banking Technology, Pondicherry University, India)
Engineering Science Reference • copyright 2023 • 432pp • H/C (ISBN: 9781668480984) • US $335.00 (our price)

Handbook of Research on AI-Based Technologies and Applications in the Era of the Metaverse

701 East Chocolate Avenue, Hershey, PA 17033, USA
Tel: 717-533-8845 x100 • Fax: 717-533-8661
E-Mail: cust@igi-global.com • www.igi-global.com

Table of Contents

Detailed Table of Contents

Chapter 1

    Ranjit Barua, Omdayal Group of Institutions, India
    Sudipto Datta, Indian Institute of Science, Bangalore, India

Medical technology powered by artificial intelligence is quickly developing into useful clinical practice solutions. Deep learning algorithms can handle the growing volumes of data produced by mobile monitoring sensors found in wearables, smartphones, and other medical devices. Currently, only a very limited number of clinical practice settings, such as the detection of atrial fibrillation, epilepsy seizures, and hypoglycemia, or the diagnosis of disease based on histopathological examination or medical imaging, benefit from the application of artificial intelligence. Patients have been waiting for the deployment of augmented medicine since it gives them more autonomy and more individualized care, but doctors have been resistant because they weren't ready for such a change in clinical practice. The purpose of this study is to glance over recent scientific material and offer a perspective on the advantages, potential benefits, and potential concerns of established artificial intelligence applications in the modern healthcare sector.

Chapter 2

    Pramod Madhavrao Kanjalkar, Vishwakarma Institute of Technology, India
    Jyoti Kanjalkar, Vishwakarma Institute of Technology, India
    Atharva Janaba Zagade, Vishwakarma Institute of Technology, India
    Vedhas Talnikar, Vishwakarma Institute of Technology, India

Identification of different plants, weeds, or any related type of vegetation is an important aspect of agricultural robotics and technologies. With the help of image processing and computer vision, multiple attempts have been made to achieve these results. These approaches made use of the shape and color of the leaf to identify a particular plant. But it can be observed that this approach has some limitations resulting in false positive and true negative errors. To overcome these limitations, the authors propose a novel approach of using Laplacian filter to extract veins morphology of leaves of a plant. This veins pattern is unique to every plant. With this Laplacian filter and data augmentation techniques, a unique dataset is developed on which a deep learning model can be trained. Based on this approach, the proposed system applies a deep learning algorithm called YOLO for plant identification. After preprocessing and YOLO training, the model is able to distinguish between plant and a weed successfully and create a bounding box for the detected type of plant.

    B. Judy Flavia, SRM Institute of Science and Technology, Ramapuram, India
    D. Pavan Kumar, SRM Institute of Science and Technology, Ramapuram, India
    R. Varun Teja, SRM Institute of Science and Technology, Ramapuram, India
    B. Lakshman, SRM Institute of Science and Technology, Ramapuram, India

Significant data privacy problems have been raised by adopting cloud computing, which has drawn much attention recently. Meanwhile, system security and cryptography offer a variety of security frameworks for protecting machine learning and maintaining privacy. Especially in the healthcare sector, cloud computing has drastically changed how we store and access data. Cloud computing has benefits but also increases the chance of data breaches and privacy abuses. Privacy protection is essential since using the cloud requires storing sensitive data on distant servers. Encrypting data and limiting access to only those with the necessary authorisation is one method to protect privacy. Data security is essential in the cloud to prevent unauthorised access, manipulation, and loss. Disaster recovery planning and routine backups are two methods we may use to maintain the previous data's security while using the BVK algorithm.

    Megha Middha, Chandigarh University, India
    Aseem Chandra Paliwal, Karnavati University, India

Almost all the sectors of the economy around the world were affected due to corona virus. Those confined in prisons were not able to reach out to courts for bail, or those who wanted to file suits found the courts closed due to lockdown. It was then that the courts decided to have hearings virtually. The chapter shall discuss how much these virtual courts have been successful in rendering justice during coronavirus. The chapter shall also try to explore if the process of rendering justice through virtual mode should continue post pandemic era also. The study shall lay emphasis upon how the criminal activities increased during the COVID-19 times and how the courts have been able to render justice in such scenarios. The chapter shall analyze the alternatives one can resort to through online mediation. The plight of migrant laborers who were left to visit their homes by foot were also denied justice. Henceforth, the research shall be based on primary data as well as secondary data available.

    N. S. Kshirsagar, Krishna Institute of Medical Sciences, India
    R. P. Patange, Krishna Institute of Medical Sciences, India

More than one million women aged 15 to 49 die annually as a result of difficulties arising during pregnancy or delivery. About half a million women lose their lives each year from complications during pregnancy, and many more have serious injuries. There are more severe outcomes for pregnant women for every maternal death that occurs. Despite international attention and efforts, poor nations continue to shoulder a disproportionate share of the load. About 19% of all maternal fatalities in these nations may be attributed to complications during labour. These risks may be greatly mitigated with vigilant monitoring for signs of aberrant development and measures to avoid a drawn-out labour process. Therefore, labour monitoring strategies are crucial for avoiding negative perinatal and maternal outcomes. To that end, using a partograph is a crucial and low-cost option. It's an easy-to-use technology that has been demonstrated to increase results when employed to monitor and control labour, and it costs very little to use.

Chapter 6

V. Vinitha, Jain University, India
R. Jayanthi, Jain University, India
S. Thirukumaran, Jain University, India
Ramchand Vedaiyan, Villa College, Maldives
G. Raja, KL Education Foundation, India

Sentiment analysis is a common technique in artificial intelligence and natural language processing. The automated assessment of consumer comments on services or products is becoming more prevalent. Multi-modal sentiment analysis has evolved as a fascinating study topic that evaluates and interprets sentiment expressions using several modalities, such as text, pictures, audio, and video. This technique enables a more thorough knowledge of human emotions by capturing the interaction of many modalities. The capacity to assess sentiment across various modalities has several advantages over unimodal techniques. Multi-modal sentiment analysis improves performance by combining text, images, audio, and video information. This allows it to catch complimentary and contextually relevant cues. Improving the performance of multi-modal sentiment analysis covers several processes, including sentiment polarity identification, multi-modal feature extraction, and fusion.

Chapter 7

R. Parvathi, Vellore Institute of Technology, Chennai, India
Savio Sajan Moloparambil, Vellore Institute of Technology, Chennai, India
Aswathi M. Kumar, Vellore Institute of Technology, Chennai, India
R. Jeyahari, Vellore Institute of Technology, Chennai, India

Automatic number plate recognition (ANPR) is a specialized image processing method that identifies the text on a given vehicle's number plate. The goal is to create a successful automatic approved vehicle identification system that makes use of the license plate. The system may be placed in many scenarios and locations, some of which may include security in prohibited areas like military and testing zones, or the vicinity of important government buildings like the Supreme Court, Parliament, etc. Using image segmentation in an image, the region containing the vehicle number plate from the image of a vehicle is extracted. Character recognition is achieved using an optical character recognition (OCR) approach in order to determine miscellaneous details like the owner of any detected vehicle, the location of registration, the address and whereabouts, etc.

Chapter 8

S. Patil Nitin, Krishna Institute of Medical Sciences, India
Paresh Patil, Krishna Vishwa Vidyapeeth, India

Tissue injury, infection, or cardiac infarction may all lead to inflammation. The restoration of normal anatomy to the joint surface and the preservation of mechanical alignment are two of the primary objectives of treatment. Ankle and subtalar range of motion must be protected and improved upon, and correct length and rotation must be maintained. Inflammation can be caused by either infectious or non-infectious triggers. When a tissue is damaged, our bodies send out a series of chemical signals to trigger reactions that promote tissue repair. All of these cues stimulate circulating leukocytes to chemotactically migrate to the site of injury. As a result of being activated, leukocytes release cytokines, which set off other inflammatory processes in the body. Inflammatory disorders can be treated with a wide variety of medications nowadays.

Chapter 9

Blood malignancies and various blood disorders can have an impact on a person. It is a major health issue in all age groups. A blood disorder, such as influence platelets, blood plasma, and white and red blood cells, can impact any of the four primary blood components. The primary goal of this chapter is to detect the cancer blood disorder. This paved the way to propose a comparative study with previous studies based on convolutional neural networks in this work. The authors propose a model for cancer blood disorder detection. It consists of five steps. The blood sample image data set is collected from the Kaggle. First, the data set is transferred for image preprocessing to remove the noise from the images. Next, it is applied to the image enhancement for clarity; the image and segmentation are performed on enhanced images. Next, feature selection is used to extract the features from the segmentation images. The convolutional neural network technique is used for classification finally.

Chapter 10

The Earth's surface has changed significantly as a result of human activity on the land expanding agriculture and population. To fulfil the growing demand for fundamental human necessities and wellbeing, it is crucial to have correct information on land use and land cover (LULC) and the best methods of using it. Large geographic regions can be found in sufficient detail in satellite photos, both qualitatively and quantitatively. The most effective methods for detecting together static and dynamic biophysical modules on the Earth's surface, which are regularly introduced for mapping LULC, are satellite depending remote sensing (RS) methods. In order to classify RS images into change/nochange classes, image pre-processing is done in this study, and the information content of the satellite images is assessed. In this work, a change detection method for identifying land cover and water bodies is proposed utilizing a stacked ensemble classifier with mean weight residual neural network (MWResNet) and entropy.

Chapter 11

Jyoti P. Kanjalkar, Vishwakarma Institute of Technology, India
Rutuja Shinde, Vishwakarma Institute of Technology, India
Tanmay Sharma, Vishwakarma Institute of Technology, India
Abhishek Tyade, Vishwakarma Institute of Technology, India
Uma Thakur, Vishwakarma Institute of Technology, India
Pramod Kanjalkar, Vishwakarma Institute of Technology, India

In 2021–2022, 5.57 crore students are expected to enroll in higher education in India, and every year, there will be close to 9 million graduates. According to estimates, there are 0.5 cases of this type of blindness per 1,000 people in India. Many children are blind or have severe visual impairment (SVI) or blindness (BL). Dealing with sight loss or low vision is just one of the difficulties that the visually impaired face in everyday life. There are many challenges in their daily life such as navigating around places, most of the information is inaccessible, finding reading material, etc. They are also facing many challenges in their educational careers as well. If any blind student has graduated and he/she wants to maintain all the original certificates, then it becomes tiresome to track these certificates and manually verify their legitimacy for them. Also, everything needs to be digitized with the principles of confidentiality, reliability, and availability in order to make the data more secure and safe.

Chapter 12

Di Wang, University of Illinois at Chicago, USA

Artificial intelligence faces a considerable challenge in automated reasoning, particularly in inferring missing data from existing observations. Knowledge graph (KG) reasoning can significantly enhance the performance of context-aware AI systems such as GPT. Deep reinforcement learning (DRL), an influential framework for sequential decision-making, exhibits strength in managing uncertain and dynamic environments. Definitions of state space, action space, and reward function in DRL directly dictate the performances. This chapter provides an overview of the pipeline and advantages of leveraging DRL for knowledge graph reasoning. It delves deep into the challenges of KG reasoning and features of existing studies. This chapter offers a comparative study of widely used state spaces, action spaces, reward functions, and neural networks. Furthermore, it evaluates the pros and cons of DRL-based methodologies and compares the performances of nine benchmark models across six unique datasets and four evaluation metrics.

Chapter 13

S. S. Vhawal, Krishna Institute of Medical Sciences, India
Bahulekar Ashitosh, Krishna Vishwa Vidyapeeth, India

In order to minimise negative perinatal outcomes, good clinical management is essential for the time of the delivery. Regular ultrasound tests using the cerebro-placental ratio and Doppler technology are examples of in utero monitoring (CPR). The pulsatility index (PI) of the MCA is divided by the UA's PI to arrive at the cardiac output rate (CPR). The umbilical artery (UA) and the middle cerebral artery (MCA) are used as indicators of placental function and foetal adjustment to placental insufficiency, respectively. It has been shown that unfavourable outcomes for neonates are linked to reduced CPR, which is an indicator of cerebral redistribution. Doppler is a safe and painless way to assess foetoplacental circulation in pregnant women. It aids in the treatment of high-risk pregnancies because of the useful information it provides regarding the foetus's hemodynamic state. Neonatal morbidity includes conditions such as birth asphyxia and low blood sugar.

Chapter 14

Shradha Vidyadhar Naik, Krishna Institute of Medical Sciences, India
V. M. Joshi, Krishna Institute of Medical Sciences, India

The use of opioids is linked to impaired gastrointestinal motility. In order to prevent postoperative ileus, opioid use should be kept to a minimum and alternative medications should be used in its place. One issue is the absence of a consistent criteria for the risk of postoperative urine retention. Opioid usage, however, is unquestionably a significant risk factor. Even though the processes are only poorly understood, efforts that reduce the use of opioids have been proven to reduce its incidence. The issue of postoperative shivering has finally, at least in part, been resolved by avoiding large opioid doses and using alpha-2 agonists. It has recently been questioned whether opioids should be used routinely during surgery, especially in cases where patients are fat. The need of opioids may be decreased by using alpha-2 agonists, which have a strong analgesic effect. The CNS and peripheral alpha-2 adrenergic receptors are bound by alpha-2 agonists. By preventing the central sympathetic outflow, they lower blood pressure.

Chapter 15

Pankaj Dwivedi, Jaypee University of Engineering and Technology, India
Dilip Kumar Sharma, Jaypee University of Engineering and Technology, India

This chapter's major goal is to examine the issue of real-world recognition to enhance species preservation. As it is a popular topic and a crucial one, the authors focus on identifying plant species. The examples are scanned specimens in traditional plant species identification, and the setting is plain. Real-world species recognition, on the other hand, is more difficult. They begin by looking at realistic species recognition and how it differs from traditional plant species recognition. Interdisciplinary teamwork based on the newest breakthroughs in technology and computer science is provided to cope with the difficult challenge. In this research, they offer a unique framework for deep learning as well as an effective data augmentation strategy. They crop the image before everyone is aware in terms of visual attention. Furthermore, they use it as a data augmentation technique. Attention cropping (AC) is the name given to a revolutionary data augmentation technique. To predict species from a significant quantity of information, fully convolutional neural networks (CNN) are constructed.

Chapter 16

Murat Şengöz, Independent Researcher, Turkey

The military command and control process refers to a process of the methods and principles to be followed in order to fulfill military missions or achieve an objective. The main components of this process are the information that has been analyzed and gathered concerning the description, classification, and evaluation of parameters and variables related to the enemy, air and land, in proportion to the available resources. This study examines the algorithms needed for strategic, operative, and tactical-level units, and the usability of algorithms produced by artificial intelligence-supported techniques such as machine learning and deep learning in military command and control processes in a way to adapt to the modern warfare environment, which requires speed, tempo, and flexibility. So, in this study, an explanation was made about the nature of the algorithms required for military command and control and preparation of the operational environment as a component, and suggestions were made for subsequent research.

Chapter 17

M. A. Balasubramani, Bharath Institute of Higher Education and Research, India
R. Venkatakrishnaiah, Bharath Institute of Higher Education and Research, India
K. V. B. Raju, Bharath Institute of Higher Education and Research, India

Numerous earth retaining and earth-supported buildings have been built during the last three decades using geogrid as reinforcement. In more recent times, it has been used to reinforce railroad sleepers in order to improve their structural integrity and use. Before conducting the experimental study on the strain and temperature sensing capabilities of the smart geogrid, a general explanation of the manufacturing process for the FBG integrated smart geogrid was provided. It has now been developed to employ an external sensor to provide a reference displacement for the Harris Hawk optimization (HHO) recommended to find the appropriate weighted coefficient in order to calibrate the reconstructed deformation. The geosynthetic-encased stone column (ESC) is a frequent ground improvement approach because of the current site circumstances (low shear strength) and the need to finish the project within the allotted time.

Chapter 18

R. Regin, SRM Institute of Science and Technology, Ramapuram, India
A. Aakash Khanna, SRM Institute of Science and Technology, Ramapuram, India
Vamsi Krishnan, SRM Institute of Science and Technology, Ramapuram, India
Muskan Gupta, SRM Institute of Science and Technology, Ramapuram, India
S. Rubin Bose, SRM Institute of Science and Technology, Ramapuram, India
S. Suman Rajest, Dhaanish Ahmed College of Engineering, India

In response to the safety concerns surrounding the IoT, an attribute-based encryption and access control scheme (ABE-ACS) has been proposed. This scheme can be more effectively implemented through the use of cutting-edge technology and incorporating attribute-based encryption (ABE) and attribute-based access control (ABAC) models with features as the point of origin. Facing Edge-IoT is a heterogeneous network made up of certain nodes with more powerful computers and the majority of resource-constrained IoT devices. The authors provide a lightweight with an upgrade to the proof-of-work consensus to address the issues of excessive resource consumption and challenging deployment of existing platforms. To protect the confidentiality of the access control policies, the limits of the tree are utilised for transformation and allocation stored. Six smart contracts are created for devices and data to implement the ABAC and punishment mechanism, which outsources ABE to edge nodes for privacy and integrity. Thus, the plan implements device-controlled access and Edge-IoT privacy protection for data.

Chapter 19

C. Patil Shilpa, Krishna Institute of Medical Sciences, India
Makarand B. Mane, Krishna Vishwa Vidyapeeth, India

Hepatic steatosis is defined as the accumulation of fat in hepatocytes, making up more than 5% of the total weight of the liver. The global incidence of obesity and the incidence of steatosis of the liver is increasing simultaneously, which represents the commonest cause of liver disease. In addition to obesity, this liver disease is also closely related to a wide range of metabolic comorbidities such as dyslipidemia, type 2 diabetes, and high blood pressure. Patients with metabolic syndrome (MetS) have a high association with NAFLD (non-alcoholic fatty liver disease). Patients with NAFLD are at greater risk to develop fibrosis/cirrhosis and hepatocellular carcinoma (HCC) which causes great morbidity. The most common form of chronic liver disease worldwide by far is NAFLD. It is estimated that around one-third of the adult population in industrialized nations is affected by it. NAFLD is an asymptomatic condition, reaching advanced stages even before being suspected or diagnosed.

Chapter 20

S. G. Lavand, Krishna Institute of Medical Sciences, India
Shailesh B. Patil, Krishna Institute of Medical Sciences, India

As the rate of preterm births continues to rise, a thorough neurological examination of newborns born too soon is more crucial than ever. As a result of advancements in NICU technology, the survival rate of babies with extremely low birth weight has also increased. There is a higher chance of neurological abnormalities occurring in the survivors. Premature infants have an increased risk of developing neurological impairments, and about 10% of these infants will go on to have substantial learning problems, motor developmental disabilities, cerebral palsy, seizures, or mental retardation. White matter injury, germinal matrix haemorrhage, intraventricular haemorrhage, periventricular leucomalacia, cerebellar haemorrhage and atrophy, and periventricular leucomalacia are all examples of brain injuries that may develop from secondary hemodynamic disturbances. Timely detection of intracranial abnormalities is critical for improving neonates' health and lowering their risk of death or disability later on.

Chapter 21

Kasi Uday Kiran, Koneru Lakshmaiah Education Foundation, India
Sandeep Dwarkanath Pande, Madras Institute of Technology, India
P. Poorna Priya, DIET College, India
K. Kalki Sai, Koneru Lakshmaiah Education Foundation, India
Nandigama Apoorva, Koneru Lakshmaiah Education Foundation, India
M. Geethika, Koneru Lakshmaiah Education Foundation, India
Sk Hasane Ahammad, Koneru Lakshmaiah Education Foundation, India

According to numerous statistics, it can be inferred that the rate of violence using firearms and dangerous weapons is rising annually, making it difficult for law enforcement organizations to address this problem promptly. There are several locations where there are high rates of crime with firearms or knives, particularly in areas with lax gun restrictions. For the security of citizens, the early identification of violent crime is crucial. We see a lot of crimes and attacks on public transportation these days. Different ways have been developed to hide the weapons to launch savage attacks on the unwary population. These criminals' primary goals are to manipulate people and harm public property. All these things only occur as a result of weapons and other dangerous items being readily transported into buses and trains. To protect the public and its assets, it is important to create and implement highly effective technologies across the nation. By spotting the existence of deadly weapons like knives and firearms, these situations can be avoided.

Preface

The future of Intelligence is being questioned as there is growing unease concerning the most recent Artificial Intelligence (AI) wave embodied in machine learning. This is not to fully discount the importance of machine learning. People shouldn't have too high of expectations from so-called Artificial Intelligence, which is intended to create intelligent automation. The following four fields, physics, knowledge, mental processes, and social science, frequently exhibit various things and objects of facts, appraisal, and occasional obligation. In contrast, the human-machine hybrid's data input, justification, and decision-making processes may not alter much, whereas the method for dealing with significance and understanding comprehension is more adaptable. Existing artificial Intelligence only addresses a small portion of the automation problem, which is significantly less than the predicted level of Intelligence. It is just formalized empirical calculation without conscious value calculation. This is true because automation and computational intelligence only address the input, processing, and output issues external to the system; they do not address more significant internal data, processing, and output issues. This book examines the intriguing but contentious interplay between machine and human Intelligence.

The media frequently discusses human Intelligence as a formless intellect that could exist without a conscious mind, an unconscious mind, or thoughts. This short book explores the situations in which robots can replace people. It shows that strong artificial Intelligence may present serious problems because it operates outside of direct human control, opening the door for various extrapolations, such as inserting chips made from silicon in the brains of a fortunate caste. It also highlights the wide gap between advocates of strong human Intelligence and those who oppose it. It helps readers comprehend and carry on this open discussion on human Intelligence, which poses practical ethical issues for which meaningful solutions are still in their infancy. It draws on mathematics, cognitive neuroscience, and philosophy concepts. Critics will point out that psychometric exams have significant flaws. Individual variations in performance on a psychometric exam don't reveal anything about many very interesting topics. An intellect quotient cannot describe creativity and other types of speciality expertise.

An intelligence quotient test is merely an attempt to evaluate a person's capacity for success in the modern world, and individual results are only somewhat predictive of future achievement. The validity of human intelligence tests was not given much concern in the early days of psychologists; instead, those in positions of social influence and those of prominence attempted to justify their positions of influence. While knowledge is the input of uncertainty, unprogrammable interpreting, and the output of uncertainty, automation is the input of determinism, configurable manufacturing, and determined output; machine learning is the input of partial determinism, configurable manufacturing, and partial deterministic output; and automation is automation. Artificial Intelligence differs from Intelligence in that the former is a function while the latter is an aptitude category. Many individuals assume that human intelligence function will enable ability, not function, to reach the goal of intelligent ability. This is the discrepancy between the ideal and the real world, and it is also the reason why people are disappointed when they mistake function for ability.

ORGANIZATION OF THE BOOK

The book is organized into 21 chapters. A brief description of each of the chapters follows:

Chapter 1 involves artificial intelligence-powered medical technology, rapidly becoming a clinical practise solution. Wearable, smartphone, and medical device mobile monitoring sensors generate large amounts of data that deep learning systems can handle. Only a few clinical practise situations, such as detecting atrial fibrillation, epileptic seizures, and hypoglycemia or diagnosing disease based on histological investigation or medical imaging, benefit from AI. Augmented medicine gives patients more autonomy and tailored care, so they've been waiting for it. Doctors were unprepared for such a clinical practise change, and they resisted. This paper reviews recent scientific literature and discusses AI applications' pros, cons, and potential issues in modern healthcare.

Chapter 2 identifies agricultural robotics and technologies that must accurately recognize plants, weeds, and vegetation. Plant identification uses image processing and computer vision, which often use leaf shape and colour. Unfortunately, these methods may produce false positives and real negatives. We present a unique Laplacian filter approach for extracting plant leaf vein forms to tackle these issues. This work creates a unique dataset using Laplacian filters and data augmentation. The dataset trains deep learning models. Our plant identification algorithm is YOLO (You Only Look Once). Pre-processing and YOLO training help the model distinguish plants from weeds and provide bounding boxes for plant categories. Our study provides promising solutions to standard plant identification systems' shortcomings. Vein patterns as discriminative traits increase plant categorization accuracy and reduce errors. Our method could be used in crop management, weed control, and precision agriculture. Thus, our study introduces a new plant identification approach to cover a gap in current methods. Laplacian filters and deep learning models will boost agricultural automation and efficiency.

Chapter 3 has highlighted serious data privacy concerns. Systems security and cryptography provide many frameworks for machine learning and privacy protection. Cloud computing has transformed data storage and access, especially in healthcare. Cloud computing has benefits but promotes data breaches and privacy violations. Cloud storage requires privacy protection since sensitive data is stored on remote servers. Encrypting data and restricting access to authorized users protects privacy. The cloud requires data security to prevent illegal access, modification, and loss. Disaster recovery planning and frequent backups can help secure earlier data using the BVK Algorithm. When users log in to the website using their current security or mobile number, the BVK Algorithm will backup data to protect patient and doctor history.

Chapter 4 discusses how coronavirus affects almost all economic sectors worldwide. Prisoners could not request bail, and those who wished to sue found the courts unavailable due to lockdown. The courts then agreed to hold virtual hearings. The paper will describe how virtual courts administered justice during the Coronavirus. The paper will also examine whether virtual justice should continue post-pandemic. The investigation will highlight how COVID-19 boosted crime and how courts have handled it. The paper will examine online mediation possibilities. Migrant labour forced to walk home were also denied justice. From now on, research will use primary and secondary data, statutes, and case laws. The researcher will analyze and describe the justice process to find ways to enhance it.

Chapter 5 reviews over one million 15-49-year-old women who die annually from pregnancy or childbirth complications. Pregnancy problems kill half a million women and injure many more. Pregnant women suffer more with every maternal death. Despite international efforts, poor nations bear a disproportionate burden. Labor difficulties account for 19% of maternal deaths in these nations. These hazards can be reduced by screening for abnormal development and avoiding lengthy labour. Thus, labour monitoring is essential to prevent neonatal and maternal harm. To that purpose, a partograph is essential and affordable. This inexpensive, easy-to-use tool has been shown to improve labour monitoring and control results. One sheet of paper lets you record all your professional experience. The velocity of cervical dilatation, presenting portion descent, uterine contraction pattern and strength are recorded. The mother's body temperature, heart rate, blood pressure, and urinalysis are monitored in the third segment.

Chapter 6 introduces natural language processing and AI use of sentiment analysis. Consumer feedback on products and services is increasingly computerized. Multi-modal sentiment analysis, which analyses and interprets sentiment expressions in text, images, audio, and video, is an interesting research area. This method captures multimodality interactions to better understand human emotions. Sentiment assessment across modalities provides significant advantages over unimodal methods. Multi-modal sentiment analysis improves performance by mixing text, images, voice, and video. This lets it catch complementary and contextual cues. Multi-modal sentiment analysis performance improvement includes sentiment polarity identification, feature extraction, and fusion. This chapter covers multi-modal sentiment analysis, including modalities, fusion categories, and novel datasets, as well as its problems and potential uses.

Chapter 7 predicts Automatic Number Plate Recognition (ANPR) uses image processing to identify car number plates. An effective licence plate-based automatic vehicle recognition system is expanded. The gadget can be used for security in banned places like the army, testing sites, and areas near important government buildings like the High Court, Parliament, etc. The vehicle's registration plate is segmented from an image. OCR is used to recognize characters. To identify recognized vehicles and locate the registration facility, among other things. The experiment uses two datasets. Large, dependable ANPR datasets that train cutting-edge models are secret and rarely made public. The second set is an arbitrary 100 Kaggle images, most of which are vehicle shots from different angles and perspectives to challenge OCR algorithms. Implementation considers datasets with ten and 100 photos. Tesseract in English gives ten photos with 10% accuracy and 100 images with 20% accuracy. PaddleOCR achieves 30% accuracy with ten photos and 80% accuracy for 100. Even with larger images, PaddleOCR output is more accurate.

Chapter 8 explains tissue injury, infection, and myocardial infarction can cause inflammation. The main goals of treatment are joint surface anatomy restoration and mechanical alignment preservation. Protect and improve ankle and subtalar range of motion and preserve optimal length and rotation. Infectious or non-infectious factors can cause inflammation. Chemical signals from our bodies stimulate tissue restoration when a tissue is injured. These stimuli cause chemotactic leukocyte migration to the damaged site. Leukocytes release cytokines when stimulated, triggering other inflammatory processes. Inflammatory illnesses are treated with many drugs nowadays. Anti-inflammatory drugs (NSAIDs) are effective. Due to serious adverse effects, their use is limited. Since this is the case, researchers are continually searching for better, safer anti-inflammatory medications.

Chapter 9 is about blood problems, and malignancies can affect a person. This is a big health issue for all ages. A blood ailment can affect platelets, plasma, white and red blood cells, and any of the four basic blood components. This paper aims to detect cancer blood problems. This allowed this effort to present a convolutional neural network comparison with earlier studies. We must propose a cancer blood disorder detecting methodology. The process has five steps. The Kaggle blood sample image data is obtained. First, the data set is transferred for picture pre-processing to reduce noise. Next, improve photographs for clarity and segment them. Next, feature selection extracts segmentation image features. The final classification method is the convolutional neural network. This study found that CNN outperforms alternative neural network models and machine learning techniques.

Chapter 10 develops how the Earth's surface has changed dramatically due to agriculture and population growth. The growing need for basic human needs and well-being requires accurate land use and land cover (LULC) information and best practises. Qualitative and quantitative satellite pictures detail large regions. Satellite-dependent remote sensing (RS) technologies are best for detecting static and dynamic biophysical modules on the Earth's surface for mapping LULC. This work uses picture pre-processing and satellite image information content to categorize RS images as change/no change. This study offers a stacked ensemble classifier with Mean Weight Residual Neural Network (MWResNet) and Entropy Parameter Optimization - Deep Belief Network to detect land cover and water body changes (EPO-DBN). This method detects water and land cover changes in three phases. MWResNet architecture for land cover classification with WLFCM segmentation is described first. Second, EPO-DBN uses multi-scale segmentation to classify land cover images. Finally, image differencing optimizes multi-scale segmentation parameters to describe the water body and land cover in Multi-scale Cat Swarm Optimisation (MCSO). The effect of textural and morphological variables on the accuracy of the Kaggle database change-detection technique using ensemble classification is compared to well-known classifiers. The approach performed well with 96.69 percent sensitivity, 96.67 percent specificity, 96.66 percent accuracy, and a 0.033 mean error rate. The approach is implemented in MATLAB.

Chapter 11 shows recently, 5.57 crore students are scheduled to enrol in higher education in India, and about 9 million will graduate annually. Indian statistics show 0.5 incidences of this type of blindness per 1,000 individuals; many youngsters are blind or have severe visual impairment (SVI) (BL). Low vision is one of the challenges the visually handicapped confront daily. They face daily problems, such as navigating, accessing information, and locating reading material. Their education also presents various obstacles. Blind graduates who want to save their original certificates find tracking and physically validating them tedious. To protect data, everything must be digitized with Confidentiality, Reliability, and Availability. This study addresses all these difficulties with blockchain technology. Our system generates and validates certificates. Each certificate will contain a hash key that businesses may use to validate its authenticity using the proposed system. The certificate is converted to Braille for blind persons to read. Blockchain reduces the risk of students losing or deleting certificates and simplifies and secures certificate validation.

Chapter 12 discusses how Artificial Intelligence faces a considerable challenge in automated reasoning, particularly inferring missing data from existing observations. Knowledge Graph (KG) reasoning can significantly enhance the performance of context-aware AI systems such as GPT. Deep Reinforcement Learning (DRL), an influential framework for sequential decision-making, exhibits strength in managing uncertain and dynamic environments. Definitions of state space, action space, and reward function in DRL directly dictate the performances. This chapter overviews the pipeline and advantages of leveraging DRL for knowledge graph reasoning. It delves deep into the challenges of KG reasoning and features of existing studies. Besides, this chapter offers a comparative study of widely used state spaces, action spaces, reward functions, and neural networks. Furthermore, it evaluates the pros and cons of DRL-based methodologies and compares the performances of nine benchmark models across six unique datasets and four evaluation metrics.

Chapter 13 detects good clinical treatment at delivery reduces perinatal outcomes. Regular cerebro-placental ratio and Doppler ultrasounds are in-utero monitoring (CPR). The cardiac output rate equals the MCA's pulsatility index (PI) divided by the UA's (CPR). The umbilical (UA) and middle cerebral artery (MCA) indicate placental function and foetal response to insufficiency. Reduced CPR, indicating cerebral redistribution, is connected to poor neonatal outcomes. Pregnant women can assess fetal-placental circulation safely and painlessly with Doppler. It helps treat high-risk pregnancies by providing hemo-dynamic information on the foetus. Asphyxia, low blood sugar, low body temperature, premature birth, high-risk caesarean sections, and NICU hospitalization are neonatal morbidities. Also, adult physical and brain growth may be hindered.

Chapter 14 analyzes how opioids inhibit gastrointestinal motility. Reduce opioid use and use other treatments to prevent postoperative ileus. Lack of consistent postoperative urine retention risk criteria is an issue. Opioids are a major risk factor. Opioid reduction has been shown to lessen its usage, even if the procedures are poorly understood. Avoiding excessive opioid doses and employing alpha-2 agonists has helped reduce postoperative shivering. Some dispute whether opioids should be routinely administered during surgery, especially in obese patients. Alpha-2 agonists, which are potent analgesics, can reduce opioid use. Alpha-2 agonists bind CNS and peripheral receptors. They lower blood pressure, heart rate, and anaesthetic and analgesic effects by blocking central sympathetic outflow. Alpha-2 agonists soothe, but recovery is shorter than opioids.

Chapter 15 focuses on real-world recognition to preserve species. As a popular and important topic, we identify plant species. The basic setting and scanned specimens are for traditional plant species identification. Real-world species recognition is harder. How does realistic species recognition vary from standard plant species recognition? Aims: Interdisciplinary teamwork using the latest technology and computer science discoveries solves complex problems. This study presents a novel deep-learning framework and data augmentation method. We crop the image before visual attention is drawn. We also utilize it to enrich data. An innovative data augmentation method is attention cropping (AC). Fully convolutional neural networks (CNN) predict species from large amounts of data. We extensively tested our technique on the standard and tailored datasets for real-world recognition. The initial experiments show that our method yields cutting-edge outcomes on numerous datasets. The AC data augmentation approach is also evaluated. Results indicate air conditioning outperforms alternative methods. Shannon's information measures leaf data and calculates for more accurate findings. AC operations are far more precise than non-AC procedures.

Chapter 16 discusses the military command and control process, which refers to the methods and principles to fulfil military missions or achieve objectives. The main components of this process are the information that has been analyzed and gathered concerning the description, classification and evaluation of parameters and variables related to the enemy, air and land, in proportion to the available resources. This study examines the algorithms needed for strategic, operative and tactical-level units and the us-ability of algorithms produced by artificial intelligence-supported techniques such as machine learning and deep learning in military command and control processes in a way to adapt to the modern warfare environment, which requires speed, tempo and flexibility. So, in this study, an explanation was made about the nature of the algorithms required for military command and control and preparation of the operational environment as a component, and suggestions were made for subsequent research.

Chapter 17 addresses Geogrid, which has reinforced several earth-retaining and earth-supported buildings in the last 30 years. Recent use has reinforced railroad sleepers to improve their structural integrity and use. The FBG-integrated smart geogrid's manufacturing process was explained briefly before the strain and temperature monitoring experiment. It uses an external sensor to provide a reference displacement for Harris Hawk Optimization (HHO) to discover the right weighted coefficient to calibrate the reconstructed deformation. The geosynthetic-encased stone column (ESC) is a common ground improvement method due to the site's low shear strength and the requirement to accomplish the project on time. Field tests, including in-depth ground soil testing, provided data for optimization models. The base isolator's inadequate sand-based Geogrid-reinforced soil foundation feeds an HHO algorithm that controls pressure. A geogrid-reinforced soil structure's bearing capacity, stiffness, and pressure were calculated numerically. The approach is implemented in MATLAB. The numerical findings reveal that improving bad soil effects significantly affects optimal geogrid-reinforced soil foundation properties. Finding the best geogrid-reinforced soil foundation qualities reduces settlement and pressure.

Chapter 18 shows IoT safety concerns have led to attribute-based encryption and access control (ABE-ACS). Cutting-edge technology, attribute-based encryption (ABE), and access control (ABAC) models employing characteristics as the point of origin can improve this technique. Facing Edge IoT includes most resource-constrained devices and strong computer nodes. Our lightweight proof-of-work consensus upgrade addresses the high resource consumption and challenging deployment of earlier platforms. Transformation and allocation storage use tree restrictions to protect access control policy confidentiality. Six smart contracts for devices and data outsource ABE to edge nodes for privacy and integrity with ABAC and penalty mechanisms. We protect data via edge-IoT privacy and device-controlled access. The provided approach is secure, and experimental results show that our LBC has faster throughput and less resource use. The encryption and decryption costs of our method are good. Administrators can protect important resources with northbound interface authentication and granular access control. Decentralized access control for each request and stringent policy enforcement may monitor network applications and prevent privileged behaviour or security policy conflicts in the proposed system. Our three modules Attribute Management, Smart Contract Layer, and BlockChain Generation create a prototype of this architecture to test its security implications and performance in typical usage scenarios. ABAC manages information system attributes like attribute-based access control. The smart contract layer controls access, enforces access rules, judges, punishes, or executes object access control, and preserves subject and object attributes. Blockchain allows all users to verify transactions and interactions between nodes without untrustworthy parties.

Chapter 19 classifies hepatic steatosis develops when liver fat exceeds 5%. The global obesity epidemic is increasing steatosis, the most frequent liver condition. Most liver diseases are caused by steatosis. Overweight, dyslipidemia, type 2 diabetes, and hypertension are associated with this liver disease. Metabolic syndrome increases the risk of NAFLD (MetS). Patients with NAFLD are more likely to develop two severe morbidities: fibrosis, cirrhosis, or HCC. NAFLD is the most common chronic liver disease worldwide. One-third of adults in wealthy countries are estimated to be affected. Because NAFLD has no symptoms, the disease often progresses before being diagnosed.

Chapter 20 discusses how preterm deliveries are rising, making neurological exams of premature babies more important than ever. NICU technology has improved the survival percentage of extremely low birth weight newborns. Survivors have an increased risk of neurological problems. About 10% of premature infants will experience learning issues, motor developmental disabilities, cerebral palsy, seizures, or mental retardation. Brain injuries caused by subsequent hemodynamic disturbances include white matter injury, germinal matrix haemorrhage, intraventricular haemorrhage, periventricular leucomalacia, cerebellar haemorrhage, and atrophy. Early intracranial abnormality identification improves infant health and reduces death and impairment. Due to its non-invasive nature, brain sonography is vital for screening and managing high-risk premature babies. Ultrasound equipment can check NICU infants at their parents' bedside in minutes. X-rays, CTs, and brain MRIs can examine newborns.

Chapter 21 shows how numerous figures show that firearm and dangerous weapon violence is rising annually, making it difficult for law enforcement to handle this issue quickly. Firearm and knife crime rates are high in places with permissive gun laws. Early violent crime detection is vital to public safety. Many crimes and attacks occur on public transit today. Different methods have been developed to hide firearms and attack the unwary. These crooks aim to influence people and damage property. Because firearms and other dangerous goods are easily transported on buses and trains, these things only happen. Developing and implementing effective technology nationwide protects the public and its assets. Detecting knives and firearms can prevent these situations. The project mainly aims to find firearms or other risky items in a vehicle.

S. Suman Rajest
Dhaanish Ahmed College of Engineering, India

Bhopendra Singh
Amity University, Dubai, UAE

Ahmed J. Obaid
University of Kufa, Iraq

R. Regin
SRM Institute of Science and Technology, Ramapuram, India

Karthikeyan Chinnusamy
Veritas, USA

Chapter 1
Artificial Intelligence in Modern Medical Science:
A Promising Practice

Ranjit Barua
https://orcid.org/0000-0003-2236-3876
Omdayal Group of Institutions, India

Sudipto Datta
https://orcid.org/0000-0003-2161-6878
Indian Institute of Science, Bangalore, India

ABSTRACT

Medical technology powered by artificial intelligence is quickly developing into useful clinical practice solutions. Deep learning algorithms can handle the growing volumes of data produced by mobile monitoring sensors found in wearables, smartphones, and other medical devices. Currently, only a very limited number of clinical practice settings, such as the detection of atrial fibrillation, epilepsy seizures, and hypoglycemia, or the diagnosis of disease based on histopathological examination or medical imaging, benefit from the application of artificial intelligence. Patients have been waiting for the deployment of augmented medicine since it gives them more autonomy and more individualized care, but doctors have been resistant because they weren't ready for such a change in clinical practice. The purpose of this study is to glance over recent scientific material and offer a perspective on the advantages, potential benefits, and potential concerns of established artificial intelligence applications in the modern healthcare sector.

1. INTRODUCTION

The core of evidence-based medicine is using historical data to inform current treatment decisions (Buch et al., 2018). By characterizing data patterns as mathematical equations, statistical methods have traditionally handled this issue. For instance, linear regression offers a "line of best fit." AI offers methods for 'machine learning' (ML) that reveal complicated correlations that are difficult to sum up in an

DOI: 10.4018/978-1-6684-9189-8.ch001

equation (Datta et al., 2019). In a manner analogous to the human brain, neural networks, for instance, encode data using a massive number of interconnected neurons. As a result, ML systems can approach difficult problem solving in the same way that a doctor could by carefully analyzing the available data and drawing valid judgments (Barua et al., 2023). These systems, as opposed to a single physician, may observe and process a virtually infinite amount of inputs concurrently. These algorithms can also learn from each incremental case and can be exposed to more cases in a short period of time than a physician could ever view in their whole career (Barua et al., 2022). This explains how an AI-driven tool can diagnose suspicious skin lesions more accurately than dermatologists' can (Esteva et al., 2017), or why AI is trusted to handle jobs where specialists frequently disagree, such categorizing pulmonary tuberculosis on chest radiographs (Lakhani et al., 2017). Despite the fact that AI is a broad area, this article only focuses on ML approaches due to their widespread use in significant biomedical and clinical applications (Barua et al., 2022). The most widespread applications of AI and ML in medicine have been in the disciplines of radiology, dermatology, cardiology, and mental health (Sabry et al., 2022). Figure 1 shows the AI used in various modern healthcare system. Given their effectiveness in certain domains of medicine, where they can occasionally surpass human doctors, AI and ML are attracting more and more attention (Barua et al., 2022).

In comparison to other medical specialties, the application of AI and ML in the orthopedic profession is still in its early stages. For AI and ML to be broadly adopted in orthopedics, more experimental research as well as structured research frameworks like cohort studies and randomized controlled trials are still required. ML makes use of statistical techniques and computer algorithms to find intricate patterns and trends in data that are otherwise indistinguishable to humans. With the help of covariate-linking models that relate covariates to a target variable of interest and models that explain a system's behavior, ML may "learn" patterns from data (Barua et al., 2022). In the realm of medicine, ML may gather information from imaging and laboratory testing, as well as electronic medical records, to assist doctors in making decisions that are more effective and fruitful (Groot et al., 2022). Depending on the objective, supervised learning and unsupervised learning are the two broad categories of ML that are typically used in medicine (Saravi et al., 2022). The main goals of supervised learning are estimating an unknown parameter and selecting a subgroup to characterize a new instance of data (Saravi et al., 2022). For instance, how a specific pattern on an EKG is related to a group of diseases, or how a lung nodule from a chest radiograph is automatically discovered (Meisel et al., 2019). Unsupervised learning, in contrast, concentrates on the patterns or groupings within the data rather than trying to forecast an outcome. Finding the data's hidden structure and learning its pattern is the aim of unsupervised learning (Barua et al., 2023). For instance, it is possible to obtain endomyocardial samples and analyses them histologically to determine the cellular makeup that can help in the development of a targeted therapy for myocarditis (Pillay et al., 2022). The type of machine learning used is determined by the patient's and the doctor's demands.

2. APPLICATION OF AI IN MEDICAL FIELD

New innovations entering the medical industry must not only show greater efficacy, but also integrate with existing procedures, receive the necessary regulatory permission, and, perhaps most crucially, motivate medical professionals and patients to adopt a new paradigm (Barua et al., 2022). A number of new trends in AI research and application are developing as a result of these difficulties. Scientific

Figure 1. Application of AI in various healthcare sectors

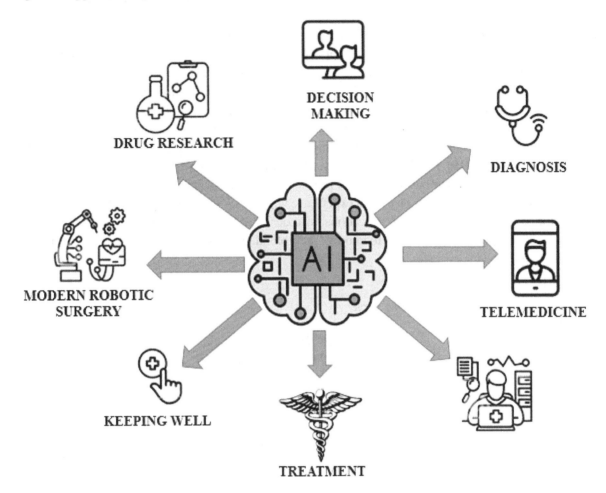

study has concentrated on areas where AI may successfully compare its performance to a human physician. These activities often contain binary outputs that are simple to validate and clearly stated inputs. A digital photograph is used as the input for classifying worrisome skin lesions, and the result is a straightforward binary classification: benign or malignant. When categorizing previously unseen photos of biopsy-validated lesions, researchers just had to show that AI had better sensitivity and specificity than dermatologists (Esteva et al., 2017). Due to the fact that machines lack human traits like empathy and compassion, patients must believe that their doctors are human and are guiding conversations. Furthermore, it is unrealistic to expect patients to instantly have faith in AI, a field shrouded in scepticism. As a result, AI frequently conducts necessary but constrained duties that leave a human doctor in charge of managing patients on a primary basis. A clinical experiment is under underway to determine whether AI can calculate target zones for head and neck radiotherapy more rapidly and correctly than a person. The final decision to provide the therapy still rests with an interventional radiologist, but AI plays a crucial supporting role in shielding the patient from dangerous radiation (Chu et al., 2016).

3. ARTIFICIAL INTELLIGENCE APPLICATIONS IN MEDICINE TODAY

Clinical nephrology has used artificial intelligence in a number of settings. For instance, it has been shown to be helpful for determining the risk for developing progressive IgA nephropathy (Kim et al., 2020), and for predicting the deterioration in glomerular filtration rate in patients with polycystic kidney disease. However, a recent review documents how the sample size required for inference currently limits research.

Patients with diabetes can examine interstitial glucose measurements in real-time using continuous glucose monitoring, which also offers data on the direction and rate of change of blood glucose levels. The smartphone-compatible Guardian glucose monitoring system from Medtronic has obtained FDA approval (Ellis et al., 2019). For their Sugar.IQ system, the business teamed up with Watson (AI created by IBM) in 2018 to help their customers better prevent hypoglycemic episodes based on repeated measurement. While a study focusing on patient experience with glucose monitoring found that participants, while expressing confidence in the notifications, also declared feelings of personal failure to regulate glucose level, it is possible for patients to improve their blood glucose control and reduce stigma associated with hypoglycemic episodes.

Figure 2. Application of AI in modern surgery

4. AI IN MODERN MEDICAL SURGERY

Medical surgery is one of the sectors where AI has become a game-changing technology. AI has made great strides in boosting surgical techniques, better patient outcomes, and revolutionizing how surgeries are carried out throughout time (Barua et al., 2020). Surgical planning, robotic surgery, image-guided surgery, decision support systems, predictive analytics, and the use of virtual reality (VR) and augmented reality (AR) will all be thoroughly discussed in this essay as they relate to AI's assistance in medical surgery (Barua et al., 2022). Any surgical operation must include careful surgical planning, and AI has shown to be an effective tool in this regard. Medical imaging data from CT scans, MRI scans, and X-rays can be analyzed by AI algorithms to find anomalies, recognize structures, and calculate exact measurements (Fritz, 2021). AI can help doctors precisely plan the procedure, choose the best strategy, and anticipate probable difficulties before they enter the operating room by utilizing machine learning techniques. This not only saves time but also lowers the chance of mistakes and enhances the success of surgeries.

The incorporation of AI has led to significant breakthroughs in robotic surgery. Robotic surgical systems, like the da Vinci Surgical System, use AI algorithms to precisely control their robotic arms. These robotic arms allow surgeons to execute difficult operations through smaller incisions since they can be controlled remotely (Yu et al., 2014). Artificial intelligence (AI) algorithms improve the surgeon's motions by minimizing tremors and enhancing dexterity (Barua et al., 2022). This results in greater accuracy, less damage to the tissues around it, quicker healing durations, and more patient satisfaction. The use of AI in image-guided surgery is another crucial application. AI algorithms can give surgeons precise guidance during surgery by fusing preoperative images with real-time intraoperative imaging technologies like ultrasound or fluoroscopy. These algorithms are able to examine the images, recognize anatomical features, and superimpose pertinent information into the surgery field. This helps surgeons to maneuver through complicated anatomical areas, find important structures, and carry out precise surgical. In the end, this enhances surgical precision and lowers the possibility of problems.

The potential influence of AI-powered decision support systems on surgical operations is enormous. AI algorithms can provide surgeons with helpful suggestions and insights during surgery by examining patient data, medical records, and live physiological signals. These technologies, for instance, can recommend probable risks based on specific patient traits, direct the best surgical strategy, and provide individualized treatment plans (Barua et al., 2022). This helps surgeons make well-informed decisions that improve surgical outcomes and patient safety. Another useful application of AI in surgery is predictive analytics (Farris et al., 2021). AI systems can find trends and forecast surgical outcomes by examining vast datasets that include patient characteristics, surgical methods, and historical data. These projections can be used by surgeons to anticipate postoperative recovery times, calculate the likelihood of complications, and improve surgical plans (Barua et al., 2022). Insights from predictive analytics can help surgeons make data-driven decisions and enhance patient care.

Virtual reality (VR) and augmented reality (AR) technologies, when combined with AI, have the potential to revolutionize surgical training and education. VR allows surgeons to practice complex procedures in a virtual environment, simulate surgical scenarios, and receive real-time feedback on their performance. This immersive training experience enhances surgical skills, reduces the learning curve, and improves patient safety (Bielsa., 2021). On the other hand, AR can overlay relevant information onto the surgeon's field of view during surgery, providing vital data and guidance without diverting attention from the surgical field. AR enhances precision, reduces errors, and streamlines surgical procedures. While the integration of AI in medical surgery offers numerous benefits, it is important to acknowledge certain challenges and considerations. Firstly, ethical concerns arise when using AI algorithms in surgical decision-making (Khanagar et al., 2021). The responsibility for patient care ultimately lies with the surgeon, and AI should be seen as a tool to augment their expertise rather than replace it. The transparency and explainability of AI algorithms are critical to ensure that surgeons understand and trust the recommendations.

Data security and privacy are particularly crucial when discussing AI in surgery. For the sake of patient confidentiality and in accordance with legal and ethical requirements, patient data used by AI algorithms must be managed with the utmost care. To protect patient information, appropriate data anonymization methods and secure storage systems should be put in place. Additionally, continual research and development are required to enhance AI algorithms and continuously verify their efficacy. To evaluate the effects of AI on surgical results, patient safety, and cost-effectiveness, extensive clinical trials and real-world implementation studies are essential. To define guidelines, standards, and best practices for the integration of AI in surgery, cooperation between surgeons, engineers, data scientists, and regulatory agencies is crucial. Overall, artificial intelligence has significantly advanced the field of surgical procedures. AI has the potential to revolutionize the way surgeries are performed, improve patient outcomes, and advance surgical training and education. AI applications in surgery range from surgical planning to robotic-assisted surgery, image-guided surgery, decision support systems, predictive analytics, and the usage of VR and AR (Barua et al., 2022). While there are difficulties, responsible and ethical deployment, continued research, and cross-disciplinary collaboration will make sure that AI continues to improve the future of surgical procedures.

5. APPLICATION OF AI IN COVID-19 PANDEMIC

The COVID-19 pandemic has involved AI (Artificial Intelligence) in many ways, from early detection and diagnosis to medical discovery and vaccine development. The impact of AI on the fight against the COVID-19 pandemic will be thoroughly examined in this essay, including its uses in epidemiology, public health, diagnostics, and screening, drug repurposing, vaccine development, and resource management.

a. **Epidemiology and Public Health:** Large-scale data analysis and precise COVID-19 spread forecasting have both benefited from artificial intelligence (AI). Machine learning algorithms have been used to model the dynamics of transmission, forecast the locations of outbreaks, and calculate the effects of various control strategies. These forecasts aid public health professionals in devoting resources wisely, carrying out focused interventions, and controlling the virus's spread.

b. **Diagnostics and Screening:** The creation of efficient and precise COVID-19 diagnostic tools has been made possible by AI. To help with disease diagnosis and categorization, machine learning algorithms have been trained on substantial datasets of COVID-19 chest X-rays and CT scans (Barua et al., 2021). AI algorithms have also been used to choose patients for testing based on their chance of infection by analyzing symptom data. Additionally, chatbots and virtual assistants powered by AI have been put to use to offer initial screening and direction to people worried about potential COVID-19 symptoms.

c. **Drug Repurposing:** By utilizing the already-existing knowledge of licensed medications and their mechanisms of action, AI has sped up the process of identifying viable pharmaceuticals for COVID-19 treatment. Large medicinal chemical databases can be analyzed by AI algorithms to forecast possible efficacy against viruses. AI systems can find prospective candidates for repurposing medications by taking into account their chemical structure and interactions, freeing researchers to concentrate on studying these drugs in clinical trials (Saravi et al., 2022).

d. **Vaccine Development:** By utilizing the already-existing knowledge of licensed medications and their mechanisms of action, AI has sped up the process of identifying viable pharmaceuticals for COVID-19 treatment. Large medicinal chemical databases can be analyzed by AI algorithms to forecast possible efficacy against viruses (Barua et al., 2022). AI systems can find prospective candidates for repurposing medications by taking into account their chemical structure and interactions, freeing researchers to concentrate on studying these drugs in clinical trials.

e. **Contact Tracing and Monitoring:** In order to identify and stop the spread of the virus, contact tracking operations have become far more effective thanks to AI. In order to find probable contacts of infected individuals, AI-powered algorithms can analyze massive datasets, including mobile phone data, social media data, and records of public transit. AI can help public health officials take prompt, focused action to stop the future spread by tracing and monitoring potential chains of transmission (Saravi et al., 2022).

f. **Misinformation Detection and Public Communication:** AI has been used to stop the transmission of false information and COVID-19-related fake news. In order to find inaccurate or misleading information, AI systems can analyze huge amounts of web content, social media messages, and news stories (Barua et al., 2021). This enables public health officials and organizations to rapidly address false information and give the public accurate information (Buch, et al., 2018).

While AI has been helpful in the fight against the COVID-19 epidemic, it's crucial to understand its limitations and difficulties. Biases in the data can produce biased results since AI systems depend on the accuracy and representativeness of the data they are trained on (Saravi et al., 2022). Furthermore, privacy issues must be taken into consideration when using personal data for contact tracking and monitoring. To ensure the moral and efficient application of AI in the fight against COVID-19, responsible use of AI, transparent algorithms, and coordination between AI experts, healthcare professionals, and policymakers are required. The COVID-19 pandemic has been impacted by AI in several ways, including epidemiology, public health, diagnostics, drug repurposing, vaccine development, and resource management. In order to successfully control the spread of the virus, diagnose patients, create treatments and vaccinations, and manage healthcare resources, researchers, healthcare practitioners, and public health authorities have benefited from the integration of AI technologies (Datta et al., 2019). A more adaptable and successful response to upcoming pandemics will result from ongoing research, innovation, and prudent application of AI (Barua et al., 2022).

6. FUTURE TRENDS OF AI IN MEDICAL FIELD

The electronic footprint of a patient will be mined by AI for key information. This will first reduce time and boost productivity, but after sufficient testing, it will also directly influence patient management. Consider a type 2 diabetic patient who is having a consultation. At the moment, a doctor must spend a lot of time reading outpatient letters, examining blood work, and getting clinical guidelines from many disjointed systems. Contrarily, AI could prepare the most significant dangers and actions automatically given the patient's clinical data. Additionally, it could automatically create a summary letter for the clinician to review and approve from the consultation's recorded dialogue. Due to the fact that neither of these programs replaces physicians but rather works in tandem with them, significant time would be saved and implementation could happen relatively rapidly (Zaharchuk et al., 2021) (Farris et al., 2022). AI-based healthcare systems will also integrate advanced diagnostic knowledge into primary care. Images might be taken at a general practitioner's office and submitted to a specialized dermatological AI system for immediate analysis if an image of a skin lesion is sufficient to accurately detect its cause. Low-risk patients would get immediate assurance, while high-risk patients would have shorter waiting periods for referrals because clinics would only be accepting chosen cases. This idea is not just applicable to skin lesions; AI has showed promise in analyzing a wide range of picture data, including retinal scans, radiography, and ultrasound, among others. A lot of these pictures can be taken using reasonably priced, easily accessible equipment. Only by cognitively synthesizing vast amounts of medical data would AI be able to conduct the research necessary for this "personalized" therapy. AI will also play a big part in preventative medicine because of its ability to monitor millions of inputs at once. Medical sciences are changing in a number of ways thanks to artificial intelligence (AI), including:

a. **Increasing diagnostic precision:** AI systems can examine medical imagery and spot patterns that human practitioners might overlook. As a result, diseases like cancer may be diagnosed earlier and with greater precision.
b. **Customizing care:** AI can assist in determining which medicines are most successful for certain patients based on their distinctive characteristics and medical history by analyzing vast datasets.
c. **Simplifying administrative work:** AI can automate activities like arranging appointments and billing, freeing up administrative staff to concentrate on more difficult jobs.
d. **Improving drug development:** By forecasting the effectiveness and safety of new drugs, AI can assist uncover novel therapeutic targets and expedite the drug discovery process.
e. **Improving patient outcomes:** AI can assist physicians in making more knowledgeable judgments about patient care, resulting in better results and shorter hospital stays.

When AI judges that the patient's risk of developing a specific diabetic condition justifies action, it could proactively recommend consultations. Contrarily, it would be impracticable to entrust a human with the duty of continuously monitoring every appointment and test result of every diabetes patient in a practice. Upcoming research on artificial intelligence should focus on a few carefully chosen tasks that, in general, follow the tendencies mentioned in this article. Building a relationship where AI can benefit clinicians by increasing their efficiency or cost-effectiveness and clinicians can provide AI with the crucial clinical exposure it needs to learn complex clinical case management is necessary for integrating these systems into clinical practice. The public's reluctance to embrace an increasingly divisive technology will be the biggest barrier to AI's mainstream adoption, thus it will be crucial to ensure that AI does not hide the human face of medicine throughout the process.

7. CONCLUSION

It is true that artificial intelligence is changing the field of medical science, but it is crucial to distinguish between its potential and its actual applications. Although AI has shown significant ability in jobs like medication research and medical imaging analysis, there are still restrictions on its application in healthcare. One significant drawback is the opaqueness of AI algorithms, which can make it challenging to comprehend how choices are made and potentially introduce bias. The application of AI in healthcare is also fraught with ethical questions, notably those related to data security and privacy. The requirement for a lot of high-quality data to train AI algorithms presents another difficulty. Despite the abundance of healthcare data that is available, information is frequently fragmented and non-standardized, which can make it challenging to use efficiently. Despite these obstacles, artificial intelligence (AI) has the power to transform healthcare by increasing the precision and effectiveness of diagnoses, treatments, and research. But it's critical to proceed cautiously when using AI in healthcare, making sure that ethical and transparency issues are taken care of and that the technology is employed to supplement, not replace, human expertise and decision-making. Instead of replacing human intelligence, AI should be viewed as a tool to support it and enable improved decision-making.

ACKNOWLEDGMENT

The authors would like to thank Centre for Healthcare Science and Technology Lab, Heaton Hall, IIEST-Shibpur.

REFERENCES

Barua, R., Bhowmik, S., Dey, A., & Mondal, J. (2023). Advances of the Robotics Technology in Modern Minimally Invasive Surgery. In *Design and Control Advances in Robotics* (pp. 91–104). IGI Global.

Barua, R., & Das, S. (2022). Improvements of Virtual and Augmented Reality for Advanced Treatments in Urology. In *Emerging Advancements for Virtual and Augmented Reality in Healthcare* (pp. 117–131). IGI Global. doi:10.4018/978-1-7998-8371-5.ch008

Barua, R., Das, S., Datta, S., Datta, P., & Roy Chowdhury, A. (2022). Analysis of surgical needle insertion modeling and viscoelastic tissue material interaction for minimally invasive surgery (MIS). *Materials Today: Proceedings*, *57*, 259–264. doi:10.1016/j.matpr.2022.02.498

Barua, R., Das, S., Datta, S., Datta, P., & Roy Chowdhury, A. (2022). Study and experimental investigation of insertion force modeling and tissue deformation phenomenon during surgical needle-soft tissue interaction. *Proceedings of the Institution of Mechanical Engineers, Part C: Journal of Mechanical Engineering Science*. 10.1177/09544062221126628

Barua, R., Das, S., Datta, S., Roy Chowdhury, A., & Datta, P. (2022). Experimental study of the robotically controlled surgical needle insertion for analysis of the minimum invasive process. In *Emergent Converging Technologies and Biomedical Systems: Select Proceedings of ETBS 2021* (pp. 473-482). Springer Singapore. 10.1007/978-981-16-8774-7_38

Barua, R., Das, S., & Mondal, J. (2022). Emerging Applications of Artificial Intelligence (AI) and Machine Learning (ML) in Modern Urology. *Exploring the Convergence of Computer and Medical Science Through Cloud Healthcare*, 117.

Barua, R., Das, S., Roy Chowdhury, A., & Datta, P. (2023). Experimental and simulation investigation of surgical needle insertion into soft tissue mimic biomaterial for minimally invasive surgery (MIS). *Proceedings of the Institution of Mechanical Engineers. Part H, Journal of Engineering in Medicine, 237*(2), 254–264. doi:10.1177/09544119221143860 PMID:36527297

Barua, R., Das, S., RoyChowdhury, A., & Datta, P. (2023, January). RoyChowdhury, A., & Datta, P. (2022). Simulation and experimental investigation of the surgical needle deflection model during the rotational and steady insertion process. *The International Journal of Artificial Organs, 46*(1), 40–51. Advance online publication. doi:10.1177/03913988221136154 PMID:36397288

Barua, R., Datta, P., Datta, S., & Roychowdhury, A. (2021). Study and Application of Machine Learning Methods in Modern Additive Manufacturing Processes. *Applications of Artificial Intelligence in Additive Manufacturing*, 75.

Barua, R., Datta, S., & Banerjee, D. (2022). Computational Study of In-Vivo CT-Based FEM Application in Bone Tissue Engineering. In Technological Adoption and Trends in Health Sciences Teaching, Learning, and Practice (pp. 300-316). IGI Global. doi:10.4018/978-1-7998-8871-0.ch014

Barua, R., Giria, H., Datta, S., Roy Chowdhury, A., & Datta, P. (2020). Force modeling to develop a novel method for fabrication of hollow channels inside a gel structure. *Proceedings of the Institution of Mechanical Engineers. Part H, Journal of Engineering in Medicine, 234*(2), 223–231. doi:10.1177/0954411919891654 PMID:31774361

Barua, R., & Mondal, J. (2022). Study of the Current Trends of CAD (Computer-Aided Detection) in Modern Medical Imaging. *Machine Learning and AI Techniques in Interactive Medical Image Analysis*, 35.

Bielsa, V. F. (2021). Virtual reality simulation in plastic surgery training. Literature review. *Journal of Plastic, Reconstructive & Aesthetic Surgery; JPRAS, 74*(9), 2372–2378. doi:10.1016/j.bjps.2021.03.066 PMID:33972199

Buch, V. H., Ahmed, I., & Maruthappu, M. (2018). Artificial intelligence in medicine: Current trends and future possibilities. *The British Journal of General Practice, 68*(668), 143–144. doi:10.3399/bjgp18X695213 PMID:29472224

Chu, C., De Fauw, J., Tomasev, N., Paredes, B. R., Hughes, C., Ledsam, J., Back, T., Montgomery, H., Rees, G., Raine, R., Sullivan, K., Moinuddin, S., D'Souza, D., Ronneberger, O., Mendes, R., & Cornebise, J. (2016). Applying machine learning to automated segmentation of head and neck tumour volumes and organs at risk on radiotherapy planning CT and MRI scans. *F1000 Research, 5*(2104), 2104. doi:10.12688/f1000research.9525.1

Datta, S., Barua, R., & Das, J. (2019). Application of artificial intelligence in modern healthcare system. *Alginates-recent uses of this natural polymer.*

Ellis, T. D., Cavanaugh, J. T., DeAngelis, T., Hendron, K., Thomas, C. A., Saint-Hilaire, M., Pencina, K., & Latham, N. K. (2019). Comparative Effectiveness of mHealth-Supported Exercise Compared With Exercise Alone for People With Parkinson Disease: Randomized Controlled Pilot Study. *Physical Therapy, 99*(2), 203–216. doi:10.1093/ptj/pzy131 PMID:30715489

Esteva, A., Kuprel, B., Novoa, R. A., Ko, J., Swetter, S. M., Blau, H. M., & Thrun, S. (2017). Dermatologist-level classification of skin cancer with deep neural networks. *Nature*, *542*(7639), 115–118. doi:10.1038/nature21056 PMID:28117445

Farris, A. B., Vizcarra, J., Amgad, M., Cooper, L. A. D., Gutman, D., & Hogan, J. (2021). Artificial intelligence and algorithmic computational pathology: An introduction with renal allograft examples. *Histopathology*, *78*(6), 791–804. doi:10.1111/his.14304 PMID:33211332

Fritz, J. (2021). Automated and Radiation-Free Generation of Synthetic CT from MRI Data: Does AI Help to Cross the Finish Line? *Radiology*, *298*(2), 350–352. doi:10.1148/radiol.2020204045 PMID:33355510

Groot, O. Q., Ogink, P. T., Lans, A., Twining, P. K., Kapoor, N. D., DiGiovanni, W., Bindels, B. J. J., Bongers, M. E. R., Oosterhoff, J. H. F., Karhade, A. V., Oner, F. C., Verlaan, J. J., & Schwab, J. H. (2022). Machine learning prediction models in orthopedic surgery: A systematic review in transparent reporting. *Journal of Orthopaedic Research*, *40*(2), 475–483. https://doi.org/ doi:10.1002/jor.25036

Khanagar, S. B., Al-Ehaideb, A., Vishwanathaiah, S., Maganur, P. C., Patil, S., Naik, S., Baeshen, H. A., & Sarode, S. S. (2021). Scope and performance of artificial intelligence technology in orthodontic diagnosis, treatment planning, and clinical decision-making - A systematic review. *Journal of Dental Sciences*, *16*(1), 482–492. doi:10.1016/j.jds.2020.05.022 PMID:33384838

Kim, Y., Seo, J., An, S. Y., Sinn, D. H., & Hwang, J. H. (2020). Efficacy and safety of an mHealth app and wearable device in physical performance for patients with hepatocellular carcinoma: Development and usability study. *JMIR mHealth and uHealth*, *8*(3), e14435. doi:10.2196/14435 PMID:32159517

Lakhani, P., & Sundaram, B. (2017). Deep Learning at Chest Radiography: Automated Classification of Pulmonary Tuberculosis by Using Convolutional Neural Networks. *Radiology*, *284*(2), 574–582. doi:10.1148/radiol.2017162326 PMID:28436741

Meisel, C., & Bailey, K. A. (2019). Identifying signal-dependent information about the preictal state: A comparison across ECoG, EEG and EKG using deep learning. *EBioMedicine*, *45*, 422–431. doi:10.1016/j.ebiom.2019.07.001 PMID:31300348

Pillay, J., Gaudet, L., Wingert, A., Bialy, L., Mackie, A. S., Paterson, D. I., & Hartling, L. (2022). Incidence, risk factors, natural history, and hypothesised mechanisms of myocarditis and pericarditis following covid-19 vaccination: Living evidence syntheses and review. *BMJ (Clinical Research Ed.)*, *378*, e069445. doi:10.1136/bmj-2021-069445 PMID:35830976

Sabry, F., Eltaras, T., Labda, W., Alzoubi, K., & Malluhi, Q. (2022). Machine Learning for Healthcare Wearable Devices: The Big Picture. *Journal of Healthcare Engineering*, *4653923*, 1–25. Advance online publication. doi:10.1155/2022/4653923 PMID:35480146

Saravi, B., Hassel, F., Ülkümen, S., Zink, A., Shavlokhova, V., Couillard-Despres, S., Boeker, M., Obid, P., & Lang, G. M. (2022). Artificial Intelligence-Driven Prediction Modeling and Decision Making in Spine Surgery Using Hybrid Machine Learning Models. *Journal of Personalized Medicine*, *12*(4), 509. doi:10.3390/jpm12040509 PMID:35455625

Yu, J., Wang, Y., Li, Y., Li, X., Li, C., & Shen, J. (2014). The safety and effectiveness of Da Vinci surgical system compared with open surgery and laparoscopic surgery: A rapid assessment. *Journal of Evidence-Based Medicine*, 7(2), 121–134. doi:10.1111/jebm.12099 PMID:25155768

Zaharchuk, G., & Davidzon, G. (2021). Artificial Intelligence for Optimization and Interpretation of PET/CT and PET/MR Images. *Seminars in Nuclear Medicine*, 51(2), 134–142. doi:10.1053/j.semnuclmed.2020.10.001 PMID:33509370

KEY TERMS AND DEFINITIONS

Artificial Intelligence: AI stands for "Artificial Intelligence," which refers to the ability of machines and computer programs to perform tasks that typically require human intelligence, such as learning, problem-solving, decision-making, and natural language processing.

Deep Learning: Basically a subset of machine learning, which is a branch of artificial intelligence. It involves training artificial neural networks with large datasets to identify patterns and make predictions or decisions based on the input data.

Digital Twins: Virtual replicas of physical objects, processes, or systems that are created using digital technologies, such as computer-aided design (CAD), simulation, and data analytics. In the context of engineering and manufacturing, digital twins are used to model and simulate products, equipment, and manufacturing processes, allowing for optimization, prediction, and analysis of performance and behavior.

Healthcare: The healthcare industry involves numerous professionals, such as doctors, nurses, pharmacists, therapists, and technicians, as well as organizations, such as hospitals, clinics, and insurance companies that provide and manage healthcare services.

Machine Learning: Machine learning is essentially the analysis of computer algorithms that automatically correct themselves through repetition. It is also referred to as an AI application.

Medical Devices: Medical devices are instruments, machines, implants, or other similar products used in the diagnosis, treatment, monitoring, or prevention of diseases and other medical conditions. Medical devices can range from simple devices, such as thermometers or blood glucose meters, to complex ones, such as MRI machines or robotic surgical systems.

Chapter 2
A Novel Approach to Identify Leaf Vein Morphology Using Laplacian Filter and Deep Learning for Plant Identification

Pramod Madhavrao Kanjalkar
Vishwakarma Institute of Technology, India

Jyoti Kanjalkar
Vishwakarma Institute of Technology, India

Atharva Janaba Zagade
Vishwakarma Institute of Technology, India

Vedhas Talnikar
Vishwakarma Institute of Technology, India

ABSTRACT

Identification of different plants, weeds, or any related type of vegetation is an important aspect of agricultural robotics and technologies. With the help of image processing and computer vision, multiple attempts have been made to achieve these results. These approaches made use of the shape and color of the leaf to identify a particular plant. But it can be observed that this approach has some limitations resulting in false positive and true negative errors. To overcome these limitations, the authors propose a novel approach of using Laplacian filter to extract veins morphology of leaves of a plant. This veins pattern is unique to every plant. With this Laplacian filter and data augmentation techniques, a unique dataset is developed on which a deep learning model can be trained. Based on this approach, the proposed system applies a deep learning algorithm called YOLO for plant identification. After preprocessing and YOLO training, the model is able to distinguish between plant and a weed successfully and create a bounding box for the detected type of plant.

DOI: 10.4018/978-1-6684-9189-8.ch002

1. INTRODUCTION

Detection and identification of multiple types of plants, crops or weeds using computer vision is an important topic in Agricultural development (Pande, et al., 2022). A typical farm consists of multiple plants and weeds growing together. To separate them, a significant amount of manual labour is required from time to time. Therefore, modern technologies such as Robotics need to be used (Gayakwad, et al., 2022). To implement such technologies for agricultural purposes, quick and real-time plant identification with good precision plays a vital role (Kulkarni, et al., 2019). This can prove beneficial for Weed removal systems or crop harvesting systems (Kanjalkar et al., 2022).

To date, a significant amount of research is already done in this field. Multiple algorithms and Image processing techniques have been implemented to get the results. But an optimised solution is yet to be found. This project presents one such approach with the help of the Laplacian filter and the YOLO Object Detection Algorithm (Kanjalkar et al., 2023a) . This project utilises an open-source CWFI dataset (Haug & Ostermann, 2015) consisting of RGB images having plants and weeds. The proposed system converts the image into a single-channel grey image and then, with a Laplacian filter, extracts the morphological vein pattern of the plant (Kanjalkar et al., 2023b). Based on this data, the YOLO algorithm is trained, which finally differentiates between the plant and the weed with an mAP score greater than 87% (Uddin, et al., 2022). The algorithm creates a bounding box above the detected plant, which records the spatial dimensions and centre coordinates of the plant with respect to the original image.

2. LITERATURE SURVEY

Recently, there has been a good amount of research and development in this sector, some of which is explained briefly below.

The aim of this study is to apply image processing techniques for agricultural plant identification, which can lead to faster and more efficient specimen identification and classification (Sonnad, et al., 2022). The proposed method uses various factors such as colour moments, vein features, texture features based on lacunarity, GIST, Local Binary Pattern (LBP), and geometric features, among others, to identify plant leaf photos. The features are normalised, and the 'Pbest-guide binary particle swarm optimisation (PBPSO)' technique is used to reduce the features. Several machine learning classifiers are evaluated, including multi-SVM, k-nearest neighbour, decision trees, and naive Bayes, and the decision tree classifier showed the best performance. The proposed method achieved an accuracy of 98.58% and 90.02% for the "Flavia" and "Folio" datasets, respectively (Keivani, et al., 2020).

The detection of invasive species in ornamental lawns and sports turf can be accomplished through the use of edge detection algorithms. In this study, 12 different edge detection filters were evaluated on collected photos. To minimise false positives, the outputs of the three most effective filters - sharpening (I), sharpening (II), and Laplacian - were combined using various cell values. Two filters were then selected for further investigation based on tests conducted with different cell sizes. To identify the optimal cell size and the most effective filter, box plots were used. The best results were obtained by applying the sharpening (I) filter with a cell size of 10 and the aggregation method with the minimum value. Finally, based on the number of false positives, false negatives, and generated indexes, a threshold value was selected to achieve the best performance in terms of Precision, Recall, and F1-Score. The results varied slightly for sports grass and ornamental turf (Parra, et al., 2020).

Computer vision plays a vital role in enabling automation and efficiency in various operations within the crop production cycle, from planting to harvesting. However, the lack of publicly available picture datasets is a significant challenge for developing and evaluating computer vision and machine learning algorithms for specific tasks. To address this bottleneck, several image databases have been created and made available to the public since 2015, including 15 datasets on weed control, ten datasets on fruit detection, and nine datasets on other applications for precision agriculture (Pandit, 2023). This paper provides a comprehensive but not exhaustive assessment of these public image datasets acquired in the field of precision agriculture. The paper reviews the main characteristics and applications of these datasets and discusses important considerations for producing high-quality public picture databases (Lu & Young, 2020).

In addition to standard object recognition issues brought on by light, stance, and orientation variations, the identification of plant types is made more difficult by variations in leaf shape over time and shifting leaf colour depending on the weather. With the right choice of representative leaf-based features, the limiting accuracy of current methods can be enhanced. In this study, various manually created visual leaf features are evaluated, along with the methods used to extract and classify them. In order to do this, a new five-step approach for classifying plant types based on leaf pictures is provided. The algorithm consists of image pre-processing, segmentation, feature extraction, dimensionality reduction, and classification steps. A self-compiled dataset of 625 leaf images and the publicly accessible standard dataset "Flavia" is used to evaluate the suggested technique (Saleem, et al., 2019).

To properly utilise the high-spatial detailed data collected by unmanned aerial vehicles (UAV) or high-resolution satellite imagers for mapping vegetation, efficient approaches are required. Convolutional neural networks (CNN) and other deep learning techniques are currently opening up new possibilities for image analysis and computer vision. To achieve fine-grained mapping of vegetation species and communities, a CNN-based segmentation strategy (U-net) is used in combination with training data that is directly produced from visual interpretation of UAV-based high-resolution RGB imagery. The results demonstrate that this approach can accurately map and segment vegetation species and communities (Kattenborn et al., 2019).

Botanical taxonomy and computer vision have both begun to focus on the multidisciplinary topic of plant image identification. The first plant image collection, which contains 10,000 photographs of 100 decorative plant species on the campus of Beijing Forestry University, was acquired by cell phone in a natural setting. For large-scale plant categorisation in a natural environment, a 26-layer deep learning model with eight leftover building components is created. On the BJFU100 dataset, the suggested model achieves a recognition rate of 91.78%, illuminating the potential of deep Learning for smart forestry (Sun, et al., 2017).

We suggest applying a deep convolutional neural network (CNN) to the issue of identifying plants from the patterns of their leaf veins. We focus on classifying the white bean, red bean, and soybean, three diverse species of legumes (Suthar, et al., 2022). By using a CNN, which is a standard component of modern pipelines, bespoke feature extractors are avoided (Priscila, et al., 2023). Additionally, the accuracy of the referred pipeline is greatly increased by this deep learning approach (Grinblat, et al., 2016).

In the medical field, X-ray images are used by clinicians to accurately diagnose disease. A similar idea was applied here. From a 2-dimensional photograph of a leaf, geometrical features and digital morphological features are retrieved. The purpose of this work is to offer acceptable leaf image elements that may be helpful in future plant identification studies (Bagal & Manza, 2016).

The paper explores the use of convolutional neural networks (CNN) to learn unsupervised feature representations for 44 different plant species gathered at the Royal Botanic Gardens, Kew, England. Instead of using a "black box" approach, the authors employ a visualisation technique based on deconvolutional networks (DN) to gain insights into the selected features from the CNN model. The study reveals that different orders of venations were selected to represent each plant species (Gunturu, et al., 2023). The results of experiments using various classifiers and these CNN features indicate consistency and superiority over state-of-the-art approaches that rely on hand-crafted features (Lee, et al., 2015).

The methods for identifying plants by analysing leaf complexity and calculating their fractal dimension are covered in this article (Tan, et al., 2020). The complexity of the inside and outward shapes of leaves was examined. To enable automatic plant identification, computational software was created to process, examine, and extract the features of leaf photographs. The results of two tests are presented: the first used fifty leaf samples from ten distinct species to identify plant species from the Brazilian Atlantic woodland and Brazilian Cerrado scrublands, and the second used twenty leaf samples from four different Passiflora species to accomplish the same (Uike, et al., 2022). Two approaches to estimating fractal dimension are contrasted (box-counting and multiscale Minkowski) (Backes, et al., 2009).

The Laplacian filter has been widely studied and adopted for various image analysis tasks, including plant identification. In a study by Fu, & Chi, (2006), the authors explored the potential of the Laplacian filter in extracting venation patterns from leaf images. Their findings demonstrated that the Laplacian filter effectively enhanced the visibility of leaf veins, enabling accurate feature extraction. This research emphasised the importance of vein patterns as reliable discriminative features for plant species classification (Ullah, et al., 2020).

Deep Learning, especially Convolutional Neural Networks (CNNs), has emerged as a dominant technique in various image recognition applications, including plant identification. In a seminal work by Boulent, et al., (2019), the authors introduced the concept of CNNs and demonstrated their capabilities in solving complex visual recognition problems. Since then, CNNs have become the go-to choice for automated plant species classification (Bansal, et al., 2022).

Despite improvements in machine learning and image processing techniques for plant identification, a crucial concern in the current study relates to the use of mediation analysis in this context. Mediation analysis can give important insights into the underlying processes by which particular variables or traits affect the accuracy of plant identification. In the context of our research, mediation analysis might assist us in identifying the causal connections between the Laplacian-extracted image features, Deep Learning-based classifiers, and the results of the plant identification process. We may better understand how the chosen strategies affect the overall effectiveness of the plant identification system by identifying the mediating elements and their relationships (Nath, et al., 2023). Various machine learning methods are used in (Pande, & Chetty, 2021) to enhance accuracies.

From this research, we understand that most of the experiments are conducted in a closed and controlled environment, which differs significantly from the natural environment (Nirmala, et al., 2023). Also, the use of Laplacian as a filter for leaf veins identification is a novel approach in our proposed system (Saxena & Chaudhary, 2023). The major focus of our proposed system is the identification of plants with good accuracy in their natural environment, with varied lighting conditions and shapes (Jeba, et al., 2023).

3. PLANT IDENTIFICATION USING COLOR AND SHAPE

In an earlier approach, we tried to identify different types of plants with the help of the design of the leaf and the RGB colour of the leaf (Alarood, et al., 2022). As different leaves have different shapes and a range of green colours, a Deep Learning model was trained to identify those leaves with their shape and colours. For this model, we created our custom dataset and tested the model on actual field images (Jeganathan, et al., 2023). A canny edge detection filter, famous for shape detection, along with a Sobel operator, was implemented to extract the shape of the leaves (Rani, et al., 2021). But it turned out that the model had a lot of issues in the identification of the exact species of the plant and rendered many faulty predictions (Vashishtha & Dhawan, 2023). The model had a higher percentage of True Negative and False Positive errors. Some of those faulty results are displayed below:

The trained model was supposed to identify the spinach crop from the weed. As we see in Fig 1. the model performed fairly to identify major parts of the spinach crop. But in some areas, the leaves went

Figure 1. True negative error if the model in which some of the leaves are not identified

undetected by the model (Cirillo, et al., 2023). This is called the True Negative error, which simply means that an object is present in the image, but the model is unable to identify it.

Now let's consider Figure 2. In this scenario, the model predicted some of the weeds as Spinach crops. This kind of error is called a False Positive error, meaning the wrong type of object is identified as a class by our model (Zannah, et al., 2023).

These were the limitations of the model training based on colour and shape. After troubleshooting, we came to an understanding that the actual images that are found in the field have a huge degree of variation in terms of colour and shape. This difference may occur due to weather conditions, sunlight, or even the position of the camera. In order to tackle this limitation, we propose a novel approach in which our proposed system tries to identify plants based on the morphological pattern of the leaves, which are unique to all species. This pattern is independent of the colour and shape of the leaf and, thus, is extremely useful for our purpose. To extract this leaf vein morphology, our system makes use of the Laplacian filter, and the YOLO Object Identification model is trained based on the Laplacian dataset. The detailed flow of our system is explained below.

Figure 2. False positive error of the model displaying the wrong plant as Spinach

4. DATA PRE-PROCESSING FOR THE PROPOSED SYSTEM

4.1. Dataset

The proposed system for Crop/Weed Identification was trained on a benchmark dataset that was specifically designed for computer vision tasks in precision agriculture. The dataset is composed of 60 images captured on a carrot farm using an autonomous field robot (Haug & Ostermann, 2015). The images show the carrot plant in its early growth stage, along with intra- and inter-row weeds that are similar in size to the crop. Moreover, the weeds and crops are growing close to each other. The dataset was created in natural conditions and is openly available (Haug & Ostermann, 2015).

As the dataset is comparatively smaller in size with respect to the standard size required to train a deep learning model, the proposed system uses data augmentation techniques to increase the size of the dataset. Also, the similarities between the plant and the weed are significant, making it even more difficult for the Deep Learning model to distinguish between them (Saleh, et al., 2021). But, because these conditions constitute the natural environment of any field, a model trained on this dataset performs better than a model developed in a controlled environment (Figures 3 and 4).

Figure 3. Images from the CWIP dataset, representing carrot crop and the weed. The carrot crop is in its early development stage and looks similar to the weed growing around it (Haug & Ostermann, 2015).

4.2. Laplacian Filter

In the original dataset, identifying plants and weeds is difficult as they look similar. To address this issue, the proposed system uses the morphological pattern of plant veins, a unique characteristic of each plant. In order to extract this pattern, the proposed system implements a Laplacian filter.

The Laplacian filter is an edge detection filter commonly used in digital image processing. It calculates the second derivative of the image, which measures the rate of change of the first derivative. This helps determine if a change in pixel values is due to an edge or a continuous progression.

The filter kernel for the Laplacian filter usually has negative values arranged in a cross pattern in the middle, with either zero or positive values at the corners. The centre value can be either positive or negative. A 3x3 kernel example for the Laplacian filter is given below:

$$\begin{bmatrix} 0 & -1 & 0 \\ -1 & 4 & -1 \\ 0 & -1 & 0 \end{bmatrix} \tag{1}$$

Equation 01 – 3x3 Laplacian Kernel Matrix

The kernel matrix of any filter performs convolutional operation with the image and obtains the results. This particular kernel can successfully extract the morphological vein patterns from an image of a leaf.

Before implementing this filter, our system clears the background from the image, keeping only the green part, essentially the plant leaves. Anything other than leaves is removed from the image. This operation is carried out using an HSV colour filter for green colour. The Original RGB format image is converted to Hue-Saturation-Value (HSV) value from which only the green-coloured HSV value is passed, and all other colour values are blocked (Figure 5).

After clearing the background using the HSV filter, the proposed system converts a three-channel RGB image to a single-channel greyscale image, as the kernel is designed to be implemented on a single-channel image for edge detection. Finally, we apply the 3x3 Laplacian kernel to the greyscale image, which gives the morphological veins pattern of all the leaves, as demonstrated in Figure 6.

These filters are applied to all 60 images in the dataset. All these images are then converted back to 3-channel images, although only one active channel exists.

Figure 4. Data pre-processing flowchart

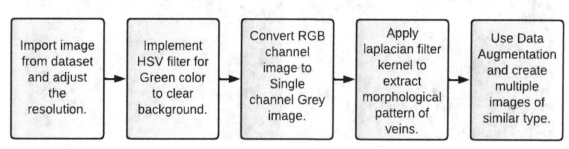

Figure 5. HSV filter for green colour is implemented on the original image to keep the green colored part, i.e., leaves and anything other than that turned into black pixels

Figure 6. The results of the Laplacian filter are shown on the right side. We can observe that the filtered image shows the veins pattern of the leaves, which is the most crucial part of our proposed system.

 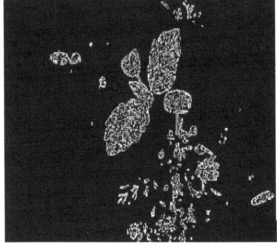

4.3. Data Augmentation

As the number of images in our dataset is significantly small, our system implements Data Augmentation techniques to increase the number of training images. These techniques include scaling up, scaling down by a factor, shifting the image to either the left or right side by a particular distance, zooming in/out, shear operation or horizontal/vertical flip. For each image, any of these operators are applied randomly to create a new image with the same dimensions as the original but with some changes. A single image may be operated by multiple operators as well to increase the amount of variation. This process is carried out on every image from the dataset after applying the Laplacian filter.

This Data Augmentation process introduces a significant amount of variation in the dataset without changing the original theme of the data. This variation ensures that the model trained isn't affected by overfitting, which is usually true when working with smaller datasets. This helps a lot in training the data, and the model works better even if some unknown variations occur while testing. This is precisely what is needed for agricultural tasks, as there are limitations on datasets with varied environmental conditions. Here, the Data Pre-processing is completed for our system, and the filters mentioned above with the augmentation ensure that our Object Detection model works as fine as possible.

5. PLANT DETECTION USING YOLO

After pre-processing, our dataset consists of 960 filtered images, on which You Only Look Once, v5 (YOLOv5) Object Detection Algorithm is trained. The dataset is divided into training and testing data. The training data consists of 85% images, while 15% are for testing.

5.1. Model Training

The model was trained using the YOLOv5 algorithm, which is a popular Object Detection Algorithm known for its fast and precise detection. Unlike previous versions of YOLO that used the TensorFlow framework, YOLOv5 is developed using the PyTorch Python framework. YOLOv5 employs a more advanced architecture called EfficientDet, based on the EfficientNet network architecture. This more sophisticated architecture allows YOLOv5 to achieve better accuracy and more robust generalisation across a broader range of object categories.

In order to train or model, it is required to create a bounding box for every image present in the complete dataset. This bounding box consists of the object's width, height and centre coordinates. Also, each object corresponds to a class, the object's name. In this case, our model consists of a single class called a plant. All this information is stored in an annotations file respective to its image. Thus, each image eventually has an annotation file which stores the class id, centre coordinates and the spatial dimensions of the objects in the image in normalised form.

Every carrot leaf with a morphological pattern is an object for our system. Any other leaf is then classified as Not-a-plant or simply weed. Therefore, we create all such bounding boxes for every image having a plant and store them correspondingly.

To train our model, our system uses Google Collaboratory and utilises the GPU provided on the cloud. The model is trained using a python Programming language. The input image resolution is 640x640 px for training. The model is compiled for 100 epochs meaning 150 iterations through the complete training dataset with a batch size 16. This implies that 16 images are loaded on the GPU simultaneously. The training was completed in 0.154 hours. The trained model is a pytorch-based file with 157 layers and a single class.

5.2. Testing and Implementation

In order to implement this trained model, the system has to load this model first with the configuration file, which defines all the hyperparameters, such as model resolution, GPU, activation functions, classes, etc. After that, we import the image on which the model will be tested (Figure 7).

Figure 7. Process flowchart for plant identification

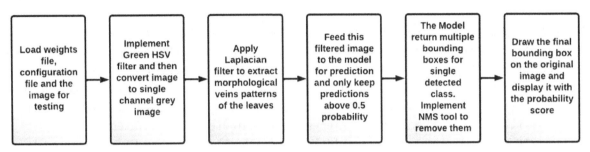

Now that the model is trained on the Laplacian filtered dataset, we also need to convert the testing image to the same filter. To do so, the proposed system implements the Green colour HSV filter and then converts the image to a single-channel grey image. Laplacian filter is applied to this 1-D image to extract the morphological veins patterns. Based on this veins pattern, the model will predict the class for each plant in the image with respective probability scores and draw the bounding boxes accordingly. Our system has defined a threshold value of 0.5 probability score. Only those bounding boxes above that threshold are shown, and others are discarded. It may happen that for a single object present in the image, multiple bounding boxes are shown. The proposed system uses a Non-max suppression tool (NMS) to remove these repetitive boxes. This works on the principle of Intersection over Union and fuses multiple bounding boxes into a single box for each object. Finally, the system draws the final bounding box on the original image and returns the image with the probability score.

Figure 8. Graphical representation of multiple training Parameters

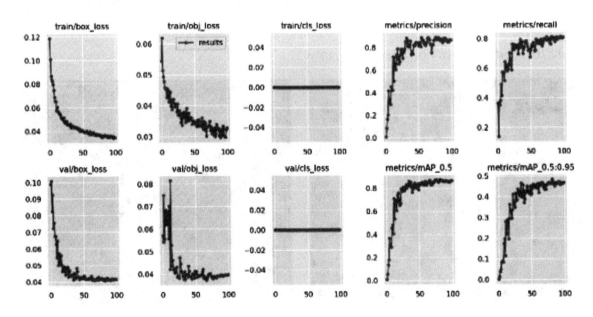

6. RESULTS AND DISCUSSION

Figure 8 explains multiple parameters that reflect the model training. We can observe that training loss is decreasing exponentially and stabilises at 0.034. This implies that the difference between actual and predicted plants is very small. The mAP50-95 score of 0.483 on a scale of 0.5 can also be stated as the model's accuracy. Also, the precision and recall values are above 85 and 80 percent, respectively and show exponential growth in the graphs. All these parameters together state that the model is suitable enough to predict classes of the plant and differentiate them from each other efficiently.

From the images displayed in Figures 9-14, it can be observed that the YOLOv5 trained model can identify the carrot crop from the weed. The carrot leaves are marked with red-coloured bounding boxes, which also display the probability of successful prediction of that crop. The probability scores are mostly between 80% to 90% in all these images. Also, the output is displayed as a Laplacian filter, which is the key parameter of our proposed system. Due to this filter, the model identifies the veins pattern, and the

Figure 9. Input Image with corresponding output

 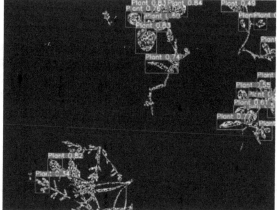

Figure 10. Input Image with corresponding output

 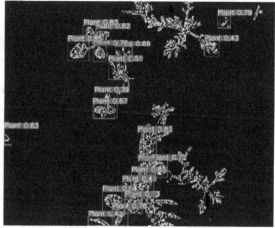

Figure 11. Input Image with corresponding output

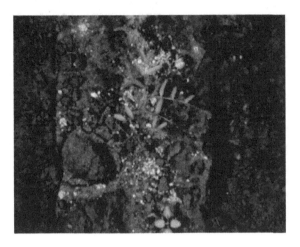
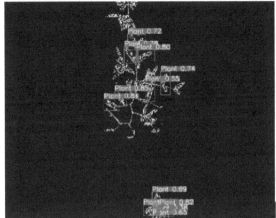

Figure 12. Input Image with corresponding output

Figure 13. Input Image with corresponding output

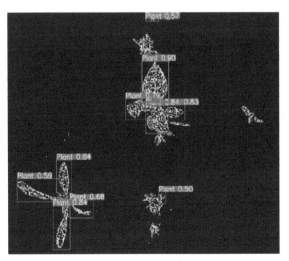

Figure 14. Input Image with corresponding output

 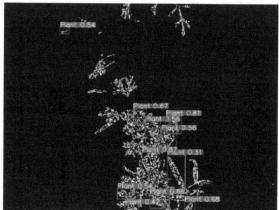

crop class is predicted. As the bounding boxes are created on all the detections, our system automatically records the centre coordinates of the detected object with spatial dimensions. This can be very beneficial for systems requiring the identified crop's location.

7. DISCUSSION

The findings of this study show the efficacy of an integrated strategy for plant identification in agricultural development that combines the Laplacian filter with deep Learning. The Laplacian filter has shown to be a useful pre-processing step, effectively increasing leaf vein patterns, which serve as essential discriminative traits for precise plant species categorization. Additionally, using CNNs, in particular, shows off Deep Learning's capacity to automatically learn complicated properties from photos, allowing the system to perform at the cutting edge of plant identification.

The accuracy and robustness of the plant identification system are greatly improved by combining the Laplacian filter and Deep Learning techniques. Our strategy outperforms utilising either method independently, illuminating the methods' complementary nature. Deep Learning efficiently learns and classifies plant species based on these properties with the help of the Laplacian filter, making extracting useful feature information easier. Combining these methods results in a comprehensive and potent plant identification solution.

The suggested approach also shows promising results for practical agricultural applications. Our method can help farmers and agricultural specialists improve crop management, find invasive species, and use precision agriculture techniques because it can quickly and reliably identify plants. Our solution increases overall efficiency in the agriculture industry by automating the process of plant identification, saving significant time and resources while reducing manual labour.

8. CONCLUSION

The proposed system is designed to implement an Object Detection model for crop identification with the help of Laplacian filters. The proposed model is based on identifying leaf morphological veins pattern using a Laplacian filter kernel. This approach works better than the earlier approach, which was dependent on leaf structure and colour pattern. The system successfully does so for the carrot crop, which is in its initial stage. Although, at this stage, the crop and the plant look very similar, our proposed model has successfully differentiated the morphological vein pattern of their leaves. This proves that using appropriate image processing tools and filters and suitable Deep learning algorithms with computer vision makes the identification of crops in real-time with high accuracy and precision possible. This identification of crops with just image processing has a wide range of applications. Multiple types of Robotic devices can make use of our proposed system. This opens a wide area of research in precision Agriculture. In the future, the proposed system will be integrated with multiple agricultural devices, which will benefit the the agricultural sector globally.

8.1. Future Scope

The integrated approach using the Laplacian filter and Deep Learning demonstrates significant promise for plant identification in agriculture. The Laplacian filter effectively enhances vein patterns, while Deep Learning achieves high accuracy by learning complex features. Their combination leads to superior performance, enabling rapid and reliable species classification. The proposed approach offers high accuracy, automation, environmental conditions adaptability, and precision agriculture support. It holds the potential for scale-up and contributes to sustainable crop management. Future research can focus on optimising filter parameters, exploring ensemble approaches, and leveraging transfer learning with limited data. Additionally, interpretable Deep Learning and mediation analysis can provide valuable insights into feature relationships, leading to a better understanding of the system.

REFERENCES

Alarood, A. A., Alsolami, E., Al-Khasawneh, M. A., Ababneh, N., & Elmedany, W. (2022). IES: Hyperchaotic plain image encryption scheme using improved shuffled confusion-diffusion. *Ain Shams Engineering Journal, 13*(3), 101583. doi:10.1016/j.asej.2021.09.010

Backes, A. R., de M. Sá Junior, J. J., Kolb, R. M., & Bruno, O. M. (2009). Plant species identification using multi-scale fractal dimension applied to images of adaxial surface epidermis. In Computer Analysis of Images and Patterns (pp. 680–688). Springer Berlin Heidelberg.

Bagal, V. C., & Manza, R. R. (2016). Feature extraction of plant species from leaf architecture. In *2016 International Conference on Electrical, Electronics, and Optimization Techniques (ICEEOT)*. IEEE. 10.1109/ICEEOT.2016.7755481

Bansal, V., Pandey, S., Shukla, S. K., Singh, D., Rathod, S. A., & Gonzáles, J. L. A. (2022). A frame work of security attacks, issues classifications and configuration strategy for IoT networks for the successful implementation. In *2022 5th International Conference on Contemporary Computing and Informatics (IC3I)*. IEEE.

Boulent, J., Foucher, S., Théau, J., & St-Charles, P.-L. (2019). Convolutional Neural Networks for the automatic identification of plant diseases. *Frontiers in Plant Science*, *10*, 941. doi:10.3389/fpls.2019.00941 PMID:31396250

Cirillo, S., Polese, G., Salerno, D., Simone, B., & Solimando, G. (2023). Towards Flexible Voice Assistants: Evaluating Privacy and Security Needs in IoT-enabled Smart Homes. *FMDB Transactions on Sustainable Computer Letters*, *1*(1), 25–32.

Fu, H., & Chi, Z. (2006). Combined thresholding and neural network approach for vein pattern extraction from leaf images. *IEE Proceedings. Vision Image and Signal Processing*, *153*(6), 881. doi:10.1049/ip-vis:20060061

Gayakwad, M., Patil, S., Joshi, R., Gonge, S., & Pande, S. D. (2022). Credibility Evaluation of User-Generated Content Using Novel Multinomial Classification Technique. *International Journal on Recent and Innovation Trends in Computing and Communication*, *10*(2s, no. 2s), 151–157. doi:10.17762/ijritcc.v10i2s.5922

Grinblat, G. L., Uzal, L. C., Larese, M. G., & Granitto, P. M. (2016). Deep learning for plant identification using vein morphological patterns. *Computers and Electronics in Agriculture*, *127*, 418–424. doi:10.1016/j.compag.2016.07.003

Gunturu, V., Bansal, V., Sathe, M., Kumar, A., Gehlot, A., & Pant, B. (2023). Wireless communications implementation using blockchain as well as distributed type of IOT. In *2023 International Conference on Artificial Intelligence and Smart Communication (AISC)*. IEEE. 10.1109/AISC56616.2023.10085249

Haug, S., & Ostermann, J. (2015). A crop/weed field image dataset for the evaluation of computer vision based precision agriculture tasks. In *Computer Vision - ECCV 2014 Workshops* (pp. 105–116). Springer International Publishing. doi:10.1007/978-3-319-16220-1_8

Jeba, J. A., Bose, S. R., & Boina, R. (2023). Exploring Hybrid Multi-View Multimodal for Natural Language Emotion Recognition Using Multi-Source Information Learning Model. *FMDB Transactions on Sustainable Computer Letters*, *1*(1), 12–24.

Jeganathan, J., Vashist, S., Nirmala, G., & Deep, R. (2023). A Cross Sectional Study on Anxiety and Depression Among Patients with Alcohol Withdrawal Syndrome. *FMDB Transactions on Sustainable Health Science Letters*, *1*(1), 31–40.

Kanjalkar, J., Kanjalkar, P., Aole, K., Ansari, A., Abak, H., & Tiwari, A. (2023a). Analysis of machine learning algorithms for COVID detection using deep learning. In *Data Management, Analytics and Innovation* (pp. 405–420). Springer Nature Singapore. doi:10.1007/978-981-99-1414-2_31

Kanjalkar, J., Kanjalkar, P., Deshmukh, T., Deshmukh, J., Dhamal, P., & Bhalerao, A. (2022). A novel system for AYUSH healthcare services using classification and regression. *International Journal on Recent and Innovation Trends in Computing and Communication, 10*(1s), 232–240. doi:10.17762/ijritcc.v10i1s.5830

Kanjalkar, P., Chinchole, P., Chitre, A., Kanjalkar, J., & Sharma, P. (2023b). Economical solution to automatic evaluation of an OMR sheet using image processing. In *Data Management, Analytics and Innovation* (pp. 665–683). Springer Nature Singapore. doi:10.1007/978-981-99-1414-2_48

Kattenborn, T., Eichel, J., & Fassnacht, F. E. (2019). Convolutional Neural Networks enable efficient, accurate and fine-grained segmentation of plant species and communities from high-resolution UAV imagery. *Scientific Reports, 9*(1), 17656. doi:10.103841598-019-53797-9 PMID:31776370

Keivani, M., Mazloum, J., Sedaghatfar, E., & Tavakoli, M. (2020). Automated analysis of leaf shape, texture, and color features for plant classification. *TS. Traitement du Signal, 37*(1), 17–28. doi:10.18280/ts.370103

Kulkarni, J. B. (2019). Depth analysis of single view image objects based on object detection and focus measure. *International Journal of Advanced Trends in Computer Science and Engineering, 5*(8), 2608–2612. doi:10.30534/ijatcse/2019/112852019

LeeS. H.ChanC. S.WilkinP.RemagninoP. (2015). *Deep-Plant: Plant Identification with convolutional neural networks*. doi:10.1109/ICIP.2015.7350839

Lu, Y., & Young, S. (2020). A survey of public datasets for computer vision tasks in precision agriculture. *Computers and Electronics in Agriculture, 178*(105760), 105760. doi:10.1016/j.compag.2020.105760

Nath, T., Caffo, B., Wager, T., & Lindquist, M. A. (2023). A machine learning based approach towards high-dimensional mediation analysis. *NeuroImage, 268*(119843), 119843. doi:10.1016/j.neuroimage.2022.119843 PMID:36586543

Nirmala, G., Premavathy, R., Chandar, R., & Jeganathan, J. (2023). An Explanatory Case Report on Biopsychosocial Issues and the Impact of Innovative Nurse-Led Therapy in Children with Hematological Cancer. *FMDB Transactions on Sustainable Health Science Letters, 1*(1), 1–10.

Pande, S. D., & Chetty, M. S. R. (2021). Fast medicinal leaf retrieval using CapsNet. In *Advances in Intelligent Systems and Computing* (pp. 149–155). Springer Singapore.

Pande, S. D., Rathod, S. B., Chetty, M. S. R., Pathak, S., Jadhav, P. P., & Godse, S. P. (2022). Shape and textural based image retrieval using K-NN classifier. *Journal of Intelligent & Fuzzy Systems, 43*(4), 4757–4768. doi:10.3233/JIFS-213355

Pandit, P. (2023). On the Context of Diabetes: A Brief Discussion on the Novel Ethical Issues of Non-communicable Diseases. *FMDB Transactions on Sustainable Health Science Letters, 1*(1), 11–20.

Parra, L., Marin, J., Yousfi, S., Rincón, G., Mauri, P. V., & Lloret, J. (2020). Edge detection for weed recognition in lawns. *Computers and Electronics in Agriculture, 176*(105684), 105684. doi:10.1016/j.compag.2020.105684

Priscila, S. S., Rajest, S. S., Tadiboina, S. N., Regin, R., & András, S. (2023). Analysis of Machine Learning and Deep Learning Methods for Superstore Sales Prediction. *FMDB Transactions on Sustainable Computer Letters*, *1*(1), 1–11.

Rani, R., Kumar, S., Kaiwartya, O., Khasawneh, A. M., Lloret, J., Al-Khasawneh, M. A., & Alarood, A. A. (2021). Towards green computing oriented security: A lightweight postquantum signature for IoE. *Sensors (Basel)*, *21*(5), 1883. doi:10.339021051883 PMID:33800227

Saleem, G., Akhtar, M., Ahmed, N., & Qureshi, W. S. (2019). Automated analysis of visual leaf shape features for plant classification. *Computers and Electronics in Agriculture*, *157*, 270–280. doi:10.1016/j.compag.2018.12.038

Saleh, M. A., Othman, S. H., Al-Dhaqm, A., & Al-Khasawneh, M. A. (2021). Common investigation process model for Internet of Things forensics. In *2021 2nd International Conference on Smart Computing and Electronic Enterprise (ICSCEE)* (pp. 84-89). IEEE. 10.1109/ICSCEE50312.2021.9498045

Saxena, D., & Chaudhary, S. (2023). Predicting Brain Diseases from FMRI-Functional Magnetic Resonance Imaging with Machine Learning Techniques for Early Diagnosis and Treatment. *FMDB Transactions on Sustainable Computer Letters*, *1*(1), 33–48.

Sonnad, S., Sathe, M., Basha, D. K., Bansal, V., Singh, R., & Singh, D. P. (2022). The integration of connectivity and system integrity approaches using internet of things (IoT) for enhancing network security. In *2022 5th International Conference on Contemporary Computing and Informatics (IC3I)*. IEEE.

Sun, Y., Liu, Y., Wang, G., & Zhang, H. (2017). Deep learning for plant identification in natural environment. *Computational Intelligence and Neuroscience*, *2017*, 1–6. doi:10.1155/2017/7361042 PMID:28611840

Suthar, V., Bansal, V., Reddy, C. S., Gonzáles, J. L. A., Singh, D., & Singh, D. P. (2022). Machine Learning Adoption in Blockchain-Based Smart Applications. In *2022 5th International Conference on Contemporary Computing and Informatics (IC3I)*. IEEE.

Tan, M., Pang, R., & Le, Q. V. (2020). EfficientDet: Scalable and Efficient Object Detection. In *2020 IEEE/CVF Conference on Computer Vision and Pattern Recognition (CVPR)*. IEEE. 10.1109/CVPR42600.2020.01079

Uddin, M. I., Ali Shah, S. A., Al-Khasawneh, M. A., Alarood, A. A., & Alsolami, E. (2022). Optimal policy learning for COVID-19 prevention using reinforcement learning. *Journal of Information Science*, *48*(3), 336–348. doi:10.1177/0165551520959798

Uike, D., Agarwalla, S., Bansal, V., Chakravarthi, M. K., Singh, R., & Singh, P. (2022). Investigating the role of block chain to secure identity in IoT for industrial automation. In *2022 11th International Conference on System Modeling & Advancement in Research Trends (SMART)*. IEEE.

Ullah, Z., Zeb, A., Ullah, I., Awan, K. M., Saeed, Y., Uddin, M. I., & Zareei, M. (2020). Certificateless proxy reencryption scheme (CPRES) based on hyperelliptic curve for access control in content-centric network (CCN). *Mobile Information Systems*, *2020*, 1–13. doi:10.1155/2020/4138516

Vashishtha, E., & Dhawan, G. (2023). Bridging Generation Gap on Analysis of Mentor-Mentee Relationship in Healthcare Setting. *FMDB Transactions on Sustainable Health Science Letters*, *1*(1), 21–30.

Zannah, A. I., Rachakonda, S., Abubakar, A. M., Devkota, S., & Nneka, E. C. (2023). Control for Hydrogen Recovery in Pressuring Swing Adsorption System Modeling. *FMDB Transactions on Sustainable Energy Sequence*, *1*(1), 1–10.

Chapter 3
A Privacy–Preserving Untraceable Group Data–Sharing Technique

B. Judy Flavia

SRM Institute of Science and Technology, Ramapuram, India

D. Pavan Kumar

SRM Institute of Science and Technology, Ramapuram, India

R. Varun Teja

SRM Institute of Science and Technology, Ramapuram, India

B. Lakshman

SRM Institute of Science and Technology, Ramapuram, India

ABSTRACT

Significant data privacy problems have been raised by adopting cloud computing, which has drawn much attention recently. Meanwhile, system security and cryptography offer a variety of security frameworks for protecting machine learning and maintaining privacy. Especially in the healthcare sector, cloud computing has drastically changed how we store and access data. Cloud computing has benefits but also increases the chance of data breaches and privacy abuses. Privacy protection is essential since using the cloud requires storing sensitive data on distant servers. Encrypting data and limiting access to only those with the necessary authorisation is one method to protect privacy. Data security is essential in the cloud to prevent unauthorised access, manipulation, and loss. Disaster recovery planning and routine backups are two methods we may use to maintain the previous data's security while using the BVK algorithm.

1. INTRODUCTION

The term "cloud computing" refers to the provision of computer services on a pay-per-use basis through the Internet, including servers, storage, databases, software, and other resources (sometimes referred

DOI: 10.4018/978-1-6684-9189-8.ch003

to as "the cloud"). In other words, rather than buying and maintaining physical gear and equipment, firms may access and use these resources as needed from third-party providers who own and control the underlying infrastructure (Uddin, et al., 2022). Businesses are only charged for the resources they use, and they can quickly and simply adjust the capacity of their cloud computing to fit changing demands (Ullah, et al., 2020). A wide range of cloud computing services from companies like Google Cloud Platform, Microsoft Azure, and Amazon Web Services (AWS) are included in eHealthcare, also known as electronic medical services or computerised medical services (Alarood, et al., 2022).

It involves the usage of telemedicine, wearable technology, mobile health applications, electronic health records (EHRs), and other technological improvements to simplify the supply and coordination of medical services. EHealthcare makes it possible for medical professionals to access and share patient data remotely, enhancing the efficiency of healthcare delivery, reducing expenses, and expanding scientific understanding. Patients may access their medical information, chat remotely with doctors and other healthcare professionals, obtain advice and data tailored to their needs, and use mobile applications and other technology platforms (Rani, et al., 2021). Virtual expert interviews, remote comprehension testing, and health data sharing networks are examples of eHealthcare initiatives that let medical practitioners safely share patient information with other medical care groups (Saleh, et al., 2021).

The infrastructure and tools provided by cloud computing enable the efficient operation of eHealthcare; as a result, the two are intertwined. Cloud computing is used by eHealthcare to manage, store, and analyse the enormous volumes of data that patients and healthcare organisations create (Mast, et al., 2021). As long as healthcare professionals have an internet connection, they may access patient data and medical records via cloud computing from any location and device (Al-Khasawneh, et al., 2018). In order to enhance patient outcomes and save expenses, healthcare providers may offer remote treatment and telemedicine (Kumar, et al., 2021). Healthcare companies may easily and quickly increase their computer capabilities as data processing and storage need rise. Consequently, healthcare providers might expand their capabilities and services without investing in new infrastructure or equipment (Zannah, et al., 2023). ORAM has an O (log n log n) cost for online communication and computing (Sabir, et al., 2022).

Information access sequence is written as A = (op1, u1, data1), (op2, u2, data2), and so on to maintain security, where creations denote the read or compose activity, ui denotes the information address, and data specifies the information contents. If a distributed storage system's entry designs can't be determined in polynomial time given two information access groups, An and A′, it is considered to have security preserved (Alam Khan, et al., 2020).

Cloud computing also provides the security and privacy features necessary to protect patient data and ensure compliance with medical regulations (Arslan, et al., 2021). Cloud service providers often offer robust security measures like multi-factor authentication and encryption to protect sensitive information from unauthorised access and internet hazards (Sharma, et al., 2021a). In order to provide patients and medical staff with high-quality, efficient, and secure medical services, cloud computing is usually required. Given the proliferation of big data, having the greatest degree of privacy and security in healthcare is crucial (Ogunmola, et al., 2021). The creation of e-healthcare platforms has been a crucial step towards ensuring the secure exchange of medical data between patients, researchers, and healthcare professionals. However, patients' private information and sensitive medical data are at risk of hacking attempts because of the present customary methods of data interchange, threatening their privacy and confidentiality (Jeba, et al., 2023). This issue may be handled by setting up a platform for anonymous group data sharing that protects patient privacy, is untraceable, and guarantees the highest level of security for patient data (Sharma, et al., 2021b). This strategy will address the problems with privacy and security that are vital in modern healthcare. The protocol uses the OTmn protocol to safeguard the two-way privacy of the parties to the conversation. The following paper discusses an innovative method for distributing group data using e-healthcare platforms.

This method protects people's identities and privacy while giving academics and medical professionals access to crucial medical data (Priscila, et al., 2023). The introduction of a secure cloud storage solution, which combines essential multi-owner data-sharing authentication support with cloud storage public audit capability, is the last stage. This method allows for the public auditability of cloud storage, protecting privacy. Overall, various recommended strategies are developed to enhance load balancing and untraceable group data sharing while protecting user privacy in cloud computing.

Privacy: When processing data in the cloud, homomorphic encryption and secret sharing, two modern cryptography approaches, ensure that the information stays private.

Enhanced Security: The private information of user commitments and the security of transactions is ensured by using blind signatures and zero-knowledge proofs. Adjusting the load, the optimal system performance is provided by load balancing, which guarantees an equitable workload distribution across all cloud servers.

Figure 1 explains the main roles that various devices play in the e-health care protocol and how they are related. Clients, patients, and doctors must have a variety of devices, connect them to networks, and log in to our application or web page before they can connect to the data server and database. As a result, we offer a variety of protocols and security measures, including ORAM, OTMN, and BVK (Sharma, et al., 2021c).

Figure 1. This is a figure that says what is the main thing in this working paper

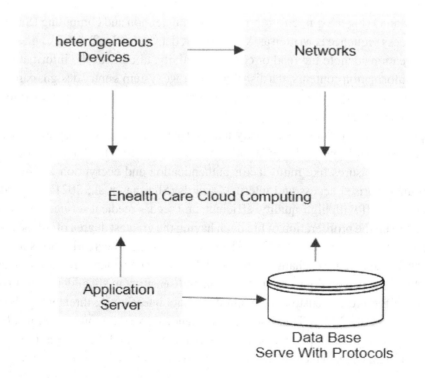

2. RELATED WORK

In order to guarantee the quality of water supplied to customers from a water treatment facility, the paper suggests a hybrid data recording system that employs blocks of cryptographic hashing based on both the Secure Hash Function 256 (SHA-256) and Message Digest 5 (MD5). Blockchain technology would store the hash functions developed at the data logging facility, making them secure and nearly uncrackable (Quist-Aphetsi and Blankson, 2019).

The Paper A cutting-edge huge data cloud solution called S2Cloud, sometimes called Smart and Safe Cloud, gives healthcare organisations a smart and safe approach to handling patient data and measurements. Through an interactive website, this cutting-edge system enables doctors to effectively monitor patients and access vital health data. S2Cloud makes it possible to maintain historical and real-time data, which enables the retrieval and visualisation of patient measurements (Stauffer and Zhang, 2021).

The paper Explains Internal and external threats that might jeopardise private electronic health records (EHRs) can affect cloud-based eHealth systems. A blockchain-assisted eHealth architecture is suggested as a solution to safeguard outsourced EHRs (Cirillo, et al., 2023). The framework is illustrated in a case study and satisfies system and security requirements. The article's conclusion covers future research directions for safe EHRs in cloud-based eHealth systems (Cao, et al., 2020).

The paper Information and communication technology (ICT) solutions, such as cloud-based healthcare services that use the Internet of Things (IoT) to access patient information, have been adopted in India due to the need for smart cities. However, data centres use a lot of energy due to mobile cloud computing offering these services. The healthcare sector's top priority now is to increase the energy efficiency of these data centres. Mobile cloud computing brings medical data to mobile devices, which enhances application speed and battery life (Agarkhed et al., 2019).

This paper reviews and discusses the processes and challenges of using cloud computing to analyse big data in healthcare. The geographic flexibility, resource sharing, and scalability of cloud computing can be advantageous for big data management and processing in the healthcare sector. Despite the numerous challenges that the introduction of big data has presented to the industry, cloud computing may be used to manage healthcare data systems effectively. The paper addresses the fundamental challenges this technology confronts and the benefits and drawbacks of cloud computing for processing big data in healthcare. The study suggests future, more efficient big data processing techniques in healthcare (Rajabion et al., 2019).

The paper says, in particular, that electronic health records (EHRs) stored in the cloud are the focus of this article's thorough assessment of e-health systems' security and privacy concerns. In order to identify important study topics and future directions, the authors evaluated and examined many EHR security and privacy facets, including cryptographic and non-cryptographic techniques. They emphasise the critical necessity for effective and all-encompassing security measures to keep patient data accurate and private in the digital era (Chenthara, et al., 2019).

The paper examines the healthcare sector's security and privacy problems with Mobile Cloud Computing (MCC). The paper suggests a solution based on Layered Modelling and the Modular Encryption Standard (MES), which performs better than other widely used algorithms in terms of both security and performance metrics. The suggested strategy might affect the system's performance, which solely takes textual data into account. Future work may integrate with quantum computing and incorporate image-oriented data to increase efficiency. To protect patient privacy, it may also be useful to investigate the usage of blockchain security models (Shabbir, et al., 2021).

This study suggests an untraceable and privacy-preserving method for group data sharing in the cloud that is secure that makes use of the proxy re-encryption algorithm and ORAM. The plan guarantees the privacy of shared data, the safety of data storage, the untraceability of stored data, and effective data access pattern concealment. The protocol can withstand multiparty collaboration and stop data manipulation by recognising malevolent users. Both theoretical and experimental investigations demonstrate the security and effectiveness of the suggested architecture (Shen, et al., 2022).

The Paper Explains By building a federated cloud infrastructure, and the health-X project seeks to enable people to access and manage their health data from various sources, such as wearables and mobile health devices. Modern, individualised health and care services may be created by unlocking this data and making it accessible. The concept emphasises giving the person control and priority over future healthcare services. The initiative will use multidisciplinary scientific research to accomplish this aim, integrating disciplines including computer science, data science, and medicine (Sharma, et al., 2021d). This strategy seeks to address the issues of data security and privacy while simultaneously encouraging innovation and cooperation in the healthcare sector. The project's ultimate objective is to provide people with better health results via greater access and control over their health data (Boll & Meyer, 2022).

The study suggests an approach for attaining accurate average agreement in dynamic load balancing and cooperative management of vehicle formations termed APPAC that protects privacy. By creating and sending random numbers based on the Paillier cryptosystem, the technique enables agents to hide their starting states. The requirements that must be met to deduce starting states are also covered in this study. Extensive simulations demonstrate the usefulness of the suggested approach (Yin, et al., 2020).

The paper offers a thorough review of the advantages and difficulties of cloud computing in healthcare, emphasising the privacy and security issues that may come up. The paper analyses several tactics and approaches used in e-Health to solve these difficulties by thoroughly examining the literature, including access control, data encryption, and user authentication. Healthcare organisations thinking about using cloud-based services are advised after a full discussion of the benefits and drawbacks of each strategy. In order to secure the confidentiality, integrity, and availability of sensitive health information in cloud-based e-Health systems, the study emphasises the significance of resolving privacy and security concerns (Sivan, & Zukarnain, 2021).

The use of cloud computing, the Internet of Things (IoT), and sensor-based cyber-physical systems (CPS) in healthcare networks is discussed in this article, with an emphasis on the difficulties posed by the storage and processing costs of mobile terminal devices as well as the security and privacy of healthcare data. The paper suggests a quick ciphertext-policy attribute-based encryption (CP-ABE) solution for mobile devices with constrained computation and storage resources to overcome these problems (Hathaliya, & Tanwar, 2020). To relieve local pressure and guarantee a constant level of straightforward local calculations, the suggested system incorporates outsourcing computationally demanding activities to a small number of partially trusted outsiders. A Boneh-Lynn-Shacham short signature technique is also incorporated into the strategy to guarantee the precision of the decryption findings (Wang et al., 2020).

"Medical Cyber-Physical Systems" (MCPS) is a cutting-edge system that integrates patient physiological data, software-controlled devices, and networking capabilities in contemporary medicine. The article discusses MCPS. Through the development of digital medical records that can be kept and accessed from a distance, MCPS has emerged as a crucial resource for several facets of healthcare, including insurance, diagnostics, and medication. Overviews of MCPS architectures, modelling Data storage and analysis, key communications, identity and sign sensing, monitoring, data security and privacy protection, and research views are covered in this article. Providing efficient healthcare services in the current medical environment requires understanding these technology features and MCPS research developments (Chen, et al., 2021).

The Article Explain A brand-new paradigm for distributing Electronic Health Records (EHRs) in mobile cloud settings is put forward in this study. The suggested architecture offers a safe and dependable platform for exchanging EHRs across various patients and healthcare professionals by fusing blockchain technology with the decentralised interplanetary file system (IPFS). The framework also has a reliable access control system based on smart contracts, which guarantees that only those with permission can access private health data. Comparing the proposed framework to current data-sharing models, empirical findings from a prototype implementation demonstrate that it offers a more practical solution for data transfers in mobile clouds with high levels of privacy and security. The system assessment and security analysis further highlight the enhancements in minimal network latency and light-weight access control architecture (Nguyen, et al., 2019).

3. PROPOSED SYSTEM

The Methods Major Ideology To guarantee the security and protection of information, the proposed security safeguarding load adjusting and bunch information sharing methodology in distributed computing perhaps utilise a mix of cryptographic procedures. The following are likely calculations: Homomorphic encryption is the capacity to compute encoded information without uncovering the basic information. Secret sharing is dispersing pieces of confidentiality among members so the whole gathering can assemble them back. Responsibility Plans: These permit the shipper to commit to a worth without unveiling it to the beneficiary, who will then, at that point, be educated regarding it. A heap adjusting approach that utilises a hereditary calculation to all the more likely to distribute assets in the cloud is recommended by the creators of "A Hereditary Calculation Based Burden Adjusting Approach for Distributed Computing" (2019). While sharing and gathering information, clients have regularly profited from obscurity because of onion directing. The creators of "An Unknown Gathering Information Sharing Plan because of Onion Directing in Distributed Computing" (2018) propose an onion steering-based bunch information sharing plan to safeguard client security. Moreover, secure multiparty figuring has empowered secure information division among a few gatherings. The creators of "Secure Multiparty Calculation for Protection Safeguarding Information Partaking in Distributed Computing" (2019) propose a solid multiparty processing framework that empowers numerous members to figure out shared information without revealing confidential data.

Task dissemination among a few servers is known as burden change, and it is finished to accomplish ideal resource use and the best throughput. It is vital for producing any fruitful organisation engineering and is expected to accomplish high accessibility and adaptability. In conventional burden-adjusting techniques, the whole effort is, as often as possible, constrained by a solitary server in a unified way. This approach could prompt a weak link and limit versatility since the incorporated server could turn into a bottleneck if it can't deal with the responsibility. To tackle these issues, current burden-adjusting procedures utilise a circulated approach. This approach utilises numerous servers, each responsible for an unmistakable part of the heap-adjusting technique. This can work on the framework's adaptability and adaptation to internal failure because the disappointment of one server will not affect the whole framework. Appropriated load adjusting may likewise support speed and empower better asset use by utilising various servers. Zero-Information Verifications: To empower a prover to show a verifier they know about a worth without uncovering it. Blind Marks: The capacity for an underwriter to sign a letter without realising what is inside (Figure 2).

The information stockpiling, recovery, and transmission periods of the heap adjusting and information sharing cycle in distributed computing may be in every way gotten utilising these strategies. White box testing, also identified as "clear box testing", "glass box testing," "straightforward box testing," and "underlying testing," is a kind of programming testing that assesses an application's inner operations rather than its usefulness. (i.e., black-box testing). Programming expertise and a framework perspective are used to design experiments for white-box testing, which examines various code pathways and predicts expected results. Analyse circuit nodes in ICT; it is comparable to testing in-circuit. Although it is typically done at the unit level, Unit, integration, and system levels can all benefit from this testing during the software testing process. The links formed during integration among units and subsystems can be examined using a system evaluation. This test design approach can reveal many flaws or problems but may also miss unmet demands or parts of the specification that haven't been implemented. These are some tactics for creating white-box tests.

- Control flow analysis
- Data flow analysis
- Branch evaluation
- Path analysis
- Statement protection
- Coverage of decisions

Figure 2. Load balancer and privacy-preserving design
Source: Toosi et al. (2014)

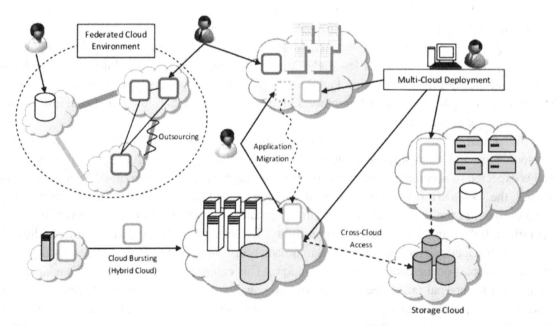

- Control Flow Analysis: Control flow testing is a software testing method directed at the sequence and flow of program statement execution to find potential bugs and guarantee good program behaviour.
- Data flow testing: By examining how data travels across the system, software testing uses data flow testing to identify potential bugs or vulnerabilities in a programme.
- Branch testing: A software testing approach called branch testing checks all conceivable iterations or branches of conditional statements in a programme to ensure they are valid and spot any potential flaws.
- Path testing: Using the control flow through a software programme as a guide, test cases are chosen and carried out as part of the software testing approach known as path testing.

"Clear-box testing" is a technique for testing an application down to the source code. The trials are conducted using the previously indicated plan methodologies: articulation inclusion, choice inclusion, altered condition/choice inclusion, control stream testing, information stream testing, branch testing, way testing, etc. These methodologies are used in "white-box testing," which takes a gander at any feeble code while spreading out an environment freed from botches Glass box testing is a strategy that depends on multiple White-box testing strategies and entails thoroughly testing an application down to the source code level to find any hidden faults. By checking every possible path in the source code, these approaches seek to eliminate mistakes and produce an environment free of defects. Figuring out which line of code is being executed and what the normal result ought to be are the two critical objectives Glass testing stages:

- White-box testing is done at the unit level before freshly tested code is integrated to ensure it works as intended. White-box unit testing helps identify issues early on and repair faults that may happen once the program's code is integrated with the rest of the application, preventing errors from occurring later.
- A Glass box testing strategy is used in the incorporation testing stage to look at the communication between various points of engagement. By evaluating the known cooperation points with white-box testing, this testing technique assesses the correctness of the behaviour in an open environment. This testing aims to confirm that every code segment has undergone extensive testing and is operating correctly in a regulated environment.
- Analysis of relapse During unit and incorporation relapse testing, reused white-box experiments are used for white-box testing.

A developer must have a solid grasp of the source code being tested to use white-box testing effectively. This enables the development of tests that account for all potential directions of execution. When the source code is accessible, it can be examined, and appropriate tests can be made. Three basic phases are normally involved in creating a test for white-box testing. Instances of sources of info are the various necessities, practical details, intensive report plans, exact source codes, and security particulars. All fundamental realities are currently set out during the white-box testing arrangement step. The Handling Unit is liable for dealing with the entire testing process, making a reasonable test plan, executing experiments, and revealing discoveries. Making experiments currently will guarantee that the application has been thoroughly assessed and that the discoveries have been appropriately archived. In the last report, notice the arrangement work and results from the previous cycles.

An approach to testing a product known as "black-box testing" involves only looking at the application's functionality, not its internal workings or structure. Unit, integration, system, and acceptance testing are just a few of the stages of software testing where this method may be applied. It is frequently used in higher-level testing, although it may also be utilised to some extent in unit testing. In contrast to white-box testing, which looks at the internal workings of the software, the approach is used.

It isn't expected to have the application's code, inward design, or programming overall in that frame of mind. Although the analyst is aware of the intended functions of the product, he or she may not be familiar with the underlying mechanisms that enable those functions. For instance, the analyst can be aware that a certain input results in a certain expected output without necessarily being aware of the underlying procedures used by the programme to produce the outcome. Investigation of a case Particulars and necessities, or what the application should perform, are utilised to fabricate experiments. Outside portrayals of the product, like necessities, are often the most important phase in the plan of experiments, details, and plan norms. Albeit utilitarian tests make up most of the tests utilised, non-practical testing can likewise be utilised. Without knowing the inner construction of the test object, the test creator picks both right and mistaken contributions to show up in the right response.

4. APPROACHES FOR TEST PLAN

Common strategies for planning black-box tests include:

- Choice table testing
- All-matches testing
- State change tables
- Comparability dividing
- Limit esteem examination

In computer programming, unit testing assesses the efficacy of specific lines of source code, collections of one or more computer programme modules and the control data associated with them, and implementation and functional processes. A unit can be conceptualised as the littlest testable component of an application. In procedural programming, a unit may be an entire module, even though it comprises one capability or cycle. In object-situated programming, a unit is often a total connection point, like a class, despite the fact that it could essentially be a solitary capability. Unit tests are composed by software engineers or, inconsistently, white box analysers as a component of the improvement interaction.

Similar to exploratory testing, functional testing is A type of quality assurance (QA) process. The tests it conducts are based on the requirements of the software component under the test. Unlike white-box testing, which considers the programme's internal workings, testing typically involves input and evaluation of the outcomes. Functional testing is frequently used to characterise the system's functionality. Regarding programming, execution testing normally alludes to testing completed to decide how a framework acts concerning responsiveness and security under a specific responsibility. It might likewise be utilised to research, survey, affirm, or rate different parts of framework quality, like adaptability, dependability, and asset usage.

Check and Approval To guarantee that a framework, administration, or item adjusts with necessities and details and satisfies the expected reason, confirmation and Approval — two unique cycles — are utilised couple. These are the fundamental components of an ISO 9000 agreeable quality administration framework. The words "Free" (or IV&V) are frequently utilised before confirmation and Approval, meaning an outsider will do those exercises unbiasedly. The advantages of mysterious gathering information sharing and protection saving burden adjusting in distributed computing are:

Security: While handling information in the cloud, current cryptography strategies like homomorphic encryption and mystery sharing guarantee that the data stays private.

Expanded Security: Using visually impaired marks and zero-information verifications safeguards the security of the exchanges and the privacy of the client's responsibilities. A Heap adjusting: By ensuring an equivalent responsibility circulation across all cloud servers, load adjusting gives ideal framework execution. Gathering Coordinated effort: The framework's mystery sharing and untraceable gathering information sharing highlights empower clients to securely trade information and work together on projects in gatherings. JavaScript just approaches treats for HTTP and structure accommodation information. JavaScript works on the client; accordingly, it can't get to server-side assets like data sets, indexes, cost data, etc. variable HTML Obviously, normal HTML can't hold dynamic data. It is very practical to further develop HTML pages that imperceptibly benefit from incorporating small amounts of dynamic information because of JSP's straightforwardness and comfort. Because of its cost, dynamic information customarily must be utilised in the luckiest conditions.

Servlets can be created naturally utilising Java Server Pages (JSP) or, then again, format motors like Web Full scale. Servlets and JSPs are broadly utilised related to the "Model 2" variation of the model-view-regulator engineering. CGI programming's response to Java innovation is servlet innovation. They are programs that work on a web server and produce Site pages. It is helpful to fabricate Website pages in a flash for many reasons. (Also, habitually finished). The client submitted information to structure the foundation of the page. This technique is utilised to make programs that handle orders for web-based business sites and web crawler results pages. Information is frequently refreshed. For example, a site that gives climate data or news titles might be built progressively and return a past rendition of the page, assuming it is still modern. The site utilises data from corporate information bases and different wellsprings of a like sort (Figure 3).

The architecture diagram explains the procedure that will be followed while processing applications and securities with specific identities. It is possible to obtain certification for machinery and equipment using do-it-yourself techniques using the vendor's training course materials and tutorials or using published guidebooks like step-by-step series if on-site qualification services are not included with purchasing such goods. DQ, IQ, OQ, and PQ templates are often available online. Software, computer operating systems, and manufacturing procedures may be independently assessed to determine their suitability. The most crucial responsibility is to create and archive machinery/equipment qualification reports for auditing reasons if regulatory compliances are required.

A cryptographic bilinear handbook's first definition Creates P so that G1 while G and GT are treated as the additive and multiplicative groups, respectively, for two groups, G1 and G2, that share the same prime request q, where q is a big prime. Weil matching or Tate matching-capable cryptographic bilinear guides will be presented in cases where a planned G1 $\times$ G1 $\rightarrow$ G2 satisfies the prerequisites.

- For any P, Q, R, G, and a, b Zq, we get e(aP, bQ) = e(P, Q) stomach muscle and e(P, Q)e(P, R) = e(P, Q + R). These equations are bilinear.

Figure 3. Architecture diagram for the server back verifying key and ORAM, OTMN

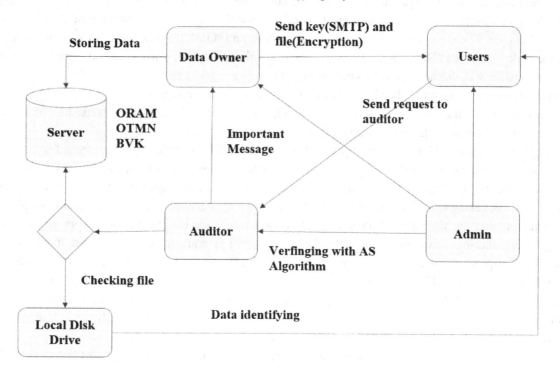

- (2Differently expressed: e (P, P) Zq is a generator of G2 in the unlikely event that P is an irregular generator of G1. Therefore, e (P, P) 6= 1 is true. Nondegeneracy has not been proven in any circumstance.
- The word "calculable" denotes the capability of computing or establishing the value of e(P, Q) for any given P and Q in G.
- The Bilinear Diffie-Hellman (BDH) issue is described as follows: In the paired configuration (G1, G2, e), given a point P in G1 and the points aP, bP, and cP (where a, b, and c are essentially random values in Zq*), determine the value of W = e(P, P)abc in G2. The procedure is claimed to solve the BDH problem in (G1, G2, e) if the probability that a computational technique An (P, aP, bP, cP) = e(P, P)abc is greater than or equal to a particular threshold. The random picks of a, b, c, and P in G1 and the random bits of algorithm A decide this probability.

In a paired context, computing a specific value is central to the BDH problem, and a computational process is said to be successful if it can do so with sufficient probability. The algorithm's success relies on several random decisions made when solving the issue. Definition 2: The BDH presumption expresses that no polynomial time calculation An enjoys a benefit of in any event in taking care of the BDH issue in (G1, G2, e), and that intends that the benefit is immaterial.

4.1. The Four Kinds of Aggressors

- A disowned client is conspiring with other collaborating clients to get the key without authorisation. Once the disowned client has the key, they will encrypt the shared data and attempt to unlock the access code by posing as a middleman.

- Despite the mediator's consent, the partially trusted cloud server may interact with a client who has renounced their membership in the client group to access encrypted information, exposing the information to the renounced client. The client may still have the subkeys required for communication even after they have been renounced and dropped from the list table, and the semi-trusted cloud server will still hold whatever information they had previously communicated with the group.

- Access operations to different information types may differ when a collecting client has access to shared information. Then, a semi-believed server might figure out the sort or significance of the information in light of various access procedures. Further, it is feasible to figure out which information the client is more intrigued by and to give data to a disavowed client to plot this information.

- The inquisitive cloud server decides the significance of scrambled information because of the quantity of information access times, so it might decide the need for information. Additionally, the interested cloud server tracks information and tries to obtain the information's content by looking into the relationship between similar or identical information and address successions being stored. A proxy is a system component between the user and the cloud server. Multiple users can securely exchange data thanks to the proxy's implementation of the OCLTORAM structure and management of the encryption process. Proxy re-encryption is the encryption technique used in this experiment. The proxy is in charge of negotiating secret key sharing with users, encrypting data, and helping to decode data. The proxy and N users negotiate the key during the proxy re-encryption phase. The two parties' key agreement mechanism generates key parameters that are then exchanged n times consecutively. This is the system's central idea.

5. RESULT AND DISCUSSION

Additionally, our proposed plan's improved load balancing mechanism ensures maximum throughput and optimal resource utilisation. We accomplish this by progressively allocating assignments to hubs because of their handling power and accessibility; This is accomplished by monitoring their capacity by determining whether the nodes are up to the task. In order to assign the task to the best node, our load-balancing algorithm considers the task's size, the number of available nodes, and the system's overall processing power. In addition, it considers the nodes' current availability to guarantee that the task is assigned to the best node. The algorithm also considers the task's priority to give tasks with a higher priority to the best nodes. The algorithm also considers the nodes' previous performance to see if they can handle the task effectively.

As a result, the system can meet its performance goals since the jobs are distributed among the most suitable nodes. In addition, the load balancing algorithm ensures that the load is distributed evenly among the nodes to maximise system efficiency. This assists with guaranteeing that the framework can meet its presentation objectives and that the errands are allocated to the most appropriate hubs. In addition, we present the concept of task migration, which permits tasks to be transferred from one node to another to ensure that resources are utilised to their full potential and that the load is distributed evenly. This is achieved through a dispersed agreement calculation that ensures adaptation to internal failure and information exactness. This algorithm works by allowing the system's nodes to communicate and agree on a single outcome. The nodes need to detect and recover from any failures or discrepancies for this to work. They also need to have a consistent view of the data.

The algorithm works by first making sure a task is legitimate and can be safely moved. During this verification process, the system's nodes check the data to see if it is consistent across the nodes. The algorithm then determines the best node to migrate the task to if the task is found to be valid and safe to do so. This is accomplished by considering the load on each system node and the current resource consumption. When the ideal objective hub has been picked, the assignment is relocated to that hub. Additionally, the algorithm guarantees the task's safe and reliable migration. Cryptographic methods like digital signatures, encryption, and authentication are used to accomplish this. These methods guarantee that the data is shielded from malicious actors and unauthorised access and manipulation. Last, the algorithm ensures that the data and the task are successfully transferred across the system. After the task has been migrated, this is accomplished by monitoring it and ensuring that the data is consistent across the nodes.

Assuming any disparities are found, the calculation will do whatever it may take to guarantee that the undertaking is effectively moved and that the information stays steady. We conducted a wide range of tests to assess the efficiency and performance of our suggested plan. Our research shows that our load-balancing method outperforms traditional throughput, reaction time, and load-balancing methods. We saw a considerable improvement in the load-balancing performance of our suggested design, which evenly spread the strain across the network. The technique could promptly recognise and adapt to network changes, considerably decreasing response time. Due to the suggested scheme's capability to successfully manage the network's burden, we also observed a large improvement in the network's throughput (figure 4).

Overall, the results of our testing show that the plan we came up with is a useful method for balancing load, reducing reaction times, and increasing throughput. Since we are confident that our findings may be applied in various other scenarios, we are eager to investigate the system's potential in more detail. Our plan also offers a comprehensive privacy and security solution for businesses and organisations that place a high importance on data protection. It safeguards privacy by preventing unauthorised access to sensitive information and enabling anonymous group data sharing, which prevents the link between shared data and its original source. Furthermore, our method ensures that data is encrypted and kept in a secure environment, preventing access to the information by any potential bad actors. We also provide a secure authentication mechanism that asks users to verify their identity before granting access to the information.

6. CONCLUSION

In conclusion, our enhanced load balancing and untraceable group data sharing scheme offer a thorough solution to the various privacy and security issues related to cloud computing. This plan aims to ensure efficient resource usage, improved load balancing, and enhanced privacy safeguards. It utilises a safe two-layer encryption mechanism to ensure the security of data storage and transfer between users. Fur-

Figure 4. Design of the work
Source: Lu et al. (2020)

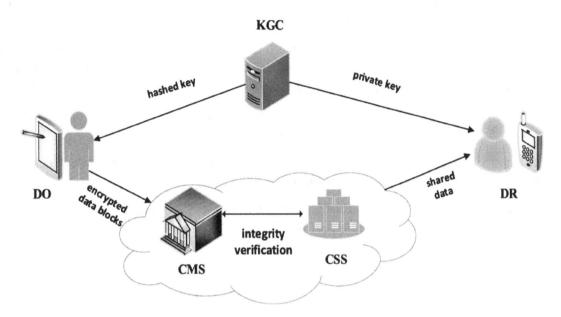

thermore, it uses a powerful load-balancing algorithm to allocate resources to users most efficiently while preserving quality of service (QoS). Various devices play the main roles in the e-health care protocol and how they are related. Clients, patients, and doctors must have a variety of devices, connect them to networks, and log in to our application or web page before they can connect to the data server and database. As a result, we offer a variety of protocols and security measures, including ORAM, OTMN, and BVK. Additionally, the proposed method guarantees that the data cannot be traced, preserving user anonymity. Finally, a distributed approach is used to make sure that the scheme is fault-tolerant, which means that it can continue working even if the system fails. Our scheme can offer its users scalability and dependability.

REFERENCES

Agarkhed, J., Ashalatha, R., & Patil, S. R. (2019). Smart healthcare systems using cloud computing environments. In *Advances in Communication, Devices and Networking* (pp. 545–552). Springer Singapore. doi:10.1007/978-981-13-3450-4_59

Al-Khasawneh, M. A., Shamsuddin, S. M., Hasan, S., & Bakar, A. A. (2018). MapReduce a comprehensive review. In *2018 International Conference on Smart Computing and Electronic Enterprise (ICSCEE)* (pp. 1-6). IEEE.

Alam Khan, Z., Feng, Z., Uddin, M. I., Mast, N., Ali Shah, S. A., Imtiaz, M., & Mahmoud, M. (2020). Optimal policy learning for disease prevention using reinforcement learning. *Scientific Programming*, *2020*, 1–13. doi:10.1155/2020/7627290

Alarood, A. A., Alsolami, E., Al-Khasawneh, M. A., Ababneh, N., & Elmedany, W. (2022). IES: Hyperchaotic plain image encryption scheme using improved shuffled confusion-diffusion. *Ain Shams Engineering Journal*, *13*(3), 101583. doi:10.1016/j.asej.2021.09.010

Arslan, F., Singh, B., Sharma, D. K., Regin, R., Steffi, R., & Suman Rajest, S. (2021). Optimization technique approach to resolve food sustainability problems. In *2021 International Conference on Computational Intelligence and Knowledge Economy (ICCIKE)*. IEEE. 10.1109/ICCIKE51210.2021.9410735

Boll, S., & Meyer, J. (2022). Health-X dataLOFT: A sovereign federated cloud for personalized health care services. *IEEE MultiMedia*, *29*(1), 136–140. doi:10.1109/MMUL.2022.3153121

Cao, S., Zhang, X., & Xu, R. (2020). Toward secure storage in cloud-based eHealth systems: A blockchain-assisted approach. *IEEE Network*, *34*(2), 64–70. doi:10.1109/MNET.001.1900173

Chen, F., Tang, Y., Wang, C., Huang, J., Huang, C., Xie, D., & Zhao, C. (2021). Medical cyber–physical systems: A solution to smart health and the state of the art. *IEEE Transactions on Computational Social Systems*, *9*(5), 1359–1386. doi:10.1109/TCSS.2021.3122807

Chenthara, S., Ahmed, K., Wang, H., & Whittaker, F. (2019). Security and privacy-preserving challenges of e-health solutions in cloud computing. *IEEE Access : Practical Innovations, Open Solutions*, *7*, 74361–74382. doi:10.1109/ACCESS.2019.2919982

Cirillo, S., Polese, G., Salerno, D., Simone, B., & Solimando, G. (2023). Towards Flexible Voice Assistants: Evaluating Privacy and Security Needs in IoT-enabled Smart Homes. *FMDB Transactions on Sustainable Computer Letters*, *1*(1), 25–32.

Hathaliya, J. J., & Tanwar, S. (2020). An exhaustive survey on security and privacy issues in Healthcare 4.0. *Computer Communications*, *153*, 311–335. doi:10.1016/j.comcom.2020.02.018

Jeba, J. A., Bose, S. R., & Boina, R. (2023). Exploring Hybrid Multi-View Multimodal for Natural Language Emotion Recognition Using Multi-Source Information Learning Model. *FMDB Transactions on Sustainable Computer Letters*, *1*(1), 12–24.

Kumar, V., Kumar, S., AlShboul, R., Aggarwal, G., Kaiwartya, O., Khasawneh, A. M., & Al-Khasawneh, M. A. (2021). Grouping and Sponsoring Centric Green Coverage Model for Internet of Things. *Sensors (Basel)*, *21*(12), 3948. doi:10.339021123948 PMID:34201100

Lu, X., Pan, Z., & Xian, H. (2020). An efficient and secure data sharing scheme for mobile devices in cloud computing. *Journal of Cloud Computing (Heidelberg, Germany)*, *9*(1), 60. Advance online publication. doi:10.118613677-020-00207-5

Mast, N., Khan, M. A., Uddin, M. I., Ali Shah, S. A., Khan, A., Al-Khasawneh, M. A., & Mahmoud, M. (2021). Channel contention-based routing protocol for wireless ad hoc networks. *Complexity*, *2021*, 1–10. doi:10.1155/2021/2051796

Nguyen, D. C., Pathirana, P. N., Ding, M., & Seneviratne, A. (2019). Blockchain for secure EHRs sharing of mobile cloud based E-health systems. *IEEE Access : Practical Innovations, Open Solutions*, *7*, 66792–66806. doi:10.1109/ACCESS.2019.2917555

Ogunmola, G. A., Singh, B., Sharma, D. K., Regin, R., Rajest, S. S., & Singh, N. (2021). Involvement of distance measure in assessing and resolving efficiency environmental obstacles. In *2021 International Conference on Computational Intelligence and Knowledge Economy (ICCIKE)*. IEEE. 10.1109/ICCIKE51210.2021.9410765

Priscila, S. S., Rajest, S. S., Tadiboina, S. N., Regin, R., & András, S. (2023). Analysis of Machine Learning and Deep Learning Methods for Superstore Sales Prediction. *FMDB Transactions on Sustainable Computer Letters*, *1*(1), 1–11.

Quist-Aphetsi, K., & Blankson, H. (2019). A hybrid data logging system using cryptographic hash blocks based on SHA-256 and MD5 for water treatment plant and distribution line. In *2019 International Conference on Cyber Security and Internet of Things (ICSIoT)*. IEEE. 10.1109/ICSIoT47925.2019.00009

Rajabion, L., Shaltooki, A. A., Taghikhah, M., Ghasemi, A., & Badfar, A. (2019). Healthcare big data processing mechanisms: The role of cloud computing. *International Journal of Information Management*, *49*, 271–289. doi:10.1016/j.ijinfomgt.2019.05.017

Rani, R., Kumar, S., Kaiwartya, O., Khasawneh, A. M., Lloret, J., Al-Khasawneh, M. A., & Alarood, A. A. (2021). Towards green computing oriented security: A lightweight postquantum signature for IoE. *Sensors (Basel)*, *21*(5), 1883. doi:10.339021051883 PMID:33800227

Sabir, M. W., Khan, Z., Saad, N. M., Khan, D. M., Al-Khasawneh, M. A., Perveen, K., & Azhar Ali, S. S. (2022). Segmentation of Liver Tumor in CT Scan Using ResU-Net. *Applied Sciences (Basel, Switzerland)*, *12*(17), 8650. doi:10.3390/app12178650

Saleh, M. A., Othman, S. H., Al-Dhaqm, A., & Al-Khasawneh, M. A. (2021). Common investigation process model for Internet of Things forensics. In *2021 2nd International Conference on Smart Computing and Electronic Enterprise (ICSCEE)* (pp. 84-89). IEEE. 10.1109/ICSCEE50312.2021.9498045

Shabbir, M., Shabbir, A., Iwendi, C., Javed, A. R., Rizwan, M., Herencsar, N., & Lin, J. C.-W. (2021). Enhancing security of health information using modular encryption standard in mobile cloud computing. *IEEE Access : Practical Innovations, Open Solutions*, *9*, 8820–8834. doi:10.1109/ACCESS.2021.3049564

Sharma, D. K., Jalil, N. A., Regin, R., Rajest, S. S., Tummala, R. K., & Thangadurai. (2021a). Predicting network congestion with machine learning. In *2021 2nd International Conference on Smart Electronics and Communication (ICOSEC)*. IEEE.

Sharma, D. K., Singh, B., Raja, M., Regin, R., & Rajest, S. S. (2021b). An Efficient Python Approach for Simulation of Poisson Distribution. In *2021 7th International Conference on Advanced Computing and Communication Systems (ICACCS)*. IEEE.

Sharma, D. K., Singh, B., Regin, R., Steffi, R., & Chakravarthi, M. K. (2021c). Efficient Classification for Neural Machines Interpretations based on Mathematical models. In *2021 7th International Conference on Advanced Computing and Communication Systems (ICACCS)*. IEEE.

Sharma, K., Singh, B., Herman, E., Regine, R., Rajest, S. S., & Mishra, V. P. (2021d). Maximum information measure policies in reinforcement learning with deep energy-based model. In *2021 International Conference on Computational Intelligence and Knowledge Economy (ICCIKE)*. IEEE. 10.1109/ICCIKE51210.2021.9410756

Shen, J., Yang, H., Vijayakumar, P., & Kumar, N. (2022). A privacy-preserving and untraceable group data sharing scheme in cloud computing. *IEEE Transactions on Dependable and Secure Computing*, *19*(4), 2198–2210. doi:10.1109/TDSC.2021.3050517

Sivan, R., & Zukarnain, Z. A. (2021). Security and privacy in cloud-based e-health system. *Symmetry*, *13*(5), 742. doi:10.3390ym13050742

Stauffer, J., & Zhang, Q. (2021). S 2 cloud: A novel cloud system for mobile health big data management. In *2021 IEEE International Conferences on Internet of Things (iThings) and IEEE Green Computing & Communications (GreenCom) and IEEE Cyber, Physical & Social Computing (CPSCom) and IEEE Smart Data (SmartData) and IEEE Congress on Cybermatics (Cybermatics)* (pp. 380–383). IEEE.

Toosi, A. N., Calheiros, R. N., & Buyya, R. (2014). Interconnected cloud computing environments: Challenges, taxonomy, and survey. *ACM Computing Surveys*, *47*(1), 1–47. doi:10.1145/2593512

Uddin, M. I., Ali Shah, S. A., Al-Khasawneh, M. A., Alarood, A. A., & Alsolami, E. (2022). Optimal policy learning for COVID-19 prevention using reinforcement learning. *Journal of Information Science*, *48*(3), 336–348. doi:10.1177/0165551520959798

Ullah, Z., Zeb, A., Ullah, I., Awan, K. M., Saeed, Y., Uddin, M. I., & Zareei, M. (2020). Certificateless proxy reencryption scheme (CPRES) based on hyperelliptic curve for access control in content-centric network (CCN). *Mobile Information Systems*, *2020*, 1–13. doi:10.1155/2020/4138516

Wang, S., Wang, H., Li, J., Wang, H., Chaudhry, J., Alazab, M., & Song, H. (2020). A fast CP-ABE system for cyber-physical security and privacy in mobile healthcare network. *IEEE Transactions on Industry Applications*, *56*(4), 4467–4477. doi:10.1109/TIA.2020.2969868

Yin, T., Lv, Y., & Yu, W. (2020). Accurate privacy preserving average consensus. IEEE Transactions on Circuits and Systems. II. *Express Briefs, 67*(4), 690–694. doi:10.1109/TCSII.2019.2918709

Zannah, A. I., Rachakonda, S., Abubakar, A. M., Devkota, S., & Nneka, E. C. (2023). Control for Hydrogen Recovery in Pressuring Swing Adsorption System Modeling. *FMDB Transactions on Sustainable Energy Sequence, 1*(1), 1–10.

Chapter 4
Access to Justice During COVID–19 Challenges and Issues Created by a Virus

Megha Middha

https://orcid.org/0000-0001-6949-2742

Chandigarh University, India

Aseem Chandra Paliwal

Karnavati University, India

ABSTRACT

Almost all the sectors of the economy around the world were affected due to corona virus. Those confined in prisons were not able to reach out to courts for bail, or those who wanted to file suits found the courts closed due to lockdown. It was then that the courts decided to have hearings virtually. The chapter shall discuss how much these virtual courts have been successful in rendering justice during coronavirus. The chapter shall also try to explore if the process of rendering justice through virtual mode should continue post pandemic era also. The study shall lay emphasis upon how the criminal activities increased during the COVID-19 times and how the courts have been able to render justice in such scenarios. The chapter shall analyze the alternatives one can resort to through online mediation. The plight of migrant laborers who were left to visit their homes by foot were also denied justice. Henceforth, the research shall be based on primary data as well as secondary data available.

1. INTRODUCTION

It seems that nature has started taking revenge on humans for what they have done to this beautiful planet. It looks as if the return gifts are being received for the harm caused to Mother Earth. In the present times, it is not a matter of astonishment to see the various new types of diseases that are turning up and affecting humans, and what is more interesting is that nobody has a proper cure or medicine available for the kind of diseases affecting humans. We, homo sapiens, were not able to come out of COVID completely,

DOI: 10.4018/978-1-6684-9189-8.ch004

and then yet another virus came along to affect us in a deadlier way, by the name of "monkeypox." The article, though, will focus on the extremes suffered during COVID times, specifically with respect to the undertrials and the migrant labourers who were not provided with adequate facilities to go home. Also, it shall discuss what kind of hardships were undergone by the police officers and medical officers during Corona. The role of courts shall also be looked upon while analysing the concept of justice delivery during COVID times.

The article shall try to highlight the injustices endured by various strata of people in detail and the role of the legal system in helping curb the menace. The research paper will try to study the success and role of technology in tough times and how the online platform has benefited people. The problems related to the online system will also be discussed in detail. Further, the article shall try to explore if the online system can be continued post-pandemic as well. Should that be adopted in normal routines? Who thought a small virus would turn the whole world upside down? The systems will have to be changed because of a small virus. The things people did not even pay serious attention to would happen have actually happened, like working from home, staying inside with a complete lockdown, telemedicine, regular online classes, faculty development programs, and, to a much bigger surprise, the online justice delivery mechanism. The world was trying to adjust to the alternate dispute resolution mechanisms, and all of a sudden, nobody thought when a new system and concept of online mediation and virtual courts turned up in no time.

Moreover, this online system has been a challenging task for many people who are not very technologically sound. But slowly and gradually, all are trying to adapt to the post-COVID scenario. There is no doubt about the fact that many new things have been learned in this pandemic, but at the same time, there cannot be a denial of the fact that many people were denied the basic rights they are entitled to. This paper, through various cases and examples, will try to analyse and explore the kind of denial of access to justice that different groups of people were subjected to. It shall read about the efforts put forth by the legislative and judicial authorities to curb the hardships being faced by people. Also, the paper will highlight the approach taken at the national and international levels to tackle the situation. The researcher, through the paper, has embodied the various aspects of justice through the instances of injustice suffered by people during colonial times. The paper, through a deep analysis of various UN reports, international conventions, scholarly articles, and national laws, shall emphasise the concept of access to justice during COVID times. The author shall explore to what extent governments around the globe have been successful in rendering the fundamental right of access to justice to their citizens.

1.1. Hypothesis

The COVID pandemic led to a violation of various human rights, thereby denying access to justice to citizens. To lessen the hardship caused by COVID, technology has played a significant role in almost every sector to make things easier for the common man.

1.2. Objectives

The objective of this paper is to highlight the instances and areas in which governments are lacking and where they need to work. Further, what hardships were suffered due to COVID and what steps were taken or could have been taken by the appropriate authorities to tackle the situation? The role played by the courts in protecting the rights of undertrials and prisoners should also be analyzed.

2. RESEARCH METHODOLOGY

The article shall be based upon secondary data, and the research applied will be analytical, descriptive, and doctrinal. The researcher shall try to study various cases that happened in Corona that led to the violation of the citizens' basic fundamental rights and the denial of access to justice. Various laws of different countries will be discussed that deal with the rights of people during the pandemic. Additionally, the steps taken by the court to provide justice to the people and the guidelines issued will be discussed in detail. The research shall be comparative study-based. The researcher has also based its study on non-doctrinal research while reaching the conclusion of the article. The population selected by the researcher is the health care professionals who were working during the COVID-19 pandemic.

2.1. Research Questions

The paper will try to explore various aspects and dimensions of justice during COVID times. The following questions will be explored:

1.   How were the children denied justice in times of conflict?
2.   How were professionals, like doctors and policemen, subjected to injustice?
3.   In what manner did the court turn up to provide access to justice to the people?
4.   Could the shortage of beds in hospitals be termed a denial of justice to patients during COVID?
5.   How has the technology been a boon in pandemic time, and could this online system be carried forward and made a part of the daily routine post-COVID also?

3. LITERATURE REVIEW

The researcher has looked into various articles and laws to reach the findings and conclusion of this research paper. An article titled "Youth Probation in the Time of COVID-19," authored by Emily Moone and Nili Bala (2020), analysed how the government has tried to curb the population of incarcerated youth inside the prisons. It has been explained how social distancing is not possible to maintain when one is incarcerated. An article by J. Jarpa Dawuni titled "The Gendered Face of COVID-19: Women and Access to Justice" has highlighted how a woman who is already a weaker section of society was more traumatised during the COVID pandemic and was denied her right to access to justice. An article by Arun Kumar et al. titled "Medicine and Law in the Times of the COVID-19 Pandemic: Understanding the Interphase" (2020) highlights very important parameters of the duties of medical practitioners during COVID-19 towards patients. It has highlighted various important provisions that provide for the protection of healthcare providers and the duties of healthcare personnel towards patients. The researcher has also reviewed various reports of the United Nations dealing with access to justice and the COVID situation.

The author has also explored the article authored by Mahak Jain, titled "Justice denied anywhere diminishes justice everywhere," which has focused on access to justice with respect to the judicial system in the country. It also refers to various causes and solutions to combat the problem of inaccessibility to justice. To study the health-related issues and injustice suffered by people during COVID, the author has analysed the article titled "Collision of Fundamental Human Rights and the Right to Health Access During the Novel Coronavirus Pandemic," authored by Santos et al (2021). The article highlights the various policy options and the implication of such policies. It highlights the right to freedom during the COVID scenario, taking into consideration the medical aspects. The present article shall seek to address whether the basic rights of those medical practitioners were ensured or were they a subject matter of injustice. In this manner, the author has tried to read and study carefully various articles related to COVID-19 and denial of access to justice to reach a conclusion about what the countries are still lacking and what more is required to be done.

3.1. Justice: Meaning

The basic objective of enacting any statute is to maintain law and order in society. The Constitution which is the norm, enlists various fundamental rights and duties of the citizens. The violation of any person's rights leads to injustice, and in order to get justice, there are various institutions established like courts, alternate dispute resolution mechanisms, etc. that help in rendering justice to the citizens of the country. Before proceeding further as to how there has been access to justice, the article will first address the meaning of justice. Justice can be described as providing people with what they deserve. Often, it has been observed that a lawful society exists only when justice is provided by its administration. The concept of justice has been enshrined under various provisions of the Indian Constitution, like Articles 14–18, which lay emphasis on equality. If individuals are not treated equally in equal circumstances, there is an absolute denial of justice.

Article 39-A, which discusses legal aid to provide to those who are indigent and can't fight a case lodged against them, The Constitution of India discusses three types of justice: social, economic, and political. By "social justice," it is meant that in society, there should be a proper, fair, and just distribution of resources. It concerns the fair manner in which the goods and liabilities that arise from collective life are shared among individuals in society (Deranty, 2016). The concept of social justice developed in the early 19th century. The purpose of this was to eliminate the exploitation of human labour and create an egalitarian society. (What is social justice?) Gender equality is an example of a social justice concept. Economic justice, on the other hand, states that merely on the basis of one's poor financial status, one should not be denied opportunities. It aims at eradicating and removing poverty from the country (Tripathi, 2022).

Political justice is a system where the government does not work on whims and caprice. In a politically just system, the government should not act arbitrarily but in a fair and just manner. Political justice provides individuals with equal political rights, like the right to vote. Legal justice is nothing but the upholding of the "rule of law." The concept of justice has also been elaborated on by John Rawls in his Theory of Justice and Amartya Sen in The Idea of Justice. His theory of justice was related to the idea of "fairness," in which he described his concept of fairness as when the citizens in a society are free and have equal rights exercised by them. There are three fundamental ideas found by Rawls that a democratic society should possess, i.e., the citizens should be free and equal, and the society should work in a fair system and with cooperation (Stanford Encyclopedia of Philosophy). The importance of the concept of justice can only be better understood by those who have suffered injustice.

Amartya Sen, who wrote the book "The Idea of Justice," contradicts Rawl's theory of justice. Amartya Sen states that instead of searching for perfect justice or the concept of justice, one should first understand the idea of justice. According to Sen, when one tries to remedy injustice, one automatically takes a step forward to attain justice (Srivastav, 2016). In COVID times, many injustices were done to different sections of the population. Children did not have access to education, and patients in hospitals were denied beds and appropriate treatment due to a lack of medical facilities. Many prisoners in jail could not avail themselves of the right to bail due to lockdown. Migrant labourers had to walk barefoot to their homes due to the shutdown of transportation. The following sections will discuss in detail the injustices done to people.

3.2. Access to Justice and Constitution

It is through Articles 32 and 226 of the Indian Constitution that the parties get access to the courts in cases of infringement of their basic fundamental rights. One of the main hindrances to having access to justice is the inability of a person to have legal advice and a pleader of his choice. Therefore, the concept of legal aid is of immense importance when one talks about access to justice. If one does not have enough means to hire a lawyer or to have his case presented in court, justice is denied to the person then and there only. Therefore, it became important to have the concept of legal aid incorporated into the various laws of the countries. Legal aid, as provided under Article 39-A of the Indian Constitution, provides that any person who, due to his financial status, is not able to have access to the courts will be provided access to the courts. The mechanism of locus standi and public interest litigation (PIL) is also a method to approach courts in this manner on behalf of some exploited sections of society.

A landmark judgement wherein legal aid and speedy justice were provided by the courts to the under-trial prisoners was the case of Hussainara Khatoon v. Home Secretary, State of Bihar (1979 AIR 1369). Access to justice is a principal part of the "Rule of Law" of any country. (Access to Justice, the United Nations, and the Rule of Law) Without this right, the authorities in position can arbitrarily exercise their powers, thereby violating the rights of other individuals and suppressing their vices in a democratic nation. But the question is, during COVID, when there was complete lockdown, how did the people have access to justice? The courts were shut in the beginning, but slowly and gradually the virtual hearings started, but only the very important cases were taken up initially. There was also the problem that many lawyers and judges were not that technologically advanced to understand the modus operandi and techniques of using technology. It was even difficult for some clients and witnesses to appear through online hearings. Therefore, access to justice became a problem during COVID, although solutions were looked for by the concerned officials so that no person had their basic fundamental rights infringementd during lockdown. Access to justice is nothing but the enjoyment of the individual's basic rights and protection from all types of violence, discrimination, injustice, etc. There have been various steps taken by many organisations around the world during the pandemic in order to protect various strata of the population from the menace of the coronavirus. One such step was taken by the Vance Center, which wrote an open letter to various international commissions like the African Commission on Human and Peoples' Rights and the Inter-American Commission on Human Rights (Cyrus R. Vance Center for International Justice).

The letters written by the centre accentuated the poor conditions of women prisoners residing in African and American regions. The kind of health and safety issues being faced by the women prisoners were not paid attention to during COVID times, and henceforth, this was a clear example of injustice having been done to the women prisoners. In India, National Legal Services Day is celebrated on November 9 every year. This day recognises the importance of rendering free legal services to the weaker section of society so that they are not deprived of justice but rather have easy access to justice. Additionally, Order XXXIII of the Civil Procedure Code also deals with indigent persons. Rule 18 of the said order clearly states that the states should be providing free legal services to indigent persons, and the same order also describes who can be considered an indigent person. (Order XXXIII, Civil Procedure Code, 1908). A similar provision to this has also been enlisted under the Criminal Procedure Code, i.e., Section 303.

3.3. Children and COVID-19

Children who are considered to be the future of nations were denied the very basic right to education during COVID-19. The schools were shut down due to lockdown, and nobody knew how to tackle the problem. After a while, the classes were conducted online, but the online system could not compete with the quality of brick-and-mortar classroom study. The right to education is part of Article 21-A of the Constitution. Though efforts were made by the concerned authorities to impart education to the children so that they were not denied this fundamental right, Additionally, the access to justice of children is a matter of concern that is looked into by UNICEF. UNICEF works in cooperation with the Convention on the Rights of the Child. UNICEF played an important role during the pandemic in order to grant the children access to justice so that they were not subjected to injustice.

Since courts were shut down initially due to the pandemic, UNICEF came forward to help children detained in prisons have access to justice. Many steps were taken by UNICEF to protect and support juveniles during COVID. For example, UNICEF, along with other major international institutions like UNDP, requested that countries like Myanmar release the children who were detained during COVID and reintegrate them with their families. It has also been observed that children have been provided with every kind of psychological support. (Access to Justice for Children in the Era of COVID-19: Notes from the Field, New York, 2020) Children have always been considered a weaker and more vulnerable section of society. Every now and then, children are subjected to different forms of violations, and with the advancement in science and technology, the violations and abuses against children have increased.

And due to COVID, when everyone was confined and locked in their homes, this violence and torture only showed a rise, as in many countries the services relating to the prevention of violence were shut down due to lockdown. (Protecting Children from Violence in the Time of COVID-19: Disruptions in Prevention and Response Services, 2020) Also, steps were taken and statements were issued in order to protect the juveniles against sexual exploitation, abuse, and other forms of violence, which increased during the pandemic when everyone was confined to their homes. (Statement by Lanzarote Committee Chairperson and Vice Chairperson on stepping up protection of children against sexual exploitation and abuse in times of the COVID-19 pandemic, 2020) Although steps were being taken at the international level, at the root level, the violence against children only rose, and there was no means of accessing justice.

3.4. Healthcare Professionals and Public Servants

What was more saddening to see was the plight of health care workers and the public servants who were serving the nation when everyone was inside their home trying to be safe. These were the people, the police officers and the health care professions, who, without caring about their own health, were ready to serve the nation. They rendered unconditional service, but what was unjust to them was that they had no access to proper precautionary and protective measures to take care of their own health. They risk their lives to protect other individuals in the country. The question is, are these people not entitled to the right to life and proper health care under Article 21 of the Constitution? Many doctors and police officers who were on duty rendered services without any PPE kits. Is that not a clear violation of their basic human rights? Forget about their rights; nobody even thought about the lives of these workers who were working selflessly.

There is not an iota of doubt that it is the duty of doctors and police officers to protect their patients and the public, respectively, but do they only possess duties and no rights? There are various laws that highlight the duties of health care professionals, like the Indian Medical Council (Professional Conduct, Etiquette, and Ethics) Regulations, 2002, etc. Clarke, in his article, justified the duties of medical professionals by stating that the duty is based on skill and that the doctors know the consequences of their actions. But at the same time, it does not mean that doctors do not have the right to protection and care for themselves during the outbreak of any infectious disease. They, being human beings, do possess some basic human rights. (Clarke). Though Section 4 of the Epidemic Diseases Act protects medical workers, It provides immunity to medical professionals for any work done by them in good faith. Additionally, Article 21 protects the rights of workers. It was seen during the pandemic that doctors were even mentally drained to see so many people dying. It was not easy for the doctors as well.

The kind of mental trauma faced by the health professionals was clearly a threat to their basic right to life under Article 21, and no attention to the said right led to its infringement. The other set of professionals who risked their lives for the public, but no attention was paid to their well-being, were the police officers. They did their jobs selflessly, subjecting themselves to the risk of viruses. The police came forward for the protection of its citizens, be they men, women, or children, in a myriad of ways. For example, in May 2020, the National Police Academy organised a webinar where it talked about the protection of children during COVID-19. (Tannishtha Dutta). Police officers themselves were stressed a lot during such times as the duty of the officers increased manifold, and they had to be more stringent and stricter in order to protect the public from being infected with the virus. Moreover, when everyone was confined to their homes, they were out on the roads to safeguard everyone, but unfortunately, no safety measures or equipment were provided to them. No PPE kits were provided to them, and many officers in charge of jails who were there to look after the prisoners were also subjected to the vulnerability of viruses. But unfortunately, these unsung heroes of the Corona were deprived of access to basic rights during the pandemic.

Due to the mishandling of the situation by the government, police officers were directed to perform such unfamiliar tasks as those of health workers (Kyprianides B. Bradford, 2022) to bring the situation under control, and these officers had no other choice but to help the country tackle the problem. Additionally, COVID-19 added stress to the lives of police officers as the shifts were altered, and for those who were provided with PPE kits, it was not possible to wear them the whole day while on duty. It was a challenging task for the police force to operate in a calm manner, and sometimes they had to use force to keep the public in control. The police officers could not come into contact with the family members, as that could pose the family of such officers to the same risk of virus. (Kyprianides B. Bradford, 2022). The heroes of Corona, therefore, had a lot of challenges to face during the pandemic, but there was a lot of mismanagement on the part of governments around the globe to tackle the problem. The basic human rights of these officers and health care professionals were not seriously taken into consideration. Therefore, it was not just the common man suffering; the life savers were at greater risk of losing their lives.

3.5. Access to Healthcare and Justice During COVID-19

It was very saddening to see the world suffering in Corona, and what was even more disheartening was that there were no beds in hospitals for the patients. The cost of basic necessities increased manifold.

Pharmaceutical companies, taking advantage of the situation, skyrocketed the prices of masks and sanitizers. Moreover, it was very difficult to get the injections required to treat the patient's corona. The medical facilities seemed to be scanty. Are these instances not enough to state that so much injustice was being inflicted upon the common man, who was not even able to avail himself of the basic facilities required for precautions and treatment? It was even observed that there was not just a shortage of beds but also a shortage of oxygen cylinders; moreover, the death toll was so high that even there was no space for cremation. (Sharma, 2021).

The right to health, which is embodied under Article 21 of the Constitution and the International Covenant on Economic, Social, and Cultural Rights, provides for both the physical and mental health of individuals. It was observed during the pandemic that not just infrastructure but also hospital staff were needed in greater numbers as the cases were only at a surge and the ratio of patient to hospital staff was very low. Moreover, the vaccination was not initially available to all people, and it was also observed that many people around the globe had no faith in the credibility of the vaccine. Therefore, a lot of difficulty was faced in terms of healthcare infrastructure, for example, a shortage of PPE kits, a shortage of hospital staff, a shortage of ventilators, etc. (Grimm, 2020). The mismanagement during the pandemic happened around the world as there was no preparedness for such a pandemic to outbreak, and the delayed response and action of WHO is also considered to be one of the reasons. The right to life is a basic, fundamental right that was denied by the states to its citizens during the pandemic. The right to health and food, safety, and nutrition all form part of the right to health, which was found missing during the pandemic (Choudhary, 2020).

Poor people had no access to proper food and nutrition, and they were also denied basic medical facilities and treatment due to a shortage of hospital infrastructure. Considering the importance of health, the right to health and the right to health care have been incorporated under Article 25 of the Universal Declaration of Human Rights (UDHR). But unfortunately, the United States failed to provide its citizens with this fundamental right. Similarly, there are many other international instruments that provide for the attainment of good physical and mental health, and during the pandemic, people suffered both physical and mental illness. Looking at the number of Corona cases and deaths that occurred during the pandemic, the members of families suffered serious mental issues. It is also observed that there is only one doctor for every 11, 000 patients, which is very low as compared to the figures provided by the WHO (Choudhary, 2020). What was even more pathetic to observe was that these health care workers themselves faced discrimination in society as they were considered corona carriers.

The cases of deaths reported were so high that hospitals even started disposing of the bodies in an arbitrary fashion and did not provide any dignity to them. Therefore, in such instances, the hon'ble Supreme Court had to take the charge, and in the case of In Re the Proper Treatment of COVID-19 Patients and Dignified Handling of Dead Bodies in Hospitals, etc., it was directed to the States that the bodies of the patients deid of Corona be disposed of in a dignified manner and not in an improper way. Following are the flow charts of the results of the survey done in 2021 by the researcher when the corona was at its peak. The data was collected from healthcare professionals online through Google Forms. 39 responses were received from them, the results of which have been depicted below (Figures 1–6).

The above charts clearly show how the doctors faced different kinds of mental harassment, as even after rendering duty during COVID times, they were not being paid enough, and additionally, they had to face the wrath of the families of the patients. The result above is clearly indicative of injustices being done to healthcare professionals. But, unfortunately, there was no one to pay heed to the basic necessities of these healthcare workers.

Figure 1. Were you on duty during Corona times?

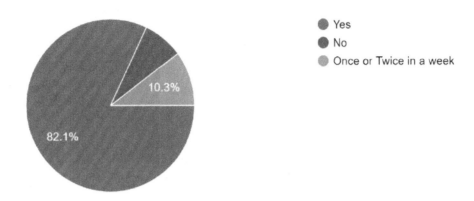

Were you on duty during Corona Times?
39 responses

Figure 2. Did you test positive while on duty?

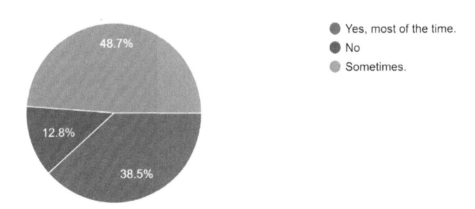

While on duty, do you have to face the wrath of the patients' families?
39 responses

4. FINDINGS AND RESULTS

4.1. Access to Justice Through Virtual Courtrooms

It is the court that helps people exercise their rights in cases of infringement, but what will a person do if he is not able to approach the court alone? The pandemic created a situation wherein people were denied access to the courts. There were many victims inside homes during lockdown; many incidents of theft, domestic violence against women and children, and many more instances of crimes were reported. But due to lockdown, no one had access to justice. It was then that the courts gradually decided to go for "virtual hearings." Although instances of judges and lawyers who belong to the older generation and are

Figure 3. Mental breakdown of doctors

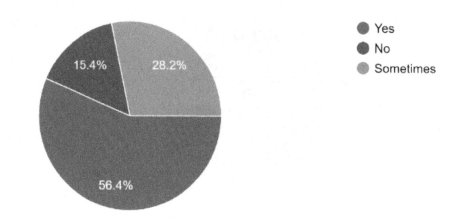

Do you face any issue with respect to income during this time?
39 responses

Figure 4. Were PPE kits issued?

Did you get PPE kits while working during these times and other necessary equipment required for your safety?
39 responses

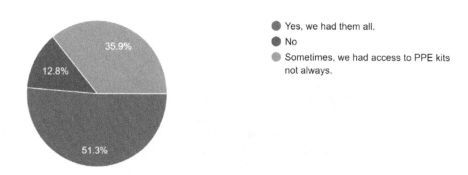

not able to use technology were heard of, with the passage of time, things improved. In fact, to lessen the burden on courts, alternate dispute resolution methods like mediation have also gained importance, and the pandemic has made legislators and authorities think about making online mediation and arbitration the new normal in dispute resolution.

However, this online mechanism of virtual hearing is not as good as it sounds. There are many difficulties and challenges surrounding this. There are still many judges and lawyers who remain conservative and are not ready to adapt to the changes of the contemporary world (Tania Sourdin, 2020). The right to justice, which is also a principle of international human rights, has been of concern during the pandemic as questions pertaining to a fair trial and whether the case can be successfully adjudged online popped up. It was also observed that, even if the courts started acting virtually, they would only take up "essential" cases. What can be termed an "essential matter" is again a question to be pondered. As for

Figure 5. Income issue

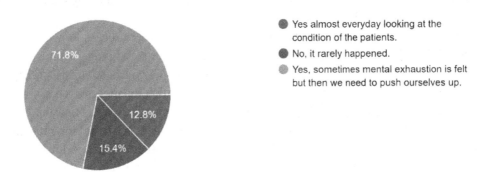

While working during this time, did you experience mental breakdown or felt mentally exhausted?
39 responses

- Yes almost everyday looking at the condition of the patients.
- No, it rarely happened.
- Yes, sometimes mental exhaustion is felt but then we need to push ourselves up.

Figure 6. Wrath of patients' families

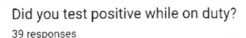

Did you test positive while on duty?
39 responses

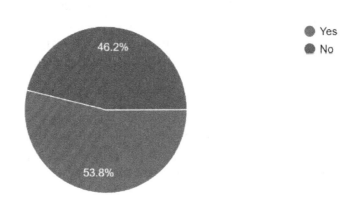

- Yes
- No

every individual looking for access to justice, not being able to reach court for any reason is a violation of that person's human rights. One of the great measures taken by China in order to take up cases online and deliver justice to its citizens was that it made the processes of the courts, like case filing, document and evidence exchanges, etc., take place online.

The plight of migrant labourers during COVID was unbearable. They walked to their home due to complete lockdown, as no work, shelter, or food was available to them, and more pathetic was the fact that no one came forward to help these migrant workers reach home. It was then that the Supreme Court came forward to help the migrant labourers by directing the governments and states to distribute rations according to the "One Nation, One Ration Card Scheme." The court, while granting the order, realised and considered the major contribution that these migrant workers made to the country's economy. The court even ordered that the workers need to be compulsorily registered under the Inter-State Migrant Workmen Act, 1979 (Bhattacharya, 2021). And looking into the environmental factors and paucity of supply of papers, this online mechanism of filing cases, documents, etc. can also help save the environment, thereby helping to achieve sustainable development. In Anita Kushwaha v. Pushpa Sudan (AIR 2016 SC 3506), the court led by CJI TS Thakur stated the various essentials of access to justice in a democratic country. It is the states' duty to provide an effective mechanism of adjudication that needs to be accessible to people irrespective of distance. It was further stated by the court that the process of adjudication should be both speedy and affordable to all.

Experiencing the dilemma of the COVID-19 scenario, where access to justice was either denied or limited, it became necessary to increase the number of courts and judges in the courts. The pre-Covid era also saw a huge pendency of cases in courts, and had the courts not turned "virtual," the burden on the judiciary would have been at its peak. Technology, in that manner, served as a boon during COVID in almost all areas. What is also required for speedy access to justice is that the courts should also be established in rural areas so that people from those areas need not travel long distances in order to get justice (Jain, n.d.). What is more saddening to see is that instead of improving the infrastructure of the courts and courtrooms, the government has reduced the budget allocation in the judicial arena (Jain, n.d.).

The judiciary is an independent organ in a democratic system, and therefore, it should remain unbiased in rendering speedy justice to the citizens. The judges, lawyers, and police officers who form part of the justice delivery system should be ready to adapt to the changes that happen in the contemporary world and be ready to impart justice to individuals. There are several international conventions dealing with judicial reform, such as the Convention on Crime and Corruption of the United Nations Office on Drugs and Crime (UNODC), and the Bangalore Principle relating to Basic Principles of Judiciary Independence. There has always been a need for the judiciary to play an active role in combating the problem of corruption. the case of the "Pharma Scam" has turned up, which has highlighted how the pharma companies have asked the doctors to prescribe Dolo medicine during COVID. It was also observed in the initial days of Corona that the prices of hand sanitizers and masks went very high; it was then that the courts came into action for the welfare of the public and directed the pharmaceutical companies to reduce the prices as they formed part of the essential commodities during Corona.

The court during the pandemic also stated that due to the outbreak of the virus, lockdown was ordered, and courts were "virtual," so the limitation period of the cases was extended. Though virtual courts have helped render justice in various instances, Hon'ble Justice Y.V. Chandrachud, while delivering a lecture in a webinar, stated that the virtual courts cannot be a substitute for "open courts." He stated that open courts in India are the spine of its legal system (Staff, 2020). There have also been technical difficulties faced by the courts during virtual hearings due to network issues. Therefore, there is a lot that is yet to be looked into before turning courts virtual. No doubt, virtual hearings have been of immense help during COVID, but looking into the pendency of cases and online dispute mechanisms, it is important to not overlook the lacunae underlying, and it is required by the concerned authorities to work upon the technical gaps existing.

4.2. Should the Online System Continue Post Pandemic?

The world has been so much adapted to the online mechanism that there is no harm in shifting to the online mechanism. But as pointed out in the above section, there are many gaps that are still required to be worked upon, and until those gaps are removed, it would become unjustified to completely rely on the online mechanism. For example, the biggest challenge posed with respect to online courts and education is the internet infrastructure; not all people in the country have access to a proper, uninterrupted internet connection. Moreover, there are still many people who are not ready to adapt and shift to the online mode; they still feel more comfortable with the offline mechanism. Moreover, the reliability of the saved online data is also questionable. There are very high chances of the technology being cracked and the system being shut down, thereby leading to the deletion of data. Also, it has been observed that during the interrogation of a witness online, it becomes very difficult to understand the body language of a person, unlike in open and non-virtual courts, wherein the judges are able to judge and decide based upon the body language of the parties and witnesses, which is not possible in virtual mode.

Same is the case in online mode teaching; for a teacher to identify which student is active and who is not, it becomes difficult in the online mode. Henceforth, there are many gaps that need to be worked upon before making or turning anything into "virtual mode." From the above sections, it can be clearly observed that during COVID, people have been deprived of their basic right to justice. If a person is not getting proper treatment, is deprived of education, or is deprived of proper healthcare facilities, then it can be clearly stated that injustice has taken place for such people. When injustice happens, people crave and long for justice. They look for courts to uphold their rights, and during COVID, it became even more difficult for people to have access to the courts. Therefore, there is a lot to be done by the governments towards the basic rights of the citizens. Access to justice is nothing but the upholding of the rule of law, and in a country where people are denied basic fundamental rights, it is really difficult to say that the rule of law can be established in such a country.

5. CONCLUSION

It is therefore important that in such a pandemic-like situation, both the centre and states come forward with the concept of cooperative federalism instead of getting indulged in political drama and corruption. The governments should look forward to learning from the failures of COVID what areas the countries are lagging behind in and what solutions can be found to overcome those problems. For example, when there is a shortage of beds and hospitals, it shows that the government needs to work in the healthcare sector, more healthcare workers need to be appointed, and more hospitals are required to be established. Similarly, in the case of minor disputes, there should be some online mechanism of courts for which parties need not travel long distances; a greater number of courts and judges should be appointed. And, finally, the boon and saviour that helped to make the lives of the people in the pandemic a little better were the "Internet facilities." The government should turn up with better internet infrastructure. There are many things that Corona has taught the whole world and many lessons that are to be learned from it.

REFERENCES

Access to Justice for Children in the era of Covid-19: Notes from the field. (2020). United Nations Children's Fund (UNICEF). Retrieved from https://www.unicef.org/media/92251/file/Access-to-Justice-COVID-19-Field-Notes-2021.pdf

Bhattacharya, D. (2021). *Making migrants count: The role of Indian Judiciary amid Covid- 19 pandemic.* Retrieved from Down to Earth: https://www.downtoearth.org.in/blog/economy/making-migrants-count-the-role-of-indian-judiciary-amid-covid-19-pandemic-78548

Choudhary, V. (2020). *Denial of Treatment to Covid-19 Patients is a Human Rights Abuse*. Retrieved from Human Rights Pulse: https://www.humanrightspulse.com/mastercontentblog/denial-of-treatment-to-covid-19-patients-is-a-human-rights-abuse

Clarke, C. C. (n.d.). In Harm's way: AMA Physicians and the Duty to Treat. *The Journal of Medicine and Philosophy of Medicine, 30*(1). Retrieved from https://academic.oup.com/jmp/article-abstract/30/1/65/893497?redirectedFrom=fulltext

Cyrus R. Vance Center for International Justice, H. R. (n.d.). *Women in Prison Amid Covid-19 Open Letters to the African Commission on Human and Peoples' Rights and the Inter-American Commission on Human Rights.* Vance Center for International Justice. Retrieved from https://www.vancecenter.org/areas-of-practice/human-rights-and-access-to-justice/

Deranty, J.-P. (2016). Social Justice. *The International Encyclopedia of Political Communication.* Retrieved from https://www.researchgate.net/publication/314581421_Social_Justice

Grimm, C. A. (2020, March). *Hospital Experiences Responding to the Covid-19 Pandemic: Results of a National Pulse Survey*. Retrieved from U.S. Department of Health and Services: https://oig.hhs.gov/oei/reports/oei-06-20-00300.pdf

Jain, M. (n.d.). *Justice denied anywhere, diminishes justice everywhere.* Retrieved from https://papers.ssrn.com/sol3/papers.cfm?abstract_id=3771945

Jo, S. B. (n.d.). Doctors during the Covid-19 pandemic: what are their duties and what is owed to them? Retrieved from https://jme.bmj.com/content/47/1/12

Kyprianides, B., Bradford, M. B.-S.-S., Beale, M., Savigar-Shaw, L., Stott, C., & Radburn, M. (2022). Policing the Covid-19 pandemic: Police officer well being and commitment to democratic modes of policing. *Policing and Society, 32*(4), 504–521. doi:10.1080/10439463.2021.1916492

Access to Justice, United Nations and the Rule of Law. (n.d.). United Nations. Retrieved from https://www.un.org/ruleoflaw/thematic-areas/access-to-justice-and-rule-of-law-institutions/access-to-justice/

Protecting Children from violence in the time of covid-19, Disruptions in prevention and response services. (2020). UNICEF Data. Retrieved from https://data.unicef.org/resources/protecting-children-from-violence-in-the-time-of-covid-19-brochure/

Sharma, N. (2021). *India: Protect Rights, Dignity Amid Covid-19 crisis*. Retrieved from https://www.hrw.org/news/2021/04/28/india-protect-rights-dignity-amid-covid-19-crisis

Srivastav, D. S. (2016). Rawl's theory of Justice Through Amartya Sen's Idea. *ILI Law Review*. Retrieved from https://www.ili.ac.in/pdf/p11_dhawal.pdf

Staff, S. (2020, May). *Despite public health crisis, it is court's duty to protect rights of citizens: Justice Chandrachud.* Retrieved from https://scroll.in/latest/962838/despite-public-health-crisis-it-is-courts-duty-to-protect-rights-of-citizens-justice-chandrachud

Stanford Encyclopedia of Philosophy. (n.d.). Retrieved from https://plato.stanford.edu/entries/rawls/

Statement by Lanzarote Committee Chairpeson and Vice Chairperson on stepping up protection of children against sexual exploitation and abuse in times of the Covid-19 pandemic. (2020). Council of Europe. Retrieved from https://rm.coe.int/covid-19-lc-statement-en-final/16809e17ae

Tania Sourdin, B. L. (2020). *Court Innovations and Access to Justice in times of crisis.* Retrieved from Health Policy Technology: https://www.ncbi.nlm.nih.gov/pmc/articles/PMC7456584/

Tannishtha Dutta, S. R. (n.d.). Re-imaging the role of police in Covid-19 times. UNICEF India. Retrieved from https://www.unicef.org/india/stories/re-imagining-role-police-covid-19-times

Tripathi, A. P. (2022). *Concept of Justice under Indian Constitution.* Retrieved from Manupatra: https://articles.manupatra.com/article-details/Concept-of-Justice-under-Indian-Constitution

What is Social Justice? (n.d.). Retrieved from https://pachamama.org/social-justice/what-is-social-justice

Chapter 5

Analyzing Partograph Data to Compare Birth Outcomes According to WHO Active-Phase Recommendations

N. S. Kshirsagar

Krishna Institute of Medical Sciences, India

R. P. Patange

Krishna Institute of Medical Sciences, India

ABSTRACT

More than one million women aged 15 to 49 die annually as a result of difficulties arising during pregnancy or delivery. About half a million women lose their lives each year from complications during pregnancy, and many more have serious injuries. There are more severe outcomes for pregnant women for every maternal death that occurs. Despite international attention and efforts, poor nations continue to shoulder a disproportionate share of the load. About 19% of all maternal fatalities in these nations may be attributed to complications during labour. These risks may be greatly mitigated with vigilant monitoring for signs of aberrant development and measures to avoid a drawn-out labour process. Therefore, labour monitoring strategies are crucial for avoiding negative perinatal and maternal outcomes. To that end, using a partograph is a crucial and low-cost option. It's an easy-to-use technology that has been demonstrated to increase results when employed to monitor and control labour, and it costs very little to use.

1. INTRODUCTION

The uterus stays relatively still throughout pregnancy in almost all women. The progesterone that is secreted by the placenta limits the natural contractility of the uterus, which helps to ensure that the foetus remains securely contained within the uterus (Bernitz et al., 2014). The cervix does not exhibit any signs of relaxing or becoming more pliable (Cohen & Friedman, 2015). However, as the baby is fully

DOI: 10.4018/978-1-6684-9189-8.ch005

developed, the cervix begins to relax, and uterine contractions become more frequent and consistent. There is a lot of mystery around the beginning stages of labour. Nevertheless, there have been a few other hypotheses put forward (Hendricks et al., 1970). Here are a few instances that illustrate my point: The concept of the optimum amount of distension the second topic is the function of the foetus and the placenta during pregnancy. Oestrogen, Progesterone, and Prostaglandins are their Chemical Names. Oxytocin Considerations from a Neurological Standpoint (Mathai, 2009).

Over one million women around the world lose their lives each year as a direct result of complications that arise during pregnancy and childbirth.

In the United States alone, pregnancy-related illnesses claim the lives of over 500,000 women each year, and many more women sustain life-threatening injuries. More women suffer significant injuries for every mother who passes away from a preventable cause. Poor nations continue to bear a disproportionate amount of the burden, despite the attention and efforts of the international community. Complications that arise during the process of labour and delivery are responsible for around 19 percent of all maternal deaths in these countries (Zhang et al., 2011). The rate of maternal death is still between 500 and 1,000 per 100,000 births in impoverished nations (Suzuki et al., 2010). This figure is based on total births (Lavender et al., 2018). Early detection of aberrant progress and the avoidance of prolonged labour both serve to significantly reduce the likelihood of these adverse outcomes occurring. Therefore, labour monitoring techniques are absolutely necessary in order to lower the chance of undesirable outcomes for both the mother and the newborn (Peisner & Rosen, 1986).

The partograph is a useful and very inexpensive piece of equipment that can be utilised for this purpose. It is a low-cost device that, when used to monitor and manage labour, has been shown to improve results while simultaneously offering a continuous visual picture. This has been demonstrated. On a single sheet of paper, all of the information that pertains to labour has been compiled. There are three things that need to be taken into consideration: the state of labour, the condition of the foetus, and the health of the mother. During labour, the health of the developing baby can be evaluated based on a number of factors, including the foetal heart rate, the status of the membranes, the quality of the fluids, and the moulding.

When it comes to supervising personnel and keeping tabs on their progress, a partograph is an indispensable tool. This one convenient sheet of paper contains all the information that must be known about a worker in its entirety. Another significant consideration is the state of the mother's and the infant's health, in addition to the development of the labour process. When you are in the process of giving birth, it is essential to monitor the baby's shape, as well as the heart rate of the foetus, the health of the membranes, and the quality of the fluids. When it comes to supervising personnel and keeping tabs on their progress, a partograph is an indispensable tool. The intensity of the uterine contractions, the rate at which the cervix is dilating, the descent of the presenting portion, and the pattern of the presenting part are all taken into consideration and recorded. In the third section, records are kept of the mother's temperature, heart rate, blood pressure, and urinalysis results.

2. AIM AND OBJECTIVES

Analysis of partograph data comparing birth outcomes under the old and new WHO active phase guidelines.
   Objectives:

1. To study maternal and fetal outcome of labour using existing definition of active phase
2. To study maternal and fetal outcome of labour using new definition of active phase

There are four physiological stages that may be used to characterise the control of uterine functions in late pregnancy and labour. Functional dormancy (stage 1) A number of inhibitors work together to keep the uterus in a state of functional quiescence throughout pregnancy. Progesterone reduces prostaglandin synthesis, which in turn inhibits the expression of connection, a protein necessary for gap junction formation, and the release of oxytocin. Prostacycline, relaxin (which serves to block myosin light chain phosphorylation and suppress uterine stimulants like oxytocin and noradrenaline), nitric oxide, parathyroid hormone, intestinal peptide hormone, and human placental lactogen are also other examples of inhibitors (Shi et al., 2016).

During the second phase, called activation or pre-labor, a number of proteins involved in contractile activity are expressed at higher levels, ion channels are functionally activated, and connexin 43 (a crucial component of gap junctions) is elevated. Transition to Stage 3 (Stimulation and Labor): When oxytocin or prostaglandin F2 are administered after the activation phase, the uterus is ready to respond. The contractions of the uterus are induced. The tubal ostia are the site from which the waves of contractions radiate down into the uterus, serving as the pacemakers of the process. Phase 4 (Involution/Puerperium): This period follows birth and is mediated by oxytocin and perhaps thrombin.

2.1. Partograph

It was because Freidman began maintaining a visual record of her cervical dilatation while she was in labour that the idea of recording labour progress was first conceived. Philpott is the one who developed further and made improvements to this system. The term "partograph" refers to a chart that allows the most important aspects of work to be represented visually and, as a result, provides the opportunity for early detection of deviations from the norm. A labour graph is something that medical professionals use to evaluate how a woman's labour is progressing in comparison to the norm in terms of cervical dilatation and foetal descent.

According to our explanation, the partograph is a device that can be utilised by the midwifery team in order to monitor the progression of labour and to indicate when intervention is required. It has been demonstrated that the use of a partograph dramatically reduces the risks to both the mother and the newborn that are associated with protracted labour. These risks include postpartum haemorrhage, septicemia, and uterine rupture (death, anoxia, infections, etc.). To whose benefit is it being used? Those who have undergone specialised midwifery training, such as nurses, midwives, medical assistants, and nurse's aids: what kinds of situations could benefit from the use of this knowledge? Assistance in making a decision about whether or not to carry out a caesarean section, a transfer, or any other procedures that may save a patient's life. Is there a manual that explains how to make use of it? After the beginning of labour is when a partogram can finally be started. The purpose of the tool is to encourage timely referral from the peripheral areas of the curriculum, as well as facilitate collaboration and ease of reference inside teaching units.

3. REVIEW OF LITERATURE

Orji, (2008) updated the WHO partograph to assess labour progress in both primiparous and multiparous women. In the active phase of labour, the proportion of women whose cervical dilatation plots reached or crossed the partograph's action line was compared between 259 nulliparous and 204 multiparous mothers in his prospective research. Indicators of success included total labour time, delivery method, the occurrence of induction, and the frequency of vaginal exams. The study's findings showed most women's cervical dilatation remained normal throughout labour, and the duration of labour was comparable across the two groups. Women who were making typical labour progress were more likely to have a vaginal birth without medical assistance, while women whose labour was stalled were more likely to undergo labour augmentation or surgical intervention. Therefore, when using the revised WHO partograph, labour progression and duration were shown to be comparable for nulliparous and multiparous women.

Research into the use of partograph with an established procedure for managing labour on the result of labour was undertaken by Thorton (2006). Many different locations participated in the research. The results mostly back up the author's assertions, but they do lend credence to the case for keeping tabs on all labours using a partogram like Philpott and Castles' that includes alert and action lines. Despite a decrease (54% in the frequency of labours boosted by oxytocin), the findings showed a decrease (41% in protracted labor) and a decrease (3%) in emergency caesarean sections. Postpartum infections, intrapartum stillbirths, and mental morbidity decreased by 59%, most likely as a result of fewer vaginal exams performed on average during labour. Partograph users in the WHO experiment reported better discipline and communication concerning management of labour and midwives' time, which may be a key factor in the partogram's effectiveness since it frees up midwives' schedules to spend more time providing companionship to labouring women.

4. METHODOLOGY

Study Setting: The study was conducted in the labour room of the Obstetrics and Gynecology department of the Krishna Institute of Medical Sciences, Karad, Maharashtra, which is a tertiary care centre.

Study population: The study was conducted among antenatal women coming to the labour room of Krishna tertiary care centre.

Period of study: The study was conducted for period of 2 years

Type of study: This was a prospective observational study.

Sampling Technique: Pregnant women who were admitted to the labour and delivery ward were randomly divided into two groups. Information was gathered by conducting a thorough history, physical, and systemic examination, as well as an obstetrical examination, on all patients admitted to the labour and delivery ward. For those who met the criteria, a partial record of the labour process was kept. The patients were split into two groups at random. Active-phase partographic recording began at 4 cm in Group A. Partographic documentation of the active phase began at 6 cm in Group B. The duration of labour, the need for interventions during labour, and the result of labour were all tracked for both groups.

5. ETHICAL CONSIDERATIONS

- The prospective participants were explained the purpose and nature of the study by me in a language they understood.
- Assent from adolescents was sought after a properly signed informed consent form was requested from the patient. In the event of juveniles or those with mental disabilities, a guardian was asked to provide consent instead.
- The participant was recruited only after the patient willingly signed the Informed Consent Form (ICF).
- The anonymity and confidentiality of the participant were maintained at all levels.
- The participant was given the right to opt out of the study at any stage without having to give any reason. This did not jeopardise his or her right to receive appropriate treatment and care.
- No participant was required to make any additional financial sacrifices for the sole purpose of this research project. The investigator was responsible for covering any additional expenses that arose specifically for the purpose of carrying out this research.
- Any modifications to the study, its protocol, or its design were discussed with and received clearance from the Institutional Ethics Committee in advance. In the event that an ethical problem develops at a later date, the ethics committee will be informed about it.

6. RESULTS

The results of comparing the progression of cervical dilatation during labour in both groups of the study are presented in Table 1. In group A, the amount of time needed to dilate from 4 cm to 6 cm was 2.3 hours (median), but in group B, the amount of time needed to dilate from 4 cm to 6 cm was 2.8 hours, which was significantly longer. This difference was statistically significant (p 0.05). It took almost the same amount of time ($p > 0.05$) for dilatation to go from 6 cm to 10 cm in group B as it did in group A. The median amount of time required was 1.7 hours.

P value was calculated using Kruskal-Wallis test.

Table 2 shows the comparison of indications for LSCS among patients in both groups. Foetal distress was the most common indication found in group A (20.6%), where 25% were due to oligohydramnios, 20% were due to thick meconium in the latent phase, and 15% were due to category III CTG as a result of cord around the neck, whereas foetal distress and malposition were the commonest indications in group B (6 (28.6%) and 5 (23.8%), respectively, where in cases posted for foetal distress, 18% were due to oligohydramnios and 10% were due to thick meconium stained liquor in the latent phase.

Table 1. Comparison of Progress of cervical dilatation during labour

Progress of Cervical Dilatation During Labour	4cm Group	6cm Group	P Value
	Median (95% CI)	Median (95% CI)	
4 cm to 6 cm	2.3(1.6 – 4.4) hrs	2.8(1.2-4.8)	0.032
6 cm to 10 cm	1.6 (1.2 – 4.7) hrs	1.7 (1.0 – 4.9) hrs	0.854
P value	0.0012	<0.001	

Table 2. Comparison of indication of LSCS among patients of both the groups

Indication of LSCS	4cm Group		6cm Group		Total	
	Cases	%	Cases	%	Cases	%
Deep Transverse Arrest	0	0.0%	2	9.5%	2	3.7%
Foetal Distress	20	60.6%	6	28.6%	26	48.1%
CPD	4	12.1%	2	9.5%	6	11.1%
Malposition	3	9.1%	5	23.8%	8	14.8%
Non-Reactive CTG	4	12.1%	4	19.0%	8	14.8%
Secondary Arrest in Cervical Dilatation	2	6.1%	2	9.5%	4	7.4%
Total	33	100.0%	21	100.0%	54	100.0%

7. DISCUSSION

In the current analysis, it was discovered that both groups had almost the same number of patients in each age bracket. The average ages of the patients in groups A and B were slightly different from one another, with group A having a mean age of 23.88 and group B's having a mean age of 23.442. There was not a significant difference between the two groups in terms of the age distribution ($p > 0.05$).

Patients who were measured at a thickness of 4 centimetres had a mean age of 24.843.49 years, whereas those who were measured at a thickness of 6 centimetres had a mean age of 24.623.70 years (Purwar et al., 2021).

According to the findings of a study that was published in 2018 by Oladapo et al., (2018) women who have already given birth (nulliparous) or will give birth in the future (multiparous) are unable to profit from any procedures that speed up labour. During the normal active time, their values for the 95th percentile varied from 0.1 to 0.5 cm/hour when measured from a dilatation of 4–10 cm.

Data from 2018 indicate that Oladapo et al., (2018) carried out a study in Sub-Saharan Africa with a total of 5606 female participants. From the beginning of labour until the fifth centimetre was reached, the median amount of time it took for a woman to advance by one centimetre was higher than one hour. This was the case for both women who had their first baby and women who had previous children. According to the 95th percentile, it can take a woman who has never given birth up to 7 hours for her cervix to move from 4 to 5 cm, and it can take her more than 3 hours for it to advance from 5 to 6 cm. Nulliparous women hospitalised at 4 cm, 5 cm, and 6 cm would have reached 10 cm within an anticipated time frame if the dilatation rate was less than 1 cm/hour. However, their respective 95th percentiles revealed that labour may take up to 14, 11, and 9 hours, respectively.

In a study by Purwar et al. (2021), the average time from 4 cm to 10 cm cervical dilatation was 5.12 2.01 hours in Group A (4 cm) and 5.21 2.16 hours in Group B (6 cm). Those in Group A required 2.57 1.31 hours, while those in Group B required 2.79 1.72 hours to progress from 6 cm to 10 cm of cervical dilatation.

According to Friedman & Kroll, (1971) research, the steepest part of the slope (from 4cm to 9cm) takes an average of 1.67 ± 1.25 hours.

The World Health Organization (2014) has, in recent times, produced evidence to support the position that it takes. During the active initial stage of labour, the National Institute for Health and Care

Excellence guidelines now prescribe a minimum rate of progress of 0.5 cm per hour. These guidelines were issued by the National Institute for Health and Care Excellence.

According to the results of the current study, the rate of LSCS was not significantly different between the two study groups (p > 0.05), despite the fact that the 4 cm group had a little higher LSCS rate than the other group. There was also no significant difference between the two groups in terms of how long the second stage of labour lasted or the perinatal outcome. This indicated that recognising up to 6 centimetres as latent phase or treating up to 4 centimetres as latent phase did not have an effect on the results for either the mother or the foetus.

When attempting to make sense of the findings of this study, it is important to keep in mind the constraints that were placed on it. This investigation was conducted in a single centre with only Indian participants. Due to the fact that different portions of the South Asian population have varying demographic and anthropometric statistics, it is important to proceed with caution when making predictions to other regions. Because of the small size of the sample, a more extensive investigation that involves multiple centres is required before the results can be generalised to the entire population.

8. SUMMARY AND CONCLUSION

There was a total of three hundred women who took part in this study, which utilised a partograph to compare the duration of labour and the outcome utilising the former WHO active period criteria (4 cm) and the current WHO active period standards (6 cm). The conclusions of the study are summed up as follows in this paragraph:

The age distribution of patients was very similar across the two groups. Almost no significant differences were found. The average ages of the patients in groups A and B were slightly different from one another, with group A having a mean age of 23.88 and group B's having a mean age of 23.442. There was no statistically discernible difference between the age distributions of the two groups.

Both groups of patients had a distribution that was comparable to one another in terms of their weight. Patients in group A had an average weight of 61.59 kilogrammes, while patients in group B had an average weight of 61.818 kg. The value of P was more than 0.05. None of the groups displayed a difference in their percentages of body fat that could be considered statistically significant.

In group A, it took an average of 4.638 hours to dilating by 10 centimetres, while in group B, it only took 3.216 hours.

During the course of the study, the rate of cervix dilatation from 4 to 10 centimetres per hour averaged 1.49 centimetres per hour in group A (4 cm). During the observation period, the cervix of women in group B (6 cm) dilated at a rate that was 2.42 centimetres per hour on average from 6 cm to 10 cm. During the course of the experiment, the pupils of group B, which measured 6 centimetres in diameter, dilated at a rate that was significantly quicker than group A's (10 cm). (p<0.01). In comparison, the growth rate for Group A was the slowest at 0.65 cm/h, while the growth rate for Group B was the fastest at 0.8 cm/h.

Differences between groups A and B that were statistically significant (p 0.001) include the fact that 74.7 percent of women in group B were on or left of the warning line, whereas only 46 percent of women in group A were in this position. While only 10 percent of Group B's members made it over the action line, 16.7 percent of Group A's members did so.

There was a statistically significant difference (p 0.05) between the median amount of time it took for group A (2.3 hours) and group B (2.8 hours) to enlarge a patient's cervix from 4 to 6 centimetres.

Group A completed the procedure in 2.3 hours. The median dilatation duration for group B was also 1.7 hours (6–10 cm), which was equal to the period seen in group A (p > 0.05).

REFERENCES

Bernitz, S., Øian, P., Rolland, R., Sandvik, L., & Blix, E. (2014). Oxytocin and dystocia as risk factors for adverse birth outcomes: A cohort of low-risk nulliparous women. *Midwifery, 30*(3), 364–370. doi:10.1016/j.midw.2013.03.010 PMID:23684697

Cohen, W. R., & Friedman, E. A. (2015). Perils of the new labor management guidelines. *American Journal of Obstetrics and Gynecology, 212*(4), 420–427. doi:10.1016/j.ajog.2014.09.008 PMID:25218127

Friedman, E. A., & Kroll, B. H. (1971). Computer analysis of labor progression. 3. Pattern variations by parity. *The Journal of Reproductive Medicine, 6*(4), 179–183. PMID:4938465

Hendricks, C. H., Brenner, W. E., & Kraus, G. (1970). Normal cervical dilatation pattern in late pregnancy and labor. *American Journal of Obstetrics and Gynecology, 106*(7), 1065–1082. doi:10.1016/S0002-9378(16)34092-3 PMID:5435658

Lavender, T., Cuthbert, A., & Smyth, R. M. D. (2018). Effect of partograph use on outcomes for women in spontaneous labour at term and their babies. *The Cochrane Library, 2018*(8). doi:10.1002/14651858.CD005461.pub5

Mathai, M. (2009). The partograph for the prevention of obstructed labor. *Clinical Obstetrics and Gynecology, 52*(2), 256–269. doi:10.1097/GRF.0b013e3181a4f163 PMID:19407533

Oladapo, O. T., Souza, J. P., Fawole, B., Mugerwa, K., Perdoná, G., Alves, D., Souza, H., Reis, R., Oliveira-Ciabati, L., Maiorano, A., Akintan, A., Alu, F. E., Oyeneyin, L., Adebayo, A., Byamugisha, J., Nakalembe, M., Idris, H. A., Okike, O., Althabe, F., & Gülmezoglu, A. M. (2018). Progression of the first stage of spontaneous labour: A prospective cohort study in two sub-Saharan African countries. *PLoS Medicine, 15*(1), e1002492. doi:10.1371/journal.pmed.1002492 PMID:29338000

Orji, E. (2008). Evaluating progress of labor in nulliparas and multiparas using the modified WHO partograph. *International Journal of Gynaecology and Obstetrics: the Official Organ of the International Federation of Gynaecology and Obstetrics, 102*(3), 249–252. doi:10.1016/j.ijgo.2008.04.024 PMID:18603248

Peisner, D. B., & Rosen, M. G. (1986). Transition from latent to active labor. *Obstetrics and Gynecology, 68*(4), 448–451. PMID:3748488

Purwar, R., Malik, S., Khanam, Z., & Mishra, A. (2021). Progression of the first stage of labour, in low risk nulliparas in a South Asian population: A prospective observational study. *Journal of Obstetrics & Gynaecology, 2*(8), 1–5. doi:10.1080/01443615.2020.1867967 PMID:33938356

Shi, Q., Tan, X.-Q., Liu, X.-R., Tian, X.-B., & Qi, H.-B. (2016). Labour patterns in Chinese women in Chongqing. *BJOG, 123*, 57–63. doi:10.1111/1471-0528.14019 PMID:27627599

Suzuki, R., Horiuchi, S., & Ohtsu, H. (2010). Evaluation of the labor curve in nulliparous Japanese women. *American Journal of Obstetrics and Gynecology*, *203*(3), 226.e1–226.e6. doi:10.1016/j.ajog.2010.04.014 PMID:20494329

Thorton, J. G. (2006). Use of partograph with an agreed protocol for Active Management of Labour. *Journal of Obstetrics & Gynaecology*, *91*, 188–196.

World Health Organisation. (2014). *WHO recommendations for augmentation of labour.* WHO.

Zhang, J., Landy, H. J., Branch, W., Burkman, R., Haberman, S., Gregory, K. D., Hatjis, C. G., Ramirez, M. M., Bailit, J. L., Gonzalez-Quintero, V. H., Hibbard, J. U., Hoffman, M. K., Kominiarek, M., Learman, L. A., Van Veldhuisen, P., Troendle, J., & Reddy, U. M. (2011). Contemporary patterns of spontaneous labor with normal neonatal outcomes. *Obstetrical & Gynecological Survey*, *66*(3), 132–133. doi:10.1097/OGX.0b013e31821685d0

Chapter 6
An Enhanced Approach for Multi-Modal Sentimental Analysis in Natural Language Processing

V. Vinitha
Jain University, India

R. Jayanthi
Jain University, India

S. Thirukumaran
Jain University, India

Ramchand Vedaiyan
Villa College, Maldives

G. Raja
(iD) https://orcid.org/0000-0002-4116-1682
KL Education Foundation, India

ABSTRACT

Sentiment analysis is a common technique in artificial intelligence and natural language processing. The automated assessment of consumer comments on services or products is becoming more prevalent. Multi-modal sentiment analysis has evolved as a fascinating study topic that evaluates and interprets sentiment expressions using several modalities, such as text, pictures, audio, and video. This technique enables a more thorough knowledge of human emotions by capturing the interaction of many modalities. The capacity to assess sentiment across various modalities has several advantages over unimodal techniques. Multi-modal sentiment analysis improves performance by combining text, images, audio, and video information. This allows it to catch complimentary and contextually relevant cues. Improving the performance of multi-modal sentiment analysis covers several processes, including sentiment polarity identification, multi-modal feature extraction, and fusion.

DOI: 10.4018/978-1-6684-9189-8.ch006

1. INTRODUCTION

Since the introduction of the Online platform, users have been more driven than ever to share their opinions and engage in online discussions on global issues (Al-Otaibi et al., 2022). Social media's growth has tremendously enhanced these operations by giving us a platform to freely share our viewpoints with people worldwide. Affective analytics includes two subcategories: sentiment analysis, also called opinion mining, is useful to gather and analyze public sentiment and viewpoints where sentiment analysis is analyzed. It has been gaining acceptance in academics, government agencies and service industries. The technique for recognizing human emotions is called sentiment recognition (Suganthi, & Sathiaseelan, 2023). Automatic detection of a person's mood or attitude is known as affective computing. Our emotions and sentiments significantly influence our daily lives (Vashishtha and Kapoor, 2023). In human-centred environments, they support decision-making, education, communication, and situation awareness (Sharma, et al., 2021a). In order to make it possible for computers to detect, evaluate, and interpret feelings and emotions in a way identical to that of humans, cognitive abilities have been a focus of research over the past 20 years.

Affective computing (Kratzwald et al., 2018) is the source of these initiatives. User reviews of products, services, and events are valuable from a business standpoint. They allow enterprises to monitor their products, strengthen their relationships with customers, innovative marketing strategies, and superior services. Consumers carefully analyze the content shared on social media and numerous web platforms before deciding whether to use or purchase any goods or services (Jin et al., 2022). It might be challenging to recognize and extract emotions from natural language. Compared to sentiment analysis, multi-modal sentiment analysis (Jin et al., 2022) generates people's emotions, opinions, and sentiments through behavioural observations and information retrieval analyses and extracts opinions from enormous amounts of text integrating techniques for data mining, information retrieval, and natural language processing. Physiological indicators, speech, written records and facial expressions are all examples of behavioural hints (Sharma, et al., 2021b). As humans and emotion are closely related, understanding emotions is essential to developing artificial intelligence that behaves like humans (Stappen et al., 2021). Natural language frequently reflects a person's emotions. Emotion detection has become widely used in NLP (Zadeh et al., 2020). Because of its capacity to conclude various publicly available conversational data on platforms like Facebook, YouTube, Reddit, Twitter, and others, multi-modal emotion detection is currently gaining importance in NLP (Shifat, et al., 2023). Additionally, it can be employed in other industries, including forensics, healthcare, understanding student frustration, and many more.

Many Big Data applications have used deep learning to enhance categorization and modelling performance. Modern deep learning algorithms can produce improved categorization modelling results; it has a wide range of applications (Bhatt et al., 2021). popular deep learning-based approach for image processing is the convolution neural network; the study of sentiment analysis conveyed across many modalities, such as text, photos, videos, and audio, is known as multi-modal sentiment analysis (Priscila, et al., 2023). This branch of natural language processing is developing significantly (Park et al., 2016). While text-based Multi-modal sentiment analysis has grown increasingly popular because it has attracted a lot of attention to sentiment analysis, it has the potential to offer a more thorough understanding of the sentiment represented in a piece of content where there are several methods for feature extraction and selection, classification models, and pre-processing techniques (Sharma, et al., 2021c).

Traditionally, sentiment analysis has concentrated on a single modality (visual, voice, or text). Text-based sentiment analysis (Chandrasekaran et al.,2021) has significantly contributed to NLP. Human facial

Figure 1. Classic multi-modal sentiment analysis model architecture

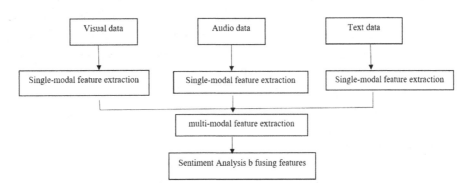

expressions and movement postures are given higher weight in vision-based sentiment analysis (Pandit, 2023). Speech-based sentiment analysis primarily drives features from speech such as pitch, timbre, and attitude for sentiment analysis. With the advancement of deep learning, these three modalities have advanced sentiment analysis (Paldi, et al., 2021). This approach is widely used in various industries, including marketing, customer service, and social media analysis.

However, sentiment analysis with one modality has limits. Single-modality emotional data is incomplete. Combining modalities may reveal deeper sentiment polarity. Analyzing one modality limits results and makes determining an action's emotion difficult. Multi-modal sentiment analysis has many models to aid. Text elements help analyse deep emotions. Visual modality extraction of emotion and step data helps text sentiment analysis and judgement. Speech modality extracts text features and voice tone to represent text state at each time point. Figure 1 shows multi-modal sentiment analysis model design. Feature extraction, fusion, and sentiment analysis make up the architecture. This work covers multi-modal sentiment analysis in detail. The evaluation summarises datasets and describes different modal fusion methods, helping researchers choose suitable datasets. Finally, we discuss multi-modal sentiment analysis challenges and potential development trajectories, offering numerous exciting study options.

2. RELATED RESEARCH

This article briefly explains the single-modal and multi-modal sentiment classification approaches.

2.1 Visual Sentiment Analysis

Early research on visual sentiment analysis was primarily concerned with hand-crafting attributes for visual feature evolutionary modelling (Machajdik, & Hanbury, 2010). Depending on psychology extracted minimal elements, including layout, texture, and colour, to forecast the emotions of images (Zhao et al., 2014) utilized artistic principles and emotional traits, such as balancing, intensity, harmony, heterogeneity, and transition, for the classification and regression of image sentiments. To find Adjective Noun Pairs (ANPs) that may be considered mid-level qualities determined by visual representations. Yuan et al., (2013) sentiment prediction of the image method makes the classification findings easier to understand. Multi-graph learning combines various attributes at various stages, including low-level features based on generic concepts and artistic elements, mid-level features based on attributes and artistic principles, and high-level features based on semantic concepts and facial expressions. Deep neural networks are frequently used in sentiment analysis in video. Deep convolutional neural networks (CNNs) were used by Yue et al., (2019) to create the DeepSentiBank visual sentiment concept classification model. Using photos tagged with website metadata, continuous training and prediction on visual sentiments was proposed. Since an image typically elicits various sentiments, local and global data for visual sentiment prediction were created to identify the sentiment mapping.

2.2 Text Sentiment Analysis

The categorization is divided into two major groups: lexicon-based models and machine-learning models; the orientation of semantic opinion phrases was predicted by considering the adjectives' preceding positive or negative polarity. The semantic Orientation calculator approach lexicon-based is described by (Taboada et al., 2011) integrates intensification negation along with dictionaries of terms with semantic orientation to analyze text sentiment where these techniques were originally used for text sentiment categorization by (Pang et al., 2015). To gather semantic and emotional data from words, Unsupervised probabilistic models of documents were presented by Santoso and Widjanadi (2016) to learn semantic similarity, and supervised models were presented to predict sentiment assessments. Considering complex sentence structure, long short-term memory was developed with a tree-like structure classifying sentence sentiment (Tang et al., 2015). This approach of obtaining sentence representations using CNN and LSTM, then utilizing neural networks to express their phrase semantics and relationships, effectively models document representation. A hierarchical attention network (HAN) was created by Stappen, et al., (2021) for the goal of document-level sentiment classification, where sentiment is incredibly complex and highly subjective. Nevertheless, because only features from a single modality are extracted in visual and textual sentiment analysis, sentiment cannot be fully represented. In actuality, sentiments expressed on social media are frequently expressed through various modalities. Hence, we focus on multi-modal sentiment analysis in this study.

2.3 Multi-modal Sentiment Analysis

Psychologists and engineers have shown a joint influence with multi-modal data to significantly determine emotion (Soleymani et al., 2017). The same image may elicit opposing feelings when accompanied by different text. Multi-modal data analysis of sentiments is essential to effectively predict sentiment. Multi-modal sentiment analysis uses characteristics from multiple modalities to estimate general sentiment, cross-media. To categorize the sentiment of micro-blogging postings, the bag-of-words model was designed, in which both text and images are presented as a single bag-of-words. A cross-modality regression technique used for evaluating simultaneous sentiment prediction that utilizes textual and visual information. Employing image captions as semantic input (Xu, 2017) devised a hierarchical semantic attentional network (HSAN) to analyze multi-modal sentiment. A deep network called MultiSentiNet was introduced to completely capture precise semantic information. It uses the image's scene and object properties are used for indication. When modelling the mutual effects of picture and text to categorize, multi-modal emotion is considered that information from two separate modalities can influence and augment each other. The most recent fusion approaches research is evaluated in the analysis of dataset generation. Each of these strategies depends on several other well-established criteria for improvisational results. Various multi-modal classification techniques are reviewed in light of the most recent developments in machine learning. It was developed to ensure that the integrated representations contain the most information from all modalities. A divide-conquer and combine strategy (Santoso, et al., 2016) created a dynamic and hierarchical cross-modality fusion method. A Multi-modal Factorization Model was applied to optimize across multi-modal data and labels. This Model incorporates features using a multi-modal discriminative variable technique and a modality-specific for generating variables.

3. IMPORTANCE OF MODALITIES

Several modalities are employed in multi-modal sentiment analysis to extract affective states from the discourse. Text, audio, and visual are the three most frequently employed modes. It helps to improve sentiment prediction, and research shows that bimodal and trimodal systems produce better results than unimodal systems. Every modality makes a significant contribution to increasing accuracy.

3.1 Text-Based Sentiment Analysis

It examines the emotions conveyed in a text document such as a tweet, review, or comment. In order to categorize the attitude depicted in the text, based sentiment analysis often comprises pre-processing the text data to eliminate noise, detecting the pertinent textual features, and categorizing the sentiment.

3.2 Image-Based Sentiment Analysis

The evaluation of the emotions conveyed by multimedia, such as photos or images, is known as image-based sentiment analysis. This can be accomplished by removing visual elements from the photographs, such as colour, texture, and shape and then classifying the sentiment shown in the images using machine learning models like convolutional neural networks (CNNs).

3.3 Video-Based Sentiment Analysis

The analysis of sentiment expressed by video content, such as movies, TV shows, or videos, is used in sentiment analysis. This is feasible by scrutinizing different aspects of the film, such as speech, body language, and facial expressions. Machine learning techniques using recurrent neural networks can be used to categorize the sentiment conveyed in the movie.

3.4 Audio-Based Sentiment Analysis

The analysis of sentiment conveyed in audio content, such as music or phone conversations, is known as audio-based sentiment analysis. This can be accomplished by looking at the audio's many characteristics, including pitch, tone, and volume and classifying the sentiment communicated in the audio using neural networks and support vector machines are examples of machine learning models.

4. MULTI-MODAL SENTIMENT ANALYSIS DATASETS

The emergence of the Internet has resulted in an era of data explosion. Multi-modal sentiment analysis has drawn much interest in recent years since it provides a more in-depth understanding of sentiment by including different modalities such as text, images, audio, and video. It overviews some of the most prominent multi-modal sentiment analysis datasets. Researchers can use these datasets to design and test multi-modal sentiment analysis models. They enable research into merging many modalities, context-aware sentiment analysis, and developing more accurate and robust models for interpreting human emotions and sentiments across several modalities.

Multi-modal Opinion Sentiment and Emotion Intensity Index (CMU-MOSEI): It is a well-known sentiment analysis dataset containing 3,228 YouTube videos (Zadeh et al., 2018). These videos are divided into 23,453 pieces and provide information in three separate modalities: text, visual, and sound. This dataset provides a varied spectrum of opinions, with contributions from 1,000 speakers and coverage of 250 distinct topics. All the movies are in English, and there are annotations for sentiment and emotion. Happy, sad, angry, afraid, disgusted, and amazed are the six emotion categories, and the sentiment strength indicators vary from very negative to strongly positive (-3 to 3). CMU-MOSEI (Arslan, et al., 2021) is a helpful resource for researchers interested in sentiment analysis across many modalities.

Interactive Emotional Dyadic Motion Capture (IEMOCAP): It is a sentiment analysis dataset (Busso et al., 2008) by the Speech Analysis and Interpretation Laboratory, is a multi-modal dataset comprising 1,039 conversational segments and a total video length of 12 hours. Participants in the study took part in five different scenarios, each with a different set of feelings. The dataset contains audio, video, and text data and facial expression and posture data gathered from additional sensors. The following emotions are assigned to data points: neutral, happy, sad, angry, shocked, afraid, disgusted, annoyed, enthusiastic, and other. IEMO-CAP is a valuable resource for educators interested in sentiment analysis across many modalities.

CMU-MOSI: A Multi-Modal Corpus of Subjectivity and Emotional Arousal The dataset consists of 93 high-quality videos from YouTube spanning a wide range of topics (Zadeh et al., 2016). These films were specifically selected such that only one speaker would be facing the camera at all times. All 89 speakers, 41 of whom were women and 48 of whom were men, spoke in English without any restrictions on camera model, distance, or speaker setting. From strongly negative to strongly favourable, the 93 videos were divided into 2,199 subjective opinion portions (-3 to 3).

Factify (Ogunmola et al., 2021) is a dataset for detecting fake news with the goal of validating implementations. It offers information in both visual and textual formats, with a total of 50,000 data sets. Most of the data's claims are related to political and governmental matters. For researchers looking into ways to spot and stop the spread of fake news, this dataset is invaluable.

Motion (Ramamoorthy et al., 2022) is a dataset of memes that covers a variety of topics, from politics and religion to sports. There are a total of 10,000 observations in the dataset, which have been subdivided into three tasks: sentiment analysis, emotion categorization, and scale/intensity of emotion classes. The subtask dictated how each data point was annotated by the annotators. Subtask 1 classifies each data point into one of three categories (negative, neutral, and positive). In the second part of the work, the information is divided into four groups (humour, sarcasm, offence, and motivation). Task 3 involves assigning labels to each data point in the range [0,4] to determine the level of emotion associated with it. Researchers now have a rare opportunity to study the impact of memes as a cultural phenomenon because to this dataset.

5. FUSION TECHNIQUES

The process of gathering, identifying, and integrating necessary features from data obtained from various sources is known as multi-modal fusion. The opinions are then derived from these facts after further processing. Data fusion, feature fusion, and decision fusion are three methods for combining or fusing data. Most work utilizes decision fusion (Poria et al., 2015). A generic feature vector is created by mixing components from several modalities, including text, audio, and visual. This vector is first categorized and normalized to the same scale before sending the resultant combined features vector. These core algorithms eliminate extraneous information from several types of material, such as audio, video, text, and contextual information from video utterances.

5.1 Early Feature Level Fusion

Each of the features from any modality, such as feature-level fusion, often referred to as early fusion, text, audio, and video, is merged into a single feature vector (Rosas et al., 2013). It is then subjected to a categorization system as a result of feature level fusion, enables early linkage between several multi-modal features, it may improve task completion. Time synchronization is a drawback of this fusion method because the features acquired can differ significantly across several places and pertain to various modalities. Hence, the characteristics must be changed into the various formats. Further fusion process could continue early feature level fusion can be carried out using straightforward approaches like concatenation or more complex ones like weighted averaging (Poria et al., 2015). It is obvious that the solution is not to combine as performed by existing classifiers, includes data fusion at the feature level, and information from audio or video are combined into a single vector. This fusion strategy cannot adequately capture the intra-modality dynamics (Figure 2).

5.2 Late Fusion

In late fusion, each modality's features are first processed and categorized separately (Cai and Xia, 2015). The sentiment prediction is then produced by merging the classification findings into the final decision vector. Late fusion refers to the process because fusing happens after classification. Most studies choose

Figure 2. Early fusion for multi-modal sentimental analysis

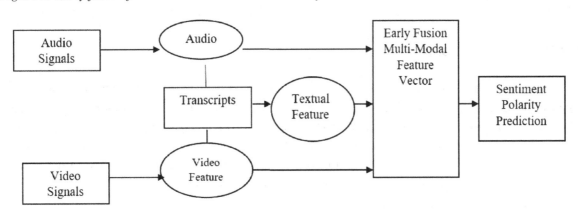

decision-level fusion where the input from each modality is modelled individually, and due to issues with early fusion, the outcomes of single recognition of modal are fused at the last stage. Pattern recognition and machine learning currently employ the technique of decision-level fusion, often known as classifier fusion. Late fusion can be carried out using straightforward strategies like averaging or more complex ones like support vector machines (SVMs).

5.3 Hybrid Fusion

This technique combines early and late fusion methods. This fusion strategy applies strategies for fusion at the feature and decision layers (Sharma, et al., 2021). It employs a hybrid fusion technique that brings together the role of texture analysis and decision-level fusion were avoiding each type of individual drawback. Techniques like multi-layer perceptrons (MLPs) or fuzzy logic systems can be used for hybrid fusion.

5.4 Bi-Modal Fusion

The separation and fusion are made possible via a unique network for fusion on pairs of modality representations to engage in a simulated conflict against one another, and the two components are trained concurrently (Wu et al., 2022). The Model accepts two bimodal pairs as input, called an information imbalance with different modalities.

5.5 Model-Level Fusion

It is investigated whether there is a relationship between the characteristics of various modalities. The appropriate Model is then developed following the study domain and problem requirement. Using this method, information creates a comfortable fusion by combining several modalities and using correlation. Researchers developed models that satisfied their research requirements while considering the event's region.

5.6 Tensor Fusion

Using a tensor fusion layer to explicitly replicate unimodal, bimodal, and trimodal interactions, this method creates a 3-fold Cartesian product utilizing modality embeddings. The quantity of training samples needed is reduced. The design of one of the tensor fusion methods

5.7 Word Level Fusion

This approach looks at interconnections between various modalities to strengthen the emotional trend. The transformer translates between several modalities and learns joint representations for utterances. The Memory Fusion Network (MFN), a recurrent model for multi-view sequential learning, consists of three parts. Long-short-term memory (LSTM) networks store the dynamics and connections unique to each view. The Delta-memory Attention Network, a particular attention mechanism in the System of LSTMs, was created to find cross-view and temporal relationships across numerous dimensions of memories. A single, integrated memory that remembers cross-view interactions across time is known as a multi-view gated memory.

6. LATEST MULTI-MODAL SENTIMENT ANALYSIS MODELS

Multi-modal Affective Generalization BERT (MAG-BERT) is a multi-modal sentiment analysis model incorporating visual, textual, and audio information for sentiment categorization. It is based on the BERT (Bidirectional Encoder Representations from Transformers) Model, a common pre-trained model for natural language processing applications. It expands BERT to handle multi-modal data by including extra modalities such as images and audio. To successfully incorporate input from many modalities, the Model employs a multi-modal fusion approach. It extracts textual information from the input text and visual and acoustic elements from images and audio files.

Multi-modal Interaction for Sentiment Analysis (MISA) refers to using multi-modal approaches in sentiment analysis. The study and interpretation of sentiments expressed by persons utilizing several modalities such as text, photos, audio, video, and other forms of data is known as multi-modal sentiment analysis. It focuses on developing models and algorithms that can successfully integrate and analyze data from diverse modalities to comprehend and interpret human feelings in the setting of "MISA," or multi-modal sentiment analysis. The goal is to capture the rich and subtle manifestations of emotion communicated through many channels.

AutoML (Automated Machine Learning) fusion is the technique of automatically learning and optimizing the fusing of multi-modal data in the context of sentiment analysis or other tasks. It entails utilizing automated machine learning algorithms to discover the ideal combination and integrate information from many modalities. Traditional fusion approaches might require manual design choices and lengthy testing to define the fusion strategy. Auto-ML-based fusion tries to automate this process using machine learning techniques to automatically learn the best fusion approach from the given multi-modal data.

Semantic feature fusion in multi-modal sentiment analysis refers to merging or fusing the semantic representations of distinct modalities to improve sentiment analysis performance. It involves gathering significant semantic elements from each modality and merging them to better understand sentiment represented in multi-modal data. The semantic features often indicate the underlying meaning or semantics of the data and can be extracted from multiple modalities such as text, pictures, audio, or video. Here are some major issues and strategies for semantic feature fusion in multi-modal sentiment analysis. ATMF-DFF refers to the suggested Model that primarily considers text and audio medium. The key contribution is the development of new multi-feature and multi-modal fusion techniques. Two parallel branches are employed to learn features for the text modality and features for the audio modality. A multi-modal attention fusion module is employed to complete the multi-modal fusion for the features of these two modalities.

7. CHALLENGES

It faces several problems (Gandhi et al., 2022), including biasing, context dependence, slag words, code-mixed data, redundancy, high dimensionality, and domain specificity. These are some of the disadvantages mentioned.

7.1 Cross Domain

Sentiment categorization is considered the domain's sensitivity since different domains express opinions differently. This problem is solved by understanding the characteristics of an unknown domain, and sentiment analysis can change according to the circumstances. Words used in any situation might not signify the same thing when used in another.

7.2 High Dimensionality

It indicates a significant feature set that suffers from computational problems and calls for appropriate feature selection techniques.

7.3 Biasing

Sentiment analysis is commonly used in industries comparable to healthcare, which handles delicate topics like counselling. It's essential to consider bias, particularly when identifying emotional cues in the many customer service calls and marketing leads from various racial and socio-economic demographics. Gender, race, age, and other factors can all be sources of bias.

7.4 Context Dependency

Depending on the subject, several sentimental expressions are used. Even seemingly neutral phrases can carry meaning when combined with other words or sentences; the same phrase can generate negative emotions.

8. APPLICATIONS

8.1 Social Media Analysis

The sentiment of data can be examined via multi-modal sentiment analysis of social media users towards a particular topic or brand. It can help businesses understand customers' opinions and feedback on their products or services. Here are a few potentials uses for multi-modal sentiment analysis on social media:

8.2 Management of Online Reputation

Social media sentiment analysis can be used to track online opinions of a certain product or business. Businesses can learn more about how the public perceives their brand by examining text, photographs, and videos on various social media sites. Businesses can use this to pinpoint areas where their reputation needs work and change their messaging accordingly.

8.3 Crisis Management

Sentiment analysis on social media can be used to track public opinion in times of crisis or disaster. Businesses can learn more about how the public responds to the crisis by examining social media posts and other internet information. This can assist companies in modifying their crisis response plans and messaging and address any concerns or questions the public may have.

8.4 Customer Service

In order to serve customers, social media sentiment analysis can be used to examine their comments on various social media sites. Businesses can use this to pinpoint areas for customer service improvement and deal with problems early on.

8.5 Marketing Analysis

Social media sentiment analysis can be used to learn more about how consumers feel about various goods and services. Businesses can learn more about what drives customers to purchase by studying social media posts and modifying their marketing efforts as necessary.

8.6 Event Monitoring

Public opinion towards various events, such as concerts, festivals, and sporting contests, can be done via social media sentiment analysis. Businesses can learn how the public responds to the event by examining social media posts, and they can modify their strategy accordingly.

Ultimately, social media multi-modal sentiment analysis can give businesses insightful information on how the general public feels about their brand or product. Businesses can develop a more thorough grasp of the sentiment towards a given topic and modify their tactics and messaging by examining text, photos, and videos across numerous social media platforms.

8.7 Recommender System

Many businesses utilize recommender systems to give users tailored recommendations based on their interests and previous actions. By combining users' emotional states and behaviour, multi-modal sentiment analysis can be utilized to improve the accuracy of recommender systems. Recommender systems can learn about users' emotional states and preferences by examining their facial expressions, tone of voice, and other physiological cues. As a result, consumers may receive more accurate and pertinent recommendations from the system, increasing their pleasure and engagement. For instance, a music streaming service could use multi-modal sentiment analysis to examine consumers' facial expressions and voice tones while they listen to music. The system can utilize this information to determine the user's emotional state and provide music that ultimately, by offering customers a more customized and emotionally intelligent experience, multi-modal sentiment analysis can potentially transform the field of recommender systems.

8.8 Healthcare

There are several potential uses for multi-modal sentiment analysis in the healthcare industry, particularly in patient care. Healthcare professionals can learn more about their patient's emotional states by examining speech patterns, facial expressions, and other physiological signs. This information can be used to improve patient outcomes and treatment plans. For example, in mental health care, multi-modal sentiment analysis can be used to monitor patients with depression or anxiety and provide targeted support and therapy based on their emotional condition. Multi-modal sentiment analysis in paediatric care might assist in identifying kids who could be at risk for mental health difficulties and offer early intervention. It can be used in elder care to recognize patients suffering from depression or other mental health disorders and offer the proper support. Ultimately, multi-modal sentiment analysis can completely transform patient care by giving medical professionals crucial information about their patient's emotional states and enabling them to tailor care to each person's specific requirements.

8.9 Education

Due to its ability to offer insightful data on students' emotional states and involvement, multi-modal sentiment analysis has the potential to completely transform the field of education. Teachers can learn more about their student's emotional states by observing speech patterns, facial expressions, and other physiological cues, and then they can adjust their teaching methods accordingly. For instance, during a class discussion, a teacher can use multi-modal sentiment analysis to track students' facial expressions and voice tones to spot those who might be disinterested or having trouble understanding the topic. The teacher can use this information to further engage the class and give those children the support and help they need. Moreover, multi-modal sentiment analysis can be utilized to track student comments on online learning environments and offer useful study advice. By giving teachers insightful information about their students' needs and emotional states, multi-modal sentiment analysis can potentially increase student engagement and academic results.

8.10 Sports Analysis

Multi-modal sentiment analysis has several uses in sports, from assessing athletes' emotional states to improving viewers' viewing experiences. Coaches can learn about an athlete's emotional state during practices and games by observing their facial expressions and body language. This can assist coaches in identifying areas where athletes might need more assistance or training regimen modifications. When used to track fan mood during sporting events, multi-modal sentiment analysis can reveal which parts of the action are most exciting for spectators and which might drive them away in displeasure. By customizing broadcasts to viewers' emotional states and preferences, this information can enhance the viewing experience for viewers. Moreover, sports betting companies can use multi-modal sentiment analysis to assess customer sentiment and modify odds. Therefore, multi-modal sentiment analysis can change the sports industry by offering insightful data on athletes' and fans' involvement and emotional condition.

8.11 Political Campaigns

Political campaigns can use multi-modal sentiment analysis as a potent technique to get important insights into voters' engagement and emotional state. Political campaigns can learn about the emotion of the electorate and modify their messaging by examining social media posts, interviews, and other contacts with voters. For instance, a political campaign could examine voter facial expressions and voice tones at a rally or debate to determine which themes resonate with people and which are not using multi-modal sentiment analysis. Future messages can be tailored using this data to connect with voters more effectively and boost engagement. Also, political campaigns can use multi-modal sentiment analysis to track online voter sentiment and modify their strategy. By examining social media posts and comments, campaigns can learn which issues are most significant to voters. They can then modify their messaging accordingly. Therefore, multi-modal sentiment analysis can transform political campaigns by offering insightful data on the emotional state and voter participation and by assisting campaigns in customizing their messaging to more effectively engage with their supporters.

9. FUTURE RESEARCH DIRECTIONS

Some promising applications of future multi-modal sentiment analysis methods are discussed below. Criminal language deception detection model, offensive language detection, and real-time multi-modal emotion analysis for assessing mental health. Researchers from a variety of fields will likely need to collaborate in the future on multi-modal sentiment analysis projects. Consider the case of an emotional humanoid robot. Ethical issues with sentiment analysis, such as privacy concerns, could be another topic of research. Emotion analysis that takes into account multiple data sources is called multi-modal emotion analysis. Sentiment analysis models that make use of multiple sources of data have been shown to greatly improve precision. There will be ongoing developments in multi-modal sentiment analysis methods. A multi-modal sentiment analysis model with many parameters that can do as well as humans in sentiment analysis might be possible in the future.

10. CONCLUSION

The multi-modal sentiment analysis study is streamlined to allow researchers to choose the best application approaches. Because different domains use a variety of languages and cultural settings, it provides domain adaptability, transfer learning, and multi-task learning. We present an overview of many aspects of multi-modal sentiment analysis, including the importance of modalities, the dataset used, Fusion Techniques the Latest Multi-modal Sentiment Analysis Models used and various applications. In this review, we Compare and analyze recent cutting-edge multi-modal sentiment analysis. Finally, we discuss the challenges of multi-modal sentiment analysis and speculate on possible future advancements. Many potential works are actively being carried out and have even been partially implemented. However, there are still issues to be solved, create a huge multi-modal sentiment dataset in several languages, Resolve the domain transfer issue for video, text, and speech data, creating of a unified, large-scale multi-modal sentence analysis model with high generalization performance, create a multi-modal sentiment analysis model capable of completing hidden sentiments which can lead to the further research directions.

REFERENCES

Al-Otaibi, S., Al-Rasheed, A. A., AlHazza, B., Khan, H. A., & AlShfloot, G., AlFaris & AlShuweishi, N. (2022). Finding Influential Users in Social Networking using Sentiment Analysis. *Informatica (Vilnius)*, *46*(5).

Arslan, F., Singh, B., Sharma, D. K., Regin, R., Steffi, R., & Rajest, S. S. (2021). Optimization technique approach to resolve food sustainability problems. In *2021 International Conference on Computational Intelligence and Knowledge Economy (ICCIKE)*. IEEE.

Bhatt, D., Patel, C., Talsania, H., Patel, J., Vaghela, R., Pandya, S., & Ghayvat, H. (2021). CNN variants for computer vision: History, architecture, application, challenges and future scope. *Electronics (Basel)*, *10*(20), 2470.

Busso, C., Bulut, M., Lee, C. C., Kazemzadeh, A., Mower, E., Kim, S., ... Narayanan, S. S. (2008). IEMOCAP: Interactive emotional dyadic motion capture database. *Language Resources and Evaluation*, *42*, 335–359.

Cai, G., & Xia, B. (2015). Convolutional neural networks for multimedia sentiment analysis. *Natural Language Processing and Chinese Computing: 4th CCF Conference, NLPCC 2015, Nanchang, China, October 9-13, 2015 Proceedings*, *4*, 159–167.

Chandrasekaran, G., Nguyen, T. N., & Hemanth, D. J. (2021). Multi-modal sentimental analysis for social media applications: A comprehensive review. *Wiley Interdisciplinary Reviews. Data Mining and Knowledge Discovery*, *11*(5), e1415.

Gandhi, A., Adhvaryu, K., Poria, S., Cambria, E., & Hussain, A. (2022). Multi-modal sentiment analysis: A systematic review of history, datasets, multi-modal fusion methods, applications, challenges and future directions. *Information Fusion*. Advance online publication. doi:10.1016/j.inffus.2022.09.025

Jin, Z., Tao, M., Zhao, X., & Hu, Y. (2022). Social Media Sentiment Analysis Based on Dependency Graph and Co-occurrence Graph. *Cognitive Computation*, *14*(3), 1039–1054.

Kratzwald, B., Ilić, S., Kraus, M., Feuerriegel, S., & Prendinger, H. (2018). Deep learning for affective computing: Text-based emotion recognition in decision support. *Decision Support Systems*, *115*, 24–35. doi:10.1016/j.dss.2018.09.002

Machajdik, J., & Hanbury, A. (2010, October). Affective image classification using features inspired by psychology and art theory. In *Proceedings of the 18th ACM international conference on Multimedia* (pp. 83-92). ACM.

Ogunmola, G. A., Singh, B., Sharma, D. K., Regin, R., Rajest, S. S., & Singh, N. (2021). Involvement of distance measure in assessing and resolving efficiency environmental obstacles. In *2021 International Conference on Computational Intelligence and Knowledge Economy (ICCIKE)*. IEEE.

Paldi, R. L., Aryal, A., Behzadirad, M., Busani, T., Siddiqui, A., & Wang, H. (2021). Nanocomposite-seeded single-domain growth of lithium niobate thin films for photonic applications. In *Conference on Lasers and Electro-Optics*. Washington, DC: Optica Publishing Group.

Pandit, P. (2023). On the Context of Diabetes: A Brief Discussion on the Novel Ethical Issues of Non-communicable Diseases. *FMDB Transactions on Sustainable Health Science Letters*, *1*(1), 11–20.

Pang, L., Zhu, S., & Ngo, C. W. (2015). Deep multi-modal learning for affective analysis and retrieval. *IEEE Transactions on Multimedia*, *17*(11), 2008–2020.

Park, S., Shim, H. S., Chatterjee, M., Sagae, K., & Morency, L. P. (2016). Multi-modal analysis and prediction of persuasiveness in online social multimedia. *ACM Transactions on Interactive Intelligent Systems*, *6*(3), 1–25.

Poria, S., Cambria, E., & Gelbukh, A. (2015, September). Deep convolutional neural network textual features and multiple kernel learning for utterance-level multi-modal sentiment analysis. In *Proceedings of the 2015 conference on empirical methods in natural language processing* (pp. 2539-2544). Academic Press.

Priscila, S. S., Rajest, S. S., Tadiboina, S. N., Regin, R., & András, S. (2023). Analysis of Machine Learning and Deep Learning Methods for Superstore Sales Prediction. *FMDB Transactions on Sustainable Computer Letters*, *1*(1), 1–11.

Ramamoorthy, S., Gunti, N., Mishra, S., Suryavardan, S., Reganti, A., Patwa, P., & Ahuja, C. (2022). Memotion 2: Dataset on sentiment and emotion analysis of memes. In *Proceedings of De-Factify: Workshop on Multi-modal Fact Checking and Hate Speech Detection, CEUR*. Academic Press.

Rosas, V. P., Mihalcea, R., & Morency, L. P. (2013). Multi-modal sentiment analysis of Spanish online videos. *IEEE Intelligent Systems*, *28*(3), 38–45.

Santoso, L. W., & Widjanadi, I. (2016). The application of New Information Economics Method on distribution company to improve the efficiency and effectiveness of performance. *International Journal of Engineering and Manufacturing*, *6*(5).

Santoso, L. W., Wilistio, A., & Dewi, L. P. (2016). Mobile Device Application to locate an Interest Point using Google Maps. *International Journal of Science and Engineering Applications*, *5*(1).

. Sharma, D. K., Jalil, N. A., Regin, R., Rajest, S. S., Tummala, R. K., & Thangadurai. (2021). Predicting network congestion with machine learning. In *2021 2nd International Conference on Smart Electronics and Communication (ICOSEC)*. IEEE.

Sharma, D. K., Singh, B., Raja, M., Regin, R., & Rajest, S. S. (2021a). An Efficient Python Approach for Simulation of Poisson Distribution. *In 2021 7th International Conference on Advanced Computing and Communication Systems (ICACCS)*. IEEE.

Sharma, D. K., Singh, B., Regin, R., Steffi, R., & Chakravarthi, M. K. (2021b). Efficient Classification for Neural Machines Interpretations based on Mathematical models. In *2021 7th International Conference on Advanced Computing and Communication Systems (ICACCS)*. IEEE.

Sharma, K., Singh, B., Herman, E., Regine, R., Rajest, S. S., & Mishra, V. P. (2021c). Maximum information measure policies in reinforcement learning with deep energy-based model. In *2021 International Conference on Computational Intelligence and Knowledge Economy (ICCIKE)*. IEEE.

Shifat, A. S. M. Z., Stricklin, I., Chityala, R. K., Aryal, A., Esteves, G., Siddiqui, A., & Busani, T. (2023). Vertical etching of scandium aluminum nitride thin films using TMAH solution. *Nanomaterials (Basel, Switzerland)*, *13*(2). Advance online publication. doi:10.3390/nano13020274 PMID:36678027

Soleymani, M., Garcia, D., Jou, B., Schuller, B., Chang, S. F., & Pantic, M. (2017). A survey of multi-modal sentiment analysis. *Image and Vision Computing*, *65*, 3–14.

Stappen, L., Baird, A., Schumann, L., & Bjorn, S. (2021). The multi-modal sentiment analysis in car reviews (muse-car) dataset: Collection, insights and improvements. *IEEE Transactions on Affective Computing*.

Suganthi, M., & Sathiaseelan, J. G. R. (2023). Image Denoising and Feature Extraction Techniques Applied to X-Ray Seed Images for Purity Analysis. *FMDB Transactions on Sustainable Health Science Letters*, *1*(1), 41–53.

Taboada, M., Brooke, J., Tofiloski, M., Voll, K., & Stede, M. (2011). Lexicon-based methods for sentiment analysis. *Computational Linguistics*, *37*(2), 267–307.

Tang, D., Qin, B., & Liu, T. (2015, September). Document modeling with gated recurrent neural network for sentiment classification. In *Proceedings of the 2015 conference on empirical methods in natural language processing* (pp. 1422-1432). Academic Press.

Vashishtha, E., & Kapoor, H. (2023). Implementation of Blockchain Technology Across International Healthcare Markets. *FMDB Transactions on Sustainable Technoprise Letters*, *1*(1), 1–12.

Wu, T., Peng, J., Zhang, W., Zhang, H., Tan, S., Yi, F., & Huang, Y. (2022). Video sentiment analysis with bimodal information-augmented multi-head attention. *Knowledge-Based Systems*, *235*, 107676.

Xu, N. (2017, July). Analyzing multi-modal public sentiment based on hierarchical semantic attentional network. In *2017 IEEE international conference on intelligence and security informatics (ISI)* (pp. 152-154). IEEE.

Yuan, J., Mcdonough, S., You, Q., & Luo, J. (2013, August). Sentribute: image sentiment analysis from a mid-level perspective. In *Proceedings of the second international workshop on issues of sentiment discovery and opinion mining* (pp. 1-8). Academic Press.

Yue, L., Chen, W., Li, X., Zuo, W., & Yin, M. (2019). A survey of sentiment analysis in social media. *Knowledge and Information Systems*, *60*, 617–663.

Zadeh, A., Cao, Y. S., Hessner, S., Liang, P. P., Poria, S., & Morency, L. P. (2020, November). CMU-MOSEAS: A multi-modal language dataset for Spanish, Portuguese, German and French. In *Proceedings of the Conference on Empirical Methods in Natural Language Processing. Conference on Empirical Methods in Natural Language Processing* (p. 1801). NIH Public Access.

Zadeh, A., Zellers, R., Pincus, E., & Morency, L. P. (2016). *Mosi: multi-modal corpus of sentiment intensity and subjectivity analysis in online opinion videos.* arXiv preprint arXiv:1606.06259.

Zadeh, A. B., Liang, P. P., Poria, S., Cambria, E., & Morency, L. P. (2018, July). Multi-modal language analysis in the wild: Cmu-mosei dataset and interpretable dynamic fusion graph. In *Proceedings of the 56th Annual Meeting of the Association for Computational Linguistics (*Volume 1*: Long Papers)* (pp. 2236-2246). Academic Press.

Zhao, S., Yao, H., Yang, Y., & Zhang, Y. (2014, November). Affective image retrieval via multi-graph learning. In *Proceedings of the 22nd ACM international conference on Multimedia* (pp. 1025-1028). ACM.

Chapter 7
Automated Vehicle Number Plate Detection Using Tesseract and Paddleocr:
Image Processing

R. Parvathi

Vellore Institute of Technology, Chennai, India

Savio Sajan Moloparambil

Vellore Institute of Technology, Chennai, India

Aswathi M. Kumar

Vellore Institute of Technology, Chennai, India

R. Jeyahari

Vellore Institute of Technology, Chennai, India

ABSTRACT

Automatic number plate recognition (ANPR) is a specialized image processing method that identifies the text on a given vehicle's number plate. The goal is to create a successful automatic approved vehicle identification system that makes use of the license plate. The system may be placed in many scenarios and locations, some of which may include security in prohibited areas like military and testing zones, or the vicinity of important government buildings like the Supreme Court, Parliament, etc. Using image segmentation in an image, the region containing the vehicle number plate from the image of a vehicle is extracted. Character recognition is achieved using an optical character recognition (OCR) approach in order to determine miscellaneous details like the owner of any detected vehicle, the location of registration, the address and whereabouts, etc.

1. INTRODUCTION

In a world where vehicles only become faster over time, accidents are more frequent, and law enforcement on motorways becomes more difficult to handle. There is the need to find the number plate of

DOI: 10.4018/978-1-6684-9189-8.ch007

a vehicle that may be breaking road laws, such as parking in the wrong area, over speeding, skipping toll gates, fender benders, or even harsh accidents. There also come certain scenarios where we need to locate vehicles of interest when the only info in hand is the number plate of the missing car. In the cases mentioned earlier, detecting the text of number plates on cars via images or video becomes vital to such cases.

In order to detect number plates of vehicles on roads, highways, streets, public places, toll gates, etc., we look towards machine learning algorithms that can know where to look in each image or frame of a video and find ways to extract text from the images. This is where the utilization of OCR comes into play, as it is the method used specifically for character extraction from said images. This paper aims to thus be able to apply such algorithms into code using Python, OpenCV, and PaddleOCR in such a way that it can take images as input and provide the text of solely the number plates of vehicles that are in the images. We use Python as the main programming language here as it is more flexible and easier to use for this application, and it comes with the benefit of supporting well-performing packages like OpenCV and PaddleOCR.

The standard techniques utilized in ANPR operations include segmenting characters, character identification, and number plate extraction. In the subsequent character segmentation stage, the entire input image is used to identify the number plate and processed further. Each character is separated and segmented during the character segmentation process. Each character is identified based on distinguishing properties in the character identification step. Number plate extraction is a challenging process because numbers typically comprise a tiny percentage of the entire image, different number plate layouts, and the effect of ambient conditions. This phase impacts the accuracy of character segmentation and recognition operations. While the primary objective of this paper is to be able to detect characters and numbers from a license plate, there, however, arises a dilemma in choosing between the two most prominent OCR libraries for such a task, namely Tesseract and PaddleOCR. In this paper, however, we shall use PaddleOCR and discuss how its results are compared to Tesseract's.

2. LITERATURE REVIEW

Lalitha (2020) established the criteria of considering the size of the image, performance rate as well as processing time, and various ANPR techniques are described. ANPR algorithms are generally divided into vehicle image capture, segmentation of characters, recognition of characters, and number plate detection.

Lubna et al. (2021) examined performance contrast of various simulated algorithms, some of which assimilate computer vision, and an extensive analysis of the methods used now and new advancements in Automatic Number Plate Recognition (ANPR) Systems. Utilizing recognition algorithms, ANPR equipment can detect and identify vehicles by their number plates.

Gnanaprakash et al. (2016) showed that the ANPR system can be developed using a deep learning library in Python called IMAGEAI and NVIDIA Jetson Nano kit to help in the training phase. According to an analysis of the algorithm's effectiveness, the system performed badly in brightly lit surroundings when morphological processing was initially used for license plate localization. The next step is to use edge detection techniques, which will improve the efficiency of the localization. At last, an IMAGEAI object identification framework that is far more effective is used.

Bhikshapathi et al. (2016) set out to increase the recognition rate of license plate characters using various techniques, including segmenting characters and extracting the license plate. The obtained data demonstrates that the recommended process combination does indeed produce a very high recognition rate. The technique has been tested using static images of automobiles sorted into several sets based on their difficulty.

Laroca et al. (2021) explained a complete, effective, and layout-independent system for reading license plates that investigates real-time-based models at every level. With post-processing rules, the recommended approach combines the identification of license plates with a categorization of layouts.

Alam et al. (2021) showed a technique for reading and identifying Bengali-written license plates on vehicles in Bangladesh. Basically, our approach uses matching templates to extract the registration plate locations using the vehicle images. A network of convolutional neural networks is used to extract features from each character and categorize the town, kind, and number of the vehicle from the segmentation character on the number plate.

Bayram (2020) reviewed the need to look into different character extraction and identification methods to increase the design efficiency of a system for recognizing license plates. Automatic Number Plate Recognition (ANPR), a type of pervasive monitoring, uses the recognition of optical characters on photos to scan license plates of moving vehicles.

Bambodkar et al. (2022) examined a technique that works well for low-resolution photos in real-time applications. It can achieve speedier recognition in challenging circumstances, particularly in low light and bad weather situations and for damaged or soiled photographs of license plates. There won't be a need to do image processing such as image denoising, picture enhancement, image segmentation, and so on under these unique situations.

Pattanaik and Balabantaray (2022) examined a convolutional neural network with three phases; the first performs license plate detection using models from the Haar cascade and canonical correlation analysis. After utilizing the bounding rectangle approach to segment, the image, in order recognize the letters in the image, a character is subsequently employed.

Shashirangana et al. (2021) displayed a mechanism for recognizing license plates that was created and intended to run on cutting-edge smartphones and can work in the dark without any extra lighting. This research also demonstrates that no past attempts have been made to identify a license plate, only modern gadgets, have been made precisely equivalent to the programs developed for use on server-grade equipment.

Madhukar & Singh (2015) showed evidence of challenges faced by automatic license plate identification on Egyptian highways, where issues exist that go beyond the capabilities of photography, picture quality, illumination levels, and alignment. This article shows that the situation's scope is more than the degree of competing jurisdictions without any coordination or planning for automated control.

Wang et al. (2022) have looked at various ALPR system ideas and employed a powerful ALPR system in a cascaded, resample-based method to increase the inference speed. The CCPD and AOLP datasets provide the best results for this method because of a new architectural design that comprises a weight-sharing classifier, an integration block, vertex estimation, and horizontal encoding. This approach also works well with PKUData and CLPD's unseen photos.

Weihong & Jiaoyang (2020) identified that the three-character recognition processes segmentation of characters, recognition of characters, and license plate detection are often separated into the process of reading license plates. The license plate recognition system offers different processing methods for complicated scenarios such as a variety of temperatures, unpredictable lighting, an unresolved filming angle, and blurred motion in real-world scenarios. These factors make it difficult for the system to identify and recognize the picture.

Shashirangana et al. (2021) showed how certain requirements and design strategies must be carefully chosen to accommodate various operational and hardware limitations while designing and developing an automated license plate recognition system. The methods and strategies currently employed in ALPR solutions have been examined and analyzed in this review. Solutions based on single-stage deep learning have demonstrated excellent performance on various datasets.

Al-batat et al. (2022) identified the steps taken for picture capture, license plate extraction, segmentation, and recognition, which are all part of the license plate recognition process. In addition to using Arabic, Libyan license plates contain a few distinctive characteristics that must be considered throughout the identification stages. Pictures of license plates were taken, and the data was then divided into smaller images, each of which included a letter, number, or word from the WHT spectrum. The coefficients and the stored database coefficients were compared. The system saved the character if the chosen coefficients matched the reference characters. This was performed for each subsequent character in the picture until the vehicle number plate was finished.

3. PROPOSED METHODOLOGY

Pre-processing, detection, identification, and searching are the four main stages of the suggested technique, as indicated in Figure 1.

The procedure known as automatic license plate recognition system consists of three main steps:

Step 1: In a given image, locate the vehicle license plate.
Step 2: Extraction of any characters from the license plate should be done after it has been located and chosen.
Step 3: Identify the extracted characters using optical character recognition (OCR) software.

3.1. Implementing OpenCV and Python

We use a Python class, PyImageSearchANPR, to provide a repeatable technique for the activities with personality OCR and number plate localization. The normal dimensions of a license plate are rectangles, with the range of aspect ratios being (maxAR - minAR).

3.2. Debugging Computer Vision Pipeline

We provide an extra method for displaying outcomes at different points in the imaging workflow while in the debugging state.

3.3. Locating Potential License Plate Candidates

The outline of the vehicle's license plate candidate can be found in an image utilizing our initial ANPR method. We require a grayscale picture with a possible license plate on it. To assist us in streamlining our ANPR pipeline, we generalize. Assume moving ahead, that the majority of the license plates possess a white backdrop (mostly reflective and blank) and a black foreground (letters). The original image

Figure 1. Methodology of the recognition system

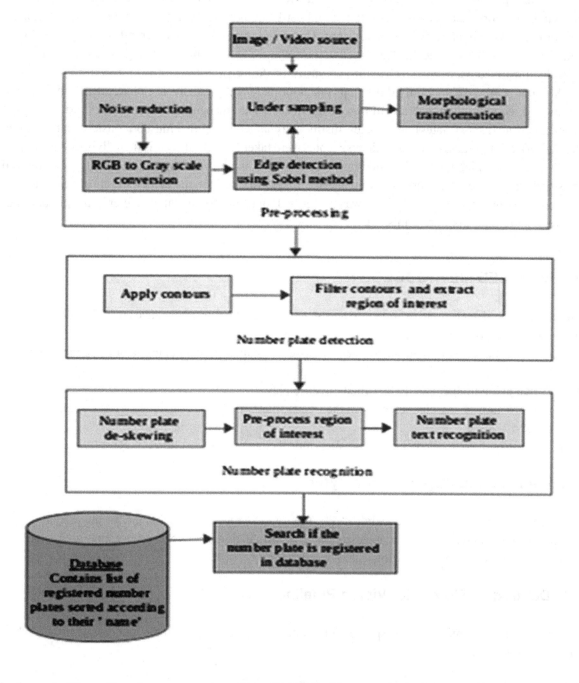

is shown in Figure 2, and pre-processing carries out a Blackhat morphological operation to make light backgrounds and dark characters (letters, numbers, and symbols) visible, as shown in Fig. 3.

The Blackhat morphological operator of OpenCV compares the numbers on the license plate with the remainder of the image on the back of the car. The majority of the surrounding noise has been drowned out, and the numbers on the license plates stand out as white characters on a black background.

Figure 2. Image before performing image processing

Figure 3. After performing Blackhat morphological operation

The characters on the license plate are mostly clear, as shown in Figure 3. We identify light areas in the image that might have characters from a license plate. We employ a small square kernel in a closure operation to fill in small gaps and help recognize more complex structures in the image. Then, using Otsu's technique, we conduct a binary black-white threshold on our image to highlight the portions of the image that may contain the letters and numbers from a license plate. The vicinity of the license plate appears to be practically one huge white surface due to Otsu's inverted binary thresholds and the closure process.

Figure 4 demonstrates how the license plate's surroundings are distinct. The edges of the image will be picked up by the Scharr gradient, bringing focus to the license plate's character limitations. We calculate the Blackhat image's x-directional Scharr gradient magnitude representation. The produced intensities are then scaled down to the range [0, 255]. Figure 5 demonstrates how the license plate characters' margins are highlighted:

The license plate's characters are clearly visible against the background, as demonstrated above. The sections that might have margins for the letters on license plates can now be seamlessly grouped. To reduce noise, the slope of the magnitude picture is blurred using the Gaussian algorithm. A closing operation is carried out once more and a binary threshold using Otsu's technique. Figure 6 shows a license plate's characters in a solid white space:

These results initially seem disorganized. In addition to the broadly defined license plate zone, there are many larger white areas. To denoise the post-threshold image, we use a sequence of erosions and dilations:

Figure 4. Closure and thresholding

Figure 5. Accentuating edges using Scharr's algorithm

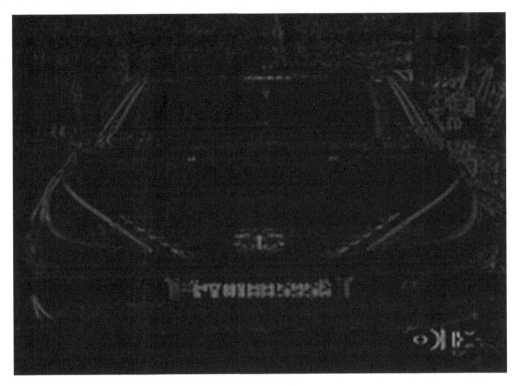

Figure 6. White area on the number plate

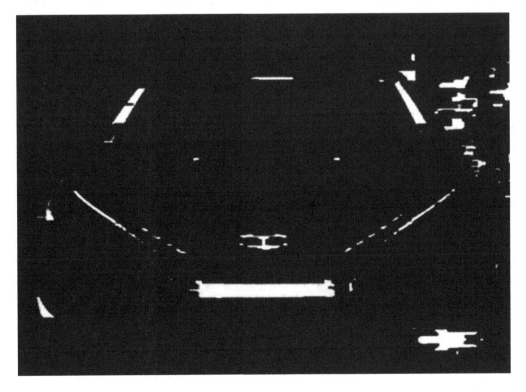

Figure 7. Cleaned-up image after dilation and erosion

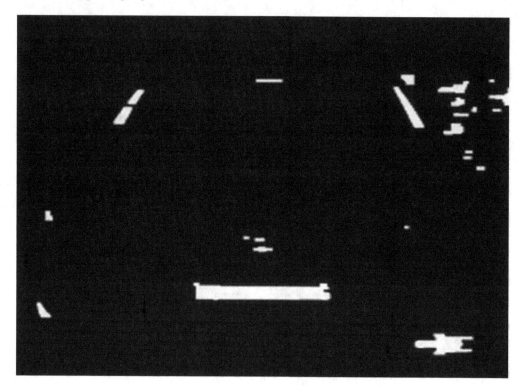

The procedure of erosion and dilation operations, as illustrated in Figure 7, significantly reduced the background noise in the prior result from Figure 6. Previously, we created a method to highlight the image's lighter regions (assuming the background is light or white and the letters are dark or black). We perform a bitwise AND on the image's post-threshold result with the luminous parts to showcase the potential license plate choices. The image is then cleaned up by using a pair of dilations and erosion processes that fills in any gaps. In Figure 8, you can see our "Final" debugging image.

The contours are found next. Accepting a grayscale image, we employ conventional image processing methods focusing on morphological processes to identify some potential license plate-containing contours. In order to locate potential license plate outlines, we employed common techniques for image processing with an emphasis on morphological evaluation and a grayscale picture as our contribution.

3.4. Pruning License Plate Candidates

We select the one with the most frequent license plate from our list of potential contours. We locate the region of interest on the license plate and recover it from the contour. We may verify that our outline has the ideal shape of a rectangle for a license plate by determining the dimension ratio of the boundary box of the contour. PaddleOCR is used to decode the characters using the output of our ANPR localization process, which is built using Python and OpenCV (Figure 9).

Figure 8. Visible contour of number plate

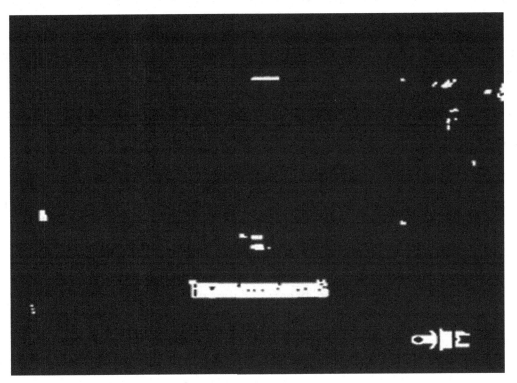

Figure 9. Outcomes of our ANPR localization workflow are based on Python and OpenCV. This sample is excellent for sending to the paddle OCR.

3.5. Optical Character Recognition Using PaddleOCR

PaddleOCR has been developed using pre-trained models of many varieties, thus crediting its reliability in text detection. Its main functionality involves text recognition, detection, and direction classifier. PaddleOCR is packaged with numerous models, including the flagship PP-OCR, and equipped with highly regarded algorithms, including SRN and NRTR. So, we create a class to implement PaddleOCR on any desired image.

3.6. Creating a Driver Script With OpenCV and PaddleOCR

- Load the input image.
- The license plate should be located anywhere in the image using image functions such as thresholding and contours.
- OCR the license plate, specifically where the license plate may be most likely found.
- Display the ANPR result in the output window.

But before that, we need to initialize a utility process. String Cleanup: since OpenCV cannot recognize special characters, it registers them as a '?'. So, to prevent special characters or symbols in a number plate from bottlenecking the process, as a safety measure, we employ a method that strips out all the characters that are alphanumeric.

4. EXPERIMENT DETAILS

There are many different sizes and styles of automatic license plate readers. Simple image processing techniques are used in ANPR under favorable conditions, including lighting and easily readable license plates. To locate license plates in images, more advanced ANPR systems employ specialized detectors for objects, including Faster R-CNN, HOG + Linear SVM, YOLO, and SSDs. Both Recurrent neural networks (RNNs) and Long Short Term Memory (LSTMs) are used in contemporary ANPR technology to improve the OCR of information directly extracted from license plate images.

4.1. Dataset Preparation

Finding a dataset to train a unique ANPR model is just one of many interrelated issues that make ANPR very difficult. Large, reliable ANPR datasets employed to train cutting-edge models are highly guarded and infrequently (if ever) made available to the general public. Such databases include on their own identifying details about the person driving the car, and the location. The staff must devote a lot of time to the laborious work of maintaining ANPR databases. Local and state governments usually engage in intense competition when awarding ANPR contracts. As a result, the collection of data that a specific company has chosen is frequently more beneficial than the model that was trained. Hence, our dataset consists of images in selected formats collected from various websites. The images are vehicles containing a license plate taken from different angles and under various conditions. For our experiment, we have procured a set of images from Kaggle, including the very images used by the authors in (Lalitha, 2020). We have selected two sets of images for our testing in the specification. The first set comprises ten images from the GitHub repository (Lalitha, 2020). The second set is an arbitrary set of 100 images collected and compiled from Kaggle, most of which are images of cars from different angles and perspectives to pose a challenging experiment for the OCR algorithms we shall be employing.

4.2. Configuring the OCR Development Environment

Installing OpenCV and virtual Python environments is advised before continuing. Pip, virtualenv, and virtualenvwrapper are all used together. Imutils, the sci-kit-image library, and the OpenCV binaries must all be installed in a Python virtual environment. Imutils, sci-kit-image, and opencv-contrib-python libraries can all be installed via pip. PaddleOCR is also required for text and character recognition. The deployment of various machine learning and computer vision algorithms will require all of these setups.

5. RESULTS AND DISCUSSION

Using Python and OpenCV, we implement automatic license plate recognition. We execute the command for our test images. These images, including either the front or rear of the car's license or number plates, demonstrate that ANPR has been successfully applied to them. The detected license plate is enclosed in a green box, and the predicted text of the license plate is also displayed, as shown in Figure 10. Our model fails in certain sets of images because it predicts inaccurately. We can also observe that PaddleOCR works better than Tesseract.

5.1. Accuracy

PaddleOCR model accuracy is low as our model makes many wrong predictions. Although the accuracy of our model is not high, it can still predict a large class of data where it works well slightly better when compared to Tesseract. There are two datasets used for the experimentation. Datasets with different images, like ten and 100 images, are considered for the implementation. Tesseract with language as English determines the accuracy for ten images as 10% and 100 images as 20%. But the using PaddleOCR implementation accuracy for ten images is 30%, and for 100 images, as 80%. The final interpretation of the output of PaddleOCR gives more accuracy even if the image size is larger, as shown in Fig. 11 and its confusion matrix is shown in Figure 12.

5.2. Implementation

With the program code now able to extract the text of vehicle license plate numbers from images of said vehicles, the final step of our work involves implementing this program in a form that takes images as input and gives the text of license plates as output. The form factor that suits this implementation would be a web application with said functionalities.

The web application constitutes two pages, one for taking the image as input and the other for returning the text extracted from the image. Since the base code of the program is in Python, the framework used in this implementation is Flask. The web pages are built and functioning properly using this framework and templates made in HTML, CSS, and Bootstrap.

Figure 10. PaddleOCR, Python, OpenCV, and automatic license/number plate recognition algorithm

Figure 11. Accuracy of Tesseract and PaddleOCR

Images Scanned	Tesseract (language = "eng")	PaddleOCR
	Accuracy	
10 (Provided in [1])	10%	30%
100 (Provided in Kaggle)	20%	80%

The home page utilizes HTML form with file input. Once uploaded to the home page, is the file Flask takes the file and saves it temporarily on the machine. It first converts the file from .jpeg/.jpg formats to .png or leaves it as is if it is already in the .png format. Once the conversion is done, it gets processed by the class imported from the file where said class implements the text extraction program discussed earlier. To avoid errors involving files not being uploaded when the form is submitted, the file input field is tagged as "required" in HTML. If the Flask application runs without any file input, an error occurs due to missing files being processed for the next page. Once the text is extracted, it is sent back into the Flask app, and then the same text is forwarded to the 2nd page as an argument along with the page template itself. The output page then showcases the image and the extracted number plate text using similar styles on the home page. Once the user's purpose is met, the home button placed on the output page can be used by the user to input another image as the button redirects to the home page, where it awaits the input of an image once more. While redirecting to the home page, the Flask app checks if

Figure 12. Confusion matrices for the performances of (a) Tesseract; (b) PaddleOCR on the first dataset (given in Lalitha, 2020) of 10 images

TESSERACT	CORRECT/PRESENT (ACTUAL)	WRONG/MISSING (ACTUAL)
CORRECT/PRESENT (PREDICTED)	1	0
WRONG/MISSING (PREDICTED)	9	0

(a)

PADDLEOCR	CORRECT/PRESENT (ACTUAL)	WRONG/MISSING (ACTUAL)
CORRECT/PRESENT (PREDICTED)	3	0
WRONG/MISSING (PREDICTED)	7	0

(b)

the temporary image file is still in the system, and when it finds the image, it deletes it as it is no longer useful to the program itself (Figure 13).

6. APPLICATIONS

Automatic Number Plate Recognition has an array of applications that prove to be very useful:

6.1. Law Enforcement

ANPR is used for law enforcement in many situations, which is seen often. Such as the technique that makes use of adjacent cameras that police utilize to determine whether a car is registered or to track down those that violate traffic laws, which snap a picture of the vehicle that is either speeding or has

Figure 13. Web page implementation of the OCR algorithm for number plate detection

crossed the red light. ANPR is used for obtaining the license plate from the image and issue the fine. Identifying vehicles also allows the authorities to track them in real time.

6.2. Smart Parking Management System

We have actively experienced this system in malls, where each vehicle requires a paid ticket to the park. Car parking management for a large number of vehicles requires a solution to detect individual vehicles and keep track of them, and this would be a very difficult task to achieve manually. Considering each car can be tracked and identified by its license plate due to ANPR, these parking garages can now have automatic parking management. It lessens the burden on the system and makes it easier for garage users to avoid managing their tickets and the time spent, preventing them from getting penalties for losing tickets or making inaccurate ticket payments.

6.3. Toll Booths

Toll Booths are something that we see commonly across India, especially in Tamil Nadu. These toll booths are manually operated, from fee collection to the opening of the boom barriers. This process is automated in some countries using various tools, including ANPR. For example, on highways with constant traffic, automation can help speed up the tollbooth procedure to help mitigate traffic. ANPR can identify the number plates, and the user can pay online, or it could be an instant auto payment.

6.4. Traffic Management

In cities with high population densities, traffic can be a perpetual issue. Especially in Indian cities, which have very high population densities. ANPR allows us to measure and analyze area-related traffic data of an entire city. Analyzing this data helps us to understand traffic congestion and aid in better traffic planning.

For example, the UK has collaborated with Siemens Traffic to regulate public and control centres using certain monitoring systems. Projects like Hampshire's ROMANSE use an interactive website with real-time city traffic updates.

7. CONCLUSION AND LIMITATIONS

7.1. Recognition Rate

The quality of videos and images taken by surveillance cameras has considerably increased over the past decade. But this alone does not guarantee perfect results in the case of Automatic Number Plate Recognition. It may be an issue with the used algorithm, which may cause failed recognition. In our case, different OCR algorithms affected the accuracy of the results. In the case of Tesseract OCR, small changes, such as clearing the foreground pixels, produced better results due to the algorithm's sensitivity.

7.2. External Factors

External factors, natural causes in specific, are hard to account for in the case of automated systems. Capturing a clear image could be difficult in the case of heavy rain, which may affect the camera lens itself, or in the case of heavy winds, which may cause objects to blow onto the camera, obstructing the view. There could also be other issues, such as the angle of sunlight, smoke, fog, snow, etc., which cannot be fixed with a small change in the algorithm. A lack of a clear image can disrupt the process, and damage to the hardware can disrupt the whole system.

7.3. Privacy

As discussed, ANPR systems allow police authorities to track vehicles to enforce the law. But it was also discussed that ANPR systems are used in malls and parking garage systems. The issue of privacy has always been principal, especially with Meta's privacy security coming into question. These systems store your license plate information; much other information is accessible with access to your license plate number. It can also become a victim of data theft.

ACKNOWLEDGMENT

Data sets were taken from the Stanford Cars dataset, Kaggle Dataset and Cars Belonging to the Travelling Agency owned by Karthi, VPJ Travels, Chennai, Tamil Nadu, India.

REFERENCES

Al-batat, R., Angelopoulou, A., Premkumar, S., Hemanth, J., & Kapetanios, E. (2022). An End-to-End Automated License Plate Recognition System Using YOLO Based Vehicle and License Plate Detection with Vehicle Classification. *Sensors (Basel)*, *22*(23), 9477. PMID:36502178

Alam, N. A., Ahsan, M., Based, M. A., & Haider, J. (2021). Intelligent System for Vehicles Number Plate Detection and Recognition Using Convolutional Neural Networks. *Technologies*, *9*(1), 9.

Bambodkar, P. R., Rahangdale, K., Dhenge, S. V., & Gondane, N. V. (2022). Helmet detection using Machine learning and automatic License Plate recognition. International Journal of Advanced Research in Science. *Tongxin Jishu*, *514–517*. Advance online publication. doi:10.48175/ijarsct-5495

Bayram, F. (2020). Automatic License Plate Recognition Based on Deep Learning. *Politeknik Dergisi*, *23*(4), 955–960.

Bhikshapathi, K., & Haribabu, D. (2016). Detection of license plate number using dynamic image processing technique. International Journal of Engineering and Computer Science. doi:10.18535/ijecs/v4i12.41

Gnanaprakash, V., Kanthimathi, N., & Saranya, N. (2021). Automatic number plate recognition using deep learning. *IOP Conference Series. Materials Science and Engineering*, *1084*(1), 012027.

Lalitha. (2020). Vehicle number plate recognition system to identify the authenticated owner of vehicles. *International Journal of Psychosocial Rehabilitation*, *24*(5), 7102–7107. doi:10.37200/ijpr/v24i5/pr2020719

Laroca, R., Zanlorensi, L. A., Gonçalves, G. R., Todt, E., Schwartz, W. R., & Menotti, D. (2021). An efficient and layout-independent automatic license plate recognition system based on the YOLO detector. *IET Intelligent Transport Systems*, *15*(4), 483–503.

Lubna, M. N., & Shah, S. A. A. (2021). Automatic number plate recognition: A detailed survey of relevant algorithms. *Sensors (Basel)*, *21*(9). Advance online publication. doi:10.339021093028 PMID:33925845

Madhukar, R., & Singh, R. R. (2015). Automatic Car license plate Recognition system using Multiclass SVM and OCR. *International Journal of Engineering Trends and Technology*, *30*(7), 369–373.

Pattanaik, A., & Balabantaray, R. C. (2022). Enhancement of license plate recognition performance using Xception with Mish activation function. *Multimedia Tools and Applications*, *82*(11), 16793–16815. PMID:36258895

Shashirangana, J., Padmasiri, H., Meedeniya, D., & Perera, C. (2021). Automated License Plate Recognition: A Survey on Methods and Techniques. *IEEE Access : Practical Innovations, Open Solutions*, *9*, 11203–11225.

Shashirangana, J., Padmasiri, H., Meedeniya, D., Perera, C., Nayak, S. R., Nayak, J., Vimal, S., & Kadry, S. (2021). License plate recognition using neural architecture search for edge devices. *International Journal of Intelligent Systems*, *37*(12), 10211–10248.

Wang, Y., Bian, Z. P., Zhou, Y., & Chau, L. P. (2022). Rethinking and Designing a High-Performing Automatic License Plate Recognition Approach. *IEEE Transactions on Intelligent Transportation Systems*, *23*(7), 8868–8880.

Weihong, W., & Jiaoyang, T. (2020). Research on License Plate Recognition Algorithms Based on Deep Learning in Complex Environment. *IEEE Access : Practical Innovations, Open Solutions*, *8*, 91661–91675.

Chapter 8

Comparative Study of One Stage V/S Two Stage Surgery for Intra–Articular Distal Tibial Pilon Fracture

S. Patil Nitin

Krishna Institute of Medical Sciences, India

Paresh Patil

Krishna Vishwa Vidyapeeth, India

ABSTRACT

Tissue injury, infection, or cardiac infarction may all lead to inflammation. The restoration of normal anatomy to the joint surface and the preservation of mechanical alignment are two of the primary objectives of treatment. Ankle and subtalar range of motion must be protected and improved upon, and correct length and rotation must be maintained. Inflammation can be caused by either infectious or non-infectious triggers. When a tissue is damaged, our bodies send out a series of chemical signals to trigger reactions that promote tissue repair. All of these cues stimulate circulating leukocytes to chemotactically migrate to the site of injury. As a result of being activated, leukocytes release cytokines, which set off other inflammatory processes in the body. Inflammatory disorders can be treated with a wide variety of medications nowadays.

INTRODUCTION

Over the past 35 years, surgeons have better appreciated the significance of the soft tissue envelope, which has led to significant advances in the surgical therapy of distal tibial fractures (De-las-Heras-Romero, et al., 2017). There is no agreement on the best treatment for these complicated wounds, even though several methods and regimens have been documented (Md, et al., 2014). Several common complications that Successful therapy relies on avoiding the many soft-tissue problems that may arise (Gardner, et al.,

DOI: 10.4018/978-1-6684-9189-8.ch008

2008). Protecting and optimising ankle and subtalar mobility and maintaining the correct length is paramount (Munshi, et al., 2019). There is no assurance that patients will have a satisfactory outcome even if these objectives are attained (Munshi, et al., 2021). Comminuted distal tibial pilon fractures may be treated surgically with either a basic distal tibial plate, a medium plating device, or an intramedullary nail for the fibula; this research will evaluate the clinical and functional outcomes of these three approaches (Masquelet, 2003). This study aims to compare the functional and clinical results of individuals who had pilon fractures treated using various surgical techniques and implant options (Nirmala, et al., 2023).

1.1. Aim of Study

The purpose of this research was to compare the outcomes of single- and double-surgery procedures for treating based on inter-distal tibial Pilon fractures.

1.2. Objectives

According to the study's abstract, the following aims were pursued: One objective is to evaluate how long it takes for a Pilon fracture to heal after a one-stage vs a two-stage operation. To compare the benefits and risks of treating a Pilon fracture in a single step vs a two-stage treatment.

2. REVIEW OF LITERATURE

While the French terms *pilon* and *plafond* are still in the *international literature*, Destot was the first to adopt the term *pilon* in 1911. To the SOFCOT in 1987, Heim (1997) presented the rationale for open internal osteosynthesis as the foundation of effective management. Two advancements have happened since Heim's (1997) time that has made it more difficult to replicate his successful outcomes the development of minimally invasive percutaneous osteosynthesis and other forms of external fixation, most notably hybrid fixing (MIPO) (Vashishtha & Dhawan, 2023). Extremely high-energy traumas (such as those sustained in the motorcycle or skiing accidents or from great heights) result in unique patterns of bone fracture osteopenia and low-impact fractures (Lavini, et al., 2014).

Articular fractures of the distal tibial weight-bearing surface are often caused by high-energy processes, such as those seen in car accidents, falls from great heights, motorcycle accidents, and on-the-job mishaps (Munshi, et al., 2018). In most cases, axial loads can be given faster than rotary forces (Pandit, 2023). Bone is viscoelastic, so it absorbs more energy before it fails, only to release all that stored energy at the moment of failure, which is then transferred to the surrounding soft tissue (Jeganathan, et al., 2023). Significant swelling and blistering can occur in these injuries even when there is no direct damage to the soft tissue envelope (Williams, et al., 2004). Injuries can fall anywhere on a continuum, some caused by axial forces and others by primarily rotating processes (Suganthi & Sathiaseelan, 2023).

2.1. Factors Affecting Outcome

No data support the claim that enhanced articular reduction improves patient outcomes. Many writers regard the degree of articular damage as the most crucial factor in determining the patient's prognosis.

Since the quality of reduction is so strongly linked to the severity of the initial injury, quantifying the relative impact of articular reduction and injury severity is challenging (Munshi, et al., 2022).

Fracture union has been demonstrated to be affected by several factors in fracture treatment, including mobility at the fracture site; surgical delay; the form of fixation; and periosteal stripping during open reduction. Univariate statistics have been employed for most of the available data from experiments and clinical trials, yet there is still debate over whether factors truly matter in predicting outcomes. The degree of skin damage, post-operative diastasis between the fracture fragments, and the location of the fracture were the most important predictors of prolonged healing time. A tibial fracture in the distal one-third of the shaft is twice as likely to mend slowly or not heal as a tibial fracture in the middle two-thirds. Surgical treatment options seemed to affect the risk of diastasis and consequent delayed union. When comparing patients who had plating done to those who had external fixation or intramedullary nailing, the latter group was more likely to have post-operative diastasis. According to certain studies, an increased risk of delayed union has also been associated with a distal fracture location on the tibial shaft. Conservative treatment with functional bracing is effective for closed distal tibia fractures in a large cohort of 450 patients.

2.2. Complications

Necrosis of the skin is common, especially with group A injuries. When it first appears, it requires aggressive care, including hospitalisation, repeated surgical cleaning, and antibiotics tailored to the specifics of the affected area. The incision can be closed when there is minimal tissue loss following excision. However, VAC therapy must be employed despite low success rates because of the poor local blood supply, or the wound must be covered when there is significant tissue loss.

2.3. Metaphyseal Malunion

It's common for the metaphysis to fail to unite properly. A delayed union may be accelerated with external stimulation (if the axes are maintained, the interfragment gap is small, and the location is stable). Autologous corticocancellous grafting and strong osteosynthesis are two examples of invasive surgical procedures that may be necessary to treat serious medical conditions using external fixation, such as a plate. Intertibial tibial grafts (ITFGs) are a tried-and-true treatment for severe bone loss (high chance of bone union, minimal risk of infection).

When the ankle is in its neutral position with its axes aligned, patients with tibiotalar arthritis often experience a remarkable improvement in their symptoms. If not, surgical intervention will likely be necessary. Arthroplasty and arthrodesis were both studied by Sanders et al. (2004) for this purpose, and their results were compared. Disappointingly low levels of mobility were observed after arthroplasty, and a significant complication rate necessitating reintervention in one patient out of every two was also observed.

3. MATERIALS AND METHODS

Study Setting: This study was conducted in the Department of Orthopaedics, Krishna Institute of Medical Sciences, Deemed University, Karad (Maharashtra), a tertiary care hospital providing services to the population in Karad and surrounding areas.

Study population: Patients who presented to the outpatient clinic (OPD) or casualty with distal tibial pilon fractures were included in this research.

Study Duration: From Dec 19-June 21

Design of study: Research participants had Pilon fractures, and the study design was a randomised controlled trial.

Sample size: The sample size was determined by using the formula n = (Z/2+Z)2 *2*2 / (s1-s2)2, where Z/2 is the critical value of the Normal distribution at /2 (e.g., for a confidence level of 95%, is 0.05 and the critical value is 1.96), Z is the critical value of the Normal distribution at (e.g., for a power of 80%, is 0.2 and the Here, S1 was determined to be an AOFAS score of 81.6 for the first set of subjects and 89.9 for the second. Twelve people were included in each category based on the calculations. There were 24 people in total in the sample.

Inclusion Criteria: The inclusion criteria for the study were as follows:

- All age groups.
- Patients of any gender.
- Patients having intraarticular distal tibial pilon fracture AO classification in type B and type C.

AO/OTA Classification initially evaluated all cases with distal tibia Pilon fracture.
Cases with the following Surgical Indications were included:

- Articular fracture displacement of >2mm
- Unstable fracture of tibial metaphysis.
- Two types of pilon fractures are recognised in medicine: open (Gustilo-Anderson type 1) and closed (Pilon fractures). Patients who met all of the requirements mentioned earlier were eventually enrolled.

Exclusion Criteria: Patients with comorbid diseases or otherwise unsuitable for surgery or anaesthesia for the reasons listed below were not included in the analysis.

- Patients who need multistage treatment for significant soft tissue damage (blister/huge edoema)
- Local Procedures
- Soft tissue transfer history
- Vascular disease in the periphery
- Anatomical Breakage and Pathology
- Two types of Gustilo-Anderson tapes, types 2 and 3 (open fracture).

4. DATA ANALYSIS

SPSS version 16 was used to do a statistical analysis of the data. Quantitative data were provided as means and standard deviations for both intervention groups, whereas qualitative variables were presented as frequencies and percentages (Patterson & Cole, 1999). The chi-square and unpaired t-test were employed to analyse the statistical significance of the observed differences between the groups.

5. RANDOMISATION

Each case that met the inclusion/exclusion criteria above was randomly allocated to either Group A or Group B.

Using a random number allocation table, all instances that met the inclusion and exclusion criteria above were divided into two groups, A and B. Strategies for Surgery: Over many decades, several skin incisions and surgical approaches to the tibial pilon have been tried, evaluated, and improved to reduce the occurrence of wound problems. As a result of the distal tibia's unstable vascular supply and high risk of wound dehiscence, extending incisions are avoided wherever possible. Tibial plafond fractures still require internal fibula fixation to maintain length and axial alignment, even though the reasons for doing so have evolved in recent years.

5.1. Post-Operative and Follow-Up Protocol

My loved one's knee was slabbed and elevated immediately after surgery. Post-operative day 3 for external fixation saw the beginning of the movement and knee exercise, whereas postoperative day 7 for final internal fixation saw the beginning of ankle movement and knee exercise. Sutures are typically removed between 12 and 15 days after the bone has healed completely. There had to be radiographic evidence of fracture union before the patient could start using a walker for partial weight-bearing walking, and full weight-bearing could resume after the fracture had healed.

6. OBSERVATION AND RESULTS

One-stage vs two-stage surgical treatment of intra-articular distal tibial pilon fractures was compared in this research of 24 patients. Data from the research was tabulated and shown in Table 1.

Patients in both groups are compared by age in Table 1. Patients' ages were distributed similarly across the two groups. The average age of patients in the first group was 44.08, whereas those in the second group were 45.16. The age distributions of the two groups did not differ significantly.

Table 1. Age-wise comparison of patients of both the groups

Age (Year)	1-Stage Procedure (n=12)	2-Stage Procedure (n=12)
10-19 years	2 (16.7%)	2 (16.7%)
20-29 years	1 (8.3%)	1 (8.3%)
30-39 years	3 (25.0%)	2 (16.7%)
40-49 years	2 (16.7%)	2 (16.7%)
≥ 50 years	4 (33.4%)	5 (41.7%)
Total	12 (100%)	12 (100%)
Mean ± Standard Deviation*	44.08±10.83 years	45.16±10.98 years
Range (Min-Max)	23-61 years	28-64 years

P value 0.964 (Non-significant) (using unpaired t-test at 95 percent CI)

7. DISCUSSION

Among the lower limb fractures, around 1% of fractures are pilon fractures; among tibial fractures, pilon fractures contribute 5-7%.82,83 Although therapy for these fractures has advanced greatly in recent years, the optimum treatment remains complex and challenging, owing to severely wounded soft tissue, a high-energy fracture pattern, and severe oedema. As a direct consequence of this, the most effective method of treatment is not yet settled upon. Open reduction and internal fixation (ORIF), closed reduction and casting, combined intramedullary nailing and plate fixation, minimally invasive plate osteosynthesis, external fixation (EF), and the two-stage treatment with EF and ORIF are all options that have been introduced as ways to treat Pilon fractures. Closed reduction and casting is the most common treatment option.

There have only been a small number of studies that compare the efficacy of the primary one-stage technique to that of the two-stage approaches in treating Pilon fractures, which has led to inconsistent results.

We wanted to see if there was a significant difference in the clinical and functional results, as well as the rate of soft tissue problems, between treating Pilon fractures with a one-stage method versus a two-stage strategy. This was a prospective trial. In the current investigation, there were a total of two patients who both suffered from an intra-articular distal tibial pilon fracture. In one group, the fracture was treated with a one-stage operation (ORIF with plates and screw fixation or MIPPO Minimally Invasive Percutaneous Plate Osteosynthesis), while in the other group, the fracture was treated with a two-stage procedure. Both groups received the same outcome (External Fixation Followed by Internal Fixation or External Fixator with Fibula fixation Followed by open reduction and Internal Fixation). Twelve patients were cared for in each of the groups. Both approaches' functional results were evaluated side by side for comparison.

Pillon fractures are infamous for being difficult to cure, even when orthopaedic surgeons put out their absolute best efforts. These wounds are renowned for being difficult to heal, and the outcomes of therapy with conventional medicine have a track record of being unsatisfactory. Because of the severe nature of the trauma that causes these fractures and the connection between them and the articular surface, a great number of patients will not achieve the goals that were anticipated for them, and a great number of patients will be forced to live with misery and suffering for the rest of their lives.

As of yet, nobody knows when or how to treat a Pilon fracture effectively. High infection rates and difficulties with wound healing after surgery are attributed to the swollen and damaged soft tissue around these fractures. Therefore, a two-step procedure was often used: external fixation of the tibia and preservation of the original fibular length; second, delayed ORIF until the soft tissue healed.

7.1. Baseline Characteristics

Patients' ages were almost evenly distributed across the two groups in the current investigation. Patients in Group 1 had a mean age of 44.08 years, whereas those in Group 2 averaged 45.16 years. The age range of participants was similar in both groups. Each group had almost the same number of male and female patients. A chi-square test with one degree of freedom and a 95% confidence interval yielded a P value 0.537. When comparing the two groups, we did not find any discernible gender differences. Patients in both groups were similarly injured. Using the chi-square test with one degree of freedom and a 95% confidence interval, we get a P value of 0.615.

No statistically significant differences in injury types between the two groups were found in the current investigation. Fibula fractures were diagnosed in 11 of 12 individuals undergoing a single-stage surgery and 9 12 patients undergoing a two-stage operation.

Three (25%) were determined to be C1 type, and three (25%) were found to be C2 type in a single-stage method. Six were considered C1 in the two-stage technique, whereas two were C2 (16.7%). Neither group differed significantly from the other. The chi-square test with 5 degrees of freedom and 95% CI yielded a P value of 0.867.

Forty-one patients were studied by Sajjid M. et al (2018), who compared the efficacy of external fixation and open reduction and internal fixation (ORIF). No statistically significant differences were found between the two groups in age, ethnicity, mechanism of fractures, or duration of follow-up in this investigation.

Neither group differed significantly from the other in the presence or absence of co-morbidities or risk factors. The two groups had very identical distributions of time between injury and treatment.

Pilon fractures are notoriously difficult to treat in the field of orthopaedics. These injuries are notoriously difficult to treat, and conventional therapies often provide poor outcomes. Even though these fractures are often the result of significant trauma and are linked with the participation of the articular surface, many people will not achieve the desired results, and they'll have to live with the anguish and suffering of this sickness for the remainder of their lives.

7.2. Union Time

There was a union rate of 66.67 percent between sixteen and 24 weeks in the group with a single-stage operation, compared to 58.33 percent in the group that underwent a two-stage treatment. Union durations in the remaining cases were more than 23 days across both groups. Union time categories were not substantially different (p>0.05) between the two groups (Çeçen, et al., 2014).

Both the one-stage (ORIF) and two-stage (ORIF) techniques for treating Pilon fractures were linked with similar fracture union times in an evaluation conducted by Richards et al (2012).

In another study, Borens, et al., (2009) used the MIPO method and found that, although it significantly reduced union time, the union rate was not statistically significant.

The findings of the two-stage method were compared to those of final external fixation by Bacon and his team. Researchers discovered that the time it took for fractures to heal in the two-stage group was much longer (1.39 to 5.24 weeks). There was no statistically significant difference between the two groups. 98

Recent research by Tang et al. (2014) reported no difference in union rates between the PORIF and delayed ORIF groups.

7.3. Hospital Stay

Hospital stays for study participants averaged 7.91.7 days for those in the first group and 19.82.8 days for those in the second group. Patients with stage one surgery would likely need less time in the hospital than those who underwent stage two therapy.

Minatorsajjadi, et al. (2018) found that the average hospital stay for the PORIF group (one stage) was 8.31.8 days, compared to 13.42.6 days for the two-stage group. When compared to the PORIF group, it was noticeably lower (P=0.027).

Delaying surgery increases the likelihood of problems like infection or the inability to achieve anatomical reduction, the length of hospital stay, the duration of treatment, and the overall cost. Due to these factors, some doctors are beginning to explore PORIF as an option for Pilon fractures.

The two-stage approach to treating Pilon fractures was deemed preferable by Abd-Almageed, et al. (2015).

Tang et al. (2014) showed that the frequency of superficial and deep infection, union rate, and mean AOFAS were all the same between the PORIF and delayed ORIF groups. By contrast, the PORIF group required less time to heal after surgery and less time in the hospital after their fractures healed.

7.4. Adverse Events After Surgery

One patient in the one-stage surgery group and two in the two-stage operation group reported developing a superficial infection during the current investigation. There were no reports of nonunion or malunion after either the one-stage or two-stage procedures. Neither group had significantly more difficulties than the other.

White and coworkers 27 treated 95 patients with PORIF for Pilon fractures. Eighty-eight percent of patients received surgery within the first 48 hours following the accident.

One patient in the PORIF group developed nonunion while receiving therapy in a mental facility due to their unwillingness to participate in their care. Malunion occurred in 2 patients in the 2-stage group and three in the PORIF group. Both groups had comparable subjective assessment outcomes (pain intensity, pleasure).

Like many other studies before it, the present one had several flaws. It seemed like there weren't enough people participating in the study groups. If the number of patients is raised, the disparity between the two groups can become statistically significant in certain respects.

The two groups of patients seemed to have a very comparable distribution of ages. The average age of patients in the first group was 44.08, whereas those in the second group were 45.16. The age range of participants was similar in both groups. Results showed that 11/12 patients had a closed type one-stage operation, whereas 8/12 patients had a closed type two-stage treatment. Using a chi-square test with 1 degree of freedom and a 95% confidence interval, the p-value was determined to be 0.131. The types of injuries sustained by patients in both groups were similar. Patients in group one had an AOFAS mean and standard deviation of 86.814.1, whereas those in group two had a score of 75.411.9. Both groups were found to have statistically significant differences. When a 95% confidence interval (CI) is applied to the results of an unpaired t-test, the resulting P value is 0.043. Patients who received stage one procedures had better functional outcomes (as measured by AOFAS) than those who underwent stage two procedures. The average length of hospitalisation for patients in group one was 7.9 1.7 days, whereas the average length for patients in group two was 19.8 2.8 days. Both groups were found to have statistically significant differences. An unpaired t-test at 95% CI yielded a p-value of 0.01. The data showed that stage one surgery patients had a much shorter hospital stay than stage two surgery patients.

The rates of arthrosis, superficial infection, and arthritis were all found to be greater in the two-stage surgery group, according to the results of the current study. Ovadia Beals's Evaluation Score (Objective Evaluation and Subjective Evaluation) Was Used To Assess The Performance. Complications occurred at a similar rate in both groups. Patients with a single-stage operation had higher functional results, as measured by the American Orthopaedic Foot and Ankle Society (AOFAS) Ankle-Hindfoot Score. Patients report less discomfort and more satisfaction with a single-stage operation than with a two-stage treatment. We favoured a single-stage surgical approach for closed fracture types b and C AO/OTA Pilon fractures due to the improved functional result and shorter hospital stay. Early mobility and anatomic restoration of the articular surface are emphasised.

Assessed by Ovadia Beals Evaluation Score - We'll take both an objective and a subjective look at your performance. The incidence of complications was likewise comparable.

On the other hand, patients who had a single-stage treatment fared better in terms of functional success, as measured by the American Orthopaedic Foot and Ankle Society (AOFAS) Ankle-Hindfoot Score. Patients report much less post-operative discomfort and higher satisfaction levels with a single-stage operation than with a two-stage one.

8. CONCLUSION

For patients with type B and type C AO/OTA Pilon fractures, the clinical, radiological, functional, and subjective outcomes of single-stage (internal fixation) and two-stage (initial external fixation followed by internal fixation) surgical surgery are comparable. Single-stage surgery involves internal fixation. Two-stage surgery involves initial external fixation followed by internal fixation. According to the findings of our investigation, neither group was able to significantly speed up the process of unionisation in comparison to the other. According to the findings of our research, a single-stage technique (internal fixation) is superior to a two-stage one for treating distal tibial pilon fractures in patients who have low-grade soft-tissue injury, limited edoema, and no blister. According to the findings of the current research, the use of external fixation was used as part of a two-stage treatment process for the purpose of preserving soft tissue and providing improved wound care for patients who had difficult wounds and poor skin conditions. According to the findings of this study, patients who got treatment in a single stage spent much less time in the hospital compared to patients who required two or more surgeries. According to the findings of this study, patients who underwent treatments that required two stages were at a greater risk of developing arthritis, superficial infections, and arthrosis. With great skin, no soft tissue injury, a sealed fracture of type b or C AO/OTA Pilon fractures, and a positive prognosis for functional recovery, a one-stage operating procedure is favoured. This is because it maximises the likelihood of a successful functional recovery. It is emphasised how important it is to achieve early mobility and anatomically precise repair of the articular surface as soon as possible.

REFERENCES

Abd-Almageed, E., Marwan, Y., Esmaeel, A., Mallur, A., & El-Alfy, B. (2015). Hybrid external fixation for Arbeitsgemeinschaft für Osteosynthesefragen (AO) 43-C tibial plafond fractures. *The Journal of Foot and Ankle Surgery: Official Publication of the American College of Foot and Ankle Surgeons, 54*(6), 1031–1036. doi:10.1053/j.jfas.2015.04.022 PMID:26215549

Borens, O., Kloen, P., Richmond, J., Roederer, G., Levine, D. S., & Helfet, D. L. (2009). Minimally invasive treatment of pilon fractures with a low profile plate: Preliminary results in 17 cases. *Archives of Orthopaedic and Trauma Surgery, 129*(5), 649–659. doi:10.100700402-006-0219-1 PMID:16951937

Çeçen, G. S., Gülabi, D., Yanık, E., Pehlivanoğlu, G., Bekler, H., & Elmalı, N. (2014). Effect of BMI on the clinical and radiological outcomes of pilon fractures. *Acta Orthopaedica et Traumatologica Turcica*, *48*(5), 570–575. doi:10.3944/AOTT.2014.14.0073 PMID:25429585

De-las-Heras-Romero, J., Lledo-Alvarez, A. M., Lizaur-Utrilla, A., & Lopez-Prats, F. A. (2017). Quality of life and prognostic factors after intra-articular tibial pilon fracture. *Injury*, *48*(6), 1258–1263. doi:10.1016/j.injury.2017.03.023 PMID:28365069

Gardner, M. J., Mehta, S., Barei, D. P., & Nork, S. E. (2008). Treatment protocol for open AO/OTA type C3 Pilon fractures with segmental bone loss. *Journal of Orthopaedic Trauma*, *22*(7), 451–457. doi:10.1097/bot.0b013e318176b8d9 PMID:18670284

Heim, U. (1997). *Fractures du pilon tibial. Conférencesd 'enseignement*. Paris: Expansion Scientique Francaise.

Jeganathan, J., Vashist, S., Nirmala, G., & Deep, R. (2023). A Cross Sectional Study on Anxiety and Depression Among Patients with Alcohol Withdrawal Syndrome. *FMDB Transactions on Sustainable Health Science Letters*, *1*(1), 31–40.

Lavini, F., Dall'Oca, C., Mezzari, S., Maluta, T., Luminari, E., Perusi, F., ... Magnan, B. (2014). Temporary bridging external fixation in distal tibial fracture. *Injury*, *45*, S58–S63. doi:10.1016/j.injury.2014.10.025 PMID:25457321

M, A., K, T., Munshi, Y, J., M, R., & M, S. (2019). Assessment of heavy metal contents in commercial feedstuffs and broiler (Gallus domesticus) meat and its impact on Swiss albino mice as an animal model. *Agricultural Science Digest - A Research Journal*. doi:10.18805/ag.d-4898

Masquelet, A. C. (2003). *Atlas des lambeaux de l'appareillocomoteur*. Saurampsmédical.

Md, N., Hasan, M., Munshi, M. H., Rahman, S. M. N., & Alam, A. (2014). Evaluation of antihyperglycemic activity of Lasia spinosa leaf extracts in Swiss albino mice. *World Journal of Pharmacy and Pharmaceutical Sciences*, *3*(10), 118–124.

Minatorsajjadi, M., Ebrahimpour, A., Okhovatpour, M. A., Karimi, A., Zandi, R., & Sharifzadeh, A. (2018). The Outcomes of Pilon Fracture Treatment: Primary Open Reduction and Internal Fixation Versus Two-stage Approach. *Archives of Bone and Joint Surgery*, *6*(5), 412–419. PMID:30320182

Munshi, M., Sohrab, M. H., Begum, M. N., Rony, S. R., Karim, M. A., Afroz, F., & Hasan, M. N. (2021). Evaluation of bioactivity and phytochemical screening of endophytic fungi isolated from Ceriops decandra (Griff.) W. Theob, a mangrove plant in Bangladesh. *Clinical Phytoscience*, *7*(1). Advance online publication. doi:10.118640816-021-00315-y

Munshi, M., Tumu, K. N., Hasan, M. N., & Amin, M. Z. (2018). Biochemical effects of commercial feedstuffs on the fry of climbing perch (Anabas testudineus) and its impact on Swiss albino mice as an animal model. *Toxicology Reports*, *5*, 521–530. doi:10.1016/j.toxrep.2018.04.004 PMID:29707493

Munshi, M., Zilani, M. N. H., Islam, M. A., Biswas, P., Das, A., Afroz, F., & Hasan, M. N. (2022). Novel compounds from endophytic fungi of Ceriops decandra inhibit breast cancer cell growth through estrogen receptor alpha in in-silico study. *Informatics in Medicine Unlocked*, *32*(101046), 101046. doi:10.1016/j.imu.2022.101046

Nirmala, G., Premavathy, R., Chandar, R., & Jeganathan, J. (2023). An Explanatory Case Report on Biopsychosocial Issues and the Impact of Innovative Nurse-Led Therapy in Children with Hematological Cancer. *FMDB Transactions on Sustainable Health Science Letters*, *1*(1), 1–10.

Pandit, P. (2023). On the Context of Diabetes: A Brief Discussion on the Novel Ethical Issues of Non-communicable Diseases. *FMDB Transactions on Sustainable Health Science Letters*, *1*(1), 11–20.

Patterson, M. J., & Cole, J. D. (1999). Two-staged delayed open reduction and internal fixation of severe Pilon fractures. *Journal of Orthopaedic Trauma*, *13*(2), 85–91. doi:10.1097/00005131-199902000-00003 PMID:10052781

Richards, J. E., Magill, M., Tressler, M. A., Shuler, F. D., Kregor, P. J., & Obremskey, W. T.The Southeast Fracture Consortium. (2012). External fixation versus ORIF for distal intra-articular tibia fractures. *Orthopedics*, *35*(6). Advance online publication. doi:10.3928/01477447-20120525-25 PMID:22691658

Sajjadi, M. M., Ebrahimpour, A., Okhovatpour, M. A., Karimi, A., Zandi, R., & Sharifzadeh, A. (2018). The Outcomes of Pilon Fracture Treatment: Primary Open Reduction and Internal Fixation Versus Two-stage Approach. *Archives of Bone and Joint Surgery*, *6*(5), 412–419. PMID:30320182

Sanders, R., Gorman, R. R., Ritter, C. A., & Walling, A. K. (2004). Replacement versus arthodesis for post-traumatic ankle arthritis. *Annual Meeting of the OTA*.

Suganthi, M., & Sathiaseelan, J. G. R. (2023). Image Denoising and Feature Extraction Techniques Applied to X-Ray Seed Images for Purity Analysis. *FMDB Transactions on Sustainable Health Science Letters*, *1*(1), 41–53.

Tang, X., Liu, L., Tu, C.-Q., Li, J., Li, Q., & Pei, F.-X. (2014). Comparison of early and delayed open reduction and internal fixation for treating closed tibial Pilon fractures. *Foot & Ankle International*, *35*(7), 657–664. doi:10.1177/1071100714534214 PMID:24842898

Vashishtha, E., & Dhawan, G. (2023). Bridging Generation Gap on Analysis of Mentor-Mentee Relationship in Healthcare Setting. *FMDB Transactions on Sustainable Health Science Letters*, *1*(1), 21–30.

Williams, T. M., Nepola, J. V., DeCoster, T. A., Hurwitz, S. R., Dirschl, D. R., & Marsh, J. L. (2004). Factors affecting outcome in tibial plafond fractures. *Clinical Orthopaedics and Related Research*, *423*(423), 93–98. doi:10.1097/01.blo.0000127922.90382.f4 PMID:15232432

Chapter 9
Comparative Study of Cancer Blood Disorder Detection Using Convolutional Neural Networks

Pulla Sujarani

Vels Institute of Science, Technology, and Advanced Studies, India

M. Yogeshwari

Vels Institute of Science, Technology, and Advanced Studies, India

ABSTRACT

Blood malignancies and various blood disorders can have an impact on a person. It is a major health issue in all age groups. A blood disorder, such as influence platelets, blood plasma, and white and red blood cells, can impact any of the four primary blood components. The primary goal of this chapter is to detect the cancer blood disorder. This paved the way to propose a comparative study with previous studies based on convolutional neural networks in this work. The authors propose a model for cancer blood disorder detection. It consists of five steps. The blood sample image data set is collected from the Kaggle. First, the data set is transferred for image preprocessing to remove the noise from the images. Next, it is applied to the image enhancement for clarity; the image and segmentation are performed on enhanced images. Next, feature selection is used to extract the features from the segmentation images. The convolutional neural network technique is used for classification finally.

1. INTRODUCTION

Anaemia, hemophilia, leukemia, lymphoma, and myeloma diseases are common blood illnesses. RBC, WBC, and platelets are the three primary types of blood cells that stem cells found in the bone marrow are classified (WebMD). Blood cancer is caused by DNA changes in blood cells (Sharma et al., 2021). Consequently, abnormal behavior in the blood cells starts to occur. Children are affected by certain kinds of blood malignancy (Sharma et al., 2021). The ability of healthy blood cells to fight off infections or stop serious bleeding is disrupted by malignant cells. Lymphoma, myeloma, and leukemia are the main

DOI: 10.4018/978-1-6684-9189-8.ch009

kinds of blood cancer. The lymphocytes' infection-fighting cells develop lymphoma. Another type of blood cancer brought on by an excessive increase in WBC is leukemia (Alanazi et al., 2021). The red blood cells and platelets are crowded out by the malignant cells and interfere with the organs' regular function. WBC counts for leukemia patients are higher than those of healthy individuals. Mortality can be decreased if the cancer sickness is identified sooner (Arslan et al., 2021).

Many types of blood diseases are numerous (Nirmala et al., 2023). The patients who suffered from blood disorders in starting stage would recover with treatment. Some are chronic and lifelong, although they do not shorten life expectancy (WHO). Other blood conditions, such as sickle cell disease and blood malignancies, can be lethal. Although screening is one type of approach, not all types of cancer can be detected with it (Ogunmola et al., 2021). There are various forms of cancer, including Any region of the body that can be affected by cancer, which develops when healthy cells turn into cancerous cells like leukemia, lymphoma, and myeloma. Cancer cells spread to entire body parts if cancer therapy is delayed (Sharma et al., 2021). The typical signs of red blood cell issues such as exhaustion, rapid heartbeat, muscle weakness, and difficulty concentrating due to a lack of oxygenated blood in the brain, and the typical signs of white blood cell disorders are weariness from ongoing illnesses, sudden weight loss and generalized sensation of ill health (Sharma et al., 2021).

Image filtering is a crucial step in the processing of images. It may be used for edge detection, blur removal, noise reduction, etc. The algorithms used for filtering include linear and non-linear filters. The appropriate filter should be used for each objective (Pandit, 2023). While a linear low-pass filter is used when the input has a high amount of noise but a low magnitude of noise, non-linear filters are used when the input has a low quantity of noise but a high magnitude of noise (Vashishtha and Dhawan, 2023). Due to their simplicity and speed, linear filters are the most used.

In contrast to non-linear filters, the linear filtering approach involves applying the algorithm to both the input and surrounding pixels of the image (Jeganathan et al., 2023). The quality of the image pixels can be improved via image filtering. It consists of operations that change the pixel values of photographs, like blurring and smoothing.

A machine learning method called deep Convolutional Neural Networks (DCNNs) allows computers to learn from picture samples and extract internal representations or attributes that underlie the grouping or categories of the images. The machine learning approach is applied for cancer blood disorder classification and recognition. Training and testing are the two segments of CNN. The database of CNN is generated based on deep feature extraction. Then based on the database, the testing image is classified and recognized using iterations.

Our paper consists of sections: Section II includes a detailed literature survey to detect the various cancer blood disorder diseases. Section III describes the proposed model. Section IV includes results and discussion, and the comparative analysis of various models is done. Finally, concludes of the paper is presented in section V.

2. LITERATURE REVIEW

A comparative analysis for cancer blood disorder detection was created based on earlier studies, and the researchers used different types of neural network methodologies and algorithms.

Alajrami et al. (2019) formulated the Just Neural Network (JNN) model to predict blood donation. Collected 973 blood sample datasets from the Blood Transfusion Service Center, and the proposed approach provided the highest outcome of 99.31% compared to the other machine learning techniques.

Vijayakumar (2019) proposed Recurrent Neural Network (RNN) to predict cancer and investigation. Breast cancer Wisconsin's original dataset was used for cancer prediction, and Compared to the other neural network models, RNN achieved high accuracy.

Kutlu et al. (2019) proposed a Regional CNN methodology to detect and classify the five types of white blood cell disorders. Combining the BCCD and LISC data sets allowed for the designed architectures. CNN architectures have the highest results in transfer learning. The accuracy percentage for identifying the different cell types was 99.52% for lymphocytes, 98.40% for monocytes, 98.48% for basophils, 96.16% for eosinophils, and 95.04% for neutrophils.

Xia et al. (2020) formulated the YOLOv3 algorithm with different learning methods to detect the Complete Blood Cell count (CBCs) testing problem. Collected 364 blood smear microscopic images of the dataset for the blood analysis of microfluidic hematology.

Alsenan et al. (2020) applied the Recurrent Neural Network approach to anticipate the penetration of substances into the CNS to address the issue of BBB permeability. The proposed method yielded the highest outcome of 96.53% and the specificity accuracy of 98.08%.

Kumar et al. (2020) handled an Optimized Dense CNN to detect white blood cancer. The proposed model accurately captured the first dataset of 94 images, and the second dataset consisted of 100 images while reproducing all the measurements. Compared to machine learning models, the suggested method had the greatest accuracy.

Ishfaque Qamar Khilji and Qamar Khilji (2020) formulated a convolutional neural network compared with resNet50, AlexNet, VGG16, and SVM methodologies to predict Acute Lymphoid Leukemia. The dataset, which has 10,000 images, was collected from the C_NMC. The suggested approach achieved the highest accuracy, 77.934% for the encrypted model and 80% of accuracy for the unencrypted model.

Yogeshwari et al. (2020) suggested novel filtering and enhancement algorithms for disease segmentation. An improved FFCMC method was utilized for clustering, and Adaptive Otsu (AO) threshold algorithm was proposed for the image threshold. In addition, comparing the proposed approaches with existing methodologies, the proposed system achieved the best segmentation outcome.

Sneha (2021) proposed a hybrid model, which is Mutual Information (MI) based and conducts segmentation (FCM), created by combining the Active Contour Model and Fuzzy C Means Algorithm. Statistical and linguistic elements are taken out of the segmented images. The retrieved features are given to the deep CNN classifier built on a chronological SCA model for leukemia identification. The best weights for the CNN model are chosen using the chronological SCA Algorithm.

Shahzad et al. (2021) handled the Deep Convolutional Encoder-Decoder Network model for semantic segmentation of anemic RBCs and collected two types of RBC datasets such as healthy and Anaemic, with each dataset consists 1000 images.

Omer Aftab et al. (2021) applied Deep Learning and Digital Image Processing (DIP) models used in medical image analytics (DL). The suggested approach is leukemia identification utilizing the convolutional neural network. Using the Spark BigDL framework and Google Net architecture to achieve 97.33% accuracy for training and 94.78% accuracy for validation. Additionally, the model is contrasted with and without BigDL GoogleNet. Validation and training accuracy are 96.42% and 92.69%.

Wang et al. (2021) handled 3D deep networks used with hyperspectral images to automatically classify five categories of typical white blood cells. Collected the dataset of 215 patients between the ages of 7 and 65 who underwent routine differential blood counts at the Ruijin 1 Hospital in Shanghai, China, which included children, adolescents, and adults.

Sagar Yeruva et al. (2021) proposed Multilayer Perceptron (MLP) classification algorithm to identify sickle cell anemia and to predict whether the patient is normal or suffering from anemia disease. This disease is classified into three classes: normal, sickle cell, and thalassemia.

Sai Pavan Kamma et al. (2021) employed to predict multiple myeloma by using 85 microscopic blood images. Images of blood were taken during the diseased patients' bone marrow aspirations. It produced the best results comparing the suggested method to the other machine learning approaches.

Yogeshwari (2021) proposed a novel 2D Adaptive Anisotropic Diffusion Filter (2D AADF) technique for image filtering to reduce noise. Adaptive Mean Adjustment (AMA) is a technique that has been proposed for better image enhancement. Clustering and threshold methods are performed for enhanced images. Finally, DCNN classification architecture is used for the detection of disease.

(Mohammad Ehtasham et al., 2022) handled the Bayesian Convolutional Neural Network (BCNN) method for classifying blood sample microscopic pictures without manual feature extraction, and 260 microscopic pictures of both malignant and non-cancerous lymphocyte cells are included in the data collection.

Jkhali and Samy (2022) formulated deep-learning techniques to diagnose and classify blood cells. The designed model yielded 98% higher accuracy than the existing method. The data set for this study includes four different types of white blood cells, with 150000 of the highest collected images.

Jambhekar and Joshi (2022) handled different existing classification techniques to detect the blood cancer diseases like Leukemia, Lymphoma, and Myeloma. This work proposed a convolutional neural network for white blood cancer detection and compared it with machine learning techniques.

Langarizadeh et al. (2022) proposed a convolutional neural network that was compared with four data mining techniques for predicting the adult's allogeneic hematopoietic stem cell transplantation. This work's data set consists of 94 patient details with 34 parameters.

Sujarani and Kalaiselvi (2018) applied a correlation feature selection as a preprocessing, a more powerful method to reduce the noise. The proposed system used 768 of the patient's dataset. For classification, a probabilistic neural network model was proposed to predict the disease, and this approach is implemented in Matlab software.

Walczak and Velanovich (2018) suggested a neural network model for enhancing prognosis and decreasing regret in treating pancreatic cancer. MLNN was created to estimate a patient's 7-month prognosis for pancreatic cancer, and MLNN produced better results. This ANN outcome prediction was used to reduce the treatment decision regret.

3. PROPOSED MODEL

This proposed work consists of five steps: image preprocessing, image enhancement, image segmentation, feature extraction, and classification. The blood sample data set is transferred through these five steps and finally detects the cancer blood disorder. Figure 1 shows the proposed architecture of blood disorder and cancer Detection.

Figure 1. Proposed architecture of cancer blood disorder detection

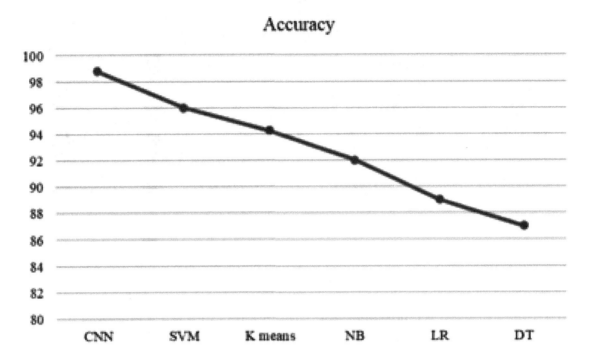

3.1. Dataset

The Cancer blood disorder dataset will be collected from Kaggle. This dataset consists of 1000 blood samples suitable for patients with Cancer blood disorder. The following Figure 2 describes the sample blood image.

3.2. Image Preprocessing

Image preprocessing is one of the important processes to be suitable for training. Without preprocessing, the neural network's training will be slow. Image processing is used in various applications and sectors to improve the image's quality after deleting unimportant visual data. So that we have to preprocess the cancer blood disorder data set. Image processing is a method used in various applications and sectors to enhance the quality of an image after deleting unimportant visual data.

To improve the visualization of the images before identifying certain diseases, it is necessary to use various image preprocessing techniques to eliminate such intrusive elements from the images. By changing the pixel values of an image source, image filters create a new image. Filters reduce noise, improve contrast, identify borders, and locate details. In this research, we have to propose a novel filtering algorithm named 2D Hybrid Wavelet Frequency Domain Bilateral Filter (2D HWFDBF) for image acquisition and filtering. The following Figure 3 shows the proposed diagram of image filtering.

Figure 2. Sample blood image

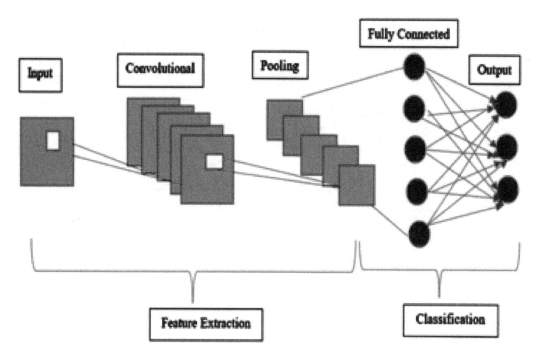

Figure 3. Proposed diagram of image filtering

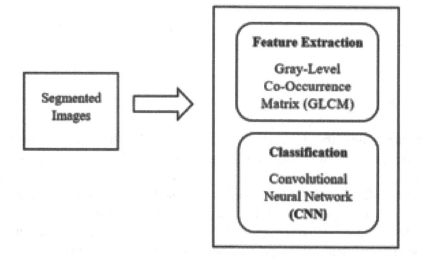

3.3. Image Enhancement

After completion of image preprocessing, the denoised images are enhanced in this step. Enhancing images involves improving their quality and informational value over the original data. It is a method of changing digital images to improve the results for presentation or further image analysis. In our work, by using denoised images, we propose 2D Edge Preservation Histogram Improvement (2D EPHI), which can be used to increase the perceived sharpness of the image. The following Figure 4 describes the proposed diagram of image enhancement.

3.4. Image Segmentation

After completion of image enhancement, the enhanced images are used for image segmentation. Segmentation separates an image into several non-overlapping areas using a set of guidelines or criteria, such as a group of related pixels or fundamental qualities like color, contrast, and texture. By splitting the original image into two groups, such as objects and backgrounds, segmentation lowers the search area of an image. In our study, we have to propose Adaptive Fast Fuzzy C Means Hybrid Clustering (AFFCMHC) Algorithm used for image segmentation. The following Figure 5 describes the proposed diagram of image segmentation.

3.5. Feature Extraction

In this step, the segmented images are transferred to feature selection. The feature extraction technique might be useful when working with huge data sets and conserving resources without losing important or relevant data. Extracting features from unprocessed raw data involves retaining the integrity of the original data set while converting it into numerical features that may be processed further. The GLCM functions to determine the frequency of pairs of pixels in an image that has particular values and is grouped in a particular spatial relationship, creating a GLCM. T From this matrix, statistical measurements are then extracted to describe an image's texture. We must suggest the Gray-Level Co Occurrence Matrix (GLCM) approach to extract the data in our study. It is calculated as

$$G\left(m,n\right) = \frac{\#\left\{\left[\left(m_1,n_1\right),\left(m_2,n_2\right)\right] \in S \left| f\left(m_1,n_1\right) = g_1 \ \& \ f\left(m_2,n_2\right) = g_2 \right.\right\}}{\# S} \tag{1}$$

Figure 4. Proposed diagram of image enhancement

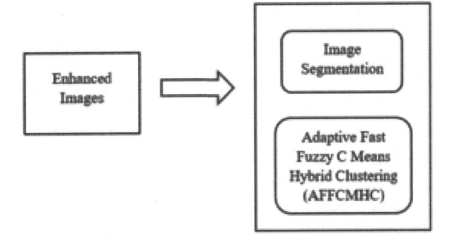

Figure 5. Proposed diagram of image segmentation

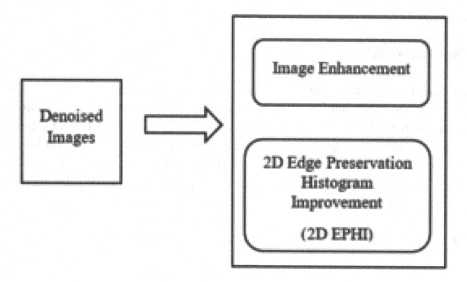

Using this technique, the GLCM matrix is produced for the entire image. The next step is to divide this GLCM matrix of size n × n. For every block, the following statistics features were extracted
Angular Second moment:
The distribution homogeneity of the picture is shown by the angular second moment. It is calculated as

$$A_{sm} = \sum_{m=1}^{M} \sum_{n=1}^{N} G(m,n)^{2} \tag{2}$$

Correlation:
The correlation value shows how similar the texture of the picture is in the horizontal and vertical dimensions, which are perpendicular to one another. It is determined as

$$C_{or} = \frac{\sum_{m=1}^{M} \sum_{n=1}^{N} (m - \bar{x})(n - \bar{y}) G(m,n)}{\sigma_{x}\sigma_{y}} \tag{3}$$

Contrast:
The difference in depth and smooth parts of the image is measured by contrast value. It is calculated as

$$C_{on} = \sum_{m=1}^{M} \sum_{n=1}^{N} (m - n)^{2} G(m,n) \tag{4}$$

Entropy:
The information content is measured by entropy, which is calculated using

$$E_{nt} = -\sum_{m=1}^{M}\sum_{n=1}^{N} G\left(m,n\right) l_{g} G\left(m,n\right) \tag{5}$$

Energy:
The sum of the squares of the components is used to calculate the energy

$$E_{ne} = \sum_{m=1}^{M}\sum_{n=1}^{N} G^{2}\left(m,n\right) \tag{6}$$

Homogeneity:
The homogeneity of a picture denotes its structural similarities. It is calculated as

$$H_{om}\left(m,n\right) = \frac{e^{-k\left(G\left(x,y\right)-G\left(m,n\right)\right)^{2}}}{\sum_{m=1}^{M}\sum_{n=1}^{N} e^{-k\left(G\left(x,y\right)-G\left(m,n\right)\right)^{2}}} \tag{7}$$

3.6. Classification

In our work, the Convolutional Neural Network approach was suggested for classifying blood images and detecting the patient's blood sample as either disease or normal (Figure 6).

3.7. Convolutional Neural Network (CNN)

This research proposes Convolutional Neural Network, a deep neural network. It is frequently employed for visual image analysis, video and image recognition, and natural language processing. CNN can recognize and classify particular aspects in images. Figure 7 depicts the Convolutional neural networks architecture.

Convolutional neural networks are a particular kind of multi-layered neural network. This network has three stages in the convolutional model's construction after loading the input data. They are

- Convolution layer: It is the important and first layer in CNN. It helps to filter the data from the input, which provides an activation function. This process can be applied repeatedly on the feature map filter. After filtering, the original image will be changed from larger to smaller.
- Pooling layer: The size of the feature maps is reduced using these layers. The main benefit of pooling is the extraction of clean, angular features.
- Fully Connected layer: It is called a neural network because every input neuron is fully connected to other output neurons, and each neuron uses a weight matrix to perform a linear transformation to the input vector.

Figure 6. Proposed diagram of classification

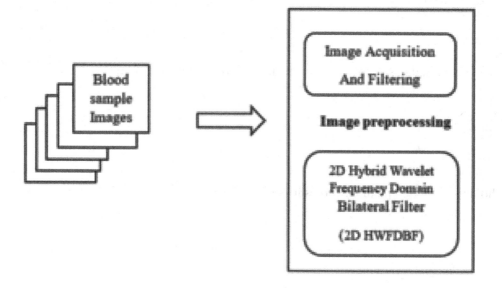

Figure 7. Convolutional neural network architecture

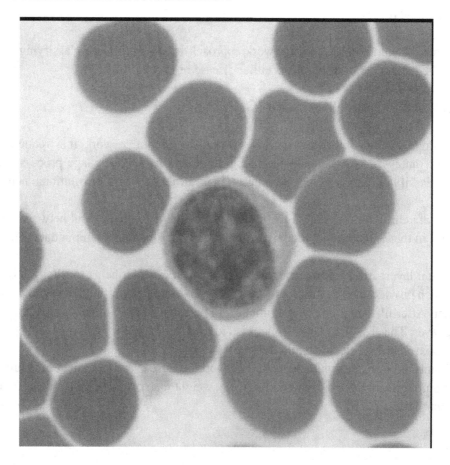

3.8. Benefits of CNN

Effective image processing: CNNs can process images effectively as one of the main advantages. CNNs are quicker and more effective than other algorithms because they may decrease the quantity of information that must be processed.

High accuracy rates: Another benefit of CNNs is their propensity for achieving high accuracy rates. This is because studying huge amounts of data may teach them to recognize intricate patterns in images.

Robust to noise: CNNs also resist noise, allowing them to detect patterns in distorted or damaged images. This is because they are more noise-resistant than other algorithms since they utilize numerous filters to extract data from images.

The proposed classification method is a convolutional neural network compared to the other machine learning algorithms such as Support Vector Machine, Naïve Bayes, Logistic regression, K means Clustering Algorithm, and Decision Tree methodologies. The proposed approach yields the highest accuracy compared to the five existing algorithms.

3.9. Support Vector Machine

The SVM approach is mostly used for classification and regression problems. The hyperplane, which must be identified, serves as the decision boundary for this strategy. When there are numerous items in a group, a decision plan is necessary to separate them into various classes. If the objects cannot be divided linearly, then the objects into different classes must be divided using sophisticated mathematical kernels. Using samples from the training data set, SVM seeks to precisely identify the objects. SVM has the following advantages: If the correct kernel function can be determined, it can handle complex functions, structured and semi-structured data, and both. The generalization approach used by SVM lowers the risk of overfitting. It can scale up with massive amounts of data. It avoids becoming stuck in a regional optimum (Ray, 2019).

3.10. Naive Bayes

The Naive Bayes classifier is commonly employed for classification applications like text categorization. It replicates the input distribution for a certain class or category and is a member of the generative learning algorithm family (Ray, 2019). This technique allows the algorithm to anticipate results quickly and precisely. Naive Bayes' advantages include its simple implementation, excellent performance, handling of continuous data, and capacity for probabilistic forecasting. Data that is continuous and discrete are managed by it. An unnecessary feature does not affect it.

3.11. Logistic Regression

Among the most popular Machine Learning algorithms, logistic regression is a component of the supervised learning approach. Logistic regression is used to forecast a categorical dependent variable's outcome. Deterministic or categorical values must thus be the outcome. Instead of the precise values of 0 and 1, it provides the probability values that fall between 0 and 1. It can be True or False, Yes or No, 0 or 1, etc. The ease of regularisation, regularisation, simplicity of implementation, and processing economy are all advantages of logistic regression. The input's features don't need to be resized. This method frequently resolves large-scale business-related problems (Ray, 2019).

3.12. K Means Clustering Algorithm

Problems involving clustering are frequently solved using the K Means Clustering Algorithm. It is a type of unsupervised learning. The method starts by choosing k starting locations, where k is the value provided to it. Each acts as the first centroid for a cluster, a physical or conceptual location that designates the cluster's center. The centroid nearest to each additional point in the dataset is then allocated to it based on distance. After that, we update our calculations of the centroids' positions. The mean value of every point in the cluster serves as the centroid's coordinate. A popular mean function for this is the arithmetic mean, the sum of all points divided by the total number of points. After recalculating the centroid positions, we may change the cluster points depending on the distance to the new sites. Until a halting condition is met, centroids are recalculated again. It offers the following advantages: It is computationally more effective than hierarchical clustering when the number of variables is large. It creates tighter groups using globular clustering and tiny k than it does using hierarchical clustering (Ray, 2019).

3.13. Decision Tree

The decision tree is one of the most efficient supervised learning techniques for classification and regression applications. Each leaf node has a class label, and each internal node specifies a test on an attribute. Each branch denotes a test result. This results in a tree structure that resembles a flowchart. Until a stopping condition is met, such as the maximum depth of the tree or the absolute minimum number of samples required to divide a node, it is formed by continually dividing the training data into subsets according to the values of the attributes. Decision trees have the following benefits: they are appropriate for classification and regression problems; they are simple to interpret; they can handle quantitative and categorical values; and they perform well because the tree traversal algorithm is effective (Ray, 2019).

4. RESULTS AND DISCUSSION

To evaluate the classification performance, initially, True Positive, True Negative, False Positive, and False Negatives were computed to assess the classification performance.

True Positive: It describes the number of cancer blood disease patients currently present and predicted to be present.

True Negative: It describes the number of cancer blood disorder patients absent or predicted.

False Positive: It describes the number of cancer blood disorder patients that are not present but predicted as diseased.

False Negative: It describes the number of cancer blood disorder patients present but not predicted as diseased.

Classification metrics, including overall accuracy, recall, precision, specificity, and F-score, were obtained from the aforementioned computed parameters.

Overall accuracy (Oa):
Overall accuracy represents the cancer blood disorder classifier's overall classification performance.

$$O_a = \frac{TP + TN}{TP + TN + FP + FN}$$

Recall (Re):
The recall demonstrates the sensitivity of cancer blood disease classification and is calculated as

$$R_e = \frac{TP}{TP + FN}$$

Precision (Pr):
Precision is measured by dividing the number of true positives by the total number of true positives and false positives.

$$P_r = \frac{TP}{TP + FP}$$

Specificity (Sp):
The specificity is the ratio of true negatives to true and false positives.

$$S_p = \frac{TN}{TN + FP}$$

F-score (Fs):
The F-score is calculated as

$$F_s = 2 \times \frac{Preciscion \times Recall}{Precision + Recall}$$

Table 1 shows the comparative study of research done by many authors and different methodologies and their accuracies. According to this performance, the proposed CNN Network gives improved accuracy compared with previous studies' accuracies. Table 1 shows a comparative Study of Blood Disorders and cancer using various techniques.

The following Figure 8 describes comparative study performance through graphical representation. According to this performance, the proposed CNN gives the highest accuracy of the other five machine-learning techniques.

Table 1. Comparative study of cancer blood disorder using various techniques

Author	Method	Resul4
Manjula, et al., (2023)	An optimized Convolutional Neural Network (OCNN) was proposed to detect cancer in the bone area.	The proposed model yielded 96.45% of accuracy.
Hossain, et.al., (2019)	Proposed CNN model and compared with five machine learning algorithms.	CNN split the ratio of 80:20 of 217 images, and the suggested approach yielded an accuracy of 97.87%.
Sohail, et al., (2021)	A CNN model for training and an automated tagger was employed across the whole framework (MP-MitDet).	According to the MP-MitDet, these metrics were 0.71 accuracies, 0.76 recall, 0.75 F1, and 0.78 area.
Mahmood, et al., (2020)	A CNN-based model was suggested, and this framework included deep CNN and the faster regional convolutional neural network (Faster R-CNN).	This technique obtained 0.841 recall, 0.858 F1, and 0.876 accuracies.
Wang et al. (2019)	An 8-layer CNN model was created using a novel model that combined--es CNN with US-ELM (CNN-GTD-ELM) for feature extraction from input images.	The CNN-GTD-ELM achieved a 0.923 AUC, 86.50% accuracy, 85.10% sensitivity, and 88.02% specificity.
Chiao, et al., (2019)	Based on ultrasound images, a mask region detection approach identified the breast cancer lesion.	This method has an average classification accuracy of 85% and a detection precision of 0.75.
Das et al. (2020)	Deep Multiple Instance Learning (MIL) was developed using the CNN breast cancer diagnostic model.	The MIL-CNN model achieved 96.63% of accuracy.
Guan (2019)	The detection of the cancer was recommended using two methods. Generative Adversarial Network (GAN) training is the first method, and the VGG model is the second method for training the images.	The accuracy of the first method was 98.85%, and the accuracy of the second method was 91.48%.
Mahbub et al. (2022)	The components of the proposed model were the developed CNN model and the fuzzy analytical hierarchy process model.	The suggested model has an accuracy rate of 98.75%.
Gonçalves, et al., (2022)	Used ResNet50, DenseNet201, and VGG16, three pre-trained CNN models. To propose a unique random forest surrogate to enhance the parameters of the pre-trained CNN models, which were created using evolutionary and particle swarm optimization techniques.	DenseNet201 and ResNet50's F1 scores increased from 0.92 to 1 and 0.85 to 0.92, respectively.
Sun et al. (2021)	The images were preprocessed via the mathematical morphology technique. The picture template matching approach was chosen to find the suspicious breast mass locations. Accuracy was increased with the PSO.	The suggested model achieved 50.81% precision, 95.38% recall, 66.31% F1 score, and 85.82% accuracy.
Huang et al. (2022)	Cancer detection was demonstrated using a compact CNN model (BM-Net). MobileNet-V3 and bilinear structure made up the lightweight CNN model. The features were extracted using the MobileNet-V3 model.	The BM-N yielded an accuracy of 0.88 and a score of 0.71.
Alanazi, et al., (2021)	To diagnose breast cancer, created a novel CNN model and employed K-nearest neighbor, logistic regression, and support vector machines as their three classifiers.	The new model has an accuracy rate of 87%, which is 9% better than machine learning techniques.

5. CONCLUSION

The main aim is to compare with other research works using convolutional neural networks. This paper consists of five steps: image preprocessing, image enhancement, image segmentation, feature extraction, and classification. In our work, we propose the best approach: CNN used for cancer blood disorder detection. The proposed approach is compared to the machine learning algorithms such as Support Vector Machine, Naïve Bayes, Logistic regression, K means Clustering Algorithm and Decision Tree methodologies. CNN approach is best for detection, and it has a fast-training process. Compared to all

Figure 8. Comparative study performance

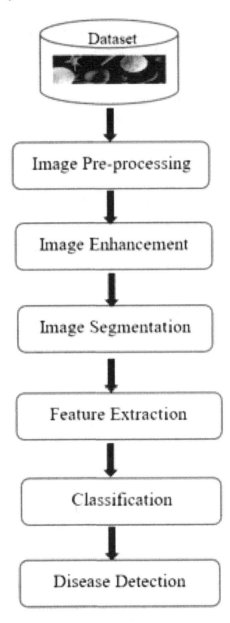

previous research neural network methods and machine learning algorithms, CNN yields the best cancer blood disorder detection accuracy.

REFERENCES

Alajrami, E., Bassem, S., Abu-Nasser, A. J., Khalil, M. M., Musleh, A. M., & Samy, S. (2019). Blood donation Prediction using Artificial Neural Network. *International Journal of Academic Engineering Research, 3*(10).

Alanazi, S. A., Kamruzzaman, M. M., Islam Sarker, M. N., Alruwaili, M., Alhwaiti, Y., Alshammari, N., & Siddiqi, M. H. (2021). Boosting breast cancer detection using convolutional neural network. *Journal of Healthcare Engineering, 5528622*. Advance online publication. doi:10.1155/2021/5528622 PMID:33884157

Alsenan, S., Al-Turaiki, I., & Hafez, A. (2020). A Recurrent Neural Network model to predict blood-brain barrier permeability. *Computational Biology and Chemistry*, 89(107377), 107377. doi:10.1016/j.compbiolchem.2020.107377 PMID:33010784

Arslan, F., Singh, B., Sharma, D. K., Regin, R., Steffi, R., & Suman Rajest, S. (2021). Optimization technique approach to resolve food sustainability problems. In *2021 International Conference on Computational Intelligence and Knowledge Economy (ICCIKE)*. IEEE.

Blood disorder types, symptoms, and treatments. (n.d.). Retrieved July 31, 2023, from WebMD website: https://www.webmd.com/cancer/lymphoma/blood-disorder-types-and-treatment

Chiao, J. Y., Chen, K. Y., Liao, K., Hsieh, P. H., & Zhang, G. (2019). Detection and classification the breast tumors using mask R-CNN on sonograms. *Medicine*, 98(19). PMID:31083152

Das, K., Conjeti, S., Chatterjee, J., & Sheet, D. (2020). Detection of breast cancer from whole slide histopathological images using deep multiple instance CNN. *IEEE Access : Practical Innovations, Open Solutions*, 8, 213502–213511.

Gonçalves, C. B., Souza, J. R., & Fernandes, H. (2022). CNN optimization using surrogate evolutionary algorithm for breast cancer detection using infrared images. In *2022 IEEE 35th International Symposium on Computer-Based Medical Systems (CBMS)*. IEEE.

Guan, S. (2019). *Using generative adversarial networks and transfer learning for breast cancer detection by convolutional neural networks*. Academic Press.

T. Hossain, F. Shadmani Shishir, M. Ashraf, M. A. A. Nasim, & M. Shah (Eds.). (2019). Brain Tumor Detection Using Convolutional Neural Network. In *International Conference on Advances in Science, Engineering and Robotics Technology (ICASERT)*. IEEE.

Huang, J., Mei, L., Long, M., Liu, Y., Sun, W., Li, X., & Lei, C. (2022). BM-Net: CNN-based MobileNet-V3 and bilinear structure for breast cancer detection in whole slide images. *Bioengineering (Basel, Switzerland)*, 9(6), 261. doi:10.3390/bioengineering9060261 PMID:35735504

Ishfaque Qamar Khilji, I., & Qamar Khilji, K. (2020). Application of Homomorphic Encryption on -Neural Network in Prediction of Acute Lymphoid Leukemia. *International Journal of Advanced Computer Science and Applications*.

Jambhekar, N. D., & Joshi, P. S. (2022). Detection of White Blood Cell Cancer diseases through classification techniques. *Vidya Bharati International Interdisciplinary Research Journal, 14*(1), 1–5.

Jeganathan, J., Vashist, S., Nirmala, G., & Deep, R. (2023). A Cross Sectional Study on Anxiety and Depression Among Patients with Alcohol Withdrawal Syndrome. *FMDB Transactions on Sustainable Health Science Letters, 1*(1), 31–40.

Jkhali, A., & Samy, S. (2022). Diagnosis of Blood Cells Using Deep Learning. *International Journal of Academic Engineering Research, 6*(2).

Kumar, D., Jain, N., Khurana, A., Mittal, S., Suresh, C., Satapathy, R., & Senkeik, J. D. (2020). Automatic Detection of White Blood Cancer From Bone Marrow Microscopic Images Using Convolutional Neural Networks. *IEEE Access : Practical Innovations, Open Solutions.*

Kutlu, H., Avci, E., & Ozyurt, F. (2019). *White blood cells detection and classification based on regional convolutional neural networks.* National Library of Science.

Langarizadeh, M., Farajollahi, B., & Hajifathali, A. (2022). Presenting a Prediction Model for Successful Allogenic Hematopoietic Stem Cell Transplantation in Adults with Acute Myeloid Leukemia. *Middle East Journal of Cancer.*

Mahbub, T. N., Yousuf, & Uddin, M. N. (2022). A modified CNN and fuzzy AHP based breast cancer stage detection system. In *International Conference on Advancement in Electrical and Electronic Engineering (ICAEEE)* (pp. 1–6). Academic Press.

Mahmood, T., Arsalan, M., Owais, M., & Park, L. (2020). Artificial intelligence-based mitosis detection in breast cancer histopathology images using faster R-CNN and deep CNNs. *Journal of Clinical Medicine, 9*(3), 749. PMID:32164298

Manjula Devi Ramasamy, R., Kumar Dhanaraj, S., Kumar Pani, R. P., Das, A. A., Movassagh, M., Gheisari, Y., Porkar, S. (2023). An improved deep convolutionary neural network for bone marrow cancer detection using image processing. *Science Direct, 38.*

Nirmala, G., Premavathy, R., Chandar, R., & Jeganathan, J. (2023). An Explanatory Case Report on Biopsychosocial Issues and the Impact of Innovative Nurse-Led Therapy in Children with Hematological Cancer. *FMDB Transactions on Sustainable Health Science Letters, 1*(1), 1–10.

Ogunmola, G. A., Singh, B., Sharma, D. K., Regin, R., Rajest, S. S., & Singh, N. (2021). Involvement of distance measure in assessing and resolving efficiency environmental obstacles. In *2021 International Conference on Computational Intelligence and Knowledge Economy (ICCIKE)*. IEEE.

Omer Aftab, M., Javed Awan, M., Khalid, S., Javed, R., & Shabir, H. (2021). Executing Spark BigDL for Leukemia Detection from Microscopic Images using Transfer Learning. In *International Conference on Artificial Intelligence and Data Analytics (CAIDA)*. IEEE.

Pandit, P. (2023). On the Context of Diabetes: A Brief Discussion on the Novel Ethical Issues of Noncommunicable Diseases. *FMDB Transactions on Sustainable Health Science Letters, 1*(1), 11–20.

Ray, S. (2019). A quick review of machine learning algorithms. In *2019 International Conference on Machine Learning, Big Data, Cloud and Parallel Computing (COMITCon)*. IEEE.

Sagar Yeruva, M., Varalakshmi, B., Gowtham, Y. H., & Chandana, P. K. (2021). Identification of Sickle Cell Anemia Using Deep Neural Networks. *Engineering Science Journal, 5*(2).

Sai Pavan Kamma, G., Chilukuri, G., & Rudra Kalyan Nayak, T. (2021). Multiple Myeloma Prediction from Bone-Marrow Blood Cell images using Machine Learning. *IEEE, Emerging Trends in Industry, 4*(0).

Shahzad, M., Umar, A. I., Shirazi, S. H., & Shaikh, I. A. (Eds.). (2021). Semantic Segmentation of Anaemic RBCs using Multilevel Deep Convolutional Encoder-Decoder Network. IEEE Access.

Sharma, D. K., Jalil, N. A., Regin, R., Rajest, S. S., Tummala, R. K., & Thangadurai. (2021). Predicting network congestion with machine learning. In *2021 2nd International Conference on Smart Electronics and Communication (ICOSEC)*. IEEE.

Sharma, D. K., Singh, B., Raja, M., Regin, R., & Rajest, S. S. (2021). An Efficient Python Approach for Simulation of Poisson Distribution. In *2021 7th International Conference on Advanced Computing and Communication Systems (ICACCS)*. IEEE.

Sharma, D. K., Singh, B., Regin, R., Steffi, R., & Chakravarthi, M. K. (2021). Efficient Classification for Neural Machines Interpretations based on Mathematical models. In *2021 7th International Conference on Advanced Computing and Communication Systems (ICACCS)*. IEEE.

Sharma, K., Singh, B., Herman, E., Regine, R., Rajest, S. S., & Mishra, V. P. (2021). Maximum information measure policies in reinforcement learning with deep energy-based model. In *2021 International Conference on Computational Intelligence and Knowledge Economy (ICCIKE)*. IEEE.

Sneha, D. (2021). Sine Cosine Algorithm Based Deep CNN for Acute Lymphocytic Leukemia Detection. *International Conference: Artificial Intelligence: Advances and Applications (ICAIAA)*.

Sohail, A., Khan, A., Wahab, N., Zameer, A., & Khan, S. (2021). A multi-phase deep CNN based mitosis detection framework for breast cancer histopathological images. *Scientific Reports, 11*(1), 1–18. PMID:33737632

Sujarani, P., & Kalaiselvi, K. (2018). Correlation Feature Selection (CFS) and Probabilistic Neural Network (PNN) for Diabetes Disease Prediction. *International Journal of Science & Technology, 7*(3).

Sun, L., Sun, H., Wang, J., Wu, S., Zhao, Y., & Xu, Y. (2021). Breast mass detection in mammography based on image template matching and CNN. *Sensors (Basel), 21*(8), 2855. doi:10.339021082855 PMID:33919623

Vashishtha, E., & Dhawan, G. (2023). Bridging Generation Gap on Analysis of Mentor-Mentee Relationship in Healthcare Setting. *FMDB Transactions on Sustainable Health Science Letters, 1*(1), 21–30.

Vijayakumar. (2019). Neural network analysis for tumor investigation and cancer prediction. *Journal of Electronics and Informatics*, (2), 89–98. doi:10.36548/jes.2019.2.004

Walczak, S., & Velanovich, V. (2018). Improving prognosis and reducing decision regret for pancreatic cancer treatment using artificial neural networks. *Elsevier Decision Support Systems, 106*, 110–118.

Wang, Q., Meizhou, Q., Li, Y., & Wen, J. (2021). A 3D attention networks for classification of white blood cells from microscopy hyperspectral images. *Optics & Laser Technology*, 139.

Wang, Z., Li, M., Wang, H., Jiang, H., & Yao, Y. (2019). Breast cancer detection using extreme learning machine based on feature fusion with CNN deep features. *IEEE Access : Practical Innovations, Open Solutions, 7*, 105146–105158.

Xia, T., Https Qing, Y., Fu, N., Jin, P., Chazot, P., & Angelov, R. (2020). AI-enabled Microscopic Blood Analysis for Microfluidic COVID-19 Hematology. *International Conference on Computational Intelligence and Applications (ICCIA)*.

Yogeshwari, M. (2020). Automatic segmentation of plant leaf disease using improved fast fuzzy C means clustering and adaptive otsu thresholding (IFFCM-AO) algorithm. *European Journal of Molecular and Clinical Medicine, 7*.

Yogeshwari, M. (2021). *Automatic Feature extraction and detection of plant leaf disease using GLCM features and Convolutional Neural Network*. Science Direct.

Chapter 10

Change Detection in Water Body Areas Through Optimization Algorithm Using High- and Low-Resolution Satellite Images

A. Sivasankari

Vels Institute of Science, Technology, and Advanced Studies, India

S. Jayalakshmi

MEASI Institute of Information Technology, India

B. Booba

Vels Institute of Science, Technology, and Advanced Studies, India

ABSTRACT

The Earth's surface has changed significantly as a result of human activity on the land expanding agriculture and population. To fulfil the growing demand for fundamental human necessities and wellbeing, it is crucial to have correct information on land use and land cover (LULC) and the best methods of using it. Large geographic regions can be found in sufficient detail in satellite photos, both qualitatively and quantitatively. The most effective methods for detecting together static and dynamic biophysical modules on the Earth's surface, which are regularly introduced for mapping LULC, are satellite depending remote sensing (RS) methods. In order to classify RS images into change/nochange classes, image pre-processing is done in this study, and the information content of the satellite images is assessed. In this work, a change detection method for identifying land cover and water bodies is proposed utilizing a stacked ensemble classifier with mean weight residual neural network (MWResNet) and entropy.

1. INTRODUCTION

In environmental research, remote sensing imageries are frequently employed to spot changes from anthropogenic or natural sources (Hussain, et al., 2013; Gregoire, et al., 2010). Change detection is "the

DOI: 10.4018/978-1-6684-9189-8.ch010

technique of finding differences in the condition of an object or phenomenon by watching it at different periods." In general, change detection methods are performed based on a two-step pattern. Feature extraction is the first step that is worked based on input images and is used to extract features, and these features are given as input for the decision step (Du, et al., 2012). In the decision step, features extracted from the previous step are classified into "change" vs. "no-change" for getting the final output (Gregoire, et al., 2010). Some methods used for the decision step change image differencing, image rationing, Principal Component Analysis (PCA), and tasseled cap transformations (Ng, et al., 2013). Classification algorithms use similarity or dissimilarity indices to categorize diverse land coverings according to their spectral characteristics (Chignell, et al., 2015). Remote sensing generally employs three classification techniques: supervised, unsupervised, and hybrid (Roy, et al., 2014). Three steps comprise the supervised approach: training the data, classifying using the trained data, and testing the classification outcomes. Instead, an unsupervised learning algorithm training dataset is not required (Shang, et al., 2019). The hybrid technique is worked based on semi-supervised and unsupervised procedures (Jia, et al., 2014). For the categorization of land use and land cover (LULC) for several applications, researchers have presented a variety of supervised and unsupervised approaches, as well as their combinations (Zalpour, et al., 2020; Samadi, et al., 2019; Acharya & Yang, 2004; Acharya, et al., 2016; Mishra & Pant, 2019).

The main Research Objectives are as follows:

Flora, mountains, hills, swamps, and water bodies cover the planet's surface (Kondraju, et al., 2014). By analyzing two or more photos of the same location taken at various times, change detection tries to find changes on the earth's surface (Salah, 2017). It can be used for various purposes, including tracking land use and cover changes, urban planning, stopping deforestation, and recovering forests (Chignell, et al., 2015). Thus, the proposed methodology offers a practical alternative that enhances RS photos' water body area change detection procedure (Uddin, et al., 2022). The following is a description of the proposed work's main goals:

- To introduce a Weighted Local Fuzzy C Means (WLFCM) Segmentation and Multi-scale Cat Swarm Optimisation (MCSO) approach to enhance the final accuracy of the change detection (Alarood, et al., 2022).
- The proposed system performs Multi-scale Segmentation to boost the overall accuracy of detection rate to variation in the spatial (Ullah, et al., 2020).
- Texture features, morphological features, and Principal Component Analysis (PCA) features were retrieved from the water body image to improve detection accuracy, shorten system runtime, and collect crucial information (Rani, et al., 2021).
- The MWResNet (Mean Weight ResNet) architecture and Entropy Parameter Optimization Deep Belief Network (EPO-DBN) approach are introduced to detection regulate to raise the detection rate of the water body, and it is capable of gathering several patterns of information from the dataset.
- MWResNet and EPO-DBN execute stacking ensemble classification to increase overall classification accuracy (Saleh, et al., 2021).

2. RELATED WORKS

Using Landsat-8 images, Du et al. (2014) suggested mapping the land surface water with a 95.00% overall accuracy, concentrating on China's Yangtze and Huaihe river basins. Spectral Angle Mapper was employed by Shen et al. (2018) to classify Landsat-8 images, and the accuracy obtained was 88.04%. Ahammad et al. (2020) developed Landsat TM (Thematic Mapper) and OLI (Operational Land Imager) data for the years 2000 to 2018; water bodies were detected, which included lakes, rivers, waterways, irrigation land, and ponds, and recognized the change in the area of the water body. The whole Landsat band and run were then used to create a PBM.

Sarp & Ozcelik, (2017) used Multi-temporal Landsat TM and ETM+ photos-based images collected from Lake Burdur from 1987 to 2011 in spatiotemporal changes. Surface water was extracted from image data using the Normalized Difference Water Index (NDWI), Modified NDWI (MNDWI), and Automated Water Extraction Index (AWEI), as well as Support Vector Machine (SVM) classification and spectral water indexing. Mishra, & Pant, (2020) presented the investigation of the water area in the Sangam region using Landsat-8 images, employing classification approaches such as the unsupervised classification method (ISODATA) and SVM-based supervised classification. The forecast of flood-like conditions in the research region benefits from estimating the water level.

Divya et al. (2018) established a method for determining shrinkage that has gradually occurred in lake water bodies over time. The study uses Landsat images from 1999 and 2009 to examine Puzhal Lake in Chennai. In these photos, classification techniques are used to extract water bodies. Additionally, utilized as a reference to verify the outcomes are topographic maps. Tv & Kn, (2021) developed a hybrid level set theory-based segmentation technique that combines edge- and region-based approaches to identify and distinguish surface water bodies in Landsat 8 images. The suggested approach was then used to analyze and detect changes to water bodies in multi-temporal Landsat data.

Li et al. (2021) proposed a goal of automatically extracting water bodies from various remote sensing images. With remote sensing photos from GF-2, GaoFen-6, Sentinel-2, and ZY-3, the proposed DLFC performed superbly. The findings show that the DLFC can automatically and quickly extract water bodies from multisource remote sensing images. Cordeiro et al. (2021) implemented a nonparametric unsupervised automatic technique such as agglomerative clustering and K means clustering for the inland water pixels' identification from multispectral satellite data. Naive Bayes (NBs) classifiers by random sub-sampling and generalization are introduced for classification.

Zeng et al. (2019) proposed contour-based regularity measurement for water segments to distinguish between aquaculture ponds and natural water. Ultimately, SVM classification based on these geometrical traits distinguishes inland lakes from aquaculture ponds. To track changes in inland aquaculture, the proposed approach can be used to extract all aquaculture ponds from all previous Landsat photos. The present study uses supervised and unsupervised approaches for categorizing the study region to achieve the best results.

3. PROPOSED METHODOLOGY

To comprehend the temporal consequences of the event on the earth's surface, the proposed approach completed three primary steps for change detection in water body areas of multi-temporal images (Mast, et al., 2021). The three major phases of water body change detection are worked depending as illustrated in Figure 1. The three main phases of the proposed system are introduced change detection in water bodies are as follows:

Figure 1. Overview of proposed system architecture

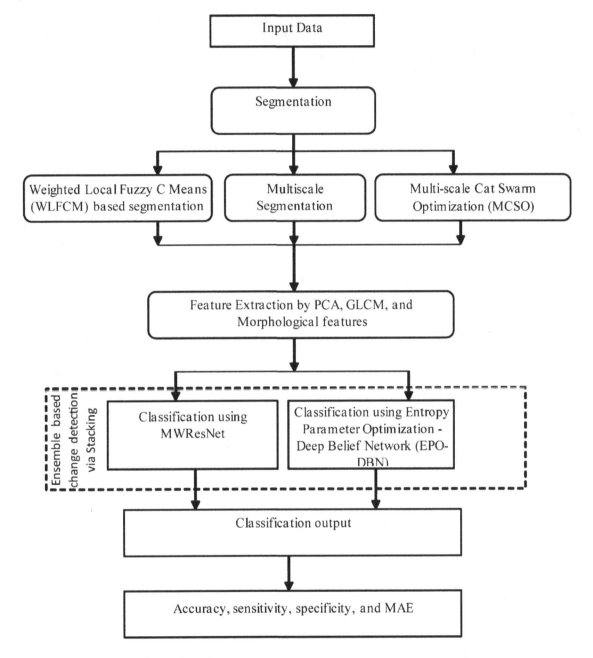

3.1. Change Detection in Water Bodies using Mean Weight Residual Neural Network (MWResNet)

Classifying land covers using the MWResNet architecture, which enables proper pre-processing of the complete model, is possible. WLFCM first does image segmentation. Analysis was done on how texture and morphological factors affected the change-detection process' accuracy (Sabir, et al., 2022).

To evaluate the effectiveness of these unsupervised learning models, a sample set of feature extraction points from MWResNet (Mean Weight ResNet) are used to test the model (Al-Khasawneh, et al., 2018).

Weighted Local FuzzyC Means (WLFCM) based Segmentation: Fuzzy clustering is the segmentation method for change detection that is most frequently employed (Chaudhary, et al., 2023). The strategy entails supplementing the conventional FCM algorithm with a weighted regularisation function. A constant or adaptive weight is used as the applied regularising weight (Alam Khan, et al., 2020). The Euclidian distance between the center prototype and the locally modified pixels mean is the adaptive weight. The clustered image is biased toward piecewise homogenous regions by the regularising function, which also seeks to smooth out additive noise (Tadiboina & Chase, 2022).

Feature Extraction by PCA: The PCA technique captures the biggest variance of a constrained set of orthogonal depending on the data correlation matrix. In this experiment, both PCA methods were used to track changes in the surface water.

Texture Features, the opening of closing by reconstruction operator by the morphological operator.

Change detection: The individual lake maps for the Mean Weight ResNet categorization have been employed for this inquiry. Water and non-water maps were separated. It was calculated first on the lake's surface and then on each class's area (Manikandan, et al., 2023). The grouped photos from various dates were then created by superimposing a lake surface map. Extinction/explosion gradients, which prohibit convergence from the start, are one of the difficulties with deep models. However, these challenges have been resolved by broadly standardized initializing and intermediate standards, enabling networks with tens of layers to converge for stochastic gradient Descent (SGD) downhill propagation. When the accuracy of deeper networks increases quickly, this issue is solved with the Deep ResNet Framework.

The core of these networks is a shortcut for identity lacking one or more steps. According to the table 1, this block is the residual block (Jain, et al., 2023). There are no parameters for this identity mapping; just the output from the previous layer is added to the subsequent layer. A linear W projection, whose residuals match the shortcut channels and can be extended, increases mapping identity. In order to add the inputs x and $F(x)$ to the following level. The connections in the Skip Layer combine the outputs from the layers above with the outputs from the levels below. Change and non-change detection is accomplished using this design. The model is then supplied and outputs a binary value indicating whether or not a sound file is available. The loss function and optimization feature using Adam Optimizer were binary cross-entropy, and the test rate was 0.001 with 32 batch sizes. In order to address the optimization problem, the study uses the following objective function:

$$f_F^* = \arg\min_f L(X, y, f) \, s.t \, f \in F \tag{1}$$

If F is the class of function f, y is the label, and X is the features from the input dataset. By taking into account the mean value of the pixels in the image dataset, the bias values in the classifier are increased, gradients are sent back to hidden layers, and the weights are adjusted appropriately. Following the computation of the weight values according to the input image samples, the mean value of the pixels for change and non-change is computed individually.

Algorithm 1. MWResNet Architecture

```
Input: Image dataset x,
Output: Water change detection results y
Step 1: Parameters initialization
Step 2: For i = 1,…N(N is the no. of samples)
Step 2.1: Perform forward propagation
For all i = 1,…N
```

Compute the predicted value x_i of via the neural network $\hat{y}_i^\theta$

Compute objective function $J(\theta) = \dfrac{1}{n} \sum\limits_{i=1}^{m} L\left(\hat{y}_i^\theta, y_i, mw_i \right)$

Where m is denoted as the size of training samples, mw_i is the mean weight of the classifier. θ the model parameters, L is the cost function

```
Step 2.2: Perform Backpropagation
```
$$\theta =: G(\theta)$$
```
Step 2.3: Compute error of the classifier, and it is considerable.
Step 3. Results change detection
```

3.2. Change Detection in Water Bodies using Entropy Parameter Optimization-Deep Belief Network (EPO-DBN)

Apply an Entropy Parameter Optimization Deep Belief Network (EPO DBN) for change detection to the challenge of unsupervised learning. The land cover photos are categorized using unlabeled data and an algorithm that has been trained in an unsupervised way. For image segmentation, multi-scale segmentation utilizing pixel differencing is introduced. Analysis was done on how texture and morphological factors affected the change-detection process' accuracy. EPO-DBN, which categorizes the uncategorized land cover and water body images from the satellite image database, provides intelligent decisions (Kumar, et al., 2021).

Multi-scale Segmentation: A pre-processing unit with sufficient spatial information is used in pixel-based image analysis as a homogenous region with pixel segmentation. This shows that the father-child relationship is on the segmented scale, which can be utilised to combine data from several levels.

Feature Extraction by PCA, texture feature extraction, opening of closing by reconstruction operator by morphological operation.

Change detection: The Deep Belief Network (DBN) is a family of deep neural networks that uses multiple layers of latent variables with connections across the levels but not between the units within each layer. It is a generative graphical model. DBNs are a compilation of basic sub-networks, where each sub-hidden network's layer acts as the next sub-visible network's layer. The following equation describes how to update weights for a single RBM using gradient descent:

$$w_{ij}(t+1) = w_{ij}(t) + \cdot\, \frac{\partial \log(p(v))}{\partial w_{ij}} \qquad (2)$$

where p(v) is the probability of a visible vector, which is given by $p(v) = \dfrac{1}{Z} \sum_{h} e^{-E(v,h)}$ . . Z is the partition function and E(v,h) is the energy function. The gradient $\dfrac{\partial \log(p(v))}{\partial w_{ij}}$ has the simple form $v_i h_{j\,data} - v_i h_{j\,model}$ where $\dots_p$ represent averages to distribution p. After n steps, the data are sampled, and that sample is used in place of $v_i h_{j\,model}$.

The full DBN preliminary structure is formed after finishing the RBM pretraining, but a labeled adjustment link to the DBN is still needed. The DBN network's final layer is configured with a Back Propagation (BP) classifier (Mahendran, et al., 2022). To increase the accuracy of the network training, the weights and biases obtained by the RBM pretraining are modified during the supervised fine-tuning procedure. This raises the network's recognition accuracy. During training, a neural network tends to learn new data while forgetting older samples, and performing too many different types of training will result in poor learning efficiency and sluggish convergence. As a result, it's important to select an appropriate momentum parameter m and learning rate η . The related update weights W and thresholds a and b will rise when the values of m and are too high, speeding up convergence. The entropy function is used to improve these values. The classifier's bias and weight are computed along with the maximum range of pixels that belong to the positive and negative classes. The classifier is evaluated using the fitness function,

$$Fitness = \frac{\left(\dfrac{TP}{TP + FN}\right)}{\left(\dfrac{TN}{FP + TN}\right)} \tag{3}$$

TP-True Positive; FN-False Negative; TN-True Negative; FP-False Positive.

Algorithm2. Entropy Parameter Optimization-Deep Belief Network (EPO-DBN) based Change Detection

1.   Create a training vector as the visible units' initial state.

2.   Train the first layer as an RBM with the visible layer modelling the input x .

3.   In light of the visible units, update the hidden units simultaneously. $p\left(h_j = 1 \| V\right) = \sigma\left(b_j + \sum_i v_i w_{ij}\right)$, σ is the sigmoid function and b_j is the bias of the hidden unit h_j

4.   In light of the hidden units, update the visible units concurrently. $p\left(v_i = 1 \| V\right) = \sigma\left(a_i + \sum_i h_j w_{ij}\right)$, a_i is the bias of the visible unit v_i .

5.   Perform weight update $\Delta w_{ij} \propto v_i, h_{j\,Data} - v_i, h_{j\,reconstruction.}$

6.   Adjust all parameters, including the momentum parameter m, learning rate η, and weight W, according to the entropy function to log-likelihood.

3.3. Multi-Scale Catswarm Optimisation (MCSO) Based Segmentation and Ensemble Classification for Water Body Change Detection

Multi-scale Cat Swarm Optimisation (MCSO) method is used to segment the land cover and water bodies in photographs. It can be carried out utilizing seeking and tracking modes, and this technique is also used to optimise the multi-scale segmentation parameters. Analysis was done on how texture and morphological factors affected the change-detection process' accuracy. EPO-DBN and MWResNet ultimately classify the images of land covers and water body images from the collected satellite images by the Stacking Ensemble Classification (SEC).

Multi-Scale Segmentation: A pre-processing unit through sufficient spatial data is used in pixel-based image analysis as a uniform region by pixel segmentation. The multi-scale segmentation approach combines the simplicity of segmenting at a rough scale with the accuracy of segmenting at a fine scale by integrating the image information from many scales. A promising multi-scale segmentation technique, Fractal Net Evolution Approach (FNEA), has just been developed. It is an object-oriented image segmentation technique that fuses image segmentation and object-oriented methodology. The region-merging technique with minimal internal heterogeneity is the foundation of FNEA. At any pixel, pixel merging begins. It initially condenses one pixel into a smaller region, earlier reducing smaller regions into polygon objects.

The segmentation scale (scale), the weight of shape heterogeneity (shape), and the weight of compactness (weight) are the segmentation parameters of FNEA (compactness). Each of the three parameters has a separate range. The Cat Swarm Optimisation (CSO) optimizes these three parameters. Cat characteristics are divided into two categories such as seeking mode and tracing mode.

3.4. Seeking Mode

Seeking Mode: It is the way of searching, and it is based on the cat's behavior, including napping, hunting, and looking for new places to roam around. The Seeking Memory Pool (SMP) symbolises the dimension of each cat's seeking memory, which displays the cat's location and the search strategy. The Selected Dimensions (SRD)stands for seeking a range of particular dimensions, which is the mutative ratio of certain dimensions. Count of Dimensions to Change (CDC) shows how many dimensions have changed. Every element operates as its principal purpose when in searching mode. The Boolean variable self-position considering (SPC) chooses to relocate the cat to a new position based on where it was previously standing.

3.5. Tracing Mode

Tracing Mode: Individual cats showing their decisions for locating various targets are named tracing mode. When a cat changes into the tracing mode, its movement is determined by its velocity in every direction. The next three steps define the method of tracing mode.

3.6. CatSwarm Optimization (CSO) Algorithm

Step 1: Create a starting population of cats using the Fractal Net Evolution Approach (FNEA) and scatter them around the M-dimensional solution space (X_i, d). At random, assign each cat a velocity inside the range of the maximum velocity value (t_i, d).

Step 2: Sprinkle the cats at random over the M, and then at random, assign each cat's velocity values that fall within the range of its maximum speed. Then randomly select several cats and put them in searching mode while setting the rest into tracing mode using Mixed Ratio (MR).

Step 3: Based on the segmentation parameters, evaluate each cat's fitness value and save the cat with the highest fitness level. The finest answer to date is represented by the location of the best cat $(Xbest)$.

Step 4: If cat_k is in searching mode, introduce the cat toward the seeking mode procedure; if not, relate it to the tracing mode procedure. Move the cats by their flags.

Step 5: Set the other cats into the searching mode, subsequently choosing several extra cats and background them into MR's tracing mode.

Step 6: Confirm the termination criteria and end the process else, repeat steps 3 to step 6.

When specific categories of items are extracted from remote sensing images, there is a difference in how the objects are distributed between the machine-segmented image and the ground truth image. Let M be the machine-segmented image, and let G be the ground truth image with N regions denoted R_{G_i} made of pixels, i = 1...N. The pixels in the region R_{G_i} may belong to K regions since over-segmentation and under-segmentation are unavoidable in a machine-segmented image. The P_{M_j} pixels that make up the K regions known as R_{M_j}. j = 1, ..., K. The smallest area in M that can encompass the region R_{G_i} is $P_{M_1} + P_{M_2} + ... + P_{M_K}$. The area total of the regions that comprise the pixels from the region R_{G_i} is the least area in M that covers the region R_{G_i} by fitness F_i:

$$F_i = \frac{P_{G_i}}{K \sum_{j=1}^{K} P_{M_j}} \quad (4)$$

Feature extraction by PCA, texture feature extraction, opening of closing by reconstruction operator by morphological.

Proposed Algorithm: For classifying RS images into change/no change classes, an ensemble classifier is presented on a single dataset of pairs of feature vectors and their classifications, stacking an ensemble merging different classifiers like EPO-DBN and MWResNet.

4. RESULTS AND ANALYSIS

The study validates the Stacking Ensemble Classifier (SEC) model in this section using well-established deep learning classifiers, such as the Adaptive Ensemble of Extreme Learning Machines (AEELM), Convolutional Neural Network (CNN), MWResNet, and EPO-DBN on the satellite images of water bodies dataset at https://www.kaggle.com/datasets/franciscoescobar/. MATLAB 2022b is used to implement these classifiers. The performance measures used to evaluate the classifiers' outputs include the following and are tabulated in Table 1:

$$Sensitivity = TP/(TP+FN) \tag{5}$$

$$Specificity = TN/(TN+FP) \tag{6}$$

$$Accuracy = (TP+TN)/(TP+TN+FP+FN) \tag{7}$$

$$MAE = \frac{1}{n}\sum_{i=1}^{n}|f_i - y_i| = \frac{1}{n}\sum_{i=1}^{n}|e_i| \tag{8}$$

Figure 2a Compares the Sensitivity of Classifiers such as SEC, AEELM, CNN, MWResNet, and EPO-DBN. The simulation results demonstrate that the proposed SEC method produces a higher sensitivity rate than current methods. The proposed classifier yields findings with a sensitivity of 96.6920%, while AEELM, CNN, MWResNet, and EPO-DBN produce results with lower values of 87.0174%, 91.0381%, 94.0109%, and 95.0588%.

The specificity of classification techniques like SEC, AEELM, CNN, MWResNet, and EPO-DBN are illustrated in Figure 2b. According to the findings, the proposed classifier has the highest specificity, at 96.6754%, while AEELM, CNN, MWResNet, and EPO-DBN have lower values, at 86.9928%, 91.0107%, 93.9953%, and 94.9887%respectively.

Figure 3a compares overall accuracy findings for several water body change detecting techniques. The proposed classifier performs with an accuracy rate of 96.6667%, while AEELM, CNN, MWResNet, and EPO-DBN produce results with lower accuracy rates of 87.00%, 91.00%, 94.00%, and 95.00%.

Results of the MAE comparison of classifiers such SEC, AEELM, CNN, MWResNet, and EPO-DBN are displayed in Figure 3b. According to simulation findings, the proposed method yields lower MAE values than existing methods. The proposed classifier produces MAE results that are lowered to 0.0333, while classifiers like AEELM, CNN, MWResNet, and EPO-DBN produce MAE values that are increased to 0.1300, 0.0900, 0.0600, and 0.0500, respectively.

Table 1. Comparison of the existing classifiers with the proposed system

Classifiers	Sensitivity %	Specificity %	Accuracy %	MAE
AEELM	87.0174	86.9928	87	0.1300
CNN	91.0381	91.0107	91	0.0900
MWResNet	94.0109	93.9953	94	0.0600
EPO-DBN	95.0588	94.9887	95	0.0500
SEC	96.692	96.6754	96.6667	0.0333

Figure 2. a) Shows Sensitivity Comparison vs. Waterbody Change Detection Methods, and b) shows specificity comparison vs. waterbody change detection methods

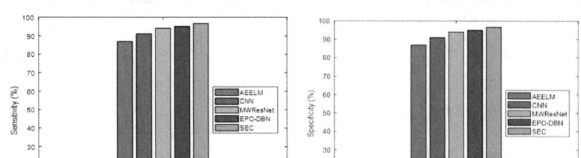

2 a   2 b

Figure 3. a) Accuracy comparison vs. waterbody change detection methods and b) shows MAE comparison vs. waterbody change detection methods

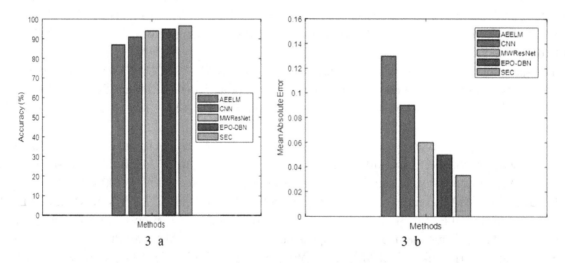

3 a   3 b

5. CONCLUSION AND FUTURE DIRECTION

Mean Weight ResNet (MWResNet) architecture, which enables the classification of land covers so that the full model is permitted with adequate pre-processing, is the initial contribution of the study. Weighted Local Fuzzy C Means (WLFCM) segmentation is used first to divide an image into its parts. Analysis was done on how texture and morphological factors affected the change-detection process' accuracy. The effectiveness of these unsupervised learning models is evaluated by using a sample of the feature-extracted points from MWResNet to test the model.

Entropy Parameter Optimization-Deep Belief Network (EPO-DBN), the work's second contribution, is presented for change detection. For image segmentation, multi-scale segmentation utilising pixel differencing is introduced. Analysis was done on how texture and morphological factors affected the change-detection process' accuracy. EPO-DBN, which categorizes land cover and water bodies from the collected satellite image database, gives higher results.

Multi-scale Cat Swarm Optimisation (MCSO) method is used to segment water bodies and land cover in photos in the work's final contribution. By using seeking and tracking modes, the CSO algorithm separates the land cover and water bodies, providing information that can be utilised to optimise segmentation parameters. Analysis was done on how texture and morphological factors affected the change-detection process' accuracy.EPO-DBN and MWResNet then classify the images of land cover and water bodies from the database using ensemble classification. The created change maps result shows that the proposed system was trained using a small fraction of the data, and it is used to classify the image's pixels into change and no-change classes. In further work, all of the pixels in the image can be further classified into change/no-change classes using the change maps generated by ensemble classification that have been trained using a large fraction of the data.

REFERENCES

Acharya, T., Lee, D., Yang, I., & Lee, J. (2016). Identification of water bodies in a Landsat 8 OLI image using a J48 decision tree. *Sensors (Basel)*, *16*(7), 1075. doi:10.339016071075 PMID:27420067

Acharya, T. D., & Yang, I. (2004). Exploring Landsat 8. *Int. J. IT Eng. Appl. Sci. Res*, (4), 4–10.

Ahammad, T., Rahaman, H., Faisal, B. R., & Sultana, N. (2020). Model based change detection of water body using Landsat imagery: A case study of Rajshahi Bangladesh. *Environment and Natural Resources Journal*, *18*(4), 345–355.

Al-Khasawneh, M. A., Shamsuddin, S. M., Hasan, S., & Bakar, A. A. (2018). MapReduce a comprehensive review. In *2018 International Conference on Smart Computing and Electronic Enterprise (ICSCEE)* (pp. 1-6). IEEE.

Alam Khan, Z., Feng, Z., Uddin, M. I., Mast, N., Ali Shah, S. A., Imtiaz, M., & Mahmoud, M. (2020). Optimal policy learning for disease prevention using reinforcement learning. *Scientific Programming*, *2020*, 1–13.

Alarood, A. A., Alsolami, E., Al-Khasawneh, M. A., Ababneh, N., & Elmedany, W. (2022). IES: Hyper-chaotic plain image encryption scheme using improved shuffled confusion-diffusion. *Ain Shams Engineering Journal*, *13*(3), 101583.

Chaudhary, J. K., Sharma, H., Tadiboina, S. N., Singh, R., Khan, M. S., & Garg, A. (2023). Applications of Machine Learning in Viral Disease Diagnosis. In *2023 10th International Conference on Computing for Sustainable Global Development (INDIACom)* (pp. 1167-1172). IEEE.

Chignell, S., Anderson, R., & Evangelista, P. (2015). Multi-temporal independent component analysis and Landsat 8 for delineating maximum extent of the 2013 Colorado front range flood. *Remote Sensing*, *7*, 9822–9843.

Cordeiro, M. C., Martinez, J. M., & Peña-Luque, S. (2021). Automatic water detection from multidimensional hierarchical clustering for Sentinel-2 images and a comparison with Level 2A processors. *Remote Sensing of Environment, 253*, 1–46.

Divya, L., Karthi, R., & Geetha, P. (2018). Temporal Change Detection in Water Body of Puzhal Lake Using Satellite Images. In *International Conference On Computational Vision and Bio Inspired Computing* (pp. 1229–1237). Cham: Springer.

Du, Z., Bin, L., Ling, F., Li, W., Tian, W., Wang, H., & Zhang, X. (2012). Estimating surface water area changes using time-series Landsat data in the Qingjiang River Basin, China". China. *Journal of Applied Remote Sensing, 6*(1), 1–17.

Du, Z., Li, W., Zhou, D., Tian, L., Ling, F., Wang, H., & Sun, B. (2014). Analysis of Landsat-8 OLI imagery for land surface water mapping. *Remote Sensing Letters, 5*(7), 672–681. doi:10.1080/215070 4x.2014.960606

Gregoire, M., Stephane, D., Emmanuel, T., & Lionel, B. (2010). Change detection in remote sensing observations. In *Digital Signal and Image Processing Series* (pp. 95–142). John Wiley & Sons Inc.

Hussain, M., Chen, D., Cheng, A., Wei, H., & Stanley, D. (2013). Change detection from remotely sensed images: From pixel-based to object-based approaches. *ISPRS Journal of Photogrammetry and Remote Sensing, 80*, 91–106.

Jain, A., Krishna, M. M., Tadiboina, S. N., Joshi, K., Chanti, Y., & Krishna, K. S. (2023). An analysis of medical images using deep learning. In *2023 3rd International Conference on Advance Computing and Innovative Technologies in Engineering (ICACITE)* (pp. 1440-1445). IEEE.

Jia, K., Wei, X., Gu, X., Yao, Y., Xie, X., & Li, B. (2014). Land cover classification using Landsat 8 Operational Land Imager data in Beijing, China. *Geocarto International, 29*(8), 941–951. doi:10.1080 /10106049.2014.894586

Kondraju, T., Mandla, V. R. B., & Mahendra, R. S. (2014). Evaluation of various image classification techniques on Landsat to identify coral reefs. *Geomatics, Natural Hazards & Risk*, (5), 173–184.

Kumar, V., Kumar, S., AlShboul, R., Aggarwal, G., Kaiwartya, O., Khasawneh, A. M., ... Al-Khasawneh, M. A. (2021). Grouping and Sponsoring Centric Green Coverage Model for Internet of Things. *Sensors (Basel), 21*(12), 3948. PMID:34201100

Li, M., Wu, P., Wang, B., Park, H., Yang, H., & Wu, Y. (2021). A deep learning method of water body extraction from high resolution remote sensing images with multisensors. *IEEE Journal of Selected Topics in Applied Earth Observations and Remote Sensing, 14*, 3120–3132.

Mahendran, R., Tadiboina, S. N., Thrinath, B. S., Gadgil, A., Madem, S., & Srivastava, Y. (2022). Application of Machine Learning and Internet of Things for Identification of Nutrient Deficiencies in Oil Palm. In *2022 5th International Conference on Contemporary Computing and Informatics (IC3I)* (pp. 2024-2028). IEEE.

Manikandan, N., Tadiboina, S. N., Khan, M. S., Singh, R., & Gupta, K. K. (2023). Automation of Smart Home for the Wellbeing of Elders Using Empirical Big Data Analysis. In *2023 3rd International Conference on Advance Computing and Innovative Technologies in Engineering (ICACITE)* (pp. 1164-1168). IEEE.

Mast, N., Khan, M. A., Uddin, M. I., Ali Shah, S. A., Khan, A., Al-Khasawneh, M. A., & Mahmoud, M. (2021). Channel contention-based routing protocol for wireless ad hoc networks. *Complexity, 2021*, 1–10.

Mishra, V. K., & Pant, T. (2019). Application of classification techniques for identification of water region in multiple sources using Landsat-8 OLI imagery. In *2019 URSI Asia-Pacific Radio Science Conference (AP-RASC).* IEEE.

Mishra, V. K., & Pant, T. (2020). Water level monitoring using classification techniques on Landsat-8 data at Sangam region, Prayagraj, India. *IET Image Processing, 14*(15), 3733–3741.

Ng, T. F., Jiang, D. H., Jiag, X., Paull, D. J., & Wang, X. H. (2013). Change detection for sustainability monitoring using satellite remote sensing data. The University of New South Wales at Canberra.

Rani, R., Kumar, S., Kaiwartya, O., Khasawneh, A. M., Lloret, J., Al-Khasawneh, M. A., & Alarood, A. A. (2021). Towards green computing oriented security: A lightweight postquantum signature for IoE. *Sensors (Basel), 21*(5), 1883. PMID:33800227

Roy, M., Ghosh, S., & Ghosh, A. (2014). A novel approach for change detection of remotely sensed images using semi-supervised multiple classifier system. *Information Sciences, 269*, 35–47. doi:10.1016/j.ins.2014.01.037

Sabir, M. W., Khan, Z., Saad, N. M., Khan, D. M., Al-Khasawneh, M. A., Perveen, K., & Azhar Ali, S. S. (2022). Segmentation of Liver Tumor in CT Scan Using ResU-Net. *Applied Sciences (Basel, Switzerland), 12*(17), 8650.

Salah, M. (2017). A survey of modern classification techniques in remote sensing for improved image classification. *Journal of Genomics, 11*(1), 1–21.

Saleh, M. A., Othman, S. H., Al-Dhaqm, A., & Al-Khasawneh, M. A. (2021). Common investigation process model for Internet of Things forensics. In *2021 2nd International Conference on Smart Computing and Electronic Enterprise (ICSCEE)* (pp. 84-89). IEEE.

Samadi, F., Akbarizadeh, G., & Kaabi, H. (2019). Change detection in SAR images using deep belief network: A new training approach based on morphological images. *IET Image Processing, 13*(12), 2255–2264.

Sarp, G., & Ozcelik, M. (2017). Water body extraction and change detection using time series: A case study of Lake Burdur, Turkey. *Journal of Taibah University for Science : JTUSCI, 11*(3), 381–391.

Shang, M., Wang, S., Zhou, Y., Du, C., & Liu, W. (2019). Object-based image analysis of suburban landscapes using Landsat-8 imagery. *International Journal of Digital Earth, 12*(6), 720–736. doi:10.1080/17538947.2018.1474959

Shen, H., Lin, Y., Tian, Q., Xu, K., & Jiao, J. (2018). A comparison of multiple classifier combinations using different voting-weights for remote sensing image classification. *International Journal of Remote Sensing, 39*(11), 3705–3722. doi:10.1080/01431161.2018.1446566

Tadiboina, S. N., & Chase, G. C. (2022). The importance and leverage of modern information technology infrastructure in the healthcare industry. *Int J Res Trends Innov*, *7*(11), 340–344.

Tv, B., & Kn, N. (2021). A Hybrid Level Set Based Approach for Surface Water Delineation using Landsat-8 Multispectral Images". Multispectral Images. *Engineering Letters*, *29*(2), 1–10.

Uddin, M. I., Ali Shah, S. A., Al-Khasawneh, M. A., Alarood, A. A., & Alsolami, E. (2022). Optimal policy learning for COVID-19 prevention using reinforcement learning. *Journal of Information Science*, *48*(3), 336–348.

Ullah, Z., Zeb, A., Ullah, I., Awan, K. M., Saeed, Y., Uddin, M. I., & Zareei, M. (2020). Certificateless proxy reencryption scheme (CPRES) based on hyperelliptic curve for access control in content-centric network (CCN). *Mobile Information Systems*, *2020*, 1–13.

Zalpour, M., Akbarizadeh, G., & Alaei-Sheini, N. (2020). A new approach for oil tank detection using deep learning features with control false alarm rate in high-resolution satellite imagery. *International Journal of Remote Sensing*, *41*(6), 2239–2262. doi:10.1080/01431161.2019.1685720

Zeng, Z., Wang, D., Tan, W., & Huang, J. (2019). Extracting aquaculture ponds from natural water surfaces around inland lakes on medium resolution multispectral images. *International Journal of Applied Earth Observation and Geoinformation*, *80*, 13–25.

Chapter 11
Certificate Authentication and Verification Using Secured Blockchain Approach for Blind People

Jyoti P. Kanjalkar
Vishwakarma Institute of Technology, India

Rutuja Shinde
Vishwakarma Institute of Technology, India

Tanmay Sharma
Vishwakarma Institute of Technology, India

Abhishek Tyade
Vishwakarma Institute of Technology, India

Uma Thakur
Vishwakarma Institute of Technology, India

Pramod Kanjalkar
Vishwakarma Institute of Technology, India

ABSTRACT

In 2021–2022, 5.57 crore students are expected to enroll in higher education in India, and every year, there will be close to 9 million graduates. According to estimates, there are 0.5 cases of this type of blindness per 1,000 people in India. Many children are blind or have severe visual impairment (SVI) or blindness (BL). Dealing with sight loss or low vision is just one of the difficulties that the visually impaired face in everyday life. There are many challenges in their daily life such as navigating around places, most of the information is inaccessible, finding reading material, etc. They are also facing many challenges in their educational careers as well. If any blind student has graduated and he/she wants to maintain all the original certificates, then it becomes tiresome to track these certificates and manually verify their legitimacy for them. Also, everything needs to be digitized with the principles of confidentiality, reliability, and availability in order to make the data more secure and safe.

DOI: 10.4018/978-1-6684-9189-8.ch011

1. INTRODUCTION

Blockchain technology has gained significant attention due to its potential to enhance security across various domains. Blockchain is a decentralized, distributed digital ledger that records transactions and data in a secure and transparent manner. Its inherent properties contribute to improved security in several ways. Blockchain technology is a cutting-edge database system that enables open information sharing inside a company network (Pande, Chetty, 2021). Data is stored in blocks that are chained together in a blockchain database. Since the chain cannot be deleted or changed without the network's approval, the data is chronologically consistent (Sonnad, et al., 2022). As a result, you can use blockchain technology to build an unchangeable or immutable ledger for keeping track of orders, payments, accounts, and other transactions (Ramesh, et al., 2017). The System is equipped with mechanisms that stop unauthorized transaction entries and establish consistency in the shared view of these transactions (Vashishtha, et al., 2020).

The first application of blockchain technology in the real world is Bitcoin, one of the most expensive digital currencies. Since the creation of the coin, Bitcoin's value has multiplied thousands of times, and this is the primary factor that accounts for blockchain's current level of popularity (Pidikiti, et al., 2023). In addition to cryptocurrencies, blockchain has also become a valuable technology that may be utilized to solve many contemporary social issues brought on by a lack of trust between various parties (Veeraiah, et al., 2022).

A phishing-resistant cryptographic method called certificate-based authentication allows computers to utilize digital certificates to securely identify one another across a network. Certificate privacy, authenticity, and anonymity are improved using blockchain technology (Ogunmola, et al., 2021). The possibility of certificate forgery is decreased by using the blockchain-based System (Gunturu, et al., 2023).

Blockchain is a foundational technology that underpins cryptocurrencies like Bitcoin, but its applications extend far beyond digital currencies (Sharma, et al., 2021). At its core, blockchain is a decentralized and distributed digital ledger that records transactions and data in a secure, transparent, and tamper-resistant manner (Sonnad, et al., 2022).

Decentralized and Distributed Ledger: Unlike traditional centralized databases where a single entity controls the data, a blockchain operates on a decentralized network of computers known as nodes. Each node has a copy of the entire ledger, ensuring redundancy and making the System resilient to failures or attacks.

Blocks and Chains: A blockchain consists of a series of "blocks," each containing a group of transactions or data. These blocks are linked together in chronological order, forming a "chain." Each block includes a unique identifier (hash) of the previous block, creating a tamper-resistant linkage between blocks.

Consensus Mechanisms: To achieve agreement on the state of the ledger and validate transactions, blockchains employ various consensus mechanisms. One common mechanism is Proof of Work (PoW), where nodes compete to solve complex mathematical puzzles to add new blocks. Another is Proof of Stake (PoS), where validators are chosen based on the amount of cryptocurrency they hold and are willing to "stake" as collateral (Uike, et al., 2022).

Immutability and Security: Once data is recorded in a block and added to the blockchain, it's extremely difficult to alter or remove. This immutability is achieved through cryptographic hashing, where each block's content is combined with the previous block's hash to form its own unique hash. If any information in a block is changed, it would invalidate subsequent blocks and be immediately noticeable (Suthar, et al., 2022).

Cryptography: Blockchain uses cryptographic techniques to secure transactions and control access. Each participant in the network has a pair of cryptographic keys: a public key (used for encryption) and a private key (used for decryption and digital signatures). This ensures secure and authenticated transactions (Gurumurthy, et al., 2021).

Transparency and Trust: The distributed nature of blockchain and the transparency of the ledger mean that all participants can view the entire transaction history. This transparency enhances accountability and trust among participants.

Smart contracts: Smart contracts are self-executing programs that run on the blockchain when specific conditions are met. They automate and enforce agreements without the need for intermediaries. Ethereum, for example, introduced the concept of smart contracts, enabling a wide range of decentralized applications.

Applications: While initially associated with cryptocurrencies, blockchain technology has found applications in various fields, including supply chain management, healthcare, finance, voting systems, energy trading, and more. It enables secure data sharing, traceability, and efficiency improvements in numerous industries (Krishna, et al., 2019).

It's important to note that while blockchain offers numerous benefits, it's not a one-size-fits-all solution, and its implementation requires careful consideration of the use case, scalability, energy consumption, and regulatory aspects (Pakala, et al., 2018). As technology evolves, newer versions of blockchain, such as permissioned blockchains and hybrid solutions, are being explored to address these considerations. According to estimates, there are 0.5 cases of this type of blindness per 1,000 people in India, and at least 210,000 children are blind or have severe visual impairment (SVI) or blindness (BL).

People who are blind or whose vision prevents them from reading printed text can use their fingers to read Braille, which consists of a pattern of raised dots. Braille is typically read with the eyes of educators, parents, and other people who are not blind. Language is not what Braille is. Instead, it is a system of writing and reading that allows languages like English or Spanish to be expressed (Bansal, et al., 2022).

People who are blind or partially sighted can learn how text is laid out on a page using Braille (Ravinder & Kulkarni, (2023a). It's important to note that while blockchain offers numerous benefits, it's not a one-size-fits-all solution, and its implementation requires careful consideration of the use case, scalability, energy consumption, and regulatory aspects. As technology evolves, newer versions of blockchain, such as permissioned blockchains and hybrid solutions, are being explored to address these considerations (Ravinder & Kulkarni, 2023b).

Certificate authentication and verification using a secured blockchain approach for blind people is a novel and innovative application that leverages the strengths of blockchain technology to address accessibility and security challenges faced by individuals with visual impairments. The key concepts and components of this approach (Pandya, et al., 2022).

Certificate authentication and verification are processes commonly used to validate the authenticity and legitimacy of documents, credentials, or certificates. These documents could include educational certificates, licenses, identification documents, and more. Ensuring the accuracy of these documents is crucial, as they often serve as proof of qualifications, skills, or legal status (Arslan, et al., 2021).

Blockchain is a decentralized and distributed digital ledger that records transactions and data in a secure, transparent, and tamper-resistant manner. It provides a way to establish trust and immutability in a network without relying on a central authority. The core principles of blockchain, such as cryptographic hashing, consensus mechanisms, and data immutability, contribute to enhancing security and transparency.

A secured blockchain approach involves utilizing blockchain technology to store and manage certificate-related data. This approach ensures that certificates are securely stored, tamper-resistant, and accessible only by authorized parties. Blockchain's decentralized nature and cryptographic features contribute to the security and trustworthiness of the process (Kulkarni, et al., 2019).

Addressing the needs of blind individuals in this context involves designing the System to be inclusive and usable for those with visual impairments. This could involve incorporating features such as screen readers, voice commands, and haptic feedback to facilitate interaction with the blockchain-based certificate authentication system.

1.1. Key Benefits

Security: Blockchain's tamper-resistant nature ensures the integrity of certificate data, preventing unauthorized changes or fraud.

Transparency: The transparency of the blockchain allows authorized parties to independently verify certificates, reducing the need for intermediaries.

Accessibility: Designing the System with accessibility features ensures that blind individuals can independently access and interact with the certification process.

Efficiency: Streamlined verification processes can reduce administrative burdens and the need for manual interventions.

Trust: The decentralized and transparent nature of blockchain technology builds trust among all parties involved in the verification process.

1.2. Challenges and Consideration

User Experience: Designing an accessible user interface that caters to the needs of blind individuals is crucial.

Data Privacy: Ensuring that sensitive personal data is handled with privacy and security in mind.

Integration: Integrating the blockchain-based System with existing certification processes and frameworks.

Education: Educating users, both blind individuals and institutions, about the benefits and usage of this innovative approach.Top of Form

2. RELATED WORK

Garba, et al. (2021) used the Hyper-ledger platform as this allows only the current users to join the network and no other. The proposed System shows how blockchain-based hash validity can be used to detect malicious and transient data changes.

Billah, et al. (2021) focus on a theoretical framework that might provide a good alternative answer for academic certificate issuance and verification. Peer-to-peer networks, digital signatures, and public/private keys are just a few of the features of blockchain technology which are used in the System.

Saleh & Osman Ghazali (2020) help to secure the certificate storage in the blockchain system. The certificate's hash code value is created using the chaotic algorithm. Additionally, these certifications are verified through the use of a mobile application.

Gayathiri, et al. (2020) emphasized and investigated the security concepts required for the blockchain verification of diplomas. For the purpose of verifying educational credentials, the Hyperledger Fabric Framework is put out as a blockchain-based framework with an emphasis on authentication, authorization, confidentiality, privacy, and ownership.

In the paper (Gupta, et al., 2014), the technique for robust voice command recognition has been represented by the authors. They employed a procedural technique that routes the voice through to the automaton, acquiring a cumulative value that must be higher than or equal to that same threshold value for successful recognition in order to provide robustness against human errors.

Kandhari, et al. (2018) benefit those who have vision impairments. This System allows users to operate it with voice commands using Speech Recognition System (SRS), and it can be reused multiple times due to speech-to-text technology.

Fonseka & Sasanka (2018) are to print out photographs in Braille after they have been converted to the Braille script. The two main methods for producing braille images are the ASCII art generation method and the graphics to braille dot map technique.

Jha & Parvathi (2019) cover a methodology to translate any scanned Hindi handwriting file to equivalent Braille. Using a histogram of directed gradients, an SVM classifier identifies Hindi character traits. The scanned documents are first converted to a printed format before being transliterated into Braille using UTF-8 codes.

In the paper (Hassan & Mohammed (2011), the author assessed the neural networks' capacity to produce Grade I Braille for people with visual impairments using scanned English-language text sheets, novels, or seminars. A minimally structured convolutional neural network was created and validated to convert English characters into grade I literary Braille coding. It is anticipated that noise will influence English characters, with a mean-variance between 0 and 0.4. The output of the Neural Network can be stored in a data document that can be sent to a Braille printer or a Braille display.

Ummuhanysifa et al. (2013) seek to create a voice-based human-machine interface for search engines (Ummuhanysifa & Banu, 2013). Users can control and command the web browser using their voice with the use of an innovative voice-based web browser and web page reader that is demonstrated. The suggested voice-based search engine intends to make utilizing the Internet easier for users, especially the blind. A computer will respond by speaking back to a user when they speak to it. While reading the materials, the user will also get assistance from the computer.

Pande & Chett, (2018) have analyzed and configured the recent flavor of CNN called the capsule network. It extracts features from input in two levels and tries to identify not only the patterns present in the input but also build the relationship among the learned features (Pande & Chetty, 2019). The authors have created their own dataset and trained the network on it. These approaches provide promising results in the testing phase. This approach could be employed for implementing certificate authentication systems (Kanjalkar, et al., 2022).

According to the literature review mentioned above, achieving higher security poses a problem, and the level of security that is attained in the survey does not meet expectations. In order to authenticate and validate data, we are suggesting the most secure blockchain technology for blind people.

3. PROPOSED METHODOLOGY

3.1. System Requirements

Our proposed methodology uses the following system requirements:

1. Web 3.0:

The World Wide Web is evolving, and the third generation of the Internet, often known as Web 3.0, represents this change. In order to create a more connected and smarter web experience for consumers, it offers a data-driven Semantic Web using a machine-based understanding of data.

2. React Js:

Facebook created the open-source React.js framework, which is a JavaScript framework and library. It's used to create interactive user interfaces and online apps quickly and effectively with a lot less code than you would with vanilla JavaScript.

3. Python:

Python is a high-level, all-purpose programming language. Code readability is given top priority, and indentation is used extensively. Python has dynamic typing and garbage collection. Programming paradigms, including functional, object-oriented, and structured programming, are all supported by it.

4. Truffle:

For creating blockchain applications, Truffle offers a world-class development environment, an asset pipeline, and a testing framework. It is a well-liked option for dApp creation on Ethereum, leading to a sizable community that supports the tool.

5. Metamask:

MetaMask is a free cryptocurrency wallet available on the web and for mobile devices that enables users to exchange and store cryptocurrencies, engage with the Ethereum blockchain ecosystem, and host an expanding number of decentralized applications (dApps). One of the most popular crypto applications exists today.

6. Ganache:

With the help of Ganache, a private Ethereum blockchain environment, you may simulate the Ethereum network and interact with private blockchain smart contracts.

7. Smart contracts:

Algorithms built on the blockchain called "smart contracts" run when specific conditions are met. They are widely used to execute agreements automatically so that all parties can be certain of the conclusion right away, without the need for an intermediary or further delay.

8.   Solidity:

On many blockchain platforms, most notably Ethereum, smart contracts are implemented using an object-oriented programming language called Solidity.

3.2. Braille Chart for the English Alphabet

There is a Braille chart for English alphabets given in Table 1.

4. PROPOSED ALGORITHM

In our proposed model, we use Ganache to create a local blockchain, and this will also give us an id and password to log in.

- Admin can log in through metamask with their id and password.
- Admin can add institutes and courses offered.

Table 1. Braille chart for the English alphabet

Character	Braille
A	⠁
B	⠃
C	⠉
D	⠙
E	⠑
F	⠋
G	⠛
H	⠓
I	⠊
J	⠚
K	⠅
L	⠇
M	⠍
N	⠝
O	⠕
P	⠏
Q	⠟

- Only the authorized institutes which are added by the admin can access the institute page after logging through metamask.
- Institute can give certificates to the appropriate students for their respective courses.
- After clicking the submit button through metamask, the certificate will get stored in the blockchain, a unique hash value will be generated corresponding to this hash value, and a certificate id will be generated.
- Users can log in and give their certificate id through text or through voice which will get converted to text (voice to text).
- The certificate id will generate a hash value, and if it matches the hash which was generated for that certificate, then the certificate is validated.
- Now the user can view and print the certificate in Braille or in plain English.
- All the actions get stored in the blockchain through metamask from logging in to clicking the submit button, and we can see the blocks in Ganache. This maintains security as each transaction is stored in the blockchain and cannot be altered, and everyone can see those transactions, so the proof of work principle is maintained.

4.1. Flowchart

Figure 1 describes the flowchart of the proposed System and about using metamask; the System starts by allocating an ID to each user and administrator. After that, we can log in using user, admin, or institute. If we log in as a user, we can use voice commands to pass the certificate identification process. If the voice commands are recognized, the certificate is verified and can then be printed in Braille or general form. For admins, we can add institutes and courses, and if we log in as an institute, we can issue certificates.

4.2. Proposed Methodology Description

We have built a local blockchain using Ganache. Ganache provides us with ten accounts for administration and the institute. Each of these accounts has a private key, an account address, and 100 either.

When using the metamask extension, we import one account in order to access and log in to the admin page. We can manage our accounts using Metamask, which allows us to import and delete accounts. We may browse and change the admin page after we've imported the account.

Administrators can add or remove courses that are available to institutions as well as verify institutes so they can award certificates to students. Each procedure has its own transaction charge and gas fee, both of which must be accepted through metamask. And you can check in Ganache to see how much was taken out of the account that we are utilizing. As a result, each transaction is recorded in the blockchain, which is visible in Ganache's block column. Each account can also check to see if the transaction is legitimate. We cannot access the website in addition to this security feature unless we log in with the correct account.

The smart contracts that were developed in Solidity were compiled and migrated using Truffle.

React, HTML and CSS are used to build the front end.

To get the account address from Metamask and put it in the JSON file, we again used Web3.

Figure 1. Flowchart of proposed system

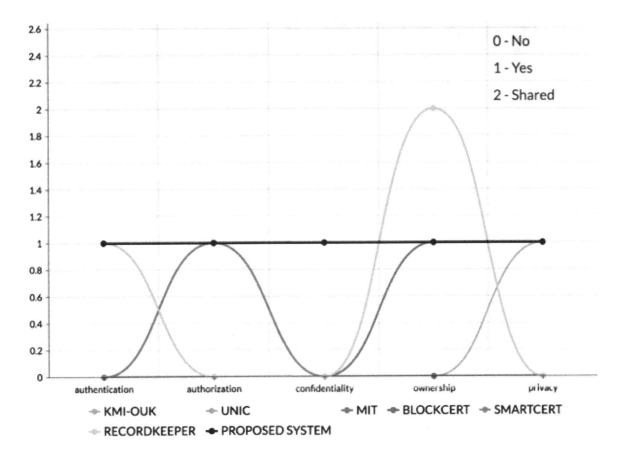

5. RESULTS AND DISCUSSIONS

Figure 2 describes viewing the braille certificate of employers by using the proposed system.

Figure 3 describes viewing the regular certificate of employers by using the proposed system.

Figure 4 describes the braille certificate of employers using the proposed system.

We have developed a blockchain-based certificate verification system for blind individuals. Therefore, we use blockchain to store certificates, and we then create braille certificates for blind individuals in addition to creating regular certificates for everyone else.

5.1. System Testing

Table 2 shows the validation process of the proposed System. ˙

The issue of phony certificates, which results in ineligible students receiving jobs and other confidentiality difficulties, is one of the reasons that despite thousands of job possibilities being created every year, many graduates still find themselves unemployed. The System is built in such a way that it introduces Digital Academic Certificates and offers a Highly Secure Blockchain-Based Storage Ar-

Figure 2. View the braille certificate page

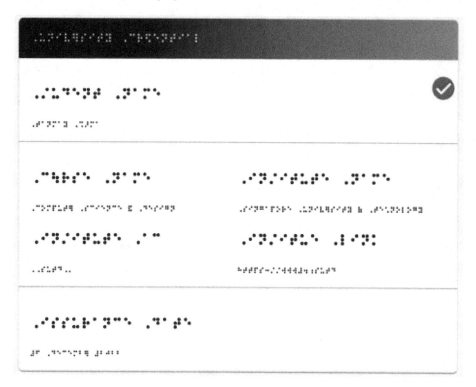

Figure 3. Regular certificate

Figure 4. Braille certificate

Table 2. System validation

Input	Expected Output
Invalid user Id	User not found
Valid user Id	Certificate Details

chitecture to store these certificates since data in a blockchain is immutable, eliminating the effect of fraudulent certificates.

The ability to create immutable ledgers is one of blockchain's primary features. This behavior helps us develop a system in which each stage of the procedure is clear and unchangeable. For our blockchain-based concept, we have proposed a paper-saving method that would let the user check and validate the certificate.

Users may easily maintain digital certificates with the help of this System, which also ensures the accuracy and security of data.

The certificate can be converted to Braille for blind people, and voice commands can be used to visit this website.

The graph in Figure 5 compares various existing works with our proposed work.

The Knowledge Media Institute (KMI) of the Open University UK has begun to use labels, certificates, and online status using blockchain as a reliable record.

Figure 5. Comparison graph

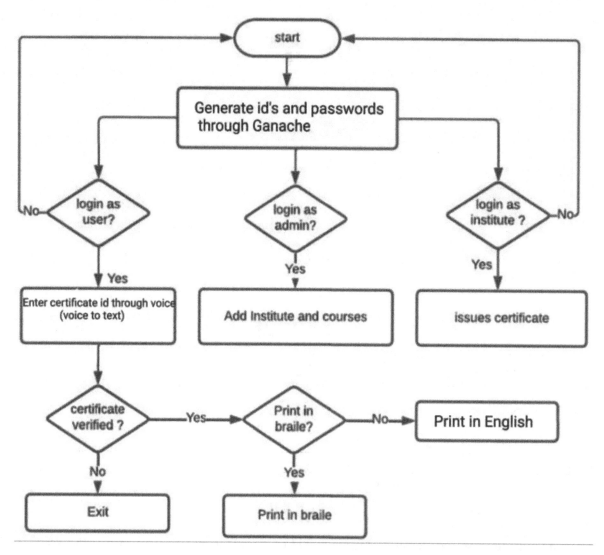

The major aims of KIM's work are to develop blockchain for use in UK higher education credentials and to pioneer blockchain projects in higher education.

The University of Nicosia (UNIC) utilizes the Bitcoin chain in a number of ways, including accepting Bitcoin as payment for the cost of any degree course and issuing academic certificates on the blockchain.

The University of Nicosia's initiative to create educational diplomas on the blockchain aims to combat financial fraud against international students.

The MIT Media Lab uses Blockcerts to provide digital certificates to student organizations, giving recipients more control over the certifications they obtain. The storing, verifying, and validating of credentials by the project's beneficiaries is not permitted to be delegated to a third-party intermediary. The blockchain transaction's hash is stored in the issuer's digital certificate after it has been signed, which is the foundation of the MIT certification architecture.

6. CONCLUSION

In a different project, apps are created using the open standard Blockcerts to validate academic credentials, professional credentials, and other types of certifications based on blockchain technology. The foundation of Blockcerts, which provides tools for creating, issuing, accessing, and verifying certificates in the blockchain, is each participant's self-sovereign identification. Blockcerts does not provide a separate service to certify the authenticity of certificates, despite the fact that certificates stored in the blockchain cannot be changed. Consequently, it is possible to forge the certificate. Another tool for verifying digital credentials based on Blockchain is SmartCert. A blockchain-based system called SmartCert was created to verify the legitimacy of academic credentials and solve the issue of false certificates. To ensure recruiting transparency, SmartCert uses cryptographic signing of educational certificates. Records Keeper is an additional blockchain-based tool for validating academic credentials. Educational institutions can issue certificates using RecordsKeeper and give the user a receipt they can use to show the certificate is genuine to a foreign entity. Using the receipt they obtained from the student, the foreign entity will examine the validity of the certificate in the RecordKeeper ledger. The proposed model can be used for future work on a test network and perform a security test on that network to identify flaws. Also, Add additional voice automation features to the current model.

REFERENCES

Arslan, F., Singh, B., Sharma, D. K., Regin, R., Steffi, R., & Suman Rajest, S. (2021). Optimization technique approach to resolve food sustainability problems. In *2021 International Conference on Computational Intelligence and Knowledge Economy (ICCIKE)*. IEEE. 10.1109/ICCIKE51210.2021.9410735

Bansal, V., Pandey, S., Shukla, S. K., Singh, D., Rathod, S. A., & Gonzáles, J. L. A. (2022). A frame work of security attacks, issues classifications and configuration strategy for IoT networks for the successful implementation. In *2022 5th International Conference on Contemporary Computing and Informatics (IC3I)*. IEEE.

Billah, S. N., Pollobe, R., Hossain, F., Abir, N. M., Zarin, A. Z., & Mridha, M. F. (2021). Blockchain based architecture for certificate authentication. SSRN *Electronic Journal*. doi:10.2139/ssrn.3842788

Fonseka, O. D., & Sasanka, N. (2018). Blind Draw-A software solution for image identification and artistic skills for visually impaired people using braille. In *2018 3rd International Conference on Information Technology Research (ICITR)* (pp. 1–6). IEEE.

Garba, A., Chen, Z., Guan, Z., & Srivastava, G. (2021). LightLedger: A novel blockchain-based domain certificate authentication and validation scheme. *IEEE Transactions on Network Science and Engineering*, *8*(2), 1698–1710. doi:10.1109/TNSE.2021.3069128

Gayathiri, A., Jayachitra, J., & Matilda, S. (2020). Certificate validation using blockchain. In *2020 7th International Conference on Smart Structures and Systems (ICSSS)*. IEEE.

Gunturu, V., Bansal, V., Sathe, M., Kumar, A., Gehlot, A., & Pant, B. (2023). Wireless communications implementation using blockchain as well as distributed type of IOT. In *2023 International Conference on Artificial Intelligence and Smart Communication (AISC)*. IEEE. 10.1109/AISC56616.2023.10085249

Gupta, A., Patel, N., & Khan, S. (2014). Automatic speech recognition technique for voice command. In *2014 International Conference on Science Engineering and Management Research (ICSEMR)*. IEEE. 10.1109/ICSEMR.2014.7043641

Gurumurthy, G., Krishna, V. B. M., & Yadlapati, K. (2021). A fractional order controller design for a class of linear systems. In *2021 IEEE Kansas Power and Energy Conference (KPEC)*. IEEE. 10.1109/KPEC51835.2021.9446215

Hassan, M. Y., & Mohammed, A. G. (2011). Conversion of English characters into braille using neural network. *IJCCCE, 11*(2), 30–37.

Jha, V., & Parvathi, K. (2019). Braille Transliteration of hindi handwritten texts using machine learning for character recognition. *Int J Sci Technol Res, 8,* 1188–1193.

Kandhari, M. S., Zulkemine, F., & Isah, H. (2018). A voice controlled E-commerce web application. In *2018 IEEE 9th Annual Information Technology, Electronics and Mobile Communication Conference (IEMCON)*. IEEE.

Kanjalkar, J., Kanjalkar, P., Deshmukh, T., Deshmukh, J., Dhamal, P., & Bhalerao, A. (2022). A Novel System for AYUSH Healthcare Services using Classification and Regression. *International Journal on Recent and Innovation Trends in Computing and Communication, 10*(1), 232–240. doi:10.17762/ijritcc.v10i1s.5830

Krishna, B. V., Jhansi, P. S., Shama, A., Boya Leelambika, C., & Prakash, B. V. V. N. (2019). Novel Solution to Improve Mental Health by Integrating Music and IoT with Neural Feedback. *Journal of Computer Information Systems, 3*(5), 234–239.

Kulkarni, J. B., Sheela, M., & Chetty, R. (2019). Depth Analysis of Single View Image Objects based on Object Detection and Focus Measure. *International Journal of Advanced Trends in Computer Science and Engineering, 5*(8), 2608–2612. doi:10.30534/ijatcse/2019/112852019

Ogunmola, G. A., Singh, B., Sharma, D. K., Regin, R., Rajest, S. S., & Singh, N. (2021). Involvement of distance measure in assessing and resolving efficiency environmental obstacles. In *2021 International Conference on Computational Intelligence and Knowledge Economy (ICCIKE)*. IEEE. 10.1109/ICCIKE51210.2021.9410765

Pakala, C., Sekhar, S., & Shinde, G. (2018). Krishna BV Murali "An Optimized Operation of Hybrid Wind/Battery/PV-System based Micro grid by using Particle Swarm Optimization Technique.". *Journal of Computer Information Systems, 14*(5), 79–84.

Pande, S., & Chetty, M. S. R. (2018). Analysis of Capsule Network (Capsnet) Architectures and Applications. *Journal of Advanced Research in Dynamical and Control Systems, 10*(10), 2765–2771.

Pande, S., & Chetty, M. S. R. (2019). Bezier Curve Based Medicinal Leaf Classification using Capsule Network. *International Journal of Advanced Trends in Computer Science and Engineering, 8*(6), 2735–2742. doi:10.30534/ijatcse/2019/09862019

Pande, S. D., & Chetty, M. S. R. (2021) Fast Medicinal Leaf Retrieval Using CapsNet. In *International Conference on Intelligent and Smart Computing in Data Analytics. Advances in Intelligent Systems and Computing* (vol. 1312). 10.1007/978-981-33-6176-8_16

Pandya, S., Gadekallu, T. R., Reddy, P. K., Wang, W., & Alazab, M. (2022). InfusedHeart: A novel knowledge-infused learning framework for diagnosis of cardiovascular events. *IEEE Transactions on Computational Social Systems*, 1–10. doi:10.1109/TCSS.2022.3151643

Pidikiti, T., Shreedevi, B, G., Subbarao, M., & Krishna, V. B. M. (2023). Design and control of Takagi-Sugeno-Kang fuzzy based inverter for power quality improvement in grid-tied PV systems. Measurement. *Sensors (Basel)*, *25*(100638). doi:10.1016/j.measen.2022.100638

Ramesh, B., Suhashini, G., Kalnoor, M., Bollapragada, D., & Rao, B. (2017). Cost Optimization by Integrating PV-System and Battery Energy Storage System into Microgrid using Particle Swarm Optimization. *International Journal of Pure and Applied Mathematics*, *114*(8), 45–55.

Ravinder, M., & Kulkarni, V. (2023a). A review on cyber security and anomaly detection perspectives of smart grid. In *2023 5th International Conference on Smart Systems and Inventive Technology (ICSSIT)*. IEEE.

Ravinder, M., & Kulkarni, V. (2023b). Intrusion detection in smart meters data using machine learning algorithms: A research report. *Frontiers in Energy Research*, *11*, 1147431. Advance online publication. doi:10.3389/fenrg.2023.1147431

Saleh, O. S., & Osman Ghazali, M. E. (2020). Blockchain based framework for educational certificates verification. *Journal of Critical Reviews*, *7*(03), 79–84.

Sharma, D. K., Jalil, N. A., Regin, R., Rajest, S. S., Tummala, R. K., & Thangadurai. (2021). Predicting network congestion with machine learning. In *2021 2nd International Conference on Smart Electronics and Communication (ICOSEC)*. IEEE.

Sonnad, S., Sathe, M., Basha, D. K., Bansal, V., Singh, R., & Singh, D. P. (2022). The integration of connectivity and system integrity approaches using internet of things (IoT) for enhancing network security. In *2022 5th International Conference on Contemporary Computing and Informatics (IC3I)*. IEEE.

Suthar, V., Bansal, V., Reddy, C. S., Gonzáles, J. L. A., Singh, D., & Singh, D. P. (2022). Machine Learning Adoption in Blockchain-Based Smart Applications. In *2022 5th International Conference on Contemporary Computing and Informatics (IC3I)*. IEEE.

Uike, D., Agarwalla, S., Bansal, V., Chakravarthi, M. K., Singh, R., & Singh, P. (2022). Investigating the role of block chain to secure identity in IoT for industrial automation. In *2022 11th International Conference on System Modeling & Advancement in Research Trends (SMART)*. IEEE.

Ummuhanysifa, U., & Banu, P. K. (2013). Voice based search engine and web page reader. *International Journal of Computational Engineering Research*, 1–5.

Vashishtha, E., Sherman, L., Sajjad, T., & Mehmood, N. (2020). Use of anti-viral therapy in treatment of Covid 19. *Journal of Advanced Medical and Dental Sciences Research*, *8*(11), 273–276.

Veeraiah, V., Pankajam, A., Vashishtha, E., Dhabliya, D., Karthikeyan, P., & Chandan, R. R. (2022). Efficient COVID-19 identification using deep learning for IoT. In *2022 5th International Conference on Contemporary Computing and Informatics (IC3I)*. IEEE.

Chapter 12
Explainable Deep Reinforcement Learning for Knowledge Graph Reasoning

Di Wang

 https://orcid.org/0000-0002-7992-7743
University of Illinois at Chicago, USA

ABSTRACT

Artificial intelligence faces a considerable challenge in automated reasoning, particularly in inferring missing data from existing observations. Knowledge graph (KG) reasoning can significantly enhance the performance of context-aware AI systems such as GPT. Deep reinforcement learning (DRL), an influential framework for sequential decision-making, exhibits strength in managing uncertain and dynamic environments. Definitions of state space, action space, and reward function in DRL directly dictate the performances. This chapter provides an overview of the pipeline and advantages of leveraging DRL for knowledge graph reasoning. It delves deep into the challenges of KG reasoning and features of existing studies. This chapter offers a comparative study of widely used state spaces, action spaces, reward functions, and neural networks. Furthermore, it evaluates the pros and cons of DRL-based methodologies and compares the performances of nine benchmark models across six unique datasets and four evaluation metrics.

INTRODUCTION

Knowledge Graphs (KG) are structured representations of entities and relationships with the graph format, which enables knowledge graphs to efficiently comprehend complicated information like human cognitive processes. The most recent application is the combination of knowledge graph reasoning and large language models (Carta et al., 2023; Meyer et al., 2023; Trajanoska et al., 2023). Knowledge graph reasoning is an inference-making and summarization process according to the structured information collected in the KG. Knowledge graph reasoning is widely applied in question-answering, information retrieval, and recommendation systems. Knowledge graph reasoning aims to find missing information in

DOI: 10.4018/978-1-6684-9189-8.ch012

the form of 'entity-relation-entity' knowledge triple (h, r, t). The head entity h has the relation r with the tail entity t. For example, given the KG and the query (h, r, ?), the value of t will be inferred. In detail, the objective is to model the probabilistic distribution and learn explicit inference formulas (Liu et al., 2022).

The difficulties and challenges in KN reasoning include the following items:

1. Knowledge graphs often include missing links and entities, which require the ability to predict the missing values.
2. Knowledge graphs often include incorrect or noisy, or misleading information for reasoning tasks.
3. The size of the knowledge graph increases exponentially as the number of entities increases. Scanning and abstracting large knowledge graphs efficiently is difficult.
4. It is necessary to infer indirect relationships. For example, if A is related to B, and B is related to C, then A is related to C.
5. The reasoning process should be logically consistent.
6. Uncertain and dynamic data are embedded in knowledge graphs.
7. The reasoning process needs to be interpretable and explainable for users' trust.

Existing research can be divided into three categories, Rule-based, Embedding-based, and Path-based algorithms, based on the way of inference (X. Wang et al., 2022). For the rule-based method, the idea is to design rules to capture patterns and dependencies for predicting missing information. The quality of predefined rules directly determines the performance of algorithms. Namely, domain knowledge is required. For the embedding-based method, the idea is to learn how to represent entities and relationships data as continuous embedding vectors within low-dimensional spaces. The following inferences and prediction works are based on the learned embedding vectors. For example, similarity methods can be taken to fetch related entities or links. A lot of related works are proposed in this research field, including translation models, graph neural networks, convolutional neural networks, attention mechanisms, and adversarial training. A lot of details will be discussed in the Section 'RELATED WORK.' For the path-based method, multiple patterns and dependencies are explored by traversing paths from one entity to another via the links. In this way, complicated and deep relationships can be learned.

On the other hand, the knowledge graph reasoning algorithms can be categorized as single-hop reasoning and multiple-hop reasoning based on the number of intermediate hops in traversing entities (Zhou et al., 2021). For the single-hop knowledge graph reasoning, only the direct connection is studied. For example, if A is related to B and B is related to C, single-hop reasoning infers the relationship between A and C without considering any intermediate nodes. For multiple-hop reasoning, multiple paths are studied. For example, if A is related to B, B is related to C, and C is related to D, multiple-hop reasoning studies the path from A to D.

Deep reinforcement learning (DRL) shows great success in many applications, like task planning (D. Wang et al., 2022; Wang et al., 2018), energy management (Mason and Grijalva, 2019; Yun et al., 2023), etc. Because of the ability to make sequential decisions, DRL shows great potential to model reasoning systems on a KG. Specifically, an agent can sequentially explore the inference path along the KG until reaching the target. As shown in Figure 1, KG serves as the environment. State space is composed of current and tail entities. Action space is defined as the relation between the current and tail entities. The reward function is well-hand-made based on the specific problem. More definitions of states, actions, and rewards are discussed later in this chapter.

Deep Reinforcement learning aims to maximize the received cumulative rewards. The mathematic basis of reinforcement learning is Markov Decision Process (MDP), involving four essential concepts, state, action, reward, and transaction. In general, the agent observes the environment to generate the state. Using tables as memory or neural networks as policy approximators, the agent takes near-optimal actions. Environments evaluate actions and give rewards to the agent. The state transition probability denotes the probability of moving the current state to the next state with the current action. Typically, it is assumed that the transition function is static in the knowledge graph reasoning problem. By taking advantage of neural networks in powerful representation abilities, Deep reinforcement learning can solve complex problems with large state space and action space (Wang, 2023). Besides, DRL has advantages in solving problems with high uncertainties and dynamics. Once the algorithm is trained, knowledge graph reasoning issues can be solved quickly.

The advantages of using DRL in KG reasoning involve the following:

1. Knowledge graph reasoning can be viewed as a sequence of decision-making processes. DRL is designed for sequential decision-making problems.
2. Knowledge graphs are embedded with uncertainty and dynamics, which may evolve with additional new entities and relationships. DRL can handle dynamics and uncertainties easily and adapt to new changes fast once the agent is well-trained.
3. DRL can solve partially observable problems. Data in knowledge graphs are often incomplete and partially observed.
4. With the power of neural networks, DRL can learn complex patterns and dependencies in the knowledge graph.
5. DRL can generate near-optimal solutions, which are important for making accurate inferences.
6. DRL is of good generalization ability, which can make inferences on unseen or scarce data. Namely, DRL can reason about entities and relationships that are not explicitly shown in the KG.

Figure 1. Schematic diagram of DRL framework for KG reasoning

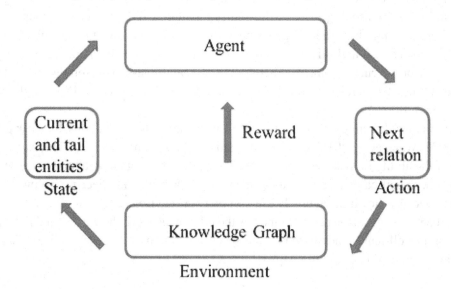

7. DRL can show users the reason for decision-making procedures through the state values or the state-action values. Especially when the graph neural networks are taken, DRL has better explanation abilities.

This chapter aims to demonstrate the pipeline and advantages of DRL-based KG reasoning. To solve practical problems with DRL, the first step is to rebuild the problem as a Markov Decision Process problem. In this step, the definitions of state space, action space, and reward functions directly determine the final performances. The second step is to select the proper algorithms and neural network architectures based on the studied problem. There are a series of DRL approaches that are designed for different applications. Besides, different neural networks have different features for solving different problems. In this chapter, different ways of state space, action space, reward functions, and neural network architectures are explored to show different characteristics.

The foundation of this chapter is as follows: Section 'RELATED WORK' presents existing research works about KG reasoning with DRL. Section 'FOUNDATION OF DEEP REINFORCEMENT LEARNING' illustrates the mathematical basics of reinforcement learning. Section 'FOUNDATION OF KNOWLEDGE GRAPH,' presents the mathematical basics of the knowledge graph. Section' KNOWLEDGE GRAPH REASONING WITH DRL' defines the state, action, reward space, and popular training architectures. Section 'RESULTS' shows performances of nine baselines on six datasets. Section 'DISCUSSION' analyzes the details of experiment results and features of each approach. Section 'LIMITATIONS' discusses the limitations of the mentioned works. Section 'CONCLUSION' summarizes this chapter and talks about future works.

RELATED WORK

Researchers introduce heuristics like logic rules into graph reasoning to boost performance. Galarraga et al. (Galárraga et al., 2013) prove that inductive logic programming can assist in building logical rules for KG. Zhou et al. (Zhou et al., 2021) propose reward reshaping functions to capture hierarchical information, including the metric of hyperbolic and a penalty strategy to constrain the sufficiency of multi-hop reasoning paths. Qu et al. (Qu et al., 2020) take logic rules as the latent variable. In the E-step of the EM algorithm, a set of high-quality rules is selected from the rule generator. In the M-step, the rule generator is updated with selected rules. Xia et al. (Xia et al., 2022) study the sparse KG problems where rules are taken to extract feasible paths, and DRL is taken to traverse these paths. Lei et al. (Lei et al., 2020) utilize symbolic-based methods to generate rules to guide reward engineering.

Deep learning increases the representation ability vastly. Translational models are an important series of approaches, including TransE(Bordes et al., 2013), TransH(Wang et al., 2014), TransR(Lin et al., 2015) and etc. These models represent relationships as translation vectors between the embeddings of the participating entities. TransE (Bordes et al., 2013) maps the head and tail entities and relations into a low-dimensional continuous vector space and then compares the distance between $\|t\text{-}h\|$ and $\|r\|$. TransD (Ji et al., 2015) is proposed for solving many-to-one or one-to-many relations. OPTransE (Zhu et al., 2019) projects the head entity and tail entity of relations into different spaces to track the order of relations in paths. Besides, multiple nonlinear combinations of path features are added through a strategy pool. The limitations of these models are discussed in detail in Section 'Limitations'.

Information can be encoded efficiently by traversing the knowledge graph. PRA (Lao et al., 2011) uses the random walk with restarts to perform multiple bounded depth-first search processes in the discrete space. The bottleneck for random walk inference is that super nodes connecting to many formulas will create huge fan-out areas that significantly slow down the inference and affect the accuracy. The limitation of random walk-based approaches is discussed in detail in Section 'LIMITATIONS.' Besides, several existing works combine DRL with path-based knowledge graph reasoning. Xiong et al. (Xiong et al., 2017) use a translation-based knowledge-based embedding method to encode the continuous state of RL. The agent takes incremental steps by sampling a relation to the extent of the path. The rewards are designed with a proposed diversity metric. Random walks are intractable with an unknown destination and combinatorial paths from a starting node. Das et al. (Das et al., 2017) navigate the graph conditioned on the input query aiming to find predictive paths with RL. Lin et al. (Lin et al., 2018) use random edge masks to boost the exploration ability and a pre-trained model to estimate the rewards. Tiwari et al. (Tiwari et al., 2021) propose a distance-aware reward shaping function to assign different rewards to the different vertex in the graph. Besides, a graph self-attention mechanism is taken to entity information effectively. Most existing works focus on relation selection. To study the impacts of entity selection, Li et al. (Li et al., 2018) utilize two agents for relation selection and entity selection, respectively, for complex path reasoning tasks. Moreover, most existing works use the pretraining strategy and lack the memory mechanism, causing reusing known paths and overfitting issues. Zhu et al. (Zhu et al., 2021) introduce the Bellman-Ford algorithm into path searching, and a Neural Bellman-Ford Network is proposed to generate paths. Wang et al. (Wang et al., 2019) propose an AttnPath model with LSTM and Graph Attention Mechanism to memory visited paths. Besides, the mean selection rate and mean replacement rate are utilized. Other temporal works include (Li et al., 2022; Mavromatis et al., 2022; Zhao et al., 2022). The limitation of DRL-based approaches is discussed in detail in Section 'LIMITATIONS.'

Recently, a momentous transformation has been unfolding worldwide, driven by the emergence of advanced generative large language models (LLMs), like GPT. The reinforcement learning from human feedback (RLHF) technique is widely used in the GPT training process (Zheng et al., 2023), which is outside of this chapter. The combination of the large language model and knowledge graph attracts increasing attention. Researchers try to use LLMs for multi-step reasoning with the technique of Chain-of-Thought (Wei et al., 2022). Specifically, Trajanoska et al. (2023) prove that LLM models, like REBEL, can improve the accuracy of extracting knowledge graphs from unstructured text. Meyer et al. (2023) study the hallucinate issue in generating KG with ChatGPT model. Carta et al. (2023) prove that even without fine-tuning and zero-shot examples, a series of appropriately defined prompts can generate a complete KG. Choudhary and Reddy (2023) propose a new method called language-guided abstract reasoning over knowledge graphs (LARK) for scanning subgraphs of KG and organizing a proper reasoning chain. Sun et al. (2023) prove that the utilization of multiple reasoning paths can further boost LLM performance.

FOUNDATION OF DEEP REINFORCEMENT LEARNING

The essential concept of DRL is the return value, which is calculated as the discounted accumulated rewards r as Eq. (1). Rewards are functions of state s and action a,

$$R_t^\gamma = \sum_{i=t}^{\infty} \gamma^{i-t} r(s_i, a_i), 0 < \gamma < 1 \tag{1}$$

where γ is the discounted coefficient. Two main approximators of the return values are the value function and the state-action value function. Different series of DRL algorithms are built on these two concepts. The difference is the existence of the initial action. In detail, value function $V^\pi(s)$ is defined as Eq. (2), and state-action value function $Q^\pi(s, a)$ is defined as Eq. (3). The transition among these two values is defined as Eq. (4) (Wang et al., 2022).

$$V^\pi(s) = \mathbb{E}[\sum_{t=0}^{\infty} \gamma^t r(s_t) \mid \pi, s_0 = s] \tag{2}$$

$$Q^\pi(s, a) = \mathbb{E}[\sum_{t=0}^{\infty} \gamma^t r(s_t, a_t) \mid \pi, s_0 = s, a_0 = a] \tag{3}$$

$$V^\pi(s) = max_a Q^\pi(s, a) \tag{4}$$

where s_0 and a_0 are the given initial state and action, π is the policy taken by the agent. Here, Deep Q-networks (DQN) and Advantage Actor Critic (A2C) are taken as examples to illustrate the training process(Wang, 2022).

DQN: DQN updates Q values by selecting the action with the maximum original Q value.

$$Q(s_t, a_t) \leftarrow Q(s_t, a_t) + \alpha[r_t + \gamma max_{a'} Q(s_{t+1}, a') - Q(s_t, a_t)] \tag{5}$$

where α is the learning rate. The Q network is parameterized by θ, which is updated by Eq. (6) with the experience replay buffer D. The target Q network is parameterized by θ'.

$$L(\theta_i) = \mathbb{E}_{(s_t, a_t, r_t, s_{t+1}) \sim D}[(r_t + \gamma max_{a'} Q_{\theta_i}(s_{t+1}, a') - Q_{\theta_i}(s_t, a_t))^2] \tag{6}$$

A2C: A2C updates policies by maximizing the log likelihood with the advantage value as Eq. (7), which can stabilize the training process.

$$\nabla_\theta J(\pi_\theta) = \mathbb{E}_{\pi_\theta}[\sum_{t=0}^{H} \nabla_\theta log \pi_\theta(a_t \mid s_t) A_\omega(s_t, a_t)] \tag{7}$$

where $A_\omega(s_t, a_t) = \mathbb{E}[r_{t+1} + \gamma V_\omega(s_{t+1}) - V_\omega(s_t)]$. The actor network is parameterized by θ while the critic network is parameterized by ω. Besides, A2C is a kind of online algorithm without the help of the experience replay buffer.

FOUNDATION OF KNOWLEDGE GRAPH

Let [X] represent the integer set {1, 2, ..., X}. The knowledge graph is represented by {(h, r, t)}, where each tuple consists of a head entity h, a relation r, and a tail entity t. The objective is to predict the target entity for a given query of source entity and relation, q: = (h, r, ?) (Bansal et al., 2019). As shown in Figure 2, a knowledge graph example with 6 entities can be represented as {(A, G, E), (B, H, E), (B, I, C), (C, J, D), (D, K, F), (E, L, F)}. Assume the current node is B, and there are two available edges, Relation H to Entity E and Relation I to Entity C. By exploring the KG, the relationship between the current node and any other node can be reasoned.

KNOWLEDGE GRAPH REASONING WITH DRL

The first step of KG reasoning is to build a Markov Decision Process model. The environment denotes the KG and keeps consistent in the training process. The definitions of the state, action, and reward functions influence performances directly. Table 1 and Table 2 present common state spaces and rewards definitions, respectively. Besides, action spaces denote the relation paths that the agent can take. Here, the invalid actions mean that the current node has no available relations. As shown in Table 1, the embeddings of the current entity node and the difference between the embeddings of the current entity node and the target entity node are necessary. Other available choices are visited paths, and KG structures. The designs of the rewards vary largely for specific problems. Some works select the simple step rewards while others design complicated episode rewards considering the matching rate of generated actions with the ground truth, the path length, and the diversity of the path.

Figure 2. A knowledge graph example

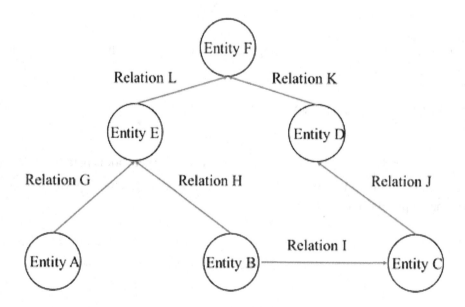

Table 1. State spaces definitions

Algorithms	State
(Xiong et al., 2017)	{embeddings of the current entity node, difference between the embeddings of the current entity node and the target entity node}
(Das et al., 2017)	{embeddings of the query, embeddings of the answer, the location of the exploration}
(Lin et al., 2018)	{visited entities, the source entity, the query relation}
(Tiwari et al., 2021)	{embeddings of the current entity node, difference between the embeddings of the current entity node and the target entity node, the graph neighborhood representation}
(Wang et al., 2019)	{embeddings of the current entity node, difference between the embeddings of the current entity node and the target entity node, the hidden state of LSTM, graph self-attention of the current entity node}
(Xia et al., 2022)	{embeddings of the current entity node, historical searching paths}

Table 2. Reward functions definitions

Algorithms	Reward
(Xiong et al., 2017)	Episode reward: global accuracy rewards + path efficiency (extra rewards for short paths)
(Das et al., 2017)	Step reward: +1, if the current node is in the correct path
(Lin et al., 2018)	Step reward: +1, if the current node is in the correct path
(Tiwari et al., 2021)	Step reward: the distance-aware factor + global reward factor $$r_i = r_{global}\left(k_1 \ln i + b\right)\left(k_2\left[\sum_{i=1}^{n} p(i)\right]^{\tau}\right)$$
(Wang et al., 2019)	Episode reward: ConvE reward (Dettmers et al., 2018) + path diversity + penalty
(Xia et al., 2022)	Step reward: +1, if the current node is in the correct path

With a well-designed MDP model, the next step is to design neural network architectures. As shown in Figure 3 (Wang et al., 2019), a three-layer long short-term memory (LSTM) memorizes actions taken before. The hidden state h_t of LSTM at time t can be calculated as Eq. (8).

$$h_t = \text{LSTM}\left(h_{t-1}, m_t\right)]$$
(8)

m_t is the concatenation of the current node's embedding and the difference between the current node's embedding and the target node's embedding. Besides, the inference should focus on relations and neighbors related to the query relations. A single-layer graph attention (GAT) calculates attention weights for the information ensemble as (9-10).

$$a_{ij} = \frac{\exp\left(\text{ReLU}\left(\vec{a}\left[w_{e_i}, w_{e_j}\right]\right)\right)}{\sum_{k \in N_i} \text{ReLU}\left(\vec{a}\left[w_{e_i}, w_{e_j}\right]\right)}$$
(9)

$$a_i = \sum_{k \in N_i} a_{ik} w_{e_k}$$
(10)

where $\vec{a}$ is shared weight vector over all entities. Figure 4 illustrates how to implement reasoning on the knowledge graph. The current node is h, while the target node is t. Leaving from the current node h, the agent explores two potential available paths. When considering the path length in the reward function, the reward of path-1 is generally higher than the one of path-2. The pseudocode is shown in Algorithm 1. According to Wang et al. (2019), the suggested embedding dimension is 100. The suggested LSTM hidden dimension is 200, and the suggested attention dimension is 100.

RESULTS

This section compares the performances of existing RL algorithms and traditional approaches on popular datasets like FB15K-237, NELL-995 NELL23K. FB15K-237 is proposed by (Toutanova et al., 2015) with 310116 triples. NELL-995 is proposed by (Xiong et al., 2017) with 154213 triples. NELL-23K is proposed

Figure 3. LSTM and graph attention as memory components

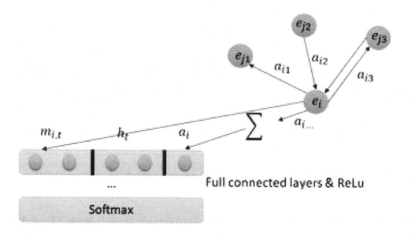

Figure 4. Schematic diagram of reasoning path

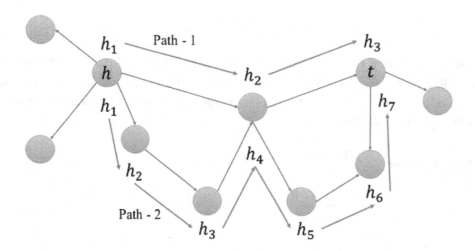

by (Lv et al., 2020). Datasets are available at https://github.com/wenhuchen/KB-Reasoning-Data. In order to simulate low-resource environments, FB15K-237-10%, FB15K-237-20%, FB15K-237-50% denote 10%, 20%, and 50% triples of data are kept, which are similar to (Xia et al., 2022). Table 3 presents the number of entities, relations, facts, and the mean values of outgoing and incoming edges of a node in the KG.

In order to evaluate the performance of state-of-art approaches, four evaluation metrics are taken to show the quality of approaches, including the mean reciprocal rank (MRR) of all correct entities and the proportion of correct entities that rank no longer than N, which are similar to (Xia et al., 2022).

$$MRR = \frac{1}{N} \sum_i \frac{1}{rank_i} \tag{11}$$

$$Hit@K = \sum_i 1(rank_i < K) / N \tag{12}$$

Where $rank_i$ denotes the rank of the correct entity i.

DISCUSSION

Table 4 shows the performances of four baselines (Das et al., 2017; Dettmers et al., 2018; Trouillon et al., 2016; Yang et al., 2014) in two datasets (FB15K-237, NELL-995). It clearly shows that the MRR

Table 3. Datasets details

	#entities	#relations	#facts	#degree avg.
NELL-995	75,492	200	154,213	4.07
NELL23K	22,927	202	35,359	2.23
FB15K-237	14,505	237	272,115	19.74
FB15K-237-10%	11,514	237	60,986	5.91
FB15K-237-20%	13,168	237	91,163	7.54
FB15K-237-50%	14,143	237	173,836	13.15

Table 4. Comparison among different methods

	Algorithm	HITS@1	HITS@3	HITS@10	MRR
FB15K-237	(Das et al., 2017)	16.9	24.8	35.7	22.7
	(Yang et al., 2014)	27.5	41.7	56.8	37.0
	(Trouillon et al., 2016)	30.3	43.4	57.2	39.4
	(Dettmers et al., 2018)	31.3	45.7	60.0	41.0
NELL-995	(Das et al., 2017)	30.0	41.7	49.7	37.1
	(Yang et al., 2014)	61.0	73.3	79.5	68.0
	(Trouillon et al., 2016)	61.2	76.1	82.7	69.4
	(Dettmers et al., 2018)	67.2	80.8	86.4	74.7

Table 5. Comparison among different methods with low-resource environments

	Algorithm	HITS@3	HITS@10	MRR
FB15K-237-10%	(Xia et al., 2022)	24.5	35.0	22.8
	(Galárraga et al., 2013)	7.0	13.1	6.3
	(Lei et al., 2020)	15.4	21.9	17.8
	(Zhu et al., 2021)	26.3	38.8	24.1
	(Lv et al., 2020)	23.9	33.7	21.8
FB15K-237-20%	(Xia et al., 2022)	27.7	39.1	25.2
	(Galárraga et al., 2013)	10.9	17.1	10.7
	(Lei et al., 2020)	24.1	31.9	22.9
	(Zhu et al., 2021)	27.8	41.7	26.0
	(Lv et al., 2020)	27.2	38.9	24.2
FB15K-237-50%	(Xia et al., 2022)	32.0	46.2	29.2
	(Galárraga et al., 2013)	19.4	25.6	18.0
	(Lei et al., 2020)	29.7	44.5	28.2
	(Zhu et al., 2021)	34.1	50.3	31.6
	(Lv et al., 2020)	32.0	45.7	29.3
NELL23K	(Xia et al., 2022)	22.2	33.9	20.3
	(Galárraga et al., 2013)	14.1	24.7	13.3
	(Lei et al., 2020)	19.9	29.9	18.3
	(Zhu et al., 2021)	28.9	46.9	27.4
	(Lv et al., 2020)	20.0	31.6	19.7

score of (Dettmers et al., 2018) is 80.6% higher than (Das et al., 2017), 10.8% higher than (Yang et al., 2014), 4.1% higher than (Trouillon et al., 2016); the HITS@10 score of (Dettmers et al., 2018) is 68.1% higher than (Das et al., 2017), 5.6% higher than (Yang et al., 2014), 4.9% higher than (Trouillon et al., 2016) in FB15K-237 dataset. Besides, the MRR score of (Dettmers et al., 2018) is 101.3% higher than (Das et al., 2017), 9.9% higher than (Yang et al., 2014), 7.6% higher than (Trouillon et al., 2016). The HITS@3 score of (Dettmers et al., 2018) is 93.8% higher than (Das et al., 2017), 10.2% higher than (Yang et al., 2014), 6.2% higher than (Trouillon et al., 2016) in NELL-995 dataset. Table 5 presents the performances of five baselines (Galárraga et al., 2013; Lei et al., 2020; Lv et al., 2020; Xia et al., 2022; Zhu et al., 2021) in four sparse KG datasets (FB15K-237-10%, FB15K-237-20%, FB15K-237-50%, NELL23K). The MRR score of (Zhu et al., 2021) is 282.5 higher than (Galárraga et al., 2013), 35.4% higher than (Lei et al., 2020), 10.6% higher than (Lv et al., 2020), 5.7% higher than (Xia et al., 2022) in FB15L-237-10% dataset. The HITS@3 score of (Zhu et al., 2021) is 75.8 higher than (Galárraga et al., 2013), 14.8% higher than (Lei et al., 2020), 6.6% higher than (Lv et al., 2020), 6.6% higher than (Xia et al., 2022) in FB15L-237-50% dataset. The HITS@10 score of (Zhu et al., 2021) is 89.9 higher than (Galárraga et al., 2013), 56.9% higher than (Lei et al., 2020), 47.0% higher than (Lv et al., 2020), 38.3% higher than (Xia et al., 2022) in NELL23K dataset.

LIMITATIONS

This section discusses the limitations of different KG reasoning approaches. The translational models, like TransE, need help learning complex relationships, especially multi-hop ones. Besides, the TransE approach has symmetric and anti-symmetric relationships. The symmetric relationship means that A is related to B, and B is related to A. The anti-symmetric relationship means that A is related to B, but B is not related to A. Similarly, TransE has the issue of learning 1-N, N-1, and N-N relationships, while TransH and TransR have solved these issues partially. Moreover, embedding methods require high-dimensional embedding spaces, while the quality of the spaces directly determines the performance of reasoning. Random walk is widely used in path-based knowledge graph reasoning approaches. However, the randomness in random walks may have unstable results. Besides, random walks can be inefficient and computationally expensive in large graphs with long Paths. Moreover, random walks ignore the edge directions and edge weights. Random walk works well for static graphs but not for dynamic graphs. For DRL-based KG reasoning approaches, reward shaping is essential to reasoning performances. Inappropriate rewards can cause failures in solving the problem. Besides, the sparse reward is a notorious headache for DRL, which can result in poor policy and slow convergence. Sparse reward means agents can only receive rewards after a sequence of actions. Moreover, balancing exploration, exploitation, and sample efficiency are other challenging issues for DRL.

CONCLUSION

Automated reasoning, inferencing missing data from observations, is challenging in artificial intelligence. Knowledge graphs can represent vast amounts of structured data. Motivated by the process of human inferencing, KG reasoning can boost context-aware AI systems, like GPT, to improve information retrieval and prediction accuracy. Deep reinforcement learning is a powerful sequential decision-making framework for uncertain and dynamic environments. Through repeated interactions between agents and environments, policies are optimized continuously with the guidance of rewards. Besides, near-optimal solutions can be found fast once the agent is well-trained. DRL is built on the Markov Decision Process, where the definitions of state space, action space, and reward function directly determine the performances of DRL approaches. DRL-based algorithms can solve knowledge graph reasoning tasks efficiently. This chapter aims to demonstrate the pipeline and advantages of using DRL to reason for missing data in the knowledge graph. Specifically, the difficulties of KG reasoning are analyzed. Categories and features of a vast amount of existing works are presented. Widely applied state spaces, action spaces, reward functions, and neural networks are compared. The advantages and disadvantages of DRL-based approaches are analyzed. Besides, the performances of nine baselines are compared with six datasets and four metrics. The combination of LLM and DRL-based KG reasoning will be studied in the future.

REFERENCES

Bansal, T., Juan, D.-C., Ravi, S., & McCallum, A. (2019). A2N: Attending to neighbors for knowledge graph inference. *Proceedings of the 57th Annual Meeting of the Association for Computational Linguistics*, 4387–4392. 10.18653/v1/P19-1431

Bordes, A., Usunier, N., Garcia-Duran, A., Weston, J., & Yakhnenko, O. (2013). Translating embeddings for modeling multi-relational data. *Advances in Neural Information Processing Systems*, 26.

Carta, S., Giuliani, A., Piano, L., Podda, A.S., Pompianu, L., & Tiddia, S.G. (2023). *Iterative Zero-Shot LLM Prompting for Knowledge Graph Construction.* arXiv Prepr. arXiv2307.01128.

Choudhary, N., & Reddy, C.K. (2023). *Complex Logical Reasoning over Knowledge Graphs using Large Language Models.* arXiv Prepr. arXiv2305.01157.

Das, R., Dhuliawala, S., Zaheer, M., Vilnis, L., Durugkar, I., Krishnamurthy, A., Smola, A., & McCallum, A. (2017). *Go for a walk and arrive at the answer: Reasoning over paths in knowledge bases using reinforcement learning.* arXiv Prepr. arXiv1711.05851.

Dettmers, T., Minervini, P., Stenetorp, P., & Riedel, S. (2018). Convolutional 2d knowledge graph embeddings. *Proceedings of the AAAI Conference on Artificial Intelligence.*

Galárraga, L. A., Teflioudi, C., Hose, K., & Suchanek, F. (2013). LEI. *Proceedings of the 22nd International Conference on World Wide Web*, 413–422.

Ji, G., He, S., Xu, L., Liu, K., & Zhao, J. (2015). Knowledge graph embedding via dynamic mapping matrix. *Proceedings of the 53rd Annual Meeting of the Association for Computational Linguistics and the 7th International Joint Conference on Natural Language Processing (Volume 1: Long Papers),* 687–696. 10.3115/v1/P15-1067

Lao, N., Mitchell, T., & Cohen, W. (2011). Random walk inference and learning in a large scale knowledge base. *Proceedings of the 2011 Conference on Empirical Methods in Natural Language Processing,* 529–539.

Lei, D., Jiang, G., Gu, X., Sun, K., Mao, Y., & Ren, X. (2020). *Learning collaborative agents with rule guidance for knowledge graph reasoning.* arXiv Prepr. arXiv2005.00571. doi:10.18653/v1/2020.emnlp-main.688

Li, Z., Guan, S., Jin, X., Peng, W., Lyu, Y., Zhu, Y., Bai, L., Li, W., Guo, J., & Cheng, X. (2022). *Complex evolutional pattern learning for temporal knowledge graph reasoning.* arXiv Prepr. arXiv2203.07782.

Li, Z., Jin, X., Guan, S., Wang, Y., & Cheng, X. (2018). Path reasoning over knowledge graph: a multi-agent and reinforcement learning based method. *2018 IEEE International Conference on Data Mining Workshops (ICDMW),* 929–936. 10.1109/ICDMW.2018.00135

Lin, X. V., Socher, R., & Xiong, C. (2018). *Multi-hop knowledge graph reasoning with reward shaping.* arXiv Prepr. arXiv1808.10568. doi:10.18653/v1/D18-1362

Lin, Y., Liu, Z., Sun, M., Liu, Y., & Zhu, X. (2015). Learning entity and relation embeddings for knowledge graph completion. *Proceedings of the AAAI Conference on Artificial Intelligence.* 10.1609/aaai.v29i1.9491

Liu, H., Zhou, S., Chen, C., Gao, T., Xu, J., & Shu, M. (2022). Dynamic knowledge graph reasoning based on deep reinforcement learning. *Knowledge-Based Systems, 241,* 108235. doi:10.1016/j.knosys.2022.108235

Lv, X., Han, X., Hou, L., Li, J., Liu, Z., Zhang, W., Zhang, Y., Kong, H., & Wu, S. (2020). *Dynamic anticipation and completion for multi-hop reasoning over sparse knowledge graph.* arXiv Prepr. arXiv2010.01899. doi:10.18653/v1/2020.emnlp-main.459

Mason, K., & Grijalva, S. (2019). A review of reinforcement learning for autonomous building energy management. *Computers & Electrical Engineering*, *78*, 300–312. doi:10.1016/j.compeleceng.2019.07.019

Mavromatis, C., Subramanyam, P. L., Ioannidis, V. N., Adeshina, A., Howard, P. R., Grinberg, T., Hakim, N., & Karypis, G. (2022). Tempoqr: temporal question reasoning over knowledge graphs. *Proceedings of the AAAI Conference on Artificial Intelligence*, 5825–5833. 10.1609/aaai.v36i5.20526

Meyer, L.-P., Stadler, C., Frey, J., Radtke, N., Junghanns, K., Meissner, R., Dziwis, G., Bulert, K., & Martin, M. (2023). *LLM-assisted Knowledge Graph Engineering: Experiments with ChatGPT.* arXiv Prepr. arXiv2307.06917.

Qu, M., Chen, J., Xhonneux, L.-P., Bengio, Y., & Tang, J. (2020). *Rnnlogic: Learning logic rules for reasoning on knowledge graphs.* arXiv Prepr. arXiv2010.04029.

Sun, J., Xu, C., Tang, L., Wang, S., Lin, C., Gong, Y., Shum, H.-Y., & Guo, J. (2023). *Think-on-Graph: Deep and Responsible Reasoning of Large Language Model with Knowledge Graph.* arXiv Prepr. arXiv2307.07697.

Tiwari, P., Zhu, H., & Pandey, H. M. (2021). DAPath: Distance-aware knowledge graph reasoning based on deep reinforcement learning. *Neural Networks*, *135*, 1–12. doi:10.1016/j.neunet.2020.11.012 PMID:33310193

Trajanoska, M., Stojanov, R., & Trajanov, D. (2023). *Enhancing Knowledge Graph Construction Using Large Language Models.* arXiv Prepr. arXiv2305.04676.

Trouillon, T., Welbl, J., Riedel, S., Gaussier, É., & Bouchard, G. (2016). Complex embeddings for simple link prediction. In *International Conference on Machine Learning*. PMLR.

Wang, D. (2022). *Meta Reinforcement Learning with Hebbian Learning. In 2022 IEEE 13th Annual Ubiquitous Computing, Electronics & Mobile Communication Conference (UEMCON)*. IEEE. doi:10.1109/UEMCON54665.2022.9965711

Wang, D. (2023). Reinforcement Learning for Combinatorial Optimization. In *Encyclopedia of Data Science and Machine Learning* (pp. 2857–2871). IGI Global.

Wang, D., & Hu, M. (2021). Deep Deterministic Policy Gradient With Compatible Critic Network. *IEEE Trans. Neural Networks Learn. Syst.*

Wang, D., Hu, M., & Gao, Y. (2018). Multi-criteria mission planning for a solar-powered multi-robot system. *International Design Engineering Technical Conferences and Computers and Information in Engineering Conference*. 10.1115/DETC2018-85683

Wang, D., Hu, M., & Weir, J.D. (2022). Simultaneous Task and Energy Planning using Deep Reinforcement Learning. *Inf. Sci.*

Wang, H., Li, S., Pan, R., & Mao, M. (2019). Incorporating graph attention mechanism into knowledge graph reasoning based on deep reinforcement learning. *Proceedings of the 2019 Conference on Empirical Methods in Natural Language Processing and the 9th International Joint Conference on Natural Language Processing (EMNLP-IJCNLP)*, 2623–2631. 10.18653/v1/D19-1264

Wang, X., Liu, K., Wang, D., Wu, L., Fu, Y., & Xie, X. (2022). Multi-level recommendation reasoning over knowledge graphs with reinforcement learning. *Proceedings of the ACM Web Conference 2022*, 2098–2108. 10.1145/3485447.3512083

Wang, Z., Zhang, J., Feng, J., & Chen, Z. (2014). Knowledge graph embedding by translating on hyperplanes. *Proceedings of the AAAI Conference on Artificial Intelligence.* 10.1609/aaai.v28i1.8870

Wei, J., Wang, X., Schuurmans, D., Bosma, M., Xia, F., Chi, E., Le, Q. V., & Zhou, D. (2022). Chain-of-thought prompting elicits reasoning in large language models. *Advances in Neural Information Processing Systems*, *35*, 24824–24837.

Xia, Y., Lan, M., Luo, J., Chen, X., & Zhou, G. (2022). Iterative rule-guided reasoning over sparse knowledge graphs with deep reinforcement learning. *Information Processing & Management*, *59*(5), 103040. doi:10.1016/j.ipm.2022.103040

Xiong, W., Hoang, T., & Wang, W. Y. (2017). *Deeppath: A reinforcement learning method for knowledge graph reasoning.* arXiv Prepr. arXiv1707.06690. doi:10.18653/v1/D17-1060

Yang, B., Yih, W., He, X., Gao, J., & Deng, L. (2014). *Embedding entities and relations for learning and inference in knowledge bases.* arXiv Prepr. arXiv1412.6575.

Yun, L., Wang, D., & Li, L. (2023). Explainable multi-agent deep reinforcement learning for real-time demand response towards sustainable manufacturing. *Applied Energy*, *347*, 121324. doi:10.1016/j.apenergy.2023.121324

Zhao, Y., Wang, X., Chen, J., Wang, Y., Tang, W., He, X., & Xie, H. (2022). Time-aware path reasoning on knowledge graph for recommendation. *ACM Transactions on Information Systems*, *41*, 1–26.

Zheng, R., Dou, S., Gao, S., Shen, W., Wang, B., Liu, Y., Jin, S., Liu, Q., Xiong, L., & Chen, L. (2023). *Secrets of RLHF in Large Language Models Part I: PPO.* arXiv Prepr. arXiv2307.04964.

Zhou, X., Wang, P., Luo, Q., & Pan, Z. (2021). Multi-hop Knowledge Graph Reasoning Based on Hyperbolic Knowledge Graph Embedding and Reinforcement Learning. *The 10th International Joint Conference on Knowledge Graphs*, 1–9. 10.1145/3502223.3502224

Zhu, Y., Liu, H., Wu, Z., Song, Y., & Zhang, T. (2019). *Representation learning with ordered relation paths for knowledge graph completion.* arXiv Prepr. arXiv1909.11864. doi:10.18653/v1/D19-1268

Zhu, Z., Zhang, Z., Xhonneux, L.-P., & Tang, J. (2021). Neural bellman-ford networks: A general graph neural network framework for link prediction. *Advances in Neural Information Processing Systems*, *34*, 29476–29490.

ADDITIONAL READING

Chen, X., Jia, S., & Xiang, Y. (2020). A review: Knowledge reasoning over knowledge graph. *Expert Systems with Applications*, *141*, 112948. doi:10.1016/j.eswa.2019.112948

Ji, S., Pan, S., Cambria, E., Marttinen, P., & Philip, S. Y. (2021). A survey on knowledge graphs: Representation, acquisition, and applications. *IEEE Transactions on Neural Networks and Learning Systems*, *33*(2), 494–514. doi:10.1109/TNNLS.2021.3070843 PMID:33900922

Tian, L., Zhou, X., Wu, Y. P., Zhou, W. T., Zhang, J. H., & Zhang, T. S. (2022). Knowledge graph and knowledge reasoning: A systematic review. *Journal of Electronic Science and Technology*, *20*(2), 100159. doi:10.1016/j.jnlest.2022.100159

KEY TERMS AND DEFINITIONS

Deep Reinforcement Learning: A Markov Decision Process based learning framework, where a series of optimal actions are made via the repeated interaction among agents and environments.

Knowledge Graph: A structured representation of entities and relationships with the graph format, which enables knowledge graph to efficiently comprehend complicated information like human cognitive processes. The most recent application is the combination of knowledge graph reasoning and large language models.

Knowledge Reasoning: An inference making and summarization process according to the structure information collected in the KG.

Markov Decision Process: A decision-making process where the system moves between different states in discrete time steps. The selection of actions based on a transition probability. The whole procedure is reward driven.

Neural Network: A framework involves interconnected layers of weighted neurons, which is motived by the human brain.

Chapter 13
Doppler Studies–Based Assessment of High-Risk Pregnancies Based on Cerebroplacental Ratios

S. S. Vhawal
Krishna Institute of Medical Sciences, India

Bahulekar Ashitosh
Krishna Vishwa Vidyapeeth, India

ABSTRACT

In order to minimise negative perinatal outcomes, good clinical management is essential for the time of the delivery. Regular ultrasound tests using the cerebro-placental ratio and Doppler technology are examples of in utero monitoring (CPR). The pulsatility index (PI) of the MCA is divided by the UA's PI to arrive at the cardiac output rate (CPR). The umbilical artery (UA) and the middle cerebral artery (MCA) are used as indicators of placental function and foetal adjustment to placental insufficiency, respectively. It has been shown that unfavourable outcomes for neonates are linked to reduced CPR, which is an indicator of cerebral redistribution. Doppler is a safe and painless way to assess foetoplacental circulation in pregnant women. It aids in the treatment of high-risk pregnancies because of the useful information it provides regarding the foetus's hemodynamic state. Neonatal morbidity includes conditions such as birth asphyxia and low blood sugar.

1.INTRODUCTION

Doppler investigations have the advantage of being non-invasive, repeatable, and safe for the foetus over other techniques. When a pregnant woman is at high risk, doppler ultrasound is crucial for spotting problems with the placenta, low oxygen levels, and their complications. Assessment of foetal circulation aids in a better understanding of the pathophysiology of high-risk pregnancies and their management.

DOI: 10.4018/978-1-6684-9189-8.ch013

Doppler is useful for identifying challenged foetuses and planning prompt deliveries, both of which are crucial for reducing foetal mortality and morbidity (Morales-Roselló et al., 2015). Doppler can be used in high-risk pregnancies to determine whether to have a longer pregnancy (stillbirth) or a chance of preterm birth (Munshi et al., 2018). Most vascular illnesses, including hypertension, diabetes, IUGR, and collagen vascular diseases, including SLE and APLA, are associated with impaired placentation. Fetal compromise can also happen when maternal anaemia and rheumatic heart conditions cause the foetus to receive less oxygen than usual. It begins with tertiary villi and ends with foetal cardiovascular symptoms (Vollgraff Heidweiller-Schreurs et al., 2018).

1.1 Doppler Velocimetry in Pregnancy

Conde-Agudelo et al. (2018) proposed use ultrasonic Doppler probes in order to obtain waveforms from the umbilical artery. In a more in-depth research that was published in 2015 DeVore, (2015). hypothesised that the assessment of a velocity waveform's systolic peak/diastolic trough (S/D) ratio would represent placental vascular resistance. This ratio would be calculated using a blood pressure monitor. Over the past few years, a significant amount of research has been conducted on the application of Doppler velocimetry in the course of a pregnancy. Early research that focused on umbilical and uterine blood flow as assessed in either uterine or arcuate artery velocimetry found that the placental bed is typically a low-resistance system. Furthermore, assessments of placental circulation resistance tend to decrease as pregnancy advances (Zohav et al., 2019). This was found to be the case. This discovery was founded on the observation that placental circulation resistance has a tendency to lessen throughout the course of pregnancy (Patil et al., 2019). In pregnancies that were complicated, having a placenta with a high barrier to blood flow was consistently related with a poor prognosis for the foetus. The latter discovery has proven to be more challenging to implement into information that is relevant to clinical practise (Moreta et al., 2019).

1.2. Objectives

The study was conducted with the following objectives: It is imperative that a method be devised for calculating the pulsatility indices of the foetal umbilical and middle cerebral arteries (Munshi et al., 2022). The relationship between the cerebroplacental ratio and the obstetrical outcome in terms of delivery mode in high-risk pregnancies between the ages of 30 and 36 weeks. The correlation between the cerebroplacental ratio in high-risk pregnancies between the ages of 30 and 36 weeks of pregnancy and the perinatal outcome in terms of birth weight, APGAR score, and admission to the NICU was studied (Khalil et al., 2017).

The following three markers are commonly used in clinical studies: In the United States, (1) the S/D ratio is the most popular metric, (2) the Pourcelot Index (S-D/S), and (3) the S/D/Mean pulsatility index. The Pourcelot index and the S/D ratio are simple to calculate, but when diastolic velocities decrease, measurement errors increase, which causes the Pourcelot index and the S/D ratio to become closer and closer to infinity (Stampalija et al., 2017). The pulsatility index is the least feasible of all the indices since it has to be digitised together with the whole waveform. The extracomputation does not appreciably affect current clinical interpretation, even if the pulsatility index comprises additional waveform data. There is no discernible difference between these indices in clinical use, despite their great correlation.

A duplex system is necessary if the vessel measurement computation calls for viewing (such as with some foetal vessels) (Figure 1).

A number of researchers have looked into the inter- and intra-observer variation. It seems that, compared to interpatient variability, interoperative variability among skilled operators is quite low. Contrary to popular belief, operator-related variation was often less than 10% and only contributed to 25% of interpatient variability (Morales-Roselló et al., 2017).

1.3. Typical Blood Flow From the Umbilical Artery

Umbilical artery velocity indices are often assessed near the placental end of the chord because they are lower there than at the foetal end of the chord. Several authors have determined normative values for blood flow through the umbilical artery during normal pregnancies. You can find these values in scholarly medical publications. Umbilical artery velocimetry has limited utility before 20 weeks of pregnancy because placental flow acts as a high-resistance bed. While there is considerable variation in the indices' levels when they are measured at different stages of gestation, all of them tend to decrease as the pregnancy progresses. After the 40th week of pregnancy, the S/D ratio typically stabilises between 1.7 and 2.4, reflecting a typical gradual decline in placental resistance. The S/D ratio may range from 3.33 to 4.33 at 20 weeks of gestation. Abnormal CPR may have its origins in certain Doppler measurement patterns.

- When an abnormally low CPR results from the UA and MCA PI being in the high and lower ranges of the distribution curve, respectively.
- When the MCA PI is reduced while the UA PI is normal, leading to an unusually low CPR.
- Atypically low CPR due to an unusually high UA PI and atypically low MCA PI.

According to the nomogram developed by Baschat and Gembruch, an aberrant CPR was defined as one that was above or below the 5th percentile for gestational age. The CPR was initially introduced in

Figure 1. Three indices of qualitative blood flow measurements

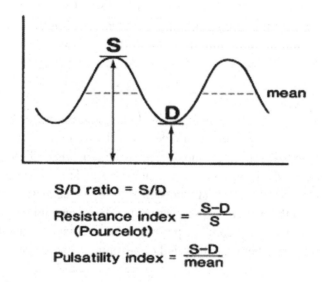

$$\text{S/D ratio} = \text{S/D}$$

$$\text{Resistance index} = \frac{S-D}{S}$$
$$\text{(Pourcelot)}$$

$$\text{Pulsatility index} = \frac{S-D}{\text{mean}}$$

the 1980s; interest in this diagnostic tool has recently grown as a result of publications linking an aberrant ratio to poor perinatal outcomes and postnatal neurological deficits. There is also evidence that some of the foetuses in a cohort of adequately grown (AGA) pregnancies with estimated weights over the 10th centile exhibit circulatory abnormalities similar to those seen in a foetus with evident growth limitation. Unfavorable obstetric and perinatal outcomes for these AGA foetuses are also more likely. A high UA PI and a low MCA PI are therefore seen in asymmetrical growth retardation. Due to this, foetuses with growth retardation have lower C/U ratios than usual. The C/U ratio and the HC/AC ratio exhibit a strong correlation. The C/U ratio provides superior diagnostic accuracy than either vessel's PI taken separately throughout the final 10 weeks of pregnancy and stays stable throughout. Ultrasonic Doppler studies may help in foetal growth restriction (FGR) to separate constitutionally tiny foetuses from those who are at risk for poor postnatal outcomes (Vashishtha et al., 2020). The clinical usefulness of umbilical artery (UA) Doppler in high-risk pregnancies has been documented in a Cochrane review of 18 randomised controlled studies, which is why current FGR guidelines suggest it as a crucial surveillance tool (Table 1).

2. LITERATURE REVIEW

Doppler ultrasounds were done on 1573 high-risk single pregnancies between December 29, 1994 and December 31, 2017 at Lund University Hospital and University Hospital of Malmö, and the results were analysed retrospectively by Bonnevier et al. (2021). Predictive value of gestational age-specific z-scores for CPR for perinatal asphyxia or mortality, birthweight small for gestational age (SGA), and two composite outcomes, appropriate for gestational age/large for gestational age liveborn infants with neonatal morbidity, and SGA liveborn infants with neonatal morbidity, were assessed using receiver operating characteristics (ROC) curves. There was no discernible improvement in performance between the three factors in predicting prenatal asphyxia or mortality. CPR and the MCA PI were able to predict baby morbidity according to gestational age, large for gestational age, and SGA infant morbidity, similar to the UA PI (P.001), but much better. In this study, none of the three Doppler readings were able to reliably predict prenatal hypoxia or mortality.

3. METHODOLOGY

Location of the Study: A tertiary care hospital's Obstetrics and Gynecology department was the setting for the research that was conducted.

Table 1. The maternal and fetal risk factors which need increased surveillance

Maternal Condition	Fetal Condition
hypertensive disorders of pregnancy	Intrauterine growth restriction
diabetes complicating pregnancy	Decreased perception of fetal movements
Antiphospholipid syndrome	Prior h / oIUD / still birth /IUGR / oligohydramnios

Data Sources: The study included pregnant women who were found to have any maternal risk factor. These ladies visited our hospital's antenatal care clinics or were admitted to our obstetrics and gynaecology ward.

The research was carried out over the course of two years after receiving approval from the relevant departmental committee and ethics board.

In this prospective observational study, the maternal and foetal outcomes of pregnant women considered to be at high risk were assessed. This was a prospective observational study, hence it was set up in this way.

Sample Size: It has been considered using formula as follows:

Sample size n = [DEFF*Np(1-p)]/ [(d2/Z21-α/2*(N-1)+p*(1-p)]

where the rate of pathological CPR (1.0) found by Grüttner et al., (2019) was used as the frequency or prevalence of the outcome factor in the population (p). In 2019, this was discovered. The design effect was assumed to be 1.0, and the confidence bounds were calculated using the formula 5 percent of 100 (absolute +/- percent) (d), respectively. At a degree of confidence equal to 99 percent, the sample size that was computed using the aforementioned technique was 139, and this number was rounded up to 150. Despite this, during the course of the study we were able to recruit a total of 146 female participants despite the stringent requirements for participation.

Eligibility Criteria: At least one of the following risk factors was present in the study group patient:

- Hypertensive disorder of pregnancy
- Gestational Diabetes mellitus
- IUGR
- Oligohydramnios
- Medical disorders in pregnancy (E.g. anemia)

Any pregnant women with any of the following conditions were excluded from the study:

- Multiple pregnancies
- Congenital anomalies in the foetus
- Normal ANC cases.

3.1. Data Collection Methods

Pregnant women who visited the obstetrics outpatient clinic or were hospitalised were assessed for maternal risk factors. Women who were pregnant at the time of recruitment had their complete demographic, medical, obstetric, and prenatal histories documented, together with notes on any difficulties that arose before or during pregnancy. Consent was sought from women who had at least one high-risk characteristic. The next step was the administration of the standard comprehensive physical examination. Every woman who volunteered for the study had her CPR evaluated using a colour Doppler USG. Doppler recordings were taken from the umbilical artery. As measured by the pulsatility index. The pulsatility index was also obtained from DOPPLER recordings of the middle cerebral artery.

Follow up: All recruited mothers were followed up until delivery to record maternal and foetal outcomes.

Maternal outcomes were recorded in terms of including mode of delivery and indication of LSCS.

Foetal outcomes were assessed in term of birth weight, APGAR Score and NICU admission rate.

3.2. Statistical Methods

The study used proper statistical procedures to examine the data, such as the mean, median, mode, and chi-square test. Both descriptive and inferential statistics were employed in this study. Results for continuous variables were reported as Mean Standard Deviation (Min-Max), while those for categorical variables were given as Number (percent). The analysis was performed at the 5% level of significance. The following assumptions were made about the data:

Assumptions: An ideal situation would have a normally distributed dependent variable, a randomly selected sample from the entire population, and independent cases within the sample. One method used to establish statistical significance between groups in an intergroup study of metric parameters was the Student t test (two-tailed, independent). The P value of a Chi-Square or Fisher Exact Test Two or more groups were compared using the precise test based on categorical study parameters. In order to examine the link between CPR and maternal and foetal outcomes, antenatal women were randomly assigned to one of two groups: CPR-1 or CPR-1

3.3. Ethical Issues

We spoke with potential participants and explained the study's goals and procedures in terms they could grasp. Adolescents' permission was requested once a signed informed consent form was obtained from their parents or legal guardians. Only after the patient signs the Informed Consent Form voluntarily will the participant be recruited (ICF). The person's privacy and anonymity were respected at all times. The subject was allowed to withdraw from the study at any time, with no explanation necessary. This did not compromise his or her entitlement to medical care and treatment. No one who participated in the study was asked to pay anything out of pocket. The researcher is responsible for any additional costs that arise as a direct result of conducting this research. The Institutional Ethics Committee was informed of and gave their blessing to any changes made to the study, protocol, or design. The ethics committee will be informed of any potential problems down the road.

4. RESULTS

The age distribution of mothers at the time of pregnancy registration is depicted in Figure 2, which can be found here.

The distribution of mothers according to their gestational age at the time of delivery is shown in Figure 3.

5. DISCUSSION

Among the 146 high-risk pregnant women in the current study, only 61.0% received CPR. This demonstrates that the CPR is not typical. CPR greater than 1 was considered usual for the remaining 39% of patients. The mean CPR value was 1.14, with a standard deviation of 0.29, and there was a total of 146 individuals. Sengodan & Mathiyalagan, (2020) found that 25 participants had a cardiac index (CPR) lower than 1, whereas the remaining 75 participants all had CPRs over 1. Grüttner et al., (2019) showed

Figure 2. Age of mother at the time of registration

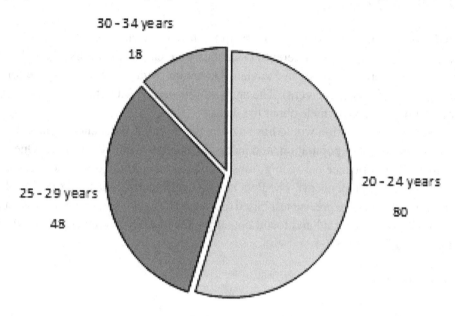

Figure 3. Distribution of mothers according to gestational age at the time of delivery

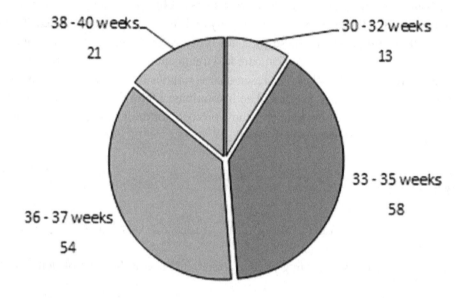

that among their cohort of patients, 126 had a CPR of 1.0, while 2144 had a CPR of >1.0. In total, 2,270 patients participated in the trial. Out of 62 cases, Shaheen et al., (2014) found that 21 (33.8%) had abnormal CPR whereas the remaining two-thirds had normal CPR. The overall rate of CPR has been found to be lower in other studies compared to this one. Possible explanations for this discrepancy include the fact that only high-risk pregnancies were included in the current study, while all pregnancies were included in the earlier trials.

According to Sengodan & Mathiyalagan, (2020) the LSCS rate was 72% in the CPR 1 group and 62% in the standard CPR group. The rate of LSCS newborns was significantly higher in the CPR1 group compared to the CPR2 group (p 0.05). According to the findings of the study, LSCS has a positive predictive value of 72%, making it the method of choice for delivery in cases of inadequate CPR even when the odds are against it. In the current study, low APGAR scores (7) were seen in 50.6% of the neonates in the CPR-1 group and in 24.6% of the neonates in the conventional CPR group. Cases with a CPR of less than one had a significantly higher percentage (p 0.01) of having an APGAR score of seven or lower than the group with a CPR of one or higher. 26.57 percent of neonates in the incorrect CPR group had an APGAR score of 7 at 5 minutes compared to 2.88 percent of neonates in the normal CPR group. A p-value of less than 0.05 indicates statistical significance. In the current study, the rate of neonatal mortality was 11.2% in the abnormal CPR group and 5.3% in the normal CPR group.

Sengodan & Mathiyalagan (2020) found that 96% of newborns survived in a sample of 100 cases, while 2 received IUDs and 2 had perinatal fatalities. Odibo et al. (2005) found a correlation between an abnormal cerebroplacental Doppler ratio and an earlier time between the last Doppler and delivery in subjects with FGR. Cases with a CPR of less than 1 had a substantially higher APGAR score of 7 than those with a CPR of 1 or greater (p 0.05). Compared to cases with a CPR of 1 or higher, the rate of admission to a neonatal intensive care unit (NICU) was significantly lower in the group of cases with a CPR of 0 or 1. (p 0.01). Given this, it might be argued that the length of time between the diagnosis of FGR and the delivery is a better predictor of worse perinatal outcomes than the mode of delivery itself. 146 high-risk pregnancies were included in the study to assess the correlation between the cerebroplacental ratio and obstetric and perinatal outcomes.

The results of the study are summarised as follows: Only 60 (41.1%) of the 146 newborns did not need to be admitted to the NICU, whereas 86 (58.9%) did. Low birth weight, respiratory distress, and premature birth were the leading indicators for NICU admission. There were 29 (33.7%) premature babies, (36.0%) infants with respiratory distress, and 43 (50.0%) children admitted due to low birth weight. At 5 minutes, 87 (59.6 percent) of 146 babies had an APGAR score of 7 or higher. There was abnormal CPR in 89 cases and normal CPR in 57 cases. Patients with CPRs less than 1 had significantly younger gestational ages than those with CPRs greater than or equal to 1. (p 0.05). There were a total of 42 cases of IUGR (47.2%), 38 cases of preeclampsia (42.7%), and 17 cases of GDM (19.1%) among the mothers in the CPR 1 group. In the CPR 1 group, the highest rates of occurrence for maternal risk factors were 23.3% for preeclampsia, 23.2% for IUGR, and 21.7% for GDM. Out of the 89 patients in the CPR 1 group, 37 (41%) were delivered through LSCS and 25 (28%) were delivered vaginally.

Twenty out of 57 (29.0%) of CPR 1 group patients gave birth via LSCS before their due date, sixteen out of 57 (23.2%) gave birth via LSCS at full term, and sixteen out of 57 (23.2%) gave birth vaginally. There is no statistically significant difference in the LSCS rate (p > 0.05) between the CPR group with CPR 1 and the CPR 1 group. There was a marked increase in the rate of preterm birth as compared to the CPR-1 group (p 0.01). In a study including 146 high-risk pregnant women, the cerebroplacental ratio was utilised to assess obstetric and perinatal outcomes. Here is a quick rundown of what we found in this investigation: Mothers between the ages of 20 and 24 made up the largest single age group (54.8 percent of all mothers). The average age of a mother was 24.83 years old, with a range of 2.93 to 32.22. Sixty-three moms, or 43.2% of the total, were between 34 and 35 weeks along in their pregnancies.

Gestational age ranged from 33.90 to 34.03 weeks on average, with a standard deviation of 1.53 weeks. Sixty-one percent of the 146 patients were in the group that received less than one CPR. Standard deviation was 0.29 for the mother's CPR, which had a mean of 1.14. There were more than 50% full-term births. Of all births, 39.7 percent happened between weeks 33 and 35 of pregnancy, whereas only 8.9 percent occurred before week 33. Maternal gestational age ranged from 35.50 2.01 weeks, with a mean of 35.50 weeks. There were 61 cases of preeclampsia (41.8%), 58 cases of IUGR (39.7%), and 32 cases of GDM (3.2%). (21.9 percent). Preterm LSCS deliveries accounted for 57 (39.0%) of the total, whereas full-term LSCS deliveries accounted for 31 (21.2%) of the total. There was a total of 30 vaginal preterm births (20.5%), followed by 28 vaginal full-term births (19.2%). There was a total of 29 cases of foetal distress (19.9%), 18 cases of failure of indication (12.3%), 15 cases of severe preeclampsia (10.3%), and 13 cases of GDM (8.1%). (8.9 percent). Sixty (41.1% of the total) patients were born weighing between 1.5 and 2.499 kg. Average birth weight was 2.18 kg (0.53 SD), and the range was narrow.

There were 146 babies in all, 76 (52.1%) of whom were male and 70 (47.1%) of them were female. There were 146 newborns, 133 (91.1%) made it, and 13 (8.9%) didn't. Of the total 146, 86 required hospitalisation to a neonatal intensive care unit (NICU), whereas 60 did not. Common reasons for admission to the neonatal intensive care unit included low birth weight, respiratory distress, and premature birth. Of these newborns, 43 (50%) were admitted because of their low birth weight, 31 (36%) were admitted because of respiratory distress, and 29 (33%) were admitted because they were born prematurely. Among the 146 infants, 87 (59.6 percent) had an APGAR score of 7 or above at 5 minutes. A total of 89 cases were found to have abnormal CPR, while 57 were found to have normal CPR. The gestational ages of babies born to mothers with a CPR of 0 or greater were significantly younger than those born to mothers with a CPR of 1 or greater (p 0.05).

In the CPR 1 group, 47.2% of the pregnant women experienced IUGR, 42.7% experienced preeclampsia, and 17.2% experienced GDM (19.1 percent). Twenty-three (33.3%) mothers in the CPR 1 group had preeclampsia, followed by IUGR (23.3%) and GDM (15.3%). (21 percent). Of the 89 patients in the CPR 1 group, 41.6% gave birth through LSCS and 28.1% gave birth vaginally. Out of 57 patients in the CPR 1 group, 20 (29.0 percent) had LSCS births at a premature stage, 16 (23.2 percent) at full term, and 16 (23.2 percent) at vaginal stage.

The LSCS rate in the CPR 1 group is not significantly different from the CPR 1 rate in the other group (p > 0.05). The CPR-1 group had a considerably greater rate of premature delivery than the control group (p 0.01). Foetal distress (19; 36.5%), gestational diabetes (9; 17.3%), and severe preeclampsia (9; 9%) were the most common reasons for LSCS in the CPR 1 group (17.3 percent). In the CPR 1 group, failure of induction accounted for 11 (30.56%) of LSCS procedures, followed by foetal distress (10) and severe preeclampsia (6%). (19.4 percent). Infants in the CPR 1 group averaged 2.16 kg, while those in the CPR 2 group weighed 2.36 kg on average. Birth weight was significantly lower in cases where the CPR was less than 1, compared to cases where the CPR was more than or equal to 1. (p 0.05). In comparison to the CPR1 group, mortality was higher in the CPR1 group. However, this difference did not warrant further statistical analysis.

In comparison to instances with a CPR of 1 or more, the rate of cases with a low APGAR score (7) was considerably higher in those with a CPR of 1. (p 0.05). Out of a total of 89 patients, 62 (69.7 percent) were admitted to the NICU while only 42.1% were admitted to the CPR 1 group. Patients with a CPR of less than 1 had a significantly greater rate of NICU admission compared to those with a CPR of 1 or higher (p 0.01). The most common reasons for NICU admissions for the CPR 1 group were low birth weight (35, 39.3 percent), IUGR (27, 30.3 percent), and respiratory distress (21, 23.6 percent). In the CPR 1 group, 12 premature infants were admitted to the NICU; 10 had respiratory distress, and 8 had low birth weight. It was shown that there was a higher rate of respiratory distress and IUGR in the CPR-1 group.

6. CONCLUSION

Our results indicate that doppler investigations of the cerebro-placental ratio (CPR1) typically reveal an unfavourable outcome in 60% of high-risk pregnancies. Preterm birth was shown to be significantly increased in high-risk pregnant women with a CPR of less than one. It's possible that the lack of an association between CPR and the rate of caesarean sections is due to the large number of premature infants in the CPR 1 group. In high-risk pregnancies, a low CPR value (CPR1) also has a major impact on the foetus's development and survival. In comparison to patients with a CPR of 1 or higher, those with a CPR of 0 or 1 had significantly lower birth weights. The CPR1 group has a higher mortality rate than the CPR2 group. A change occurred, but it was too small to be detected statistically. However, if obstetric conditions indicate that a birth within 6-12 hours would be more likely if one waited for natural labour, then one should opt for an LSCS delivery rather than prolonging the duration of labour by waiting for natural labour. An obstetrician may consider this while deciding whether or not to do LSCS on an infant with FGR for reasons unrelated to the pregnancy.

REFERENCES

Bonnevier, A., Maršál, K., Brodszki, J., Thuring, A., & Källén, K. (2021). Cerebroplacental ratio as predictor of adverse perinatal outcome in the third trimester. *Acta Obstetricia et Gynecologica Scandinavica, 100*(3), 497–503. doi:10.1111/aogs.14031 PMID:33078387

Conde-Agudelo, A., Villar, J., Kennedy, S. H., & Papageorghiou, A. T. (2018). Predictive accuracy of cerebroplacental ratio for adverse perinatal and neurodevelopmental outcomes in suspected fetal growth restriction: systematic review and meta-analysis: CPR predicts perinatal death in suspected FGR. *Ultrasound in Obstetrics & Gynecology, 52*(4), 430–441. doi:10.1002/uog.19117 PMID:29920817

DeVore, G. R. (2015). The importance of the cerebroplacental ratio in the evaluation of fetal well-being in SGA and AGA fetuses. *American Journal of Obstetrics and Gynecology, 213*(1), 5–15. doi:10.1016/j.ajog.2015.05.024 PMID:26113227

Grüttner, B., Ratiu, J., Ratiu, D., Gottschalk, I., Morgenstern, B., Abel, J. S., Eichler, C., Pahmeyer, C., Ludwig, S., Mallmann, P., & Thangarajah, F. (2019). Correlation of cerebroplacental ratio (CPR) with adverse perinatal outcome in singleton pregnancies. *In Vivo (Athens, Greece), 33*(5), 1703–1706. doi:10.21873/invivo.11659 PMID:31471427

Khalil, A., Morales-Rosello, J., Khan, N., Nath, M., Agarwal, P., Bhide, A., Papageorghiou, A., & Thilaganathan, B. (2017). Is cerebroplacental ratio a marker of impaired fetal growth velocity and adverse pregnancy outcome? *American Journal of Obstetrics and Gynecology, 216*(6), 606.e1–606.e10. doi:10.1016/j.ajog.2017.02.005 PMID:28189607

Morales-Roselló, J., Khalil, A., Alba-Redondo, A., Martinez-Triguero, L., Akhoundova, F., Perales-Marín, A., & Thilaganathan, B. (2017). Protein S100β in late-pregnancy fetuses with low birth weight and abnormal cerebroplacental ratio. *Fetal Diagnosis and Therapy, 41*(1), 15–22. doi:10.1159/000445114 PMID:27104871

Morales-Roselló, J., Khalil, A., Alberola-Rubio, J., Hervas-Marín, D., Morlando, M., Bhide, A., Papageorghiou, A., Perales-Marín, A., & Thilaganathan, B. (2015). Neonatal acid-base status in term fetuses: Mathematical models investigating cerebroplacental ratio and birth weight. *Fetal Diagnosis and Therapy*, *38*(1), 55–60. doi:10.1159/000368829 PMID:25660123

Moreta, D., Vo, S., Eslick, G. D., & Benzie, R. (2019). Re-evaluating the role of cerebroplacental ratio in predicting adverse perinatal outcome. *European Journal of Obstetrics, Gynecology, and Reproductive Biology*, *242*, 17–28. doi:10.1016/j.ejogrb.2019.06.033 PMID:31526912

Munshi, M., Tumu, K. N., Hasan, M. N., & Amin, M. Z. (2018). Biochemical effects of commercial feedstuffs on the fry of climbing perch (Anabas testudineus) and its impact on Swiss albino mice as an animal model. *Toxicology Reports*, *5*, 521–530. doi:10.1016/j.toxrep.2018.04.004 PMID:29707493

Munshi, M., Zilani, M. N. H., Islam, M. A., Biswas, P., Das, A., Afroz, F., & Hasan, M. N. (2022). Novel compounds from endophytic fungi of Ceriops decandra inhibit breast cancer cell growth through estrogen receptor alpha in in-silico study. *Informatics in Medicine Unlocked*, *32*(101046), 101046. doi:10.1016/j.imu.2022.101046

Odibo, A.O., Riddick, C., Pare, E., Stamilio, D. M., & Macones, G.A. (2005). Cerebroplacental Doppler ratio and adverse perinatal outcomes in intrauterine growth restriction: evaluating the impact of using gestational agespecific reference values. *J Ultrasound Med.*, (9), 1223-8. doi:.2005.24.9.1223 doi:10.7863/jum

Patil, V., Gowda, S., Das, S., Suma, K. B., Hiremath, R., Shetty, S., Raj, V., & Shashikumar, M. R. (2019). Cerebro-placental ratio in women with hypertensive disorders of pregnancy: A reliable predictor of neonatal outcome. *Journal of Clinical and Diagnostic Research*. Advance online publication. doi:10.7860/JCDR/2019/41185.12862

Sengodan, S. S., & Mathiyalagan, S. (2020). Doppler study (cerebroplacental ratio) as a predictor of adverse perinatal outcome. *International Journal of Reproduction, Contraception, Obstetrics and Gynecology*, *9*(12), 5068–5074. doi:10.18203/2320-1770.ijrcog20205249

Shaheen, S., Imam, B., Ibne, A., & Singh, A. (2014). Doppler Cerebroplacental Ratio and Adverse Perinatal Outcome. *Journal of South Asian Federation of Obstetrics and Gynecology*, *6*(1), 25–27. doi:10.5005/jp-journals-10006-1262

Stampalija, T., Arabin, B., Wolf, H., Bilardo, C. M., Lees, C., Brezinka, C., Derks, J. B., Diemert, A., Duvekot, J. J., Ferrazzi, E., Frusca, T., Ganzevoort, W., Hecher, K., Kingdom, J., Marlow, N., Marsal, K., Martinelli, P., Ostermayer, E., Papageorghiou, A. T., & Zimmermann, A. (2017). Is middle cerebral artery Doppler related to neonatal and 2-year infant outcome in early fetal growth restriction? *American Journal of Obstetrics and Gynecology*, *216*(5), 521.e1–521.e13. doi:10.1016/j.ajog.2017.01.001 PMID:28087423

Vashishtha, E., Sherman, L., Sajjad, T., & Mehmood, N. (2020). Use of anti-viral therapy in treatment of Covid 19. *Journal of Advanced Medical and Dental Sciences Research*, *8*(11), 273–276.

Vollgraff Heidweiller-Schreurs, C. A., De Boer, M. A., Heymans, M. W., Schoonmade, L. J., Bossuyt, P. M. M., Mol, B. W. J., De Groot, C. J. M., & Bax, C. J. (2018). Prognostic accuracy of cerebroplacental ratio and middle cerebral artery Doppler for adverse perinatal outcome: Systematic review and meta-analysis. *Ultrasound in Obstetrics & Gynecology, 51*(3), 313–322. doi:10.1002/uog.18809 PMID:28708272

Zohav, E., Zohav, E., Rabinovich, M., Alasbah, A., Shenhav, S., Sofer, H., Ovadia, Y. S., Anteby, E. Y., & Grin, L. (2019). Third-trimester reference ranges for cerebroplacental ratio, middle cerebral artery, and umbilical artery pulsatility index in normal-growth singleton fetuses in the Israeli population. *Rambam Maimonides Medical Journal, 10*(4), e0025. doi:10.5041/RMMJ.10379 PMID:31675306

Chapter 14
Evaluating Intraoperative Infusion of Low Dose Ketamine vs. Low Dose Ketamine and Dexmedetomidines Perioperatively in Head and Neck Surgeries

Shradha Vidyadhar Naik
Krishna Institute of Medical Sciences, India

V. M. Joshi
Krishna Institute of Medical Sciences, India

ABSTRACT

The use of opioids is linked to impaired gastrointestinal motility. In order to prevent postoperative ileus, opioid use should be kept to a minimum and alternative medications should be used in its place. One issue is the absence of a consistent criteria for the risk of postoperative urine retention. Opioid usage, however, is unquestionably a significant risk factor. Even though the processes are only poorly understood, efforts that reduce the use of opioids have been proven to reduce its incidence. The issue of postoperative shivering has finally, at least in part, been resolved by avoiding large opioid doses and using alpha-2 agonists. It has recently been questioned whether opioids should be used routinely during surgery, especially in cases where patients are fat. The need of opioids may be decreased by using alpha-2 agonists, which have a strong analgesic effect. The CNS and peripheral alpha-2 adrenergic receptors are bound by alpha-2 agonists. By preventing the central sympathetic outflow, they lower blood pressure.

1. INTRODUCTION

Head and neck surgeries are very complicated and can go for long hours. There may be severe blood loss and fluctuation in haemodynamic parameters (Miller, 2010). The perioperative period is very important.

DOI: 10.4018/978-1-6684-9189-8.ch014

Appropriate intraoperative maintenance of anaesthesia is an utmost priority without the fluctuations in vitals (Stoelting, 2006). Postoperative sedation and analgesia add to the outcome of the surgery and also improve the prognosis; the patient should be comfortable without any possible side effects of the drugs used intraoperatively (Munshi, et al., 2019). The immediate postoperative period is very important because severe agitation and cough during emergence from anaesthesia can lead to wide fluctuations in blood pressure and heart rate, which may be fatal for major vascular surgeries of the brain like aneurysmal clipping etc. Extubation must be smooth, and extubation response should be minimal to avoid wide fluctuations in heart rate and blood pressure (Andjelković, et al., 2018).

Clinical anaesthesia often involves the use of opioids. Postoperative nausea and vomiting, dizziness, constipation, respiratory depression, shivering, tolerance, physical dependency, ileus, and urinary retention are all possible adverse reactions (Boenigk, et al., 2019).

There is some evidence to suggest that opioid usage reduces gastrointestinal motility. As a result, additional medications should be used instead of or in addition to opioids to avoid postoperative ileus. One issue with assessing postoperative urinary retention risk is the absence of a universally accepted definition (Bajwa, et al., 2012). However, there is no denying that opioid usage is a major contributing element (Savola & Virtanen, 1991). Postoperative nausea and vomiting occurred in a significant number of patients (Md, et al., 2014). Although the processes are only partly known, opioid-sparing techniques have been demonstrated to reduce its occurrence (Munshi, et al., 2022). Finally, the issue of postoperative shivering has been somewhat resolved by the avoidance of excessive dosages of opioids and the use of alpha-2 agonists (Peng, et al., 2017).

The usual perioperative use of opioids has lately been questioned, particularly in obese patients, because of the substantial adverse effects of the opioids. There is promising evidence that the use of opioids may be reduced with the use of medicines known as alpha-2 agonists, which have significant analgesic effectiveness. Both the central nervous system (CNS) and peripheral alpha-2 adrenergic receptors are targets for alpha-2 agonists. Due to their ability to dampen the central sympathetic outflow, anaesthetics and pain relievers are being used with more restraint. In the postoperative phase, alpha-2 agonists give analgesia without the common opioid side effects of sedation and respiratory depression. Intraoperatively, dexmedetomidine has been shown to be an effective substitute for the synthetic opioid fentanyl. Despite their sedative effects, alpha-2 agonists do not significantly slow recovery compared to opioids (Munshi, et al., 2021).

Opioid usage is unquestionably a significant risk factor. Postoperative nausea and vomiting were extremely common. Even though the processes are only poorly understood, efforts that reduce the use of opioids have been proven to reduce its incidence (Munshi, et al., 2018). The new alpha-2 agonist dexmedetomidine has an affinity for alpha-2 adrenoceptors that is eight times higher than that of clonidine. Although it is just a partial agonist, it is known to reduce plasma catecholamine levels and inhibit catecholamine release. El Sharkawy, (2019) conducted a prospective randomised cohort study comparing the effectiveness of dexmedetomidine and low-dosage ketamine to that of propofol and low-dose ketamine. Sixty people between the ages of 18 and 60 who had received general anaesthesia were enlisted for the study, and they were randomly split into two groups. D-K (n = 30) was administered a bolus over the course of 10 minutes consisting of 0.5 mg/kg of ketamine and one ug/kg of dexmedetomidine. The next step was a continuous infusion of ketamine (0.5 mg/kg) and dexmedetomidine (1 ug/kg). A bolus dose of 1 mg/kg propofol and 0.5 mg/kg ketamine was given to the second group (P-K group; n = 30) over the course of 10 minutes. Then a ketamine infusion of 0.5 mg/kg/min was followed by a propofol infusion of 1 mg/kg/min.

Sixty adults were included in a randomised controlled clinical trial that compared the efficacy of supplementary analgesia with dexmedetomidine (DG), lidocaine (LG), and a placebo (CG). Lidocaine (Xylocaine; AstraZeneca; London, UK) was infused into the LG group at a rate of 1.5 mg/kg/h, dexmedetomidine (Dexdor; Orion Pharma; Espoo, Finland) was infused into the DG group at a rate of 0.5 mg/kg/h, and normal saline was infused into the CG group before surgery. They stopped the infusion of dexmedetomidine and lidocaine after they were done with the procedure (Jeganathan, et al., 2023). The study found that intravenous lidocaine reduced the need for opioid pain relievers on the first postoperative day and in the long run (Pandit, 2023). Dexmedetomidine with lidocaine infusion helped reduce the need for propofol during surgery (Nirmala, et al., 2023).

Aim: This study compared the effects of low doses of ketamine and low doses of ketamine combined with dexmedetomidine on the need for perioperative opioids in head and neck procedures.

1.1. Objectives

1.1.1. Primary Objective

- To assess the total amount of opioids required perioperatively.
- The time to the first dose of opioid perioperatively.

1.1.2. Secondary Objective

- We used the Riker Sedation-Agitation Scale to evaluate the effects of intraoperative ketamine infusions alone and in combination with dexmedetomidine.
- This Modified Aldrete score analysis is intended to determine how well the patient has recovered.
- To investigate postoperative blood pressure and heart rate variations.
- For the purpose of making a direct comparison between the time required for written and vocal responses in minutes.
- With the aim of contrasting the potentially dangerous side effects of various pharmaceuticals.

2. REVIEW OF LITERATURE

The effects of intra- and postoperative dexmedetomidine (DEX) + sufentanil infusions on postoperative analgesia in patients having neurosurgery were evaluated in retrospective research by Su et al. (2016) Patients recovering after neurosurgery were divided into two groups: Group D (DEX infusion at 0.5 g/kg for 10 min, subsequently lowered to 0.3 g/kg/hr till incision suturing) and Group ND (no DEX infusion) (no DEX infusion during surgery). Patient-controlled analgesia (Group D: 0.02 g/kg/hr sufentanil with DEX 0.021 g/kg/hr; Group ND: 0.02 g/kg/hr sufentanil) was used for 72 hours after surgery in this retrospective study (Vashishtha & Dhawan, 2023). This research suggests that administering sufentanil (0.02) and DEX (0.02 mcg/kg/hr) combined can reduce pain after surgery without the use of opioids or their potentially dangerous side effects. The effects of RSS or BCS did not appear until after the first 72 hours had passed after neurosurgery.

Mitra et al. (2017) conducted a randomised controlled experiment on 42 patients aged 18 to 60 who were scheduled to undergo elective lumbar spine instrumentation (surgery at two or more spinal levels). Patients were categorised as male or female and as having ASA Status I or II. Computer-generated randomisation was used to place patients into one of three treatment groups. Patients were randomly assigned to one of three groups using an opaque seal on envelopes: Group K received a 0.5 mg/kg bolus of racemic ketamine, whereas Group D received a 0.5 mcg/kg bolus of dexmedetomidine, and Group S received a saline (placebo) infusion (Group S). Analgesia after lumbar instrumentation surgery can be enhanced with the use of either ketamine or dexmedetomidine, as demonstrated in this study of 42 individuals. A greater sample size is necessary to prove that one medication is superior to another.

Abdalla et al. (2015) did a randomised controlled trial comparing group-DP and group-KP, with 30 patients in each. Sixty adults (20-50 years old) with planned diagnostic or therapeutic ERCP were involved in this research. Dexmedetomidine (1 mcg/kg loading dose), propofol (0.5 mcg/kg/hr infusion), and propofol (5 mg/kg/hr infusion) were administered intravenously to the dexmedetomidine/propofol (DP) group. Group KP (ketamine/propofol) was given an IV infusion of ketamine (5 mg/kg/hr) and propofol (1 mg/kg loading). The study found that throughout the procedure, there were statistically significant variations in HR and MAP between the two groups, with lower values in the DP group (p 0.01 or 0.001). During the post-procedural period, the DP group had a significantly lower HR and MAP. Both groups consumed propofol at similar rates (268.0 122.3 mg in the DP group versus 304.7 142.0 mg in the KP group). When compared to the KP group's (22.2 8.2 min), the DP group's post-procedural recovery time was significantly lower (5.7 1.7 min; p 0.01).

3. MATERIALS AND METHODS

Sample Size: According to the available literature, to detect the influence of intraoperative infusion of low-dose ketamine vs combination of low-dose ketamine and dexmedetomidine on reduction of perioperative opioid consumption by 30% for an alpha value of 0.05 and power of 90%, I calculated the sample size according to the following formula.

$N = 4 \times SD2 / (\bar{x} \times \varepsilon)2$

$\bar{x}$ - mean

ε - precision

SD- standard deviation

The study was conducted on a sample size of 60 patients, with 30 patients in each group.

Study Duration: Eighteen months (after approval of the institutional ethical committee) between January 2020 and June 2021.

Study Design: Prospective randomised Comparative Study.

4. SAMPLING TECHNIQUE

The use of Excel for randomisation was used. All the forms were randomly divided into two groups, K and KD, and will be stored separately. The research included taking the envelope one at a time in a sequential fashion.

5. SOURCE OF DATA

Having received clearance from the Krishna Institute of Medical Sciences' Institutional Ethical Committee, this trial was set to begin in Karad, Maharashtra. The study lasted from January 2020 to June 2021 and took place at KIMSDU's Department of Anaesthesiology in Karad.

The following criteria were used to identify patients to participate in the research.

5.1. Inclusion criteria

- Age group of 18-60 years of both sexes
- ASA physical status I or II
- Patients are coming for elective Head and Neck surgeries under general anaesthesia.

5.2. Exclusion criteria

- Patients on alpha-2 antagonist treatment or on monoamine oxidase inhibitors.
- Patients with uncontrolled hypertension.
- Patients with heart block.
- Patients with a history of alcohol/drug abuse.
- Patients with known/suspected allergy to alpha two adrenergic agonists or NSAIDs.
- Patients with cognitive impairment.
- Patients with coagulation disorders, respiratory or pulmonary disorders.
- Pregnancy.
- Patients with Full stomach/patients with risk of regurgitation-aspiration.
- Patients with increased intracranial/intraocular pressure.
- BMI >30kg/m2

6. DATA ANALYSIS

Interpretation of the data was carried out and analysed using Microsoft Excel and the software Statistical Package for Social Sciences SPSS version 20.0. The standard formula was used for data analysis. We used a standard t-test for statistical analysis, and $P \leq 0.05$ was considered statistically significant.

6.1. Method of Collection of Data

Patients in the 18-to-60-year-old age range who had ASA physical status I or II and were having elective head and neck procedures were chosen at random. The 60 people in the sample were split in half to create two groups of 30.

Group K – ketamine

Group KD – ketamine-Dexmedetomidine

6.2. Procedure

The pre-anaesthetic evaluation was undergone. Potential participants underwent one day prior to surgery. Basic laboratory investigations like FBS or RBS, Hb%, blood urea, serum creatinine and ECG were carried out routinely in all the patients. The entire procedure was explained in detail in their own local language to every patient.

Premedication: All the patients were premedicated with Inj. ondansetron 0.15mg/kg and Inj. midazolam 0.05 mg/kg 30 mins before induction.

Induction: Medications and pieces of equipment necessary for resuscitation and general anaesthesia were kept at hand. The patient's baseline blood pressure (SBP, DBP, MAP), heart rate (HR), oxygen saturation, respiratory rate, and electrocardiogram (ECG) were monitored.

After a 5-minute monitoring period, patients in Group K were given a continuous infusion of Inj and ketamine at a rate of 10 mcg/kg/min and patients in Group KD were given. (200 mcg of dexmedetomidine was diluted in 50ml normal saline to give a concentration of 4 mcg/ml). Both drugs are administered through separate syringe pumps. General anaesthesia was induced by using in. thiopentone at 5 mg/kg after preloading with 4 ml/kg of crystalloid solution. Inj. Succinylcholine 1mg/kg was used for endotracheal intubation. Anaesthesia was maintained on sevoflurane and N2O: O2 (50:50). Inj. vecuronium was used as muscle relaxant. A bi-spectral index was used for the target of BIS between 40 and 50. Additional monitors after intubation have consisted of Heart rate, spo2, NIBP, end-tidal carbon dioxide (EtCO2) and ECG.

Mechanical ventilation was maintained with a tidal volume of 6-8 ml/kg, and ventilation frequency was set to maintain ETco2 between 35-40 mm Hg. Anaesthesia was maintained with sevoflurane which was regulated at 0.8-1.8 volume % adjusted minimal alveolar concentration (MAC). Inj. Diclofenac 1mg/kg IV (max dose-75 mg) was given at the completion of closure to all the participants of either group.

Once the surgery was complete, Infusions of the study drugs were stopped, oral suctioning was performed and Inj. Glycopyrrolate 0.5 mg and Inj. Neostigmine 2.5 mg was given to reverse the action of neuromuscular blockage after affirming the return of some neuromuscular function.

Inhalational agent cut-off (defined as time '0' in the emergence process) in either group ventilation was changed to manual ventilation at 6-8 L /min. Except for continuous verbal requests to open their eyes and occasional glabellar tap, the patient was not disturbed. All other stimuli were averted. When the patient began to breathe spontaneously, extubation was initiated regularly till the patient was in a position to respond to verbal commands.

7. RESULTS

The mean total dose of fentanyl required perioperatively in group K and group KD

The average amount of fentanyl that was needed in both groups, K and KD, was 3.17 + 9.868. It was determined to be statistically significant (p 0.05) using an unpaired t-test (table 1).

The mean time for the first dosage of fentanyl to be administered in groups K and KD following intubation.

The average amount of time needed to administer the first dosage of fentanyl after intubation was 5.60 + 0.675 in group K and 83.33 + 25.74 in group KD. Unpaired t-test analysis revealed that it was statistically insignificant (p 0.05) (table 2).

According to our findings, neither the K nor the KD groups vary from one another in terms of age, gender, or weight at the outset (P>0.05). Mitra et al. (2017) conducted a prospective randomised comparative study comparing intraoperative low-dose ketamine and dexmedetomidine as an anaesthetic adjuvant in lumbar spine instrumentation surgery for the postoperative analgesic requirement. Additionally, they discovered no statistically significant change in the baseline demographics of age, gender, and weight across the ketamine, dexmedetomidine, and saline groups (P>0.05). In our current investigation, group K and Group KD's demographic profiles were so comparable.

In this investigation, we discovered that there was a statistically significant difference in the average amount of time needed to provide the initial opioid dose (P = 0.001). The average amount of time needed to administer the first dosage of fentanyl after intubation was 5.60 + 0.675 in group K and 83.33 + 25.74 in group KD. The mean time needed to administer the first dosage of opioid was much longer in group KD, possibly as a result of the dexmedetomidine infusion. We gave all of the patients in group K inj. fentanyl two mcg/kg immediately following intubation because there was an increase in heart rate and blood pressure in that group immediately following intubation, which may have been caused by an intubation pressure reaction. To determine the impact of dexmedetomidine on opioid use and pain management, Liu et al. (2021) performed a meta-analysis of randomised controlled trials of patients who underwent laparoscopic cholecystectomy. In terms of outcomes, eight trials reported

Table 1. Mean total dose of fentanyl required perioperatively in group K and group KD

	The Mean Total Dose of Fentanyl					
	Mean	SD	Maximum	Minimum	t-Value	P Value
Group K	113.67	16.07	140	100	58.43	0.0001*
Group KD	3.17	9.868	40	0		

Table 2. Mean time for administration of the first dose of fentanyl after intubation in Group K and Group KD

	Mean Time the First Dose of Fentanyl					
	Mean	SD	Maximum	Minimum	t-Value	P Value
Group K	5.60	0.675	7	5	5.026	0.001
Group KD	83.33	25.74	100	0		

opioid consumption in the first 24 hours following surgery, five trials reported the time of the patient's first request for analgesia, seven trials reported the time of the patient's first request for analgesia, and four trials reported the incidence of patient need for rescue analgesics. The period between the initial request for analgesia and the DEX infusion was dramatically extended. DEX dramatically decreased the amount of opioids consumed in the first 24 hours following surgery, according to research done on 577 registered participants. As a result, our findings regarding the meantime for the initial opioid dose were in line with those of the earlier research.

A large portion of group K patients experienced distress after being extubated. As evidenced in the majority of our patients in group KD, dexmedetomidine's ability to inhibit CNS sympathetic activity allows for a seamless transition from the time of reversal administration to the post-extubation phase, resulting in a high quality of extubation. The mean Riker sedation agitation score was considerably lower in the dexmedetomidine group compared to the control group in a randomised controlled trial evaluating the sevoflurane-sparing effect of dexmedetomidine in patients having laparoscopic cholecystectomy by Ahuja et al., (2017).

8. DISCUSSION

The anesthesiologist community has a constant need for the widespread availability of a medicine capable of reliably and irreversibly blocking all potentially lethal reactions to unpleasant stimuli. In order to determine whether the addition of dexmedetomidine would reduce the dose of opioids and anaesthetics for attenuation of haemodynamic response during laryngoscopy, tracheal intubation, surgery, and extubation, we devised a prospective randomised comparative study with a focus on dexmedetomidine's multidimensional features.

We examined the perioperative opioid demand in head and neck procedures between low-dose ketamine and low-dose ketamine-dexmedetomidine combo in a retrospective, randomised, comparative research.

We have administered Inj. fentanyl (1-2 mcg), when the blood pressure is more than 140/90 mm of Hg or the heart rate is more than 110 beats per minute in the two consecutive readings 5 minutes apart.

Demographics: In our study, we found that there is no statistically significant difference in baseline demographics like age, gender and weight between group K and group KD (P>0.05). Similarly, Mitra et al. (2017) conducted a prospective randomised comparative study between intraoperative low-dose ketamine and dexmedetomidine as an anaesthetic adjuvant in lumbar spine instrumentation surgery for the postoperative analgesic requirement.

Requirement of opioids: In our study, the mean total dose of fentanyl required in group K was $113 + 16.07$, and in the group, KD was $3.17 + 9.868$ (p=0.0001), which was statistically very significant. From the statistical analysis, we found that dexmedetomidine has the opioid-sparing property. In our study, we administered a loading dose of inj. Dexmedetomidine with one mcg/kg over a period of 10 minutes and maintenance dose of inj. Dexmedetomidine at the rate of 0.5 mcg/kg/hr and received a continuous infusion of inj. Ketamine at a rate of 10 mcg/kg/min till the end of the surgery in group KD. In group KD, out of 30 subjects, only three patients only required inj. fentanyl intraoperatively. Whereas in group K, all the patients required inj. fentanyl immediately after intubation to make the patient haemodynamically stable.

Haemodynamic parameters: When comparing group K with group KD, we looked at mean heart rate, systolic blood pressure, diastolic blood pressure, and mean arterial pressure. Parameters in group K were found to vary significantly from those in group KD (p 0.05). When comparing group K with group

KD from 10 minutes before intubation to 6 hours after arrival at the post anaesthesia care unit, group KD had considerably lower mean heart rate, systolic blood pressure, diastolic blood pressure, and mean arterial pressure (PACU). Patients who had undergone neurosurgery were the focus of a retrospective investigation by Su et al. (2016). Both the D group (in which dexmedetomidine was infused at a rate of 0.5 g/kg for 10 minutes before being lowered to 0.3 g/kg/h till incision suturing) and the ND group (in which no anaesthetic was administered) had similar outcomes (no dexmedetomidine infusion during surgery). Heart rate (HR) in group D was considerably reduced from intubation to 20 minutes after arrival at the after-anaesthesia care unit (PACU), and mean arterial pressure (MAP) in group D was significantly reduced from intubation to 5 minutes after arrival at the PACU, compared with group ND.

Emergence and agitation: In our study, the grading of emergence agitation was assessed using the Riker sedation agitation scale. It was observed that there was a statistically significant difference in the Riker sedation agitation scale between group K and group KD (p=0.001). Most of the patients in group KD were calm, cooperative and sedated after extubation. Most of the patients in group K were agitated after extubation. Dexmedetomidine, by suppressing the CNS sympathetic activity, enables a smooth transition from the time of administration of reversal to the post-extubation phase, leading to a high quality of extubation, as was observed in the majority of our patients in group KD.

Quality of recovery: In our study, the Modified Aldrete score was used to assess the recovery one hour after surgery. It was observed that there was no statistically significant difference in the modified Aldrete score between group K and group KD (p=0.156). The effect of intraoperative dexmedetomidine infusion on improving the quality of recovery has not been studied widely. Many studies concluded that dexmedetomidine infusion doesn't affect the quality of recovery.

Cough during emergence: The severity of coughing during emergence was measured using the cough scale in our research. The difference between K and KD was not statistically significant (P = 0.247). Studying the effectiveness of a single dosage of dexmedetomidine for cough suppression during anaesthetic emergence, Hilly, et al., (2016) drew their conclusions. Dexmedetomidine patients had a much lower coughing rate than placebo patients. The dexmedetomidine group also had a decreased median cough grade upon extubation.

Tidal volume was kept at 6–8 ml/kg, and ventilation frequency was chosen to keep ETco2 at 35–40 mm Hg during mechanical ventilation. Sevoflurane, which was controlled at an adjusted minimal alveolar concentration of 0.8–1.8 volume%, was used to maintain anaesthesia (MAC). When the patient started breathing on his or her own, extubation was started and continued until the patient was able to respond to spoken directions. In our research, we used the Riker scale to measure the level of sedation agitation experienced by participants.

9. CONCLUSION

At the conclusion of closure, all individuals in either group received an IV injection of diclofenac 1 mg/kg (max dose: 75 mg). Immediately following the procedure, once some neuromuscular function had been confirmed to have returned, the study medications' intravenous infusions were halted, oral suctioning was carried out, and injections of glycopyrrolate 0.5 mg and neostigmine 2.5 mg were administered to end the action of neuromuscular blockade. Both groups' ventilation switched to manual ventilation at a rate of 6–8 L/min after the inhalational agent cut-off, which is represented by time '0' in the emerging process. The patient wasn't disturbed other than by constant verbal commands to open their eyes and the occasional tapping of the glabella. Significant differences were seen between groups K and KD on the Riker Sedation Agitation Scale (p 001). Heart rate, systolic blood pressure, diastolic blood pressure, and mean arterial pressure were measured and compared between groups K and KD after extubation. It was observed that there was a statistically significant difference (p 0.05) in the parameters between the K and KD groups. Throughout the perioperative period, the KD group maintained consistent vital signs, including heart rate, systolic blood pressure, diastolic blood pressure, and mean arterial pressure on average.

REFERENCES

Abdalla, M. W., El Shal, S. M., El Sombaty, A. I., Abdalla, N. M., & Zeedan, R. B. (2015). Propofol dexmedetomidine versus propofol ketamine for anesthesia of endoscopic retrograde cholangiopancreatography (ERCP) (A randomised comparative study). *Egyptian Journal of Anaesthesia, 31*(2), 97–105. doi:10.1016/j.egja.2014.12.008

Ahuja, V., Sharma, P., Gombar, S., Jain, A., & Dalal, U. (2017). Sevoflurane sparing effect of dexmedetomidine in patients undergoing laparoscopic cholecystectomy: A randomized controlled trial. *Journal of Anaesthesiology, Clinical Pharmacology, 33*(4), 496. doi:10.4103/joacp.JOACP_144_16 PMID:29416243

Andjelković, L., Novak-Janković, V., Požar-Lukanovič, N., Bosnić, Z., & Spindler-Vesel, A. (2018). Influence of dexmedetomidine and lidocaine on perioperative opioid consumption in laparoscopic intestine resection: A randomised controlled clinical trial. *The Journal of International Medical Research, 46*(12), 5143–5154. doi:10.1177/0300060518792456 PMID:30209962

Bajwa, S. J. S., Kaur, J., Singh, A., Parmar, S., Singh, G., Kulshrestha, A., Gupta, S., Sharma, V., & Panda, A. (2012). Attenuation of pressor response and dose sparing of opioids and anaesthetics with pre-operative dexmedetomidine. *Indian Journal of Anaesthesia, 56*(2), 123–128. doi:10.4103/0019-5049.96303 PMID:22701201

Boenigk, K., Echevarria, G. C., Nisimov, E., von Bergen Granell, A. E., Cuff, G. E., Wang, J., & Atchabahian, A. (2019). Low-dose ketamine infusion reduces postoperative hydromorphone requirements in opioid-tolerant patients following spinal fusion: A randomised controlled trial: A randomised controlled trial. *European Journal of Anaesthesiology, 36*(1), 8–15. doi:10.1097/EJA.0000000000000877 PMID:30113350

El Sharkawy, R. A. (2019). Efficacy of adding low-dose ketamine to dexmedetomidine versus low-dose ketamine and propofol for conscious sedation in patients undergoing awake fiber-optic intubation. *Anesthesia, Essays and Researches, 13*(1), 73–78. doi:10.4103/aer.AER_181_18 PMID:31031484

Hilly, J., Bellon, M., Le, A., Daphne, B., Maesani, M., & Brasher, C. (2016). *Efficacy of Intraoperative Dexmedetomidine Compared with Placebo for Postoperative Pain Management : A Meta-Analysis of Published Studies*. Academic Press.

Jeganathan, J., Vashist, S., Nirmala, G., & Deep, R. (2023). A Cross Sectional Study on Anxiety and Depression Among Patients with Alcohol Withdrawal Syndrome. *FMDB Transactions on Sustainable Health Science Letters, 1*(1), 31–40.

Liu, Y., Zhao, G., Zang, X., Lu, F., Liu, P., & Chen, W. (2021). Effect of dexmedetomidine on opioid consumption and pain control after laparoscopic cholecystectomy: A meta-analysis of randomized controlled trials. *Wideochirurgia i Inne Techniki Malo Inwazyjne*, *16*(3), 491–500. doi:10.5114/wiitm.2021.104197 PMID:34691300

M, A., K, T., Munshi, Y, J., M, R., & M, S. (2019). Assessment of heavy metal contents in commercial feedstuffs and broiler (Gallus domesticus) meat and its impact on Swiss albino mice as an animal model. *Agricultural Science Digest - A Research Journal*. doi:10.18805/ag.D-4898

Md, N., Hasan, M., Munshi, M. H., Rahman, S. M. N., & Alam, A. (2014). Evaluation of antihyperglycemic activity of Lasia spinosa leaf extracts in Swiss albino mice. *World Journal of Pharmacy and Pharmaceutical Sciences*, *3*(10), 118–124.

Miller, R. D. (2010). *Anaesthesia* (7th ed.). Churchill Livingstone.

Mitra, R., Prabhakar, H., Rath, G., Bithal, P., & Khandelwal, A. (2017). A comparative study between intraoperativelow-dose ketamine and dexmedetomidine, as an anaesthetic adjuvant in lumbar spine instrumentation surgery for the postoperative analgesic requirement. *Journal of Neuroanaesthesiology and Critical Care*, *4*(2), 91–98. doi:10.4103/jnacc-jnacc-3.17

Munshi, M., Sohrab, M. H., Begum, M. N., Rony, S. R., Karim, M. A., Afroz, F., & Hasan, M. N. (2021). Evaluation of bioactivity and phytochemical screening of endophytic fungi isolated from Ceriops decandra (Griff.) W. Theob, a mangrove plant in Bangladesh. *Clinical Phytoscience*, *7*(1), 81. Advance online publication. doi:10.118640816-021-00315-y

Munshi, M., Tumu, K. N., Hasan, M. N., & Amin, M. Z. (2018). Biochemical effects of commercial feedstuffs on the fry of climbing perch (Anabas testudineus) and its impact on Swiss albino mice as an animal model. *Toxicology Reports*, *5*, 521–530. doi:10.1016/j.toxrep.2018.04.004 PMID:29707493

Munshi, M., Zilani, M. N. H., Islam, M. A., Biswas, P., Das, A., Afroz, F., & Hasan, M. N. (2022). Novel compounds from endophytic fungi of Ceriops decandra inhibit breast cancer cell growth through estrogen receptor alpha in in-silico study. *Informatics in Medicine Unlocked*, *32*(101046), 101046. doi:10.1016/j.imu.2022.101046

Nikoubakht, N., Alimian, M., Faiz, S. H. R., Derakhshan, P., & Sadri, M. S. (2021). Effects of ketamine versus dexmedetomidine maintenance infusion in posterior spinal fusion surgery on acute postoperative pain. *Surgical Neurology International*, *12*(192), 192. doi:10.25259/SNI_850_2020 PMID:34084620

Nirmala, G., Premavathy, R., Chandar, R., & Jeganathan, J. (2023). An Explanatory Case Report on Biopsychosocial Issues and the Impact of Innovative Nurse-Led Therapy in Children with Hematological Cancer. *FMDB Transactions on Sustainable Health Science Letters*, *1*(1), 1–10.

Pandit, P. (2023). On the Context of Diabetes: A Brief Discussion on the Novel Ethical Issues of Noncommunicable Diseases. *FMDB Transactions on Sustainable Health Science Letters*, *1*(1), 11–20.

Peng, K., Zhang, J., Meng, X., Liu, H., & Ji, F. (2017). Optimisation of Postoperative Intravenous Patient-Controlled Analgesia with Opioid-Dexmedetomidine Combinations : An Updated Meta-Analysis with Trial Sequential Analysis of Randomiz. *Optimisation of Postoperative Intravenous Patient - Controlled Analgesi.*

Savola, J.-M., & Virtanen, R. (1991). Central α2-adrenoceptors are highly stereoselective for dexmedetomidine, the dextro enantiomer of medetomidine. *European Journal of Pharmacology*, *195*(2), 193–199. doi:10.1016/0014-2999(91)90535-X PMID:1678707

Stoelting, R. K. (2006). Pharmacology and physiology in anaesthesia practice Lippincott-Raven.

Su, S., Ren, C., Zhang, H., Liu, Z., & Zhang, Z. (2016). *The Opioid-Sparing Effect of Perioperative Dexmedetomidine Plus Sufentanil Infusion during Neurosurgery : A Retrospective Study*. Academic Press.

Vashishtha, E., & Dhawan, G. (2023). Bridging Generation Gap on Analysis of Mentor-Mentee Relationship in Healthcare Setting. *FMDB Transactions on Sustainable Health Science Letters*, *1*(1), 21–30.

Chapter 15

Plant Species Classification Using Information Measure and Deep Learning for an Actual Environmental Problem

Pankaj Dwivedi

Jaypee University of Engineering and Technology, India

Dilip Kumar Sharma

Jaypee University of Engineering and Technology, India

ABSTRACT

This chapter's major goal is to examine the issue of real-world recognition to enhance species preservation. As it is a popular topic and a crucial one, the authors focus on identifying plant species. The examples are scanned specimens in traditional plant species identification, and the setting is plain. Real-world species recognition, on the other hand, is more difficult. They begin by looking at realistic species recognition and how it differs from traditional plant species recognition. Interdisciplinary teamwork based on the newest breakthroughs in technology and computer science is provided to cope with the difficult challenge. In this research, they offer a unique framework for deep learning as well as an effective data augmentation strategy. They crop the image before everyone is aware in terms of visual attention. Furthermore, they use it as a data augmentation technique. Attention cropping (AC) is the name given to a revolutionary data augmentation technique. To predict species from a significant quantity of information, fully convolutional neural networks (CNN) are constructed.

1. INTRODUCTION

Plants are important in our environment, and they have a direct impact on a variety of areas like ecological systems, agriculture, climate, etc. Furthermore, they constitute the primary food supply for human existence and growth. Many issues, such as global warming, ecosystem damage, environmental

DOI: 10.4018/978-1-6684-9189-8.ch015

degradation, species extinction, habitat loss, etc. are linked to plant conservation. Identification of plant species is required for protection. There have been a lot of studies done on the subject. The picture classification approach is currently thought to be useful in improving plant taxonomy. As described in (Goeau, et al., 2016), it is one of the most promising options among the relevant study effort. It has also been a popular study topic for a long time. Flowers and fruits of plants are seasonal, many experts feel leaves are a better way to identify them. Leaves were widely employed for computer-aided plant species categorization in the early days. Leaf pictures were used in most suggested image-based identification algorithms and assessment data (Kumar, et al., 2012; Backes, et al., 2009; Cerutti, et al., 2011). Sun et al., (2022) provides two new species of Glossophyllum are described and 12 species are recognized. Many leaf photos, on the other hand, are specimens or were scanned at the time.

The procedure for obtaining samples is very precise. Following that, flowers are used (Cerutti, et al., 2011). Approaches based (Nilsback, & Zisserman, 2008; Xu, et al., 2021; Nilsback, & Zisserman, 2006) solely on leaves or flowers are unsatisfactory when it comes to protection and realistic identification of the plant. For correct identification, many different sections of plants must be evaluated, especially when plants cannot see their leaves throughout the year. The backdrop in those datasets where the camera is close to targets when individuals snap images is simple when compared to images captured in actual ways. We feel those are not real-world recognizance tasks. We concentrate on plant species identification in this paper, particularly realistic recognition. Plant picture examples should comprise multiple components, such as fruits, branches, and full plants, in addition to leaves and flowers, plant identification task for the real world. Simultaneously, the process of creating and acquiring plant photos should not be rigid. They can take snapshots at different times and in other locations, and users can do so at their leisure. Image examples may have a cluttered backdrop.

Furthermore, the scenario combines both interior and outdoor elements. We feel these are appropriate plant identification for the real world. Identification of species is more challenging than standard species identification, but it is also more valuable. We can only achieve better, more convenient, and comprehensive plant protection if we recognize real-world species. Several programs and organizations, such as Botanica and naturalist, have been able to generate huge volumes of biodiversity data in recent years. In comparison to the past, large amounts of biodiversity data may be more easily accessible (Agarwal, et al., 2006). Because the great majority of people find it handy to take photos of plants using their mobile phones (Suganthi & Sathiaseelan, 2023). The process of creating and acquiring plant photos gets simpler and more like that of a real-world situation. Furthermore, individuals like sharing them and conversing with one another on their social networks. We begin by reviewing related work about plant species recognition in this publication. We cover how to identify traditional species using leaf and flower identification methods. To solve the challenge of realistic recognition, we provide an effective data augmentation strategy and a new framework. We employ deep learning to perform our research because deep convolutional neural networks (CNNs) are a powerful tool for large-scale picture categorization.

As mentioned in (Klein, et al., 2021; Neisser, et al., 2022), our human visual attention is focused on the prominent things that must be identified in a picture. We call the procedure attention cropping (AC) because we crop the image based on our visual attention. The saliency detection technique is used to achieve AC using the obtained saliency map. Data augmentation is a crucial operation in deep learning, as we all know. We use AC in this paper for deep learning as a data augmentation strategy. Figure 1, (Figure 3, Figure 5) depicts a schematic representation of our architecture. Several comparisons confirm our suggested technique, and the findings reveal that superior outcomes are produced (Saxena & Chaudhary, 2023). This study identifies and categorize a plant species based on a photograph. We return a description of the plant and indicate an eventual illness after the categorization is complete (Ogunmola, et al., 2021).

The development of food crops is significantly impacted by the different plant diseases. The Irish potato famine of 1845–1849, which claimed 1.2 million lives is one well-known example (Sharma, et al., 2021a). It requires time, effort, and specialised knowledge for humans to identify plant diseases according to their expertise and by studying the disease's characteristics on leaves and stems (Sankaran, et al., 2010). Due to the diversity of plants, various crops also exhibit diverse disease features, which adds a great deal of complexity to the categorization of plant illnesses. In the meanwhile, several research has concentrated on the machine learning-based categorization of plant diseases (Priscila, et al., 2023). The three main steps in using machine learning methods for recognizing plant diseases are as follows: Firstly, removing historical information or segmenting the afflicted region using pre-processing techniques; second, collecting the distinguishing characteristics for further analysis; and finally, classifying the features employing automated classification or unsupervised algorithms for clustering (Barbedo 2014; Feng, et al., 2016; Omrani, et al., 2014; Barbedo Arnal, 2017). A large portion of machine learning research has focused on classifying plant diseases using characteristics like the texture (Mokhtar, et al., 2015), type (Rumpf, et al., 2010), and colour (Hossain, et al., 2019) of images of plant leaves. The three main classification methods are support vector machines (Rumpf, et al., 2010). K-nearest neighbours (Hossain, et al., 2019), and random forests (Hossain, et al., 2019). Following is a list of these techniques' main drawbacks:

Poor performance (Türkoğlu & Hanbay, 2019): Because the performance they attained was subpar, real-time categorization was impossible. Professional database (Arivazhagan, et al., 2013): The datasets they used included photos of plants that were challenging to find in real life. In the instance of Plant Village, the dataset was collected in an ideal laboratory setting where each image only contained one plant leaf and the surrounding environment had no impact on the photograph. Seldom utilized (Jiang, et al., 2020; Gao, et al., 2020). They frequently need to manually develop and extract characteristics, which necessitates professional skills from research employees (Arslan, et al., 2021). Necessitating the use of segmented operation (Athanikar and Badar, 2016): To get research datasets, plants must be cut off from their roots (Cirillo, et al., 2023). This process obviously isn't suitable for real-time applications (Sharma, et al., 2021b). The majority of conventional machine learning algorithms were developed under laboratory circumstances and lack the resilience required for real-world agricultural applications. Convolutional neural network (CNN)-based deep learning (DL) techniques, in particular, are finding a lot of use in the agricultural sector nowadays for tasks like plant disease diagnosis (Bansal, et al., 2021), weed detection (Yu, et al., 2019), and crop pest categorization (Sharma, et al., 2021c).

A machine learning study area is deep learning. Traditional machine learning techniques' issues with lack of actual pictures (Arivazhagan, et al., 2013), poor performance (Türkoğlu & Hanbay, 2019), and segmented operation (Athanikar & Badar, 2016) have been resolved, at least in part (Sharma, et al., 2021d). The key benefit of DL models is their ability to extract features without the need for segmented operations while still achieving acceptable performance. Automatic feature extraction from the underlying data occurs for each item (Jeba, et al., 2023). The Neocognitron, created by Kunihiko Fukushima in 1980, served as the foundation for CNNs (Wang and Raj, 2017). Plant disease categorization systems are now more effective and automated because to the development of CNNs.

The study are structured as: In part 2, we looked at the most recent CNN networks that were pertinent to categorising plant leaf diseases. In section 3, we provided a summary of CNN, Shannon's Information Measures, and Deep Learning ideas. In section 4, we detailed the main problems and suitable CNN solutions utilised for categorising plant diseases and provided results. In section 5, we discussed about the potential developments in the categorization of plant diseases. Finally, in section 6 includes the conclusion of study.

2. DATASET

The new plant diseases dataset is from Kaggle, and it has been rigorously tested by many users. It contains no mistakes or incorrectly categorized photos. This Dataset is made up of leaves that have been spread out on a consistent background as given in Figure 7. And contains around 87,000 images of leaves diseased and healthy. Those pictures represent 14 plants over 38 classes:

The percentage distribution and classification of disease given in Figure 7 continue as Tomato, Strawberry, Squash, Soyabean, Raspberry, Potato, Bell paper, Peach, Orange, Grape, Corn Maize, Cherry, Blueberry, Apple.

The distribution is as per above. The dataset has been recreated using offline augmentation from another dataset, thus as we can see in the prior graph the classes are well balanced (with around 3% for each class's external layer).

Figure 1. Sample of Swedish leaf, samples of Flavia leaf, and Oxford flower. Illustration of image classification of our proposed method in a general way.

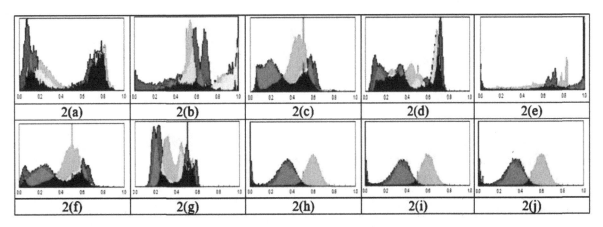

Figure 2. Histogram of image classification of Figure 1

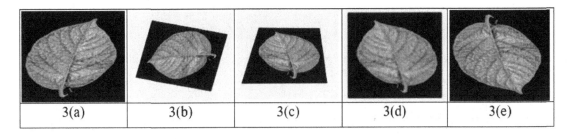

Figure 3. Classification of the image in the proposed method in a general way

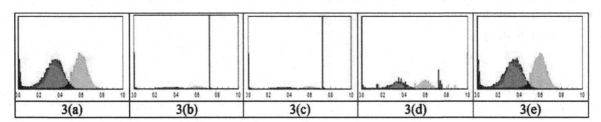

Figure 4. Histogram of image classification of Figure 3

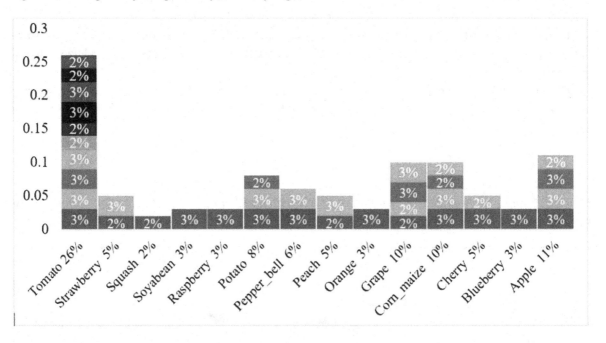

3. SHANNON'S INFORMATION MEASURES, DEEP LEARNING, AND CONVOLUTION NEURAL NETWORK MODELS

Shannon's Information: Suppose $\Delta_n^+ = \left\{ p = (p_1, p_2, \ldots\ldots p_n); p_i \geq 0, \sum_i^n p_i = 1 \right\}$, are a collection of all potential discrete distributions of likelihood.

Shannon (1948), first investigated and characterized, through certain postulates, a measure of information given by

$$H(P) = -\sum_{i=1}^{n} p_i \log p_i \qquad (1)$$

For all $p_1, p_2, \ldots\ldots p_n \in \Delta_n^+$

Figure 5. Classification of the image in the proposed method in a general way

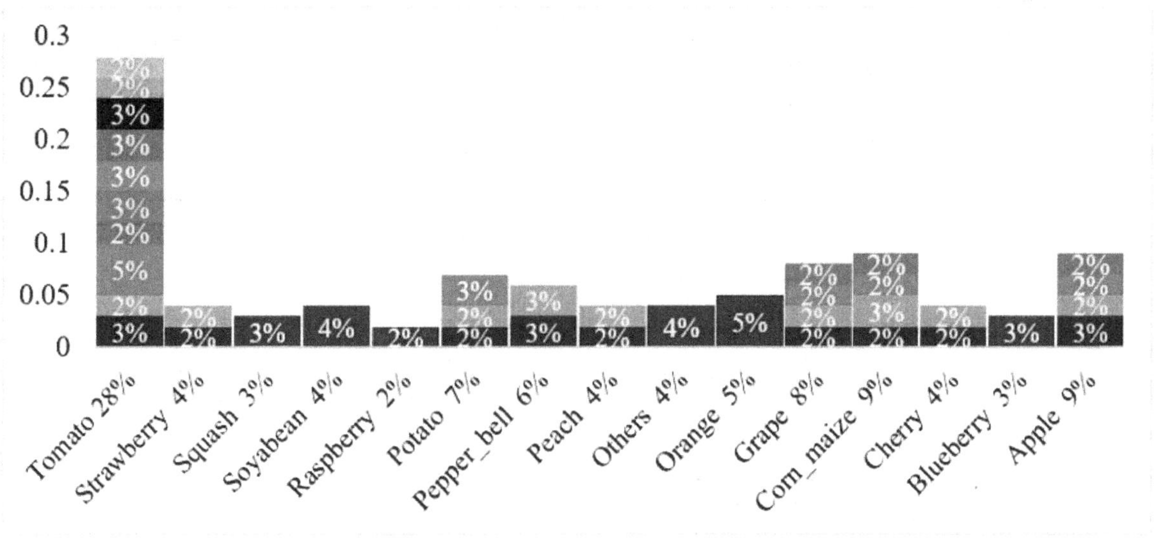

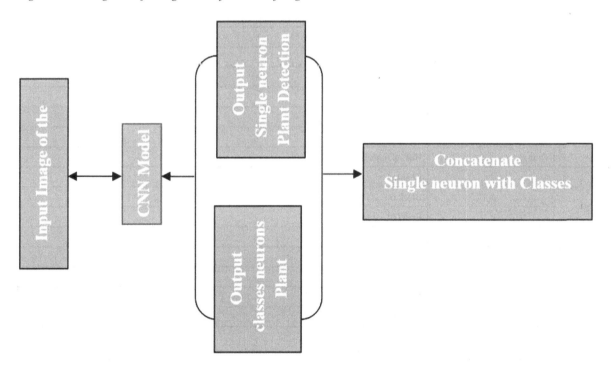

Figure 6. Histogram of image classification of Figure 5

Shannon's entropy is the term used in the literature to describe $H(P)$ in Equation (1).

Remarks. It is assumed that all logarithms are in base 2 throughout these notes, and $0.\log 0 = 0$.

Equation (1) is also known as an uncertainty measure. It determines how much information is included in a distribution, i.e., how much uncertainty there is about the outcome of an experiment. Several

Table 1. Diseases per plant

S.N.	Plants	Diseases
1	Tomato	Healthy
		Bacterial spot
		Early blight
		Late blight
		Leaf Mold
		Septoria leaf spot
		Spider mites Two-spotted spider mite
		Target spot
		Tomato mosaic virus
		Tomato Yellow Leaf Curl Virus
2	Strawberry	Healthy
		Leaf Scorch
3	Squasch	Powdery mildew
4	Soyabean	Healthy
5	Raspberry	Healthy
6	Potato	Healthy
		Early blight
		Late blight
7	Bell paper	Healthy
		Bacterial spot
8	Peach	Healthy
		Bacterial spot
9	Orange	Huanglongbing
10	Grape	Healthy
		Black rot
		Esca (Black Measles)
		Leaf blight
11	Corn Maize	Healthy
		Cercosporin Leaf spot
		Common rust
		Northern Leaf Blight
12	Cherry	Healthy Powdery mildew
13	Blueberry	Healthy
14	Apple	Healthy
		Apple scab
		Black rot
		Cedar Apple rust

Figure 7. Distribution of the classes in the dataset and their percentages

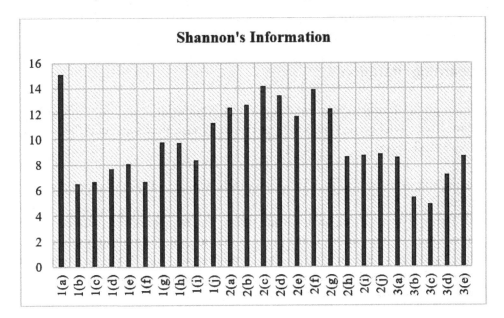

authors, beginning with Shannon (1948), have demonstrated the measure of the quantity of information [Eq. (1)] is uniquely defined by natural postulates. Dwivedi and Sharma (2021) provides 'Useful' Renyi Information Rate.

Deep Learning: Modern state-of-the-art for solving most picture classification problems is Deep Learning (DL), constituting the most extensive study field in this discipline, and obtaining results that are equivalent to or better than humans. Some works utilizing DL for plant identification can be found in the literature, including a couple published in the grapevine setting.

Convolution Neural Network: When compared to convolutional neural networks, recurrent neural networks (RNNs) are less often utilised in classification and computer vision applications. Identifying things in photos before CNNs necessitated the use of time-consuming feature extraction methods. Convolutional neural networks are more extensible for image processing and object recognition applications because they leverage linear algebra techniques, particularly matrix multiplication, to discover patterns within an image. We used a web scraping script to retrieve photos from "Google Images" to test our model on photographs of leaves in a vegetal setting. This test dataset has 38 classes as well as a class called "Others" that represents photos without plants.

When compared to the original Dataset, the photos from the test set do not follow the same format (one leaf per image).

4. RESULT

In this section, we calculate new plant diseases from the dataset by deep learning, and the information measure plant diseases from the dataset Shannon's entropy by of various plant leaves which are mentioned in Figure 1, Figure 3, and Figure 5 with their histogram data from Figure 2, Figure 4, and Figure 6 respectively. We used a web scraping script to retrieve photos from "Google Images" to test our model on photographs of leaves in a vegetal setting. This test dataset has 38 classes as well as a class called "Others" that represents photos without plants. When compared to the original Dataset, the photos from the test set do not follow the same format (one leaf per image).

4.1 Deep Learning: Iteration 1

In the first phase, we use TensorFlow to create our own CNN model:

Tensor Flow: This model is composed of three convolutional blocks and one classification block. Convolutional block layers:

- **Image size:** Images are scaled to 128x128x3 pixels, which is a fair balance between processing time and data loss.
- **Conv2D:** Extract patterns from photos using filters. The number of filters for each Conv2D layer has been increased in comparison to the previous one to capture a broader variety of patterns.
- **Activation function:** Use Relu, which is the most often used for CNN, to apply non-linearity.
- **Batch Normalization (BN)** is a technique for normalizing the output of preceding layers. It improves CNN's speed, and stability, and reduces overfitting.
- **MaxPool2D:** Reduce the dimensionality of pictures by reducing the number of pixels, which decreases the number of model parameters and gives the internal representation a modest scale invariance.

Layers of classification blocks:

- **Dense:** For categorization, three completely linked layers are employed.
- **Dropout:** Avoid overfitting by disregarding chosen neurons at random during training.

Layer between Conv blocks and classification blocks:

- **GlobalAveragePooling2D (GAP):** It calculates the average of each feature Map's values. Unlike the "flatten" layer, "GAP" eliminates a significant number of trainable parameters, offers translation invariance, and hence decreases overfitting.

Regularization: We utilized L2 regularization, which adds the sum of squared parameters (weights) to the loss function to prevent overfitting.

The following is the model code:

On the validation dataset, this model has a **99.3** percent accuracy.

The test dataset, however, makes very poor predictions, with an accuracy of **13.2** percent.

An Overview of Iteration 1:

- Dataset: "new-plant-diseases-dataset," which consists of photos of leaves on a consistent backdrop.
- Excellent Validation Dataset prediction — Val accuracy > 99 percent.
- Poor predictions on the Test Dataset, which consists of photographs of leaves in a natural setting.
- Plants are predicted by the model even when there are no plants in the picture.

Our model was trained with a dataset of leaves photographs on a uniform background, which is the major cause for poor predictions of leaves images in a real context. Furthermore, because no photos in the training dataset are without plants, our model will be unable to predict that no plant would be present in the images if this occurs.

4.2 Deep Learning: Iteration 2

We sought to enhance our models in a second iteration by adding a vegetative backdrop to the leaf's photos. We changed our dataset and utilized the Kaggle plant village dataset, which is identical to our initial dataset (leaves photos on a uniform backdrop) but does not include any data augmentation. Consequently, the dataset is severely uneven (with more than 5000 photos in some classes and less than 200 images in others), but it does contain segmented leaves images that might be used to create vegetal backdrops. To rebalance this dataset, a data augmentation was performed following the transformations described hereafter. The distribution of the classes in the Dataset after data augmentation is Illustrated in Figure 8.

To detect the absence of plants in the images, we add another class "Others" to our dataset using random images from the "Image-net" dataset. After data augmentation and adding the new class "Others," this dataset contains 114 077 images distributed as follows:

To import photographs and provide a backdrop, we utilized a "custom Dataset," which replaced black pixels in segmented pictures with our background pixels. The function "tf.where" replaces a pixel in the leaf image with one of the background pictures if the value of the pixel in the left image is less than a set threshold. It is worth noting that in the second version, we only utilized ONE backdrop for each plant kind. For example, the background for all tomato classes is the same tomato plants.

We compared the results from both iterations using the identical model, with the exception that the last Dense layer's output shape is 39 (38 plants + Others).

On the new validation dataset, this model has a **95.1** percent accuracy.

Figure 8. Distribution of the classes in the dataset after data augmentation

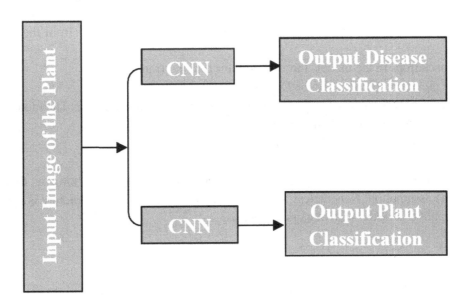

However, with an accuracy of **10.5** percent on the test dataset, it makes very poor predictions.
An overview of iteration 2:

- Dataset "Plant Village" with data enhancements and new classes added from dataset "Image-Net."
- Adding backdrops to the models throughout their training (only one background per plant type).
- Accurate picture predictions for the Dataset.
- Although there was a little increase in the predictions on the test dataset, the performance was still below expectations, particularly with photographs where the leaves could not be seen entirely.
- The model appears to be able to tell whether the image is of a plant.
- The model appears to be concentrating on the backdrop rather than the leaf itself.

Our model learned to utilize the backdrop instead of the leaves during iteration 2, therefore we produced iteration "2-bis" using the same model and technique, but instead of having a single background per plant, we generated a collection of backgrounds per plant that would be picked at random each time.

As a result, we produced one folder per plant (there are 14 plants in our Dataset), with the following information in each folder:

- 5 photos of the real plant (i.e.: potato plants for all potato classes).
- Each folder will have 4 photographs of plants, lawns, and forests.

This should aid the model's development.:

- Do not put too much emphasis on the backdrop image.
- Perform better in a real-world setting.

On the validation dataset, this model (2-bis) has a **98.4** percent accuracy.
However, with an accuracy of **18.1** percent on the test dataset, it makes very poor predictions.
An overview of the iteration 2-Bis:

- Dataset: "Plant Village" with data augmentation and additional classes from the "Image-Net" dataset.
- Adding backdrops to the models throughout their training (randomly).
- Accurate picture predictions for the Dataset.
- Predictions on the test dataset improved somewhat compared to iteration 2. The model is not concentrating on the background since it is random.
- The model appears to be able to tell whether the image is of a plant.

We can see some improvement in the forecast execution on our test dataset, however, the outcome is still beneath the assumption. Nonetheless, this model can anticipate whether a picture is a plant, which is an improvement contrasted with our first emphasis.

4.3 Deep Learning: Iteration 3

During Iteration 2, we incorporate another Class called "Others" and address pictures of "anything". This drive was to assist the model with trying not to anticipate a plant when there is none in the picture. However, we can see that the outcomes are not quite so great true to form on the test dataset. One arrangement is to anticipate the likelihood of a plant in a picture. One result addresses whether the picture is containing a plant, and the subsequent Output addresses the Plant Classification. The Iteration 3 model demonstrate in Figure 9.

Hereafter, the code of the model we used the Functional Model:

To evaluate how well our model predicts a dataset, we need to create a custom Loss Function:

$$Loss = \alpha_{Other} \times BinaryCrossEntropy + \alpha_{Plant} \times CatrgoricalCrossEntropy$$

Custom Loss function with $\alpha_{Other} = \{0,1\}$, whether the image is a plant (=1) or not (=0). The Categorical Cross entropy is not calculated if the image is not a plant.

As per our model, the first neuron represents whether the image contains a plant or not, and the 38 other neurons represent the plant classification. This model (3) gives an accuracy on the validation dataset of **97.4** percent. However, it gives very bad predictions on the test dataset with an accuracy of **19.2** percent. But predictions of images without plants (Class: Others) on the test Dataset are better than the ones done with the iteration 2-bis models.

An overview of iteration 3:

- Dataset: "Plant Village" with data augmentation and adding new classes from dataset "Image-Net."
- Excellent prediction on the Validation Dataset valid accuracy > 99%.
- Predictions on the Test Dataset are still bad.
- Better predictions of images without a plant (Class: Others) on the test Dataset.

Figure 9. Model Iteration 3

4.4 Shannon's Entropy

In the following Table 2, Table 3, and Table 4, we measure Shannon's information on the dataset.

The combine Shannon's Information on the leaves from Table 1, Table 2, and Table 3, and their data is represented in Figure 10.

Improvement

1. **New Dataset with Images in a real environment:** As we discovered during several testing stages, the model is doing incredible on pictures with just one leaf and uniform foundation yet cannot foresee pictures in normal spots. We attempted to fix this issue by adding a foundation, yet we can in any case see a few imperfections in the result. Making a full dataset from pictures taken straight-

Table 2. Shannon's information of images of Figure 1

S.N.	Images	Shannon's Information of Images $H = -\sum_{i=1}^{n} p_i \log p_i$
1	1(a)	15.09961
2	1(b)	6.52096
3	1(c)	6.69123
4	1(d)	7.65364
5	1(e)	8.10802
6	1(f)	6.66043
7	1(g)	9.73681
8	1(h)	9.70434
9	1(i)	8.37060
10	1(j)	11.28664

Table 3. Shannon's information of images of Figure 3

S.N.	Images	Shannon's Information of Images $H = -\sum_{i=1}^{n} p_i \log p_i$
1	2(a)	12.46423
2	2(b)	12.70497
3	2(c)	14.15058
4	2(d)	13.40404
5	2(e)	11.81646
6	2(f)	13.90879
7	2(g)	12.39568
8	2(h)	8.60063
9	2(i)	8.69906
10	2(j)	8.82883

Table 4. Shannon's information of images of Figure 5

S.N.	Images	Shannon's Information of Images $H = -\sum_{i=1}^{n} p_i \log p_i$
1	3(a)	8.56913
2	3(b)	5.40256
3	3(c)	4.92045
4	3(d)	7.17908
5	3(e)	8.64331

Figure 10. Data illustration of Shannon's information

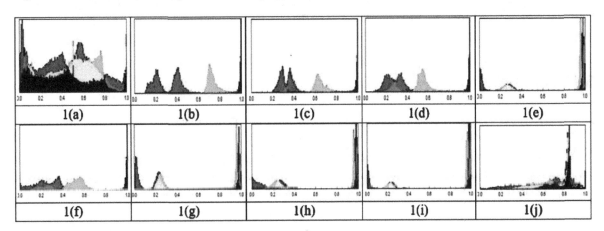

forwardly in a genuine climate (or a blend of both) may assist with working on the unwavering quality of the outcomes. This should be possible by utilizing Web Scraping.

2. **Concatenation of 2 models (multi-output)**: In the current Dataset, a few plants have a similar illness (i.e.: Bacterial Spot infection for tomato and peach leaves, or Late Blight sickness for potato and tomato leaves). In an indigenous habitat, our model appears to recognize the right illness yet not the right plant. One arrangement is to make a multi-yield model:
   ○ One model focuses on the leave classification.
   ○ One model focuses on Disease classification.

With this method, we can predict separately the plant and the disease. So, this can improve the model and might be able to predict known diseases on the new plant i.e.: Bacterial Spot (known disease) on Apple. The Multi-output of the Plant Disease and plant classification is represented in Figure 11.

3. **Semantic Segmentation:** To work on the expectation in a regular habitat, the utilization of a semantic division model like UNET, would assist with separating the pixels of the leaves, and afterwards, we would utilize the Leaves Classification model to foresee the actual plant.

Figure 11. Multi-output model

5. DISCUSSION

Due to the rapid development of intelligent devices such as smartphones, personal computers, fixed cameras, along with UAVs today, image categorization projects have grown more useful and highly intelligent. He and his co-workers put out a plan that relied on the widespread use of Android clients and servers. The plan is divided into two parts: (1) a mobile phone client that allows users to submit the gathered photographs to the server; (2) a server-side programme that processes the images and provides the user with the classification consequences. To make it easier for users to query, the server must additionally store the pertinent results in the database (He, et al., 2020). It is simple to implement the functionality of capturing images to identify pests and counting insects using the cloud platform. The use of deep learning in daily life will expand rapidly with the swift development of intelligent products. Yet, rural areas might occasionally be located distant from urban centres. Mobile clients and Edge devices, which may be deployed offline and don't need to transfer data to the server, could be excellent measures in this situation. It is possible to use the electrical impulses output produced by plants to identify plant illnesses in real-time, according to several studies (Shre, 2017; Najdenovska, et al., 2021). Plants use electrical impulses to sense their environment (Chatterjee, et al., 2015) and fundamentally signify alterations in basic physiological systems. While under the influence of stress (such as disease), the metabolic activities of many plant tissues and cells are unstable, which will be represented in physiologically electrical characteristics. Hence, a useful study approach for the categorization of plant illnesses would be the extraction of significant features from the generating electrical signals and the utilisation of such extracted features (Chatterjee, et al., 2018). We talked about the potential avenues for future research in plant disease categorization, such as plant electrophysiology and the coupling of a server-side application with a mobile phone client. Due to the challenges in detecting precise tree placements and crown extensions, independent validated spatially explicit reference data on tree species occurrence are scarce (Fassnacht et al., 2016). Locally acquired and gridded products utilising the study's suggested method could aid in bridging this gap. Vijayaraghavareddy et al. (2022) examined rice and wheat to explore the variations in drought-adaptive processes at the species level as wheat is known to endure drought better than rice in their study. Erik and Alexandra's study (Murchie & Burgess, 2022) examined how architectural features impact photosynthesis and light absorption. They also talk about the future of agricultural study, including the idea of the perfect plant species, the traits to look for, and potential social restrictions on crop building.

6. CONCLUSION

In this work, we deal with a real-world species detection challenge, which is more difficult and seems more reasonable. Pictures are edited as far as visual consideration before being perceived. AC assists us with zeroing in on our truly intrigued target and eliminating the impedances. What is more, we apply it as an information expansion strategy. It is the first ideal opportunity to edit pictures in quite a while of visual consideration for information expansion even though there have been numerous information increase techniques in profound learning local area. A broad similar examination is completed on various kinds of datasets including Oxford Blossom which is a conventional dataset and Plant CLEF which is a particular dataset for true distinguishing proof. Tests show that new cutting-edge results have been given. What is more significant, contrastive outcomes demonstrate that unrivalled improvement is gotten by utilizing AC. Also, the exhibition is very huge, particularly in re-sensible recognizable proof. Is worth focusing on that AC can be applied to other acknowledgement assignments and application scenes in the vision local area although we essentially centre around true plant species acknowledgement in this paper. Moreover, concerning future work, it would be intriguing to examine an issue that the acknowledgement framework can direct obscure and never seen classes. Furthermore, new advances in AI save the future possible jobs for the interdisciplinary exploration field of species acknowledgement including certifiable species ID for the following, not many years.

Models created through those three emphases are making amazing forecasts on the Validation dataset, with an aftereffect of up to 97%. It was a characteristic decision to test those models on pictures in a regular habitat, to address a genuine business case. Yet, we found rapidly that even though we attempted however much we could work on our model to distinguish pictures in a genuine climate, we were unable to accomplish this objective. We can change the model quite far; it can just foresee what it was prepared with pictures of leaves on a uniform foundation. We had the option to approve some speculation location of pictures without plants, the grouping of pictures with uniform foundations, and reject the way that adding foundations would assist with further developing the model robustness. There is still an opportunity to get better of this model as proposed already yet before anything more, we ought to consider utilizing a Dataset that is nearer to the risky anticipate plant infection from any photography. The results obtained after Shannon's information and Entropy study show that the leaf which has the highest Shannon's information is less likely to get sick while those with less Shannon's information are the leaf more likely to get sick.

REFERENCES

Agarwal, G., Belhumeur, P., Feiner, S., Jacobs, D., Kress, W. J., Ramamoorthi, R., Bourg, N. A., Dixit, N., Ling, H., Mahajan, D., Russell, R., Shirdhonkar, S., Sunkavalli, K., & White, S. (2006). First steps toward an electronic field guide for plants. *Taxon*, *55*(3), 597–610. doi:10.2307/25065637

Arivazhagan, S., Shebiah, R. N., Ananthi, S., & Varthini, S. V. (2013). Detection of unhealthy region of plant leaves and classification of plant leaf diseases using texture features. *Agricultural Engineering International: CIGR Journal, 15*, 211–217.

Arslan, F., Singh, B., Sharma, D. K., Regin, R., Steffi, R., & Suman Rajest, S. (2021). Optimization technique approach to resolve food sustainability problems. In *2021 International Conference on Computational Intelligence and Knowledge Economy (ICCIKE)*. IEEE. 10.1109/ICCIKE51210.2021.9410735

Athanikar, G., & Badar, P. (2016). Potato leaf diseases detection and classification system. *Int. J. Comput. Sci. Mob. Comput., 5*, 76–88.

Backes, A. R., Casanova, D., & Bruno, O. M. (2009). Plant leaf identification based on volumetric fractal dimension. *International Journal of Pattern Recognition and Artificial Intelligence, 23*(06), 1145–1160. doi:10.1142/S0218001409007508

Bansal, P., Kumar, R., & Kumar, S. (2021). Disease detection in apple leaves using deep convolutional neural network. *Agriculture, 11*(7), 617. doi:10.3390/agriculture11070617

Barbedo Arnal, J. G. (2014). An Automatic Method to Detect and Measure Leaf Disease Symptoms Using Digital Image Processing. *Plant Disease, 98*(12), 1709–1716. doi:10.1094/PDIS-03-14-0290-RE PMID:30703885

Barbedo Arnal, J. G. (2017). A new automatic method for disease symptom segmentation in digital photographs of plant leaves. *European Journal of Plant Pathology, 147*(2), 349–364. doi:10.100710658-016-1007-6

Cerutti, G., Tougne, L., Vacavant, A., & Coquin, D. (2011). A parametric active polygon for leaf segmentation and shape estimation. In *Advances in Visual Computing* (pp. 202–213). Springer Berlin Heidelberg. doi:10.1007/978-3-642-24028-7_19

Chatterjee, S. K., Das, S., Maharatna, K., Masi, E., Santopolo, L., Mancuso, S., & Vitaletti, A. (2015). Exploring strategies for classification of external stimuli using statistical features of the plant electrical response. *Journal of the Royal Society, Interface, 12*(104), 20141225. doi:10.1098/rsif.2014.1225 PMID:25631569

Chatterjee, S. K., Malik, O., & Gupta, S. (2018). Chemical sensing employing plant electrical signal response-classification of stimuli using curve fitting coefficients as features. *Biosensors (Basel), 8*(3), 83. Advance online publication. doi:10.3390/bios8030083 PMID:30201898

Cirillo, S., Polese, G., Salerno, D., Simone, B., & Solimando, G. (2023). Towards Flexible Voice Assistants: Evaluating Privacy and Security Needs in IoT-enabled Smart Homes. *FMDB Transactions on Sustainable Computer Letters, 1*(1), 25–32.

Dwivedi, P. P., & Sharma, D. K. (2021). Lower and upper bounds for 'useful' Renyi information rate. In *Communications in Computer and Information Science* (pp. 271–280). Springer International Publishing.

Fassnacht, F. E., Latifi, H., Stereńczak, K., Modzelewska, A., Lefsky, M., Waser, L. T., Straub, C., & Ghosh, A. (2016). Review of studies on tree species classification from remotely sensed data. *Remote Sensing of Environment, 186*, 64–87. doi:10.1016/j.rse.2016.08.013

Feng, Q., Dongxia, L., Bingda, S., Liu, R., Zhanhong, M., & Haiguang, W. (2016). Identification of Alfalfa Leaf Diseases Using Image Recognition Technology. *PLoS One*, 11. PMID:27977767

Gao, J., French, A. P., Pound, M. P., He, Y., Pridmore, T. P., & Pieters, J. G. (2020). Deep convolutional neural networks for image-based Convolvulus sepium detection in sugar beet fields. *Plant Methods*, *16*(1), 29. doi:10.118613007-020-00570-z PMID:32165909

Garcia-Barreda, S., Sangüesa-Barreda, G., García-González, M. D., & Camarero, J. J. (2022). Sex and tree rings: Females neither grow less nor are less water-use efficient than males in four dioecious tree species. *Dendrochronologia*, *73*(125944), 125944. doi:10.1016/j.dendro.2022.125944

Goeau, H., Bonnet, P., & Joly, A. (2016). Plant identification in an open-world. In Working Notes of CLEF 2016-Conference and Labs of the Eval- uation forum (pp. 428–439). Academic Press.

He, Y., Zhou, Z., Tian, L., Liu, Y., & Luo, X. (2020). Brown rice planthopper (Nilaparvata lugens Stal) detection based on deep learning. *Precision Agriculture*, *21*(6), 1385–1402. doi:10.100711119-020-09726-2

Hossain, E., Hossain, M. F., & Rahaman, M. A. (2019). A color and texture based approach for the detection and classification of plant leaf disease using KNN classifier. *2019 International Conference on Electrical, Computer and Communication Engineering (ECCE)*. 10.1109/ECACE.2019.8679247

Jeba, J. A., Bose, S. R., & Boina, R. (2023). Exploring Hybrid Multi-View Multimodal for Natural Language Emotion Recognition Using Multi-Source Information Learning Model. *FMDB Transactions on Sustainable Computer Letters*, *1*(1), 12–24.

Jiang, F., Lu, Y., Chen, Y., Cai, D., & Li, G. (2020). Image recognition of four rice leaf diseases based on deep learning and support vector machine. *Computers and Electronics in Agriculture*, *179*(105824), 105824. doi:10.1016/j.compag.2020.105824

Klein, H. S., Vanneste, S., & Pinkham, A. E. (2021). The limited effect of neural stimulation on visual attention and social cognition in individuals with schizophrenia. *Neuropsychologia*, *157*, 107880. doi:10.1016/j.neuropsychologia.2021.107880 PMID:33961863

Kumar, N., Belhumeur, P. N., Biswas, A., Jacobs, D. W., Kress, W. J., Lopez, I. C., & Soares, J. V. B. (2012). Leafsnap: A computer vision system for automatic plant species identification. In Computer Vision – ECCV 2012 (pp. 502–516). Springer Berlin Heidelberg. doi:10.1007/978-3-642-33709-3_36

Mokhtar, U., El Bendary, N., Hassenian, A. E., Emary, E., Mahmoud, M. A., Hefny, H., & Tolba, M. F. (2015). SVM-based detection of tomato leaves diseases. In *Advances in Intelligent Systems and Computing* (pp. 641–652). Springer International Publishing.

Murchie, E. H., & Burgess, A. J. (2022). Casting light on the architecture of crop yield. *Crop and Environment*, *1*(1), 74–85. doi:10.1016/j.crope.2022.03.009

Najdenovska, E., Dutoit, F., Tran, D., Plummer, C., Wallbridge, N., Camps, C., & Raileanu, L. E. (2021). Classification of plant electrophysiology signals for detection of spider mites infestation in tomatoes. *Applied Sciences (Basel, Switzerland)*, *11*(4), 1414. doi:10.3390/app11041414

Neisser, U. (1967). Cognitive psychology. appleton-century-crofts. [aac] nelson, k. (2003) self and social functions: Individual autobiographical memory and collective narrative. *Memory (Hove, England)*, *11*(2).

Nilsback, M.-E., & Zisserman, A. (2006). A visual vocabulary for flower classification. Computer Vision and Pattern Recognition. IEEE Computer Society Conference On, 2, 1447–1454. doi:10.1109/CVPR.2006.42

Nilsback, M.-E., & Zisserman, A. (2008). Automated flower classification over a large number of classes. *2008 Sixth Indian Conference on Computer Vision, Graphics & Image Processing*. 10.1109/ICVGIP.2008.47

Ogunmola, G. A., Singh, B., Sharma, D. K., Regin, R., Rajest, S. S., & Singh, N. (2021). Involvement of distance measure in assessing and resolving efficiency environmental obstacles. In *2021 International Conference on Computational Intelligence and Knowledge Economy (ICCIKE)*. IEEE. 10.1109/ICCIKE51210.2021.9410765

Omrani, E., Khoshnevisan, B., Shamshirband, S., Saboohi, H., Anuar, N. B., & Nasir, M. H. N. M. (2014). Potential of radial basis function-based support vector regression for apple disease detection. Measurement. *Measurement, 55*, 512–519. doi:10.1016/j.measurement.2014.05.033

Priscila, S. S., Rajest, S. S., Tadiboina, S. N., Regin, R., & András, S. (2023). Analysis of Machine Learning and Deep Learning Methods for Superstore Sales Prediction. *FMDB Transactions on Sustainable Computer Letters, 1*(1), 1–11.

Rumpf, T., Mahlein, A.-K., Steiner, U., Oerke, E.-C., Dehne, H.-W., & Plümer, L. (2010). Early detection and classification of plant diseases with Support Vector Machines based on hyperspectral reflectance. *Computers and Electronics in Agriculture, 74*(1), 91–99. doi:10.1016/j.compag.2010.06.009

Sankaran, S., Mishra, A., Ehsani, R., & Davis, C. (2010). A review of advanced techniques for detecting plant diseases. *Computers and Electronics in Agriculture, 72*(1), 1–13. doi:10.1016/j.compag.2010.02.007

Saxena, D., & Chaudhary, S. (2023). Predicting Brain Diseases from FMRI-Functional Magnetic Resonance Imaging with Machine Learning Techniques for Early Diagnosis and Treatment. *FMDB Transactions on Sustainable Computer Letters, 1*(1), 33–48.

Shannon, C. E. (1948). A mathematical theory of communication. *The Bell System Technical Journal, 27*(3), 379–423. doi:10.1002/j.1538-7305.1948.tb01338.x

Sharma, D. K., Jalil, N. A., Regin, R., Rajest, S. S., Tummala, R. K., & Thangadurai. (2021a). Predicting network congestion with machine learning. In *2021 2nd International Conference on Smart Electronics and Communication (ICOSEC)*. IEEE.

Sharma, D. K., Singh, B., Raja, M., Regin, R., & Rajest, S. S. (2021b). An Efficient Python Approach for Simulation of Poisson Distribution. In *2021 7th International Conference on Advanced Computing and Communication Systems (ICACCS)*. IEEE.

Sharma, D. K., Singh, B., Regin, R., Steffi, R., & Chakravarthi, M. K. (2021c). Efficient Classification for Neural Machines Interpretations based on Mathematical models. In *2021 7th International Conference on Advanced Computing and Communication Systems (ICACCS)*. IEEE.

Sharma, K., Singh, B., Herman, E., Regine, R., Rajest, S. S., & Mishra, V. P. (2021d). Maximum information measure policies in reinforcement learning with deep energy-based model. In *2021 International Conference on Computational Intelligence and Knowledge Economy (ICCIKE)*. IEEE. 10.1109/ICCIKE51210.2021.9410756

Shre, K. C. (2017). *An Approach towards Plant Electrical Signal Based External Stimuli Monitoring System*. Academic Press.

Suganthi, M., & Sathiaseelan, J. G. R. (2023). Image Denoising and Feature Extraction Techniques Applied to X-Ray Seed Images for Purity Analysis. *FMDB Transactions on Sustainable Health Science Letters*, *1*(1), 41–53.

Sun, Y., Deng, S., Lu, Y., Fan, R., Ma, X., & Lü, D. (2022). Emendation of the Triassic plant species Glossophyllum shensiense (Ginkgoales) with a review of the genus Glossophyllum Kräusel. *Review of Palaeobotany and Palynology*, *301*(104657), 104657. doi:10.1016/j.revpalbo.2022.104657

Türkoğlu, M., & Hanbay, D. (2019). Plant disease and pest detection using deep learning-based features. *Turkish Journal of Electrical Engineering and Computer Sciences*, *27*(3), 1636–1651. doi:10.3906/elk-1809-181

Vijayaraghavareddy, P., Lekshmy, S. V., Struik, P. C., Makarla, U., Yin, X., & Sreeman, S. (2022). Production and scavenging of reactive oxygen species confer to differential sensitivity of rice and wheat to drought stress. *Crop and Environment*, *1*(1), 15–23. doi:10.1016/j.crope.2022.03.010

Wang, H., & Raj, B. (2017). *On the origin of deep learning*. arXiv 2017, arXiv:1702.07800.

Xu, Z., Shi, H., Lin, P., & Liu, T. (2021). Integrated lithology identification based on images and elemental data from rocks. *Journal of Petroleum Science Engineering*, *205*(108853), 108853. doi:10.1016/j.petrol.2021.108853

Yu, J., Sharpe, S. M., Schumann, A. W., & Boyd, N. S. (2019). Deep learning for image-based weed detection in turfgrass. European Journal of Agronomy. *European Journal of Agronomy*, *104*, 78–84. doi:10.1016/j.eja.2019.01.004

Chapter 16
On Algorithms Required to Be Used in Military Command and Control Processes

Murat Şengöz
https://orcid.org/0000-0001-6597-0161
Independent Researcher, Turkey

ABSTRACT

The military command and control process refers to a process of the methods and principles to be followed in order to fulfill military missions or achieve an objective. The main components of this process are the information that has been analyzed and gathered concerning the description, classification, and evaluation of parameters and variables related to the enemy, air and land, in proportion to the available resources. This study examines the algorithms needed for strategic, operative, and tactical-level units, and the usability of algorithms produced by artificial intelligence-supported techniques such as machine learning and deep learning in military command and control processes in a way to adapt to the modern warfare environment, which requires speed, tempo, and flexibility. So, in this study, an explanation was made about the nature of the algorithms required for military command and control and preparation of the operational environment as a component, and suggestions were made for subsequent research.

INTRODUCTION

Today, thanks to the developments in information technologies, management sciences are becoming more and more digitized, and managers benefit from engineering applications more and more. In this context, artificial intelligence-supported systems are still used as primary or complementary technologies in the development of combat platforms such as manned and unmanned land, air and naval vehicles, in internal security and cyber defense applications, in the provision of transportation and logistics services, in target recognition and identification, in the provision of battlefield first aid and treatment, and in the development of combat simulation and training (Akgül, 2015: 263-267). At this point, the critical issue is to define the needs clearly and precisely, to determine the models and algorithms for the solution,

DOI: 10.4018/978-1-6684-9189-8.ch016

and to form project teams in an interdisciplinary manner. In this context, in order to address problems through artificial intelligence-supported systems, it should be ensured that an awareness of the solution and solution methodologies is established as a corporate culture. In the near future, the national security, warfare and conflict environment will undoubtedly become more complex with the more visible introduction of AI-enabled systems and insights. Therefore, these systems will enable faster, more agile and lethal operations for the relatively superior parties. For this reason, artificial intelligence-supported systems and technologies are becoming a phenomenon that needs to be taken into consideration in terms of their ethical and legal consequences as well as their areas of expertise.

As a matter of fact, military command and control, in essence, is the processing, analysis, combination or separation of all data inputs and all other factors affecting the issue in a holistic and orderly manner and analyzing, combining or separating all data inputs and all other factors affecting the issue in order to reveal, define and describe the existence of all parameters and variables related to the operation, and to determine the measures for the solution, and to produce results by making the necessary evaluations. In this context, artificial intelligence (AI) can make positive contributions to increasing the effectiveness and efficiency of effective decision support systems and management processes (Ergen, 2019; Kayaönü, 2000: 90). As a matter of fact, today, "artificial intelligence applications that mimic the functioning of the human brain without the risk factors that affect decision-making and save time and costs, which are the most important resources, are gaining importance" (İnce, et al., 2021:52).

In this sense, "technologies such as artificial intelligence, internet of things, big data, machine learning, deep learning, natural language processing, augmented and virtual reality, blockchain and Mesh Technology, especially artificial intelligence, are becoming mandatory areas to follow" (İyigün, 2021: 675). Moreover, a digitized decision support system helps facilitate decision-making based on data. Artificial intelligence capabilities take this one step further and automate decision-making as an expert system. AI works by creating artificial neural networks, a set of algorithms that can mimic the way the human brain works, identifying relationships and patterns in data. AI systems can then create optimization methods to help organizations make informed decisions. In this context, AI algorithms can be utilized to improve various aspects of military command and control processes, such as decision-making, planning and resource allocation. For example, AI algorithms can be used to analyze large amounts of sensor data to identify potential threats and predict the consequences of different courses of action. AI can be very helpful in optimizing logistics and resource allocation, such as determining the most efficient routes for supplies and personnel. In addition, AI can be utilized in the development of military training and simulation systems. In general, the use of artificial intelligence can help military organizations make more informed decisions and operate more efficiently, but it is critical to clearly outline the desired command and control algorithms and frame the demand.

Indeed, an algorithm is a set of instructions or steps that are followed to solve a problem or perform a task. It is a specific set of steps that can be followed to achieve a particular result or outcome. Algorithms are used in many different fields such as computer science, mathematics and engineering. They can be simple or complex and can be expressed in many different forms, such as natural language, pseudocode or programming languages. An AI algorithm is a set of instructions that enables a computer to perform tasks that typically require human intelligence, such as understanding natural language and recognizing objects in images or making decisions. There are many different types of AI algorithms, including supervised learning, unsupervised learning and reinforcement learning. Some examples of commonly used AI algorithms include neural networks, decision trees and genetic algorithms. Military command and control algorithms are computer programs and techniques used to aid decision-making and coordination in military operations. These algorithms can be used for tasks such as route planning, target tracking and resource allocation. They can also be used to simulate and analyze different scenarios and provide commanders with real-time information about the battlefield. The specific algorithms will vary depending on the task and the available technology.

In this context, this study will examine the usability of algorithms generated by AI-powered systems, especially in the context of military command and control. As a matter of fact, this study is a pioneering study in this respect and needs to be finalized with some other studies of this nature. In this context, this study will first provide an explanation of the nature of the algorithms needed by strategic, operative and tactical-level military units, and in this context, the issues needed for the use of algorithms produced by machine learning and deep learning techniques in military command and control processes will be revealed and suggestions will be made for further research.

ON THE ALGORITHMS REQUIRED BY ANALYZING AND UNDERSTANDING THE SITUATIONAL AWARENESS AND THE BATTLEFIELD

It is very critical in a military planning process to analyze and understand the situational awareness in a given area of operations with artificial intelligence and all other means of intelligence. It helps military planners understand the physical, social, economic, and cultural factors that influence military operations. This process helps military leaders identify potential threats and opportunities, and make informed decisions about how to best employ their resources to achieve their objectives. Analyzing and understanding the operational environment is a continuous process that evolves as the situation changes and new information becomes available. This is the process of analyzing variables within the mission such as the weather, terrain, considerations of civilians in the area of interest, and the enemy. These factors are important in determining their effects on the operations on the battlefield. Analyzing and understanding the operational environment and the battlefield consists of the following steps:

Definition of the environment of operation – this lays out the characteristics of the area within which the operations of the battle will be located. The characteristics of the area of operation explain the factors that may influence the operations of the enemy and its allies. The battlefield environment should provide an easy framework for the success of the military (Powell, 1995). This is done by carrying out an in-depth evaluation of the effects of the weather and the demographic and logistical infrastructure on the enemies and friendly operations. The environment of the operation should also establish limits for the area of interest. This is done by facilitating efforts in gathering intelligence and analytical frameworks from the geographical area involved in military operations are carried out by looking at the location of the battlefield and its nature and how it will influence military operations. Defining the battlefield also helps to identify the gaps in specific and current intelligence. It helps to identify the missing factors on the battlefield that can be added. The commander's knowledge of the battlefield helps to fill the gaps detected in the battlefield environment, and it is based on the specific intelligence gathered. Once the commander approves the specific intelligence, the ratified solutions assessed for the threats in the situation lay the ground for the initial intelligence requirements provided by the commander.

The next step describes the effects of the battlefield on the operations. It describes how the characteristics related to the terrain, the weather and the enemy affect friendly operations. This comes after the analysis of the information provided by intelligence staff in step one of analyzing and understanding the operational environment and the battlefield. These analyzed factors describe how they influence the operations of allies. Step two also takes into consideration the effects of these factors on the operations of the enemy. This evaluation helps to enhance the next step of analyzing and understanding the operational environment and the battlefield. The effects of the battlefield on operations help the military to ascertain the effect of the terrain on the allies and enemies as well. What is more, the characteristics of the geography of the battlefield facilitate putting into context factors such as the local population, civil press, politics, and demographics. This occurs by giving an overlay of the status of the number of people within that area. It also helps to give a depiction of the aspects of the military and the relevant effects of the terrain. Lastly, it helps to give an analysis matrix of the weather patterns and their effect on personnel (Paul and Landree, 2008).

The third step in analyzing and understanding the operational environment and the battlefield is an evaluation of the threat or adversary (Powell, 1995). The evaluation of a threat or adversary is conducted to establish strategies to counter the operations of the enemy, as well as to study the effect of the enemies' undertakings on friendly operations. The allies use this information to support analyzing and understanding the operational environment and the battlefield. The information might be recorded for future threats or adversaries in order to develop a similar model or the current one. Where an adversary or threat is not available such as in the case of a natural disaster, the nature of the terrain may help in developing a model to counter the disaster.

The last step is determining the threat and the course of action. This comes after reviewing the mode of operation of the enemy. The intelligence staff identifies and develops courses of action based on an adversary or a threat. These are based on the likelihood of the factors associated with the adversary in the mission of the allies. The need to study the adversary or the threat arises in order to prevent a surprise attack. The intelligence on the adversary or threat also helps in the identification of civil issues that need to be taken into consideration. These are factors that affect the operational environment based on the activities of local populations, allied forces, and the adversary or threat. It helps to shape the best tactic to mitigate and counter the threat (Paul and Landree, 2008).

Analyzing and understanding the operational environment and the battlefield can be conducted with artificial intelligence and all other means of intelligence by intelligence officers and in a coordination with the following people within an army. In this respect, an army commander at all levels considers the actions of the enemy's troops that he may engage with as well as the effect of the terrain on the course of action of the enemy and on them fulfilling their objective in the mission, and a rifleman, who may also consider the actions that he may deploy in war within an infantry team by reconsidering the effects of the weather and the terrain on himself and the enemy.

Analyzing and understanding the operational environment and the battlefield also follows a set of principles in order to serve its purpose: the evaluation of the effect of the battlefield on the enemy and friendly operations; the identification of the assets that a threat or adversary needs to incorporate for the success of a course of action; and the identification of activities or locations that the adversary or threat will adopt in the implementation of their course of action. Next comes the determination of possible threats and the probable courses of action of the adversary. Analyzing and understanding the operational environment and the battlefield also relates to various steps in the military command and control process. In the mission analysis process, analyzing and understanding the operational environment and the battlefield helps a commander to assess and make assumptions on the battlefield based on the interaction of the allied and enemy forces. It helps to identify the capabilities and the vulnerabilities of the enemy relative to the mission analysis step of the military command and control process as well. This helps to make assumptions about the capabilities of the command of the allied forces and the enemies.

In addition, it helps to identify any gaps in the knowledge of the threat or battlefield environment that the command may not know about.

Analyzing and understanding the operational environment and the battlefield also helps the development and execution of the course of action. This is realized by helping allies base their courses of action on assumptions and facts used by the mission analysis. Incorporating the results from these two processes ensures taking advantage of opportunities in the environment. Analyzing and understanding the operational environment and the battlefield additionally helps with the analysis and comparison of the courses of action. The wargaming session in this stage is incorporated to predict a course of action that an adversary may develop.

Analyzing and understanding the operational environment and the battlefield, especially with artificial intelligence and all other means of intelligence helps in decision-making and in the implementation orders. At this point, it is critical to design the desired information sets and algorithms for analyzing and understanding the operational environment and the battlefield clearly and precisely in order to obtain and process the all necessary information about the enemy and the operational area on the battlefield. This is because the list of requirements that are associated with the course of action may be identified from analyzing and understanding the operational environment and the battlefield. A commander applies the result of analyzing and understanding the operational environment in the implementation and development of a course of action. The progress of analyzing and understanding the operational environment and the battlefield helps in the execution of a military operation. This is done through the new intelligence acquired from the battlefield that helps a military force to adapt to an ongoing operation. It also acts as guidance to the commands that are developed in the course of action.

In essence, the military command and control process describes an algorithm for the form, sequence, procedures and principles that must be followed in order to fulfill the tasks undertaken for the command and control of military organizations in the campaign or to achieve a goal. The main components of this algorithm are the analyzed and compiled information on the description, classification and evaluation of parameters and variables related to the enemy, air and terrain, to the extent of available resources. The basic principle in the planning and execution of military command and control is to carry out situation assessments and situation judgments in the context of the fulfillment of the assigned mission, to reveal the possible courses of action that the enemy may adopt and to determine the courses of action of friendly elements. The aim is to ensure that decision-makers reach the most optimal decisions. As a result of a properly executed military decision-making process, the mission, the enemy's possible courses of action and our own courses of action are determined and operational endpoints, critical sensitivities and activities that must be carried out in a synchronized and orchestrated manner are revealed, success criteria and decision points are determined, critical issues are identified, areas of influence and interest, criteria for response safety times are defined, and lines of operation for each battlefield main function area are planned and assembled in a synchronized and orchestrated manner. In this context, military command and control consist of the translation of the envisioned operational architecture into the real situation, i.e. the translation of doctrine to the terrain and the creation of an understandable algorithm to match it with the adversary forces. This process is carried out within the framework of a set of planning factors and formats that are traditionally operated.

In military organizations, the strategic level is the level at which military operations are militarized by linking them to the desired political end state or desired high-level political objectives. In this sense, strategic-level units may be high-level joint commands, or they may be a combination of offensive air assets, weapons systems that can fire blindly, and a team of special troops to execute a specific mission, or any combination of these. Basically, operative-level units are the units responsible for the primary monitoring and formulation of the joint tactical picture of the operation and the transfer of strategic-level military decisions, i.e., in a way, envisioning the envisioned operation, transforming it into a practicable form that is compatible with military doctrines, and transferring it as clear orders and requests to the tactical-level elements actually deployed in the field. Tactical-level units, on the other hand, are generally organizations that fulfill the tasks assigned to them, subject to military doctrine and standard operating procedures. For strategic and operative-level units, the fulfillment of the purpose of the mission is of primary importance, while for tactical-level military elements, it is more important how to fulfill the assigned tasks within the framework. In this respect, while strategic and operative-level military organizations deal with more vague and conceptual issues, tactical-level military elements deal with more concrete tasks. In this respect, the command and control processes operated in military organizations differ according to the level of the military organization. In this context, some of the parameters that form the basis for the information needs of strategic, operative and tactical-level military organizations in their command and control processes are shown in Table-1.

In this context, in general, strategic and operative-level organizations focus on issues that are much more difficult to determine, but much more vital for achieving victory, such as mission formulation, desired end state, lines of operation, critical sensitivities, decisive points, decision points, the center of gravity analyses, and high-value targets. Indeed, tactical successes in a military operation cannot cover strategic mistakes. However, operations at the tactical level are usually guided by doctrine and standard operating procedures. Tactical-level elements, regardless of whether they are primary or secondary assault units, are focused solely on accomplishing their assigned mission, surviving, destroying the enemy or capturing an objective.

Military command and control differ according to the level of the units. Therefore, the information sets and processing processes required by the units also differ. In this context, while strategic and operative-level units need algorithms for the deployment and organization of main subordinate units in the field and the establishment of mission organizations, tactical-level units select their weapons and equipment in accordance with the type of operation they will carry out following with the standard application procedures already in place. In this context, they require practical information that is immediately needed at the tactical level, such as the identification, allocation and division of targets in the tactical area, the selection of counter-weapons, and the utilization of terrain that provides cover and concealment for friendly forces. In other words, tactical-level units need practical approaches and applications that have been tested and confirmed rather than complex intuitive or mathematical algorithms and formulas (Karakaşoğlu, 2008: 8).

In this context, it can be said that tactical-level units need systems that will support them in the allocation and allocation of targets and that will provide them with practical information about the enemy in real time, allowing them to use their resources in the most optimum way. Strategic and operative-level military organizations, on the other hand, require first-order satellite and aerial imagery and signals intel-

Table 1. Strategic, operational, and tactical-level focal points

Strategic-Level	Operative-Level	Tactical-Level
Imagination	Envision	Execution
Development of War Concepts	Preparation of Doctrines	Development of Standard Operation Procedures
Preparation of Military Assets	Organization of Missions and Tasks	Completion of Organizations for Combat

ligence, supported by other intelligence data, such as biographical intelligence on enemy decision-makers and commanders, to understand the enemy's intentions and intentions, and to enable a realistic analysis of enemy capabilities and capabilities, and may use complex mathematical algorithms and formulas. At this point, a broader explanation of the distinction between strategic, operational and tactical-level units will not be attempted. This is because the purpose of the explanations at this point is only to emphasize the importance and necessity of the information sets and analysis needs of strategic, operative and tactical-level units in the command and control processes, and the importance and necessity of rapidly translating strategic-level decisions into operative and tactical-level orders and objectives. To this end, it can be said that the information technology systems required by tactical-level units are different from those required by higher-level units. While tactical-level units need longbow-like robotic and computer vision and robotic ready-made products, higher-level units need a set of dynamic algorithms and decision support templates and algorithms that are specially and precisely prepared and produced in the context of contributing to the command and control processes together with and in addition to ready-made prescriptions and package programs.

ON THE ADAPTATION OF ARTIFICIAL INTELLIGENCE ALGORITHMS TO MILITARY COMMAND AND CONTROL PROCESSES

In the context of determining the enemy's war strategies and possible courses of action through artificial intelligence-based models, analyses that take into account the knowledge acquis by enemy commanders in certain aspects, such as their ability to take risks, take initiatives, and deal with uncertainty, as well as their emotional engagement and previous attitudes and behaviors can be very helpful (Howard, 2019: 921). Of course, this requires defining, describing and analyzing the capacity of the analyzed individuals and entities to work together and the organizational climate they create. In this context, algorithms produced by utilizing techniques such as data science in general and machine learning and deep learning, in particular, can be very useful (Blair, et al., 2021: 247). In particular, algorithms produced through machine learning and deep learning models can enable the creation of realistic algorithms and the processing of a wide variety of information in this context by modeling the problems allegorically and as a machine learning and deep learning technique in the form of a multi-layer neural network (Mitchell, 1997, MacKay, 2021). Of course, in order to achieve this goal, it is critical to create the model properly and to select the appropriate algorithms. If this is not the case, predictions for solving the desired problems or obtaining target information will not be successful.

Nowadays, especially due to the developments in warfare technologies and the dynamic nature of warfare, military decision-makers have to consider many more parameters and variables than in the past (Schubert, et al., 2018). In this context, this section will provide an explanation of the use of artificial intelligence-supported systems and technologies in military decision-making processes by utilizing secondary data. Machine learning, neural learning and deep learning are at the forefront of these technologies (Bozinovski, 2014: 255-263). Such systems basically describe the activity of collecting the data needed within the scope of decision-based information needs from sources, cleaning and processing them and making them suitable for analysis, analyzing the data made suitable for analysis by using relevant techniques and creating algorithms (Jarrahi, 2018: 5).

As a matter of fact, algorithms are models for classifying, describing and explaining the data obtained through abstractly constructed structures in order to understand an issue, event, phenomenon or system.

In other words, the path designed to produce a solution to a problem or to achieve the determined goal and the successive process steps is called algorithms (Enes, 2017). For an algorithm to be functional, it should be simple, as short, concise and understandable as possible (Semiz, 2017). In this context, the algorithm prepared to solve a problem should describe all the steps necessary for the solution in a sequential manner (Semiz, 2017). These models help to understand the influence and mutual causal relationships that will allow us to explain the degree of some relationships or the relationships and differences between categorical data sets by the nature of the variables included in the algorithm. However, since the aggregated data sets are hypothetical, non-physical, they cannot be directly measured and cannot be fully verified. For this reason, systems, events or phenomena with a complex network of relationships consisting of many overt and covert variables that do not have directly observable deterministic relationships between them are designed and modeled as if they were organic (living) beings within the artificial intelligence paradigm. In this context, algorithms offer a simple method for solving a specific problem and these methods are translated into codes in the computer environment, creating a software language (Toprak, 2020: 49).

In this respect, artificial intelligence-based systems essentially allow for the production of models that are closer to reality by processing and analyzing much more data and operating repetitive processes compared to classical statistical modeling and measurement apparatus (Russell & Norvig, 2009). In this respect, artificial intelligence-based systems can produce more accurate and holistic information about the accuracy, reliability, validity and structural integrity of the models produced compared to classical statistical methods.

Indeed, an algorithm is typically a finite set of rigorous instructions used to solve a particular class of problems or perform a computation. Algorithms are used as specifications for performing calculations and processing data. More advanced algorithms can perform automatic deductions (called automated reasoning) and use mathematical and logical tests to guide code execution in various ways (called automated decision-making). Effectively, an algorithm can be expressed in a well-defined formal language within a finite amount of space and time to compute a function. Because the transition from one state to another is not necessarily deterministic, some algorithms, known as randomized algorithms, involve random input.

Algorithm design refers to a method or mathematical process for problem-solving and engineering algorithms (Bleakley, 2020). The design of algorithms is part of many solution theories of operations research, such as dynamic programming and divide and conquer. Techniques for designing and implementing algorithm designs are also called algorithm design patterns, with examples including the template method pattern and the decorator pattern. Typical steps in algorithm development are: defining the problem, developing a model, determining the parameters and variables of the algorithm, designing the algorithm, checking and analyzing its correctness, implementing and testing the algorithm, and preparing documentation (Harel, 2004).

The Military Command and Control Process is basically a six-stage process that begins with the assignment of the mission for military decision-making in both tactical and garrison environments. These are assignment of the mission, analysis of the mission, determination of the enemy's likely courses of action, development of one's own courses of action, analysis of courses of action, comparison of courses of action, and issuance of the order. In this respect, this process can essentially be classified into three parts. These are collecting and analyzing data, making plans and executing. At this point, through artificial intelligence-based systems, a large amount of information on the enemy, terrain and weather conditions from a wide variety of sources can be gathered and processed in a certain automated manner, and rendered meaningful for analysis. These information sets can then be analyzed through certain algorithms and transformed into data that can be applied to decision support systems, and finally, the effectiveness and efficiency of the courses of action produced can be evaluated relatively and comparatively.

In this way, plans for military operations can be prepared through machine learning techniques and instant evaluations can be made for the execution of existing plans. However, in this context, a practice in which the planning and execution processes of military operations are operated within an artificial intelligence architecture has not yet been fully experienced. However, in several countries such as the United States, China, South Korea and Sweden, simulations are being prepared and command post-exercises are being planned for the integrated execution of command and control of military operations with artificial intelligence-based systems (Brynielsson, 2007: 1454-1463; Svenmarck, et al.: 2018: 1-5).

ON THE ADAPTATION OF MACHINE LEARNING AND DEEP LEARNING TECHNIQUES TO COMMAND AND CONTROL PROCESSES

Basically, there is a widespread assumption that the use of artificial intelligence (AI) in warfare and especially in command and control (C2) applications can provide advantages in terms of faster information processing, but the nature of the algorithms created for the application of machine learning techniques and the information sets selected is critical (Bishop, 2004: Murphy, 2021). In fact, machine learning algorithms can be classified into two parts (MacKay, 2021). One is supervised machine learning and the other is unsupervised machine learning. However, nowadays, machine learning is evolving towards deep learning, especially in terms of enabling it to work with more dense information sets and algorithms in multiple evolutionary layers. In this context, the basic algorithms used in supervised, and unsupervised machine learning and deep learning techniques are summarized in Table-2.

Supervised machine learning algorithms are mainly used to solve regression, logistic regression and classification problems, to determine the proportion of influence between dependent and independent variables and to predict the relationships, to create the linear combination that best predicts the dependent variable, The hypothesis gives successful results in terms of predicting causal relationships between the variables in the model, determining whether there is a significant difference between group means, and creating a combination of dependent variables that will maximize the difference between group means (Russell and 2009).

Unsupervised machine learning algorithms are useful in solving clustering and dimensional reduction problems (Alpaydın, 2004). Unlike classical regression and classification algorithms, unsupervised machine learning algorithms also allow clustering and discriminant analysis between categorical and mixed variables (Jordan and Bishop, 2004). Unsupervised machine learning algorithms are also successful in generating the best linear combinations for predicting group membership, using linear combinations of observed variables representing the latent variable, i.e. exploratory and factor analysis. The difference

Table 2. Basic machine learning algorithms

Supervised Machine Learning	Unsupervised Machine Learning	Deep Learning
Regression Analysis Logistic Regression Classification	Cluster Analysis Discriminant Analysis Dimensional Reduction	Evolutionary Neural Networks Recurrent Neural Networks

between regression and classification algorithms is that in classical regression analyses the dependent and independent variables are quantitative, whereas in logistic regression analyses the independent variables can be quantitative or categorical, i.e. mixed, and the dependent variable can be categorical. In classification analyses, categorical data are used for the dependent variable and independent variables. In linear regressions, the dependent variable is a linear function of the independent variable or variables (Bzdok, et al., 2018).

In summary, machine learning involves the efforts to create data processing models within the discipline of data science using a set of algorithms, computational and statistical methods and models created from data sets collected for a purpose (Friedman, 1998:3-9). In this context, machine learning is basically classified into two categories: supervised and unsupervised machine learning. Supervised machine learning is concerned with classifying and categorizing the properties of the measured data and explaining the effects of the data on each other with their properties. Indeed, outputs corresponding to inputs are called labels. In this context, labels are used to train algorithms. Unsupervised machine learning, on the other hand, refers to the process of clustering and dimensionality reduction by labeling the features of the data. If the data set lacks labels, unsupervised machine learning techniques are used so that hidden patterns in the unlabeled data can be found and the data can be grouped.

Within the scope of classification analysis created within the scope of supervised machine learning; decision trees, logistic regression, and support vector machine algorithms are used (Cortes and Vapnik, 1995). In regression analysis, linear regression analysis and artificial neural network techniques can be used. For unsupervised machine learning, clustering, principal component analysis, and k-means can be used to reduce the size of the data.

In addition, machine learning allows working with smaller data sets than deep learning (Pedro, 2015). As data sets grow in size, machine learning algorithms evolve into deep learning algorithms. Deep learning is an algorithm that consists of multiple evolutionary layers, especially in areas such as computer vision and object detection. Deep learning mainly uses evolutionary neural networks and recurrent neural network techniques. In this respect, this technique is utilized in the development of target detection systems and radars, and the development of smart firing systems. The recurrent neural network technique is used to predict the future using time series and sequential data. In practice, machine learning allows working with small and medium-sized data sets, while deep learning allows working with larger data sets. For this reason, deep learning requires both more capacity computer hardware and a longer time to teach the data to the algorithms needed for analysis (Schmidhuber, 2014: 85-117). While the nature of the models of the algorithms in machine learning is clear, the models of the algorithms used in deep learning are not explainable.

In this context, machine learning and deep learning techniques can be used to analyze the discourse of the leaders of the adversary country at the strategic level to determine their possible courses of action and strategic choices, the attitudes and preferences of the people of the adversary or target country on certain issues, assessments of weapons and means of warfare within the scope of relative power comparisons, military and security strategies of the adversary or target country, their strengths, vulnerabilities, and vulnerabilities. In addition to this, in order to implement the doctrine adopted at the operational level, it is possible to determine operational directions and defense lines, establish logistic corridors, and ensure uninterrupted supply flow with algorithms to be created through machine learning and deep learning techniques in evaluations of enemy, terrain and weather conditions, Artificial Intelligence (AI)-based systems can be utilized for seamless coordination and organization of transportation activities, obtaining, processing and drawing meaningful conclusions from simultaneous and accurate intelligence information on the adversary and the target country, and using unmanned warfare systems and apparatuses in coordination, and the process can be carried out in a hybrid manner in this way. However, at this point, there is a need to develop robust, reliable, and guaranteed artificial intelligence (AI), machine learning, and system autonomy technologies, especially for command and control, surveillance and reconnaissance, and logistics systems to be used within the scope of military command and control. For this purpose, hybrid artificial intelligence algorithms should be developed and the need should be demonstrated.

CONCLUSION

The predictive functionality of AI is what makes it a great decision support tool, taking raw data and turning it into actionable recommendations. In this context, AI decision support systems in general regulate the command and control process by processing the required datasets and predicting outcomes based on large amounts of data, making recommendations based on large datasets of both internal and external data, and contributing to the generation of various optimization models, In particular, it can suggest various courses of action to decision-makers and help them resolve issues based on a specific problem or issue, draw roadmaps describing the process to be followed to achieve the desired end state, and help them plan work more efficiently or anticipate contingencies or minimize uncertainty.

However, for this to happen, it is first necessary to prepare the algorithms needed for military command and control nationally, taking into account the capabilities and limitations of technologies such as machine learning and deep learning, i.e. to explain how the algorithms and architecture needed for command and control can be realized holistically through machine learning and deep learning techniques in order to harmonize demand with supply, and to form an eclectic working group by publishing the need as a project definition document.

In this context, in future studies, an examination can be made of the algorithms that can be utilized in the processes of situation assessments and situation judgments carried out within the scope of the command and control of military operations and the formation of operational orders. Thus, the effectiveness and success of classical decision-making processes and synthetic or semi-synthetic decision-making processes carried out through algorithms produced by artificial intelligence-supported systems can be tested with a simulation-supported command post-exercise.

REFERENCES

Akgül, A. (2015). Artificial Intelligence Military Applications. *Journal of Ankara University Faculty of Political Sciences*, 45(1), 255–271.

Alpaydın, E. (2004). *Introduction to Machine Learning*. MIT Press.

Bishop, C. M. (2006). *Pattern Recognition and Machine Learning*. Springer.

Blair, A., Duguid, P., Goeing, A. S., & Grafton, A. (2021). *Information: A Historical Companion*. Princeton University Press. doi:10.1515/9780691209746

Bleakley, C. (2020). *Poems that Solve Puzzles: The History and Science of Algorithms*. Oxford University Press. doi:10.1093/oso/9780198853732.001.0001

Bozinovski, S. (2014). Modeling mechanisms of cognition-emotion interaction in artificial neural networks, since 1981. *Procedia Computer Science*, *41*, 255–263. doi:10.1016/j.procs.2014.11.111

Brynielsson, J. (2007). Using AI and Games For Decision Support in Command and Control. *Decision Support Systems*, *43*(4), 1454–1463. doi:10.1016/j.dss.2006.06.012

Bzdok, D., Altman, N., & Krzywinski, M. (2018). Statistics Versus Machine Learning. *Nature Methods*, *15*(4), 233–234. doi:10.1038/nmeth.4642 PMID:30100822

Cortes, C., & Vapnik, V. N. (1995). Support-vector networks. *Machine Learning*, *20*(3), 273–297. doi:10.1007/BF00994018

Enes, K. (2017, February 2). Algoritma Nedir? https://www.eneskamis.com/%EF%BB%BFalgoritma-nedir-algoritma-ne-ise-yarar

Ergen, M. (2019). What is Artificial Intelligence? Technical Considerations and Future Perception. *The Anatolian Journal of Cardiology*, *22*(2), 5–7. doi:10.14744/AnatolJCardiol.2019.79091 PMID:31670719

Friedman, J. H. (1998). Data Mining and Statistics: What's the connection? *Computing Science and Statistics.*, *29*(1), 3–9.

Harel, D., & Feldman, Y. (2004). *Algorithmics: The Spirit of Computing*. Addison-Wesley.

Howard, J. (2019). Artificial Intelligence: Implications for The Future of Work. *American Journal of Industrial Medicine*, *62*(11), 917–926. doi:10.1002/ajim.23037 PMID:31436850

İnce, H., İmamoğlu, S. E., & İmamoğlu, S. Z. (2021). Yapay Zekâ Uygulamalarının Karar Verme Üzerine Etkileri: Kavramsal Bir Çalışma. *International Review of Economics and Management*, *9*(1), 50–63. doi:10.18825/iremjournal.866432

İyigün, N. Ö. (2021). Yapay Zekâ ve Stratejik Yönetim. *TRT Akademi*, *6*(13), 675–679. doi:10.37679/trta.1002518

Jarrahi, M. H. (2018). Artificial Intelligence and The Future of Work: Human-AI Symbiosis in Organizational Decision Making. *Business Horizons*, *61*(4), 577–586. doi:10.1016/j.bushor.2018.03.007

Jordan, M. I., & Bishop, C. M. (2004). Neural Networks. In Computer Science Handbook, Second Edition (Section VII: Intelligence Systems). Chapman & Hall/CRC Press LLC.

Karakaşoğlu, N. (2008). *Bulanık Çok Kriterli Karar Verme Yöntemleri ve Uygulama* [Unpublished master's thesis]. Pamukkale University Institute of Social Sciences.

Kayaönü, E. (2000). *Yapay Zekânın Teorik Temelleri* [Unpublished master's thesis]. Istanbul Technical University Institute of Science and Technology.

MacKay, D. J. C. (2021). *Information Theory, Inference, and Learning Algorithms*. Cambridge University Press.

Mitchell, T. (1997). *Machine Learning*. McGraw Hill.

Murphy, K. P. (2021). *Probabilistic Machine Learning: An Introduction*. MIT Press.

Paul, C., & Landree, E. (2008). Defining Terrorists' Information Requirements: The Modified Intelligence Preparation of the Battlefield (ModIPB) Framework. *Journal of Homeland Security and Emergency Management, 5*(1), 1–18. doi:10.2202/1547-7355.1433

Pedro, D. (2015). *The Master Algorithm: How the Quest for the Ultimate Learning Machine Will Remake Our World*. Basic Books.

Powell, C. L., & Persico, J. E. (1995). *My American Journey*. Random House.

Russell, S., & Norvig, P. (2009). *Artificial Intelligence – A Modern Approach*. Pearson.

Schmidhuber, J. (2015). Deep Learning in Neural Networks: An Overview. *Neural Networks, 61*, 85–117. doi:10.1016/j.neunet.2014.09.003 PMID:25462637

Schubert, J., Brynielsson, J., Nilsson, M., & Svenmarck, P. (2018). Artificial Intelligence for Decision Support in Command and Control Systems. *23rd International Command and Control Research & Technology Symposium "Multi-Domain C2"*.

Semiz, T. Y. (2017, December 26). Algoritma Nedir? https://maker.robotistan.com/algoritma

Svenmarck, P., Luotsinen, L., Nilsson, M., & Schubert, J. (2018). Possibilities and Challenges for Artificial Intelligence in Military Applications. In *Proceedings of the NATO Big Data and Artificial Intelligence for Military Decision Making Specialists' Meeting*. NATO Research and Technology Organisation.

Toprak, A. (2020). Yapay Zekâ Algoritmalarının Dijital Enstalasyona Dönüşmesi. *Ege University Faculty of Communication New Thoughts Peer-reviewed E-Journal*, (14), 47–59.

Chapter 17
Harris Hawk Optimization Study of Geosynthetic-Encased Stone Columns Supporting a Railway Embankment in Soft Clay

M. A. Balasubramani
Bharath Institute of Higher Education and Research, India

R. Venkatakrishnaiah
Bharath Institute of Higher Education and Research, India

K. V. B. Raju
Bharath Institute of Higher Education and Research, India

ABSTRACT

Numerous earth retaining and earth-supported buildings have been built during the last three decades using geogrid as reinforcement. In more recent times, it has been used to reinforce railroad sleepers in order to improve their structural integrity and use. Before conducting the experimental study on the strain and temperature sensing capabilities of the smart geogrid, a general explanation of the manufacturing process for the FBG integrated smart geogrid was provided. It has now been developed to employ an external sensor to provide a reference displacement for the Harris Hawk optimization (HHO) recommended to find the appropriate weighted coefficient in order to calibrate the reconstructed deformation. The geosynthetic-encased stone column (ESC) is a frequent ground improvement approach because of the current site circumstances (low shear strength) and the need to finish the project within the allotted time.

1. INTRODUCTION

The ability of the subgrade soil to support the load that is being placed on it has a significant impact on the layout of the pavement that is going to be constructed. The enhancement of the soil subgrade

DOI: 10.4018/978-1-6684-9189-8.ch017

through the use of geosynthetic reinforcement is a method that is not only economical but also safe for the surrounding environment (Lazorenko, et al., 2019; Kempfert & Raithel, 2005). The use of geosynthetics makes the pavement more resilient and extends its lifespan by reducing the amount of pavement deformation that is caused by the weight of moving vehicles (Arslan, et al., 2021). This results in an increased amount of time that the pavement can be used (Pandya, et al., 2022). In order to ensure the long-term stability of geotechnical materials, it is imperative to employ techniques that are appropriate for reinforcing geotechnical materials (Ogunmola, et al., 2021). Reinforcing railroad ballast with geogrids is an additional method that can effectively reduce ballast deformation while also being efficient in terms of cost (Sharma, et al., 2021).

Geogrids have the capability of containing ballast laterally as well as vertically, which lessens the possibility of particle fragmentation and lessens the effects of settling (Sol-Sánchez & D'Angelo, 2017; Liu, et al., 2018; Deshpande, et al., 2021; Woodward, et al., 2014). In the research that is currently available in the body of published work, the performance of reinforced ballast has been the topic of discussion. According to the findings of these studies, the proper use of geogrid reinforcement has the potential to slow down the rate of permanent deformation brought on by the spreading of lateral ballast (Lai, et al., 2014). It is common practise to attribute the reinforcing effect to the tensile strain that was generated as a result of the interlocking action of the geogrid and the surrounding aggregate (Fan, et al., 2021; Schary, 2020). This is done because it is believed that this strain contributed to the generation of the tensile strain that was responsible for the effect (Lazorenko, et al., 2020).

Increasing the load-bearing capacity of shallow foundations and utilising waste materials as a component in the production of building materials such as concrete and geopolymer bricks are two areas that have been the focus of investigation by a number of researchers (Banu, et al., 2022). There isn't much research on railways that supports employing waste materials, either alone or in combination with recycled glass and mixed recovered plastic, as subballast in lieu of natural aggregates like recycled concrete aggregates (Buragadda, et al., 2022). Bricks that have been broken up and used as subballast and a combination of coal wash, slag from steel furnaces, and rubber crumbs used as ballast are two additional options (Pandit, 2023). The stress distribution that is caused by a train track running over geogrid-reinforced clay-based ballast was demonstrated by Fattah et al. (2018). In order to carry out the tests, a half-scale railroad consisting of two tracks measuring 800 millimetres in length and three hardwood sleepers was constructed (900 mm, 10 mm, 10 mm). During the testing, three different thicknesses of ballast were utilised: 200, 300, and 400 millimetres (Diwedar, et al., 2019).

The ballast was placed on top of a layer of solid and soft clay that measured 500 millimeters in thickness. Fattah et al. (2018) conducted research on the impact of load amplitude and load frequency on the behavior of reinforced and unreinforced ballast layers. The researchers were interested in how these factors affected the behavior of the ballast layers. In order to conduct the tests, a train that was only one-half the size of the actual one was constructed. It consisted of two tracks that were 800 millimeters long and three wooden sleepers that were 900 millimeters tall and 90 millimeters broad. On top of the ballast was a clay layer that was 500 millimeters in thickness. The testing was carried out within a securely fastened steel box that measured 1.5 meters in length, 1 meter in width, and 1 meter in height. Both of them used geogrid reinforcement, however one of them used it without the other. Esmaeili et al. (2018) were able to demonstrate the influence that geogrid has on the stability and settlement of high railway embankments through the use of laboratory testing and finite element modeling. (Ali, et al., 2014) This was achieved by stacking equally five sets of 50-cm-high embankments that were produced at a scale of 1:20 on the crest of a loading chamber that was 240 cm x 235 cm x 220 cm in size.

There were no geogrid layers used to reinforce the initial set of embankments when they were built. When we compare the reinforced case to the unreinforced one while applying the same load, Ziegler, (2017) has demonstrated an increase in bearing capacity as well as a significant reduction in displacements (Ashour, et al., 2021). It was demonstrated that these effects could perhaps be related to the limiting and interlocking properties of the geogrid reinforcement, which transform the more or less linear deviatoric stress path in the reinforced case into a more isotropic one (Abdelhaleem, et al., 2021).

Yu et al. (2019) conducted research in which ballasted railroad track samples were put through combined vertical and horizontal cycle loads while moving at high relative train speeds. We evaluated the performance benefits of placing geogrid at the ballast-subballast contact, the subballast-subgrade interface, and the influence of subgrade stiffness on geogrid performance at the subballast-subgrade interface. This was done in order to better understand how geogrid can improve performance.

The primary objective of this study is to gain an understanding of the role that geogrid reinforcement layers play in the functioning of high railway embankments (Gowtham et al., 2022). According to Zannah et al.'s 2023 research, the focus of this study is mostly on preventing sliding in the embankment mass and minimizing crest settling, both of which are important factors in determining the serviceability of railway embankments. Using the findings from the preliminary numerical modeling as well as the findings from all of the reinforced numerical models, the suitable level at which to insert the geogrid layers was determined. According to Nirmala et al. 2023, the first set of embankments was constructed without any further geogrid reinforcement, and the second through fifth sets of embankments were strengthened using one to four components of geogrid. This was done in order to accomplish this goal.

2. PROPOSED METHODOLOGY

2.1. Scaling Law

For the purpose of conducting a subsurface test for weak formation between Madurai and Tuticorin, an embankment with a height of ten meters, a crest width of four meters and a sideslope of one and one-half was selected as the embankment. It was built in compliance with the norms that govern the Iranian railway system. After then, the formula for scaling was used on the aforementioned embankment, but this time at a scale of 1:20 for the laboratory experiment program. This was done in accordance with the method that HHO had recommended. Taking into account the height of the loading chamber and the 10 cm course of the hydraulic card, the embankment was constructed with a maximum height of 50 centimeters and a thickness of 60 centimeters of foundation soil (subgrade) at the chamber (Indraratna, et al., 2017). This allowed for a total height of 60 centimeters.

In order to prevent the chamber walls from having an influence on the carrying capacity of the embankment and potential elevation on the sides of the laboratory model (2.35–2.4 meters), a space allowance of 50 centimeters was allowed on each side of the wall, despite the fact that space was limited within the available loading chamber. Because of these restrictions and because it was expected that the breadth of the crest would be 24 centimeters, the side slope for the laboratory model was determined to be 1:1. It is important to note that the chosen slope exerts a greater amount of strain on the sliding stability of the embankment when subjected to the vertical load than the average slope of 1:1.5 does. In addition to this, it highlights the benefits of employing geogrid to stabilize embankments in a more clear and concise manner.

2.2. Characteristics of Substandard Materials

The subgrade material utilised in this project was standard sand 06 (sand with a maximum grain size of 6 mm), poorly graded (SP), with uniformity coefficients (CU) of 1.45 and curvature coefficients (CC) of 1.08. The UIC Code 719R assigns a QS2 rating to this soil. According to ASTM D4254 and D4253, this sand's lowest specific weight in the lab was determined to be 14.3 kN/m³, and its greatest specific weight was found to be 16.9 kN/m³. A 12 kg laboratory roller was ran nine times over the 5 cm subgrade soil strata in this investigation to achieve a 70% compaction ratio (Heidari, 2019). In line with ASTM D1556-82, the in-place density measurement utilising a sand cone was used to manage the compaction ratio (Saxena & Chaudhary, 2023). However, several direct shear tests on remoulded samples under drained conditions were carried out in accordance with ASTM D3080 to ascertain the shear strength properties of the subgrade soil (Ahmed, et al., 2014).

2.3. Multi-Objective Function

The multi-objective function should decrease the error pressure and settlement by carefully choosing the control parameters and the Geogrid reinforced soil foundation. The required multi-objective function is defined by the following equation (1).

$$FF = Max\left(P_S, P_{BC}\right) \tag{1}$$

Where, P_S is the weak sand's stability and P_{BC} is the sand's ability to bearing capacity on a railroad track. Since choosing the optimal controller may be applied to highways, railroads, and other systems, these would be the four objective functions that need to be improved. The comparator that serves as the HHO algorithm's input is employed in the proposed technique to assess these objective functions (Siva Ramkumar, et al., 2022). The performance of the HHO algorithm is analysed and the equivalent outputs are enhanced largely using a Geogrid controller. The proposed HHO algorithm improves the Geogrid controller's performance (Chakravarthi & Venkatesan, 2021).

2.4. Control of Pressure in Bearing Capacity-Based Geogrid Using HHO Algorithm

In this section, the suggested and described architecture of the HHO optimization algorithm-based Geogrid is used to forecast settlement, bearing capacity, and stability of reinforced foundations. The data must initially be divided into training and testing groups as the first phase in the model creation process. Once the incorrect numbers for pressure, soil density, bearing capacity, and settlement are established (Kamboj, et al., 2020), an HHO is produced. The root mean square error (RMSE) between the actual and predicted values is then reduced using the HHO technique. Following validation using a range of statistical indicators, robustness and generalisation, and independent test data prediction, the final model is selected. In the training phase, parameter optimization is used to lessen the discrepancy between the reference value and the actual value. The HHO algorithm is used to reduce the error value. In Figure 1, the suggested architecture is shown.

Figure 1. Proposed scheme for HHO method-based geogrid

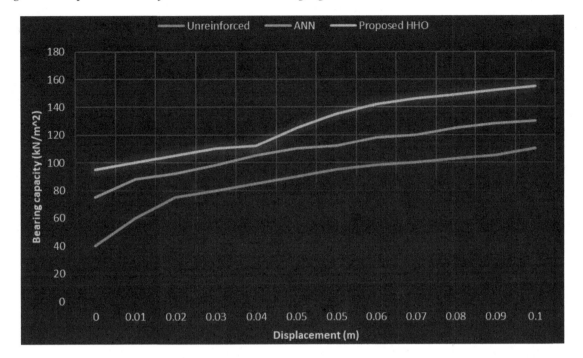

The suggested method should make it easier to assess how much of that material has been forgotten. The following information requires an algorithm to find: (1) Flexible performance settlement after finding the optimal methods for determining bearing capacity (2) Determine if the test number or model best represents the degree of impairment; The goal of the software in this book is to analyse how Harris smart weapons behave while looking for explosives. The HHO paradigm includes algorithm testing and distribution methods that make it easier to research, surprise, and use distinctive attack methods on Harry Hawks' victims.

Steps of HHO Algorithm

Step 1: HHO's first stage is parameter initialization. The parameters of a geogrid controller are arbitrary. Here, the starting values for bearing capacity, pressure, and density are set. It is expected that the initialized system parameters are a function (t+1) It is possible to represent Harris' peregrine prey statistically while taking into consideration the fact that pilgrims wait for prey in various locations (Xie, et al., 2020).

$$X(t+1) = \begin{cases} X_{arb}(t) - r_1 \left| X_{arb}(t) - 2r_2 X(t) \right| & q \geq 0.5 \\ (X_{prey}(t) - X_m(t)) - r_3 \left(\text{LB} + r_4 \left(UB - \text{LB} \right) \right) & q < 0.5 \end{cases} \tag{2}$$

Step 2: Average Number of Solutions

It is possible to define the X_m is as the average number of solutions discovered in the given N number.

$$X_m(t) = \frac{1}{N}\sum_{j=1}^{N} X_j(t) \tag{3}$$

$X_m(t)$ denotes the typical number of replies received during the current iteration. N stands for all potential solutions. Each answer based on mental retardation in repetition is referred to as $X_j(t)$. The same idea often holds true for equation (2), when a hawk utilises information from random thieves to capture its target. Regarding the second rule, all the Falcons collaborate admirably with a highly paid eagle.

Step 3: Exploration of the Transitional Phase of Operation

The progression of HHO from experimental to powerful is described in this section (E). According to the approach of equation (1) from [1, -1], the exhaust gas energy of the victim decreases with beginning energy E_0.

$$E = 2E_0\left(1 - \frac{t}{T_{max}}\right) E_0 \in [-1, 1] \tag{4}$$

Where, T_{max} max is the highest possible number and t is the current cycle.

The tetragon rot tempo (MHHOS) as pursuit may change the escaping energy for the productive combination of the optimum worth.

$$E = 2E_0\left(1 - \frac{t^2}{T_{max}^2}\right) \tag{5}$$

During the research and commissioning stages, the major equipment is compared to the avoided power description of the intended purpose.

Step 4: Exploitation Phase

In the use phase, the hawks' position is modified in accordance with the energy usage determined by equation (5). The Hawks assault method employs four different strategies to take advantage of the HHO, including soft siege, hard siege, soft siege with progressive fast dives, and heavy siege with progressive rapid immersion. These methods rely on two variables, r and |E|, which define the method used. A light barrier is one with an emitted energy of $E \geq 0.5$, whereas a strong barrier is one with <0.5. Case location access is explained in the following:

$$X(t+1) = \begin{cases} \Delta X(t) - E|JX_{prey}(t) - X(t)| & E \geq 0.5 \\ X_{prey}(t) - E|\Delta X(t)| & E < 0.5 \end{cases} \tag{6}$$

$$\Delta X(t) = X_{prey}(t) - X(t) \tag{7}$$

where J=2(1-r^5) and r5in has any value (0, 1). As a result, using the established summary instructions from the preceding mathematical representation, the controller settings may be adjusted properly (Figure 2).

Figure 2. Flowchart of HHO algorithm

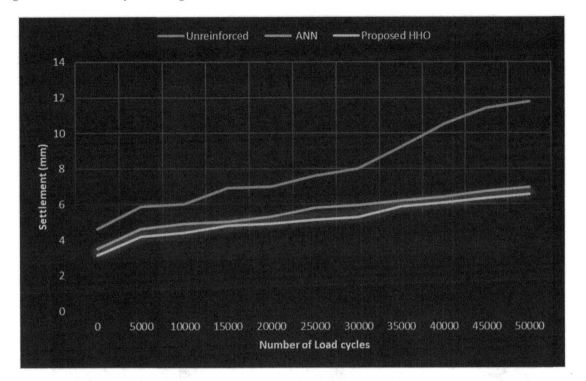

3. RESULTS AND DISCUSSION

When defining nondimensional improvement factors for the ultimate loading capacity and different levels of footing settlement in order to assess the performance of railway tracks with weak sand-based Geogrid foundations, improvements in the bearing capacity and footing settlement are indicated. However, the bulk of foundation designs are predicated on the acceptable amount of settlement rather than the actual carrying capacity. Using the MATLAB platform, the HHO model is created to forecast how geogrid-reinforced sand foundations would settle. The concept behind the proposed HHO technique is that adding geosynthetics to unpaved railway tracks will enhance the sand's poor bearing capacity. Unpaved railway lines are regularly built for remote settlements. It is crucial to know how to react to loads that are below the poor sand's maximum bearing capability. The input parameters for the geogrid are shown in Table 1. As shown in Figure 3, spherical-shaped balls were bonded together to represent geogrids with apertures of 40 mm x 40 mm, similar to those tested in the lab. The balls' radii were 2 mm at the ribs and 4 mm at the intersections.

3.1. Statistical Analysis

To evaluate performance on both taught and unseen data, three statistical indices—mean absolute error (MAE), Root Mean Square Error (RMSE), and Coefficient of Efficiency (E)—were generated (i.e., testing input that the network hasn't encountered during the training process). The "quality of fit" is evaluated by contrasting the actual and anticipated values. The mathematical relationships are as follows:

Table 1. Components of geogrid

Soil Properties	Values
Aperture Size of Mesh (mm)	10 x 10
Shape of Aperture (mm)	Square
Tensile Strength (kN/m)	12.5
Color	Black
Structure	Bi-directional
Elongation at maximum load (%)	20.5
Thickness of Sheet (mm)	4
Raw Material	Polypropylene

Figure 3. MATLAB simulation for direct shear test geogrid

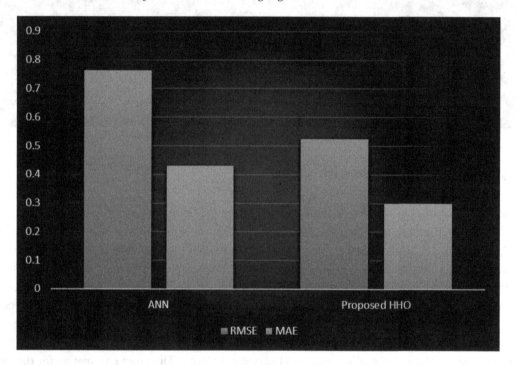

$$RMSE = \sqrt{\frac{1}{n} \sum_{i=1}^{n} \left(O_S^i - P_S^i \right)^2} \tag{8}$$

$$MAE = \frac{1}{n} \sum_{i=1}^{n} \left| P_S^i - O_S^i \right| \tag{9}$$

$$E = 1 - \frac{\sum_{i=1}^{n} \left(P_S^i - O_S^i \right)^2}{\sum_{i=1}^{n} \left(P_S^i - \bar{O}_S^i \right)^2} \tag{10}$$

Where, O_S^i, P_S^i and n stands for i^{th} the observed value of settlement, i^{th} the anticipated value of settlement, and the quantity of data samples, respectively. Tables 2 include the MAE, RMSE, and E values for the testing portion, which were obtained using Equation (8) to (10).

Based on the performance data presented in Table 1, it is possible to draw the conclusion that HHO models perform better than ANN (artificial neural network) models during the testing phase in both models of Geogrid (Figure 4). This is due to the fact that HHO models initially recall the patterns better than ANN models. During the testing phase, however, the HHO models fared better than the ANN model. This is due to the fact that this is the criterion that is used to determine which algorithm or model is the best to utilize in the first place. According to the findings of this study, HHO models produced the greatest outcomes for both of the geogrid techniques that are currently in use. The only drawback of these models is that they require additional trial and error in order to be improved.Based on the performance data presented in Table 1, it is possible to draw the conclusion that HHO models perform better than ANN (artificial neural network) models during the testing phase in both models of Geogrid. This is due to the fact that HHO models initially recall the patterns better than ANN models. During the testing phase, however, the HHO models fared better than the ANN model. This is due to the fact that this is the criterion that is used to determine which algorithm or model is the best to utilize in the first

Table 2. Performance of proposed and existing models based on statistical indices

Statistical Index	ANN	Proposed HHO
RMSE	0.763	0.524
MAE	0.43	0.298
Efficiency	0.96	0.97

Figure 4. Performance analysis of statistical measurement

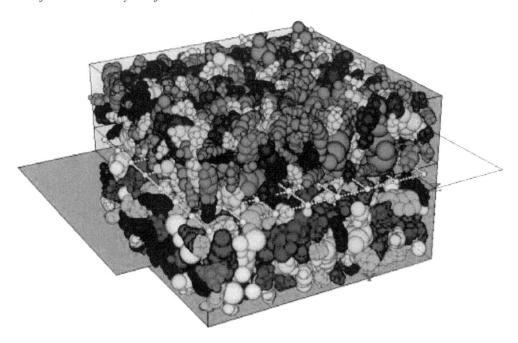

place. According to the findings of this study, HHO models produced the greatest outcomes for both of the geogrid techniques that are currently in use. The only drawback of these models is that they require additional trial and error in order to be improved.

The settling variance for a 50 mm thick granular subbase layer with several geosynthetic reinforcement layer types is typically shown in Figure 5. The findings demonstrated that the poor sand had a relatively high initial modulus, which dropped over time as settlement increased with the number of cycles until it

Figure 5. Results of settlement with number of load repetitions

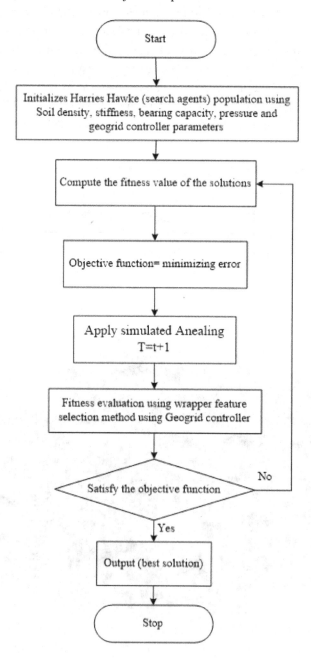

ultimately stabilised at a constant value after 25000 cycles. The effect of geosynthetics on bearing capacity after the construction of the first two embankment lifts is shown in Figure 6. The asymptotic limitation value corresponds to the maximum carrying capacity of ANNs and unreinforced techniques. The bearing capacity of the proposed HHO technique, however, increases with displacement. This improvement in maximum bearing capacity, which increases by 91% from 108 kN/m² for unreinforced structures to 153 kN/m² for suggested HHO structures, is shown in Figure 6. This improvement in bearing capacity has had a significant positive impact on progress and compaction control.

4. CONCLUSION

In this research, the investigation of the improvement effect of geogrid-reinforced sand under static stress was advised using the Harris Hawk Optimization approach. The effects of the mechanical properties of the geogrid on the bearing pressure-settlement response of the depleted sand are studied when reinforcing material with a range of specifications is used to create the geogrid. It has been shown via extensive research and associated geogrid development that employing geogrids to increase track bed stiffness would enhance the long-term performance of the railway line above. Only a full-scale evaluation based on both numerical analysis studies may realistically be used to compare the potential advantages of various geogrid designs. Biaxial geogrids and the more recently developed multiaxial geogrids have different

Figure 6. Results of geogrid on the improvement of bearing capacity

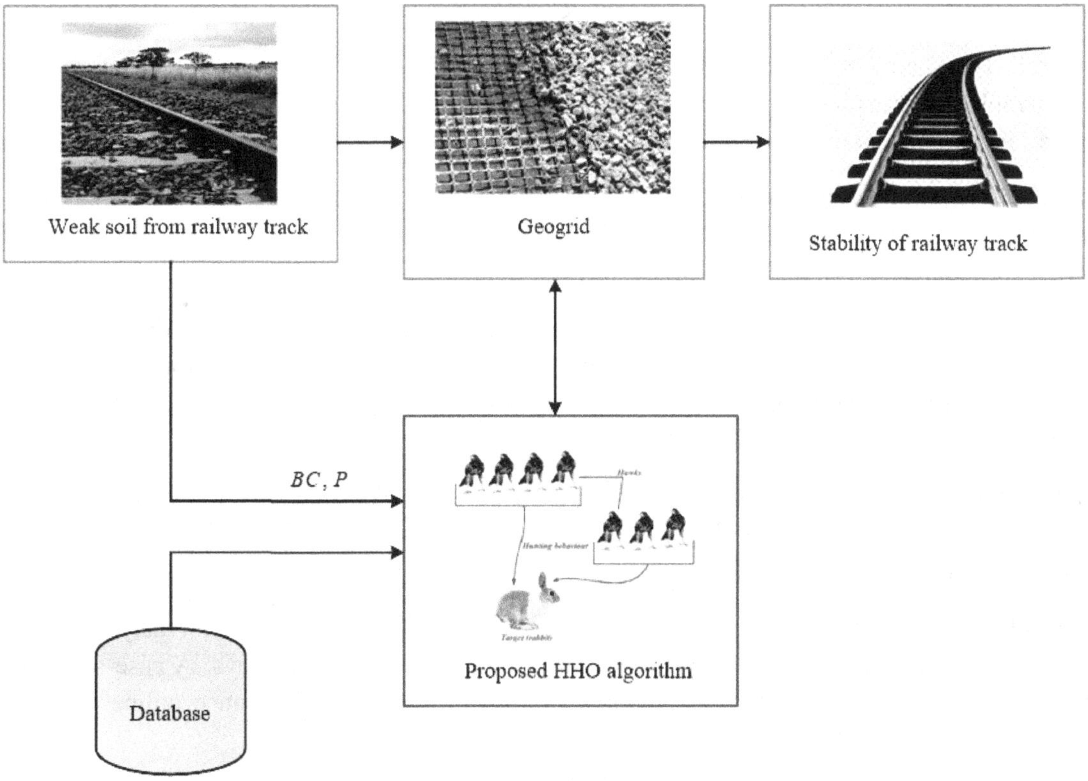

relative performances, which suggests that judging a product just on its basic product characteristics would not provide an appropriate estimate of the performance of the eventual track bed construction. Innovative geogrid technology has the potential to perform better than more established technologies, giving rail engineers greater chances to add value to their projects. Research into the effectiveness of these products, nevertheless, keeps demonstrating and quantifying their advantages.

REFERENCES

Abdelhaleem, F. S., Basiouny, M., Ashour, E., & Mahmoud, A. (2021). Application of remote sensing and geographic information systems in irrigation water management under water scarcity conditions in Fayoum, Egypt. *Journal of Environmental Management, 299*, 113683. doi:10.1016/j.jenvman.2021.113683 PMID:34526284

Ahmed, H. M. A., El Gendy, M., Mirdan, A. M. H., Ali, A. A. M., & Haleem, F. S. F. A. (2014). Effect of corrugated beds on characteristics of submerged hydraulic jump. *Ain Shams Engineering Journal, 5*(4), 1033–1042. doi:10.1016/j.asej.2014.06.006

Ali, H. M., El Gendy, M. M., Mirdan, A. M. H., Ali, A. A. M., & Abdelhaleem, F. S. F. (2014). Minimizing downstream scour due to submerged hydraulic jump using corrugated aprons. *Ain Shams Engineering Journal, 5*(4), 1059–1069. doi:10.1016/j.asej.2014.07.007

Arslan, F., Singh, B., Sharma, D. K., Regin, R., Steffi, R., & Suman Rajest, S. (2021). Optimization technique approach to resolve food sustainability problems. In *2021 International Conference on Computational Intelligence and Knowledge Economy (ICCIKE)*. IEEE. 10.1109/ICCIKE51210.2021.9410735

Ashour, E. H., Ahemd, S. E., Elsayed, S. M., Basiouny, M. E., & Abdelhaleem, F. S. (2021). Integrating geographic information system, remote sensing, and Modeling to enhance reliability of irrigation network. *Water and Energy International, 64*(1), 6–13.

Banu, A., Naidu, S. M., Vinjamuri, S. N., Dattu, G., Sridevi, M., & Chakravarthi, N. R. (2022). Experimentally investigating the influence of static mixers on the performance of a solar water heater. *Materials Today: Proceedings, 62*(4), 2370–2375. doi:10.1016/j.matpr.2022.04.851

Buragadda, S., Rani, K. S., Vasantha, S. V., & Chakravarthi, M. K. (2022). HCUGAN: Hybrid Cyclic UNET GAN for Generating Augmented Synthetic Images of Chest X-Ray Images for Multi Classification of Lung Diseases. *International Journal of Engineering Trends and Technology, 70*(2), 229–238. doi:10.14445/22315381/IJETT-V70I2P227

Chakravarthi, M. K., & Venkatesan, N. (2021). Experimental Transfer Function Based Multi-Loop Adaptive Shinskey PI Control For High Dimensional MIMO Systems. *Journal of Engineering Science and Technology, 16*(5), 4006–4015.

Deshpande, T. D., Kumar, S., Begum, G., Basha, S. A. K., & Rao, B. H. (2021). Analysis of railway embankment supported with geosynthetic-encased stone columns in soft clays: A case study. *International Journal of Geosynthetics and Ground Engineering, 7*(2), 43. Advance online publication. doi:10.100740891-021-00288-5

Diwedar, A. I., Abdelhaleem, F. S., & Ali, A. M. (2019). Wave parameters influence on breakwater stability. *IOP Conference Series. Earth and Environmental Science*, *326*(1), 012013. doi:10.1088/1755-1315/326/1/012013

Esmaeili, M., Naderi, B., Neyestanaki, H. K., & Khodaverdian, A. (2018). Investigating the effect of geogrid on stabilization of high railway embankments. *Soil and Foundation*, *58*(2), 319–332. doi:10.1016/j.sandf.2018.02.005

Fan, S., Song, Z., Xu, T., Wang, K., & Zhang, Y. (2021). Tunnel deformation and stress response under the bilateral foundation pit construction: A case study. *Archives of Civil and Mechanical Engineering*, *21*(3), 109. Advance online publication. doi:10.100743452-021-00259-7

Fattah, M. Y., Mahmood, M. R., & Aswad, M. F. (2018). Experimental and numerical behavior of railway track over geogrid reinforced ballast underlain by soft clay. In *Sustainable Civil Infrastructures* (pp. 1–26). Springer International Publishing.

Fattah, M. Y., Mahmood, M. R., & Aswad, M. F. (2019). Stress distribution from railway track over geogrid reinforced ballast underlain by clay. *Earthquake Engineering and Engineering Vibration*, *18*(1), 77–93. doi:10.100711803-019-0491-z

Gowtham, S., Ch, T., Kumar, N. S. M. P., Devi, M., Chakravarthi, S., Kumar, R., Harishchander Anandaram, N. M., & Kumar, K. (2022). A Survey on Additively Manufactured Nanocomposite Biomaterial for Orthopaedic Applications. *Journal of Nanomaterials*, *2022*, 2022. doi:10.1155/2022/8998451

Heidari, A., Mirjalili, S., Faris, H., Aljarah, I., Mafarja, M., & Chen, H. (2019). Harris hawks' optimization: Algorithm and applications. *Future Generation Computer Systems*, *97*, 849–872. doi:10.1016/j.future.2019.02.028

Indraratna, B., Sun, Q., Ngo, N. T., & Rujikiatkamjorn, C. (2017). Current research into ballasted rail tracks: Model tests and their practical implications. *Australian Journal of Structural Engineering*, *18*(3), 204–220. doi:10.1080/13287982.2017.1359398

Kamboj, V. K., Nandi, A., Bhadoria, A., & Sehgal, S. (2020). An intensify Harris Hawks optimizer for numerical and engineering optimization problems. *Applied Soft Computing*, *89*(106018), 106018. doi:10.1016/j.asoc.2019.106018

Kempfert, H.-G., & Raithel, M. (2005). Soil improvement and foundation systems with encased columns and reinforced bearing layers. In *Ground Improvement — Case Histories* (pp. 923–946). Elsevier. doi:10.1016/S1571-9960(05)80035-7

Lai, H.-J., Zheng, J.-J., Zhang, J., Zhang, R.-J., & Cui, L. (2014). DEM analysis of "soil"-arching within geogrid-reinforced and unreinforced pile-supported embankments. *Computers and Geotechnics*, *61*, 13–23. doi:10.1016/j.compgeo.2014.04.007

Lazorenko, G., Kasprzhitskii, A., Khakiev, Z., & Yavna, V. (2019). Dynamic behavior and stability of soil foundation in heavy haul railway tracks: A review. *Construction & Building Materials*, *205*, 111–136. doi:10.1016/j.conbuildmat.2019.01.184

Lazorenko, G., Kasprzhitskii, A., Kukharskii, A., Kochur, A., & Yavna, V. (2020). Failure analysis of widened railway embankment with different reinforcing measures under heavy axle loads: A comparative FEM study. *Transportation Engineering*, *2*(100028). doi:10.1016/j.treng.2020.100028

Liu, K., Su, Q., Ni, P., Zhou, C., Zhao, W., & Yue, F. (2018). Evaluation on the dynamic performance of bridge approach backfilled with fibre reinforced lightweight concrete under high-speed train loading. *Computers and Geotechnics*, *104*, 42–53. doi:10.1016/j.compgeo.2018.08.003

Nirmala, G., Premavathy, R., Chandar, R., & Jeganathan, J. (2023). An Explanatory Case Report on Biopsychosocial Issues and the Impact of Innovative Nurse-Led Therapy in Children with Hematological Cancer. *FMDB Transactions on Sustainable Health Science Letters*, *1*(1), 1–10.

Ogunmola, G. A., Singh, B., Sharma, D. K., Regin, R., Rajest, S. S., & Singh, N. (2021). Involvement of distance measure in assessing and resolving efficiency environmental obstacles. In *2021 International Conference on Computational Intelligence and Knowledge Economy (ICCIKE)*. IEEE. 10.1109/ICCIKE51210.2021.9410765

Pandit, P. (2023). On the Context of Diabetes: A Brief Discussion on the Novel Ethical Issues of Noncommunicable Diseases. *FMDB Transactions on Sustainable Health Science Letters*, *1*(1), 11–20.

Pandya, S., Gadekallu, T. R., Reddy, P. K., Wang, W., & Alazab, M. (2022). InfusedHeart: A novel knowledge-infused learning framework for diagnosis of cardiovascular events. *IEEE Transactions on Computational Social Systems*, 1–10. doi:10.1109/TCSS.2022.3151643

Saxena, D., & Chaudhary, S. (2023). Predicting Brain Diseases from FMRI-Functional Magnetic Resonance Imaging with Machine Learning Techniques for Early Diagnosis and Treatment. *FMDB Transactions on Sustainable Computer Letters*, *1*(1), 33–48.

Schary, Y. (2020). Case studies on geocell-based reinforced roads, railways and ports. In *Geocells* (pp. 387–411). Springer Singapore. doi:10.1007/978-981-15-6095-8_15

Sharma, D. K., Jalil, N. A., Regin, R., Rajest, S. S., Tummala, R. K., & Thangadurai. (2021). Predicting network congestion with machine learning. In *2021 2nd International Conference on Smart Electronics and Communication (ICOSEC)*. IEEE.

Siva Ramkumar, M., Priya, R., Rajakumari, R. F., Valsalan, P., Chakravarthi, M., Charlyn Pushpa Latha, G., Mathupriya, S., & Rajan, K. (2022). Review and Evaluation of Power Devices and Semiconductor Materials Based on Si, SiC, and Ga-N. *Journal of Nanomaterials*, *2022*, 2022. doi:10.1155/2022/8648284

Sol-Sánchez, M., & D'Angelo, G. (2017). Review of the design and maintenance technologies used to decelerate the deterioration of ballasted railway tracks. *Construction & Building Materials*, *157*, 402–415. doi:10.1016/j.conbuildmat.2017.09.007

Woodward, P. K., Kennedy, J., Laghrouche, O., Connolly, D. P., & Medero, G. (2014). Study of railway track stiffness modification by polyurethane reinforcement of the ballast. *Transportation Geotechnics*, *1*(4), 214–224. doi:10.1016/j.trgeo.2014.06.005

Xie, W., Xing, C., Wang, J., Guo, S., Guo, M.-W., & Zhu, L.-F. (2020). Hybrid Henry gas solubility optimization algorithm based on the Harris hawk optimization. *IEEE Access : Practical Innovations, Open Solutions*, *8*, 144665–144692. doi:10.1109/ACCESS.2020.3014309

Yu, Z., Woodward, P. K., Laghrouche, O., & Connolly, D. P. (2019). True triaxial testing of geogrid for high speed railways. *Transportation Geotechnics*, *20*(100247), 100247. doi:10.1016/j.trgeo.2019.100247

Zannah, A. I., Rachakonda, S., Abubakar, A. M., Devkota, S., & Nneka, E. C. (2023). Control for Hydrogen Recovery in Pressuring Swing Adsorption System Modeling. *FMDB Transactions on Sustainable Energy Sequence*, *1*(1), 1–10.

Ziegler, M. (2017). Application of geogrid reinforced constructions: History, recent and future developments. *Procedia Engineering*, *172*, 42–51. doi:10.1016/j.proeng.2017.02.015

Chapter 18
Information Design and Unifying Approach for Secured Data Sharing Using Attribute-Based Access Control Mechanisms

R. Regin
SRM Institute of Science and Technology, Ramapuram, India

Muskan Gupta
SRM Institute of Science and Technology, Ramapuram, India

A. Aakash Khanna
SRM Institute of Science and Technology, Ramapuram, India

S. Rubin Bose
SRM Institute of Science and Technology, Ramapuram, India

Vamsi Krishnan
SRM Institute of Science and Technology, Ramapuram, India

S. Suman Rajest
(iD) https://orcid.org/0000-0001-8315-3747
Dhaanish Ahmed College of Engineering, India

ABSTRACT

In response to the safety concerns surrounding the IoT, an attribute-based encryption and access control scheme (ABE-ACS) has been proposed. This scheme can be more effectively implemented through the use of cutting-edge technology and incorporating attribute-based encryption (ABE) and attribute-based access control (ABAC) models with features as the point of origin. Facing Edge-IoT is a heterogeneous network made up of certain nodes with more powerful computers and the majority of resource-constrained IoT devices. The authors provide a lightweight with an upgrade to the proof-of-work consensus to address the issues of excessive resource consumption and challenging deployment of existing platforms. To protect the confidentiality of the access control policies, the limits of the tree are utilised for transformation and allocation stored. Six smart contracts are created for devices and data to implement the ABAC and punishment mechanism, which outsources ABE to edge nodes for privacy and integrity. Thus, the plan implements device-controlled access and Edge-IoT privacy protection for data.

DOI: 10.4018/978-1-6684-9189-8.ch018

1. INTRODUCTION

Cloud technology is now one of the most notable technologies due to its accessibility and scalability. Large corporations are accustomed to using a variety of service platforms, including iCloud from Apple, EC2 from Amazon, and Google Apps from Google (Arslan et al., 2021). According to Indalecio and his coworkers, distributed (cloud) computing is a system that enables universal, advantageous, on-demand network access to processing resources, such as computer systems, memory devices, connections, and solutions that are mutually adjustable (Ogunmola et al., 2021). This may be rapidly introduced and then withdrawn by making only a few service-associated initiatives or contacting a service operator (Sharma et al., 2021). The general public can save their records for a reasonable fee or free of charge (Arunadevi et al., 2021). Users can choose not to claim the infrastructure for certain processing features (Buddhi et al., 2022).

In actuality, they may be used to access data from any computer situated anywhere in the world (Jain et al., 2022). This provides great flexibility compared to prior processing methods because it consolidates the parts that provide high adaptability and occupancy (Kumar et al., 2022). A newer technology, cloud computing, depends on sharing computing resources (Mawle et al., 2022). Since the cloud provider cannot be trusted, group data sharing is not secure (Nagarathna et al., 2022). Data security, sharing, resource scheduling, and energy consumption are the primary challenges faced by cloud providers when using distributed computing (Pandiyarajan et al., 2022). This project's primary contributions are the creation of transactions, the creation of blockchains, and the deployment of blockchains (Priscila et al., 2023). Cloud-based private and public data security using the Key Aggregate Cryptosystem With the help of virtual machine (VM) provisioning, cloud service providers may more efficiently employ the resources they have at their disposal and reap more benefits (Rao et al., 2021). Distributed storage offers the most efficient, versatile, and secure way for group members to exchange information resources (figure 1). The project's primary goal is:

- To develop automated, adaptable data-sharing mechanisms.
- To automate and make critical distribution, verification, and discovery easier depending on the material.
- To effectively update stated access policies. to lower user-side computational burden.
- To carry out the simultaneous collection of data related to a data owner.

The financial services industry has already begun to see disruption from the blockchain network, which powers bitcoin transactions (Reddy Madduri et al., 2022) to blockchain technology, the financial

Figure 1. The attribute-based authorisation system as represented by a system

⊞ Results ▤ Messages

	userID	emailid	password	userName	roleID	isactive
1	1	1@1.com	1	Mary Brown	1	1
2	4	test@test.com	1	a111	1	NULL
3	1004	aakash@gmail.com	NULL	abcd	4	NULL

sector can communicate directly and carry out transactions via the internet without the assistance of a third party (Sattaru et al., 2022). By encrypting the identifying information, such blockchain transactions produce a transaction record without disclosing any personal information about the participants (Singh et al., 2022). The most fascinating aspect of blockchain is how much it lowers the likelihood of a data leak (Shynu et al., 2022). In contrast to conventional methods, blockchain uses several shared copies of the same database, which makes it more difficult to launch a cyberattack or data breach attempt (Rupapara et al., 2023).

With its many anti-fraud characteristics, block chain technology has the potential to revolutionise many industries by making business processes smarter, safer, more transparent, and more effective than those used in the past (Regin, & Shynu, 2023). Data sharing capabilities may be enabled through cloud systems, and this can benefit users in a variety of ways (Regin, et al., 2023). There is currently pressure on IT businesses to step up their efforts to share data (Steffi et al., 2023). A study by InformationWeek found that almost all firms shared data in some way, with 84% sharing it with clients and 55% sharing it with suppliers (Shynu et al., 2023). A quarter of the businesses polled place the exchange of data as a major priority. Increased efficiency is one of the advantages that data sharing can bring to firms (Priscila et al., 2023). When several users from other businesses contribute to data in the cloud, it will take considerably less time and money than if data had to be manually exchanged, which would result in a jumble of redundant and sometimes outdated papers (Rajest et al., 2023). The advantages of sharing data with social networking services like Facebook are numerous (Nirmala et al., 2023). This enhances one's level of happiness in life and can enrich some people's lives, as they are amazed at how many people are interested in their lives and well-being (Figure 2).

The policy decision point (PDP), policy enforcement point (PEP), policy administration point (PAP), and policy information point (PIP) make up the ABAC framework (Vashishtha & Dhawan, 2023). The following is a description of these points (Pandit, 2023).

- PEP: Charged with processing the subject's first access request and carrying out the necessary action in accordance with the PDP's judgement outcome.
- PDP: The PEP's access request is evaluated in accordance with the access control policy, and the outcome is communicated back to the PEP.
- PAP: In charge of overseeing the access control regulations and providing PDP judgements with authority determinations.
- PIP: In charge of overseeing topic, resource, and environment attribute data.

Figure 2. Basic ABAC architecture

⊞ Results ▣ Messages

	cloudProviderID	cloudProviderName	storageSpace	usageCostPerGB	ipAddress
1	1	Microsoft Azure	100	110	NULL
2	2	iCloud	2000	90	NULL
3	1003	abc	64	30.5	NULL
4	1004	abc	64	1655	NULL

2. LITERATURE SURVEY

ABAC is a sort of access control system that makes use of characteristics to decide whether or not a user is permitted to utilise a given resource or carry out a particular operation (Suganthi & Sathiaseelan, 2023). With the help of ABAC, organisations may build intricate access controls that take into consideration a variety of contextual elements (Anand et al., 2023).

Koyasako et al., (2021) suggested that there was a growing need for the movement control of Internet of Things gadgets, including industrial machinery and drones. Utilizing systems with minimal latency, such as edge computing, is advantageous because the performance of the control is negatively impacted by the delay between communication devices. Networks that use optical access design and control for motion control, however, are the subject of no other study. On an administrative headquarters server at the edge, we wish to provide real-time motion control. System control and access edge structures that offer, depending on lag information, time-dependent latency correction are described in this work. We evaluate how well our method controls under conditions of heavy network traffic, growing delays, and packet loss. We show that the suggested technique yields 2.7 and 8.0 second motor control settling times, respectively; the motor cannot be controlled by the conventional technique in either case if the resulting downstream load rises to 9 Gbps from 10 Gbps (Jeba et al., 2023).

Shi et al., (2020), facets of human life are changing and getting better thanks to the Internet of Things (IoT). Attackers are taking advantage of the destabilisation of Internet apps and devices to damage user devices and data and gain illegal access. They achieve this by taking advantage of lax access control and authentication protocols on various IoT apps and devices. Access control is a crucial security tool for safeguarding the ecology of the IOT, which comprises smart devices, cloud computing, and edge computing services. Today's leading cloud and IoT service providers, such as Amazon Web Services (AWS), Google Cloud Platform (GCP), and Azure, use specific role-based access control (RBAC) models in combination with particular approval policies made possible by policy-based access control models. It is urgently necessary to provide access control that is adaptable and dynamic for protecting smart gadgets, information, and resources within the enabled IoT system in order to allow precise access control and overcome the limitations of the current access control architecture. In this work, we formalise the previously created access control model for AWS IoT. We make use of the AWS IOT platform and a use case for commercial IOT to illustrate the viability of our proposed approach. In addition to incorporating AWS IoT's current features, our suggested fine-grained model adds additional characteristics for IoT entities and attribute-based policies to enable expressive access control in AWS IoT. To demonstrate the viability of our model on a real-world platform, we also evaluate how well our model performs on the AWS cloud and IoT platform using a case study for potential smart sectors.

In order to regulate low speed, which is linear ultrasonic motor (LUSM) at the micron scale, Rooney & Hinders, (2021) suggested a novel control approach that combined step control with fuzzy proportional-integral-derivative (PID). Unlike a typical PID controller, a fuzzy PID controller's control parameters were affected by environmental factors. When the desired speed is below 1 mm/s through conventional means, the linear ultrasonic motor's ability to regulate in the shape of a butterfly is not excellent. An approach to tightly integrated control employing step control and fuzzy PID control was presented to enhance the linear ultrasonic motor's low-speed controlling features. The controller was built with the ability to manage speed in a closed-loop manner by varying the amplitude of the stepping driving mode's driving voltage. These were used to identify the step-regulating parameters that corresponded. Different target speeds were used in extensive tests of the developed control strategy. At the goal speed of 10 m/s, there was a maximum speed error of 24.5%; however, 16.4% and 0.10 s, respectively, for the variance coefficient and the reaction time The greatest speed tracking errors for triangular or sinusoidal waves with amplitudes of 1 mm/s were, respectively, 0.18 mm/s and 0.4 mm/s. In conclusion, effective speed monitoring was successful. The findings indicate the method's functionality and promise a low-speed, precise method of controlling proportional ultrasonic motors (Cirillo et al., 2023).

In order to distinguish between transmissions controlled by CSMA and TDMA protocols, Ghaffari et al., (2021) used the usual frequency of network broadcasts implementing a based-on reservation in the TDMA protocol. The ability to distinguish the network's method of media access control may make it simpler to incorporate cognitive radio into an existing network by emphasising a crucial component of network activity. Since one of the most apparent distinctions between reservation-based and contention-based media access control techniques is how users access the electromagnetic spectrum, In order to distinguish between transmissions controlled using TDMA and transmissions controlled by contention-based CSMA procedures, the initial component of this study leverages the predictable timing of broadcasts from networks using TDMA protocols with reservations. With the use of modular arithmetic, our approach detects periodicity in transmission timing by employing a supervised k-means algorithm to produce distinctive CSMA and TDMA clusters. We study a number of fields in the field of supervised machine learning methods in order to create a protocol classifier. Then, we show how to distinguish between transmissions from networks based on frequency division multiple access (FDMA) with numerous channels and those from networks with a single channel. Automatic machine learning clustering is used in this technique to get a rough estimate of true centre channel frequencies. A network uses this data to verify that it is utilising FDMA procedures to obtain electromagnetic spectrum access (Abbassy & Abo-Alnadr, 2019).

Aftab et al., (2020) suggested method's key objective is to provide a modular and adaptable access control system. The demand for implementing scalable access control systems has been underscored by the sharp increase in the provision of internet-based services, simplifying service authorization for qualified users. Current centralised solutions are troublesome due to their potential inability, not being scalable, and heavy computing load. These techniques also require consumers to pay the service provider individually to obtain a particular feature, which increases the user's expense. New business approaches are needed to solve these concerns. Complex access control approaches that take into account the needs of all those that seek to These models must be used in order to: 1) enter an application; 2) offer that support; and 3) supply the connection to the network. Blockchain is a facilitating technology that offers innovative decentralised access control mechanisms for new business models with potential that was previously unfathomable. We propose an attribute-based access control method that makes use of blockchain to engage in resource exchange between networking suppliers and providers of services. Our approach provides flexible access based on the needs of the parties and meets reliability, responsibility, and the immutability of It also brings down the overall cost of the service, benefiting both parties. With the help of our solution, suppliers are able to outsource the access control processes without the need for a trustworthy third party. These tests demonstrate that the system can provide a rapid, thorough, and expandable security monitoring system (Saxena & Chaudhary, 2023).

Gan et al., (2020) focused on latency and administrative costs. Therefore, An overlapping access control scheme that employs COI dynamically at the role level was proposed in this paper. Researchers in academia and business are becoming more interested in the secure localization of cars, especially in light of the global internet of things' (IoT) growth. Circuitry that allows communication is typically installed in current automobiles. The development of IoT, satellite, and 5G-based autonomous or driverless cars has increased the difficulty of safe localization and positioning. Some IoT and satellite-based localization techniques make use of access control, semantic segmentation, and machine learning. Access control prohibits unauthorised users while granting access to authorised users and providing a secure information sharing method, which is essential for security and privacy (Abbassy et al., 2020). Prior to now, access control for security purposes was COI-based. The least tolerated factor in the contemporary Internet of Things is execution delay, which is caused by excesses and administrative overload in static COI-based access control (Fabela et al., 2017).

TBAC, a unique mechanism built using the ACT, was presented by Shi et al., (2020). It is inspired by blockchains, smart contracts, and ABAC. TBAC provides certain comparative benefits over conventional centralised access control in terms of security, credibility, circulation, currency, etc. Traditional centralised access control has various drawbacks in terms of durability, reliability, and circulation. The benefits of trust and fault tolerance for blockchains Flexible expansion and automated execution are features of smart contracts. Tokens can simply capture and transfer credential information. The drawbacks of conventional access control are addressed in this study by integrating blockchain, smart contracts, and tokens. Access control, decentralised ledger contracts with logic, and tokens are first briefly explained. This work proposes a solution in two ways: first, by presenting the access control token's vast structure of data; second, by describing equivalent requirements, breaking down combine, and confirmation algorithms; and third, by describing the token-based access control's overall architecture. Research concludes by utilising a modelling system to show that token-based control of access offers assured comparative advantages. benefits in terms of resilience, reliability, movement, acceptance, and other variables (Derindere Köseoğlu et al., 2022).

A blockchain-based permission-based unauthorised delegation vulnerability was proposed by Leander et al., (2021). The security research concludes by demonstrating that the two suggested systems may address the permission delegation-related vulnerability for unauthorised access and by conducting an experimental investigation of algorithm performance. Transferring privileges for access control gives an individual a second means to get item access in addition to authorization. This is important, especially whenever there is a rift between the manager and owner of the thing. With the growth of the IOT, consistency between item managers and their owners is becoming increasingly prevalent, even if study over authorization assignment utilising blockchain-based access control is not ideal. It is controlled solely through the authorization of the token's holder. An unauthorised person might take the token and use it to get another one. Therefore, it is suggested to use a blockchain-based permission-based unauthorised delegation vulnerability. The vulnerability's important feature is subject A's desire to transfer the authorization to another subject B once it has been given via the object. It must guarantee that subject B, the recipient of the licence, is authorised to use it. After verification, the delegate passes the token and may do so to an unauthorised user. TCPDA and PRPDA, two permission algorithms, are then suggested as solutions to the issue.

Hu et al., (2022) controlled and supervised by industrial control systems. As part of the transition known as Industry 4.0, which is characterised by greater connection and flexibility, these systems are presently experiencing a metamorphosis. As a result, the landscape of cybersecurity threats for industrial control systems is changing. The access control methods now employed in industrial control systems are rather simple. It is obvious that employing more precise access control measures will help alleviate some of the rising cybersecurity dangers associated with Industry 4.0. In this article, we analyse and outline some access control tactics that may be applied in industrial systems. Using a variety of attack scenarios, we simulate an experiment to evaluate the techniques. A method for automatically generating policies based on engineering data is also described, and it is in accordance with one of the most effective tactics (Table 1).

Gartner forecasts that 70% of businesses will employ ABAC to secure vital assets by 2020, despite the fact that the RBAC approach is well-established (Lu et al., 2020). The sources (Hur, 2013; Luo & Ma, 2019; Song, et al., 2020) also offer a few clear limitations for the RBAC approach, such as:

- Rules cannot be using parameters that the system is unaware of.
- Only user roles may be given permissions; operations and objects cannot.
- The RBAC model being what it built mostly with fixed organisational roles, most of the issues with certain designs when it is necessary to make dynamic AC decisions.
- Access to certain system activities can be restricted, but not to the data model.

3. PROPOSED SYSTEM

User data is sent back and forth between data centres on a cloud server. If the user is real, they can register and authenticate (Jeganathan et al., 2023). The file can be uploaded to the server by authorised users. The file is generated by the server automatically; it is then encrypted and kept on the servers. Any user can request to download a file by first determining whether it is available and whether there are sufficient resources. The authorised user can then download the file by providing his private key. Another copy of the file kept in the dispersed data centre can be accessible if the original file is compromised by any attacker (Ead & Abbassy, 2018). In this case, we produce code from corrupted files using a regenerative function. The majority of file accesses are driven by client requests. The following equation represents the hash function:

$$dist\left(X,Y\right) = \left(\sum_{i=1}^{N}\left|hash\left(x_i\right) - hash\left(y_i\right)\right|^2\right)^{\frac{1}{2}}$$

A function known as a hash creates a single, unique value from any input or output with a specified size for the hash key. The hash function being used determines the precise formula for producing the

Table 1. Comparison between (RBAC) role-based access control and (ABAC) attribute-based access control

Features	RBAC	ABAC
Access control	Roles or groups are the foundation.	The foundation of access control is on user's or resource's qualities.
Flexibility	restricted adaptability	more freedom in defining access control policies.
Complexity	simple to manage and install	can be challenging to manage and implement, especially at scale.
Granularity	Coarse-grained	Fine-grained, enabling more individualised access control rules.
Resource allocation	Based on a pre-established roles or a collection of roles	Access is determined by certain characteristics of the assigned function or collection of responsibilities. the resource or user.
Dynamic access control	based on pre-established positions or groupings, less dynamic	enhanced by access control Based on real-time resource or service qualities, policies can be changed.

hash result. For instance, a 256-bit hash value is produced using the SHA-256 hash algorithm, which is frequently employed in blockchain technology. When using SHA-256, the hash value is created by padding the message to an aggregate of 512 bytes, dividing the message padding into 512-bit segments, initialising eight 32-bit variables to predetermined constants, and then performing a series of intricate operations on those variables for each block of the message. The 256-bit hash value is produced by adding the values of the eight variables.

3.1. Proposed Algorithm

Smart contracts are used to carry out the permission determination policy. The subject identification (UUID_SUB), object analyzer (ID_OBJ), and Type of operation (Ty_Op) are the inputs for our permission determination algorithm, which delivers the judgement result ("True" or "False") based on the design. the object's and the subject's identifier provide the subject's attribute (Att_Sub) and object's attribute (Att_Obj) to lines 1 and 2, respectively. The purpose of line 3 is in order to purchase PPC for access control using the received sub, obj, and the type of operating characteristics. Through the acquired subject attribute and the type of operation, line 4 is where EPC is acquired for controlling access. The access request is evaluated using PPC and EPC in line 5 through 13. The request of access won't be judged by EPC until it passes through PPC review.

Algorithm 1 Permission decision policy (PDP):

```
Load: Att_Obj, Att_Sub, Type of Opertaion
Output: True or False
1: Sub Attribute ← Get Attribute (Att_Sub);
2: Obj Attribute ← Get Attribute (Att_Obj);
3:PublicContract ← Fetch Public Contract();
4:PrivateContract ← Fetch Private Contract(Att_Obj);
5: if Public Contract Verify Public Contract(Att_Sub, Att_Obj,Operate)=True,
6: if Private Contract (Verify Public Contract(Att_Sub, Operate) = True,
7: return (True);
8: else:
9: return (False);
10: end Condition.
11: else:
12: return (False);
13: end
```

We build the policy on public access control by utilising a smart contract in accordance with PAC(2 Algorithm), which accepts the operation, the relevant quality of subject (Sub Attribute), the features of the Attribute of Object (Object), and judgement outcome ("True" or "False") as inputs. The Euclidean distance calculation function is used in lines 2 through 13 to assess how comparable the subject characteristics and the object features are. We may determine a hash value based on those characteristics by performing a series of computations using the knowledge we have about the discovered subject attribute. Based on the details we have about the acquired object property, we can also get a hash value. When the object attributes' hash key and the subject attributes' hash key are computed by the differences using Euclidean function, It is demonstrated that the subject and the object have enough characteristics.

Algorithm 2 Public access control policy(PAC)

```
Load: Sub Attribute, Object Attribute, Type of operation
Output: 0(True) or 1(False)
1: sum of Distance = 0 num = 1, Tvalue = Threshold Value;
2: for i = num; i <= n; i++ do:
3: sub-Attribute Hash key ← hash(subAtt[i]);
4: object Attribute Hash key ← hash(objAt[i]);
5: hash Distance ← sub Attribute Hash - object Attribute Hash;
6: powDist ← powfi hash Distance, 2fi;
7: sum of Distance = sum of Distance + pow of Distance ;
8: end loop:
9: distance = square root of (sum of Distance) ;
10: if distance <= Tvalue then
11: return 0;
12: else:
13: return 1;
14: end condition
```

3.2. Architecture Diagram

The following is an architecture diagram for a system that enables safe data exchange with attribute-based access control (ABAC) (Figure 3):

User Interface: This part offers the user interface for sharing and accessing data. Users are given the option to log in, see data, and carry out operations including data uploading, downloading, and sharing.

Attribute-Based Access Control (ABAC) Engine: The technique for enforcing access controls is provided by this component. It accepts input from the user interface and checks the desired action against properties related to the user, data, and policy to determine if it is allowed or not.

Policy Management: This part controls access policies that outline who has access to what information and when. It offers an interface for adding, changing, and removing policies. Additionally, it stores policies in a file system or database.

Data management: The system's data is managed by this part. It offers a user interface for adding, removing, and downloading data. Data metadata, including the owner, creation date, and access control rules, is also stored.

Security Services: This subsystem offers encryption, decryption, and authentication, among other security services. It makes sure authorised. The system is accessible to users, and that data is safe from hacking and unauthorised access.

Services for integration with external systems and applications are provided by this component. It enables the system to communicate with other systems using established protocols or APIs to exchange data.

Figure 3. Basic ABAC architecture

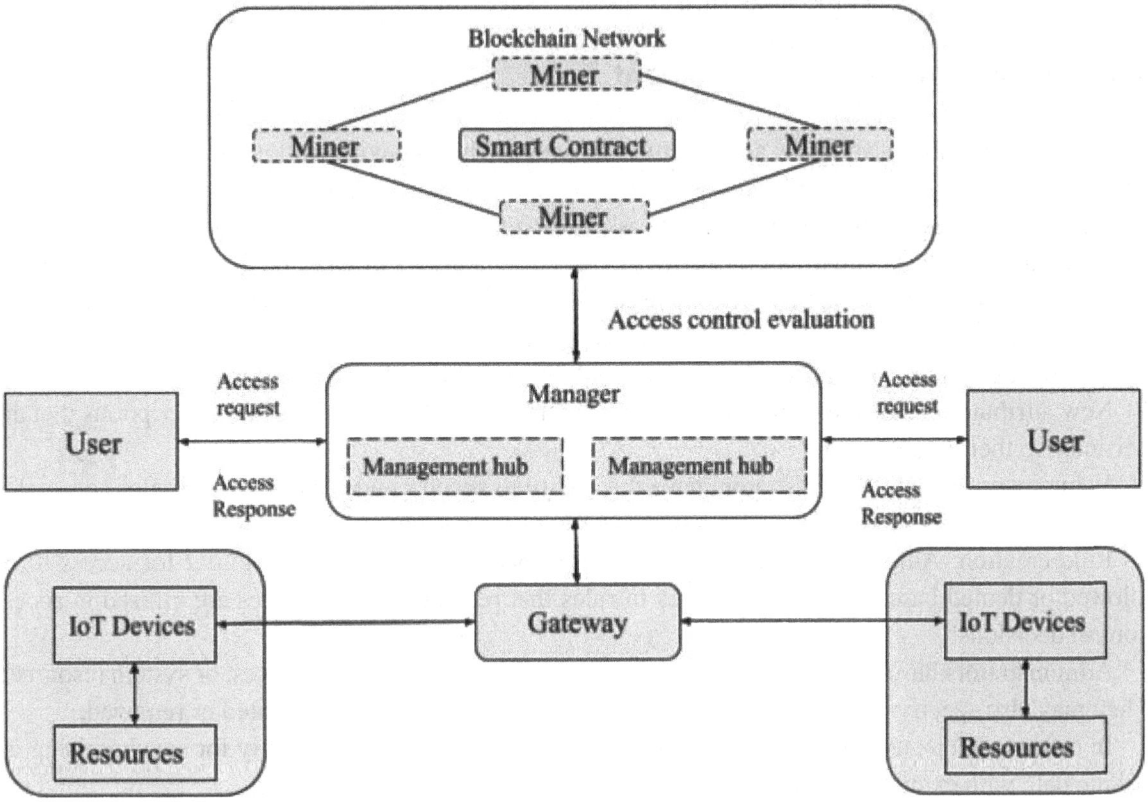

Overall, this architecture offers a safe and adaptable method of exchanging data, enabling users to only access the information to which they have been granted access based on their qualities and the access control criteria.

4. METHODOLOGY

According to the ABAC paradigm, topic features, asset attributes, authoritative attributes, and environmental attributes are crucial factors in deciding whether to provide access authorization. The heart of the ABAC model is comprised of attributes, which could be displayed as five or six tuples consisting of topic, tool, governing body, and setting attributes. Following are descriptions of the topic, tool, governing body, and setting attributes:

- Topic: The party who requested access, which might be a person, a process, etc.
- Resource: The person who received the access request is the resource. IoT device, process, file resource, etc.
- Authority: The actions a subject is capable of carrying out on resources (such opening, reading, or deleting).

- Environment: The environmental data that the subject of the access request transmitted to the resource during that procedure, such as the access request's time stamp.

4.1. Module 1: Attribute Management

To offer a decentralised, versatile, and granular Internet of Things device authorization, management of characteristics (such as location, date, time, etc.) is important. The use of attributes to specify specific rules for target access determines whether the asked-for item has prerequisite access rights, which makes them important. In these situations, the use of blockchain enables legitimate and trustworthy credentials. The blockchain's ability to regulate verifiable cooperation mechanisms through edge IoT devices makes this conceivable. In addition, characteristics are recorded and distributed via blockchain to prevent data fraud and single points of failure. The module could include the following features:

New attributes can be created by administrators with particular data kinds and descriptions that are pertinent to their organisation.

Value management: Administrators have the ability to specify and control the range of acceptable values for each property as well as the connections between various attributes.

Rule creation: Administrators can define criteria that must be satisfied in order for access to be allowed or denied based on attribute values in rules that regulate how attributes are utilised in access control decisions.

Administrators have the ability to assign attributes to various individuals, roles, or system resources. They may also specify the circumstances under which an attribute may be granted or removed.

In order to keep attribute data current, the module may include functionality for synchronising attribute data with external data sources like LDAP or HR systems.

Reporting and auditing: The module can include reporting and auditing features to follow how attributes are used by the ABAC system, including access control choices based on attribute values (Figures 4 and 5).

Figure 4. Cloud provider data

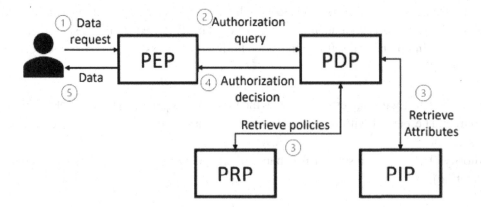

Figure 5. User data stored in server

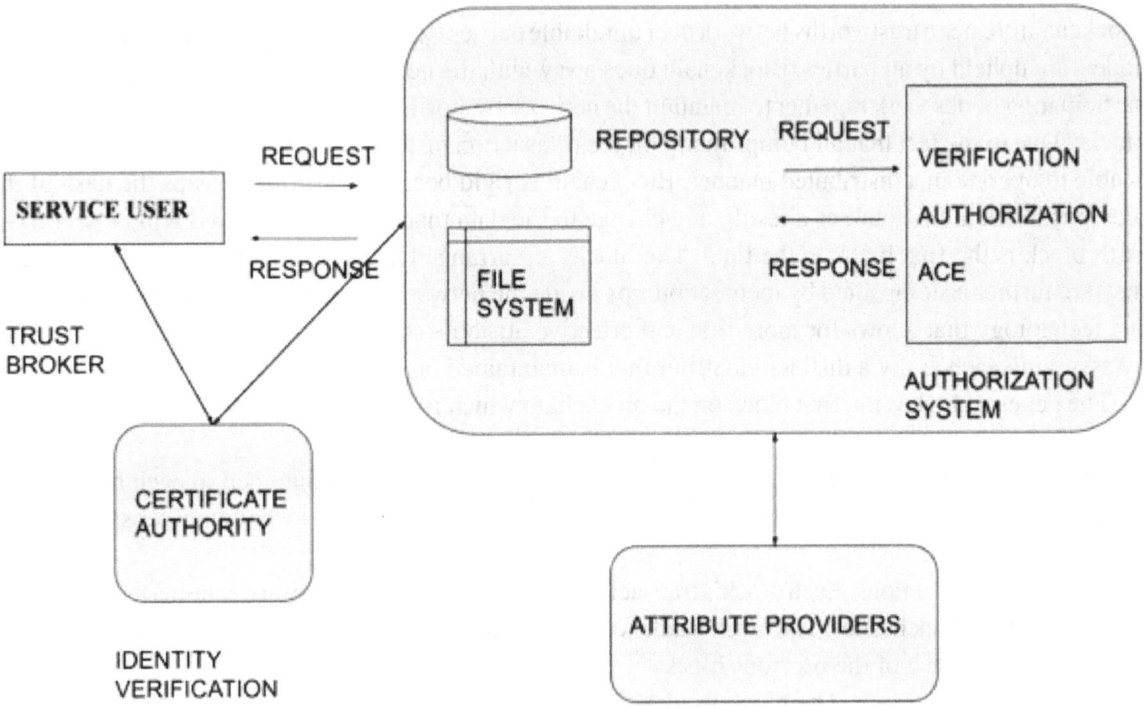

4.2. Module 2: Smart Contract Layer

The layer of smart contracts is the mechanism that ensures access control implementation, maintenance of access rules, judgement, penalties, or the carrying out of object access management, among other things. It is used to offer encryption policies for data owners and to oversee control of access regulations that were translated into the matrix from the cut-off tree, including amending, removing, and rewriting. Data attribute-based encryption and decryption are carried out using it by edge nodes. For instance, you might encrypt and safeguard the policy document's ontology attribute that corresponds to a certain object, then decode it according to the attribute of the subject.

Functionalities like policy administration, attribute validation, decision-making for access control, execution and enforcement, and auditing and reporting may all be found in the smart contract layer module. Smart contracts that enforce access choices based on user and resource traits can be used by administrators to set access control rules. Smart contracts may be used to verify the accuracy, coherence, and currentness of properties related to people and resources. The properties linked with people and resources, as well as additional contextual data like the time of day or location, may all be used by smart contracts to make access control choices. Access control decisions, permitting or denying access to resources according to established policies, may be executed and enforced using smart contracts. Access control choices made by smart contracts, such as access given or refused, and the characteristics and policies that were used to make the decision, may be tracked using the module's reporting and auditing features.

4.3. Module 3: Blockchain Generation

Blockchain creates a trustworthy network over unreliable parties where transactions, or dispatches between nodes, are upheld by all parties. Blockchain does away with the need for centralised authorities since all participating nodes work together to maintain the network by storing and validating new transactions and blocks. Due to the fact that all bumps maintain the transaction history as chained blocks, the blockchain is able to operate in a distributed manner. Blockchain is rigid because each block keeps the hash of the previous block in the total; as a result, any change to the data that was initially saved will be seen. The birth block is the first block in the total. The blocks are arranged according to logical time prints, and they are further accompanied by member bumps inside the network. Decentralized identification (DID) is a technology that allows for more safe and effective attribute sharing between various organisations by assigning each entity a distinct identifier that is maintained on a blockchain.

The genesis block is the first block on the blockchain which is empty of transactions. The blockchain is initialised using it.

Blocks are added to the blockchain: A collection of transactions are contained in each block of the blockchain. The following actions are done in order adding an additional block to the computer's blockchain:

a. Validate transactions: Each block's transactions are checked to see if they are genuine and unaltered.
b. Produce a block header: The block header contains details about the block, including the timestamp, nonce, and hash of the previous block.
c. Track down a nonce: The block header's nonce is a random integer. Finding a nonce that, when combined with the block header, generates a hash value that satisfies particular requirements is the aim. Mining is the procedure in question.

Block the blockchain after adding it: The block is appended to the blockchain after a valid nonce has been discovered. A chain of blocks is produced by adding the block hash to the following block header.

The blockchain is verified to make sure that each block is connected to the preceding block correctly and that the transactions included inside the block are genuine.

Distribute the blockchain: The network's nodes are all given access to the blockchain. Every node has a copy of the blockchain and is capable of validating and adding new transactions to it.

Consensus: A consensus method is used to make sure that every node in the network agrees on the blockchain's actual situation. The most prevalent consensual technique is evidence of work, which requires nodes to carry out a computationally demanding activity (mining) in order to approve new transactions and add them to the blockchain. Different methods are employed by various other algorithms for reaching consensus, including delegation of proof in stake and evidence in stake, to reach consensus (Figure 6).

5. RESULT AND DISCUSSION

In this work, we propose an information architecture and unified approach for safe data sharing using the mechanism. We discussed the restrictions imposed by traditional ABAC techniques and emphasised how ABAC might circumvent these limitations. Additionally, we offered a comprehensive strategy for reliably and coherently implementing ABAC across various systems. We also discussed how important it is to install ABAC using a consistent approach. Overall, our approach provides a complete solution

Figure 6. Blockchain hash key generation

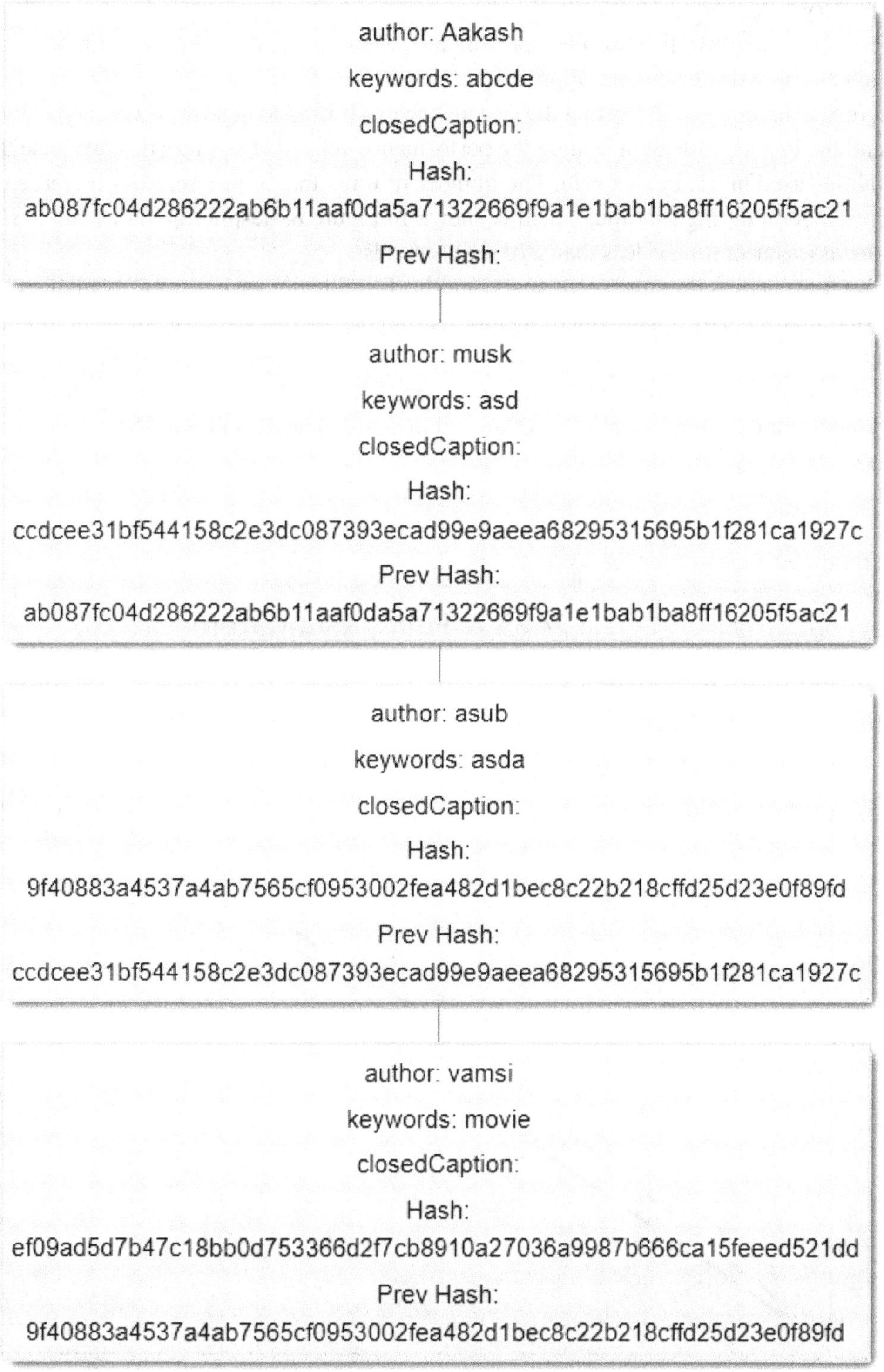

author: Aakash

keywords: abcde

closedCaption:

Hash:
ab087fc04d286222ab6b11aaf0da5a71322669f9a1e1bab1ba8ff16205f5ac21

Prev Hash:

---

author: musk

keywords: asd

closedCaption:

Hash:
ccdcee31bf544158c2e3dc087393ecad99e9aeea68295315695b1f281ca1927c

Prev Hash:
ab087fc04d286222ab6b11aaf0da5a71322669f9a1e1bab1ba8ff16205f5ac21

---

author: asub

keywords: asda

closedCaption:

Hash:
9f40883a4537a4ab7565cf0953002fea482d1bec8c22b218cffd25d23e0f89fd

Prev Hash:
ccdcee31bf544158c2e3dc087393ecad99e9aeea68295315695b1f281ca1927c

---

author: vamsi

keywords: movie

closedCaption:

Hash:
ef09ad5d7b47c18bb0d753366d2f7cb8910a27036a9987b666ca15feeed521dd

Prev Hash:
9f40883a4537a4ab7565cf0953002fea482d1bec8c22b218cffd25d23e0f89fd

for implementing ABAC in a way that is consistent and coherent across several systems. Since your file (or any other piece of data) is secured by hashing using an encryption algorithm, it would be difficult for anyone to try to authorise the file.

Businesses may improve their security posture and allow secure data sharing with other companies and individuals using this technique (Figure 7).

In Figure 8, a directory of PCAs that the system accepts is used to determine the applicable PCA. To comprehend the impact, instead of scaling the performance-related characteristics, we raise the amount on the qualities used in each index rule. The number of traits that are present has increased from 4 to 11,000. presentation during runtime, which is shown in Figure 8, despite the index rule's 100 characteristics, the assessment time is less than 270 milliseconds.

In Figure 9, we assess the time spent analysing the TAPS using various total available policy numbers. We find that the TAPS assessment method is roughly 4–8 times faster than the traditional way when employing the list of index rules to assess relevant regulations. This would be crucial in huge organisational systems with numerous policy directives. We note that the system assessment time in our suggested model starts at a relatively low value and increases linearly (Figure 10).

Figure 7. Blockchain cloud user file

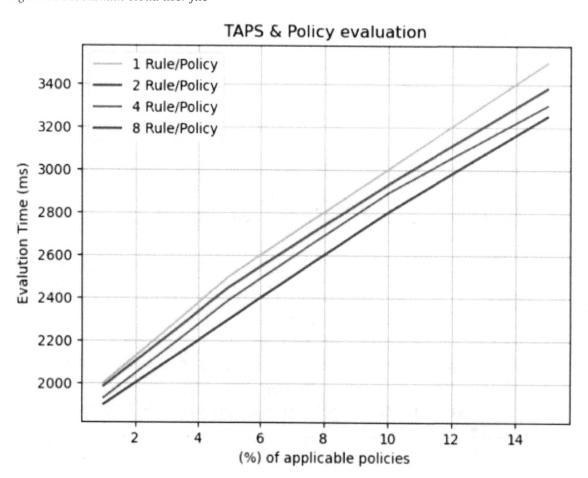

Figure 8. Evaluation in relation to the quantity of characteristics per index rule.

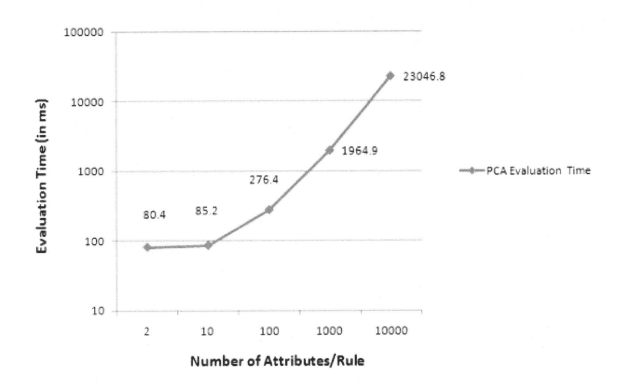

Figure 9. Time spent evaluating vs the entire amount of plans accessible

6. CONCLUSION

The attribute-based encryption and access control method (ABE-ACS) is suggested. In this research, Our plan establishes distributed, reliable access management and outsources decryption based on edge computing to address the security concerns of edge IoT. Multiple smart contracts work together to implement access control and punishment in our scheme. Improved consensus mechanisms guarantee the accuracy of outsourced decryption without raising user-side compute and transmission expenses. The threshold tree combined with the policy's privacy protection In conclusion, attribute-based access control (ABAC) is an efficient means of protecting data sharing in a range of settings, such as cloud computing and applications for smart cities. ABAC enables access to sensitive data to be provided based on a user's qualities rather than their identity, providing for fine-grained control over access. The creation of effective encryption and decryption algorithms, the formation of reliable key management

Figure 10. Blockchain generation

My Project   Home   Cloud Provider   Video Data   Blockchain ▾   Reports ▾   System ▾   Logout

Blockchain Generation

No of Blocks Are Created   4

No of Blocks Yet to be Created   0

[Generate Blocks] [Cancel]

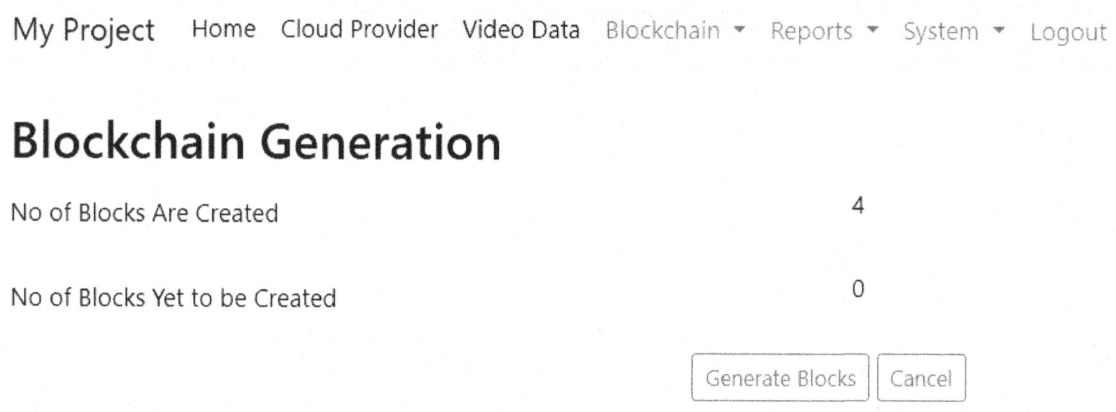

systems, and the choice of relevant characteristics are just a few of the numerous factors that must be carefully considered when designing a safe and effective ABAC scheme. ABAC solutions have been developed as a result of this research, including attribute-based encryption and access control systems, privacy-preserving methods, and enhanced key management systems.

REFERENCES

Abbassy, M., & Abo-Alnadr, A. (2019). Rule-based emotion AI in Arabic customer review. *International Journal of Advanced Computer Science and Applications, 10*(9). doi:10.14569/ijacsa.2019.010093

Abbassy, M., & Ead, W. M. (2020). Intelligent Greenhouse Management System. In *2020 6th International Conference on Advanced Computing and Communication Systems (ICACCS).* IEEE.

Aftab, M. U., Munir, Y., Oluwasanmi, A., Qin, Z., Aziz, M. H., Zakria, Son, N. T., & Tran, V. D. (2020). A hybrid access control model with dynamic COI for secure localization of satellite and IoT-based vehicles. *IEEE Access: Practical Innovations, Open Solutions, 8*, 24196–24208. 10.1109/ACCESS.2020.2969715

Anand, P. P., Kanike, U. K., Paramasivan, P., Rajest, S. S., Regin, R., & Priscila, S. S. (2023). Embracing Industry 5.0: Pioneering Next-Generation Technology for a Flourishing Human Experience and Societal Advancement. *FMDB Transactions on Sustainable Social Sciences Letters, 1*(1), 43–55.

Arslan, F., Singh, B., Sharma, D. K., Regin, R., Steffi, R., & Rajest, S. S. (2021). Optimization technique approach to resolve food sustainability problems. In *2021 International Conference on Computational Intelligence and Knowledge Economy (ICCIKE).* IEEE. 10.1109/ICCIKE51210.2021.9410735

Arunadevi, B., Saravanan, D., Villallba-Condori, K., Srivastava, K., Chakravarthi, M. K., & Rajan, R. (2021). Orthographic comparison revealed by ambient sentiment classification. *2021 5th International Conference on Electronics, Communication and Aerospace Technology (ICECA).*

Buddhi, D., Varghese, L. J., Neeraja, Hamid, S. S., Ramya, D., & Chakravarthi, M. K. (2022). Harmonic Distortion reduction in Power System to improve Reliability and power quality. *2022 International Conference on Innovative Computing, Intelligent Communication and Smart Electrical Systems (ICSES)*. 10.1109/ICSES55317.2022.9914129

Cirillo, S., Polese, G., Salerno, D., Simone, B., & Solimando, G. (2023). Towards Flexible Voice Assistants: Evaluating Privacy and Security Needs in IoT-enabled Smart Homes. *FMDB Transactions on Sustainable Computer Letters*, *1*(1), 25–32.

Derindere Köseoğlu, S., Ead, W. M., & Abbassy, M. M. (2022). Basics of Financial Data Analytics. In *Financial Data Analytics* (pp. 23–57). Springer International Publishing. doi:10.1007/978-3-030-83799-0_2

Ead, W., & Abbassy, M. (2018). Intelligent systems of machine learning approaches for developing E-services portals. *EAI Endorsed Transactions on Energy Web*, *167292*. Advance online publication. doi:10.4108/eai.2-12-2020.167292

Fabela, O., Patil, S., Chintamani, S., & Dennis, B. H. (2017). *Estimation of effective thermal conductivity of porous media utilizing inverse heat transfer analysis on cylindrical configuration* (Vol. 8). Heat Transfer and Thermal Engineering. doi:10.1115/IMECE2017-71559

Gan, G., Chen, E., Zhou, Z., & Zhu, Y. (2020). Token-Based Access Control. *IEEE Access : Practical Innovations, Open Solutions*, *8*, 54189–54199. doi:10.1109/ACCESS.2020.2979746

Ghaffari, F., Bertin, E., Crespi, N., Behrad, S., & Hatin, J. (2021). A novel access control method via smart contracts for internet-based service provisioning. *IEEE Access : Practical Innovations, Open Solutions*, *9*, 81253–81273. doi:10.1109/ACCESS.2021.3085831

Hu, H., Cao, Z., & Dong, X. (2022). Autonomous path identity-based broadcast proxy re-encryption for data sharing in clouds. *IEEE Access : Practical Innovations, Open Solutions*, *10*, 87322–87332. doi:10.1109/ACCESS.2022.3200084

Hur, J. (2013). Attribute-based secure data sharing with hidden policies in smart grid. IEEE Transactions on Parallel and Distributed Systems: A Publication of the IEEE. *IEEE Transactions on Parallel and Distributed Systems*, *24*(11), 2171–2180. doi:10.1109/TPDS.2012.61

Jain, B., Sirdeshpande, S., Gowtham, M. S., Josephson, P. J., Chakravarthi, M. K., & Pant, B. (2022). Exploratory data analysis based on micro grids generation for control communication and monitoring via wireless sensor network. *2022 2nd International Conference on Advance Computing and Innovative Technologies in Engineering (ICACITE)*.

Jeba, J. A., Bose, S. R., & Boina, R. (2023). Exploring Hybrid Multi-View Multimodal for Natural Language Emotion Recognition Using Multi-Source Information Learning Model. *FMDB Transactions on Sustainable Computer Letters*, *1*(1), 12–24.

Jeganathan, J., Vashist, S., Nirmala, G., & Deep, R. (2023). A Cross Sectional Study on Anxiety and Depression Among Patients with Alcohol Withdrawal Syndrome. *FMDB Transactions on Sustainable Health Science Letters*, *1*(1), 31–40.

Koyasako, Y., Suzuki, T., Kim, S.-Y., Kani, J.-I., & Terada, J. (2021). Motion control system with time-varying delay compensation for access edge computing. *IEEE Access : Practical Innovations, Open Solutions*, 9, 90669–90676. doi:10.1109/ACCESS.2021.3091707

Kumar, T. C. A., Dixit, G. K., Singh, R., Narukullapati, B. K., Chakravarthi, M. K., & Gangodkar, D. (2022). Wireless sensor network using control communication and monitoring of smart grid. *2022 2nd International Conference on Advance Computing and Innovative Technologies in Engineering (ICACITE)*.

Leander, B., Causevic, A., Hansson, H., & Lindstrom, T. (2021). Toward an ideal access control strategy for industry 4.0 manufacturing systems. *IEEE Access : Practical Innovations, Open Solutions*, 9, 114037–114050. doi:10.1109/ACCESS.2021.3104649

Lu, X., Pan, Z., & Xian, H. (2020). An efficient and secure data sharing scheme for mobile devices in cloud computing. *Journal of Cloud Computing (Heidelberg, Germany)*, 9(1), 60. Advance online publication. doi:10.118613677-020-00207-5

Luo, W., & Ma, W. (2019). Secure and efficient data sharing scheme based on certificateless hybrid signcryption for cloud storage. *Electronics (Basel)*, 8(5), 590. doi:10.3390/electronics8050590

Mawle, P. P., Dhomane, G. A., Narukullapati, B. K., Venkatesh, P. M., Chakravarthi, M. K., & Shukla, S. K. (2022). A Novel Framework For Data Visualization Via Power System Monitoring Control And Protection Based On Wireless Communication. In *2022 2nd International Conference on Advance Computing and Innovative Technologies in Engineering (ICACITE)* (pp. 1056–1060). 10.1109/ICACITE53722.2022.9823492

Nagarathna, S. B., Gehlot, A., Tiwari, M., Tiwari, T., Chakravarthi, M. K., & Verma, D. (2022). A review of bio-cell culture processes in real-time monitoring approach with cloud computing techniques. *2022 2nd International Conference on Advance Computing and Innovative Technologies in Engineering (ICACITE)*.

Nirmala, G., Premavathy, R., Chandar, R., & Jeganathan, J. (2023). An Explanatory Case Report on Biopsychosocial Issues and the Impact of Innovative Nurse-Led Therapy in Children with Hematological Cancer. *FMDB Transactions on Sustainable Health Science Letters*, 1(1), 1–10.

Ogunmola, G. A., Singh, B., Sharma, D. K., Regin, R., Rajest, S. S., & Singh, N. (2021). Involvement of distance measure in assessing and resolving efficiency environmental obstacles. In *2021 International Conference on Computational Intelligence and Knowledge Economy (ICCIKE)*. IEEE. 10.1109/ICCIKE51210.2021.9410765

Pandit, P. (2023). On the Context of Diabetes: A Brief Discussion on the Novel Ethical Issues of Non-communicable Diseases. *FMDB Transactions on Sustainable Health Science Letters*, 1(1), 11–20.

Pandiyarajan, M., Thimmiaraja, J., Ramasamy, J., Tiwari, M., Shinde, S., & Chakravarthi, M. K. (2022). Medical image classification for disease prediction with the aid of deep learning approaches. *2022 2nd International Conference on Advance Computing and Innovative Technologies in Engineering (ICACITE)*.

Priscila, S. S., Rajest, S., Regin, R., Shynu, T., & Steffi, R. (2023). Classification of Satellite Photographs Utilizing the K-Nearest Neighbor Algorithm. *Central Asian Journal of Mathematical Theory and Computer Sciences*, 4(6), 53–71.

Priscila, S. S., Rajest, S. S., Tadiboina, S. N., Regin, R., & András, S. (2023). Analysis of Machine Learning and Deep Learning Methods for Superstore Sales Prediction. *FMDB Transactions on Sustainable Computer Letters*, *1*(1), 1–11.

Rajest, S. S., Silvia Priscila, S., Regin, R., Shynu, T., & Steffi, R. (2023). Application of Machine Learning to the Process of Crop Selection Based on Land Dataset. *International Journal on Orange Technologies*, *5*(6), 91–112.

Rao, K. S., Pradeep, D. J., Pavan Kumar, Y. V., Chakravarthi, M. K., & Reddy, C. P. (2021). Quantitative analysis on open-loop PI tuning methods for liquid level control. *2021 4th International Symposium on Advanced Electrical and Communication Technologies (ISAECT)*.

Reddy Madduri, G. P., Kumar, D., Muniappan, A., Kumar, Y., Karthick, M. R., & Chakravarthi, M. K. (2022). Rapid computer-aided manufacturing tools including computerized motion control. *2022 2nd International Conference on Advance Computing and Innovative Technologies in Engineering (ICACITE)*.

Regin, R., Rajest, S. S., Shynu, T., & Steffi, R. (2023). The application of machine learning to the prediction of heart attack. *International Journal of Human-Computer Studies*, *5*(4), 5–25. https://journals.researchparks.org/index.php/IJHCS/article/view/4259

Regin, R., & Shynu, T. (2023). Principal Component Analysis for ATM Facial Recognition Security. *Central Asian Journal of Medical and Natural Science*, *4*(3), 292–311.

Rooney, M. M., & Hinders, M. K. (2021). Machine learning for medium access control protocol recognition in communications networks. *IEEE Access : Practical Innovations, Open Solutions*, *9*, 110762–110771. doi:10.1109/ACCESS.2021.3102859

Rupapara, V., Rajest, S. S., Rajan, R., Steffi, R., Shynu, T., & Christabel, G. J. A. (2023). A Dynamic Perceptual Detector Module-Related Telemonitoring for the Intertubes of Health Services. In P. Agarwal, K. Khanna, A. A. Elngar, A. J. Obaid, & Z. Polkowski (Eds.), *Artificial Intelligence for Smart Healthcare. EAI/Springer Innovations in Communication and Computing*. Springer. doi:10.1007/978-3-031-23602-0_15

Sattaru, N. C., Baker, M. R., Umrao, D., Pandey, U. K., Tiwari, M., & Chakravarthi, M. K. (2022). Heart attack anxiety disorder using machine learning and artificial neural networks (ANN) approaches. *2022 2nd International Conference on Advance Computing and Innovative Technologies in Engineering (ICACITE)*.

Saxena, D., & Chaudhary, S. (2023). Predicting Brain Diseases from FMRI-Functional Magnetic Resonance Imaging with Machine Learning Techniques for Early Diagnosis and Treatment. *FMDB Transactions on Sustainable Computer Letters*, *1*(1), 33–48.

Sharma, D. K., Jalil, N. A., Regin, R., Rajest, S. S., Tummala, R. K., & Thangadurai. (2021). Predicting network congestion with machine learning. In *2021 2nd International Conference on Smart Electronics and Communication (ICOSEC)*. IEEE.

Shi, J., Li, R., & Hou, W. (2020). A mechanism to resolve the unauthorized access vulnerability caused by permission delegation in blockchain-based access control. *IEEE Access : Practical Innovations, Open Solutions*, *8*, 156027–156042. doi:10.1109/ACCESS.2020.3018783

Shi, Y., Zhang, J., Lin, Y., & Wu, W. (2020). Improvement of low-speed precision control of a butterfly-shaped linear ultrasonic motor. *IEEE Access: Practical Innovations, Open Solutions, 8*, 135131–135137. doi:10.1109/ACCESS.2020.3007773

Shynu, O. A. J., Singh, B., Rajest, S. S., Regin, R., & Priscila, S. S. (2022). Sustainable intelligent outbreak with self-directed learning system and feature extraction approach in technology. *International Journal of Intelligent Engineering Informatics, 10*(6), 484-503. doi:10.1504/IJIEI.2022.10054270

Shynu, T., Rajest, S. S., & Regin, R. (2023). OTP As a Service in the Cloud Allows for Authentication of Multiple Services. *International Journal on Orange Technologies, 5*(4), 94–112.

Singh, T., Rastogi, P., Pandey, U. K., Geetha, A., Tiwari, M., & Chakravarthi, M. K. (2022). Systematic healthcare smart systems with the integration of the sensor using cloud computing techniques. *2022 2nd International Conference on Advance Computing and Innovative Technologies in Engineering (ICACITE)*.

Song, L., Li, M., Zhu, Z., Yuan, P., & He, Y. (2020). Attribute-based access control using smart contracts for the internet of things. *Procedia Computer Science, 174*, 231–242. doi:10.1016/j.procs.2020.06.079

Steffi, S. R. S., Rajest, R., Shynu, T., & Priscila, S. S. (2023). Analysis of an Interview Based on Emotion Detection Using Convolutional Neural Networks. *Central Asian Journal of Theoretical and Applied Science, 4*(6), 78–102.

Suganthi, M., & Sathiaseelan, J. G. R. (2023). Image Denoising and Feature Extraction Techniques Applied to X-Ray Seed Images for Purity Analysis. *FMDB Transactions on Sustainable Health Science Letters, 1*(1), 41–53.

Vashishtha, E., & Dhawan, G. (2023). Bridging Generation Gap on Analysis of Mentor-Mentee Relationship in Healthcare Setting. *FMDB Transactions on Sustainable Health Science Letters, 1*(1), 21–30.

Chapter 19
Shear–Wave Elastography for Metabolic Syndrome Patients' Non–Alcoholic Fatty Liver Disease (NAFLD) Assessment

C. Patil Shilpa
Krishna Institute of Medical Sciences, India

Makarand B. Mane
Krishna Vishwa Vidyapeeth, India

ABSTRACT

Hepatic steatosis is defined as the accumulation of fat in hepatocytes, making up more than 5% of the total weight of the liver. The global incidence of obesity and the incidence of steatosis of the liver is increasing simultaneously, which represents the commonest cause of liver disease. In addition to obesity, this liver disease is also closely related to a wide range of metabolic comorbidities such as dyslipidemia, type 2 diabetes, and high blood pressure. Patients with metabolic syndrome (MetS) have a high association with NAFLD (non-alcoholic fatty liver disease). Patients with NAFLD are at greater risk to develop fibrosis/ cirrhosis and hepatocellular carcinoma (HCC) which causes great morbidity. The most common form of chronic liver disease worldwide by far is NAFLD. It is estimated that around one-third of the adult population in industrialized nations is affected by it. NAFLD is an asymptomatic condition, reaching advanced stages even before being suspected or diagnosed.

1. INTRODUCTION

Steatosis, fibrosis, and chronic structural inflammatory alterations are all hallmarks of nonalcoholic fatty liver disease (NAFLD), which can range from simple steatosis (fat accumulation in hepatocytes) to NASH (Cordero, et al., 2017). Liver steatosis, fibrosis, and chronic structural inflammatory altera- tions cover a broad spectrum of diseases (non-alcoholic steatohepatitis). Cirrhosis of the liver and, in

DOI: 10.4018/978-1-6684-9189-8.ch019

extremely rare instances, hepatocellular cancer can develop in up to twenty percent of people who have NASH. The degree of fibrosis in the liver is one of the most important factors that plays a role in determining the prognosis and clinical course of NAFLD (Krishnamoorthy, et al., 2020). People who have low-grade lobular inflammation or fibrosis and steatosis are also at a higher risk for developing non-alcoholic steatohepatitis (NASH) (Munshi, et al., 2022). It is estimated that between 5 and 20 percent of people who have non-alcoholic fatty liver disease also have NASH with fibrosis (Yamaguchi, et al., 2007). This becomes especially apparent whenever the metabolic condition deteriorates over the course of time (Munshi, et al., 2019).

A biopsy of the liver is still the most accurate method of diagnosis that can be performed (Kuk & Ardern, 2010). Histology is the only method that can differentiate between NASH and NAFL and determine the level of fibrosis that has occurred (Meigs, et al., 2006). Due to the invasive nature of a liver biopsy, there is a risk of bleeding that cannot be controlled, as well as injury to vascular structures, other organs, and difficulties with the anaesthesia (Md, et al., 2014). Given that the sample for the biopsy is taken at random, it is highly unlikely that it will be representative of the liver as a whole (Munshi, et al., 2021).

2. REVIEW OF LITERATURE

DGAT2- Genetic elimination of diacylglycerol acyltransferase 2) in mouse models provides additional support for the hepatotoxicity of saturated fatty acids, such that (Munshi, et al., 2018).

As a consequence of this, the NASH model exhibits a separation of hepatic steatosis and hepatic fibrosis.

Hepatotoxicity caused by saturated FFAs does not only harm liver cells; it also affects other cell types. It is possible for it to affect pancreatic beta cells, which can then lead to beta cell malfunction (frequently observed in T2DM).

This disease, which affects both liver and pancreatic -cells, plays a very significant role in the process of determining plasma glucose levels.

The following is a summary (table 1) of the cytokines, growth factors, and inflammatory mediators that play an essential role in NAFLD:

Between sixty percent and ninety percent of all cases of incidental abnormal LFTs are caused by nonalcoholic fatty liver disease (NAFLD) (Vashishtha, & Sherman, 2018). The fact that almost 80% of patients diagnosed with NAFLD have normal liver function tests is one of the most remarkable characteristics of this condition. Despite this, there is no difference in the histological severity of the condition between patients who have normal or abnormal liver function tests (Veeraiah, et al., 2022). Because of their close connection, patients who have established cardiovascular diseases, polycystic ovarian syndrome (PCOS), and obstructive sleep apnea should have NAFLD suspected and ruled out as a possible cause of their conditions (OSA) (Vashishtha, et al., 2020).

3. CLINICAL FEATURES OF NAFLD

NAFLD is an asymptomatic condition, reaching advanced stages before being suspected or diagnosed. The symptoms reported in about 50% of patients but being uncommon modes of presentation are:

Table 1. Cytokines, growth factors, and inflammatory mediators vital to NAFLD

Mediator/ Pathway	Observation/Proposed Mechanism
Adiponectin	Anti-inflammatory and anti-fibrotic. Serum levels decreased in NAFLD/NASH patients. Plasma adiponectin in NAFLD is associated to hepatic IR and lipids, not liver disease severity.
Ghrelin	Serum levels dropped in NAFLD/NASH patients, unrelated to histology. In animal models of high-fat diet-induced NAFLD, it reduces oxidative stress, inflammation, and apoptosis.
Leptin	Higher in NASH patients.
Resist in	Serum levels significantly higher in patients with NAFLD and NASH.
TNF – α	Principal mediator of the inflammatory response. In patients with NASH, serum levels were higher. Because it was found to be higher in obese people compared to patients with a normal weight, it was found to be connected with IR.
IL – 6	Patients diagnosed with NASH have been shown to have elevated plasma levels as well as liver expression. Plays a significant part in the development of NASH, IR, and DM.
FGF – 19	In obese teenagers, the development of NAFLD is linked to a decrease in fasting levels of the growth factor FGF-19.
Galectin – 3	β-galactoside-binding lectin has many functions. It is a receptor for advanced lipoxidation endproducts and affects inflammation, fibrosis, and cancer. Galectin inhibitors reduce fibrosis in thioacetamide-induced liver disease animals. GR-MD-02 Galectin inhibitor phase 1 study in NASH and advanced fibrosis patients.
Notch – mTOR pathway	Liver-specific ablation of Notch signalling. Its acute inhibition with a decoy Notch-1 receptor helps in preventing hepatosteatosis. Constitutive activation of mTorc1 enables notch gain of function to induce NAFL.
TGF – β	This is a major growth factor as well as inductor of hepatic stellate cell activation as well as hepatic fibrosis. It is suggested that this contributes to hepatocyte death and lipid accumulation via Smadsignaling.

- Discomfort in the right upper quadrant
- Fatigue
- Lethargy

When performing a routine checkup on a patient, if it is discovered that the patient has hepatomegaly or abnormal liver function tests (LFTs), then the patient is most likely diagnosed with having this disease. It is also possible for this to happen during drug testing (e.g., statin therapy). Between sixty percent and ninety percent of all cases of incidental abnormal LFTs are caused by nonalcoholic fatty liver disease (NAFLD).

The fact that almost 80% of patients diagnosed with NAFLD have normal liver function tests is one of the most remarkable characteristics of this condition (Pandit, 2023). Despite this, there is no difference in the histological severity of the condition between patients who have normal or abnormal liver function tests (Nirmala, et al., 2023).

Because of their close connection, patients who have established cardiovascular diseases, polycystic ovarian syndrome (PCOS), and obstructive sleep apnea should have NAFLD suspected and ruled out as a possible cause of their conditions (OSA) (Jeganathan, et al., 2023).

When taking a history, the focus should be on determining whether or not there is an association between the diseases that have been previously mentioned and primary NAFLD – metabolic syndrome components, cardiovascular disease, and OSA (Suganthi & Sathiaseelan, 2023). It should also concentrate on excluding potential alternative causes of steatosis, such as excessive alcohol consumption, a history of abdominal surgery, and medications that cause nonalcoholic fatty liver disease (NAFLD) (Example.: amiodarone and tamoxifen).

4. MATERIAL AND METHODS

This was a descriptive, observational, cross-sectional study that was carried out in patients who were admitted to the various wards of our institute. The study was done in a single centre hospital.

4.1. Sample Size Calculation

According to a study by Godoy-Matos, et al., (2020) the prevalence of NAFLD in metabolic syndrome was found to be 43.2%.

N = z2pq/l2, Z = standard constant value at 95% CI = 1.96, P = proportional rate of Non-alcoholic fatty liver disease in metabolic syndrome = 43.2%, Q = no proportion = 56.8%, L = allowable error = 10%

N = (1.96)2 (43.2) (56.8) / (10)2, = 3.84 x 2445.53 / 100, = 9422/100, = ~94 (100).

According to the formula, a total 100 subjects were taken in the present cross-sectional study.

Participants in the study included a total of one hundred people who were hospitalised and were admitted to wards.

The time frame of this study was one that spanned a total of one year and eighteen months (October 2019 to March 2021).

The participants in this study had to meet all of the NCEP-ATP III criteria in order to be considered metabolically healthy. syndrome of the age ≥18 years at Krishna Hospital and Medical Research Centre, Karad.

Inclusion Criteria:

- All patients with Metabolic Syndrome.
- Age ≥18 years.

Exclusion Criteria:

- Those who have a history of drinking more than 40 grammes of alcohol per week (for males) or 20 grammes of alcohol per week (for females).
- Patients who are pregnant.
- Patients with inborn errors of metabolism.
- Patients on tamoxifen, methotrexate, estrogens, corticosteroids, and tetracyclines.

The Institutional Ethics Committee provided its approval for this study to continue, thus it can now be carried out (IEC). Each participant was required to provide a copy of their written and informed consent, first translated into their mother tongue, and then translated into English before they were allowed to take part in the research. The patient's physical state was evaluated in great detail throughout the examination that took place. A mercury sphygmomanometer that had been meticulously calibrated was used to acquire a reading of the patient's blood pressure while they were in the supine position (Diamond BP MR-120 Mercurial BP Deluxe). Readings were taken with a break of one minute in between each one, and then an average of all of the measurements was recorded. Readings were taken at a minimum of two different sites. Additional characteristics, such as the pace at which the patient's pulse was being taken, were observed for the duration of the minute in the radial artery.

5. RESULTS AND DISCUSSION

The demographic profile of participants with metabolic syndrome as well as the frequency distribution of their ages were analysed. The criteria for metabolic syndrome (MetS) were met by 100 of the subjects who participated in this cross-sectional study. Eleven of these subjects were in the age range of 18-35 years, and of these 11 subjects, 10 (90.9%) were males and 1 (9.1%) was female. The total number of subjects who met the criteria for metabolic syndrome was 100. 21 of the 30 respondents in the age range of 36-55 years were male, which accounts for 70% of the total, and 9 of the subjects were female, which accounts for 30%. 18 (54.5% of the total) of the 33 participants that fell into the age range of 51 to 65 years were male, while 15 (45.5% of the total) were female. 19 (73.1% of all subjects) of the 26 people who were at least 66 years old were male, whereas 7 (26.9% of all subjects) were female. The average age of the participants was 55.80 years old (with a standard deviation of 15.347) (table 2).

5.1. Body Mass Index and Frequency Distribution of Gender of Subjects With Metabolic Syndrome

The present study measured the body mass index (BMI) of all the subjects. It was observed that none of the subjects had a body mass index (BMI) <18.5. Of the 16 subjects with BMI between 18.5-24.99, 9 (56.3%) were males, and 7 (43.8%) were females. Of the 38 subjects with BMI between 25-29.99, 23 (60.5%) were males, and 15 (39.5%) were females. Of the 46 subjects who had BMI ≥30, 36 (78.3%) were males and 10 (21.7%) were females. The mean BMI of the subjects was 29.85 (SD ± 4.65).

Body Mass Index and frequency distribution of age of subjects with metabolic syndrome: In the present study, the body mass index (BMI) of all the subjects was measured. It was observed that none of the subjects had a body mass index (BMI) <18.5 (table 3).

Of the 16 subjects which had BMI between 18.5-24.99, 1 (6.3%) subject was in the age group 18 to 35 years, 6 (37.5%) subjects were in the age group of 36 to 50 years, 5 (31.3%) subjects were in the age

Table 2. Demographic profile and frequency distribution of age in subjects with metabolic syndrome

Age Group	Number of Subjects (n=100)	
	Male	**Female**
18 – 35	10 (90.9%)	1 (9.1%)
36 – 50	21 (70%)	9 (30%)
51 – 65	18 (54.5%)	15 (45.5%)
66 & above	19 (73.1%)	7 (26.9%)
Total	68	3

Table 3. Body mass index and frequency distribution of gender of subjects with metabolic syndrome

BMI	Number of Subjects (n=100)		Percent
	Male	**Female**	
18.5 – 24.99 (Normal)	9 5 (6.3%)	7 (43.8%)	16%
25 – 29.99 (Overweight)	23 (60.5%)	15 (39.5%)	38%
30 & above (Obese)	36 (78.3%)	10 (21.7%)	46%
Total	68	32	

group 51 to 65 years and 4 (25%) subjects were in the age group of 66 years and above. Of a total of 38 subjects which had BMI between 25- 29.99, 5 (13.2%) subjects were in the age group 18 to 35 years, 9 (23.7%) subjects were in the age group of 36 to 50 years, 15 (39.5%) subjects were in the age group 51 to 65 years and 9 (23.7%) subjects were in the age group of 66 years and above. Of the 46 subjects which had BMI ≥30, 5 (10.9%) subjects were in the age group 18 to 35 years, 15 (32.6%) subjects were in the age group of 36 to 50 years, 13 (28.3%) subjects were in the age group 51 to 65 years and 13 (28.3%) subjects were in the age group 66 years and above. The mean BMI of the subjects was 29.85 (SD $\pm$ 4.65). NAFLD on USG and frequency distribution of gender of subjects with metabolic syndrome (table 4).

There was a significant positive correlation between NAFLD on USG and liver fibrosis by SWE amongst those with MetS that was found in the current study (r = 0.248 [Spearman's rho]; p = 0.013). (Vashishtha & Dhawan, 2023). These findings were comparable to those found in the research conducted by Koc and Sumbul (2019), who found that a higher risk of liver fibrosis was associated with the presence of steatosis of the liver at any severity level (mild, moderate, or severe), as well as hypertension and a larger waist circumference. Steatosis of the liver, which has been suggested to influence ultrasound elastography measurements, demonstrated negligible effects on the normal reference range of liver elasticity in a study that was conducted by Suh et al., (2014). It is important to note, however, that the study was not conducted specifically on those subjects with MetS in contrast to the study that is being compared to it (table 5).

According to the findings of this study, the mean NAFLD fibrosis score for grade 1 fatty liver was -0.66 with a standard deviation of 1.79, the mean NAFLD fibrosis score for grade 2 fatty liver was 0.30 with a standard deviation of 1.4, and the mean NAFLD fibrosis score for grade 3 fatty liver was -0.31 with a standard deviation of 2.0. Kakrani et al. (2013) conducted a study in which they compared the grades of fibrosis seen on conventional USG to the average NAFLD fibrosis scoring seen in each group. According to the findings of a study that was carried out by Kakrani et al. (2013), the mean NAFLD

Table 4. Body mass index and frequency distribution of age of subjects with metabolic syndrome

BMI	Number of Subjects (n=100)				Percent
	18-35	**36-50**	**51-65**	**66 and Above**	
18.5 – 24.99(Normal)	1 (6.3%)	6 (37.5%)	5 (31.3%)	4 (25%)	16%
25 – 29.99(Overweight)	5 (13.2%)	9 (23.7%)	15 (39.5%)	9 (23.7%)	38%
30 &above(Obese)	5 (10.9%)	15 (32.6%)	13 (28.3%)	13 (28.3%)	46%
Total	11	30	33	26	

Table 5. NAFLD on USG and frequency distribution of gender of subjects with metabolic syndrome

NAFLD on USG	Number of Subjects (n=100)		Percent
	Male	Female	
No fatty liver	33 (64.7%)	18 (35.3%)	51%
Grade 1 fatty liver	14 (73.7%)	5 (26.3%)	19%
Grade 2 fatty liver	11 (78.6%)	3 (21.4%)	14%
Grade 3 fatty liver	10 (62.5%)	6 (37.5%)	16%
Total	68	32	

fibrosis score for grade 1 fatty liver was -0.44 1.25, the mean NAFLD fibrosis score for grade 2 fatty liver was -0.13 1.35, and the mean NAFLD fibrosis score for grade 3 fatty liver was 0.15 1.06.

The current study found that there was a correlation (r = 0.076 [Spearman's rho]; p = 0.451) between the grading of fatty liver on USG and NAFLD fibrosis scores. This correlation was positive. The research carried out by Kakrani et al. (2013) came to comparable conclusions (r = 0.99; p = 0.12). However, the results of both studies showed no significant correlation between the presence of fatty liver on USG and the NAFLD Fibrosis Score. This suggests that the two factors are not significantly related. The current investigation discovered a significant link between fibrosis as measured by SWE and NAFLD-fibrosis scoring in subjects diagnosed with MetS (r = 0.023 [Spearman's rho]; p = 0.819). On the other hand, it was of no consequence.

They also reported that glycosylated haemoglobin and alkaline phosphatase did correlate with liver stiffness independently (p < 0.05). Every 1% increase in HbA1c was associated with a 68% increased likelihood of liver fibrosis; however, significant correlations were not observed in the present study. Ghamar-Chehreh et al. (2012) reported a significant association between grade of fatty liver, triglycerides, body weight, greater fasting blood sugar, and transaminases, thus, indirectly with the components of MetS similar to the present study.

Zhang et al (2018) reported that the body mass index, fasting glucose, 2-hour postprandial glucose, triglyceride, total cholesterol, low-density lipoprotein, and alanine aminotransferase in those with NAFLD were significantly great than those not having NAFLD similar to the present study. Sanyal et al (2015) (2-15) reported that ALT, GGT, and AST are markers of liver injury and may be useful surrogate measures of NAFLD, however, such similar findings could be observed in the present study. Petrović et al (2016) reported that those with type 2 diabetes mellitus or raised fasting blood glucose as a metabolic factor was most common in those patients with grade 3 fatty liver on USG finding, in comparison to grade 1 fatty liver on USG (p <0.05) similar to the present study.

The current research's results were found to be consistent with those of a study by Mohan et al. (2009), which revealed that NAFLD was related to MetS after controlling for age, gender, and circumference of the waist (OR: 2.0, 95% C.I.: 1.3–3.1, p < 0.001).

The consequences of nonalcoholic fatty liver disease are connected to the presence of metabolic syndrome (MetS). After controlling for factors such as age, gender, or the presence of steatosis on USG, participants with higher degrees of fibrosis had a greater proportion of components of MetS when compared to those with a lower level of fibrosis. Recent research has established a connection between the MetS and NAFLD. Our findings were weighed against those obtained from earlier studies, both in India and elsewhere. The geographical, cultural, and racial diversity of people who have been diagnosed with metabolic syndrome may help explain differences found in different studies. In addition, the patients who were in hospitals were the primary subjects of this investigation.

6. CONCLUSION

The prevalence of metabolic syndrome (MetS) as well as non-alcoholic fatty liver disease has been on the rise in recent years (NAFLD). In the current study, which involved 100 people with MetS: Triglycerides and fibrosis as measured by SWE were found to have a significant positive correlation (r = 0.291 [Spearman's rho]; p = 0.003 respectively). There was a connection between prothrombin time/international normalised ratio (r = 0.217 [Spearman's rho]; p = 0.03) and fibrosis grade as determined by SWE. This connection was positive. The grade of nonalcoholic fatty liver disease (NAFLD) on ultrasonography was found to have a positive correlation with post-prandial blood sugar (r = 0.232 [Spearman's rho]; p = 0.02). Triglyceride levels and the severity of nonalcoholic fatty liver disease (NAFLD) as measured by ultrasonography were found to have a positive correlation (r = 0.295 [Spearman's rho]; p = 0.003). There was a connection between the grade of NAFLD on ultrasonography and the prothrombin time/ international normalised ratio (r = 0.260 [Spearman's rho]; p = 0.009; there was a positive correlation between the two variables). It was found that those who had grade 3 fatty liver (steatosis) on ultrasonography had a 3.39 times greater chance of having significant fibrosis or cirrhosis (F3-F4) by SWE than those who did not have fatty liver (steatosis) on USG independently (odds ratio: 3.39, 95% confidence interval: 1.03–11.09, p = 0.043). This was determined after taking into account age and gender. With lower grades of fatty liver, it was not possible to recognise any significant associations.

REFERENCES

Cordero, P., Li, J., & Oben, J. A. (2017). Bariatric surgery as a treatment for metabolic syndrome. *Journal of the Royal College of Physicians of Edinburgh*, 47(4), 364–368. doi:10.4997/jrcpe.2017.414 PMID:29537411

Ghamar-Chehreh, M. E., Khedmat, H., Amini, M., & Taheri, S. (2012). Predictive Factors for Ultrasono-graphic Grading of Nonalcoholic Fatty Liver Disease. *Hepatitis Monthly*, 12(11), e6860. PMID:23346150

Godoy-Matos, A. F., Silva Júnior, W. S., & Valerio, C. M. (2020). NAFLD as a continuum: From obesity to metabolic syndrome and diabetes. *Diabetology & Metabolic Syndrome*, 12(1), 60. doi:10.118613098-020-00570-y PMID:32684985

Jeganathan, J., Vashist, S., Nirmala, G., & Deep, R. (2023). A Cross Sectional Study on Anxiety and Depression Among Patients with Alcohol Withdrawal Syndrome. *FMDB Transactions on Sustainable Health Science Letters*, 1(1), 31–40.

Kakrani, A., Sharma, Z., Thind, S., & Gokhale, V. (2013). Correlation of NAFLD Fibrosis Score and BARD Score with Ultrasonographic Evidence of Nonalcoholic Fatty Liver Disease in Overweight Patients: A Prospective Study. *International Journal of Medicine and Public Health*, 3(2), 111–114. doi:10.4103/2230-8598.115183

Koc, A. S., & Sumbul, H. E. (2019). Prediabetes Is Associated With Increased Liver Stiffness Identified by Noninvasive Liver Fibrosis Assessment: ElastPQ Ultrasound Shear Wave Elastography Study. *Ultrasound Quarterly*, *35*(4), 330–338. doi:10.1097/RUQ.0000000000000419 PMID:30724873

Krishnamoorthy, Y., Rajaa, S., Murali, S., Rehman, T., Sahoo, J., & Kar, S. S. (2020). Prevalence of metabolic syndrome among adult population in India: A systematic review and meta-analysis. *PLoS One*, *15*(10), e0240971. doi:10.1371/journal.pone.0240971 PMID:33075086

Kuk, J. L., & Ardern, C. I. (2010). Age and Sex Differences in the Clustering of Metabolic Syndrome Factors. *Diabetes Care*, *33*(11), 2457–2461. doi:10.2337/dc10-0942 PMID:20699434

M, A., K, T., Munshi, Y, J., M, R., & M, S. (2019). Assessment of heavy metal contents in commercial feedstuffs and broiler (Gallus domesticus) meat and its impact on Swiss albino mice as an animal model. *Agricultural Science Digest - A Research Journal*. doi:10.18805/ag.D-4898

Md, N., Hasan, M., Munshi, M. H., Rahman, S. M. N., & Alam, A. (2014). Evaluation of antihyperglycemic activity of Lasia spinosa leaf extracts in Swiss albino mice. *World Journal of Pharmacy and Pharmaceutical Sciences*, *3*(10), 118–124.

Meigs, J. B., Wilson, P. W. F., Fox, C. S., Vasan, R. S., Nathan, D. M., Sullivan, L. M., & D'Agostino, R. B. (2006). Body mass index, metabolic syndrome, and risk of type 2 diabetes or cardiovascular disease. *The Journal of Clinical Endocrinology and Metabolism*, *91*(8), 2906–2912. doi:10.1210/jc.2006-0594 PMID:16735483

Mohan, V., Farooq, S., Deepa, M., Ravikumar, R., & Pitchumoni, C. S. (2009). Prevalence of non-alcoholic fatty liver disease in urban south Indians about different glucose intolerance and metabolic syndrome grades. *Diabetes Research and Clinical Practice*, *84*(1), 84–91. doi:10.1016/j.diabres.2008.11.039 PMID:19168251

Munshi, M., Sohrab, M. H., Begum, M. N., Rony, S. R., Karim, M. A., Afroz, F., & Hasan, M. N. (2021). Evaluation of bioactivity and phytochemical screening of endophytic fungi isolated from Ceriops decandra (Griff.) W. Theob, a mangrove plant in Bangladesh. *Clinical Phytoscience*, *7*(1), 81. Advance online publication. doi:10.118640816-021-00315-y

Munshi, M., Tumu, K. N., Hasan, M. N., & Amin, M. Z. (2018). Biochemical effects of commercial feedstuffs on the fry of climbing perch (Anabas testudineus) and its impact on Swiss albino mice as an animal model. *Toxicology Reports*, *5*, 521–530. doi:10.1016/j.toxrep.2018.04.004 PMID:29707493

Munshi, M., Zilani, M. N. H., Islam, M. A., Biswas, P., Das, A., Afroz, F., & Hasan, M. N. (2022). Novel compounds from endophytic fungi of Ceriops decandra inhibit breast cancer cell growth through estrogen receptor alpha in in-silico study. *Informatics in Medicine Unlocked*, *32*(101046), 101046. doi:10.1016/j.imu.2022.101046

Nirmala, G., Premavathy, R., Chandar, R., & Jeganathan, J. (2023). An Explanatory Case Report on Biopsychosocial Issues and the Impact of Innovative Nurse-Led Therapy in Children with Hematological Cancer. *FMDB Transactions on Sustainable Health Science Letters*, *1*(1), 1–10.

Pandit, P. (2023). On the Context of Diabetes: A Brief Discussion on the Novel Ethical Issues of Noncommunicable Diseases. *FMDB Transactions on Sustainable Health Science Letters*, *1*(1), 11–20.

Petrović, G., Bjelaković, G., Benedeto-Stojanov, D., Nagorni, A., Brzački, V., & Marković-Živković, B. (2016). Obesity and metabolic syndrome are risk factors for developing non-alcoholic fatty liver disease as diagnosed by ultrasound. *Vojnosanitetski Pregled. Military-Medical and Pharmaceutical Review*, *73*(10), 910–920. doi:10.2298/VSP150514093P PMID:29327896

Sanyal, D., Mukherjee, P., Raychaudhuri, M., Ghosh, S., Mukherjee, S., & Chowdhury, S. (2015). Profile of liver enzymes in non-alcoholic fatty liver disease in patients with impaired glucose tolerance and newly detected untreated type 2 diabetes. *Indian Journal of Endocrinology and Metabolism*, *19*(5), 597–601. doi:10.4103/2230-8210.163172 PMID:26425466

Suganthi, M., & Sathiaseelan, J. G. R. (2023). Image Denoising and Feature Extraction Techniques Applied to X-Ray Seed Images for Purity Analysis. *FMDB Transactions on Sustainable Health Science Letters*, *1*(1), 41–53.

Suh, C. H., Kim, S. Y., Kim, K. W., Lim, Y. S., Lee, S. J., Lee, M. G., Lee, J. B., Lee, S.-G., & Yu, E. (2014). Determination of Normal Hepatic Elasticity by Using Real-time Shear-wave Elastography. *Radiology*, *271*(3), 895–900. doi:10.1148/radiol.14131251 PMID:24555633

Vashishtha, E., & Dhawan, G. (2023). Bridging Generation Gap on Analysis of Mentor-Mentee Relationship in Healthcare Setting. *FMDB Transactions on Sustainable Health Science Letters*, *1*(1), 21–30.

Vashishtha, E., & Sherman, L. (2018). Socioeconomic Status and Childhood Obesity. *International Journal of Physical and Social Sciences*, *8*(11), 184–194.

Vashishtha, E., Sherman, L., Sajjad, T., & Mehmood, N. (2020). Use of anti-viral therapy in treatment of Covid 19. *Journal of Advanced Medical and Dental Sciences Research*, *8*(11), 273–276.

Veeraiah, V., Pankajam, A., Vashishtha, E., Dhabliya, D., Karthikeyan, P., & Chandan, R. R. (2022). Efficient COVID-19 identification using deep learning for IoT. In *2022 5th International Conference on Contemporary Computing and Informatics (IC3I)*. IEEE.

Vishram, J. K. K., Borglykke, A., Andreasen, A. H., Jeppesen, J., Ibsen, H., Jørgensen, T., Palmieri, L., Giampaoli, S., Donfrancesco, C., Kee, F., Mancia, G., Cesana, G., Kuulasmaa, K., Salomaa, V., Sans, S., Ferrieres, J., Dallongeville, J., Söderberg, S., Arveiler, D., ... Olsen, M. H.The MORGAM Prospective Cohort Project. (2014). Impact of Age and Gender on the Prevalence and Prognostic Importance of the Metabolic Syndrome and Its Components in Europeans. The MORGAM Prospective Cohort Project. *PLoS One*, *9*(9), e107294. doi:10.1371/journal.pone.0107294 PMID:25244618

Yamaguchi, K., Yang, L., McCall, S., Huang, J., Yu, X. X., Pandey, S. K., Bhanot, S., Monia, B. P., Li, Y.-X., & Diehl, A. M. (2007). Inhibiting triglyceride synthesis improves hepatic steatosis but exacerbates liver damage and fibrosis in obese mice with nonalcoholicsteato hepatitis. *Hepatology (Baltimore, Md.)*, *45*(6), 1366–1374. doi:10.1002/hep.21655 PMID:17476695

Zhang, Z., Wang, J., & Wang, H. (2018). Correlation of blood glucose, serum chemerin and insulin resistance with NAFLD in patients with type 2 diabetes mellitus. *Experimental and Therapeutic Medicine*, *15*(3), 2936–2940. doi:10.3892/etm.2018.5753 PMID:29456698

Chapter 20
Ultrasound Imaging of the Brain of Premature Infants for the Diagnosis of Neurological Disorders

S. G. Lavand

Krishna Institute of Medical Sciences, India

Shailesh B. Patil

Krishna Institute of Medical Sciences, India

ABSTRACT

As the rate of preterm births continues to rise, a thorough neurological examination of newborns born too soon is more crucial than ever. As a result of advancements in NICU technology, the survival rate of babies with extremely low birth weight has also increased. There is a higher chance of neurological abnormalities occurring in the survivors. Premature infants have an increased risk of developing neurological impairments, and about 10% of these infants will go on to have substantial learning problems, motor developmental disabilities, cerebral palsy, seizures, or mental retardation. White matter injury, germinal matrix haemorrhage, intraventricular haemorrhage, periventricular leucomalacia, cerebellar haemorrhage and atrophy, and periventricular leucomalacia are all examples of brain injuries that may develop from secondary hemodynamic disturbances. Timely detection of intracranial abnormalities is critical for improving neonates' health and lowering their risk of death or disability later on.

1. INTRODUCTION

The first attempt at sonography of the head was made in 1955, and it used the utilisation of Amode to detect midline structure and obtain a rough estimate of ventricular size. It wasn't until 1963 that the two-dimensional bidirectional echoencephalogram was developed (Back & Rivkees, 2004). This was a significant technical achievement because it improved the information that could be gathered on ven-

DOI: 10.4018/978-1-6684-9189-8.ch020

tricular size as well as the spatial relationships inside the brain (Bowie et al., 1983). Two-dimensional imaging of the baby skull became possible with the development of the Octoson and sector-format real-time ultrasonic sensors.

Resolution and picture display are comparable to what can be achieved with computerised tomography and even appear to be higher in some instances. Because neonatal brains have a higher proportion of water than adult brains do, CT is not the modality of choice because it cannot differentiate between grey and white matter as effectively. In most cases, computed tomography (CT) and magnetic resonance imaging (MRI) are being phased out in favour of ultrasonography because to its portability, low cost, absence of ionising radiation, quick examination periods, and absence of the requirement for sedation. In 1980, it was advised that sonography be used as the primary method for detecting cerebral bleeding in premature infants (McGuinness & Smith, 1984).

This method detects subependymal germinal matrix haemorrhage, intraventricular haemorrhage, and ventriculomegaly with a high level of sensitivity while maintaining a high level of specificity. Studies that are satisfactory can be carried out at the bedside of the infant with very little danger to the child. In order to investigate the frequency of subependymal germinal matrix haemorrhage as well as its sonographic appearance, a prospective study involving 25 consecutive premature newborns weighing less than 1,500 grammes was carried out (Leksee, 1956). The haemorrhage was originally observed in the region that is directly anterior to the caudothalamic groove in each and every one of the 12 cases in whom the sonography was positive. It is important to pay particular attention to this region since doing so enables the early detection of germinal matrix bleeding (London et al., 1980).

Neurosonography of neonates should be regarded as incomplete until this region has been scanned in its whole. 112 neonates who were born one after the other and with birth weights ranging from 1,551 to 2,000 grammes were subjected to cerebral ultrasonography screening for the duration of a research project that lasted for fourteen months (DeVlieger and Ridder, 1959). Nineteen patients, or seventeen percent, had scans that were abnormal (Rumack & Drose, 2011). There were 14 germinal matrix haemorrhages and/or intraventricular haemorrhages among these anomalies, which accounts for 13 percent of the total (Volpe, 1995). More over fifty percent of the haemorrhages that were found were severe, meaning that they were grades III and IV. Over the course of nine months, 96 newborns weighing less than 1500 grammes each had a neurosonogram conducted on them (Singh et al., 2007). Twenty-two of the infants, which is twenty-three percent of the total, experienced intracranial subependymal or intraventricular haemorrhage. 13 of these patients, or 59 percent, experienced ventricular enlargement as a result of the haemorrhage. In 77 percent of the instances, this enlargement occurred within two weeks of the haemorrhage.

1.1. Brain Anatomy

The brain is separated from the rest of the body by the skull, which contains the cranial cavity. The foramen magnum connects the brain to the spinal cord. From the outside in, it is protected by three distinct layers of meninges, which are referred to as the dura matter, the arachnoid matter, and the pia matter. The forebrain, the midbrain, the hindbrain, and the spinal cord make up the three major divisions that may be found in the human brain (Govaert and DeVries, 2010). The diencephalon and the cerebrum make up the forebrain (Martin et al., 2002). The diencephalon is located in the middle of the forebrain. The medulla oblongata, the pons, and the cerebellum are the three major components that make up the hind brain (Skullerud and Wester, 1986).

1.2. Ventricular System

The cerebrospinal fluid (CSF) and the choroid plexus are contained within the brain's ventricles. The lateral ventricles each account for one-third and one-fourth of the brain's total volume. Both cerebral hemispheres have lateral ventricles that communicate with the third ventricle through the formen of Monro. Located between the two thalami, the third ventricle resembles a slit. It connects to the fourth ventricle via the Sylvius aqueduct of the brain (Figure 1).

The cerebellum is located in front of the fourth ventricle, which is located behind the pons and the medulla. It connects with the central canal of the spinal cord distally and with the subarachnoid space ventrally via three foramina in its roof. The cerebrospinal fluid (CSF) is made in a specialised organ called the choroid plexus. The cerebrospinal fluid (CSF) circulates between the ventricles and the subarachnoid space to nourish the neurological system. The arachnoid villi absorb the majority of the cerebrospinal fluid, which is then drained into the superior sagittal sinus (Figure 2).

1.3. Blood Vessels of Brain

A pair of internal carotid arteries and a pair of vertebral arteries are responsible for supplying the brain with oxygen-rich blood via the arterial system. The bailar artery is formed when the two vertebral arteries come together at the base of the pons to form a single larger vessel (Jagtap, 2021).

The circle of Willis, also known as the circulus arteriosus, is the name given to the arterial circle that is formed by the interconnection of the main arteries near the base of the brain. Because it is a direct arterial anastomosis, it makes it easier to control the arterial pressure on both sides (Figure 3).

Figure 1. Diagrammatic representation of gross anatomy of brain in the mid sagittal image

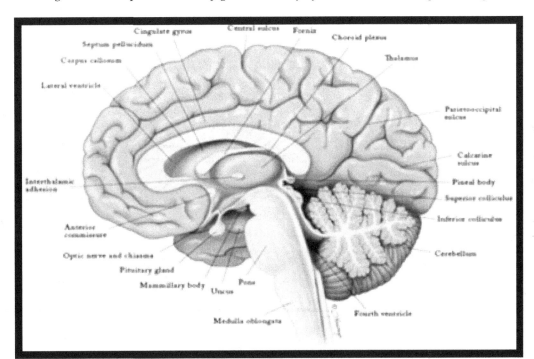

Figure 2. Diagrammatic representation of the ventricular system
Source: Craniosacral rhythm (2018)

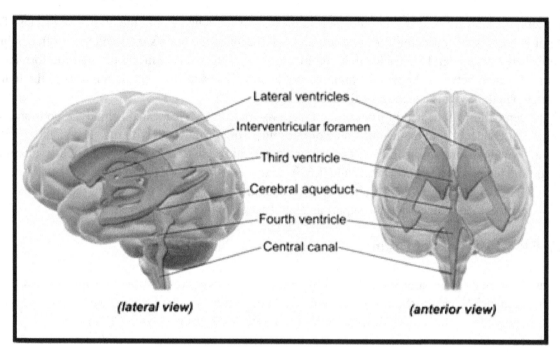

Figure 3. Arterial blood supply of brain
Source: Craniosacral rhythm (2018)

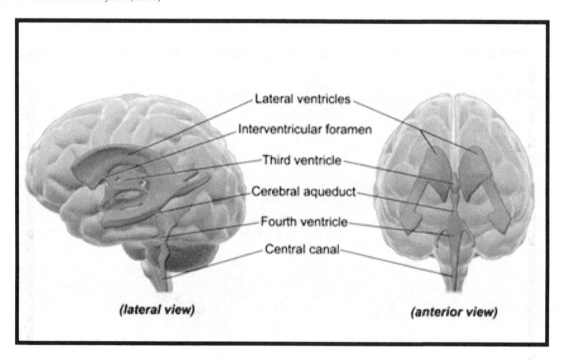

Branches of the Main Arteries: Cerebral part of the internal carotid artery gives off:

- Ophthalmic artery
- Anterior cerebral artery
- Middle cerebral artery
- Posterior communicating artery
- Anterior choroidal artery-it may arise from middle cerebral artery.

Fourth part of vertebral artery gives off:

- Meningeal artery
- Posterior spinal artery
- Anterior spinal artery
- Posterior inferior cerebellar artery
- Medullary artery

Basilar artery gives off:

- Pontinearteries
- Labyrinthine artery
- Anterior inferior cerebellar artery
- Superior cerebellar artery
- Posterior cerebral artery

The superficial (cortical) veins and the deep veins make up the cerebral venous system. The cerebral venous system is separated into these two types of veins. The cavernous and superior sagittal sinuses get drainage from the superficial veins, also known as cortical veins. These veins are located on the lateral surface of the cerebral hemispheres. The medullary veins, subependymal veins, basal veins, and the vein of Galen are all included in the group of veins known as the deep cerebral veins. The majority of the most profound layers of the cerebral hemisphere are the ones that are drained into the straight sinus (Figure 4).

1.4. Aim and Objectives

The purpose of this research is to investigate the role that preterm newborns' neurosonograms have in the diagnosis of a variety of intracranial abnormalities, including as cerebral haemorrhage, periventricular leukomalacia, ventriculomegaly, and other types of evolutionary changes.

2. LITERATURE REVIEW

The developing brain has a lissencephalic smooth surface on both hemispheres and a germinal matrix of primitive cells surrounds each lateral ventricle (DeReuck, 1984).

Figure 4. Venous system of brain
Source: Themes (2017)

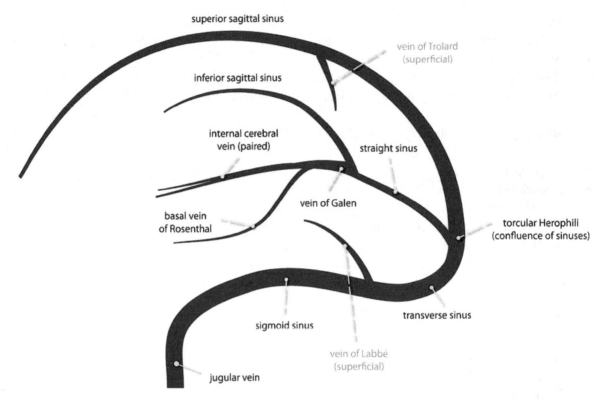

These germinal matrix cells generate progeny, which divide, migrate "inside-out" to the cerebral cortex, and differentiate into neurons and glia. It is believed that the germinal matrix is formed around week 7 of pregnancy and involutes around week 28 to 30, but that it persists in the form of clusters of cells until weeks 36 to 39. During the sixth and seventh months of development, the surface of the cerebral hemispheres develops primitive gyri and sulci. (Jagtap, 2021)

Thus, the adult brain pattern can be identified as the due date approaches. Fibre tracts, including commissural fibres, are being formed at the same time. Seventy-five infants were born early (at 34 weeks or later) in a study meant to be scientifically rigorous, and all of them weighed more than 1500 grammes at birth (range 1500 g to 2500 g). Ultrasounds of the brain were performed on all newborns to check for intraventricular haemorrhaging (PIVH). Low Apgar scores, the need for resuscitation, and/or assisted breathing were common immediately after birth in infants with cerebral haemorrhage (Creed & Haber, 1984).

2.1. History of Ultrasound

The piezoelectric effect was discovered in 1880 and is the fundamental principle of ultrasonography. In the year 1880, Pierre and Jacques Curie were the pioneers who proved this phenomenon for the first time. Before its first major attempt at practical usage was made in the hunt for the sunken Titanic in the

North Atlantic, which was unsuccessful, the technology that produced ultrasound was known for many years. After that, Paul Langevin was the first person to employ the pulse echo technique for the purpose of locating submarines. The very first application that was effective was called SONAR, which stands for "Sound Navigation and Ranging." Karl Kursik made the first use of ultrasound in medicine in 1942 when he sought to find brain tumours using two opposing ultrasonic transducers. This was the first time that ultrasound was used in medicine.

2.2. Normal Ultrasonic Appearance of Neonatal Brain

It is vital to have a comprehensive grasp of the typical ultrasonic architecture of the newborn brain in order to use ultrasound to identify and evaluate the different disorders that affect the brain. A preterm baby's brain has a smooth surface because the gyri and sulci are not fully developed at this point in their development. The ventricles that are located on the body's sides. Most of the time, the lateral ventricles are asymmetrical. In most cases, the left ventricle as well as the occipital horns are significantly larger than the right ventricle as well as the frontal horns. In premature infants, the ventricles, which are fluid-filled structures that resemble commas, are frequently larger than those in term infants. Term infants have ventricles that are completely formed. Between the two frontal horns of the lateral ventricles is where you'll find the cavum septum pellucidum in the brain. The cavum vergae is the area behind the cavum septum pellucidi. The lateral ventricle bodies are separated by the cavum vergae. These two cavum segments can be distinguished from one another by the foramen of Monro. The cerebrospinal fluid (CSF) in the ventricles is produced by the choroidal plexus. It covers the whole inside of the brain, from the horns at the top and bottom of each lateral ventricle to the rest of the brain. The glomus, the greatest part of the choroidal plexus, is located in the trigones of the lateral ventricle.

Beginning from the glomus, the choroidal plexus tapers off toward the anterior third ventricle roof and the posterior temporal horns of each lateral ventricle. Choroid plexus terminates in the caudothalamic groove, not the frontal or occipital horns of the lateral ventricles, as is commonly believed. Growing beneath the ependyma, the germinal matrix gives rise to the neurons and glia that will eventually become the cerebral cortex and basal ganglia. (Jagtap, 2021)

These cells are in the process of multiplying but have a poor cell structure. It possesses the most densely perfused vascular bed of any part of the developing brain. In this region, you might be able to spot a juvenile vascular rete made up of teeny-tiny capillaries, paper-thin veins, and larger, more crooked blood vessels.

The germinal matrix is an essential anatomic location where haemorrhage occurs in preterm babies. However, it is not visible on sonography because it is placed above the caudo-thalamic groove and under the ependymal lining of the ventricles. As a result, the germinal matrix cannot be seen. A normal finding in almost all infants is referred to as periventricular white matter echogenicity. This is an echogenic boundary that runs parallel to the posterior region of the lateral ventricles and is considered to be an echogenic boundary. The echogenic zone that surrounds the ventricles is referred to as the "periventricular halo" in medical terminology. The echogenicity of the abnormal choroidal plexus should be less than or at least similar to that of the normal choroidal plexus. The brush strokes that make up the halo should all appear the same. A cerebral haemorrhage or periventricular leukomalacia are two more conditions that might give rise to periventricular echogenicity. If the periventricular halo is symmetrical or if it has a higher echogenicity than the choroidal plexus, then one should investigate whether or not one of these illnesses is present.

2.3. Brain Damage in Preterm Babies

The phrase "preterm infant" is used to describe a newborn who enters the world before 37 weeks of gestation (or 259 days). The negative health implications of premature delivery extend far into adulthood, making it one of the leading causes of infant mortality and illness. Preterm birth can happen at any time during pregnancy. When compared to full-term infants, premature babies are more likely to experience health problems such cerebral palsy, sensory impairments, cognitive challenges, and respiratory infections. Premature birth is associated with a higher risk of morbidity, especially in later life. Brain injuries in premature infants can cause a wide variety of symptoms, from mild morbidity and cognitive abnormalities to severe spastic motor deficits like spastic diplegia and spastic quadriplegia, which are linked to severe learning disabilities. It is estimated that 28% of all newborn deaths (defined as deaths within the first seven days of life) are attributable to causes other than congenital abnormalities.

The occurrence and what led to it: Up to 12.9 million infants are born prematurely every year; that's 9.6 percent of the global population. Premature births make up about 21% of the total birth rate in India. Germinal matrix haemorrhage remains at an incredible 55 percent, even if the prevalence of PVL has fallen from the previous prevalence range of 25-40 percent in children delivered at less than 32 weeks of gestation and in neonates with extremely low birth weight. Improvements in prenatal steroid use and baby respiratory treatment, especially surfactant therapy, have led to a 7 percent drop in the incidence of PVL and a 25 percent drop in the number of reported cases of GMH.

All of these price drops can be traced back to this cause. The research into the root causes of GMH has found an intricate web of interconnected variables. Hypoxia, hypertension, hypercapnia, hypernatremia, fast volume rise, and pneumothorax are only few of the conditions that are often seen in premature infants. Maternal chorioamnionitis may produce PVL after a severe hemodynamic shock characterised by cardiorespiratory failure resulting in hypotension, acute hypoxia, and ischaemia. Infection and inflammation of the chorioamnion membrane are additional causes of maternal chorioamnionitis.

2.4. Pathophysiology

Damage to the brain of a preterm newborn may occur over the course of time rather than as a direct consequence of a single traumatic event. If the brain displays characteristics of immature development, such as a reduced ability to adjust to change, it may be more susceptible to harm both within and outside of the womb. This is because the brain is more susceptible to damage when it is young.

In unfavourable clinical settings, insufficient cerebral blood flow and arterial oxygen delivery in the brain are caused by the structural and functional immaturity of the organs responsible for breathing and circulation in a premature newborn. This immaturity can lead to conditions such as cerebral ischemia and ischemic stroke. (Jagtap, 2021)

Immature vascular architecture, particular aspects of development in cerebral circulation, innate cell sensitivity, and a number of toxic processes are all common risk factors for brain injury.

3. MATERIALS AND METHODS

At the Department of Radio Diagnostics at the Krishna Institute of Medical Sciences and Hospital in Karad, Maharashtra, a prospective observational study was conducted with the participation of one hundred premature neonates. All of the premature infants, but notably the ones whose brain injury was feared, were taken to the radiology department to have a neuro-ultrasonography performed.

Patient preparation:

- All premature infants were safely brought to the ultrasonography department by snuggling them up in warm blankets.
- The infant was well-fed before to the assessment.
- The infant should have been with her mother or another close relative.
- There was no anaesthetic administered.
- The infant lay supine

Both the examiner's hands and the transducer probes were sterilised before beginning.

Equipment: Each baby in this investigation was scanned using an ultrasound machine equipped with a Siemens Accuson Juniper, which was equipped with both a curvilinear transducer and a linear assay high-frequency transducer.

3.1. Technique

After that, the newborns were inspected using ultrasound technology, which required them to be transported to a separate room. It was important that the subject have a full stomach before undergoing any form of medical or psychological assessment. Warm blankets were used to wrap infants, who were at risk of developing hypothermia, in order to protect them. The infant is lying on its back in the supine position. The ultrasonic transducer and the media gel (profuse coupling agent) were placed on the newborn head's anterior fontanelle in order to gather images in the coronal and sagittal planes. At the beginning of the examination, the probe was angled so that it faced the front of the body. This is because the investigation began in the coronal plane along the coronal suture. By moving the transducer from the front to the rear of the head, a variety of coronal planes of the brain may be scanned. After the investigation of the coronal plane was completed, photographs of the sagittal and parasagittal planes were taken. The transducer was placed on the anterior fontanelle at a right angle to the coronal plane. It was then moved in a sweeping motion from the midline through the lateral ventricles to the cerebral parenchyma on each side of the head. Because the dense and echogenic choroid plexus on both sides could potentially confuse diagnostic imaging of subependymal haemorrhage, we took extra precautions to ensure that the scan was perfectly symmetrical throughout the entire process.

Average time 10 to 15mins.

During the first week of the newborn's life, a cranial ultrasonogram was performed. During this examination, special consideration was given to the echogenicity of the cerebral parenchyma, the size of the ventricles, the symmetry of the ventricles, any haemorrhage, any focal echodense or cystic changes, and PVE. (Jagtap, 2021)

4. OBSERVATIONS AND RESULTS

The distribution of the different types of deliveries and clinical characteristics that were observed in the study there were a total of one hundred infants engaged in the research. The study included a total of 102 participants, with 52 males and 48 females. The gender breakdown of the youngsters who participated in the research is presented in Table 1.

The subjects are broken down according to their gestational ages in the following Table 2.

According to the findings of the study, the lowest birth weight recorded was 1 kg, while the highest birth weight recorded was 2.5 kg (Table 3). The observed mean birth weight is 2.15 0.21 kilogrammes. The following graph presents the birth weight distribution found in the study (Table 4).

Eighty-eight point eight percent of the subjects had grade one GMH, fifteen point four percent of the subjects had grade three GMH, and three point eight percent of the subjects had grade four GMH. The plot that follows depicts the same thing.

Within the scope of the study, a total of 44 LSCS deliveries and 36 vaginal deliveries were observed (Table 5). 27 percent of the patients in the study didn't have any complaints in clinical features, and

Table 1. Distribution of gender

Gender	Number of Subjects (%)
Male	52 (52%)
Female	48 (48%)

Table 2. Subject distribution by gestational age

Gestational Age (in Weeks)	Number of Subjects (%)
28-30 weeks	10(10%)
30-32 weeks	30(30%)
32-34 weeks	35(35%)
34-36 weeks	25(25%)

Table 3. Birth weight distribution of subjects

Birth Weight (in Kgs)	Number of Subjects (%)
1.5-2 Kg	15 (15%)
2-2.5 Kg	85 (85%)

Table 4. Distribution of grade of GMH lesions

Grade of GMH	Number of Subjects (%)
Grade 1 GMH	21 (80.8%)
Grade 3 GMH	4 (15.4%)
Grade 4 GMH	1 (3.8%)

Table 5. Clinical characteristics and delivery type distribution

Variables		Number of Subjects (%)	
Type of delivery	Forceps	20	(20%)
	LSCS	44	(44%)
	Vaginal	36	(36%)
Clinical features	Seizure	1	(1%)
	Poor suckling	5	(5%)
	Hypotonia	7	(7%)
	Low saturation	8	(8%)
	Excessive cry	11	(11%)
	Delayed cry	13	(13%)
	No complaints	27	(27%)
	Lethargy	28	(28%)

28 percent of them reported lethargy. These percentages are from the total study. The plot that follows depicts the same thing.

5. DISCUSSION

One hundred infants who have only recently been born are taking part in this prospective observational study. The investigation includes a total of 102 neonates, with 52 males and 48 females participating. All of the newborns analysed were delivered at a gestational age of between 28 and 36 weeks. Ten percent (10%) of the people were at the point in their pregnancies where they were between 28 and 30 weeks along. There were thirty infants born between the ages of 30 and 32 weeks (representing 30 percent of the total), thirty-five infants born between the ages of 32 and 34 weeks (representing 35 percent of the total), and twenty-three infants born between the ages of 34 and 36 weeks (representing 25 percent of the total).

It was between 28 and 30 weeks of pregnancy when the bulk of abnormal sonograms were performed. Six of the children, or sixty percent, had GMH, and four of the children, or forty percent, had PVL; therefore, one hundred percent of the scans performed at this stage of gestation were abnormal. At the time of delivery, the infants who took part in the study ranged in weight from 1.5 to 2.5 kg (low birth weight). There are records of both 1 kg and 2.5 kg as the highest possible birth weight. The average birth weight for this population is 2.15 0.21 kilogrammes. The birth weights of 15 (fifteen percent) of the newborns and 85 (eighty-five percent) of the total were between 2 and 2.5 kilogrammes when they were recorded.

The birth weight range of 1.5 to 2 kilogrammes was related with the highest incidence of aberrant neurosonograms, whereas the birth weight range of 2 to 2.5 kilogrammes was associated with the highest prevalence of normal neurosonograms. According to the findings of our study, the most common clinical sign of neonatal brain injury is lethargy, which accounts for 28 percent, followed by delayed crying (13 percent). 7 percentage of patients additionally presented with hypotonia, 8 percentage of patients presented with low saturation, 5 percentage of patients presented with poor feeding, and 1 percentage of patients presented with seizures. The childbirth experiences of each of the infants that are highlighted here have been taken into consideration.

LSCS was the most prevalent way of delivery, accounting for 44 percent of all births, followed by vaginal delivery (36 percent), and then delivery with the assistance of forceps (20 percent). During the first week of life, an ultrasound was performed, and then another one was performed at the end of the first month. The fact that only 45 of the 55 neonates who received their initial neurosonogram within seven days of birth had normal results suggests that there was a problem with the procedure. In the first examination, germinal matrix haemorrhage was the anomaly that was found to be present the majority of the time (26 percent).

The Papile classification system was used to determine students' placement in Grades I through IV. This was consistent with what was discovered in the study that Paneth N. and colleagues conducted on preterm newborns. A total of twenty-four newborns, or eighty percent, were discovered to have GMH of Grade I, while four infants, or fifteen percent, had GMH of Grade 2, and one infant, or three percent, had GMH of Grade 3.

The quality of the majority of the results ranged from poor to average. This was consistent with the findings of the study that Kadri and his colleagues published in 2006. PVL was the second most common neurosonogram abnormality, accounting for 19 percent of all abnormalities found in the study. 15 of the questions had a PVL of grade 1, while 3 (15.8 percent) had a PVL of grade 2, and 1 (5.3 percent) had a PVL of grade 3 among the themes. This was related to the work that Skullred and his colleagues did. After a month, despite receiving therapy, four children who had GMH and one infant who had PVL had passed away. Two of the neonates who were included in the follow-up investigation and were later determined to have abnormalities had their neurosonograms unaltered, despite the fact that they had initially been scanned and confirmed to have normal conditions.

During the initial screening, it was determined that a total of 21 persons exhibited Grade 1 GMH. One of these 21 patients could not be located for further examination, two had developed grade 2 GMH, nine had the same grade of lesions, and the neurosonograms of the remaining nine patients were normal. Four infants tested positive for GMH of grade 3. A GMH diagnosis of Grade 4 was given to one infant, but sadly, this child did not live long enough to have the follow-up examination.

At birth, 19 children were found to have perventricular leukomalacia, with 15 having Grade I, 3 having Grade 2, and 1 having Grade 4. At the end of the month's scan, there were three Grade I patients who had not received follow-up care. After the initial diagnosis of grade, I PVL, seven people showed signs of improvement, whereas four patients continued to show signs of improvement after the original diagnosis. At the end of the month, the results were still evident in three people who had PVL of grade 2. However, one guy who had PVL grade 3 did not make it through the ordeal.

According to the findings of our research, abnormal scans are most prevalent in children who are delivered between the ages of 28 and 32 weeks of pregnancy. but the risk of having an anomaly between 32 and 36 weeks of pregnancy was relatively low. Because of this, we are able to draw the conclusion that it is in everyone's best interest to notice abnormal neurosonogram results as early in the pregnancy as possible. This corroborates the findings of a number of earlier investigations, including the ones conducted by Koksal et al., (2022). The birth weights of the infants who participated in our study ranged between 1.5 and 2.5 kg. The largest incidence of abnormal neurosonograms was seen in newborns with a body mass index (BMI) ranging from 1.5 to 2.0. This, in turn, helps establish the association between low birth weight and an increased risk of abnormal neurosonograms, both of which are associated with a shorter gestational age. Both of these factors are correlated with having a shorter gestational age. Numerous studies have all arrived at the same conclusions.

Germinal matrix haemorrhage is the intracranial abnormality that occurs most frequently in preterm infants, who are at the highest risk of acquiring intracranial abnormalities. The Grade IV GMH and the Grade 3 PVL are associated with the highest level of mortality, and this is especially true in neonates who were born with a low birth weight. The early evaluation of preterm newborns, which should take place within the first week of life, is helpful in the diagnosis of underlying intracranial problems. The various grades of cerebral haemorrhage and PVL are the lesions that are observed the most frequently in preterm newborns. Both of these conditions can be identified as early as during the first 24 hours after birth.

6. CONCLUSION

Neurosonography is a very significant primary screening technology that plays an essential role in the early evaluation of the many neurological diseases that might affect neonates. The low cost, excellent efficiency, and lightning-fast response time are just some of the many benefits that it offers. In the first examination of high-risk preterm children who are suspected of having germinal matrix haemorrhage or intraventricular haemorrhage, as well as in subsequent scans to monitor for the progression of these conditions, neurosonography is especially beneficial because of its non-invasive and effective properties. This is especially true when compared to other diagnostic methods. Patients who are believed to have sustained brain injuries typically receive treatment in a timely manner as a result of the widespread availability of modern NICU services and equipment. As a direct result of this, there is a lower probability of undesirable consequences occurring. One of the few downsides associated with neurosonography is the fact that it can be difficult to determine whether or not a lesion that has a thick echo in the parenchyma is bleeding. Despite its greater accuracy and sensitivity in distinguishing hemorrhagic from non-hemorrhagic diseases, the use of CT in routine screening of vulnerable newborns is restricted due to transport, sedation, IV contrast administration, temperature management, and the risk of ionising radiation. This is the case despite the fact that CT has a better ability to detect hemorrhagic diseases. As a result, the neurosonogram is the primary non-invasive instrument of choice when it comes to analysing the brain of a newborn baby. In conclusion, the technique is efficient in terms of cost, helps in the early detection of preterm neonates and supports their treatment, and contributes to the reduction of neonatal morbidity, mortality, and future maldevelopment.

REFERENCES

Back, S. A., & Rivkees, S. A. (2004). Emerging concepts in periventricular white matter injury. *Seminars in Perinatology*, *28*(6), 405–414. doi:10.1053/j.semperi.2004.10.010 PMID:15693397

Bowie, J. D., Kirks, D. R., Rosenberg, E. R., & Clair, M. R. (1983). Caudothalamic groove: Value in identification of germinal matrix hemorrhage by sonography in preterm neonates. *AJR. American Journal of Roentgenology*, *141*(6), 1317–1320. doi:10.2214/ajr.141.6.1317 PMID:6606337

Craniosacral rhythm. (2018). *John Dalton Therapy*. https://www.johndaltontherapy.com/craniosacral-rhythm/

Creed, L., & Haber, K. (1984). Ultrasonic evaluation of the infant head. *Critical Reviews in Diagnostic Imaging*, *21*(1), 37–84. PMID:6373149

DeReuck, J. L. (1984). Cerebral angioarchitecture and perinatal brain lesions in premature and full term infants. *Acta Neurologica Scandinavica*, *70*(6), 391–395. doi:10.1111/j.1600-0404.1984.tb00843.x PMID:6516787

DeVlieger, M., & Ridder, H. J. (1959). Use of echoencephalography. *Neurology*, *9*(4), 216–223. doi:10.1212/WNL.9.4.216 PMID:13644550

Govaert, P., & DeVries, L. S. (2010). An atlas of neonatal brain sonography (2nd ed.). MacKeith Press.

Jagtap, A. (2021). *The role of cranial ultrasonography in detecting neurological abnormalities in preterm neonates the role of cranial ultrasonography in detecting neurological abnormalities in preterm neonates*. Grin Verlag.

Koksal, N., Bayton, B., Bayram, Y., & Nacorkucuk, E. (2002). Risk factors for intraventricular hemorrhage in very low birth weight infants. *Indian Journal of Pediatrics*, *69*(7), 561–564. doi:10.1007/BF02722677 PMID:12173693

Leksee, L. (1956). Echo- encephalography In detection of intracranial complications following head injury. *Acta Chirurgica Scandinavica*, (110), 301–305. PMID:13292078

London, D. A., Carroll, B. A., & Enzmann, D. R. (1980). Sonography of ventricular size and germinal matrix hemorrhage in premature infants. *AJNR. American Journal of Neuroradiology*, *1*, 295–300. PMID:6773378

Martin, J. A., Hamilton, B. E., Ventura, S. J., Menacker, F., & Park, M. M. (2002). Births: Final data for 2000. *National Vital Statistics Reports*, *50*, 1–101. PMID:11876093

McGuinness, G.A., Smith, W.L., (1984). Head ultrasound screening in premature neonates weighing more than 1,500 g at birth. *Am J Dis Child, 138*(9), 817-20.

Rumack, C. M., & Drose, J. A. (2011). Neonatal and infant brain imaging. In *Diagnostic ultrasound* (4th ed., pp. 1558–163). Elsevier, Mosby.

Singh, U., Singh, N., & Shikha, S. (2007). A prospective analysis of etiology and outcome of preterm labour. *Journal of Obstetrics and Gynaecology of India*, *57*(1), 48.

Skullerud, K., & Wester, B. (1986). Frequency and prognostic significance of germinal matrix hemorrhage, periventricular leukomalacia, and pontosubicular necrosis in preterm neonates. *Acta Neuropathologica*, *70*(3-4), 257–261. doi:10.1007/BF00686080 PMID:3766126

Themes, U. F. O. (2017). *49 72-year-old female with a 2-day history of progressively worsening headache, nausea, and vomiting*. Radiology Key. https://radiologykey.com/49-72-year-old-female-with-a-2-day-history-of-progressively-worsening-headache-nausea-and-vomiting/(Accessed by 12 March, 2023)

Volpe, J. J. (1995). Neurological evaluation; hypoxic-ischemic encephalopathy; and intracranial hemorrhage. In *Neurology of the newborn* (3rd ed., pp. 95–463). W.B. Saunders Company.

Chapter 21
Smart Weapon Detection System Using Thermal Imaging Through Machine Learning Algorithms

Kasi Uday Kiran
*Koneru Lakshmaiah Education Foundation,
India*

Sandeep Dwarkanath Pande
(iD) https://orcid.org/0000-0001-6969-0423
Madras Institute of Technology, India

P. Poorna Priya
DIET College, India

K. Kalki Sai
*Koneru Lakshmaiah Education Foundation,
India*

Nandigama Apoorva
*Koneru Lakshmaiah Education Foundation,
India*

M. Geethika
*Koneru Lakshmaiah Education Foundation,
India*

Sk Hasane Ahammad
*Koneru Lakshmaiah Education Foundation,
India*

ABSTRACT

According to numerous statistics, it can be inferred that the rate of violence using firearms and dangerous weapons is rising annually, making it difficult for law enforcement organizations to address this problem promptly. There are several locations where there are high rates of crime with firearms or knives, particularly in areas with lax gun restrictions. For the security of citizens, the early identification of violent crime is crucial. We see a lot of crimes and attacks on public transportation these days. Different ways have been developed to hide the weapons to launch savage attacks on the unwary population. These criminals' primary goals are to manipulate people and harm public property. All these things only occur as a result of weapons and other dangerous items being readily transported into buses and trains. To protect the public and its assets, it is important to create and implement highly effective technologies across the nation. By spotting the existence of deadly weapons like knives and firearms, these situations can be avoided.

DOI: 10.4018/978-1-6684-9189-8.ch021

1. INTRODUCTION

Rail transportation is an important mode of travel for both people and goods in the majority of countries across the world. The government is in charge of the majority of the railroad operations across the country (Gosain, 2021). Indian Railways is a state-owned corporation that is owned by the Ministry of Railways, which at one time had its own separate budget from the government (Myla et al., 2019). Between 2019 and 2020, the Indian Railways network was utilised by many millions of passengers on a daily basis. The trains in Kolkata and the Chennai Metro are just two examples of the many suburban and urban trains that are operated by various locally owned public corporations around the country (Peng et al., 2002; Xue and Blum, 2003). However, as of right now, there are just a few private sector operations for cargo trains and railroads, and they are primarily for non-passenger usage. In the year 2020, new measures were launched to encourage private sector involvement in running passenger trains (Reddy et al., 2019). India's national rail network is the fourth largest in the world, coming in behind only that of the United States, Russia, and China (Fazil et al., 2023).

The railroad network is essential to the transportation industry (Ahammad et al., 2020). The majority of travellers find that travelling by train is enjoyable, and the convenience that railways provide to logistics cannot be overstated (Kaya et al., 2021). As a result of the fact that the majority of people in our country frequently use railroads as their mode of transportation, there are a great deal of potential for a catastrophe to take place. This suggests that a significant number of criminal organisations or terrorist groups will attempt to attack specific individuals as well as the wider community (Sathyaseelan et al., 2021). They will use firearms and other lethal objects to enable them in their assaults and murders of innocent persons (Thakare, 2018; Elsner et al., 2018; Yu & Chen, 2020). It was in one of these examples that we first became aware of the concept. The critical step in putting a halt to all of the attacks is learning how to identify them so that we can avoid being hurt. Terrorists of today receive extensive training, and they have devised cunning methods to conceal their weapons while still allowing others to see them. This enables them to carry out lethal attacks on innocent people. They frequently carry out these activities while dressed inconspicuously. It is critical to design and put into action monitoring systems that are exceptionally efficient on a global scale if one wishes to shield the general populace and the assets it possesses (Yousef et al., 2023).

The highly developed surveillance systems all come equipped with a multitude of cameras, which are helpful for swiftly monitoring, locating, and recognising whatever is in the field of view (Jolly et al., 2016). Over the course of the past few years, there have been a number of incidents involving the discharge of potentially lethal firearms in public settings. After carrying out attacks on a number of mosques in New Zealand over the course of the previous year, the perpetrator hit the Christchurch AL-Noor Mosque at 1:40 p.m. on March 15, 2019, taking the lives of approximately 44 worshippers who were unarmed and did not pose a threat. On the same day, at 1:55 p.m., a second attack took place, which resulted in the deaths of seven more persons (Wikipedia, 2019). It is essential to provide people with hope and to put an end to acts of terrorism, but law enforcement officials need to be able to recognise weapons that are concealed beneath people's clothing in order to prevent more attacks. Eliminating potential dangers as soon as possible is absolutely necessary in order to be safe (Yuenyong et al., 2018).

As a result of this issue, walk-through detection gates or manual screening procedures have been implemented in high-traffic areas such as airports, train stations, metro stations, bus stops, stadiums, educational institutions, movie theatres, and shopping malls. These locations see a significant amount of foot traffic. However, there have been instances that have resulted in fatalities in which traditional scanners failed to detect the presence of weapons and explosives, so allowing attackers to bypass detection barriers and cause catastrophic damage (Ahammad, et al., 2020). The operator of the security system can realise benefits from a thermal image processing system by enhancing the relevant information present in the picture, which subsequently makes it possible to differentiate between important image elements (Gonzalez & Woods, 2002). The more advanced imaging systems can automatically recognise potential dangers and alert the human operator to their presence (Prasad, 2017). In order to accomplish these responsibilities, specialised algorithms are implemented for the purpose of detecting and tracking objects inside a picture. Because tracking and vision systems that work in visible light are unable to directly use detection algorithms for the analysis of thermal images (Holst, 1998) specialised techniques have been developed for the detection and tracking of objects on thermal images. These techniques allow for the detection and tracking of objects on thermal images (Karthik et al., 2021).

2. LITERATURE SURVEY

The provision of adequate security and the reduction of life-threatening activities are challenging challenges in every location. Because of this, a large number of researchers have begun using object detection in order to monitor a wide variety of behaviours and actions (Pavlidis & Symosek, 2002). The framework of a smart surveillance system is typically developed on three levels. The first level is designed to extract low-level information such as features engineering and object tracking. The second level is designed to identify unusual human activities, behaviour, or detection of any weapon. The third level is designed to identify high-level decision-making such as abnormal event detection or any anomaly (Chen et al., 2005). When knives or firearms are recognised automatically in CCTV footage, an algorithm developed by Gupta et al., (2023) notifies the security guard or operator (Grega et al., 2016). Concentrating largely on lessening the number of false alarms and providing a real-time application, with the algorithm having a specificity of 94.93 percent for detecting knives and a sensitivity of 81.18 percent for doing so. In addition, the fire detection system has a specificity of 96.69 percent and a sensitivity of 34.98 percent for the various things seen in the movie (Sekhar, & Kranthi, 2017).

The histogram of directed tracklets is a video classifier that was created by Mousavi and colleagues in (Mousavi et al., 2015). This classifier is also used to recognise irregular circumstances in challenging images (Vaishna, 2016). As an alternative to the standard approaches based on optical flow, which only measure edge features from the two frames that follow it, descriptors have been expanding over long-range motion projections that are known as tracklets. Sequences of spatial-temporal cuboid imagery are statistically collected on the tracklets that cross them (Bendes and Aslantas, 2015). E. M. Upadhyay and colleagues came up with the idea of using image fusion as a CWD approach. They employed infrared photos and visual fusion to find hidden weapons when there was an image of the scene over and under exposed portions. The method that they used entailed applying a homomorphic filter on visible and infrared images that were captured at a range of different exposure levels (Upadhyay & Rana, 2014). The current methods achieve a high level of accuracy by utilising various combinations of extractors and detectors. This can be done through the application of straightforward techniques such as boundary detection, pattern matching, and straightforward intensity descriptors (Gesick et al., 2009), or through the application of more complex techniques such as cascade classifiers with boosting.

3. RELATED WORK

The problem of identifying and classifying objects in real time became apparent following significant developments in the disciplines of surveillance, processing technology, and deep learning models. There hasn't been a lot of research done in this area, and the majority of it has been centred on finding weapons that are being hidden (CWD). Beginning with concealed weapon detection (CWD), it was based on imaging technology and utilised for airport security, luggage control, and other uses such as millimeter-wave and infrared imaging (Alfaifi & Khan, 2022). [CWD] stands for concealed weapon detection. In the past, it was utilised for the detection of weapons. Imaging methods that are based on a combination of sensor technologies and processing could provide a solution to a major part of the problem associated with the detection of concealed objects (such as pistols). The Mili-Meter Wave (MMW) system, which finds concealed weapons by employing terahertz imaging (Lee et al., 2009), has been developed specifically for this purpose (Chang & Johnson, 2001).

A select few individuals put out a CWD strategy predicated on a multi-scale decomposition method that combines colour and visual picture with the incorporation of infrared (IR) light. And the others suggested a CWD method that was based on the combining of visual and IR, or millimetre wave, images using a multi-resolution mosaic technique to bring attention to the covert weapon that was hidden in the target image. It was hypothesised by Thi et al., (2011) that fusing infrared and visible images together for robust person detection would be beneficial. They talked about the image fusion methodology for recognising humans and gave ways for finding persons in FIR images. A study titled "Multi-scale Fusion of Visible and Thermal IR Images for Illumination-Invariant Face Recognition" was conducted by Kong et al., (2007). The title of the paper is "Multi-scale Fusion of Visible and Thermal IR Images for Illumination-Invariant Face Recognition." They proposed an innovative software-based method for the registration and merging of visible and thermal infrared (IR) image data for face identification in challenging working situations with variable illumination (Khan & Alajmi, 2019).

4. METHODOLOGY

Applications that deal with computer vision and image processing frequently make use of the Gaussian blur method, which is a specific kind of picture smoothing algorithm. It gets its name from the Gaussian distribution, a mathematical function that defines the probability distribution of a random variable. The Gaussian distribution inspired the naming of this phenomenon. The image is convolved with a Gaussian kernel, which is a two-dimensional matrix of values that corresponds to the Gaussian function, as part of the operation that makes up the Gaussian blur algorithm. The Gaussian kernel is normally in the shape of a square, and it always has an odd number of rows and columns.

The element in the centre of the square has the greatest possible value. When the image is convolved with the Gaussian kernel, the pixel values that are produced are a weighted average of the pixel values that are neighbouring, with the weights being determined by the values that are contained within the

Gaussian kernel. When the value of the kernel is higher at a particular position, the contribution of the pixel that is associated with that location is increased relative to the final value. When developing a grayscale algorithm to convert a thermal image to grayscale, a straightforward method that may be used is to map the temperature values to the grayscale values using a linear scaling or thresholding technique. For instance, you may select a temperature range that is of particular interest to you, map the lowest and highest temperatures in that range to the minimum and maximum grayscale values (0 and 255, respectively), and then linearly interpolate the grayscale values for the remaining temperatures. You also have the option of selecting a temperature threshold and assigning the colour white to all pixels whose temperatures are higher than the threshold, and black to all pixels whose temperatures are lower than the threshold (Figure 1).

The thermal image that we obtain from a thermal camera is converted into a grayscale image. In the BGR colour space, an image is represented using three colour channels: blue, green, and red. The grayscale conversion replaces each pixel value in the image with a single intensity value, representing the brightness of the pixel. After this conversion, the resulting grayscale image will contain a grayscale version of the original image with one colour channel instead of three, which can be used for further filtering, edge detection, and segmentation. There can be a lot of background noise in the grayscale image, which makes it difficult to extract the necessary features. The Gaussian algorithm is a technique used to reduce noise and smooth an image by convolving it with a Gaussian filter kernel.

The filter kernel is a matrix of weights that represents the shape of a Gaussian distribution. The blur is applied to the image by calculating the weighted average of the surrounding pixel values, with the weight determined by the Gaussian function. The amount of blur is controlled by the size of the kernel

Figure 1. Flow chart of methodology

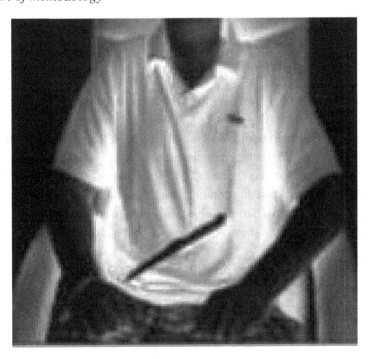

and the standard deviation of the Gaussian function. And the blur image obtained after the Gaussian algorithm is subjected to applying the threshold to segment the image based on pixel intensity values. It involves creating a binary image from a grayscale or colour image by setting pixel values above or below a threshold value to 1 or 0, respectively. By applying thresholding, we can segment an image into regions of interest based on pixel intensity values, which can be useful for object detection and feature extraction. And in this case, 100 is the threshold value used to separate the foreground (pixels with intensity greater than or equal to the threshold) from the background (pixels with intensity less than the threshold). 255 is the maximum pixel value to be used for pixels that are above the threshold. In this case, the maximum value of 255 indicates that pixels that pass the threshold will be set to white. The contour detection technique is applied to the segmented image to detect the contours on the image, where a contour is a curve that joins the points along the boundary of an object having the same intensity or color. "Detecting contours" refers to the process of identifying and extracting the boundaries of objects or regions in an image.

By detecting and manipulating contours, information can be extracted about the shape and structure of objects in an image. And the contours are drawn on the image, which will be used to detect objects in the image. Then each contour in the image is verified with existing or predefined weapon detection criteria. Different types of weapons with different shapes and sizes have been observed and verified, and the criteria have been defined and verified with the contours detected on the image. The shape and size criteria are defined by the conditions that the contour width (w) is greater than the height (h), the width is greater than 30 pixels, and the height is greater than 10 pixels. So, each contour is verified with the criteria, and if the properties of the contour satisfy the weapon detection criteria, a rectangle box is drawn around the contour where the weapon is detected, and the image with the box will be displayed along with the text "Weapon Detected." If no contour satisfies the weapon detection criteria, then the image will be displayed along with the text "Weapon not detected."

5. COMPARATIVE ANALYSIS

5.1. Result Analysis and Discussion

Figures 2, 5, and 8 are the RGB images of persons, which are helpful to know the identity of the person if any weapon is detected with him. Figures 3, 6, and 9 are the thermal images of the persons to whom the algorithms are applied. The methodology as provided first detects the objects from the thermal image. After detecting the objects, contours are drawn around them. Then each contour is compared with the weapon criteria as mentioned in the methodology. The contours that do not satisfy weapon criteria are considered harmless objects. When any contour satisfies the weapon detection criteria as mentioned (Figure 11), the object is considered a harmful object or weapon, and a rectangular box is drawn around the detected weapon and displayed as shown in Figures 4, 7, and 10.

Accuracy = TP + TN / TP + FP + FN + TN = 90.62%

Precision = TP / TP + FP = 83.45%

Figure 2. RGB image of person with gun

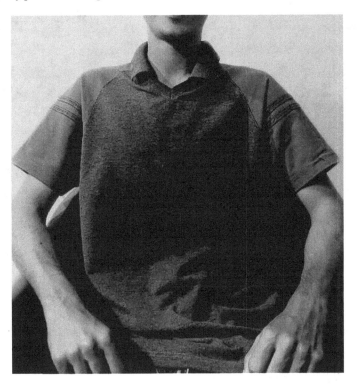

Figure 3. Thermal/IR image of person with gun

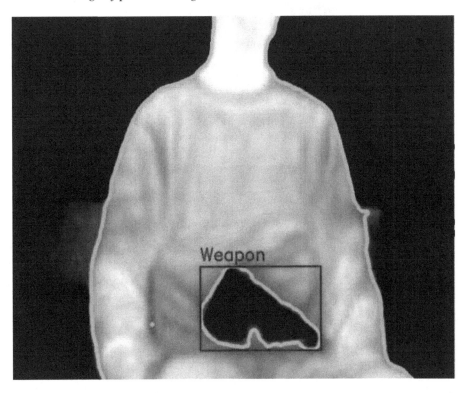

Figure 4. Weapon detected

Figure 5. RGB image of person with gun

Figure 6. Thermal image of person with gun

Figure 7. Weapon detected

Figure 8. RGB image of person with knife

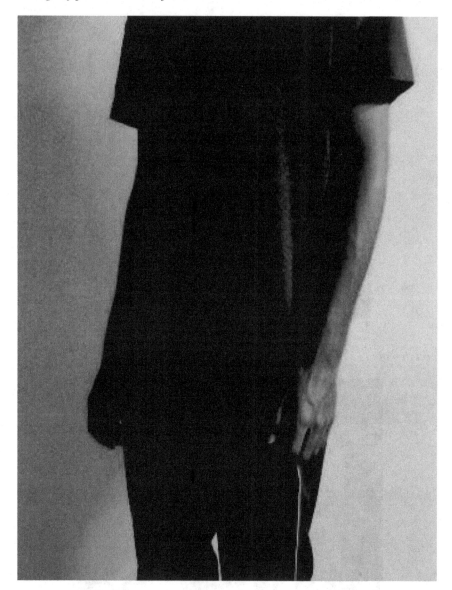

6. CONCLUSION

This research was conducted with the intention of developing a practical automated method for discovering concealed firearms. We are able to quickly neutralise a potential threat by utilising the wearer's facial characteristics while simultaneously locating and isolating a hidden weapon with the assistance of image processing techniques. This allows us to determine whether the item in question is a weapon or not, all the while maintaining the wearer's identity. Machine learning is utilised in order to identify hidden items and determine whether or not they are weapons with the least amount of work required from humans. The study of monitoring and governance improvement is advanced by the results of this experiment.

Figure 9. Thermal image of person with knife

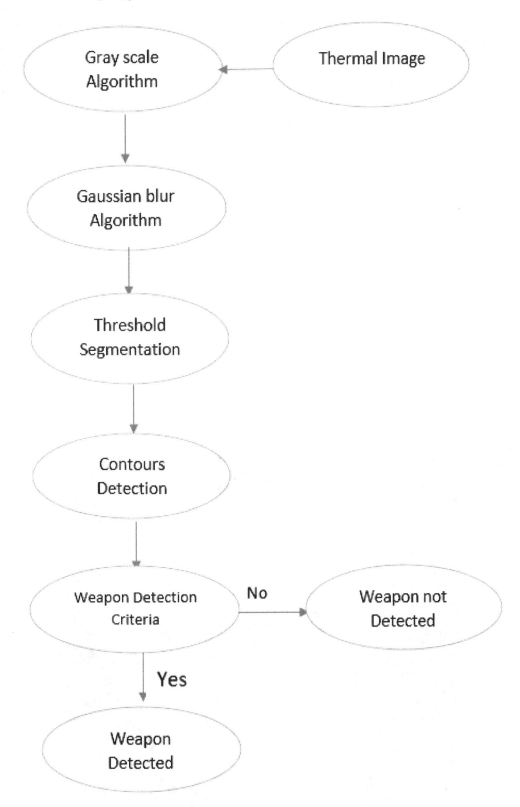

Figure 10. Weapon detected

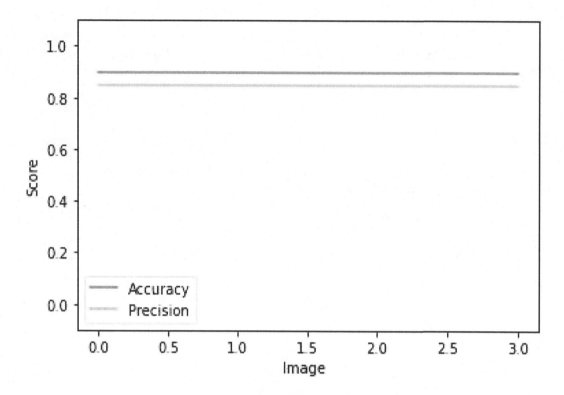

Figure 11. Accuracy and precision

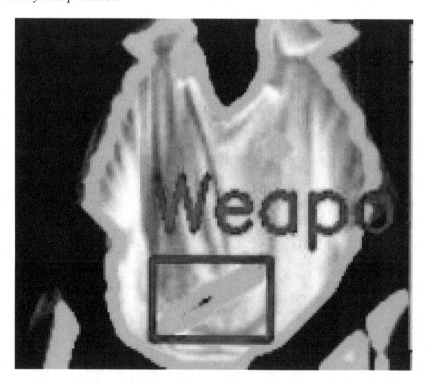

REFERENCES

Ahammad, S. H., Rajesh, V., Rahman, M. Z. U., & Lay-Ekuakille, A. (2020). A hybrid CNN-based segmentation and boosting classifier for real time sensor spinal cord injury data. *IEEE Sensors Journal, 20*(17), 10092–10101. doi:10.1109/JSEN.2020.2992879

Alfaifi, A. A., & Khan, S. G. (2022). Utilizing data from Twitter to explore the UX of "Madrasati" as a Saudi e-learning platform compelled by the pandemic. *Arab Gulf Journal of Scientific Research*, 200–208. doi:10.51758/AGJSR-03-2021-0025

Bendes, E., & Aslantas, V. (2015). The sum of the correlations of differences is a new picture quality metric for image fusion. *AEÜ. International Journal of Electronics and Communications, 69*(12), 1890–1896. doi:10.1016/j.aeue.2015.09.004

Chang, Y-W., Johnson, M. (2001). *Portable Concealed Weapon Detection Using Millimeter Wave FMCW Radar Imaging.* 189918: August 30, 1998-DT-CXK001.

Chen, H.-M., Lee, S., Rao, R. M., Slamani, M.-A., & Varshney, P. K. (2005). Imaging for concealed weapon detection: A tutorial overview of development in imaging sensors and processing. *IEEE Signal Processing Magazine, 22*(2), 52–61. doi:10.1109/MSP.2005.1406480

Elsner, J., Fritz, T., Henke, L., Jarrousse, O., Taing, S., & Uhlenbrock, M. (2018). Automatic Weapon Detection in Social Media Image Data using a Two-Pass Convolutional Neural Network. *European Law Enforcement Research Bulletin*, (4), 61-65. Retrieved from http://bulletin.cepol.europa.eu/index.php/bulletin/article/view/323

Fazil, M., Khan, S., Albahlal, B. M., Alotaibi, R. M., Siddiqui, T., & Shah, M. A. (2023). Attentional Multi-Channel Convolution With Bidirectional LSTM Cell Toward Hate Speech Prediction. *IEEE Access : Practical Innovations, Open Solutions, 11*, 16801–16811. doi:10.1109/ACCESS.2023.3246388

Gesick, R., Saritac, C., & Hung, C.-C. (2009). Automatic image analysis process for the detection of concealed weapons. *Proceedings of the 5th Annual Workshop on Cyber Security and Information Intelligence Research: Cyber Security and Information Intelligence Challenges and Strategies.* 10.1145/1558607.1558630

Gonzalez, R. C., & Woods, R. E. (2002). *Digital image processing* (2nd ed.). Prentice-Hall.

Gosain, S. (2021). Concealed weapon detection using image processing and machine learning. *International Journal for Research in Applied Science and Engineering Technology, 9*(12), 1374–1384. doi:10.22214/ijraset.2021.39506

Grega, M., Matiolański, A., Guzik, P., & Leszczuk, M. (2016). Automated detection of firearms and knives in a CCTV image. *Sensors (Basel), 16*(1), 47. doi:10.339016010047 PMID:26729128

Gupta, G., Khan, S., Guleria, V., Almjally, A., Alabduallah, B. I., Siddiqui, T., Albahlal, B. M., Alajlan, S. A., & Al-Subaie, M. (2023). DDPM: A dengue disease prediction and diagnosis model using sentiment analysis and machine learning algorithms. *Diagnostics (Basel), 13*(6), 1093. Advance online publication. doi:10.3390/diagnostics13061093 PMID:36980401

Holst, G. C. (1998). *Testing and evaluating of infrared imaging systems*. SPIE Optical Engineering Press.

Jolly, A. R., & Chakravarthi, M. K. (2016). A Standalone Data Logger For Fibre Optic Vibration Measurement System Using Beagle bone. *International Conference on Intelligent Systems and Control*.

Karthik, M. V., Chakravarthi, M. K., Yapanto, L. M., Selvapandian, D., Harish, R., & Subramani, K. (2021). Optical Analysis of the UPQC using PI Controller in Power flow System. *2021 7th International Conference on Advanced Computing and Communication Systems (ICACCS)*.

Kaya, V., Tuncer, S., & Baran, A. (2021). Detection and Classification of Different Weapon Types Using Deep Learning. *Applied Sciences (Basel, Switzerland)*, *11*(16), 7535. doi:10.3390/app11167535

Khan, S., & Alajmi, M. F. (2019). A Review on Security Concerns in Cloud Computing and their Solutions. *International Journal of Computer Science Network Security*, *19*(2).

Kong, S. G., Heo, J., Boughorbel, F., Zheng, Y., Abidi, B. R., Koschan, A., Yi, M., & Abidi, M. A. (2007). Multiscale fusion of visible and thermal IR images for illumination-invariant face recognition. *International Journal of Computer Vision*, *71*(2), 215–233. doi:10.100711263-006-6655-0

Lee, D.-S., Yeom, S., Son, J.-Y., & Kim, S.-H. (2009). Image segmentation of concealed objects detected by passive millimeter wave imaging. *2009 34th International Conference on Infrared, Millimeter, and Terahertz Waves*.

Mousavi, H., Mohammadi, S., Perina, A., Chellali, R., & Murino, V. (2015). Analyzing tracklets for the detection of abnormal crowd behavior. *2015 IEEE Winter Conference on Applications of Computer Vision*. 10.1109/WACV.2015.27

Myla, S., Marella, S. T., Swarnendra Goud, A., Hasane Ahammad, S., Kumar, G. N. S., & Inthiyaz, S. (2019). Design decision taking system for student career selection for accurate academic system. *International Journal of Recent Technology and Engineering*, *8*(9), 2199–2206.

Pavlidis, I., & Symosek, P. (2002). The imaging issue in an automatic face/disguise detection system. Proceedings *IEEE Workshop on Computer Vision Beyond the Visible Spectrum: Methods and Applications* (Cat. No.PR00640).

Peng, C.-Y. J., Lee, K. L., & Ingersoll, G. M. (2002). An introduction to logistic regression analysis and reporting. *The Journal of Educational Research*, *96*(1), 3–14. doi:10.1080/00220670209598786

Prasad, C. H. (2017). Failure analysis and prediction for metal jobs using fuzzy computation. In *International Conference on Intelligent Computing, Instrumentation and Control Technologies (ICICICT)* (pp. 1159–1163). IEEE.

Reddy, A. P. C., Kumar, D. M. S., Krishna, B. M., Inthiyaz, S., & Ahammad, S. H. (2019). Physical Unclonable Function based Design for Customized Digital Logic Circuit. *International Journal of Advanced Science and Technology*, *28*(8), 206–221.

Sathyaseelan, M. P., Amit, P., & Sudipta, S. (2021). IoT based COVID De-Escalation System using Bluetooth Low Level Energy. In *6th International Conference on Inventive Computation Technologies (ICICT)* (pp. 174–177). IEEE.

Sekhar, C., & Kranthi, K. (2017). Traffic signal breach vehicle stop system using IOT. In *IEEE International Conference on Nextgen Electronic Technologies: Silicon to Software (ICNETS2)* (pp. 296–300). IEEE.

Thakare, A. (2018). Concealed Weapon Detection Using Image Processing. *International Journal of Electronics, Communication and Soft Computing Science and Engineering*, 31–34.

Thi, T., Takahashi, H., Toriu, T., & Ham, H. (2011). Fusion of Infrared and Visible Images for Robust Person Detection. Graduate School of Engineering, Osaka City University. doi:10.5772/14173

Upadhyay, E. M., & Rana, N. K. (2014). Exposure fusion for concealed weapon detection. *2014 2nd International Conference on Devices, Circuits and Systems (ICDCS)*.

Vaishna, S., & Kumar, M. K. (2016). MSP430 Data Logger: An Implementation for Stress Measurement in Concrete Structures. *International Conference on Intelligent Systems and Control*.

Wikipedia. (2019). *Christchurch mosque shootings*. Available:https://en.wikipedia.org/wiki/Christchurch_mosque_shootings

Xue, Z., & Blum, R. (2003). Colour image fusion for the detection of hidden weapons. *FUSION 2003: Proceedings of the Sixth International Conference on Information Fusion*. 10.1109/ICIF.2003.177504

Yousef, R., Khan, S., Gupta, G., Albahlal, B. M., Alajlan, S. A., & Ali, A. (2023). Bridged-U-Net-ASPP-EVO and Deep Learning Optimization for Brain Tumor Segmentation. *Diagnostics (Basel)*, *13*(16), 2633. doi:10.3390/diagnostics13162633 PMID:37627893

Yu, S., & Chen, X. (2020). Infrared and visible image fusion based on a latent low-rank representation nested with multiscale geometric transform. *IEEE Access : Practical Innovations, Open Solutions*, *8*, 110214–110226. doi:10.1109/ACCESS.2020.3001974

Yuenyong, S., Hnoohom, N., & Wongpatikaseree, K. (2018). Automatic detection of knives in infrared images. *2018 International ECTI Northern Section Conference on Electrical, Electronics, Computer and Telecommunications Engineering (ECTI-NCON)*. 10.1109/ECTI-NCON.2018.8378283

Compilation of References

. Sharma, D. K., Jalil, N. A., Regin, R., Rajest, S. S., Tummala, R. K., & Thangadurai. (2021). Predicting network congestion with machine learning. In *2021 2nd International Conference on Smart Electronics and Communication (ICOSEC)*. IEEE.

Abbassy, M., & Abo-Alnadr, A. (2019). Rule-based emotion AI in Arabic customer review. *International Journal of Advanced Computer Science and Applications, 10*(9). doi:10.14569/ijacsa.2019.010093

Abbassy, M., & Ead, W. M. (2020). Intelligent Greenhouse Management System. In *2020 6th International Conference on Advanced Computing and Communication Systems (ICACCS)*. IEEE.

Abdalla, M. W., El Shal, S. M., El Sombaty, A. I., Abdalla, N. M., & Zeedan, R. B. (2015). Propofol dexmedetomidine versus propofol ketamine for anesthesia of endoscopic retrograde cholangiopancreatography (ERCP) (A randomised comparative study). *Egyptian Journal of Anaesthesia, 31*(2), 97–105. doi:10.1016/j.egja.2014.12.008

Abd-Almageed, E., Marwan, Y., Esmaeel, A., Mallur, A., & El-Alfy, B. (2015). Hybrid external fixation for Arbeitsgemeinschaft für Osteosynthesefragen (AO) 43-C tibial plafond fractures. *The Journal of Foot and Ankle Surgery: Official Publication of the American College of Foot and Ankle Surgeons, 54*(6), 1031–1036. doi:10.1053/j.jfas.2015.04.022 PMID:26215549

Abdelhaleem, F. S., Basiouny, M., Ashour, E., & Mahmoud, A. (2021). Application of remote sensing and geographic information systems in irrigation water management under water scarcity conditions in Fayoum, Egypt. *Journal of Environmental Management, 299*, 113683. doi:10.1016/j.jenvman.2021.113683 PMID:34526284

Access to Justice for Children in the era of Covid-19: Notes from the field. (2020). United Nations Children's Fund (UNICEF). Retrieved from https://www.unicef.org/media/92251/file/Access-to-Justice-COVID-19-Field-Notes-2021.pdf

Access to Justice, United Nations and the Rule of Law . (n.d.). United Nations. Retrieved from https://www.un.org/ruleoflaw/thematic-areas/access-to-justice-and-rule-of-law-institutions/access-to-justice/

Acharya, T. D., & Yang, I. (2004). Exploring Landsat 8. *Int. J. IT Eng. Appl. Sci. Res*, (4), 4–10.

Acharya, T., Lee, D., Yang, I., & Lee, J. (2016). Identification of water bodies in a Landsat 8 OLI image using a J48 decision tree. *Sensors (Basel), 16*(7), 1075. doi:10.339016071075 PMID:27420067

Aftab, M. U., Munir, Y., Oluwasanmi, A., Qin, Z., Aziz, M. H., Zakria, Son, N. T., & Tran, V. D. (2020). A hybrid access control model with dynamic COI for secure localization of satellite and IoT-based vehicles. *IEEE Access: Practical Innovations, Open Solutions, 8*, 24196–24208. 10.1109/ACCESS.2020.2969715

Agarkhed, J., Ashalatha, R., & Patil, S. R. (2019). Smart healthcare systems using cloud computing environments. In *Advances in Communication, Devices and Networking* (pp. 545–552). Springer Singapore. doi:10.1007/978-981-13-3450-4_59

Agarwal, G., Belhumeur, P., Feiner, S., Jacobs, D., Kress, W. J., Ramamoorthi, R., Bourg, N. A., Dixit, N., Ling, H., Mahajan, D., Russell, R., Shirdhonkar, S., Sunkavalli, K., & White, S. (2006). First steps toward an electronic field guide for plants. *Taxon*, *55*(3), 597–610. doi:10.2307/25065637

Ahammad, S. H., Rajesh, V., Rahman, M. Z. U., & Lay-Ekuakille, A. (2020). A hybrid CNN-based segmentation and boosting classifier for real time sensor spinal cord injury data. *IEEE Sensors Journal*, *20*(17), 10092–10101. doi:10.1109/JSEN.2020.2992879

Ahammad, T., Rahaman, H., Faisal, B. R., & Sultana, N. (2020). Model based change detection of water body using Landsat imagery: A case study of Rajshahi Bangladesh. *Environment and Natural Resources Journal*, *18*(4), 345–355.

Ahmed, H. M. A., El Gendy, M., Mirdan, A. M. H., Ali, A. A. M., & Haleem, F. S. F. A. (2014). Effect of corrugated beds on characteristics of submerged hydraulic jump. *Ain Shams Engineering Journal*, *5*(4), 1033–1042. doi:10.1016/j.asej.2014.06.006

Ahuja, V., Sharma, P., Gombar, S., Jain, A., & Dalal, U. (2017). Sevoflurane sparing effect of dexmedetomidine in patients undergoing laparoscopic cholecystectomy: A randomized controlled trial. *Journal of Anaesthesiology, Clinical Pharmacology*, *33*(4), 496. doi:10.4103/joacp.JOACP_144_16 PMID:29416243

Akgül, A. (2015). Artificial Intelligence Military Applications. *Journal of Ankara University Faculty of Political Sciences*, *45*(1), 255–271.

Alajrami, E., Bassem, S., Abu-Nasser, A. J., Khalil, M. M., Musleh, A. M., & Samy, S. (2019). Blood donation Prediction using Artificial Neural Network. *International Journal of Academic Engineering Research, 3*(10).

Alam Khan, Z., Feng, Z., Uddin, M. I., Mast, N., Ali Shah, S. A., Imtiaz, M., & Mahmoud, M. (2020). Optimal policy learning for disease prevention using reinforcement learning. *Scientific Programming*, *2020*, 1–13. doi:10.1155/2020/7627290

Alam, N. A., Ahsan, M., Based, M. A., & Haider, J. (2021). Intelligent System for Vehicles Number Plate Detection and Recognition Using Convolutional Neural Networks. *Technologies*, *9*(1), 9.

Alanazi, S. A., Kamruzzaman, M. M., Islam Sarker, M. N., Alruwaili, M., Alhwaiti, Y., Alshammari, N., & Siddiqi, M. H. (2021). Boosting breast cancer detection using convolutional neural network. *Journal of Healthcare Engineering*, *5528622*. Advance online publication. doi:10.1155/2021/5528622 PMID:33884157

Alarood, A. A., Alsolami, E., Al-Khasawneh, M. A., Ababneh, N., & Elmedany, W. (2022). IES: Hyper-chaotic plain image encryption scheme using improved shuffled confusion-diffusion. *Ain Shams Engineering Journal*, *13*(3), 101583. doi:10.1016/j.asej.2021.09.010

Al-batat, R., Angelopoulou, A., Premkumar, S., Hemanth, J., & Kapetanios, E. (2022). An End-to-End Automated License Plate Recognition System Using YOLO Based Vehicle and License Plate Detection with Vehicle Classification. *Sensors (Basel)*, *22*(23), 9477. PMID:36502178

Alfaifi, A. A., & Khan, S. G. (2022). Utilizing data from Twitter to explore the UX of "Madrasati" as a Saudi e-learning platform compelled by the pandemic. *Arab Gulf Journal of Scientific Research*, 200–208. doi:10.51758/AGJSR-03-2021-0025

Ali, H. M., El Gendy, M. M., Mirdan, A. M. H., Ali, A. A. M., & Abdelhaleem, F. S. F. (2014). Minimizing downstream scour due to submerged hydraulic jump using corrugated aprons. *Ain Shams Engineering Journal*, *5*(4), 1059–1069. doi:10.1016/j.asej.2014.07.007

Al-Khasawneh, M. A., Shamsuddin, S. M., Hasan, S., & Bakar, A. A. (2018). MapReduce a comprehensive review. In *2018 International Conference on Smart Computing and Electronic Enterprise (ICSCEE)* (pp. 1-6). IEEE.

Al-Otaibi, S., Al-Rasheed, A. A., AlHazza, B., Khan, H. A., & AlShfloot, G., AlFaris & AlShuweishi, N. (2022). Finding Influential Users in Social Networking using Sentiment Analysis. *Informatica (Vilnius)*, *46*(5).

Alpaydın, E. (2004). *Introduction to Machine Learning*. MIT Press.

Alsenan, S., Al-Turaiki, I., & Hafez, A. (2020). A Recurrent Neural Network model to predict blood-brain barrier permeability. *Computational Biology and Chemistry*, *89*(107377), 107377. doi:10.1016/j.compbiolchem.2020.107377 PMID:33010784

Anand, P. P., Kanike, U. K., Paramasivan, P., Rajest, S. S., Regin, R., & Priscila, S. S. (2023). Embracing Industry 5.0: Pioneering Next-Generation Technology for a Flourishing Human Experience and Societal Advancement. *FMDB Transactions on Sustainable Social Sciences Letters*, *1*(1), 43–55.

Andjelković, L., Novak-Janković, V., Požar-Lukanovič, N., Bosnić, Z., & Spindler-Vesel, A. (2018). Influence of dexmedetomidine and lidocaine on perioperative opioid consumption in laparoscopic intestine resection: A randomised controlled clinical trial. *The Journal of International Medical Research*, *46*(12), 5143–5154. doi:10.1177/0300060518792456 PMID:30209962

Arivazhagan, S., Shebiah, R. N., Ananthi, S., & Varthini, S. V. (2013). Detection of unhealthy region of plant leaves and classification of plant leaf diseases using texture features. *Agricultural Engineering International: CIGR Journal*, *15*, 211–217.

Arslan, F., Singh, B., Sharma, D. K., Regin, R., Steffi, R., & Suman Rajest, S. (2021). Optimization technique approach to resolve food sustainability problems. In *2021 International Conference on Computational Intelligence and Knowledge Economy (ICCIKE)*. IEEE. 10.1109/ICCIKE51210.2021.9410735

Arunadevi, B., Saravanan, D., Villallba-Condori, K., Srivastava, K., Chakravarthi, M. K., & Rajan, R. (2021). Orthographic comparison revealed by ambient sentiment classification. *2021 5th International Conference on Electronics, Communication and Aerospace Technology (ICECA)*.

Ashour, E. H., Ahemd, S. E., Elsayed, S. M., Basiouny, M. E., & Abdelhaleem, F. S. (2021). Integrating geographic information system, remote sensing, and Modeling to enhance reliability of irrigation network. *Water and Energy International*, *64*(1), 6–13.

Athanikar, G., & Badar, P. (2016). Potato leaf diseases detection and classification system. *Int. J. Comput. Sci. Mob. Comput.*, *5*, 76–88.

Backes, A. R., de M. Sá Junior, J. J., Kolb, R. M., & Bruno, O. M. (2009). Plant species identification using multi-scale fractal dimension applied to images of adaxial surface epidermis. In Computer Analysis of Images and Patterns (pp. 680–688). Springer Berlin Heidelberg.

Backes, A. R., Casanova, D., & Bruno, O. M. (2009). Plant leaf identification based on volumetric fractal dimension. *International Journal of Pattern Recognition and Artificial Intelligence*, *23*(06), 1145–1160. doi:10.1142/S0218001409007508

Back, S. A., & Rivkees, S. A. (2004). Emerging concepts in periventricular white matter injury. *Seminars in Perinatology*, *28*(6), 405–414. doi:10.1053/j.semperi.2004.10.010 PMID:15693397

Bagal, V. C., & Manza, R. R. (2016). Feature extraction of plant species from leaf architecture. In *2016 International Conference on Electrical, Electronics, and Optimization Techniques (ICEEOT)*. IEEE. 10.1109/ICEEOT.2016.7755481

Bajwa, S. J. S., Kaur, J., Singh, A., Parmar, S., Singh, G., Kulshrestha, A., Gupta, S., Sharma, V., & Panda, A. (2012). Attenuation of pressor response and dose sparing of opioids and anaesthetics with pre-operative dexmedetomidine. *Indian Journal of Anaesthesia*, *56*(2), 123–128. doi:10.4103/0019-5049.96303 PMID:22701201

Bambodkar, P. R., Rahangdale, K., Dhenge, S. V., & Gondane, N. V. (2022). Helmet detection using Machine learning and automatic License Plate recognition. International Journal of Advanced Research in Science. *Tongxin Jishu*, *514–517*. Advance online publication. doi:10.48175/ijarsct-5495

Bansal, V., Pandey, S., Shukla, S. K., Singh, D., Rathod, S. A., & Gonzáles, J. L. A. (2022). A frame work of security attacks, issues classifications and configuration strategy for IoT networks for the successful implementation. In *2022 5th International Conference on Contemporary Computing and Informatics (IC3I)*. IEEE.

Bansal, P., Kumar, R., & Kumar, S. (2021). Disease detection in apple leaves using deep convolutional neural network. *Agriculture*, *11*(7), 617. doi:10.3390/agriculture11070617

Bansal, T., Juan, D.-C., Ravi, S., & McCallum, A. (2019). A2N: Attending to neighbors for knowledge graph inference. *Proceedings of the 57th Annual Meeting of the Association for Computational Linguistics*, 4387–4392. 10.18653/v1/P19-1431

Banu, A., Naidu, S. M., Vinjamuri, S. N., Dattu, G., Sridevi, M., & Chakravarthi, N. R. (2022). Experimentally investigating the influence of static mixers on the performance of a solar water heater. *Materials Today: Proceedings*, *62*(4), 2370–2375. doi:10.1016/j.matpr.2022.04.851

Barbedo Arnal, J. G. (2014). An Automatic Method to Detect and Measure Leaf Disease Symptoms Using Digital Image Processing. *Plant Disease*, *98*(12), 1709–1716. doi:10.1094/PDIS-03-14-0290-RE PMID:30703885

Barbedo Arnal, J. G. (2017). A new automatic method for disease symptom segmentation in digital photographs of plant leaves. *European Journal of Plant Pathology*, *147*(2), 349–364. doi:10.100710658-016-1007-6

Barua, R., & Mondal, J. (2022). Study of the Current Trends of CAD (Computer-Aided Detection) in Modern Medical Imaging. *Machine Learning and AI Techniques in Interactive Medical Image Analysis*, 35.

Barua, R., Das, S., & Mondal, J. (2022). Emerging Applications of Artificial Intelligence (AI) and Machine Learning (ML) in Modern Urology. *Exploring the Convergence of Computer and Medical Science Through Cloud Healthcare*, 117.

Barua, R., Das, S., Datta, S., Datta, P., & Roy Chowdhury, A. (2022). Study and experimental investigation of insertion force modeling and tissue deformation phenomenon during surgical needle-soft tissue interaction. *Proceedings of the Institution of Mechanical Engineers, Part C: Journal of Mechanical Engineering Science*. 10.1177/09544062221126628

Barua, R., Das, S., Datta, S., Roy Chowdhury, A., & Datta, P. (2022). Experimental study of the robotically controlled surgical needle insertion for analysis of the minimum invasive process. In *Emergent Converging Technologies and Biomedical Systems: Select Proceedings of ETBS 2021* (pp. 473-482). Springer Singapore. 10.1007/978-981-16-8774-7_38

Barua, R., Datta, P., Datta, S., & Roychowdhury, A. (2021). Study and Application of Machine Learning Methods in Modern Additive Manufacturing Processes. *Applications of Artificial Intelligence in Additive Manufacturing*, 75.

Barua, R., Datta, S., & Banerjee, D. (2022). Computational Study of In-Vivo CT-Based FEM Application in Bone Tissue Engineering. In Technological Adoption and Trends in Health Sciences Teaching, Learning, and Practice (pp. 300-316). IGI Global. doi:10.4018/978-1-7998-8871-0.ch014

Barua, R., Bhowmik, S., Dey, A., & Mondal, J. (2023). Advances of the Robotics Technology in Modern Minimally Invasive Surgery. In *Design and Control Advances in Robotics* (pp. 91–104). IGI Global.

Barua, R., & Das, S. (2022). Improvements of Virtual and Augmented Reality for Advanced Treatments in Urology. In *Emerging Advancements for Virtual and Augmented Reality in Healthcare* (pp. 117–131). IGI Global. doi:10.4018/978-1-7998-8371-5.ch008

Barua, R., Das, S., Datta, S., Datta, P., & Roy Chowdhury, A. (2022). Analysis of surgical needle insertion modeling and viscoelastic tissue material interaction for minimally invasive surgery (MIS). *Materials Today: Proceedings, 57*, 259–264. doi:10.1016/j.matpr.2022.02.498

Barua, R., Das, S., Roy Chowdhury, A., & Datta, P. (2023). Experimental and simulation investigation of surgical needle insertion into soft tissue mimic biomaterial for minimally invasive surgery (MIS). *Proceedings of the Institution of Mechanical Engineers. Part H, Journal of Engineering in Medicine, 237*(2), 254–264. doi:10.1177/09544119221143860 PMID:36527297

Barua, R., Das, S., Roy Chowdhury, A., & Datta, P. (2023, January). Roy Chowdhury, A., & Datta, P. (2022). Simulation and experimental investigation of the surgical needle deflection model during the rotational and steady insertion process. *The International Journal of Artificial Organs, 46*(1), 40–51. Advance online publication. doi:10.1177/03913988221136154 PMID:36397288

Barua, R., Giria, H., Datta, S., Roy Chowdhury, A., & Datta, P. (2020). Force modeling to develop a novel method for fabrication of hollow channels inside a gel structure. *Proceedings of the Institution of Mechanical Engineers. Part H, Journal of Engineering in Medicine, 234*(2), 223–231. doi:10.1177/0954411919891654 PMID:31774361

Bayram, F. (2020). Automatic License Plate Recognition Based on Deep Learning. *Politeknik Dergisi, 23*(4), 955–960.

Bendes, E., & Aslantas, V. (2015). The sum of the correlations of differences is a new picture quality metric for image fusion. *AEÜ. International Journal of Electronics and Communications, 69*(12), 1890–1896. doi:10.1016/j.aeue.2015.09.004

Bernitz, S., Øian, P., Rolland, R., Sandvik, L., & Blix, E. (2014). Oxytocin and dystocia as risk factors for adverse birth outcomes: A cohort of low-risk nulliparous women. *Midwifery, 30*(3), 364–370. doi:10.1016/j.midw.2013.03.010 PMID:23684697

Bhattacharya, D. (2021). *Making migrants count: The role of Indian Judiciary amid Covid-19 pandemic*. Retrieved from Down to Earth: https://www.downtoearth.org.in/blog/economy/making-migrants-count-the-role-of-indian-judiciary-amid-covid-19-pandemic-78548

Bhatt, D., Patel, C., Talsania, H., Patel, J., Vaghela, R., Pandya, S., & Ghayvat, H. (2021). CNN variants for computer vision: History, architecture, application, challenges and future scope. *Electronics (Basel), 10*(20), 2470.

Bhikshapathi, K., & Haribabu, D. (2016). Detection of license plate number using dynamic image processing technique. International Journal of Engineering and Computer Science. doi:10.18535/ijecs/v4i12.41

Bielsa, V. F. (2021). Virtual reality simulation in plastic surgery training. Literature review. *Journal of Plastic, Reconstructive & Aesthetic Surgery; JPRAS, 74*(9), 2372–2378. doi:10.1016/j.bjps.2021.03.066 PMID:33972199

Billah, S. N., Pollobe, R., Hossain, F., Abir, N. M., Zarin, A. Z., & Mridha, M. F. (2021). Blockchain based architecture for certificate authentication. SSRN *Electronic Journal*. doi:10.2139/ssrn.3842788

Bishop, C. M. (2006). *Pattern Recognition and Machine Learning*. Springer.

Blair, A., Duguid, P., Goeing, A. S., & Grafton, A. (2021). *Information: A Historical Companion*. Princeton University Press. doi:10.1515/9780691209746

Bleakley, C. (2020). *Poems that Solve Puzzles: The History and Science of Algorithms*. Oxford University Press. doi:10.1093/oso/9780198853732.001.0001

Blood disorder types, symptoms, and treatments. (n.d.). Retrieved July 31, 2023, from WebMD website: https://www.webmd.com/cancer/lymphoma/blood-disorder-types-and-treatment

Boenigk, K., Echevarria, G. C., Nisimov, E., von Bergen Granell, A. E., Cuff, G. E., Wang, J., & Atchabahian, A. (2019). Low-dose ketamine infusion reduces postoperative hydromorphone requirements in opioid-tolerant patients following spinal fusion: A randomised controlled trial: A randomised controlled trial. *European Journal of Anaesthesiology*, *36*(1), 8–15. doi:10.1097/EJA.0000000000000877 PMID:30113350

Boll, S., & Meyer, J. (2022). Health-X dataLOFT: A sovereign federated cloud for personalized health care services. *IEEE MultiMedia*, *29*(1), 136–140. doi:10.1109/MMUL.2022.3153121

Bonnevier, A., Maršál, K., Brodszki, J., Thuring, A., & Källén, K. (2021). Cerebroplacental ratio as predictor of adverse perinatal outcome in the third trimester. *Acta Obstetricia et Gynecologica Scandinavica*, *100*(3), 497–503. doi:10.1111/aogs.14031 PMID:33078387

Bordes, A., Usunier, N., Garcia-Duran, A., Weston, J., & Yakhnenko, O. (2013). Translating embeddings for modeling multi-relational data. *Advances in Neural Information Processing Systems*, 26.

Borens, O., Kloen, P., Richmond, J., Roederer, G., Levine, D. S., & Helfet, D. L. (2009). Minimally invasive treatment of pilon fractures with a low profile plate: Preliminary results in 17 cases. *Archives of Orthopaedic and Trauma Surgery*, *129*(5), 649–659. doi:10.100700402-006-0219-1 PMID:16951937

Boulent, J., Foucher, S., Théau, J., & St-Charles, P.-L. (2019). Convolutional Neural Networks for the automatic identification of plant diseases. *Frontiers in Plant Science*, *10*, 941. doi:10.3389/fpls.2019.00941 PMID:31396250

Bowie, J. D., Kirks, D. R., Rosenberg, E. R., & Clair, M. R. (1983). Caudothalamic groove: Value in identification of germinal matrix hemorrhage by sonography in preterm neonates. *AJR. American Journal of Roentgenology*, *141*(6), 1317–1320. doi:10.2214/ajr.141.6.1317 PMID:6606337

Bozinovski, S. (2014). Modeling mechanisms of cognition-emotion interaction in artificial neural networks, since 1981. *Procedia Computer Science*, *41*, 255–263. doi:10.1016/j.procs.2014.11.111

Brynielsson, J. (2007). Using AI and Games For Decision Support in Command and Control. *Decision Support Systems*, *43*(4), 1454–1463. doi:10.1016/j.dss.2006.06.012

Buch, V. H., Ahmed, I., & Maruthappu, M. (2018). Artificial intelligence in medicine: Current trends and future possibilities. *The British Journal of General Practice*, *68*(668), 143–144. doi:10.3399/bjgp18X695213 PMID:29472224

Buddhi, D., Varghese, L. J., Neeraja, Hamid, S. S., Ramya, D., & Chakravarthi, M. K. (2022). Harmonic Distortion reduction in Power System to improve Reliability and power quality. *2022 International Conference on Innovative Computing, Intelligent Communication and Smart Electrical Systems (ICSES)*. 10.1109/ICSES55317.2022.9914129

Buragadda, S., Rani, K. S., Vasantha, S. V., & Chakravarthi, M. K. (2022). HCUGAN: Hybrid Cyclic UNET GAN for Generating Augmented Synthetic Images of Chest X-Ray Images for Multi Classification of Lung Diseases. *International Journal of Engineering Trends and Technology*, *70*(2), 229–238. doi:10.14445/22315381/IJETT-V70I2P227

Busso, C., Bulut, M., Lee, C. C., Kazemzadeh, A., Mower, E., Kim, S., ... Narayanan, S. S. (2008). IEMOCAP: Interactive emotional dyadic motion capture database. *Language Resources and Evaluation*, *42*, 335–359.

Bzdok, D., Altman, N., & Krzywinski, M. (2018). Statistics Versus Machine Learning. *Nature Methods*, *15*(4), 233–234. doi:10.1038/nmeth.4642 PMID:30100822

Cai, G., & Xia, B. (2015). Convolutional neural networks for multimedia sentiment analysis. *Natural Language Processing and Chinese Computing: 4th CCF Conference, NLPCC 2015, Nanchang, China, October 9-13, 2015 Proceedings*, *4*, 159–167.

Cao, S., Zhang, X., & Xu, R. (2020). Toward secure storage in cloud-based eHealth systems: A blockchain-assisted approach. *IEEE Network*, *34*(2), 64–70. doi:10.1109/MNET.001.1900173

Carta, S., Giuliani, A., Piano, L., Podda, A.S., Pompianu, L., & Tiddia, S.G. (2023). *Iterative Zero-Shot LLM Prompting for Knowledge Graph Construction*. arXiv Prepr. arXiv2307.01128.

Çeçen, G. S., Gülabi, D., Yanık, E., Pehlivanoğlu, G., Bekler, H., & Elmalı, N. (2014). Effect of BMI on the clinical and radiological outcomes of pilon fractures. *Acta Orthopaedica et Traumatologica Turcica*, *48*(5), 570–575. doi:10.3944/AOTT.2014.14.0073 PMID:25429585

Cerutti, G., Tougne, L., Vacavant, A., & Coquin, D. (2011). A parametric active polygon for leaf segmentation and shape estimation. In *Advances in Visual Computing* (pp. 202–213). Springer Berlin Heidelberg. doi:10.1007/978-3-642-24028-7_19

Chakravarthi, M. K., & Venkatesan, N. (2021). Experimental Transfer Function Based Multi-Loop Adaptive Shinskey PI Control For High Dimensional MIMO Systems. *Journal of Engineering Science and Technology*, *16*(5), 4006–4015.

Chandrasekaran, G., Nguyen, T. N., & Hemanth, D. J. (2021). Multi-modal sentimental analysis for social media applications: A comprehensive review. *Wiley Interdisciplinary Reviews. Data Mining and Knowledge Discovery*, *11*(5), e1415.

Chang, Y-W., Johnson, M. (2001). *Portable Concealed Weapon Detection Using Millimeter Wave FMCW Radar Imaging*. 189918: August 30, 1998-DT-CXK001.

Chatterjee, S. K., Das, S., Maharatna, K., Masi, E., Santopolo, L., Mancuso, S., & Vitaletti, A. (2015). Exploring strategies for classification of external stimuli using statistical features of the plant electrical response. *Journal of the Royal Society, Interface*, *12*(104), 20141225. doi:10.1098/rsif.2014.1225 PMID:25631569

Chatterjee, S. K., Malik, O., & Gupta, S. (2018). Chemical sensing employing plant electrical signal response-classification of stimuli using curve fitting coefficients as features. *Biosensors (Basel)*, *8*(3), 83. Advance online publication. doi:10.3390/bios8030083 PMID:30201898

Chaudhary, J. K., Sharma, H., Tadiboina, S. N., Singh, R., Khan, M. S., & Garg, A. (2023). Applications of Machine Learning in Viral Disease Diagnosis. In *2023 10th International Conference on Computing for Sustainable Global Development (INDIACom)* (pp. 1167-1172). IEEE.

Chen, F., Tang, Y., Wang, C., Huang, J., Huang, C., Xie, D., & Zhao, C. (2021). Medical cyber–physical systems: A solution to smart health and the state of the art. *IEEE Transactions on Computational Social Systems*, *9*(5), 1359–1386. doi:10.1109/TCSS.2021.3122807

Chen, H.-M., Lee, S., Rao, R. M., Slamani, M.-A., & Varshney, P. K. (2005). Imaging for concealed weapon detection: A tutorial overview of development in imaging sensors and processing. *IEEE Signal Processing Magazine*, *22*(2), 52–61. doi:10.1109/MSP.2005.1406480

Chenthara, S., Ahmed, K., Wang, H., & Whittaker, F. (2019). Security and privacy-preserving challenges of e-health solutions in cloud computing. *IEEE Access : Practical Innovations, Open Solutions*, *7*, 74361–74382. doi:10.1109/ACCESS.2019.2919982

Chiao, J. Y., Chen, K. Y., Liao, K., Hsieh, P. H., & Zhang, G. (2019). Detection and classification the breast tumors using mask R-CNN on sonograms. *Medicine*, *98*(19). PMID:31083152

Chignell, S., Anderson, R., & Evangelista, P. (2015). Multi-temporal independent component analysis and Landsat 8 for delineating maximum extent of the 2013 Colorado front range flood. *Remote Sensing, 7*, 9822–9843.

Choudhary, N., & Reddy, C.K. (2023). *Complex Logical Reasoning over Knowledge Graphs using Large Language Models.* arXiv Prepr. arXiv2305.01157.

Choudhary, V. (2020). *Denial of Treatment to Covid-19 Patients is a Human Rights Abuse.* Retrieved from Human Rights Pulse: https://www.humanrightspulse.com/mastercontentblog/denial-of-treatment-to-covid-19-patients-is-a-human-rights-abuse

Chu, C., De Fauw, J., Tomasev, N., Paredes, B. R., Hughes, C., Ledsam, J., Back, T., Montgomery, H., Rees, G., Raine, R., Sullivan, K., Moinuddin, S., D'Souza, D., Ronneberger, O., Mendes, R., & Cornebise, J. (2016). Applying machine learning to automated segmentation of head and neck tumour volumes and organs at risk on radiotherapy planning CT and MRI scans. *F1000 Research, 5*(2104), 2104. doi:10.12688/f1000research.9525.1

Cirillo, S., Polese, G., Salerno, D., Simone, B., & Solimando, G. (2023). Towards Flexible Voice Assistants: Evaluating Privacy and Security Needs in IoT-enabled Smart Homes. *FMDB Transactions on Sustainable Computer Letters, 1*(1), 25–32.

Clarke, C. C. (n.d.). In Harm's way: AMA Physicians and the Duty to Treat. *The Journal of Medicine and Philosophy of Medicine, 30*(1). Retrieved from https://academic.oup.com/jmp/article-abstract/30/1/65/893497?redirectedFrom=fulltext

Cohen, W. R., & Friedman, E. A. (2015). Perils of the new labor management guidelines. *American Journal of Obstetrics and Gynecology, 212*(4), 420–427. doi:10.1016/j.ajog.2014.09.008 PMID:25218127

Conde-Agudelo, A., Villar, J., Kennedy, S. H., & Papageorghiou, A. T. (2018). Predictive accuracy of cerebroplacental ratio for adverse perinatal and neurodevelopmental outcomes in suspected fetal growth restriction: systematic review and meta-analysis: CPR predicts perinatal death in suspected FGR. *Ultrasound in Obstetrics & Gynecology, 52*(4), 430–441. doi:10.1002/uog.19117 PMID:29920817

Cordeiro, M. C., Martinez, J. M., & Peña-Luque, S. (2021). Automatic water detection from multidimensional hierarchical clustering for Sentinel-2 images and a comparison with Level 2A processors. *Remote Sensing of Environment, 253*, 1–46.

Cordero, P., Li, J., & Oben, J. A. (2017). Bariatric surgery as a treatment for metabolic syndrome. *Journal of the Royal College of Physicians of Edinburgh, 47*(4), 364–368. doi:10.4997/jrcpe.2017.414 PMID:29537411

Cortes, C., & Vapnik, V. N. (1995). Support-vector networks. *Machine Learning, 20*(3), 273–297. doi:10.1007/BF00994018

Craniosacral rhythm. (2018). *John Dalton Therapy.* https://www.johndaltontherapy.com/craniosacral-rhythm/

Creed, L., & Haber, K. (1984). Ultrasonic evaluation of the infant head. *Critical Reviews in Diagnostic Imaging, 21*(1), 37–84. PMID:6373149

Cyrus R. Vance Center for International Justice, H. R. (n.d.). *Women in Prison Amid Covid-19 Open Letters to the African Commission on Human and Peoples' Rights and the Inter-American Commission on Human Rights.* Vance Center for International Justice. Retrieved from https://www.vancecenter.org/areas-of-practice/human-rights-and-access-to-justice/

Das, R., Dhuliawala, S., Zaheer, M., Vilnis, L., Durugkar, I., Krishnamurthy, A., Smola, A., & McCallum, A. (2017). *Go for a walk and arrive at the answer: Reasoning over paths in knowledge bases using reinforcement learning.* arXiv Prepr. arXiv1711.05851.

Das, K., Conjeti, S., Chatterjee, J., & Sheet, D. (2020). Detection of breast cancer from whole slide histopathological images using deep multiple instance CNN. *IEEE Access : Practical Innovations, Open Solutions, 8*, 213502–213511.

Datta, S., Barua, R., & Das, J. (2019). Application of artificial intelligence in modern healthcare system. *Alginates-recent uses of this natural polymer.*

De-las-Heras-Romero, J., Lledo-Alvarez, A. M., Lizaur-Utrilla, A., & Lopez-Prats, F. A. (2017). Quality of life and prognostic factors after intra-articular tibial pilon fracture. *Injury, 48*(6), 1258–1263. doi:10.1016/j.injury.2017.03.023 PMID:28365069

Deranty, J.-P. (2016). Social Justice. *The International Encyclopedia of Political Communication.* Retrieved from https://www.researchgate.net/publication/314581421_Social_Justice

DeReuck, J. L. (1984). Cerebral angioarchitecture and perinatal brain lesions in premature and full term infants. *Acta Neurologica Scandinavica, 70*(6), 391–395. doi:10.1111/j.1600-0404.1984.tb00843.x PMID:6516787

Derindere Köseoğlu, S., Ead, W. M., & Abbassy, M. M. (2022). Basics of Financial Data Analytics. In *Financial Data Analytics* (pp. 23–57). Springer International Publishing. doi:10.1007/978-3-030-83799-0_2

Deshpande, T. D., Kumar, S., Begum, G., Basha, S. A. K., & Rao, B. H. (2021). Analysis of railway embankment supported with geosynthetic-encased stone columns in soft clays: A case study. *International Journal of Geosynthetics and Ground Engineering, 7*(2), 43. Advance online publication. doi:10.100740891-021-00288-5

Dettmers, T., Minervini, P., Stenetorp, P., & Riedel, S. (2018). Convolutional 2d knowledge graph embeddings. *Proceedings of the AAAI Conference on Artificial Intelligence.*

DeVlieger, M., & Ridder, H. J. (1959). Use of echoencephalography. *Neurology, 9*(4), 216–223. doi:10.1212/WNL.9.4.216 PMID:13644550

DeVore, G. R. (2015). The importance of the cerebroplacental ratio in the evaluation of fetal well-being in SGA and AGA fetuses. *American Journal of Obstetrics and Gynecology, 213*(1), 5–15. doi:10.1016/j.ajog.2015.05.024 PMID:26113227

Divya, L., Karthi, R., & Geetha, P. (2018). Temporal Change Detection in Water Body of Puzhal Lake Using Satellite Images. In *International Conference On Computational Vision and Bio Inspired Computing* (pp. 1229–1237). Cham: Springer.

Diwedar, A. I., Abdelhaleem, F. S., & Ali, A. M. (2019). Wave parameters influence on breakwater stability. *IOP Conference Series. Earth and Environmental Science, 326*(1), 012013. doi:10.1088/1755-1315/326/1/012013

Du, Z., Bin, L., Ling, F., Li, W., Tian, W., Wang, H., & Zhang, X. (2012). Estimating surface water area changes using time-series Landsat data in the Qingjiang River Basin, China". China. *Journal of Applied Remote Sensing, 6*(1), 1–17.

Du, Z., Li, W., Zhou, D., Tian, L., Ling, F., Wang, H., & Sun, B. (2014). Analysis of Landsat-8 OLI imagery for land surface water mapping. *Remote Sensing Letters, 5*(7), 672–681. doi:10.1080/2150704x.2014.960606

Dwivedi, P. P., & Sharma, D. K. (2021). Lower and upper bounds for 'useful' Renyi information rate. In *Communications in Computer and Information Science* (pp. 271–280). Springer International Publishing.

Ead, W., & Abbassy, M. (2018). Intelligent systems of machine learning approaches for developing E-services portals. *EAI Endorsed Transactions on Energy Web, 167292.* Advance online publication. doi:10.4108/eai.2-12-2020.167292

El Sharkawy, R. A. (2019). Efficacy of adding low-dose ketamine to dexmedetomidine versus low-dose ketamine and propofol for conscious sedation in patients undergoing awake fiber-optic intubation. *Anesthesia, Essays and Researches, 13*(1), 73–78. doi:10.4103/aer.AER_181_18 PMID:31031484

Ellis, T. D., Cavanaugh, J. T., DeAngelis, T., Hendron, K., Thomas, C. A., Saint-Hilaire, M., Pencina, K., & Latham, N. K. (2019). Comparative Effectiveness of mHealth-Supported Exercise Compared With Exercise Alone for People With Parkinson Disease: Randomized Controlled Pilot Study. *Physical Therapy*, *99*(2), 203–216. doi:10.1093/ptj/pzy131 PMID:30715489

Elsner, J., Fritz, T., Henke, L., Jarrousse, O., Taing, S., & Uhlenbrock, M. (2018). Automatic Weapon Detection in Social Media Image Data using a Two-Pass Convolutional Neural Network. *European Law Enforcement Research Bulletin*, (4), 61-65. Retrieved from http://bulletin.cepol.europa.eu/index.php/bulletin/article/view/323

Enes, K. (2017, February 2). Algoritma Nedir? https://www.eneskamis.com/%EF%BB%BFalgoritma-nedir-algoritma-ne-ise-yarar

Ergen, M. (2019). What is Artificial Intelligence? Technical Considerations and Future Perception. *The Anatolian Journal of Cardiology*, *22*(2), 5–7. doi:10.14744/AnatolJCardiol.2019.79091 PMID:31670719

Esmaeili, M., Naderi, B., Neyestanaki, H. K., & Khodaverdian, A. (2018). Investigating the effect of geogrid on stabilization of high railway embankments. *Soil and Foundation*, *58*(2), 319–332. doi:10.1016/j.sandf.2018.02.005

Esteva, A., Kuprel, B., Novoa, R. A., Ko, J., Swetter, S. M., Blau, H. M., & Thrun, S. (2017). Dermatologist-level classification of skin cancer with deep neural networks. *Nature*, *542*(7639), 115–118. doi:10.1038/nature21056 PMID:28117445

Fabela, O., Patil, S., Chintamani, S., & Dennis, B. H. (2017). *Estimation of effective thermal conductivity of porous media utilizing inverse heat transfer analysis on cylindrical configuration* (Vol. 8). Heat Transfer and Thermal Engineering. doi:10.1115/IMECE2017-71559

Fan, S., Song, Z., Xu, T., Wang, K., & Zhang, Y. (2021). Tunnel deformation and stress response under the bilateral foundation pit construction: A case study. *Archives of Civil and Mechanical Engineering*, *21*(3), 109. Advance online publication. doi:10.100743452-021-00259-7

Farris, A. B., Vizcarra, J., Amgad, M., Cooper, L. A. D., Gutman, D., & Hogan, J. (2021). Artificial intelligence and algorithmic computational pathology: An introduction with renal allograft examples. *Histopathology*, *78*(6), 791–804. doi:10.1111/his.14304 PMID:33211332

Fassnacht, F. E., Latifi, H., Stereńczak, K., Modzelewska, A., Lefsky, M., Waser, L. T., Straub, C., & Ghosh, A. (2016). Review of studies on tree species classification from remotely sensed data. *Remote Sensing of Environment*, *186*, 64–87. doi:10.1016/j.rse.2016.08.013

Fattah, M. Y., Mahmood, M. R., & Aswad, M. F. (2018). Experimental and numerical behavior of railway track over geogrid reinforced ballast underlain by soft clay. In *Sustainable Civil Infrastructures* (pp. 1–26). Springer International Publishing.

Fattah, M. Y., Mahmood, M. R., & Aswad, M. F. (2019). Stress distribution from railway track over geogrid reinforced ballast underlain by clay. *Earthquake Engineering and Engineering Vibration*, *18*(1), 77–93. doi:10.100711803-019-0491-z

Fazil, M., Khan, S., Albahlal, B. M., Alotaibi, R. M., Siddiqui, T., & Shah, M. A. (2023). Attentional Multi-Channel Convolution With Bidirectional LSTM Cell Toward Hate Speech Prediction. *IEEE Access : Practical Innovations, Open Solutions*, *11*, 16801–16811. doi:10.1109/ACCESS.2023.3246388

Feng, Q., Dongxia, L., Bingda, S., Liu, R., Zhanhong, M., & Haiguang, W. (2016). Identification of Alfalfa Leaf Diseases Using Image Recognition Technology. *PLoS One*, 11. PMID:27977767

Fonseka, O. D., & Sasanka, N. (2018). Blind Draw-A software solution for image identification and artistic skills for visually impaired people using braille. In *2018 3rd International Conference on Information Technology Research (ICITR)* (pp. 1–6). IEEE.

Friedman, E. A., & Kroll, B. H. (1971). Computer analysis of labor progression. 3. Pattern variations by parity. *The Journal of Reproductive Medicine, 6*(4), 179–183. PMID:4938465

Friedman, J. H. (1998). Data Mining and Statistics: What's the connection? *Computing Science and Statistics., 29*(1), 3–9.

Fritz, J. (2021). Automated and Radiation-Free Generation of Synthetic CT from MRI Data: Does AI Help to Cross the Finish Line? *Radiology, 298*(2), 350–352. doi:10.1148/radiol.2020204045 PMID:33355510

Fu, H., & Chi, Z. (2006). Combined thresholding and neural network approach for vein pattern extraction from leaf images. *IEE Proceedings. Vision Image and Signal Processing, 153*(6), 881. doi:10.1049/ip-vis:20060061

Galárraga, L. A., Teflioudi, C., Hose, K., & Suchanek, F. (2013). LEI. *Proceedings of the 22nd International Conference on World Wide Web,* 413–422.

Gandhi, A., Adhvaryu, K., Poria, S., Cambria, E., & Hussain, A. (2022). Multi-modal sentiment analysis: A systematic review of history, datasets, multi-modal fusion methods, applications, challenges and future directions. *Information Fusion*. Advance online publication. doi:10.1016/j.inffus.2022.09.025

Gan, G., Chen, E., Zhou, Z., & Zhu, Y. (2020). Token-Based Access Control. *IEEE Access : Practical Innovations, Open Solutions, 8*, 54189–54199. doi:10.1109/ACCESS.2020.2979746

Gao, J., French, A. P., Pound, M. P., He, Y., Pridmore, T. P., & Pieters, J. G. (2020). Deep convolutional neural networks for image-based Convolvulus sepium detection in sugar beet fields. *Plant Methods, 16*(1), 29. doi:10.118613007-020-00570-z PMID:32165909

Garba, A., Chen, Z., Guan, Z., & Srivastava, G. (2021). LightLedger: A novel blockchain-based domain certificate authentication and validation scheme. *IEEE Transactions on Network Science and Engineering, 8*(2), 1698–1710. doi:10.1109/TNSE.2021.3069128

Garcia-Barreda, S., Sangüesa-Barreda, G., García-González, M. D., & Camarero, J. J. (2022). Sex and tree rings: Females neither grow less nor are less water-use efficient than males in four dioecious tree species. *Dendrochronologia, 73*(125944), 125944. doi:10.1016/j.dendro.2022.125944

Gardner, M. J., Mehta, S., Barei, D. P., & Nork, S. E. (2008). Treatment protocol for open AO/OTA type C3 Pilon fractures with segmental bone loss. *Journal of Orthopaedic Trauma, 22*(7), 451–457. doi:10.1097/bot.0b013e318176b8d9 PMID:18670284

Gayakwad, M., Patil, S., Joshi, R., Gonge, S., & Pande, S. D. (2022). Credibility Evaluation of User-Generated Content Using Novel Multinomial Classification Technique. *International Journal on Recent and Innovation Trends in Computing and Communication, 10*(2s, no. 2s), 151–157. doi:10.17762/ijritcc.v10i2s.5922

Gayathiri, A., Jayachitra, J., & Matilda, S. (2020). Certificate validation using blockchain. In *2020 7th International Conference on Smart Structures and Systems (ICSSS)*. IEEE.

Gesick, R., Saritac, C., & Hung, C.-C. (2009). Automatic image analysis process for the detection of concealed weapons. *Proceedings of the 5th Annual Workshop on Cyber Security and Information Intelligence Research: Cyber Security and Information Intelligence Challenges and Strategies.* 10.1145/1558607.1558630

Ghaffari, F., Bertin, E., Crespi, N., Behrad, S., & Hatin, J. (2021). A novel access control method via smart contracts for internet-based service provisioning. *IEEE Access : Practical Innovations, Open Solutions, 9*, 81253–81273. doi:10.1109/ACCESS.2021.3085831

Ghamar-Chehreh, M. E., Khedmat, H., Amini, M., & Taheri, S. (2012). Predictive Factors for Ultrasonographic Grading of Nonalcoholic Fatty Liver Disease. *Hepatitis Monthly, 12*(11), e6860. PMID:23346150

Gnanaprakash, V., Kanthimathi, N., & Saranya, N. (2021). Automatic number plate recognition using deep learning. *IOP Conference Series. Materials Science and Engineering, 1084*(1), 012027.

Godoy-Matos, A. F., Silva Júnior, W. S., & Valerio, C. M. (2020). NAFLD as a continuum: From obesity to metabolic syndrome and diabetes. *Diabetology & Metabolic Syndrome, 12*(1), 60. doi:10.118613098-020-00570-y PMID:32684985

Goeau, H., Bonnet, P., & Joly, A. (2016). Plant identification in an open-world. In Working Notes of CLEF 2016-Conference and Labs of the Eval- uation forum (pp. 428–439). Academic Press.

Gonçalves, C. B., Souza, J. R., & Fernandes, H. (2022). CNN optimization using surrogate evolutionary algorithm for breast cancer detection using infrared images. In *2022 IEEE 35th International Symposium on Computer-Based Medical Systems (CBMS).* IEEE.

Gonzalez, R. C., & Woods, R. E. (2002). *Digital image processing* (2nd ed.). Prentice-Hall.

Gosain, S. (2021). Concealed weapon detection using image processing and machine learning. *International Journal for Research in Applied Science and Engineering Technology, 9*(12), 1374–1384. doi:10.22214/ijraset.2021.39506

Govaert, P., & DeVries, L. S. (2010). An atlas of neonatal brain sonography (2nd ed.). MacKeith Press.

Gowtham, S., Ch, T., Kumar, N. S. M. P., Devi, M., Chakravarthi, S., Kumar, R., Harishchander Anandaram, N. M., & Kumar, K. (2022). A Survey on Additively Manufactured Nanocomposite Biomaterial for Orthopaedic Applications. *Journal of Nanomaterials, 2022*, 2022. doi:10.1155/2022/8998451

Grega, M., Matiolański, A., Guzik, P., & Leszczuk, M. (2016). Automated detection of firearms and knives in a CCTV image. *Sensors (Basel), 16*(1), 47. doi:10.339016010047 PMID:26729128

Gregoire, M., Stephane, D., Emmanuel, T., & Lionel, B. (2010). Change detection in remote sensing observations. In *Digital Signal and Image Processing Series* (pp. 95–142). John Wiley & Sons Inc.

Grimm, C. A. (2020, March). *Hospital Experiences Responding to the Covid-19 Pandemic: Results of a National Pulse Survey.* Retrieved from U.S. Department of Health and Services: https://oig.hhs.gov/oei/reports/oei-06-20-00300.pdf

Grinblat, G. L., Uzal, L. C., Larese, M. G., & Granitto, P. M. (2016). Deep learning for plant identification using vein morphological patterns. *Computers and Electronics in Agriculture, 127*, 418–424. doi:10.1016/j.compag.2016.07.003

Groot, O. Q., Ogink, P. T., Lans, A., Twining, P. K., Kapoor, N. D., DiGiovanni, W., Bindels, B. J. J., Bongers, M. E. R., Oosterhoff, J. H. F., Karhade, A. V., Oner, F. C., Verlaan, J. J., & Schwab, J. H. (2022). Machine learning prediction models in orthopedic surgery: A systematic review in transparent reporting. *Journal of Orthopaedic Research, 40*(2), 475–483. https://doi.org/ doi:10.1002/jor.25036

Grüttner, B., Ratiu, J., Ratiu, D., Gottschalk, I., Morgenstern, B., Abel, J. S., Eichler, C., Pahmeyer, C., Ludwig, S., Mallmann, P., & Thangarajah, F. (2019). Correlation of cerebroplacental ratio (CPR) with adverse perinatal outcome in singleton pregnancies. *In Vivo (Athens, Greece), 33*(5), 1703–1706. doi:10.21873/invivo.11659 PMID:31471427

Guan, S. (2019). *Using generative adversarial networks and transfer learning for breast cancer detection by convolutional neural networks.* Academic Press.

Gunturu, V., Bansal, V., Sathe, M., Kumar, A., Gehlot, A., & Pant, B. (2023). Wireless communications implementation using blockchain as well as distributed type of IOT. In *2023 International Conference on Artificial Intelligence and Smart Communication (AISC)*. IEEE. 10.1109/AISC56616.2023.10085249

Gupta, A., Patel, N., & Khan, S. (2014). Automatic speech recognition technique for voice command. In *2014 International Conference on Science Engineering and Management Research (ICSEMR)*. IEEE. 10.1109/ICSEMR.2014.7043641

Gupta, G., Khan, S., Guleria, V., Almjally, A., Alabduallah, B. I., Siddiqui, T., Albahlal, B. M., Alajlan, S. A., & Al-Subaie, M. (2023). DDPM: A dengue disease prediction and diagnosis model using sentiment analysis and machine learning algorithms. *Diagnostics (Basel)*, *13*(6), 1093. Advance online publication. doi:10.3390/diagnostics13061093 PMID:36980401

Gurumurthy, G., Krishna, V. B. M., & Yadlapati, K. (2021). A fractional order controller design for a class of linear systems. In *2021 IEEE Kansas Power and Energy Conference (KPEC)*. IEEE. 10.1109/KPEC51835.2021.9446215

Harel, D., & Feldman, Y. (2004). *Algorithmics: The Spirit of Computing*. Addison-Wesley.

Hassan, M. Y., & Mohammed, A. G. (2011). Conversion of English characters into braille using neural network. *IJCCCE*, *11*(2), 30–37.

Hathaliya, J. J., & Tanwar, S. (2020). An exhaustive survey on security and privacy issues in Healthcare 4.0. *Computer Communications*, *153*, 311–335. doi:10.1016/j.comcom.2020.02.018

Haug, S., & Ostermann, J. (2015). A crop/weed field image dataset for the evaluation of computer vision based precision agriculture tasks. In *Computer Vision - ECCV 2014 Workshops* (pp. 105–116). Springer International Publishing. doi:10.1007/978-3-319-16220-1_8

Heidari, A., Mirjalili, S., Faris, H., Aljarah, I., Mafarja, M., & Chen, H. (2019). Harris hawks' optimization: Algorithm and applications. *Future Generation Computer Systems*, *97*, 849–872. doi:10.1016/j.future.2019.02.028

Heim, U. (1997). *Fractures du pilon tibial. Conférencesd 'enseignement*. Paris: Expansion Scientique Francaise.

Hendricks, C. H., Brenner, W. E., & Kraus, G. (1970). Normal cervical dilatation pattern in late pregnancy and labor. *American Journal of Obstetrics and Gynecology*, *106*(7), 1065–1082. doi:10.1016/S0002-9378(16)34092-3 PMID:5435658

He, Y., Zhou, Z., Tian, L., Liu, Y., & Luo, X. (2020). Brown rice planthopper (Nilaparvata lugens Stal) detection based on deep learning. *Precision Agriculture*, *21*(6), 1385–1402. doi:10.100711119-020-09726-2

Hilly, J., Bellon, M., Le, A., Daphne, B., Maesani, M., & Brasher, C. (2016). *Efficacy of Intraoperative Dexmedetomidine Compared with Placebo for Postoperative Pain Management : A Meta-Analysis of Published Studies*. Academic Press.

Holst, G. C. (1998). *Testing and evaluating of infrared imaging systems*. SPIE Optical Engineering Press.

Hossain, E., Hossain, M. F., & Rahaman, M. A. (2019). A color and texture based approach for the detection and classification of plant leaf disease using KNN classifier. *2019 International Conference on Electrical, Computer and Communication Engineering (ECCE)*. 10.1109/ECACE.2019.8679247

T. Hossain, F. Shadmani Shishir, M. Ashraf, M. A. A. Nasim, & M. Shah (Eds.). (2019). Brain Tumor Detection Using Convolutional Neural Network. In *International Conference on Advances in Science, Engineering and Robotics Technology (ICASERT)*. IEEE.

Howard, J. (2019). Artificial Intelligence: Implications for The Future of Work. *American Journal of Industrial Medicine*, *62*(11), 917–926. doi:10.1002/ajim.23037 PMID:31436850

Huang, J., Mei, L., Long, M., Liu, Y., Sun, W., Li, X., & Lei, C. (2022). BM-Net: CNN-based MobileNet-V3 and bilinear structure for breast cancer detection in whole slide images. *Bioengineering (Basel, Switzerland)*, *9*(6), 261. doi:10.3390/bioengineering9060261 PMID:35735504

Hu, H., Cao, Z., & Dong, X. (2022). Autonomous path identity-based broadcast proxy re-encryption for data sharing in clouds. *IEEE Access : Practical Innovations, Open Solutions*, *10*, 87322–87332. doi:10.1109/ACCESS.2022.3200084

Hur, J. (2013). Attribute-based secure data sharing with hidden policies in smart grid. IEEE Transactions on Parallel and Distributed Systems: A Publication of the IEEE. *IEEE Transactions on Parallel and Distributed Systems*, *24*(11), 2171–2180. doi:10.1109/TPDS.2012.61

Hussain, M., Chen, D., Cheng, A., Wei, H., & Stanley, D. (2013). Change detection from remotely sensed images: From pixel-based to object-based approaches. *ISPRS Journal of Photogrammetry and Remote Sensing*, *80*, 91–106.

İnce, H., İmamoğlu, S. E., & İmamoğlu, S. Z. (2021). Yapay Zekâ Uygulamalarının Karar Verme Üzerine Etkileri: Kavramsal Bir Çalışma. *International Review of Economics and Management*, *9*(1), 50–63. doi:10.18825/iremjournal.866432

Indraratna, B., Sun, Q., Ngo, N. T., & Rujikiatkamjorn, C. (2017). Current research into ballasted rail tracks: Model tests and their practical implications. *Australian Journal of Structural Engineering*, *18*(3), 204–220. doi:10.1080/13287982.2017.1359398

Ishfaque Qamar Khilji, I., & Qamar Khilji, K. (2020). Application of Homomorphic Encryption on -Neural Network in Prediction of Acute Lymphoid Leukemia. *International Journal of Advanced Computer Science and Applications*.

İyigün, N. Ö. (2021). Yapay Zekâ ve Stratejik Yönetim. *TRT Akademi*, *6*(13), 675–679. doi:10.37679/trta.1002518

Jagtap, A. (2021). *The role of cranial ultrasonography in detecting neurological abnormalities in preterm neonates the role of cranial ultrasonography in detecting neurological abnormalities in preterm neonates.* Grin Verlag.

Jain, A., Krishna, M. M., Tadiboina, S. N., Joshi, K., Chanti, Y., & Krishna, K. S. (2023). An analysis of medical images using deep learning. In *2023 3rd International Conference on Advance Computing and Innovative Technologies in Engineering (ICACITE)* (pp. 1440-1445). IEEE.

Jain, B., Sirdeshpande, S., Gowtham, M. S., Josephson, P. J., Chakravarthi, M. K., & Pant, B. (2022). Exploratory data analysis based on micro grids generation for control communication and monitoring via wireless sensor network. *2022 2nd International Conference on Advance Computing and Innovative Technologies in Engineering (ICACITE)*.

Jain, M. (n.d.). *Justice denied anywhere, diminishes justice everywhere.* Retrieved from https://papers.ssrn.com/sol3/papers.cfm?abstract_id=3771945

Jambhekar, N. D., & Joshi, P. S. (2022). Detection of White Blood Cell Cancer diseases through classification techniques. *Vidya Bharati International Interdisciplinary Research Journal*, *14*(1), 1–5.

Jarrahi, M. H. (2018). Artificial Intelligence and The Future of Work: Human-AI Symbiosis in Organizational Decision Making. *Business Horizons*, *61*(4), 577–586. doi:10.1016/j.bushor.2018.03.007

Jeba, J. A., Bose, S. R., & Boina, R. (2023). Exploring Hybrid Multi-View Multimodal for Natural Language Emotion Recognition Using Multi-Source Information Learning Model. *FMDB Transactions on Sustainable Computer Letters*, *1*(1), 12–24.

Jeganathan, J., Vashist, S., Nirmala, G., & Deep, R. (2023). A Cross Sectional Study on Anxiety and Depression Among Patients with Alcohol Withdrawal Syndrome. *FMDB Transactions on Sustainable Health Science Letters*, *1*(1), 31–40.

Jha, V., & Parvathi, K. (2019). Braille Transliteration of hindi handwritten texts using machine learning for character recognition. *Int J Sci Technol Res*, *8*, 1188–1193.

Jia, K., Wei, X., Gu, X., Yao, Y., Xie, X., & Li, B. (2014). Land cover classification using Landsat 8 Operational Land Imager data in Beijing, China. *Geocarto International*, *29*(8), 941–951. doi:10.1080/10106049.2014.894586

Jiang, F., Lu, Y., Chen, Y., Cai, D., & Li, G. (2020). Image recognition of four rice leaf diseases based on deep learning and support vector machine. *Computers and Electronics in Agriculture*, *179*(105824), 105824. doi:10.1016/j.compag.2020.105824

Ji, G., He, S., Xu, L., Liu, K., & Zhao, J. (2015). Knowledge graph embedding via dynamic mapping matrix. *Proceedings of the 53rd Annual Meeting of the Association for Computational Linguistics and the 7th International Joint Conference on Natural Language Processing (*Volume 1*: Long Papers),* 687–696. 10.3115/v1/P15-1067

Jin, Z., Tao, M., Zhao, X., & Hu, Y. (2022). Social Media Sentiment Analysis Based on Dependency Graph and Co-occurrence Graph. *Cognitive Computation*, *14*(3), 1039–1054.

Jkhali, A., & Samy, S. (2022). Diagnosis of Blood Cells Using Deep Learning. *International Journal of Academic Engineering Research*, *6*(2).

Jo, S. B. (n.d.). Doctors during the Covid-19 pandemic: what are their duties and what is owed to them? Retrieved from https://jme.bmj.com/content/47/1/12

Jolly, A. R., & Chakravarthi, M. K. (2016). A Standalone Data Logger For Fibre Optic Vibration Measurement System Using Beagle bone. *International Conference on Intelligent Systems and Control.*

Jordan, M. I., & Bishop, C. M. (2004). Neural Networks. In Computer Science Handbook, Second Edition (Section VII: Intelligence Systems). Chapman & Hall/CRC Press LLC.

Kakrani, A., Sharma, Z., Thind, S., & Gokhale, V. (2013). Correlation of NAFLD Fibrosis Score and BARD Score with Ultrasonographic Evidence of Nonalcoholic Fatty Liver Disease in Overweight Patients: A Prospective Study. *International Journal of Medicine and Public Health*, *3*(2), 111–114. doi:10.4103/2230-8598.115183

Kamboj, V. K., Nandi, A., Bhadoria, A., & Sehgal, S. (2020). An intensify Harris Hawks optimizer for numerical and engineering optimization problems. *Applied Soft Computing*, *89*(106018), 106018. doi:10.1016/j.asoc.2019.106018

Kandhari, M. S., Zulkemine, F., & Isah, H. (2018). A voice controlled E-commerce web application. In *2018 IEEE 9th Annual Information Technology, Electronics and Mobile Communication Conference (IEMCON).* IEEE.

Kanjalkar, J., Kanjalkar, P., Aole, K., Ansari, A., Abak, H., & Tiwari, A. (2023a). Analysis of machine learning algorithms for COVID detection using deep learning. In *Data Management, Analytics and Innovation* (pp. 405–420). Springer Nature Singapore. doi:10.1007/978-981-99-1414-2_31

Kanjalkar, J., Kanjalkar, P., Deshmukh, T., Deshmukh, J., Dhamal, P., & Bhalerao, A. (2022). A novel system for AYUSH healthcare services using classification and regression. *International Journal on Recent and Innovation Trends in Computing and Communication*, *10*(1s), 232–240. doi:10.17762/ijritcc.v10i1s.5830

Kanjalkar, P., Chinchole, P., Chitre, A., Kanjalkar, J., & Sharma, P. (2023b). Economical solution to automatic evaluation of an OMR sheet using image processing. In *Data Management, Analytics and Innovation* (pp. 665–683). Springer Nature Singapore. doi:10.1007/978-981-99-1414-2_48

Karakaşoğlu, N. (2008). *Bulanık Çok Kriterli Karar Verme Yöntemleri ve Uygulama* [Unpublished master's thesis]. Pamukkale University Institute of Social Sciences.

Karthik, M. V., Chakravarthi, M. K., Yapanto, L. M., Selvapandian, D., Harish, R., & Subramani, K. (2021). Optical Analysis of the UPQC using PI Controller in Power flow System. *2021 7th International Conference on Advanced Computing and Communication Systems (ICACCS).*

Kattenborn, T., Eichel, J., & Fassnacht, F. E. (2019). Convolutional Neural Networks enable efficient, accurate and fine-grained segmentation of plant species and communities from high-resolution UAV imagery. *Scientific Reports*, *9*(1), 17656. doi:10.103841598-019-53797-9 PMID:31776370

Kayaönü, E. (2000). *Yapay Zekânın Teorik Temelleri* [Unpublished master's thesis]. Istanbul Technical University Institute of Science and Technology.

Kaya, V., Tuncer, S., & Baran, A. (2021). Detection and Classification of Different Weapon Types Using Deep Learning. *Applied Sciences (Basel, Switzerland)*, *11*(16), 7535. doi:10.3390/app11167535

Keivani, M., Mazloum, J., Sedaghatfar, E., & Tavakoli, M. (2020). Automated analysis of leaf shape, texture, and color features for plant classification. *TS. Traitement du Signal*, *37*(1), 17–28. doi:10.18280/ts.370103

Kempfert, H.-G., & Raithel, M. (2005). Soil improvement and foundation systems with encased columns and reinforced bearing layers. In *Ground Improvement — Case Histories* (pp. 923–946). Elsevier. doi:10.1016/S1571-9960(05)80035-7

Khalil, A., Morales-Rosello, J., Khan, N., Nath, M., Agarwal, P., Bhide, A., Papageorghiou, A., & Thilaganathan, B. (2017). Is cerebroplacental ratio a marker of impaired fetal growth velocity and adverse pregnancy outcome? *American Journal of Obstetrics and Gynecology*, *216*(6), 606.e1–606.e10. doi:10.1016/j.ajog.2017.02.005 PMID:28189607

Khanagar, S. B., Al-Ehaideb, A., Vishwanathaiah, S., Maganur, P. C., Patil, S., Naik, S., Baeshen, H. A., & Sarode, S. S. (2021). Scope and performance of artificial intelligence technology in orthodontic diagnosis, treatment planning, and clinical decision-making - A systematic review. *Journal of Dental Sciences*, *16*(1), 482–492. doi:10.1016/j.jds.2020.05.022 PMID:33384838

Khan, S., & Alajmi, M. F. (2019). A Review on Security Concerns in Cloud Computing and their Solutions. *International Journal of Computer Science Network Security*, *19*(2).

Kim, Y., Seo, J., An, S. Y., Sinn, D. H., & Hwang, J. H. (2020). Efficacy and safety of an mHealth app and wearable device in physical performance for patients with hepatocellular carcinoma: Development and usability study. *JMIR mHealth and uHealth*, *8*(3), e14435. doi:10.2196/14435 PMID:32159517

Klein, H. S., Vanneste, S., & Pinkham, A. E. (2021). The limited effect of neural stimulation on visual attention and social cognition in individuals with schizophrenia. *Neuropsychologia*, *157*, 107880. doi:10.1016/j.neuropsychologia.2021.107880 PMID:33961863

Koc, A. S., & Sumbul, H. E. (2019). Prediabetes Is Associated With Increased Liver Stiffness Identified by Noninvasive Liver Fibrosis Assessment: ElastPQ Ultrasound Shear Wave Elastography Study. *Ultrasound Quarterly*, *35*(4), 330–338. doi:10.1097/RUQ.0000000000000419 PMID:30724873

Koksal, N., Bayton, B., Bayram, Y., & Nacorkucuk, E. (2002). Risk factors for intraventricular hemorrhage in very low birth weight infants. *Indian Journal of Pediatrics*, *69*(7), 561–564. doi:10.1007/BF02722677 PMID:12173693

Kondraju, T., Mandla, V. R. B., & Mahendra, R. S. (2014). Evaluation of various image classification techniques on Landsat to identify coral reefs. *Geomatics, Natural Hazards & Risk*, (5), 173–184.

Kong, S. G., Heo, J., Boughorbel, F., Zheng, Y., Abidi, B. R., Koschan, A., Yi, M., & Abidi, M. A. (2007). Multiscale fusion of visible and thermal IR images for illumination-invariant face recognition. *International Journal of Computer Vision*, *71*(2), 215–233. doi:10.100711263-006-6655-0

Koyasako, Y., Suzuki, T., Kim, S.-Y., Kani, J.-I., & Terada, J. (2021). Motion control system with time-varying delay compensation for access edge computing. *IEEE Access : Practical Innovations, Open Solutions*, *9*, 90669–90676. doi:10.1109/ACCESS.2021.3091707

Kratzwald, B., Ilić, S., Kraus, M., Feuerriegel, S., & Prendinger, H. (2018). Deep learning for affective computing: Text-based emotion recognition in decision support. *Decision Support Systems*, *115*, 24–35. doi:10.1016/j.dss.2018.09.002

Krishna, B. V., Jhansi, P. S., Shama, A., Boya Leelambika, C., & Prakash, B. V. V. N. (2019). Novel Solution to Improve Mental Health by Integrating Music and IoT with Neural Feedback. *Journal of Computer Information Systems*, *3*(5), 234–239.

Krishnamoorthy, Y., Rajaa, S., Murali, S., Rehman, T., Sahoo, J., & Kar, S. S. (2020). Prevalence of metabolic syndrome among adult population in India: A systematic review and meta-analysis. *PLoS One*, *15*(10), e0240971. doi:10.1371/journal.pone.0240971 PMID:33075086

Kuk, J. L., & Ardern, C. I. (2010). Age and Sex Differences in the Clustering of Metabolic Syndrome Factors. *Diabetes Care*, *33*(11), 2457–2461. doi:10.2337/dc10-0942 PMID:20699434

Kulkarni, J. B. (2019). Depth analysis of single view image objects based on object detection and focus measure. *International Journal of Advanced Trends in Computer Science and Engineering*, *5*(8), 2608–2612. doi:10.30534/ijatcse/2019/112852019

Kumar, N., Belhumeur, P. N., Biswas, A., Jacobs, D. W., Kress, W. J., Lopez, I. C., & Soares, J. V. B. (2012). Leafsnap: A computer vision system for automatic plant species identification. In Computer Vision – ECCV 2012 (pp. 502–516). Springer Berlin Heidelberg. doi:10.1007/978-3-642-33709-3_36

Kumar, T. C. A., Dixit, G. K., Singh, R., Narukullapati, B. K., Chakravarthi, M. K., & Gangodkar, D. (2022). Wireless sensor network using control communication and monitoring of smart grid. *2022 2nd International Conference on Advance Computing and Innovative Technologies in Engineering (ICACITE)*.

Kumar, D., Jain, N., Khurana, A., Mittal, S., Suresh, C., Satapathy, R., & Senkeik, J. D. (2020). Automatic Detection of White Blood Cancer From Bone Marrow Microscopic Images Using Convolutional Neural Networks. *IEEE Access : Practical Innovations, Open Solutions*.

Kumar, V., Kumar, S., AlShboul, R., Aggarwal, G., Kaiwartya, O., Khasawneh, A. M., & Al-Khasawneh, M. A. (2021). Grouping and Sponsoring Centric Green Coverage Model for Internet of Things. *Sensors (Basel)*, *21*(12), 3948. doi:10.339021123948 PMID:34201100

Kutlu, H., Avci, E., & Ozyurt, F. (2019). *White blood cells detection and classification based on regional convolutional neural networks*. National Library of Science.

Kyprianides, B., Bradford, M. B.-S.-S., Beale, M., Savigar-Shaw, L., Stott, C., & Radburn, M. (2022). Policing the Covid-19 pandemic: Police officer well being and commitment to democratic modes of policing. *Policing and Society*, *32*(4), 504–521. doi:10.1080/10439463.2021.1916492

Lai, H.-J., Zheng, J.-J., Zhang, J., Zhang, R.-J., & Cui, L. (2014). DEM analysis of "soil"-arching within geogrid-reinforced and unreinforced pile-supported embankments. *Computers and Geotechnics*, *61*, 13–23. doi:10.1016/j.compgeo.2014.04.007

Lakhani, P., & Sundaram, B. (2017). Deep Learning at Chest Radiography: Automated Classification of Pulmonary Tuberculosis by Using Convolutional Neural Networks. *Radiology*, *284*(2), 574–582. doi:10.1148/radiol.2017162326 PMID:28436741

Lalitha. (2020). Vehicle number plate recognition system to identify the authenticated owner of vehicles. *International Journal of Psychosocial Rehabilitation, 24*(5), 7102–7107. doi:10.37200/ijpr/v24i5/pr2020719

Langarizadeh, M., Farajollahi, B., & Hajifathali, A. (2022). Presenting a Prediction Model for Successful Allogenic Hematopoietic Stem Cell Transplantation in Adults with Acute Myeloid Leukemia. *Middle East Journal of Cancer.*

Lao, N., Mitchell, T., & Cohen, W. (2011). Random walk inference and learning in a large scale knowledge base. *Proceedings of the 2011 Conference on Empirical Methods in Natural Language Processing*, 529–539.

Laroca, R., Zanlorensi, L. A., Gonçalves, G. R., Todt, E., Schwartz, W. R., & Menotti, D. (2021). An efficient and layout-independent automatic license plate recognition system based on the YOLO detector. *IET Intelligent Transport Systems, 15*(4), 483–503.

Lavender, T., Cuthbert, A., & Smyth, R. M. D. (2018). Effect of partograph use on outcomes for women in spontaneous labour at term and their babies. *The Cochrane Library, 2018*(8). doi:10.1002/14651858.CD005461.pub5

Lavini, F., Dall'Oca, C., Mezzari, S., Maluta, T., Luminari, E., Perusi, F., ... Magnan, B. (2014). Temporary bridging external fixation in distal tibial fracture. *Injury, 45*, S58–S63. doi:10.1016/j.injury.2014.10.025 PMID:25457321

Lazorenko, G., Kasprzhitskii, A., Khakiev, Z., & Yavna, V. (2019). Dynamic behavior and stability of soil foundation in heavy haul railway tracks: A review. *Construction & Building Materials, 205*, 111–136. doi:10.1016/j.conbuildmat.2019.01.184

Lazorenko, G., Kasprzhitskii, A., Kukharskii, A., Kochur, A., & Yavna, V. (2020). Failure analysis of widened railway embankment with different reinforcing measures under heavy axle loads: A comparative FEM study. *Transportation Engineering, 2*(100028). doi:10.1016/j.treng.2020.100028

Leander, B., Causevic, A., Hansson, H., & Lindstrom, T. (2021). Toward an ideal access control strategy for industry 4.0 manufacturing systems. *IEEE Access : Practical Innovations, Open Solutions, 9*, 114037–114050. doi:10.1109/ACCESS.2021.3104649

Lee, D.-S., Yeom, S., Son, J.-Y., & Kim, S.-H. (2009). Image segmentation of concealed objects detected by passive millimeter wave imaging. *2009 34th International Conference on Infrared, Millimeter, and Terahertz Waves.*

LeeS. H.ChanC. S.WilkinP.RemagninoP. (2015). *Deep-Plant: Plant Identification with convolutional neural networks.* doi:10.1109/ICIP.2015.7350839

Lei, D., Jiang, G., Gu, X., Sun, K., Mao, Y., & Ren, X. (2020). *Learning collaborative agents with rule guidance for knowledge graph reasoning.* arXiv Prepr. arXiv2005.00571. doi:10.18653/v1/2020.emnlp-main.688

Leksee, L. (1956). Echo- encephalography In detection of intracranial complications following head injury. *Acta Chirurgica Scandinavica*, (110), 301–305. PMID:13292078

Li, Z., Guan, S., Jin, X., Peng, W., Lyu, Y., Zhu, Y., Bai, L., Li, W., Guo, J., & Cheng, X. (2022). *Complex evolutional pattern learning for temporal knowledge graph reasoning.* arXiv Prepr. arXiv2203.07782.

Li, M., Wu, P., Wang, B., Park, H., Yang, H., & Wu, Y. (2021). A deep learning method of water body extraction from high resolution remote sensing images with multisensors. *IEEE Journal of Selected Topics in Applied Earth Observations and Remote Sensing, 14*, 3120–3132.

Lin, X. V., Socher, R., & Xiong, C. (2018). *Multi-hop knowledge graph reasoning with reward shaping.* arXiv Prepr. arXiv1808.10568. doi:10.18653/v1/D18-1362

Lin, Y., Liu, Z., Sun, M., Liu, Y., & Zhu, X. (2015). Learning entity and relation embeddings for knowledge graph completion. *Proceedings of the AAAI Conference on Artificial Intelligence.* 10.1609/aaai.v29i1.9491

Liu, H., Zhou, S., Chen, C., Gao, T., Xu, J., & Shu, M. (2022). Dynamic knowledge graph reasoning based on deep reinforcement learning. *Knowledge-Based Systems, 241,* 108235. doi:10.1016/j.knosys.2022.108235

Liu, K., Su, Q., Ni, P., Zhou, C., Zhao, W., & Yue, F. (2018). Evaluation on the dynamic performance of bridge approach backfilled with fibre reinforced lightweight concrete under high-speed train loading. *Computers and Geotechnics, 104,* 42–53. doi:10.1016/j.compgeo.2018.08.003

Liu, Y., Zhao, G., Zang, X., Lu, F., Liu, P., & Chen, W. (2021). Effect of dexmedetomidine on opioid consumption and pain control after laparoscopic cholecystectomy: A meta-analysis of randomized controlled trials. *Wideochirurgia i Inne Techniki Malo Inwazyjne, 16*(3), 491–500. doi:10.5114/wiitm.2021.104197 PMID:34691300

Li, Z., Jin, X., Guan, S., Wang, Y., & Cheng, X. (2018). Path reasoning over knowledge graph: a multi-agent and reinforcement learning based method. *2018 IEEE International Conference on Data Mining Workshops (ICDMW), 929–936.* 10.1109/ICDMW.2018.00135

London, D. A., Carroll, B. A., & Enzmann, D. R. (1980). Sonography of ventricular size and germinal matrix hemorrhage in premature infants. *AJNR. American Journal of Neuroradiology, 1,* 295–300. PMID:6773378

Lubna, M. N., & Shah, S. A. A. (2021). Automatic number plate recognition:A detailed survey of relevant algorithms. *Sensors (Basel), 21*(9). Advance online publication. doi:10.339021093028 PMID:33925845

Luo, W., & Ma, W. (2019). Secure and efficient data sharing scheme based on certificateless hybrid signcryption for cloud storage. *Electronics (Basel), 8*(5), 590. doi:10.3390/electronics8050590

Lu, X., Pan, Z., & Xian, H. (2020). An efficient and secure data sharing scheme for mobile devices in cloud computing. *Journal of Cloud Computing (Heidelberg, Germany), 9*(1), 60. Advance online publication. doi:10.118613677-020-00207-5

Lu, Y., & Young, S. (2020). A survey of public datasets for computer vision tasks in precision agriculture. *Computers and Electronics in Agriculture, 178*(105760), 105760. doi:10.1016/j.compag.2020.105760

Lv, X., Han, X., Hou, L., Li, J., Liu, Z., Zhang, W., Zhang, Y., Kong, H., & Wu, S. (2020). *Dynamic anticipation and completion for multi-hop reasoning over sparse knowledge graph.* arXiv Prepr. arXiv2010.01899. doi:10.18653/v1/2020.emnlp-main.459

M, A., K, T., Munshi, Y, J., M, R., & M, S. (2019). Assessment of heavy metal contents in commercial feedstuffs and broiler (Gallus domesticus) meat and its impact on Swiss albino mice as an animal model. *Agricultural Science Digest - A Research Journal.* doi:10.18805/ag.D-4898

M, A., K, T., Munshi, Y, J., M, R., & M, S. (2019). Assessment of heavy metal contents in commercial feedstuffs and broiler (Gallus domesticus) meat and its impact on Swiss albino mice as an animal model. *Agricultural Science Digest - A Research Journal.* doi:10.18805/ag.d-4898

Machajdik, J., & Hanbury, A. (2010, October). Affective image classification using features inspired by psychology and art theory. In *Proceedings of the 18th ACM international conference on Multimedia* (pp. 83-92). ACM.

MacKay, D. J. C. (2021). *Information Theory, Inference, and Learning Algorithms.* Cambridge University Press.

Madhukar, R., & Singh, R. R. (2015). Automatic Car license plate Recognition system using Multiclass SVM and OCR. *International Journal of Engineering Trends and Technology, 30*(7), 369–373.

Mahbub, T. N., Yousuf, & Uddin, M. N. (2022). A modified CNN and fuzzy AHP based breast cancer stage detection system. In *International Conference on Advancement in Electrical and Electronic Engineering (ICAEEE)* (pp. 1–6). Academic Press.

Mahendran, R., Tadiboina, S. N., Thrinath, B. S., Gadgil, A., Madem, S., & Srivastava, Y. (2022). Application of Machine Learning and Internet of Things for Identification of Nutrient Deficiencies in Oil Palm. In *2022 5th International Conference on Contemporary Computing and Informatics (IC3I)* (pp. 2024-2028). IEEE.

Mahmood, T., Arsalan, M., Owais, M., & Park, L. (2020). Artificial intelligence-based mitosis detection in breast cancer histopathology images using faster R-CNN and deep CNNs. *Journal of Clinical Medicine*, 9(3), 749. PMID:32164298

Manikandan, N., Tadiboina, S. N., Khan, M. S., Singh, R., & Gupta, K. K. (2023). Automation of Smart Home for the Wellbeing of Elders Using Empirical Big Data Analysis. In *2023 3rd International Conference on Advance Computing and Innovative Technologies in Engineering (ICACITE)* (pp. 1164-1168). IEEE.

Manjula Devi Ramasamy, R., Kumar Dhanaraj, S., Kumar Pani, R. P., Das, A. A., Movassagh, M., Gheisari, Y., Porkar, S. (2023). An improved deep convolutionary neural network for bone marrow cancer detection using image processing. *Science Direct, 38*.

Martin, J. A., Hamilton, B. E., Ventura, S. J., Menacker, F., & Park, M. M. (2002). Births: Final data for 2000. *National Vital Statistics Reports*, 50, 1–101. PMID:11876093

Mason, K., & Grijalva, S. (2019). A review of reinforcement learning for autonomous building energy management. *Computers & Electrical Engineering*, 78, 300–312. doi:10.1016/j.compeleceng.2019.07.019

Masquelet, A. C. (2003). *Atlas des lambeaux de l'appareillocomoteur*. Saurampsmédical.

Mast, N., Khan, M. A., Uddin, M. I., Ali Shah, S. A., Khan, A., Al-Khasawneh, M. A., & Mahmoud, M. (2021). Channel contention-based routing protocol for wireless ad hoc networks. *Complexity*, 2021, 1–10. doi:10.1155/2021/2051796

Mathai, M. (2009). The partograph for the prevention of obstructed labor. *Clinical Obstetrics and Gynecology*, 52(2), 256–269. doi:10.1097/GRF.0b013e3181a4f163 PMID:19407533

Mavromatis, C., Subramanyam, P. L., Ioannidis, V. N., Adeshina, A., Howard, P. R., Grinberg, T., Hakim, N., & Karypis, G. (2022). Tempoqr: temporal question reasoning over knowledge graphs. *Proceedings of the AAAI Conference on Artificial Intelligence*, 5825–5833. 10.1609/aaai.v36i5.20526

Mawle, P. P., Dhomane, G. A., Narukullapati, B. K., Venkatesh, P. M., Chakravarthi, M. K., & Shukla, S. K. (2022). A Novel Framework For Data Visualization Via Power System Monitoring Control And Protection Based On Wireless Communication. In *2022 2nd International Conference on Advance Computing and Innovative Technologies in Engineering (ICACITE)* (pp. 1056–1060). 10.1109/ICACITE53722.2022.9823492

McGuinness, G.A., Smith, W.L., (1984). Head ultrasound screening in premature neonates weighing more than 1,500 g at birth. *Am J Dis Child, 138*(9), 817-20.

Md, N., Hasan, M., Munshi, M. H., Rahman, S. M. N., & Alam, A. (2014). Evaluation of antihyperglycemic activity of Lasia spinosa leaf extracts in Swiss albino mice. *World Journal of Pharmacy and Pharmaceutical Sciences*, 3(10), 118–124.

Meigs, J. B., Wilson, P. W. F., Fox, C. S., Vasan, R. S., Nathan, D. M., Sullivan, L. M., & D'Agostino, R. B. (2006). Body mass index, metabolic syndrome, and risk of type 2 diabetes or cardiovascular disease. *The Journal of Clinical Endocrinology and Metabolism*, 91(8), 2906–2912. doi:10.1210/jc.2006-0594 PMID:16735483

Meisel, C., & Bailey, K. A. (2019). Identifying signal-dependent information about the preictal state: A comparison across ECoG, EEG and EKG using deep learning. *EBioMedicine*, 45, 422–431. doi:10.1016/j.ebiom.2019.07.001 PMID:31300348

Meyer, L.-P., Stadler, C., Frey, J., Radtke, N., Junghanns, K., Meissner, R., Dziwis, G., Bulert, K., & Martin, M. (2023). *LLM-assisted Knowledge Graph Engineering: Experiments with ChatGPT.* arXiv Prepr. arXiv2307.06917.

Miller, R. D. (2010). *Anaesthesia* (7th ed.). Churchill Livingstone.

Minatorsajjadi, M., Ebrahimpour, A., Okhovatpour, M. A., Karimi, A., Zandi, R., & Sharifzadeh, A. (2018). The Outcomes of Pilon Fracture Treatment: Primary Open Reduction and Internal Fixation Versus Two-stage Approach. *Archives of Bone and Joint Surgery*, *6*(5), 412–419. PMID:30320182

Mishra, V. K., & Pant, T. (2019). Application of classification techniques for identification of water region in multiple sources using Landsat-8 OLI imagery. In *2019 URSI Asia-Pacific Radio Science Conference (AP-RASC).* IEEE.

Mishra, V. K., & Pant, T. (2020). Water level monitoring using classification techniques on Landsat-8 data at Sangam region, Prayagraj, India. *IET Image Processing*, *14*(15), 3733–3741.

Mitchell, T. (1997). *Machine Learning.* McGraw Hill.

Mitra, R., Prabhakar, H., Rath, G., Bithal, P., & Khandelwal, A. (2017). A comparative study between intraoperative low-dose ketamine and dexmedetomidine, as an anaesthetic adjuvant in lumbar spine instrumentation surgery for the postoperative analgesic requirement. *Journal of Neuroanaesthesiology and Critical Care*, *4*(2), 91–98. doi:10.4103/jnacc-jnacc-3.17

Mohan, V., Farooq, S., Deepa, M., Ravikumar, R., & Pitchumoni, C. S. (2009). Prevalence of non-alcoholic fatty liver disease in urban south Indians about different glucose intolerance and metabolic syndrome grades. *Diabetes Research and Clinical Practice*, *84*(1), 84–91. doi:10.1016/j.diabres.2008.11.039 PMID:19168251

Mokhtar, U., El Bendary, N., Hassenian, A. E., Emary, E., Mahmoud, M. A., Hefny, H., & Tolba, M. F. (2015). SVM-based detection of tomato leaves diseases. In *Advances in Intelligent Systems and Computing* (pp. 641–652). Springer International Publishing.

Morales-Roselló, J., Khalil, A., Alba-Redondo, A., Martinez-Triguero, L., Akhoundova, F., Perales-Marín, A., & Thilaganathan, B. (2017). Protein S100β in late-pregnancy fetuses with low birth weight and abnormal cerebroplacental ratio. *Fetal Diagnosis and Therapy*, *41*(1), 15–22. doi:10.1159/000445114 PMID:27104871

Morales-Roselló, J., Khalil, A., Alberola-Rubio, J., Hervas-Marín, D., Morlando, M., Bhide, A., Papageorghiou, A., Perales-Marín, A., & Thilaganathan, B. (2015). Neonatal acid-base status in term fetuses: Mathematical models investigating cerebroplacental ratio and birth weight. *Fetal Diagnosis and Therapy*, *38*(1), 55–60. doi:10.1159/000368829 PMID:25660123

Moreta, D., Vo, S., Eslick, G. D., & Benzie, R. (2019). Re-evaluating the role of cerebroplacental ratio in predicting adverse perinatal outcome. *European Journal of Obstetrics, Gynecology, and Reproductive Biology*, *242*, 17–28. doi:10.1016/j.ejogrb.2019.06.033 PMID:31526912

Mousavi, H., Mohammadi, S., Perina, A., Chellali, R., & Murino, V. (2015). Analyzing tracklets for the detection of abnormal crowd behavior. *2015 IEEE Winter Conference on Applications of Computer Vision.* 10.1109/WACV.2015.27

Munshi, M., Sohrab, M. H., Begum, M. N., Rony, S. R., Karim, M. A., Afroz, F., & Hasan, M. N. (2021). Evaluation of bioactivity and phytochemical screening of endophytic fungi isolated from Ceriops decandra (Griff.) W. Theob, a mangrove plant in Bangladesh. *Clinical Phytoscience*, *7*(1). Advance online publication. doi:10.118640816-021-00315-y

Munshi, M., Tumu, K. N., Hasan, M. N., & Amin, M. Z. (2018). Biochemical effects of commercial feedstuffs on the fry of climbing perch (Anabas testudineus) and its impact on Swiss albino mice as an animal model. *Toxicology Reports*, *5*, 521–530. doi:10.1016/j.toxrep.2018.04.004 PMID:29707493

Munshi, M., Zilani, M. N. H., Islam, M. A., Biswas, P., Das, A., Afroz, F., & Hasan, M. N. (2022). Novel compounds from endophytic fungi of Ceriops decandra inhibit breast cancer cell growth through estrogen receptor alpha in in-silico study. *Informatics in Medicine Unlocked*, *32*(101046), 101046. doi:10.1016/j.imu.2022.101046

Murchie, E. H., & Burgess, A. J. (2022). Casting light on the architecture of crop yield. *Crop and Environment*, *1*(1), 74–85. doi:10.1016/j.crope.2022.03.009

Murphy, K. P. (2021). *Probabilistic Machine Learning: An Introduction*. MIT Press.

Myla, S., Marella, S. T., Swarnendra Goud, A., Hasane Ahammad, S., Kumar, G. N. S., & Inthiyaz, S. (2019). Design decision taking system for student career selection for accurate academic system. *International Journal of Recent Technology and Engineering*, *8*(9), 2199–2206.

Nagarathna, S. B., Gehlot, A., Tiwari, M., Tiwari, T., Chakravarthi, M. K., & Verma, D. (2022). A review of bio-cell culture processes in real-time monitoring approach with cloud computing techniques. *2022 2nd International Conference on Advance Computing and Innovative Technologies in Engineering (ICACITE)*.

Najdenovska, E., Dutoit, F., Tran, D., Plummer, C., Wallbridge, N., Camps, C., & Raileanu, L. E. (2021). Classification of plant electrophysiology signals for detection of spider mites infestation in tomatoes. *Applied Sciences (Basel, Switzerland)*, *11*(4), 1414. doi:10.3390/app11041414

Nath, T., Caffo, B., Wager, T., & Lindquist, M. A. (2023). A machine learning based approach towards high-dimensional mediation analysis. *NeuroImage*, *268*(119843), 119843. doi:10.1016/j.neuroimage.2022.119843 PMID:36586543

Neisser, U. (1967). Cognitive psychology. appleton-century-crofts. [aac] nelson, k. (2003) self and social functions: Individual autobiographical memory and collective narrative. *Memory (Hove, England)*, *11*(2).

Ng, T. F., Jiang, D. H., Jiag, X., Paull, D. J., & Wang, X. H. (2013). Change detection for sustainability monitoring using satellite remote sensing data. The University of New South Wales at Canberra.

Nguyen, D. C., Pathirana, P. N., Ding, M., & Seneviratne, A. (2019). Blockchain for secure EHRs sharing of mobile cloud based E-health systems. *IEEE Access : Practical Innovations, Open Solutions*, *7*, 66792–66806. doi:10.1109/ACCESS.2019.2917555

Nikoubakht, N., Alimian, M., Faiz, S. H. R., Derakhshan, P., & Sadri, M. S. (2021). Effects of ketamine versus dexmedetomidine maintenance infusion in posterior spinal fusion surgery on acute postoperative pain. *Surgical Neurology International*, *12*(192), 192. doi:10.25259/SNI_850_2020 PMID:34084620

Nilsback, M.-E., & Zisserman, A. (2006). A visual vocabulary for flower classification. Computer Vision and Pattern Recognition. IEEE Computer Society Conference On, 2, 1447–1454. doi:10.1109/CVPR.2006.42

Nilsback, M.-E., & Zisserman, A. (2008). Automated flower classification over a large number of classes. *2008 Sixth Indian Conference on Computer Vision, Graphics & Image Processing*. 10.1109/ICVGIP.2008.47

Nirmala, G., Premavathy, R., Chandar, R., & Jeganathan, J. (2023). An Explanatory Case Report on Biopsychosocial Issues and the Impact of Innovative Nurse-Led Therapy in Children with Hematological Cancer. *FMDB Transactions on Sustainable Health Science Letters*, *1*(1), 1–10.

Odibo, A.O., Riddick, C., Pare, E., Stamilio, D. M., & Macones, G.A. (2005). Cerebroplacental Doppler ratio and adverse perinatal outcomes in intrauterine growth restriction: evaluating the impact of using gestational agespecific reference values. *J Ultrasound Med.*, (9), 1223-8. doi:.2005.24.9.1223 doi:10.7863/jum

Ogunmola, G. A., Singh, B., Sharma, D. K., Regin, R., Rajest, S. S., & Singh, N. (2021). Involvement of distance measure in assessing and resolving efficiency environmental obstacles. In *2021 International Conference on Computational Intelligence and Knowledge Economy (ICCIKE)*. IEEE. 10.1109/ICCIKE51210.2021.9410765

Oladapo, O. T., Souza, J. P., Fawole, B., Mugerwa, K., Perdoná, G., Alves, D., Souza, H., Reis, R., Oliveira-Ciabati, L., Maiorano, A., Akintan, A., Alu, F. E., Oyeneyin, L., Adebayo, A., Byamugisha, J., Nakalembe, M., Idris, H. A., Okike, O., Althabe, F., & Gülmezoglu, A. M. (2018). Progression of the first stage of spontaneous labour: A prospective cohort study in two sub-Saharan African countries. *PLoS Medicine*, *15*(1), e1002492. doi:10.1371/journal.pmed.1002492 PMID:29338000

Omer Aftab, M., Javed Awan, M., Khalid, S., Javed, R., & Shabir, H. (2021). Executing Spark BigDL for Leukemia Detection from Microscopic Images using Transfer Learning. In *International Conference on Artificial Intelligence and Data Analytics (CAIDA)*. IEEE.

Omrani, E., Khoshnevisan, B., Shamshirband, S., Saboohi, H., Anuar, N. B., & Nasir, M. H. N. M. (2014). Potential of radial basis function-based support vector regression for apple disease detection. Measurement. *Measurement*, *55*, 512–519. doi:10.1016/j.measurement.2014.05.033

Orji, E. (2008). Evaluating progress of labor in nulliparas and multiparas using the modified WHO partograph. *International Journal of Gynaecology and Obstetrics: the Official Organ of the International Federation of Gynaecology and Obstetrics*, *102*(3), 249–252. doi:10.1016/j.ijgo.2008.04.024 PMID:18603248

Pakala, C., Sekhar, S., & Shinde, G. (2018). Krishna BV Murali "An Optimized Operation of Hybrid Wind/Battery/PV-System based Micro grid by using Particle Swarm Optimization Technique.". *Journal of Computer Information Systems*, *14*(5), 79–84.

Paldi, R. L., Aryal, A., Behzadirad, M., Busani, T., Siddiqui, A., & Wang, H. (2021). Nanocomposite-seeded single-domain growth of lithium niobate thin films for photonic applications. In *Conference on Lasers and Electro-Optics*. Washington, DC: Optica Publishing Group.

Pande, S. D., & Chetty, M. S. R. (2021) Fast Medicinal Leaf Retrieval Using CapsNet. In *International Conference on Intelligent and Smart Computing in Data Analytics. Advances in Intelligent Systems and Computing* (vol. 1312). 10.1007/978-981-33-6176-8_16

Pande, S. D., & Chetty, M. S. R. (2021). Fast medicinal leaf retrieval using CapsNet. In *Advances in Intelligent Systems and Computing* (pp. 149–155). Springer Singapore.

Pande, S. D., Rathod, S. B., Chetty, M. S. R., Pathak, S., Jadhav, P. P., & Godse, S. P. (2022). Shape and textural based image retrieval using K-NN classifier. *Journal of Intelligent & Fuzzy Systems*, *43*(4), 4757–4768. doi:10.3233/JIFS-213355

Pande, S., & Chetty, M. S. R. (2018). Analysis of Capsule Network (Capsnet) Architectures and Applications. *Journal of Advanced Research in Dynamical and Control Systems*, *10*(10), 2765–2771.

Pande, S., & Chetty, M. S. R. (2019). Bezier Curve Based Medicinal Leaf Classification using Capsule Network. *International Journal of Advanced Trends in Computer Science and Engineering*, *8*(6), 2735–2742. doi:10.30534/ijatcse/2019/09862019

Pandit, P. (2023). On the Context of Diabetes: A Brief Discussion on the Novel Ethical Issues of Non-communicable Diseases. *FMDB Transactions on Sustainable Health Science Letters*, *1*(1), 11–20.

Pandiyarajan, M., Thimmiaraja, J., Ramasamy, J., Tiwari, M., Shinde, S., & Chakravarthi, M. K. (2022). Medical image classification for disease prediction with the aid of deep learning approaches. *2022 2nd International Conference on Advance Computing and Innovative Technologies in Engineering (ICACITE)*.

Pandya, S., Gadekallu, T. R., Reddy, P. K., Wang, W., & Alazab, M. (2022). InfusedHeart: A novel knowledge-infused learning framework for diagnosis of cardiovascular events. *IEEE Transactions on Computational Social Systems*, 1–10. doi:10.1109/TCSS.2022.3151643

Pang, L., Zhu, S., & Ngo, C. W. (2015). Deep multi-modal learning for affective analysis and retrieval. *IEEE Transactions on Multimedia*, *17*(11), 2008–2020.

Park, S., Shim, H. S., Chatterjee, M., Sagae, K., & Morency, L. P. (2016). Multi-modal analysis and prediction of persuasiveness in online social multimedia. *ACM Transactions on Interactive Intelligent Systems*, *6*(3), 1–25.

Parra, L., Marin, J., Yousfi, S., Rincón, G., Mauri, P. V., & Lloret, J. (2020). Edge detection for weed recognition in lawns. *Computers and Electronics in Agriculture*, *176*(105684), 105684. doi:10.1016/j.compag.2020.105684

Patil, V., Gowda, S., Das, S., Suma, K. B., Hiremath, R., Shetty, S., Raj, V., & Shashikumar, M. R. (2019). Cerebro-placental ratio in women with hypertensive disorders of pregnancy: A reliable predictor of neonatal outcome. *Journal of Clinical and Diagnostic Research*. Advance online publication. doi:10.7860/JCDR/2019/41185.12862

Pattanaik, A., & Balabantaray, R. C. (2022). Enhancement of license plate recognition performance using Xception with Mish activation function. *Multimedia Tools and Applications*, *82*(11), 16793–16815. PMID:36258895

Patterson, M. J., & Cole, J. D. (1999). Two-staged delayed open reduction and internal fixation of severe Pilon fractures. *Journal of Orthopaedic Trauma*, *13*(2), 85–91. doi:10.1097/00005131-199902000-00003 PMID:10052781

Paul, C., & Landree, E. (2008). Defining Terrorists' Information Requirements: The Modified Intelligence Preparation of the Battlefield (ModIPB) Framework. *Journal of Homeland Security and Emergency Management*, *5*(1), 1–18. doi:10.2202/1547-7355.1433

Pavlidis, I., & Symosek, P. (2002). The imaging issue in an automatic face/disguise detection system. Proceedings *IEEE Workshop on Computer Vision Beyond the Visible Spectrum: Methods and Applications* (Cat. No.PR00640).

Pedro, D. (2015). *The Master Algorithm: How the Quest for the Ultimate Learning Machine Will Remake Our World*. Basic Books.

Peisner, D. B., & Rosen, M. G. (1986). Transition from latent to active labor. *Obstetrics and Gynecology*, *68*(4), 448–451. PMID:3748488

Peng, K., Zhang, J., Meng, X., Liu, H., & Ji, F. (2017). Optimisation of Postoperative Intravenous Patient-Controlled Analgesia with Opioid-Dexmedetomidine Combinations : An Updated Meta-Analysis with Trial Sequential Analysis of Randomiz. *Optimisation of Postoperative Intravenous Patient - Controlled Analgesi*.

Peng, C.-Y. J., Lee, K. L., & Ingersoll, G. M. (2002). An introduction to logistic regression analysis and reporting. *The Journal of Educational Research*, *96*(1), 3–14. doi:10.1080/00220670209598786

Petrović, G., Bjelaković, G., Benedeto-Stojanov, D., Nagorni, A., Brzački, V., & Marković-Živković, B. (2016). Obesity and metabolic syndrome are risk factors for developing non-alcoholic fatty liver disease as diagnosed by ultrasound. *Vojnosanitetski Pregled. Military-Medical and Pharmaceutical Review*, *73*(10), 910–920. doi:10.2298/VSP150514093P PMID:29327896

Pidikiti, T., Shreedevi, B, G., Subbarao, M., & Krishna, V. B. M. (2023). Design and control of Takagi-Sugeno-Kang fuzzy based inverter for power quality improvement in grid-tied PV systems. Measurement. *Sensors (Basel)*, *25*(100638). doi:10.1016/j.measen.2022.100638

Pillay, J., Gaudet, L., Wingert, A., Bialy, L., Mackie, A. S., Paterson, D. I., & Hartling, L. (2022). Incidence, risk factors, natural history, and hypothesised mechanisms of myocarditis and pericarditis following covid-19 vaccination: Living evidence syntheses and review. *BMJ (Clinical Research Ed.)*, *378*, e069445. doi:10.1136/bmj-2021-069445 PMID:35830976

Poria, S., Cambria, E., & Gelbukh, A. (2015, September). Deep convolutional neural network textual features and multiple kernel learning for utterance-level multi-modal sentiment analysis. In *Proceedings of the 2015 conference on empirical methods in natural language processing* (pp. 2539-2544). Academic Press.

Powell, C. L., & Persico, J. E. (1995). *My American Journey*. Random House.

Prasad, C. H. (2017). Failure analysis and prediction for metal jobs using fuzzy computation. In *International Conference on Intelligent Computing, Instrumentation and Control Technologies (ICICICT)* (pp. 1159–1163). IEEE.

Priscila, S. S., Rajest, S. S., Tadiboina, S. N., Regin, R., & András, S. (2023). Analysis of Machine Learning and Deep Learning Methods for Superstore Sales Prediction. *FMDB Transactions on Sustainable Computer Letters*, *1*(1), 1–11.

Priscila, S. S., Rajest, S., Regin, R., Shynu, T., & Steffi, R. (2023). Classification of Satellite Photographs Utilizing the K-Nearest Neighbor Algorithm. *Central Asian Journal of Mathematical Theory and Computer Sciences*, *4*(6), 53–71.

Protecting Children from violence in the time of covid-19, Disruptions in prevention and response services. (2020). UNICEF Data. Retrieved from https://data.unicef.org/resources/protecting-children-from-violence-in-the-time-of-covid-19-brochure/

Purwar, R., Malik, S., Khanam, Z., & Mishra, A. (2021). Progression of the first stage of labour, in low risk nulliparas in a South Asian population: A prospective observational study. *Journal of Obstetrics & Gynaecology*, *2*(8), 1–5. doi:10.1080/01443615.2020.1867967 PMID:33938356

Qu, M., Chen, J., Xhonneux, L.-P., Bengio, Y., & Tang, J. (2020). *Rnnlogic: Learning logic rules for reasoning on knowledge graphs.* arXiv Prepr. arXiv2010.04029.

Quist-Aphetsi, K., & Blankson, H. (2019). A hybrid data logging system using cryptographic hash blocks based on SHA-256 and MD5 for water treatment plant and distribution line. In *2019 International Conference on Cyber Security and Internet of Things (ICSIoT)*. IEEE. 10.1109/ICSIoT47925.2019.00009

Rajabion, L., Shaltooki, A. A., Taghikhah, M., Ghasemi, A., & Badfar, A. (2019). Healthcare big data processing mechanisms: The role of cloud computing. *International Journal of Information Management*, *49*, 271–289. doi:10.1016/j.ijinfomgt.2019.05.017

Rajest, S. S., Silvia Priscila, S., Regin, R., Shynu, T., & Steffi, R. (2023). Application of Machine Learning to the Process of Crop Selection Based on Land Dataset. *International Journal on Orange Technologies*, *5*(6), 91–112.

Ramamoorthy, S., Gunti, N., Mishra, S., Suryavardan, S., Reganti, A., Patwa, P., & Ahuja, C. (2022). Memotion 2: Dataset on sentiment and emotion analysis of memes. In *Proceedings of De-Factify: Workshop on Multi-modal Fact Checking and Hate Speech Detection, CEUR*. Academic Press.

Ramesh, B., Suhashini, G., Kalnoor, M., Bollapragada, D., & Rao, B. (2017). Cost Optimization by Integrating PV-System and Battery Energy Storage System into Microgrid using Particle Swarm Optimization. *International Journal of Pure and Applied Mathematics*, *114*(8), 45–55.

Rani, R., Kumar, S., Kaiwartya, O., Khasawneh, A. M., Lloret, J., Al-Khasawneh, M. A., & Alarood, A. A. (2021). Towards green computing oriented security: A lightweight postquantum signature for IoE. *Sensors (Basel)*, *21*(5), 1883. doi:10.339021051883 PMID:33800227

Rao, K. S., Pradeep, D. J., Pavan Kumar, Y. V., Chakravarthi, M. K., & Reddy, C. P. (2021). Quantitative analysis on open-loop PI tuning methods for liquid level control. *2021 4th International Symposium on Advanced Electrical and Communication Technologies (ISAECT)*.

Ravinder, M., & Kulkarni, V. (2023a). A review on cyber security and anomaly detection perspectives of smart grid. In *2023 5th International Conference on Smart Systems and Inventive Technology (ICSSIT)*. IEEE.

Ravinder, M., & Kulkarni, V. (2023b). Intrusion detection in smart meters data using machine learning algorithms: A research report. *Frontiers in Energy Research, 11*, 1147431. Advance online publication. doi:10.3389/fenrg.2023.1147431

Ray, S. (2019). A quick review of machine learning algorithms. In *2019 International Conference on Machine Learning, Big Data, Cloud and Parallel Computing (COMITCon)*. IEEE.

Reddy Madduri, G. P., Kumar, D., Muniappan, A., Kumar, Y., Karthick, M. R., & Chakravarthi, M. K. (2022). Rapid computer-aided manufacturing tools including computerized motion control. *2022 2nd International Conference on Advance Computing and Innovative Technologies in Engineering (ICACITE)*.

Reddy, A. P. C., Kumar, D. M. S., Krishna, B. M., Inthiyaz, S., & Ahammad, S. H. (2019). Physical Unclonable Function based Design for Customized Digital Logic Circuit. *International Journal of Advanced Science and Technology, 28*(8), 206–221.

Regin, R., Rajest, S. S., Shynu, T., & Steffi, R. (2023). The application of machine learning to the prediction of heart attack. *International Journal of Human-Computer Studies, 5*(4), 5–25. https://journals.researchparks.org/index.php/IJHCS/article/view/4259

Regin, R., & Shynu, T. (2023). Principal Component Analysis for ATM Facial Recognition Security. *Central Asian Journal of Medical and Natural Science, 4*(3), 292–311.

Richards, J. E., Magill, M., Tressler, M. A., Shuler, F. D., Kregor, P. J., & Obremskey, W. T.The Southeast Fracture Consortium. (2012). External fixation versus ORIF for distal intra-articular tibia fractures. *Orthopedics, 35*(6). Advance online publication. doi:10.3928/01477447-20120525-25 PMID:22691658

Rooney, M. M., & Hinders, M. K. (2021). Machine learning for medium access control protocol recognition in communications networks. *IEEE Access : Practical Innovations, Open Solutions, 9*, 110762–110771. doi:10.1109/ACCESS.2021.3102859

Rosas, V. P., Mihalcea, R., & Morency, L. P. (2013). Multi-modal sentiment analysis of Spanish online videos. *IEEE Intelligent Systems, 28*(3), 38–45.

Roy, M., Ghosh, S., & Ghosh, A. (2014). A novel approach for change detection of remotely sensed images using semi-supervised multiple classifier system. *Information Sciences, 269*, 35–47. doi:10.1016/j.ins.2014.01.037

Rumack, C. M., & Drose, J. A. (2011). Neonatal and infant brain imaging. In *Diagnostic ultrasound* (4th ed., pp. 1558–163). Elsevier, Mosby.

Rumpf, T., Mahlein, A.-K., Steiner, U., Oerke, E.-C., Dehne, H.-W., & Plümer, L. (2010). Early detection and classification of plant diseases with Support Vector Machines based on hyperspectral reflectance. *Computers and Electronics in Agriculture, 74*(1), 91–99. doi:10.1016/j.compag.2010.06.009

Rupapara, V., Rajest, S. S., Rajan, R., Steffi, R., Shynu, T., & Christabel, G. J. A. (2023). A Dynamic Perceptual Detector Module-Related Telemonitoring for the Intertubes of Health Services. In P. Agarwal, K. Khanna, A. A. Elngar, A. J. Obaid, & Z. Polkowski (Eds.), *Artificial Intelligence for Smart Healthcare. EAI/Springer Innovations in Communication and Computing*. Springer. doi:10.1007/978-3-031-23602-0_15

Russell, S., & Norvig, P. (2009). *Artificial Intelligence – A Modern Approach*. Pearson.

Sabir, M. W., Khan, Z., Saad, N. M., Khan, D. M., Al-Khasawneh, M. A., Perveen, K., & Azhar Ali, S. S. (2022). Segmentation of Liver Tumor in CT Scan Using ResU-Net. *Applied Sciences (Basel, Switzerland)*, *12*(17), 8650. doi:10.3390/app12178650

Sabry, F., Eltaras, T., Labda, W., Alzoubi, K., & Malluhi, Q. (2022). Machine Learning for Healthcare Wearable Devices: The Big Picture. *Journal of Healthcare Engineering*, *4653923*, 1–25. Advance online publication. doi:10.1155/2022/4653923 PMID:35480146

Sagar Yeruva, M., Varalakshmi, B., Gowtham, Y. H., & Chandana, P. K. (2021). Identification of Sickle Cell Anemia Using Deep Neural Networks. *Engineering Science Journal, 5*(2).

Sai Pavan Kamma, G., Chilukuri, G., & Rudra Kalyan Nayak, T. (2021). Multiple Myeloma Prediction from Bone-Marrow Blood Cell images using Machine Learning. *IEEE, Emerging Trends in Industry, 4*(0).

Salah, M. (2017). A survey of modern classification techniques in remote sensing for improved image classification. *Journal of Genomics*, *11*(1), 1–21.

Saleem, G., Akhtar, M., Ahmed, N., & Qureshi, W. S. (2019). Automated analysis of visual leaf shape features for plant classification. *Computers and Electronics in Agriculture*, *157*, 270–280. doi:10.1016/j.compag.2018.12.038

Saleh, M. A., Othman, S. H., Al-Dhaqm, A., & Al-Khasawneh, M. A. (2021). Common investigation process model for Internet of Things forensics. In *2021 2nd International Conference on Smart Computing and Electronic Enterprise (ICSCEE)* (pp. 84-89). IEEE.

Saleh, M. A., Othman, S. H., Al-Dhaqm, A., & Al-Khasawneh, M. A. (2021). Common investigation process model for Internet of Things forensics. In *2021 2nd International Conference on Smart Computing and Electronic Enterprise (ICSCEE)* (pp. 84-89). IEEE. 10.1109/ICSCEE50312.2021.9498045

Saleh, O. S., & Osman Ghazali, M. E. (2020). Blockchain based framework for educational certificates verification. *Journal of Critical Reviews*, *7*(03), 79–84.

Samadi, F., Akbarizadeh, G., & Kaabi, H. (2019). Change detection in SAR images using deep belief network: A new training approach based on morphological images. *IET Image Processing*, *13*(12), 2255–2264.

Sanders, R., Gorman, R. R., Ritter, C. A., & Walling, A. K. (2004). Replacement versus arthodesis for post-traumatic ankle arthritis. *Annual Meeting of the OTA.*

Sankaran, S., Mishra, A., Ehsani, R., & Davis, C. (2010). A review of advanced techniques for detecting plant diseases. *Computers and Electronics in Agriculture*, *72*(1), 1–13. doi:10.1016/j.compag.2010.02.007

Santoso, L. W., & Widjanadi, I. (2016). The application of New Information Economics Method on distribution company to improve the efficiency and effectiveness of performance. *International Journal of Engineering and Manufacturing*, *6*(5).

Santoso, L. W., Wilistio, A., & Dewi, L. P. (2016). Mobile Device Application to locate an Interest Point using Google Maps. *International Journal of Science and Engineering Applications*, *5*(1).

Sanyal, D., Mukherjee, P., Raychaudhuri, M., Ghosh, S., Mukherjee, S., & Chowdhury, S. (2015). Profile of liver enzymes in non-alcoholic fatty liver disease in patients with impaired glucose tolerance and newly detected untreated type 2 diabetes. *Indian Journal of Endocrinology and Metabolism*, *19*(5), 597–601. doi:10.4103/2230-8210.163172 PMID:26425466

Saravi, B., Hassel, F., Ülkümen, S., Zink, A., Shavlokhova, V., Couillard-Despres, S., Boeker, M., Obid, P., & Lang, G. M. (2022). Artificial Intelligence-Driven Prediction Modeling and Decision Making in Spine Surgery Using Hybrid Machine Learning Models. *Journal of Personalized Medicine*, *12*(4), 509. doi:10.3390/jpm12040509 PMID:35455625

Sarp, G., & Ozcelik, M. (2017). Water body extraction and change detection using time series: A case study of Lake Burdur, Turkey. *Journal of Taibah University for Science : JTUSCI*, *11*(3), 381–391.

Sathyaseelan, M. P., Amit, P., & Sudipta, S. (2021). IoT based COVID De-Escalation System using Bluetooth Low Level Energy. In *6th International Conference on Inventive Computation Technologies (ICICT)* (pp. 174–177). IEEE.

Sattaru, N. C., Baker, M. R., Umrao, D., Pandey, U. K., Tiwari, M., & Chakravarthi, M. K. (2022). Heart attack anxiety disorder using machine learning and artificial neural networks (ANN) approaches. *2022 2nd International Conference on Advance Computing and Innovative Technologies in Engineering (ICACITE)*.

Savola, J.-M., & Virtanen, R. (1991). Central α2-adrenoceptors are highly stereoselective for dexmedetomidine, the dextro enantiomer of medetomidine. *European Journal of Pharmacology*, *195*(2), 193–199. doi:10.1016/0014-2999(91)90535-X PMID:1678707

Saxena, D., & Chaudhary, S. (2023). Predicting Brain Diseases from FMRI-Functional Magnetic Resonance Imaging with Machine Learning Techniques for Early Diagnosis and Treatment. *FMDB Transactions on Sustainable Computer Letters*, *1*(1), 33–48.

Schary, Y. (2020). Case studies on geocell-based reinforced roads, railways and ports. In *Geocells* (pp. 387–411). Springer Singapore. doi:10.1007/978-981-15-6095-8_15

Schmidhuber, J. (2015). Deep Learning in Neural Networks: An Overview. *Neural Networks*, *61*, 85–117. doi:10.1016/j.neunet.2014.09.003 PMID:25462637

Schubert, J., Brynielsson, J., Nilsson, M., & Svenmarck, P. (2018). Artificial Intelligence for Decision Support in Command and Control Systems. *23rd International Command and Control Research & Technology Symposium "Multi-Domain C2"*.

Sekhar, C., & Kranthi, K. (2017). Traffic signal breach vehicle stop system using IOT. In *IEEE International Conference on Nextgen Electronic Technologies: Silicon to Software (ICNETS2)* (pp. 296–300). IEEE.

Semiz, T. Y. (2017, December 26). Algoritma Nedir? https://maker.robotistan.com/algoritma

Sengodan, S. S., & Mathiyalagan, S. (2020). Doppler study (cerebroplacental ratio) as a predictor of adverse perinatal outcome. *International Journal of Reproduction, Contraception, Obstetrics and Gynecology*, *9*(12), 5068–5074. doi:10.18203/2320-1770.ijrcog20205249

Shabbir, M., Shabbir, A., Iwendi, C., Javed, A. R., Rizwan, M., Herencsar, N., & Lin, J. C.-W. (2021). Enhancing security of health information using modular encryption standard in mobile cloud computing. *IEEE Access : Practical Innovations, Open Solutions*, *9*, 8820–8834. doi:10.1109/ACCESS.2021.3049564

Shaheen, S., Imam, B., Ibne, A., & Singh, A. (2014). Doppler Cerebroplacental Ratio and Adverse Perinatal Outcome. *Journal of South Asian Federation of Obstetrics and Gynecology*, *6*(1), 25–27. doi:10.5005/jp-journals-10006-1262

Shahzad, M., Umar, A. I., Shirazi, S. H., & Shaikh, I. A. (Eds.). (2021). Semantic Segmentation of Anaemic RBCs using Multilevel Deep Convolutional Encoder-Decoder Network. IEEE Access.

Shang, M., Wang, S., Zhou, Y., Du, C., & Liu, W. (2019). Object-based image analysis of suburban landscapes using Landsat-8 imagery. *International Journal of Digital Earth*, *12*(6), 720–736. doi:10.1080/17538947.2018.1474959

Shannon, C. E. (1948). A mathematical theory of communication. *The Bell System Technical Journal*, 27(3), 379–423. doi:10.1002/j.1538-7305.1948.tb01338.x

Sharma, D. K., Jalil, N. A., Regin, R., Rajest, S. S., Tummala, R. K., & Thangadurai. (2021). Predicting network congestion with machine learning. In *2021 2nd International Conference on Smart Electronics and Communication (ICOSEC)*. IEEE.

Sharma, D. K., Jalil, N. A., Regin, R., Rajest, S. S., Tummala, R. K., & Thangadurai. (2021a). Predicting network congestion with machine learning. In *2021 2nd International Conference on Smart Electronics and Communication (ICOSEC)*. IEEE.

Sharma, D. K., Singh, B., Raja, M., Regin, R., & Rajest, S. S. (2021). An Efficient Python Approach for Simulation of Poisson Distribution. In *2021 7th International Conference on Advanced Computing and Communication Systems (ICACCS)*. IEEE.

Sharma, D. K., Singh, B., Raja, M., Regin, R., & Rajest, S. S. (2021a). An Efficient Python Approach for Simulation of Poisson Distribution. *In 2021 7th International Conference on Advanced Computing and Communication Systems (ICACCS)*. IEEE.

Sharma, D. K., Singh, B., Raja, M., Regin, R., & Rajest, S. S. (2021b). An Efficient Python Approach for Simulation of Poisson Distribution. In *2021 7th International Conference on Advanced Computing and Communication Systems (ICACCS)*. IEEE.

Sharma, D. K., Singh, B., Regin, R., Steffi, R., & Chakravarthi, M. K. (2021). Efficient Classification for Neural Machines Interpretations based on Mathematical models. In *2021 7th International Conference on Advanced Computing and Communication Systems (ICACCS)*. IEEE.

Sharma, D. K., Singh, B., Regin, R., Steffi, R., & Chakravarthi, M. K. (2021b). Efficient Classification for Neural Machines Interpretations based on Mathematical models. In *2021 7th International Conference on Advanced Computing and Communication Systems (ICACCS)*. IEEE.

Sharma, D. K., Singh, B., Regin, R., Steffi, R., & Chakravarthi, M. K. (2021c). Efficient Classification for Neural Machines Interpretations based on Mathematical models. In *2021 7th International Conference on Advanced Computing and Communication Systems (ICACCS)*. IEEE.

Sharma, N. (2021). *India: Protect Rights, Dignity Amid Covid-19 crisis*. Retrieved from https://www.hrw.org/news/2021/04/28/india-protect-rights-dignity-amid-covid-19-crisis

Sharma, K., Singh, B., Herman, E., Regine, R., Rajest, S. S., & Mishra, V. P. (2021d). Maximum information measure policies in reinforcement learning with deep energy-based model. In *2021 International Conference on Computational Intelligence and Knowledge Economy (ICCIKE)*. IEEE. 10.1109/ICCIKE51210.2021.9410756

Shashirangana, J., Padmasiri, H., Meedeniya, D., & Perera, C. (2021). Automated License Plate Recognition: A Survey on Methods and Techniques. *IEEE Access : Practical Innovations, Open Solutions*, 9, 11203–11225.

Shashirangana, J., Padmasiri, H., Meedeniya, D., Perera, C., Nayak, S. R., Nayak, J., Vimal, S., & Kadry, S. (2021). License plate recognition using neural architecture search for edge devices. *International Journal of Intelligent Systems*, 37(12), 10211–10248.

Shen, H., Lin, Y., Tian, Q., Xu, K., & Jiao, J. (2018). A comparison of multiple classifier combinations using different voting-weights for remote sensing image classification. *International Journal of Remote Sensing*, 39(11), 3705–3722. doi:10.1080/01431161.2018.1446566

Shen, J., Yang, H., Vijayakumar, P., & Kumar, N. (2022). A privacy-preserving and untraceable group data sharing scheme in cloud computing. *IEEE Transactions on Dependable and Secure Computing, 19*(4), 2198–2210. doi:10.1109/TDSC.2021.3050517

Shifat, A. S. M. Z., Stricklin, I., Chityala, R. K., Aryal, A., Esteves, G., Siddiqui, A., & Busani, T. (2023). Vertical etching of scandium aluminum nitride thin films using TMAH solution. *Nanomaterials (Basel, Switzerland), 13*(2). Advance online publication. doi:10.3390/nano13020274 PMID:36678027

Shi, J., Li, R., & Hou, W. (2020). A mechanism to resolve the unauthorized access vulnerability caused by permission delegation in blockchain-based access control. *IEEE Access : Practical Innovations, Open Solutions, 8*, 156027–156042. doi:10.1109/ACCESS.2020.3018783

Shi, Q., Tan, X.-Q., Liu, X.-R., Tian, X.-B., & Qi, H.-B. (2016). Labour patterns in Chinese women in Chongqing. *BJOG, 123*, 57–63. doi:10.1111/1471-0528.14019 PMID:27627599

Shi, Y., Zhang, J., Lin, Y., & Wu, W. (2020). Improvement of low-speed precision control of a butterfly-shaped linear ultrasonic motor. *IEEE Access : Practical Innovations, Open Solutions, 8*, 135131–135137. doi:10.1109/ACCESS.2020.3007773

Shre, K. C. (2017). *An Approach towards Plant Electrical Signal Based External Stimuli Monitoring System*. Academic Press.

Shynu, O. A. J., Singh, B., Rajest, S. S., Regin, R., & Priscila, S. S. (2022). Sustainable intelligent outbreak with self-directed learning system and feature extraction approach in technology. *International Journal of Intelligent Engineering Informatics, 10*(6), 484-503. doi:10.1504/IJIEI.2022.10054270

Shynu, T., Rajest, S. S., & Regin, R. (2023). OTP As a Service in the Cloud Allows for Authentication of Multiple Services. *International Journal on Orange Technologies, 5*(4), 94–112.

Singh, T., Rastogi, P., Pandey, U. K., Geetha, A., Tiwari, M., & Chakravarthi, M. K. (2022). Systematic healthcare smart systems with the integration of the sensor using cloud computing techniques. *2022 2nd International Conference on Advance Computing and Innovative Technologies in Engineering (ICACITE)*.

Singh, U., Singh, N., & Shikha, S. (2007). A prospective analysis of etiology and outcome of preterm labour. *Journal of Obstetrics and Gynaecology of India, 57*(1), 48.

Siva Ramkumar, M., Priya, R., Rajakumari, R. F., Valsalan, P., Chakravarthi, M., Charlyn Pushpa Latha, G., Mathupriya, S., & Rajan, K. (2022). Review and Evaluation of Power Devices and Semiconductor Materials Based on Si, SiC, and Ga-N. *Journal of Nanomaterials, 2022*, 2022. doi:10.1155/2022/8648284

Sivan, R., & Zukarnain, Z. A. (2021). Security and privacy in cloud-based e-health system. *Symmetry, 13*(5), 742. doi:10.3390ym13050742

Skullerud, K., & Wester, B. (1986). Frequency and prognostic significance of germinal matrix hemorrhage, periventricular leukomalacia, and pontosubicular necrosis in preterm neonates. *Acta Neuropathologica, 70*(3-4), 257–261. doi:10.1007/BF00686080 PMID:3766126

Sneha, D. (2021). Sine Cosine Algorithm Based Deep CNN for Acute Lymphocytic Leukemia Detection. *International Conference: Artificial Intelligence: Advances and Applications (ICAIAA)*.

Sohail, A., Khan, A., Wahab, N., Zameer, A., & Khan, S. (2021). A multi-phase deep CNN based mitosis detection framework for breast cancer histopathological images. *Scientific Reports, 11*(1), 1–18. PMID:33737632

Soleymani, M., Garcia, D., Jou, B., Schuller, B., Chang, S. F., & Pantic, M. (2017). A survey of multi-modal sentiment analysis. *Image and Vision Computing, 65*, 3–14.

Sol-Sánchez, M., & D'Angelo, G. (2017). Review of the design and maintenance technologies used to decelerate the deterioration of ballasted railway tracks. *Construction & Building Materials, 157*, 402–415. doi:10.1016/j.conbuildmat.2017.09.007

Song, L., Li, M., Zhu, Z., Yuan, P., & He, Y. (2020). Attribute-based access control using smart contracts for the internet of things. *Procedia Computer Science, 174*, 231–242. doi:10.1016/j.procs.2020.06.079

Sonnad, S., Sathe, M., Basha, D. K., Bansal, V., Singh, R., & Singh, D. P. (2022). The integration of connectivity and system integrity approaches using internet of things (IoT) for enhancing network security. In *2022 5th International Conference on Contemporary Computing and Informatics (IC3I)*. IEEE.

Srivastav, D. S. (2016). Rawl's theory of Justice Through Amartya Sen's Idea. *ILI Law Review*. Retrieved from https://www.ili.ac.in/pdf/p11_dhawal.pdf

Staff, S. (2020, May). *Despite public health crisis, it is court's duty to protect rights of citizens: Justice Chandrachud.* Retrieved from https://scroll.in/latest/962838/despite-public-health-crisis-it-is-courts-duty-to-protect-rights-of-citizens-justice-chandrachud

Stampalija, T., Arabin, B., Wolf, H., Bilardo, C. M., Lees, C., Brezinka, C., Derks, J. B., Diemert, A., Duvekot, J. J., Ferrazzi, E., Frusca, T., Ganzevoort, W., Hecher, K., Kingdom, J., Marlow, N., Marsal, K., Martinelli, P., Ostermayer, E., Papageorghiou, A. T., & Zimmermann, A. (2017). Is middle cerebral artery Doppler related to neonatal and 2-year infant outcome in early fetal growth restriction? *American Journal of Obstetrics and Gynecology, 216*(5), 521.e1–521.e13. doi:10.1016/j.ajog.2017.01.001 PMID:28087423

Stanford Encyclopedia of Philosophy. (n.d.). Retrieved from https://plato.stanford.edu/entries/rawls/

Stappen, L., Baird, A., Schumann, L., & Bjorn, S. (2021). The multi-modal sentiment analysis in car reviews (muse-car) dataset: Collection, insights and improvements. *IEEE Transactions on Affective Computing*.

Statement by Lanzarote Committee Chairpeson and Vice Chairperson on stepping up protection of children against sexual exploitation and abuse in times of the Covid-19 pandemic. (2020). Council of Europe. Retrieved from https://rm.coe.int/covid-19-lc-statement-en-final/16809e17ae

Stauffer, J., & Zhang, Q. (2021). S 2 cloud: A novel cloud system for mobile health big data management. In *2021 IEEE International Conferences on Internet of Things (iThings) and IEEE Green Computing & Communications (GreenCom) and IEEE Cyber, Physical & Social Computing (CPSCom) and IEEE Smart Data (SmartData) and IEEE Congress on Cybermatics (Cybermatics)* (pp. 380–383). IEEE.

Steffi, S. R. S., Rajest, R., Shynu, T., & Priscila, S. S. (2023). Analysis of an Interview Based on Emotion Detection Using Convolutional Neural Networks. *Central Asian Journal of Theoretical and Applied Science, 4*(6), 78–102.

Stoelting, R. K. (2006). Pharmacology and physiology in anaesthesia practice Lippincott-Raven.

Su, S., Ren, C., Zhang, H., Liu, Z., & Zhang, Z. (2016). *The Opioid-Sparing Effect of Perioperative Dexmedetomidine Plus Sufentanil Infusion during Neurosurgery : A Retrospective Study.* Academic Press.

Suganthi, M., & Sathiaseelan, J. G. R. (2023). Image Denoising and Feature Extraction Techniques Applied to X-Ray Seed Images for Purity Analysis. *FMDB Transactions on Sustainable Health Science Letters, 1*(1), 41–53.

Suh, C. H., Kim, S. Y., Kim, K. W., Lim, Y. S., Lee, S. J., Lee, M. G., Lee, J. B., Lee, S.-G., & Yu, E. (2014). Determination of Normal Hepatic Elasticity by Using Real-time Shear-wave Elastography. *Radiology, 271*(3), 895–900. doi:10.1148/radiol.14131251 PMID:24555633

Sujarani, P., & Kalaiselvi, K. (2018). Correlation Feature Selection (CFS) and Probabilistic Neural Network (PNN) for Diabetes Disease Prediction. *International Journal of Science & Technology, 7*(3).

Sun, J., Xu, C., Tang, L., Wang, S., Lin, C., Gong, Y., Shum, H.-Y., & Guo, J. (2023). *Think-on-Graph: Deep and Responsible Reasoning of Large Language Model with Knowledge Graph.* arXiv Prepr. arXiv2307.07697.

Sun, L., Sun, H., Wang, J., Wu, S., Zhao, Y., & Xu, Y. (2021). Breast mass detection in mammography based on image template matching and CNN. *Sensors (Basel), 21*(8), 2855. doi:10.339021082855 PMID:33919623

Sun, Y., Deng, S., Lu, Y., Fan, R., Ma, X., & Lü, D. (2022). Emendation of the Triassic plant species Glossophyllum shensiense (Ginkgoales) with a review of the genus Glossophyllum Kräusel. *Review of Palaeobotany and Palynology, 301*(104657), 104657. doi:10.1016/j.revpalbo.2022.104657

Sun, Y., Liu, Y., Wang, G., & Zhang, H. (2017). Deep learning for plant identification in natural environment. *Computational Intelligence and Neuroscience, 2017*, 1–6. doi:10.1155/2017/7361042 PMID:28611840

Suthar, V., Bansal, V., Reddy, C. S., Gonzáles, J. L. A., Singh, D., & Singh, D. P. (2022). Machine Learning Adoption in Blockchain-Based Smart Applications. In *2022 5th International Conference on Contemporary Computing and Informatics (IC3I).* IEEE.

Suzuki, R., Horiuchi, S., & Ohtsu, H. (2010). Evaluation of the labor curve in nulliparous Japanese women. *American Journal of Obstetrics and Gynecology, 203*(3), 226.e1–226.e6. doi:10.1016/j.ajog.2010.04.014 PMID:20494329

Svenmarck, P., Luotsinen, L., Nilsson, M., & Schubert, J. (2018). Possibilities and Challenges for Artificial Intelligence in Military Applications. In *Proceedings of the NATO Big Data and Artificial Intelligence for Military Decision Making Specialists' Meeting.* NATO Research and Technology Organisation.

Taboada, M., Brooke, J., Tofiloski, M., Voll, K., & Stede, M. (2011). Lexicon-based methods for sentiment analysis. *Computational Linguistics, 37*(2), 267–307.

Tadiboina, S. N., & Chase, G. C. (2022). The importance and leverage of modern information technology infrastructure in the healthcare industry. *Int J Res Trends Innov, 7*(11), 340–344.

Tang, D., Qin, B., & Liu, T. (2015, September). Document modeling with gated recurrent neural network for sentiment classification. In *Proceedings of the 2015 conference on empirical methods in natural language processing* (pp. 1422-1432). Academic Press.

Tang, X., Liu, L., Tu, C.-Q., Li, J., Li, Q., & Pei, F.-X. (2014). Comparison of early and delayed open reduction and internal fixation for treating closed tibial Pilon fractures. *Foot & Ankle International, 35*(7), 657–664. doi:10.1177/1071100714534214 PMID:24842898

Tania Sourdin, B. L. (2020). *Court Innovations and Access to Justice in times of crisis.* Retrieved from Health Policy Technology: https://www.ncbi.nlm.nih.gov/pmc/articles/PMC7456584/

Tan, M., Pang, R., & Le, Q. V. (2020). EfficientDet: Scalable and Efficient Object Detection. In *2020 IEEE/CVF Conference on Computer Vision and Pattern Recognition (CVPR).* IEEE. 10.1109/CVPR42600.2020.01079

Tannishtha Dutta, S. R. (n.d.). Re-imaging the role of police in Covid-19 times. UNICEF India. Retrieved from https://www.unicef.org/india/stories/re-imagining-role-police-covid-19-times

Thakare, A. (2018). Concealed Weapon Detection Using Image Processing. *International Journal of Electronics, Communication and Soft Computing Science and Engineering*, 31–34.

Themes, U. F. O. (2017). *49 72-year-old female with a 2-day history of progressively worsening headache, nausea, and vomiting.* Radiology Key. https://radiologykey.com/49-72-year-old-female-with-a-2-day-history-of-progressively-worsening-headache-nausea-and-vomiting/(Accessed by 12 March, 2023)

Thi, T., Takahashi, H., Toriu, T., & Ham, H. (2011). Fusion of Infrared and Visible Images for Robust Person Detection. Graduate School of Engineering, Osaka City University. doi:10.5772/14173

Thorton, J. G. (2006). Use of partograph with an agreed protocol for Active Management of Labour. *Journal of Obstetrics & Gynaecology, 91*, 188–196.

Tiwari, P., Zhu, H., & Pandey, H. M. (2021). DAPath: Distance-aware knowledge graph reasoning based on deep reinforcement learning. *Neural Networks, 135*, 1–12. doi:10.1016/j.neunet.2020.11.012 PMID:33310193

Toosi, A. N., Calheiros, R. N., & Buyya, R. (2014). Interconnected cloud computing environments: Challenges, taxonomy, and survey. *ACM Computing Surveys, 47*(1), 1–47. doi:10.1145/2593512

Toprak, A. (2020). Yapay Zekâ Algoritmalarının Dijital Enstalasyona Dönüşmesi. *Ege University Faculty of Communication New Thoughts Peer-reviewed E-Journal*, (14), 47–59.

Trajanoska, M., Stojanov, R., & Trajanov, D. (2023). *Enhancing Knowledge Graph Construction Using Large Language Models.* arXiv Prepr. arXiv2305.04676.

Tripathi, A. P. (2022). *Concept of Justice under Indian Constitution.* Retrieved from Manupatra: https://articles.manupatra.com/article-details/Concept-of-Justice-under-Indian-Constitution

Trouillon, T., Welbl, J., Riedel, S., Gaussier, É., & Bouchard, G. (2016). Complex embeddings for simple link prediction. In *International Conference on Machine Learning*. PMLR.

Türkoğlu, M., & Hanbay, D. (2019). Plant disease and pest detection using deep learning-based features. *Turkish Journal of Electrical Engineering and Computer Sciences, 27*(3), 1636–1651. doi:10.3906/elk-1809-181

Tv, B., & Kn, N. (2021). A Hybrid Level Set Based Approach for Surface Water Delineation using Landsat-8 Multispectral Images". Multispectral Images. *Engineering Letters, 29*(2), 1–10.

Uddin, M. I., Ali Shah, S. A., Al-Khasawneh, M. A., Alarood, A. A., & Alsolami, E. (2022). Optimal policy learning for COVID-19 prevention using reinforcement learning. *Journal of Information Science, 48*(3), 336–348. doi:10.1177/0165551520959798

Uike, D., Agarwalla, S., Bansal, V., Chakravarthi, M. K., Singh, R., & Singh, P. (2022). Investigating the role of block chain to secure identity in IoT for industrial automation. In *2022 11th International Conference on System Modeling & Advancement in Research Trends (SMART)*. IEEE.

Ullah, Z., Zeb, A., Ullah, I., Awan, K. M., Saeed, Y., Uddin, M. I., & Zareei, M. (2020). Certificateless proxy reencryption scheme (CPRES) based on hyperelliptic curve for access control in content-centric network (CCN). *Mobile Information Systems, 2020*, 1–13. doi:10.1155/2020/4138516

Ummuhanysifa, U., & Banu, P. K. (2013). Voice based search engine and web page reader. *International Journal of Computational Engineering Research*, 1–5.

Upadhyay, E. M., & Rana, N. K. (2014). Exposure fusion for concealed weapon detection. *2014 2nd International Conference on Devices, Circuits and Systems (ICDCS)*.

Vaishna, S., & Kumar, M. K. (2016). MSP430 Data Logger: An Implementation for Stress Measurement in Concrete Structures. *International Conference on Intelligent Systems and Control*.

Vashishtha, E., & Dhawan, G. (2023). Bridging Generation Gap on Analysis of Mentor-Mentee Relationship in Healthcare Setting. *FMDB Transactions on Sustainable Health Science Letters*, *1*(1), 21–30.

Vashishtha, E., & Kapoor, H. (2023). Implementation of Blockchain Technology Across International Healthcare Markets. *FMDB Transactions on Sustainable Technoprise Letters*, *1*(1), 1–12.

Vashishtha, E., & Sherman, L. (2018). Socioeconomic Status and Childhood Obesity. *International Journal of Physical and Social Sciences*, *8*(11), 184–194.

Vashishtha, E., Sherman, L., Sajjad, T., & Mehmood, N. (2020). Use of anti-viral therapy in treatment of Covid 19. *Journal of Advanced Medical and Dental Sciences Research*, *8*(11), 273–276.

Veeraiah, V., Pankajam, A., Vashishtha, E., Dhabliya, D., Karthikeyan, P., & Chandan, R. R. (2022). Efficient CO-VID-19 identification using deep learning for IoT. In *2022 5th International Conference on Contemporary Computing and Informatics (IC3I)*. IEEE.

Vijayakumar. (2019). Neural network analysis for tumor investigation and cancer prediction. *Journal of Electronics and Informatics*, (2), 89–98. doi:10.36548/jes.2019.2.004

Vijayaraghavareddy, P., Lekshmy, S. V., Struik, P. C., Makarla, U., Yin, X., & Sreeman, S. (2022). Production and scavenging of reactive oxygen species confer to differential sensitivity of rice and wheat to drought stress. *Crop and Environment*, *1*(1), 15–23. doi:10.1016/j.crope.2022.03.010

Vishram, J. K. K., Borglykke, A., Andreasen, A. H., Jeppesen, J., Ibsen, H., Jørgensen, T., Palmieri, L., Giampaoli, S., Donfrancesco, C., Kee, F., Mancia, G., Cesana, G., Kuulasmaa, K., Salomaa, V., Sans, S., Ferrieres, J., Dallongeville, J., Söderberg, S., Arveiler, D., ... Olsen, M. H.The MORGAM Prospective Cohort Project. (2014). Impact of Age and Gender on the Prevalence and Prognostic Importance of the Metabolic Syndrome and Its Components in Europeans. The MORGAM Prospective Cohort Project. *PLoS One*, *9*(9), e107294. doi:10.1371/journal.pone.0107294 PMID:25244618

Vollgraff Heidweiller-Schreurs, C. A., De Boer, M. A., Heymans, M. W., Schoonmade, L. J., Bossuyt, P. M. M., Mol, B. W. J., De Groot, C. J. M., & Bax, C. J. (2018). Prognostic accuracy of cerebroplacental ratio and middle cerebral artery Doppler for adverse perinatal outcome: Systematic review and meta-analysis. *Ultrasound in Obstetrics & Gynecology*, *51*(3), 313–322. doi:10.1002/uog.18809 PMID:28708272

Volpe, J. J. (1995). Neurological evaluation; hypoxic-ischemic encephalopathy; and intracranial hemorrhage. In *Neurology of the newborn* (3rd ed., pp. 95–463). W.B. Saunders Company.

Walczak, S., & Velanovich, V. (2018). Improving prognosis and reducing decision regret for pancreatic cancer treatment using artificial neural networks. *Elsevier Decision Support Systems*, *106*, 110–118.

Wang, D., & Hu, M. (2021). Deep Deterministic Policy Gradient With Compatible Critic Network. *IEEE Trans. Neural Networks Learn. Syst.*

Wang, D., Hu, M., & Gao, Y. (2018). Multi-criteria mission planning for a solar-powered multi-robot system. *International Design Engineering Technical Conferences and Computers and Information in Engineering Conference*. 10.1115/DETC2018-85683

Wang, D., Hu, M., & Weir, J.D. (2022). Simultaneous Task and Energy Planning using Deep Reinforcement Learning. *Inf. Sci.*

Wang, H., & Raj, B. (2017). *On the origin of deep learning*. arXiv 2017, arXiv:1702.07800.

Wang, D. (2022). *Meta Reinforcement Learning with Hebbian Learning. In 2022 IEEE 13th Annual Ubiquitous Computing, Electronics & Mobile Communication Conference (UEMCON)*. IEEE. doi:10.1109/UEMCON54665.2022.9965711

Wang, D. (2023). Reinforcement Learning for Combinatorial Optimization. In *Encyclopedia of Data Science and Machine Learning* (pp. 2857–2871). IGI Global.

Wang, H., Li, S., Pan, R., & Mao, M. (2019). Incorporating graph attention mechanism into knowledge graph reasoning based on deep reinforcement learning. *Proceedings of the 2019 Conference on Empirical Methods in Natural Language Processing and the 9th International Joint Conference on Natural Language Processing (EMNLP-IJCNLP)*, 2623–2631. 10.18653/v1/D19-1264

Wang, Q., Meizhou, Q., Li, Y., & Wen, J. (2021). A 3D attention networks for classification of white blood cells from microscopy hyperspectral images. *Optics & Laser Technology*, 139.

Wang, S., Wang, H., Li, J., Wang, H., Chaudhry, J., Alazab, M., & Song, H. (2020). A fast CP-ABE system for cyber-physical security and privacy in mobile healthcare network. *IEEE Transactions on Industry Applications*, *56*(4), 4467–4477. doi:10.1109/TIA.2020.2969868

Wang, X., Liu, K., Wang, D., Wu, L., Fu, Y., & Xie, X. (2022). Multi-level recommendation reasoning over knowledge graphs with reinforcement learning. *Proceedings of the ACM Web Conference 2022*, 2098–2108. 10.1145/3485447.3512083

Wang, Y., Bian, Z. P., Zhou, Y., & Chau, L. P. (2022). Rethinking and Designing a High-Performing Automatic License Plate Recognition Approach. *IEEE Transactions on Intelligent Transportation Systems*, *23*(7), 8868–8880.

Wang, Z., Li, M., Wang, H., Jiang, H., & Yao, Y. (2019). Breast cancer detection using extreme learning machine based on feature fusion with CNN deep features. *IEEE Access : Practical Innovations, Open Solutions*, *7*, 105146–105158.

Wang, Z., Zhang, J., Feng, J., & Chen, Z. (2014). Knowledge graph embedding by translating on hyperplanes. *Proceedings of the AAAI Conference on Artificial Intelligence.* 10.1609/aaai.v28i1.8870

Weihong, W., & Jiaoyang, T. (2020). Research on License Plate Recognition Algorithms Based on Deep Learning in Complex Environment. *IEEE Access : Practical Innovations, Open Solutions*, *8*, 91661–91675.

Wei, J., Wang, X., Schuurmans, D., Bosma, M., Xia, F., Chi, E., Le, Q. V., & Zhou, D. (2022). Chain-of-thought prompting elicits reasoning in large language models. *Advances in Neural Information Processing Systems*, *35*, 24824–24837.

What is Social Justice? (n.d.). Retrieved from https://pachamama.org/social-justice/what-is-social-justice

Wikipedia. (2019). *Christchurch mosque shootings*. Available:https://en.wikipedia.org/wiki/Christchurch_mosque_shootings

Williams, T. M., Nepola, J. V., DeCoster, T. A., Hurwitz, S. R., Dirschl, D. R., & Marsh, J. L. (2004). Factors affecting outcome in tibial plafond fractures. *Clinical Orthopaedics and Related Research*, *423*(423), 93–98. doi:10.1097/01.blo.0000127922.90382.f4 PMID:15232432

Woodward, P. K., Kennedy, J., Laghrouche, O., Connolly, D. P., & Medero, G. (2014). Study of railway track stiffness modification by polyurethane reinforcement of the ballast. *Transportation Geotechnics*, *1*(4), 214–224. doi:10.1016/j.trgeo.2014.06.005

World Health Organisation. (2014). *WHO recommendations for augmentation of labour*. WHO.

Wu, T., Peng, J., Zhang, W., Zhang, H., Tan, S., Yi, F., & Huang, Y. (2022). Video sentiment analysis with bimodal information-augmented multi-head attention. *Knowledge-Based Systems*, *235*, 107676.

Xia, T., Https Qing, Y., Fu, N., Jin, P., Chazot, P., & Angelov, R. (2020). AI-enabled Microscopic Blood Analysis for Microfluidic COVID-19 Hematology. *International Conference on Computational Intelligence and Applications (ICCIA)*.

Xia, Y., Lan, M., Luo, J., Chen, X., & Zhou, G. (2022). Iterative rule-guided reasoning over sparse knowledge graphs with deep reinforcement learning. *Information Processing & Management*, *59*(5), 103040. doi:10.1016/j.ipm.2022.103040

Xie, W., Xing, C., Wang, J., Guo, S., Guo, M.-W., & Zhu, L.-F. (2020). Hybrid Henry gas solubility optimization algorithm based on the Harris hawk optimization. *IEEE Access : Practical Innovations, Open Solutions*, *8*, 144665–144692. doi:10.1109/ACCESS.2020.3014309

Xiong, W., Hoang, T., & Wang, W. Y. (2017). *Deeppath: A reinforcement learning method for knowledge graph reasoning*. arXiv Prepr. arXiv1707.06690. doi:10.18653/v1/D17-1060

Xu, N. (2017, July). Analyzing multi-modal public sentiment based on hierarchical semantic attentional network. In 2017 IEEE international conference on intelligence and security informatics (ISI) (pp. 152-154). IEEE.

Xue, Z., & Blum, R. (2003). Colour image fusion for the detection of hidden weapons. *FUSION 2003: Proceedings of the Sixth International Conference on Information Fusion*. 10.1109/ICIF.2003.177504

Xu, Z., Shi, H., Lin, P., & Liu, T. (2021). Integrated lithology identification based on images and elemental data from rocks. *Journal of Petroleum Science Engineering*, *205*(108853), 108853. doi:10.1016/j.petrol.2021.108853

Yamaguchi, K., Yang, L., McCall, S., Huang, J., Yu, X. X., Pandey, S. K., Bhanot, S., Monia, B. P., Li, Y.-X., & Diehl, A. M. (2007). Inhibiting triglyceride synthesis improves hepatic steatosis but exacerbates liver damage and fibrosis in obese mice with nonalcoholicsteato hepatitis. *Hepatology (Baltimore, Md.)*, *45*(6), 1366–1374. doi:10.1002/hep.21655 PMID:17476695

Yang, B., Yih, W., He, X., Gao, J., & Deng, L. (2014). *Embedding entities and relations for learning and inference in knowledge bases*. arXiv Prepr. arXiv1412.6575.

Yin, T., Lv, Y., & Yu, W. (2020). Accurate privacy preserving average consensus. IEEE Transactions on Circuits and Systems. II. *Express Briefs, 67*(4), 690–694. doi:10.1109/TCSII.2019.2918709

Yogeshwari, M. (2020). Automatic segmentation of plant leaf disease using improved fast fuzzy C means clustering and adaptive otsu thresholding (IFFCM-AO) algorithm. *European Journal of Molecular and Clinical Medicine, 7*.

Yogeshwari, M. (2021). *Automatic Feature extraction and detection of plant leaf disease using GLCM features and Convolutional Neural Network*. Science Direct.

Yousef, R., Khan, S., Gupta, G., Albahlal, B. M., Alajlan, S. A., & Ali, A. (2023). Bridged-U-Net-ASPP-EVO and Deep Learning Optimization for Brain Tumor Segmentation. *Diagnostics (Basel)*, *13*(16), 2633. doi:10.3390/diagnostics13162633 PMID:37627893

Yuan, J., Mcdonough, S., You, Q., & Luo, J. (2013, August). Sentribute: image sentiment analysis from a mid-level perspective. In *Proceedings of the second international workshop on issues of sentiment discovery and opinion mining* (pp. 1-8). Academic Press.

Yue, L., Chen, W., Li, X., Zuo, W., & Yin, M. (2019). A survey of sentiment analysis in social media. *Knowledge and Information Systems*, *60*, 617–663.

Yuenyong, S., Hnoohom, N., & Wongpatikaseree, K. (2018). Automatic detection of knives in infrared images. *2018 International ECTI Northern Section Conference on Electrical, Electronics, Computer and Telecommunications Engineering (ECTI-NCON)*. 10.1109/ECTI-NCON.2018.8378283

Yu, J., Sharpe, S. M., Schumann, A. W., & Boyd, N. S. (2019). Deep learning for image-based weed detection in turfgrass. European Journal of Agronomy. *European Journal of Agronomy*, *104*, 78–84. doi:10.1016/j.eja.2019.01.004

Yu, J., Wang, Y., Li, Y., Li, X., Li, C., & Shen, J. (2014). The safety and effectiveness of Da Vinci surgical system compared with open surgery and laparoscopic surgery: A rapid assessment. *Journal of Evidence-Based Medicine, 7*(2), 121–134. doi:10.1111/jebm.12099 PMID:25155768

Yun, L., Wang, D., & Li, L. (2023). Explainable multi-agent deep reinforcement learning for real-time demand response towards sustainable manufacturing. *Applied Energy, 347*, 121324. doi:10.1016/j.apenergy.2023.121324

Yu, S., & Chen, X. (2020). Infrared and visible image fusion based on a latent low-rank representation nested with multiscale geometric transform. *IEEE Access : Practical Innovations, Open Solutions, 8*, 110214–110226. doi:10.1109/ACCESS.2020.3001974

Yu, Z., Woodward, P. K., Laghrouche, O., & Connolly, D. P. (2019). True triaxial testing of geogrid for high speed railways. *Transportation Geotechnics, 20*(100247), 100247. doi:10.1016/j.trgeo.2019.100247

Zadeh, A. B., Liang, P. P., Poria, S., Cambria, E., & Morency, L. P. (2018, July). Multi-modal language analysis in the wild: Cmu-mosei dataset and interpretable dynamic fusion graph. In *Proceedings of the 56th Annual Meeting of the Association for Computational Linguistics* (Volume 1*: Long Papers*) (pp. 2236-2246). Academic Press.

Zadeh, A., Zellers, R., Pincus, E., & Morency, L. P. (2016). *Mosi: multi-modal corpus of sentiment intensity and subjectivity analysis in online opinion videos.* arXiv preprint arXiv:1606.06259.

Zadeh, A., Cao, Y. S., Hessner, S., Liang, P. P., Poria, S., & Morency, L. P. (2020, November). CMU-MOSEAS: A multi-modal language dataset for Spanish, Portuguese, German and French. In *Proceedings of the Conference on Empirical Methods in Natural Language Processing. Conference on Empirical Methods in Natural Language Processing* (p. 1801). NIH Public Access.

Zaharchuk, G., & Davidzon, G. (2021). Artificial Intelligence for Optimization and Interpretation of PET/CT and PET/MR Images. *Seminars in Nuclear Medicine, 51*(2), 134–142. doi:10.1053/j.semnuclmed.2020.10.001 PMID:33509370

Zalpour, M., Akbarizadeh, G., & Alaei-Sheini, N. (2020). A new approach for oil tank detection using deep learning features with control false alarm rate in high-resolution satellite imagery. *International Journal of Remote Sensing, 41*(6), 2239–2262. doi:10.1080/01431161.2019.1685720

Zannah, A. I., Rachakonda, S., Abubakar, A. M., Devkota, S., & Nneka, E. C. (2023). Control for Hydrogen Recovery in Pressuring Swing Adsorption System Modeling. *FMDB Transactions on Sustainable Energy Sequence, 1*(1), 1–10.

Zeng, Z., Wang, D., Tan, W., & Huang, J. (2019). Extracting aquaculture ponds from natural water surfaces around inland lakes on medium resolution multispectral images. *International Journal of Applied Earth Observation and Geoinformation, 80*, 13–25.

Zhang, J., Landy, H. J., Branch, W., Burkman, R., Haberman, S., Gregory, K. D., Hatjis, C. G., Ramirez, M. M., Bailit, J. L., Gonzalez-Quintero, V. H., Hibbard, J. U., Hoffman, M. K., Kominiarek, M., Learman, L. A., Van Veldhuisen, P., Troendle, J., & Reddy, U. M. (2011). Contemporary patterns of spontaneous labor with normal neonatal outcomes. *Obstetrical & Gynecological Survey, 66*(3), 132–133. doi:10.1097/OGX.0b013e31821685d0

Zhang, Z., Wang, J., & Wang, H. (2018). Correlation of blood glucose, serum chemerin and insulin resistance with NAFLD in patients with type 2 diabetes mellitus. *Experimental and Therapeutic Medicine, 15*(3), 2936–2940. doi:10.3892/etm.2018.5753 PMID:29456698

Zhao, S., Yao, H., Yang, Y., & Zhang, Y. (2014, November). Affective image retrieval via multi-graph learning. In *Proceedings of the 22nd ACM international conference on Multimedia* (pp. 1025-1028). ACM.

Zhao, Y., Wang, X., Chen, J., Wang, Y., Tang, W., He, X., & Xie, H. (2022). Time-aware path reasoning on knowledge graph for recommendation. *ACM Transactions on Information Systems*, *41*, 1–26.

Zheng, R., Dou, S., Gao, S., Shen, W., Wang, B., Liu, Y., Jin, S., Liu, Q., Xiong, L., & Chen, L. (2023). *Secrets of RLHF in Large Language Models Part I: PPO*. arXiv Prepr. arXiv2307.04964.

Zhou, X., Wang, P., Luo, Q., & Pan, Z. (2021). Multi-hop Knowledge Graph Reasoning Based on Hyperbolic Knowledge Graph Embedding and Reinforcement Learning. *The 10th International Joint Conference on Knowledge Graphs*, 1–9. 10.1145/3502223.3502224

Zhu, Y., Liu, H., Wu, Z., Song, Y., & Zhang, T. (2019). *Representation learning with ordered relation paths for knowledge graph completion*. arXiv Prepr. arXiv1909.11864. doi:10.18653/v1/D19-1268

Zhu, Z., Zhang, Z., Xhonneux, L.-P., & Tang, J. (2021). Neural bellman-ford networks: A general graph neural network framework for link prediction. *Advances in Neural Information Processing Systems*, *34*, 29476–29490.

Ziegler, M. (2017). Application of geogrid reinforced constructions: History, recent and future developments. *Procedia Engineering*, *172*, 42–51. doi:10.1016/j.proeng.2017.02.015

Zohav, E., Zohav, E., Rabinovich, M., Alasbah, A., Shenhav, S., Sofer, H., Ovadia, Y. S., Anteby, E. Y., & Grin, L. (2019). Third-trimester reference ranges for cerebroplacental ratio, middle cerebral artery, and umbilical artery pulsatility index in normal-growth singleton fetuses in the Israeli population. *Rambam Maimonides Medical Journal*, *10*(4), e0025. doi:10.5041/RMMJ.10379 PMID:31675306

About the Contributors

S. Suman Rajest is currently working as Dean of Research and Development (R&D) & International Student Affairs (ISA) at Dhaanish Ahmed College of Engineering, Chennai, Tamil Nadu, India. He is an Editor in Chief of the International Journal of Human Computing Studies and The International Journal of Social Sciences World, He is the Chief Executive Editor of the International Journal of Advanced Engineering Research and Science, International Journal of Advanced Engineering, Management and Science, The International Journal of Health and Medicines, The International Journal of Management Economy and Accounting Fields and The International Journal of Technology Information and Computer and also he is an Editorial Board Member in International Journal of Management in Education, Scopus, Inderscience, EAI Endorsed Transactions on e-Learning, and Bulletin of the Karaganda university Pedagogy series. He is also a Book Series Editor in IGI Global Publisher, Springer, etc. All of his writing, including his research, involves elements of creative nonfiction in the Human Computing learning system. He is also interested in creative writing and digital media, Learning, AI, student health learning, etc. He has published 155 papers in peer-reviewed international journals. He has authored and co-authored several scientific book publications in journals and conferences and is a frequent reviewer of international journals and international conferences and also, he is also a reviewer in Inderscience, EAI Journals, IGI Global, Science Publications, etc.

Bhopendra Singh is an Associate Professor in Engineering & Architecture Department, Amity University Dubai, UAE, from October 2011 to date, respectively. He is a competent & versatile professional with 25 years of experience in Strategic Planning, Academic Operations, Teaching & Mentoring. He is currently serving as a Head of Industry Relations-Engineering and senior faculty at Amity University in Dubai. He is an individual with a proactive attitude, thinking out of the box and generating new design solutions and ideas. His research parts are actively involved in accreditation like IET, WASAC, DQA Award, and HCERF Visits. Signed several MOU with industries like Cisco, Emircom, Tele logic, Siemens, Dewa R&D. Coordinating with other reputed institutions like IIT Indore for research and student's internship. Organizing industry visit industry Guest lectures for engineering students. Organizing training for engineering students. Arranging internship for engineering students since July 2018. Coordinator of Board of Studies (2011 to 2014). Member of IQAC (2012-2014). Developed and installed lab for engineering programs (2011-2012). Member of sports committee from (2011-2015). He teaches as per academic curriculum to students, recognizing and nurturing each student's creative potential. Teach students using a systematic instructional methodology comprising lecture plans (following the credit allotted to each subject), discussion groups, seminars, case studies, field assignments, and independent and/or group projects. Recently, he has been the technique program committee, the technique reviews, and the track chair for international conferences published by Springer-ASIC/LNAI Series. He is serving as the editor in chief of the editorial board of international journals, and he authored/edited different books by Springer, Wiley, CRC Press, and filed many Patents. Finally, he is a member of ISTE, IET, IEEE, etc.

Ahmed J. Obaid is an Asst. Professor at the Department of Computer Science, Faculty of Computer Science and Mathematics, University of Kufa, Iraq. Dr. Ahmed holds a Bachelor in Computer Science, degree in – Information Systems from College of Computers, University of Anbar, Iraq (2001-2005), and a Master Degree (M. TECH) of Computer Science Engineering (CSE) from School of Information Technology, Jawaharlal Nehru Technological University, Hyderabad, India (2010-2013), and a Doctor of Philosophy (PhD) in Web Mining from College of Information Technology, University of University of Babylon, Iraq (2013-2017). He is a Certified Web Mining Consultant with over 14 years of experience in working as Faculty Member in University of Kufa, Iraq. He has taught courses in Web Designing, Web Scripting, JavaScript, VB.Net, MATLAB Toolbox's, and other courses on PHP, CMC, and DHTML from more than 10 international organizations and institutes from USA, and India. Dr. Ahmed is a member of Statistical and Information Consultation Center (SICC), University of Kufa, Iraq.

R. Regin is currently working as an Assistant Professor in the Department of Computer Science and Engineering at the SRM Institute of Science and Technology, Chennai, Tamil Nadu, India. He has a specialization in the branch of information and communication. He holds experience of 10+ years in teaching faculty and research. He has also published papers in 55 reputed international journals, 40 international conferences, and 15 national conferences. He is a member of professional bodies like IE and IETE. He is also a Book Series Editor for IGI Global Publisher, Springer, etc. He is the Editor-in-Chief of the International Journal of Technology Information and Computers, Growing Scholar USA, and a member of the Journal Ilmiah Teunuleh's Editorial Advisory Board. He does research work in the fields of VANET, WSN, MANET, Cloud Computing, Network Security, and Information Security. He is a reviewer for many reputed journals like Springer, Inderscience, etc.

Karthikeyan Chinnusamy is Sr Principal with more than 25 years of experience in IT, Product Dev, R&D and Education fields. Fellow IETE, Fellow IE, Sr Member IEEE, Sr Member ACM, Project management Institute (PMI), Reviewer, Editorial Board Member of R&D Journals. Board Member & Program Director SF DAMA. SME in Data Governance, GDPR, HIPAA Compliance, Data Management, Data Architecture, Master Data, Data Quality, AI/ML, Analytics and reporting in Payment processing, Customer, Finance, CRM and License domains. Mentor in SFDC Mig, Data.com, ERP, Architecture, R&D, Embedded systems, VLSI, Adv Information processing. I am also reviewer for IEEE Silicon Valley Sr Member Elevation and Speaker, Volunteer for SFBay ACM. Reviewer of Journals in Springer Nature.

* * *

Savio S. Moloparambil is a student in Vellore Institute of Technology, Chennai, India. He is currently pursuing his 3rd year for his B.Tech. in Computer Science and Engineering with specialization in AI and Robotics. His research interests include Data Analytics, Machine Learning and Web Design.

Aseem Chandra Paliwal is working as an Associate Professor in Law at the Karnavati University Gandhinagar, Gujarat, India. He holds an LL.M from the University of Rajasthan, Jaipur, and L.L.B from Dr B.R .Ambedkar University, Agra. He completed his PhD from the University of Rajasthan, titled "Legislative trends related to reservation in India in education and private employment". Dr. Paliwal has more than 18 years of experience as an academician and has held various administrative positions in different institutions. Dr. Paliwal has undertaken various academic and professional responsibilities throughout his career, including being the Head of the Department,, NAAC coordinator, editor of the Journal of the School of Law, member of the Board of Studies, supervisor of three PhD research scholars, and guide of several LL.M scholars. He has participated and presented papers in several seminars, conferences, workshops, and conducted special lectures.

Parvathi R. is a Professor of School of Computing Science and Engineering at VIT University, Chennai since 2011. She received the Doctoral degree in the field of spatial data mining in the same year. Her teaching experience in the area of computer science includes more than two decades and her research interests include data mining, big data and computational biology.

Murat Sengöz holds a Bachelor's degree in Engineering and postgraduate degrees in Management and Finance, as well as a doctorate in Business Administration. He is the author of several academic and non-academic monographs and research papers. His researches focus on critical and reflective philosophical studies in organizational behavior, strategic management, management philosophy, and national security.

Di Wang is a Ph.D. student in the Department of Mechanical and Industrial Engineering at the University of Illinois at Chicago, IL, USA. He received his B.S. and M.S. degrees in electrical engineering from Fuzhou University, China, in 2014 and Tianjin University, China, in 2017. His current research interests include smart manufacturing, multi-agent systems, large language model, and energy management.

Index

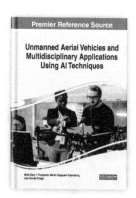

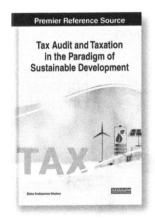

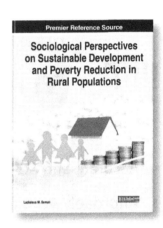

Printed in the United States
by Baker & Taylor Publisher Services